Concise European Copyright Law

Concise European Copyright Law

Second Edition

Edited by:
Thomas Dreier
P. Bernt Hugenholtz

General Series Editors:
Thomas Dreier
Charles Gielen
Richard Hacon

Published by Kluwer Law International B.V.
P.O. Box 316, 2400 AH Alphen aan den Rijn, The Netherlands
sales@kluwerlaw.com
http://www.wklawbusiness.com

Sold and distributed in North, Central and South America by
Wolters Kluwer Legal & Regulatory U.S.
7201 McKinney Circle, Frederick, MD 21704, USA

Sold and distributed in all other countries by
Turpin Distribution Services Ltd.,
Stratton Business Park,
Pegasus Drive, Biggleswade,
Bedfordshire SG18 8TQ, United Kingdom

Suggested citation:
[Author name], in Dreier/Hugenholtz, *Concise Copyright* (2nd ed.), [Document name], art. […], note […]

Disclaimer:
The chapters do not necessarily reflect the views of the contributors' law firms.

© 2016 Kluwer Law International
ISBN 978-90-411-2879-9

Printed in the United Kingdom

PREFACE

'Concise IP' is the short name given to a series of five volumes of commentary on European intellectual property legislation. The five volumes cover: Patents and related matters, Trademarks and designs, Copyrights and neighbouring rights, IT and a general volume including jurisdictional issues. The series is based on a successful formula used for a Dutch publication, a series called Tekst & Commentaar (Text & Commentary) and on the equivalent German publication, Kurz Kommentar (Short Commentary). Since their first publication, these have won a prominent place among Dutch and German legal publications with each volume becoming an authority in the field.

Concise IP aims to offer the reader a rapid understanding of all the provisions of intellectual property law in force in Europe enacted by European and other international institutions. The volumes take the form of an article-by-article commentary on the relevant regulations and other legal instruments. It is intended to provide the reader with a short and straightforward explanation of the principles of law to be drawn from each article, rule or other provision. Where appropriate, this is done by reference to the construction of that provision by senior courts. Usually only judgments of the European Court of Justice, higher national courts or other senior tribunals such as the Board of Appeal of the European Patent Office are cited, though there are exceptions where an important point has only so far be considered by a lower tribunal. The citations do not include an analysis of the facts of the case, only the relevant point of law.

In order to keep the commentaries clear, they are in a form that is as brief as the subject-matter allows. For in-depth analysis and discussion the reader will need to move on to specialist text books. Concise IP also differs from other publications in the form of commentaries, such as those in looseleaf format, by reason of its shorter, more direct style. The idea is that the reader will find it easy to gain a rapid appreciation of the meaning and effect of the provision of interest and thereafter be in a position to look in the right direction should further information be needed. The editors and authors are all prominent specialists (academics and/or practitioners) in their fields.

It is the intention of the editors and publisher to publish new editions every two to three years.

March 2006

Karlsruhe,	Amsterdam,	London,
Thomas Dreier	Charles Gielen	Richard Hacon

ABOUT THE AUTHORS

Christina Angelopoulos, Institute for Information Law (IVIR), University of Amsterdam

Stefan Bechtold, ETH Zurich

Lionel Bently, Centre for Intellectual Property and Information Law, University of Cambridge

Fabienne Brison, Hoyng Monegier ; Faculty of Law, Vrije Universiteit Brussel

Thomas Dreier, Institut für Informations- und Wirtschaftsrecht, Karlsruhe Institute of Technology (KIT), Karlsruhe

Stef van Gompel, Institute for Information Law (IVIR), University of Amsterdam

Lucie Guibault, Institute for Information Law (IVIR), University of Amsterdam

Bernt Hugenholtz, Institute for Information Law (IVIR), University of Amsterdam

Judica Krikke, Stibbe, Amsterdam

Yin Harn Lee, Faculty of Law, University of Sheffield

Martin Senftleben, Faculty of Law, VU University Amsterdam; Bird & Bird, The Hague

Hendrik Vanhees, Faculty of Law, University of Antwerp; Faculty of Law, University of Ghent

ABOUT THE AUTHORS

TABLE OF CONTENTS

Table of Contents

ABOUT THE EDITORS

Prof. Dr. Thomas Dreier, M.C.J.

Thomas DREIER studied law and art history at the Universities of Bonn, Geneva and Munich, and obtained his M.C.J.-degree from New York University School of Law. He is Professor of Law at the Karlsruhe Institute of Technology (KIT), Karlsruhe, Germany, where he is the Director of the Institute for Information and Economic Law, and Honorary Professor at the Law Faculty of the University of Freiburg. His main focus is on copyright law and new technologies. Before joining the KIT, Prof. Dreier has been working at the Max-Planck-Institute for Innovation and Competition in Munich, Germany. He has been an advisor to both the European Commission and the Council of Europe on copyright matters. Professor Dreier has also taught intellectual property as visiting professor at the New York University, School of Law. Prof. Dreier is vice-president of the Association littéraire et artistique internationale (ALAI), chairman of the copyright expert committee of the German Association for the Protection of Intellectual Property (GRUR) and Senior Fellow of the Käte Hamburger Center for Advanced Study in the Humanities "Law as Culture". He is the author of numerous publications in the field of copyright, amongst them Dreier/Schulze, *Urheberrecht* (Beck, 5th ed., 2015), and Kur/Dreier, *European Intellectual Property Law* (Elgar, 2013).

Prof. Dr. P. Bernt Hugenholtz

Bernt HUGENHOLTZ studied law at the University of Groningen. He is Professor of Law at the Institute for Information Law (IViR) of the University of Amsterdam, Faculty of Law, and also teaches at the University of Bergen (Norway) and the Munich Intellectual Property Law Center in Munich. In 1989 he received his doctorate cum laude from the University of Amsterdam. He was a member of the Amsterdam Bar from 1990 to 1998, and is now an adjunct judge at the Court of Appeals in Arnhem. He has acted as an advisor to WIPO, the European Commission, the European Parliament and the Ministry of Justice of the Netherlands. Professor Hugenholtz has published widely on a vast range of copyright-related issues. He is the co-author, with Professor Paul Goldstein (Stanford University), of *International Copyright Law* (Oxford University Press, 3rd ed., 2013). He is also the General Editor of the *Information Law Series*, published by Kluwer Law International. He is one of the founders of the Wittem Group that drafted the European Copyright Code, and co-founder and member of the European Copyright Society.

INTRODUCTION

1. General. This book is a concise commentary on the European Union directives adopted in the field of copyright and neighbouring (related) rights, and on the main international conventions in this field with relevance for the EU. This chapter introduces and provides some background to the harmonization process and the relevant international legal framework. **(a) No unitary copyright.** Despite extensive harmonization the Member States of the EU have remained autonomous in the field of copyright and neighbouring rights. No unitary Union-wide copyright, like the Community trademark or Community design right, presently exists. The 2010 Treaty on the Functioning of the European Union (TFEU) has introduced a specific competence to establish a regime of unified intellectual property protection throughout the Union (art. 118). In the future this might provide the basis for unitary rules on copyright that would replace national copyright laws. **(b) Legislative competence of the EU in the field of copyright.** The EU legislature derives its main legislative competence in the field of copyright and related rights from its general mandate to establish an internal market by way of approximation (i.e. harmonization) of national laws, as provided by art. 114 TFEU, formerly art. 95 of the EC Treaty. The Member States of the EU are obliged to transpose the rules of a directive within the time limits specified therein. Directives bind Member States only 'as to the results to be achieved [...], but shall leave to the national authorities the choice of form and methods' (art. 288 TFEU). In other words, implementation into national law need not be done literally. The norms of the directives are primarily addressed to the Member States, and are not directly binding upon the citizens of the EU. However, national courts are generally obliged to interpret national law in line with the norms of the directives. In appropriate cases national courts may ask preliminary questions to the Court of Justice of the European Union (ECJ) as to the meaning and interpretation of certain provisions of a directive. The decisions of the ECJ constitute an important source of EU copyright law (see the cases listed in the Appendix). **(c) No discrimination.** Art. 18 of the TFEU, prohibiting discrimination within the European Union on grounds of nationality, requires Member States to offer the same level of protection to all citizens and residents of the EU even in situations where discrimination by requiring reciprocity would not violate the national treatment rules of international copyright and neighbouring rights conventions. In *Phil Collins,* the ECJ held that this non-discrimination clause (formerly art. 7 of the EC Treaty) barred Germany from denying neighbouring rights protection to a British national under circumstances in which it would have given protection to a German national; see also *Ricordi* (ECJ) and *Tod's* (ECJ)).

2. International treaties. The EU and its Member States are bound by a number of international treaties in the field of copyright law and related rights. Besides the TRIPS Agreement, the main conventions in the area of copyright are the Berne Convention and the 1996 WIPO Copyright Treaty (WCT). In the field of neighbouring rights (for performing artists, phonogram producers and broadcasting organizations) the main treaties are the Rome Convention (1961), the Geneva Convention (1971) and the WIPO Performances and Phonograms Treaty (WPPT, 1996). Noteworthy are also two more recent WIPO treaties, the Beijing Treaty on Audiovisual Performances (2012), and the Marrakesh Treaty to Facilitate Access to Published Works for Persons Who Are Blind, Visually Impaired or Otherwise Print Disabled (2013). Both these treaties have not yet entered into force, and are therefore not included in this volume. All countries of the European Union belong to the Berne Union, adhere to the Rome Convention, and, through membership of the WTO, are bound by the TRIPS Agreement. On December 14, 2009, the European Union and its Member States also ratified the WIPO Treaties.

3. Harmonization of copyright and related rights in the EU. (a) Copyright and the free movement of goods and services. There is a clear tension between, on the one hand, the territorial exclusivity of intellectual property rights, which enables rightholders to partition the single market of the EU, and the principle of free movement of goods and services on the other. Applying arts. 28 and 30 EC Treaty (formerly arts. 30 and 36 EC Treaty, currently arts. 34 and 36 TFEU), the ECJ has established the principle of Union-wide exhaustion of the exclusive right to distribute works in material form after they are first placed on the market (*Deutsche Grammophon* (ECJ) and *Musik-Vertrieb Membran* (ECJ)). By contrast, there is no exhaustion of the exclusive rental right after first sale (*Metronome Musik* (ECJ)) or first rental (*Laserdisken* (ECJ)). Moreover, there is no exhaustion of the exclusive right of communication to the public (*Coditel I* (ECJ)). In the absence of EU-wide harmonization the ECJ has in several other cases accepted violation of the freedom of movement of goods resulting from differences in national copyright laws (*Christiansen* regarding national rental rights, and *Patricia* concerning differences in national terms of protection). In *Tournier* the ECJ upheld a requirement under national law of payment of an additional fee for the public performance of musical works by means of sound recordings imported from another Member State, where copyright royalties had already been paid. The rule of Union-wide exhaustion of the distribution right was eventually codified in art. 4(2) of the Information Society Directive of 2001.
(b) History of harmonization. The harmonization of the law of copyright and neighbouring (related) rights in the EU has occurred in roughly two stages. *First generation directives*. The 'first generation' directives have their roots in the European Commission's Green Paper on Copyright and the Challenge of Technology (1988). The Green Paper set out an ambitious harmonization agenda to remove disparities in the laws on copyright and neighbouring rights of the Member States that might negatively affect the internal market, with special focus on emerging information technologies. Much of this work program materialized in the course of the 1990s. The first directive in the field of copyright, the Computer Programs Directive, was

adopted in 1991, closely followed by the Rental Right Directive of 1992 that also harmonized the neighbouring rights of performers, phonogram producers, broadcasting organizations and film producers. Two more directives were adopted in 1993: the Satellite and Cable Directive, which was anticipated by the 1984 Green Paper on Television without Frontiers, and the Term Directive that harmonized the terms of protection of copyright and neighbouring rights. The Database Directive, adopted in 1996, harmonized copyright protection for databases and introduced sui generis protection for databases that are the result of substantial investment. In 2001, the Resale Right Directive that harmonized – and for many EU Member States introduced – resale royalties for works of art was finally adopted, after a long journey between the Commission, the European Parliament, and the European Council. The work program set out in the 1988 Green Paper was largely completed by the adoption in 2004 of the Enforcement Directive, which provides for harmonized remedies against piracy and other acts of infringement of intellectual property rights, including copyright, neighbouring rights and the database right. *Second generation directives.* The 'second generation' directives originated in the 1995 Green Paper on Copyright and Related Rights in the Information Society, which was mostly inspired by the challenges of the internet. At the same time, ongoing discussions at WIPO on a possible revision of the Berne Convention accelerated, which in 1996 led to the WIPO Copyright Treaty and the WIPO Performers and Phonograms Treaty. The two treaties were signed by the Commission on behalf of the European Union, reflecting a commitment to implement the new international norms in a harmonized fashion. This gave an impetus to what eventually became the Information Society Directive of 2001. After almost a decade of standstill the process of harmonization of copyright and neighbouring rights in the EU resumed in 2011 with the Term Extension Directive, followed in 2012 by the Orphan Works Directive and the Collective Rights Management Directive of 2014.

4. Areas of copyright not (yet) covered by the acquis. Whereas the law of copyright and neighbouring rights in the EU has by now been extensively harmonized, certain areas remain where harmonization has not (as yet) occurred, such as moral rights, performance and adaptation rights, and author's contracts.

5. Copyright and competition law. Dealings in copyright and neighbouring rights are not exempt from the application of competition law. **(a) Contractual restrictions.** Although decisions with regard to contractual restrictions in the area of copyright are rare, clauses of an exclusive license agreement concluded between a copyright holder and a broadcaster that obliged the broadcaster not to supply decoding devices enabling access to that rightholder's protected subject-matter outside the territory covered by the licence agreement, were held to constitute a restriction on competition prohibited by art. 101 TFEU (*Football Association Premier League and* *others* (ECJ)). **(b) Abuse of a dominant market position.** As regards abuse of a dominant market position (art. 102 TFEU), the ECJ has held that, in general, the mere exercise of the exclusive rights under copyright is not as such in violation of EU competition law. However, the exercise of an exclusive right by a rightholder who is in a dominant market position may, under exceptional circumstances, amount to abusive conduct, in particular if the refusal to license prevents the appearance on the market of a new product for which there is potential consumer demand (*Magill* (ECJ), *Microsoft* (CFI)), or if the refusal is not justified and results in reserving the after-market to the rightholder, excluding competition in a market other than the market of the original product (*IMS Health* (ECJ)). According to the Court of First Instance, general competition law rules may apply in tandem with specific harmonized rules, such as art. 6 of the Computer Programs Directive regarding decompilation of protected computer programs (*Microsoft* (CFI)). **(c) Collecting societies.** Collective rights management, the usefulness of which has been expressly recognized in several directives (see arts. 3(2), (4) and 9 Satellite and Cable Directive, and more generally the Collective Rights Management Directive), and the monopolistic licensing practices of the collecting societies have been the object of intensive scrutiny by the European Commission (the EU competition authority) and the European courts. The ECJ has so far been rather sympathetic to the basic elements of collective management of rights by collecting societies, although it does not regard collecting societies as 'undertakings entrusted with the operation of services of economic interest' benefiting from the special regime laid down in art. 106(2) TFEU (formerly art. 86(2) EC Treaty) (*GVL* (ECJ)). However, the ECJ did on several occasions redress certain instances of unjustified behaviour of the societies, both vis-à-vis their licensees (*SABAM II* (ECJ) and *GVL* (ECJ)), and in their dealings with other societies (*Tournier* (ECJ) and *Lucazeau* (ECJ)). Regarding the transborder management of rights in the field of online music licensing by collecting societies, which also gave rise to litigation (*CISAC* (CFI)), the EU enacted the Collective Rights Management Directive in 2014.

6. Other issues. There are a number of additional issues which a practitioner usually has to deal with when litigating a copyright case that touches upon one or more EU Member States. These issues include the following. **(a) Jurisdiction and enforcement.** Jurisdiction and enforcement of transborder disputes in the area of copyright are regulated by Regulation (EU) No 1215/2012 on jurisdiction and the recognition and enforcement of judgments in civil and commercial matters (formerly Regulation (EC) No. 44/2001). **(b) Applicable law.** Whenever copyright is infringed and the infringement is connected with more than one Member State, the question arises as to which national copyright law governs the infringement. Since 2007 the law applicable to cases of infringement of intellectual property rights is governed by Regulation (EC) No. 864/2007 on the law applicable to non-contractual obligations. Art. 8(1) of the Regulation provides: 'The law applicable to a non-contractual obligation arising from an infringement of an intellectual property right shall be the law of the country for which protection is claimed.' According to the Regulation's recital 26, this reflects 'the universally acknowledged principle of the lex loci protectionis.' Derogation by contract from this rule is prohibited (art. 8(3)). However, it is as yet unclear to what extent the lex loci protectionis applies to issues other than those closely related to infringement, such as first ownership and transferability of rights. Note that the rules on transborder satellite broadcasting of the Satellite and Cable Directive do not regulate applicable law, but merely determine in which country an act of transborder satellite broadcasting takes place. **(c) Interpretation of EU law.** National courts are bound to give effect to EU legislation (so-called 'effet utile') by way of an EU-friendly interpretation of national law. Moreover, according to art. 267 TFEU (formerly art. 234 EC Treaty), whenever a national court is of the opinion that a decision on the interpretation of primary or secondary Union law is necessary in order to decide a case, this court may – or, if it is a court against whose decisions there is no judicial remedy under national law, it must – request the ECJ to give a preliminary ruling thereon. The ECJ thus has the last word in interpreting both primary and secondary EU law, and in judging the conformity of national law norms with EU law. In several instances the ECJ has considered terms of the directives as autonomous concepts which must be interpreted in a uniform manner throughout the territory of the European Union, thus reserving for itself not only the ultimate, but likewise the exclusive competency to interpret these concepts. Arguably, in doing so the ECJ has in some cases gone beyond strict interpretation of secondary law by filling in gaps left by the EU legislature (e.g., as regards the concept of 'originality' for works in general, *Infopaq International* (ECJ) and *Painer* (ECJ)). **(e) Non-compliance with the provisions of a directive.** If a Member State fails to implement all or part of a directive in due time, upon application by the Commission, the ECJ in a first step may require the Member State to take the necessary measures to comply with its judgment and, if the ECJ finds that the Member State has not complied with its judgment, it may impose a financial penalty (arts. 258-260 TFEU). In addition, Member States may be held liable for any damage which the non-implementation has caused to individuals, provided the provision of the directive in question is so unambiguous that the damage would not have occurred had the directive been properly implemented in due time (*Francovich* (ECJ)). Although a directive is not itself directly applicable, its provisions may have direct effect between private parties (*Marleasing* and *Faccini Dora* (ECJ)). **(f) Newly acceding Member States.** Newly acceding Member States are generally under an obligation to implement the existing directives in their national law, even before the final date of accession to, and full membership of, the EU. **(g) European Economic Area.** Pursuant to the EEA Agreement the non-EU Member States of the European Economic Area, i.e. Iceland, Liechtenstein and Norway, are bound by the EU's directives in the field of copyright and related rights.

7. Treaties and directives covered. (a) International treaties. Part I of this volume covers the main international conventions in the field of copyright and neighbouring rights: the Berne Convention for the Protection of Literary and Artistic Works (BC), the WIPO Copyright Treaty (WCT), the Rome Convention for the Protection of Performers, Producers of Phonograms and Broadcasting Organizations (RC), the Convention for the Protection of Producers of Phonograms Against Unauthorized Duplication of Their Phonograms (Geneva Convention), the WIPO Performances and Phonograms Treaty (WPPT) and relevant provisions of the Agreement on Trade-Related Aspects of Intellectual Property Rights (TRIPS). **(b) Directives.** The European legislature has enacted nine directives that harmonize the national law of the EU Member States on copyright and rights related to copyrights. These directives are in the order of their adoption: Directive 91/250/EEC on the legal protection of computer programs (Computer Programs Directive); Directive 92/100/EEC on rental right and lending right and on certain rights related to copyright in the field of intellectual property (Rental Right Directive); Directive 93/83/EEC on the coordination of certain rules concerning copyright and related rights to copyright applicable to satellite broadcasting and cable retransmission (Satellite and Cable Directive); Directive 93/98/EEC harmonizing the term of protection of copyright and certain related rights (Term Directive); Directive 96/9/EC on the legal protection of databases (Database Directive); Directive 2001/29/EC on the harmonization of certain aspects of copyright and related rights in the information society (Information Society Directive), Directive 2001/84/EC on the resale right for the benefit of the author of an original work of art (Resale Right Directive), Directive 2012/28/EU on certain permitted uses of orphan works (Orphan Works Directive) and Directive 2014/26/EU of the European Parliament and of the Council of 26 February 2014 on collective management of copyright and related rights and multi-territorial licensing of rights in musical works for online use in the internal market (Collective Rights Management Directive). So-called codified versions of the Term Directive (Directive 2006/116/EC) and the Rental Right Directive (Directive 2006/115/EC) were enacted in 2006, updating and renumbering certain provisions without however changing the norms of the original directives. The Term Directive was eventually revised by the Term Extension Directive (Directive 2011/77/EU) of 2011. In 2009 a codified version of the Computer Programs Directive (Directive 2009/24/EC) was enacted. Directive 2004/48/EC on the enforcement of intellectual property rights (Enforcement Directive) also has a bearing on copyright, as does Regulation (EU) No. 608/2013 concerning customs enforcement of intellectual property rights (Regulation on Customs Enforcement). However, since the Enforcement Directive and the Regulation are not limited in scope to copyright, but affect all EU intellectual property rights alike, they are not covered in this volume. **(c) Appendices.** The appendices to this volume contain a list of abbreviations, a comprehensive listing of treaties, directives, cases and other documents cited in this volume, as well as an index.

BERNE CONVENTION FOR THE PROTECTION OF LITERARY AND ARTISTIC WORKS

of September 9, 1886,

completed at Paris on May 4, 1896,

revised at Berlin on November 13, 1908,

completed at Berne on March 20, 1914,

revised at Rome on June 2, 1928,

at Brussels on June 26, 1948,

at Stockholm on July 14, 1967,

and at Paris on July 24, 1971,

and amended on September 28, 1979

1. Introduction. As a matter of principle, national copyright laws which grant exclusive rights to authors of literary and artistic works only have effect within the territory of the State which enacted them. Although copyright works are intangible and ubiquitous, until now there exists no universal copyright. Rather, absent international treaties to the contrary, it depends on each individual State's national policy whether or not it grants copyright protection, and if so, how broad the exclusive rights conferred upon authors shall be. Moreover, absent the belief in a natural right of the individual author to enjoy copyright protection, no State is under a duty to grant protection to foreign authors. However, at a relatively early stage in the history of copyright, the need became apparent for authors who were nationals of States which did grant them copyright protection to receive some sort of protection for their domestic works abroad. At the same time, foreign authors of state B reciprocally asked for some kind of protection for their works abroad. In the second half of the 19th century, this led to numerous bilateral treaties based on the principle of material reciprocity, that is, foreign authors from state B were reciprocally granted copyright protection in state A because – and to the extent that – national authors of state A were protected within state B.

2. The birth of the Berne Convention; fundamental principles. Soon, however, the system of bilateral treaties became rather impractical. Hence, as early as 1886, nine mainly European States met in Berne, Switzerland, in order to conclude a multilateral agreement based on formal rather than on material reciprocity. **(a) National treatment.** In essence, any author who is a national of one of the contracting States should receive in any other contracting State the same protection as this other State grants its own nationals (principle of national treatment, art. 5(1) BC). National treatment under the BC is a principle of formal rather than of material reciprocity because protection of an author in another Member State of the BC merely depends upon both States adhering to the BC and not on the level of copyright protection which the home country of the author grants to authors of that other country. **(b) Minimum rights.** In order to ensure that national protection abroad does not fall below a certain level, the BC also provides for a set of so-called minimum rights which a foreign author is entitled to even if the national law of the foreign State grants less protection to its own nationals (art. 5(1) BC). As a matter of fact, the BC is not concerned with the protection granted by its Member States to their own nationals. However, it was generally expected that the granting of certain minimum rights to foreign authors would incite Member States to grant the same rights also to their own nationals, if they had not already done so before the minimum rights were adopted under the BC. Moreover, Member States are free to grant protection to foreign authors greater than that laid down in the minimum rights (art. 19 BC). Over time, in the course of regular revision conferences, the list of minimum rights has steadily increased. This increase of the level of protection reflected the consensus of the BC Member States with regard to what acts should be subject to authorization by the author in view of emerging new technologies such as phonogram, radio and film. It was only later, after the period of decolonization, that BC Member States could no longer agree upon an appropriate level of minimum rights. Hence, the last Revision Conference of the BC was held in Paris in 1971. **(c) Foreign protection independent of national protection; rule of no formalities.** The principle of national treatment and the minimum rights are supported by two other fundamental principles. Firstly, protection of a particular work abroad is independent of any protection granted in the country of origin of the work. Second, protection abroad is not subject to any formalities (art. 5(2) BC). It follows that due to the interplay of national treatment and the rule of no formalities, an author who is a national of one of the BC Member States, receives, by the very fact of creation of his or her work, a bundle of national copyrights throughout the territories of all BC Member States.

3. Universal Copyright Convention (UCC); TRIPS; WCT and the Marrakesh Treaty. In 1952, another international copyright Convention similar to the BC was created in the form of the Universal Copyright Convention (UCC). Its main aim was to integrate both the US and Russia into the international copyright system. At that time, neither state was Member of the BC, the US because the US-Copyright Act of 1909 and later the Copyright Act of 1976 provided for registration as a prerequisite of protection, and the Soviet Union because its copyright system differed from the western property system of copyright. However, after the adherence by the US to the BC in 1989, which led to the abandoning of registration as a prerequisite for statutory copyright protection in the US, and the accession of Russia to the BC in 1995, the UCC has by and large lost its importance. This is all the more true since art. 9(1) TRIPS requires all TRIPS Members to adhere to the substantive rules of the BC in its latest version. Consequently, by now almost all major States have become BC Members. However, only a limited number of them could agree on a minimum level of protection higher than the so-called Berne-plus approach adopted in 1995 by TRIPS which, in addition to the minimum rights of the BC, provides for copyright protection for computer programs and databases, for a rental right for computer programs and cinematographic works as well as for a limitation on Member States' freedom to create copyright exceptions and limitations. Hence, in 1996, the WIPO Copyright Treaty (WCT) was concluded as a special agreement, and not part of, the BC. In particular, the WCT provides as a minimum right the right to make protected works publicly available, legal anti-circumvention protection and protection of rights management information. In addition, in 2013, the Marrakesh Treaty Contracting to Facilitate Access to Published Works for Persons Who Are Blind, Visually Impaired, or Otherwise Print Disabled, not yet in force, the first international Treaty on limitations to the exclusive right, made it mandatory for its Member States to provide in their national copyright laws for a limitation or exception to the right of reproduction, the right of distribution, and the right of making available to the public as provided by the WCT, to facilitate the availability of works in accessible format copies for beneficiary persons. Contracting Parties may also provide a limitation or exception to the right of public performance to facilitate access to works for beneficiary persons.

4. The BC and the EU. All EU Member States are also Member States of the BC. Moreover, since all EU Member States are bound by TRIPS, they have all adhered to the Paris Act of the BC of 1971. It should be noted, however, that copyright protection in the EU Member States goes beyond what is prescribed as the minimum standard by the BC. This is due principally to the high level harmonization of copyright achieved by the EU harmonizing Directives, and the intent of the adherence of the EU along with its Member States to the WCT on 14 March 2010, after the Information Society Directive was fully implemented into national law by all EU Member States.

[Bibliography]

J. Blomqvist, *Primer on International Copyright and Related Rights* (Elgar 2014)

A. Dietz, 'The Concept of Author under the Berne Convention' (1993) 155 RIDA 2-56

M. Ficsor, *Guide to the Copyright and Related Rights Treaties Administered by WIPO And Glossary Of Copyright And Related Rights Terms* (WIPO 2003) <http://www.wipo.int/edocs/pubdocs/en/copyright/891/wipo_pub_891.pdf>

P. Geller, 'Introduction' in P. Geller and L. Bently (eds.), *International Copyright Law and Practice* (LexisNexis 2015)

P. Geller, 'Copyright Protection in the Berne Union: Analyzing the Issues' (1989) *Columbia-VLA Journal of Law* 435-476

P. Goldstein and P.B. Hugenholtz, *International Copyright* (3rd edn., Oxford University Press 2012)

A. Kerever, 'The Rule of 'National Treatment' or the Principle of Assimilation' (1993) 158 RIDA 74-130

S. von Lewinski, *International Copyright Law and Policy* (Oxford University Press 2008)

C. Masouyé, *Guide to the Berne Convention for the Protection of Literary and Artistic Works* (WIPO 1978)

W. Nordemann, K. Vinck, P. Hertin and G. Meyer, *International Copyright and Neighboring Right Law: Commentary* (Weinheim 1990)

S. Ricketson and J. Ginsburg, *International Copyright and Neighbouring Rights: The Berne Convention and Beyond* (2nd edn., Oxford University Press 2006)

L. Sobel, *International Copyright Law* (CreateSpace Independent Publishing Platform 2009)

J. Sterling, *World Copyright Law* (2nd edn., Thomson/Sweet&Maxwell 2003)

S. Stewart, *International Copyright and Neighbouring Rights* (2nd edn., Butterworths 1989)

[Preamble]

The countries of the Union, being equally animated by the desire to protect, in as effective and uniform a manner as possible, the rights of authors in their literary and artistic works,

Recognizing the importance of the work of the Revision Conference held at Stockholm in 1967,

Have resolved to revise the Act adopted by the Stockholm Conference, while maintaining without change Articles 1 to 20 and 22 to 26 of that Act.

Consequently, the undersigned Plenipotentiaries, having presented their full powers, recognized as in good and due form, have agreed as follows:

[Establishment of a Union]

Article 1

The countries to which this Convention applies constitute a Union for the protection of the rights of authors in their literary and artistic works.

1. Union. Since 1982, the Berne Union has been recognized as a legal entity under Swiss law, and is now administered by WIPO. However, the exact legal status of the union formed by art. 1 is unclear. According to one view, as a Union the Berne Union enjoys the status of a separate legal entity under international law. According to another view, a Union only differs from any other multilateral treaty amongst independent States by the fact that the designation as Union emphasises the intended permanent duration (see art. 35(1) BC) and continued existence if individual States withdraw from the BC (see art. 35(2) BC). Another question is whether each Act has constituted a Union of its own, or whether there is a single Union the Members of which are bound by different texts of the BC. This issue was resolved in the sense of the latter by the wording which was given to art. 32 at the 1967 Stockholm Revision Conference.

2. For the protection of the rights of authors. The BC is not concerned with the legal protection of authors as such, nor of the works of all Union authors. Rather, the BC aims at protecting the rights of authors with regard to their works in States other than the country of origin of the works. In other words, the BC does not regulate the legal protection authors enjoy for their works in the country of origin which is regularly their home country, but only regulates the legal protection relating to works outside of the country of origin and of foreign authors.

[Protected works]

Article 2

(1) The expression 'literary and artistic works' shall include every production in the literary, scientific and artistic domain, whatever may be the mode or form of its expression, such as books, pamphlets and other writings; lectures, addresses, sermons and other works of the same nature; dramatic or dramatico-musical works; choreographic works and entertainments in dumb show; musical compositions with or without words; cinematographic works to which are assimilated works expressed by a process analogous to cinematography; works of drawing, painting, architecture, sculpture, engraving and lithography; photographic works to which are assimilated works expressed by a process analogous to photography; works of applied art; illustrations, maps, plans, sketches and three-dimensional works relative to geography, topography, architecture or science.

(2) It shall, however, be a matter for legislation in the countries of the Union to prescribe that works in general or any specified categories of works shall not be protected unless they have been fixed in some material form.

(3) Translations, adaptations, arrangements of music and other alterations of a literary or artistic work shall be protected as original works without prejudice to the copyright in the original work.

(4) It shall be a matter for legislation in the countries of the Union to determine the protection to be granted to official texts of a legislative, administrative and legal nature, and to official translations of such texts.

(5) Collections of literary or artistic works such as encyclopaedias and anthologies which, by reason of the selection and arrangement of their contents, constitute intellectual creations shall be protected as such, without prejudice to the copyright in each of the works forming part of such collections.

(6) The works mentioned in this Article shall enjoy protection in all countries of the Union. This protection shall operate for the benefit of the author and his successors in title.

(7) Subject to the provisions of Article 7(4) of this Convention, it shall be a matter for legislation in the countries of the Union to determine the extent of the application of their laws to works of applied art and industrial designs and models, as well as the conditions under which such works, designs and models shall be protected. Works protected in the country of origin solely as designs and models shall be entitled in another country of the Union only to such special protection as is granted in that country to designs and models; however, if no such special protection is granted in that country, such works shall be protected as artistic works.

(8) The protection of this Convention shall not apply to news of the day or to miscellaneous facts having the character of mere items of press information.

1. General. (a) General rules. Art. 2 BC defines the 'literary and artistic works' covered by the BC by way of a list of non-exhaustive ('includes') examples (para. 1). In addition, it clarifies that adaptations, translations and other alterations enjoy a copyright of their own which is independent of the copyright in the underlying work (para. 3). The same is true for collections of literary and artistic works (para. 5). However, protection shall not apply to news of the day and mere facts (para. 8). Moreover, Member States are free to protect all works or certain categories of works only if these works have been fixed in some material form (para. 2). In addition, Member States are free to exempt official legal and administrative texts from copyright (para. 4). A further exemption concerns works of applied art and industrial designs and models. Here, Member States are free to grant protection and also to choose the scheme of protection (copyright, design law, or both). This is coupled with limited reciprocity, that is, if a foreign country protects certain works only as industrial designs and models, then the other BC Member States are only obliged to grant design protection to such works of the author of this particular foreign country. Only if the second country does not provide for design protection, such works shall be protected by copyright (para. 7). Apart from these exceptions, the works covered by the BC enjoy copyright protection throughout the Union to the benefit of the author and, after his or her death, to the successors in title (para. 5). **(b) European legislation.** So far, the European legislature has not harmonized copyright law as such. Rather, harmonization has only taken place with regard to two categories of works, namely computer programs (Computer Programs Directive) and databases (Database Directive) and the term of protection (Term Directive). In addition, the rights to be granted to works protected by copyright have been harmonized (Information Society Directive with regard to the reproduction, public communication and distribution rights; Satellite and Cable Directive with regard to satellite transmission and cable retransmission; Rental Right Directive with regard to lending and rental; Resale Right Directive with regard to the droit de suite/resale royalty right of originals of works of art, and Orphan Works Directive with regard to certain uses permitted of orphan works). Finally, as far as art. 2 para. 7 is concerned, mention should be made of both the Designs Directive harmonizing the legal protection of designs and Regulation (EC) No. 6/2002 creating a Community Design.

2. Literary and artistic works (para. 1). (a) Definition. The BC does not contain a proper definition of what is to be considered a work. Rather, it describes the works protected as 'literary and artistic works'. Thus, the BC is concerned with creations in the field of literature and the arts. If para. 1 likewise mentions productions in the 'scientific' domain, this clarifies that creative works which deal with scientific subject matter are also covered, such as an article or a film about a scientific subject. It does not mean, however, that the BC also covers scientific inventions and discoveries. Rather, these creations are covered mainly by the Paris Convention (patents and trademarks, as well as acts of unfair competition) and other international conventions for the protection of industrial property. Folklore is a special case, since it cannot be traced back to an individual author and often 'belongs' to a group rather than an individual author. Although some countries protect works of folklore by copyright (see art. 15(4) BC), the WIPO Intergovernmental Committee on Intellectual Property and Genetic Resources, Traditional Knowledge and Folklore has as its objective to reach an agreement on an international legal instrument, which will ensure the effective protection of traditional knowledge, traditional cultural expressions and genetic resources. **(b) List of categories of works.** Para. 1 contains a quite complete, but nevertheless non-exhaustive ('such as') list of categories of works. As textual material, books, pamphlets and other writings, lectures, addresses, sermons and other works of the same nature are mentioned. As sound material, musical compositions with or without words are mentioned. The visual field includes works of drawing, painting, architecture, sculpture, engraving and lithography; photographic and cinematographic works to which are assimilated works expressed by a process analogous to photography or cinematography (which includes digital photography as well as television films and other audiovisual works), illustrations, maps, plans, sketches and three-dimensional works relative to geography, topography, architecture or science, and works of applied art. Finally, dramatic and dramatico-musical works, choreographic works and entertainments in dumb show are explicitly mentioned. The distinction is only of importance to the extent that the BC limits certain rights and exceptions to certain categories of works (see, e.g., arts. 11 and 11ter BC). **(c) Works not mentioned.** This leaves open the question of how other categories of works are to be treated. The question can be posed with regard to other creative performances such as, for example, circus acts (explicitly protected, e.g., in France) or sports games (protected in no country under a copyright regime). Most importantly, however, the issue has been raised with regard to computer programs and databases as new objects of protection. On the one hand, it can be argued that because the list of para. 1 is non-exhaustive, and because the drafters wanted the most comprehensive coverage possible, new objects automatically are covered by the BC, provided they fall under the definition of 'literary and artistic works'. On the other hand, no single country or single group of countries has the authority to impose its own interpretation of the BC as binding upon other BC Member States. Consequently, it can be concluded that new objects are not covered by the BC as long as they have not unanimously been incorporated into the BC by either a revision conference or by common State practice (which would have to be ascertained by national courts in the same way as the drafting history, see arts. 31 et seq. Vienna Convention). Therefore, in cases of doubt, Member States appear to be free to include or exclude new works from copyright protection. Moreover, with regard to computer programs and databases, the conclusion that they are excluded as copyright works under the BC may be drawn from the fact that computer programs and databases compiling facts are now expressly covered by arts. 10(1) and (2) TRIPS, as well as arts. 4 and 5 WCT. Another question is whether a BC Member State, the national legislation of which treats new objects of protection as copyrightable subject matter and hence grants copyright protection to its own authors, will have to grant the same protection to foreign Union authors under the principle of national treatment (art. 5(1) BC; see also art. 19 BC). On the one hand, it can be argued that no such obligation exists, since the individual Member State has no obligation to grant any protection with regard to new objects of protection whatsoever. On the other hand, it may be argued that by granting copyright protection to new objects created by its own nationals, this Member State considers the new object as covered by copyright and hence cannot escape the consequences of international copyright protection. Of course, within the EU, both computer programs and databases are now protected by virtue of the Computer Programs and the Database Directives, and the issue of treatment of

Dreier

foreigners is regulated, as far as EU nationals are concerned, by the principle of non-discrimination (art. 18 TFEU) which is applicable to copyright (*Phil Collins* (ECJ), *Land Hessen v Ricordi* (ECJ) and *Tod's* (ECJ)). Moreover, most states are now under an obligation to protect both computer programs and databases under the TRIPS Agreement. **(d) Originality.** The criterion for copyrightability of literary and artistic works is usually 'originality'. However, art. 2 BC does not mention the criterion of originality as a prerequisite for copyright protection, since the drafters of the BC thought it unnecessary to state that a personal intellectual creation is required to obtain copyright protection. An exception is para. 5 which mentions the 'intellectual creation' as a prerequisite for copyright protection with regard to selection and arrangement of the materials collected. However, what exactly is required as the prerequisite for copyright protection differed widely amongst BC Member States. Traditionally, UK law had a rather low standard since it protected any work which was not a copy of another work and the creation of which involved some degree of skill and labour; French law, for example, required that a creation bears the imprint of the personality of its author; and German law, in addition to requiring that a creation be individual and personal, required a level of protection which varied from category to category (see now, however, *Geburtstagszug* (Germany), requiring the same level of originality for works of applied art as for all other works). However, within the EU, the formula of 'the author's own intellectual creation', which was first defined in art. 1(3) of the Computer Programs Directive, was subsequently adopted in art. 6 of the Term Directive for photographic works, and in art. 3(1) of the Database Directive. This criterion is intended to be situated between low and high level prerequisites of protection, not requiring too much creative activity to be shown. In addition, the ECJ seems to have adopted the standard of 'the author's own intellectual creation' for all works covered by the Information Society Directive (see *Infopaq international* (ECJ), *Football Association Premier League and others* (ECJ), *Painer* (ECJ), *Football Dataco and others* (ECJ) and *Nintendo and others* (ECJ)). Because what constitutes an original work of authorship is left to the national laws of the BC Member States, an author who obtains protection for one of his or her works in his or her home country may not be entitled to copyright protection in another BC Member State. **(e) Irrespective of mode or form.** It makes no difference in which mode or form the works covered by the BC are expressed. A sound recording of music is an expression of the musical work, as are the computer storage of its digital bytes and bits and the notation of the musical work as sheet music. **(f) Parts of works.** Although para. 1 does not mention the protection of parts of works, the common understanding is that parts are also protected provided they are protected as such by virtue of art. 2, that is, if by themselves they fulfil the requirement of originality (see above, note 2(d)). Here also, the national laws of Member States provide for quite different standards with regard to the protectability of parts of copyrighted works.

3. Optional requirement of fixation (para. 2). Some countries, in particular common law countries, provide that copyright protection only applies to works once they have been fixed in some material form. This leaves works that are orally communicated unprotected by copyright against unauthorized fixation. However, in these countries, which make copyright protection dependent on first fixation, this gap is often closed by other legal means, such as common law, the author's personality rights or right to privacy. Moreover, art. 3(1)(a) BC protects authors who are nationals of a BC Member State also with regard to their unpublished works. Under EU law, no such fixation requirement exists.

4. Adaptations, etc. (para. 3). Para. 3 merely states what is obvious today, namely, that translations, adaptations, arrangements of music and other alterations enjoy copyright protection of their own, provided, of course, that they fulfil the criterion of originality (which is not expressly stated in the text of art. 2(3), but see above, note 2(d)). Copyright in any such adaptation and so on is independent of the copyright of the underlying work. The adaptation right is granted to authors of the underlying work in art. 12 BC and may be licensed to others. Consequently, whoever wishes to use an adaptation in way that would infringe copyright needs the consent of the author(s) of both the adaptation and the work adapted.

5. Official texts (para. 4). According to para. 4, official texts which are of a legislative, administrative and legal nature, as well as official translations of such texts can be exempt of copyright. The reason is that information about legal sources and administrative acts shall not be hindered by copyright. If BC Member States are free to withhold copyright protection from these texts at all, then they are also allowed to limit protection granted by way of a statutory limitation. For exclusion from protection of political speeches and speeches delivered in the course of legal proceedings see art. 2bis(1) BC, and for other possible restrictions of the exercise of rights with regard to certain categories of works see art. 2bis(2) BC and the exceptions and limitations as provided for in the articles granting the exclusive rights.

6. Collections (para. 5). (a) Copyright of their own. In stating that collections of literary or artistic works shall be protected as works which enjoy a copyright of their own, provided they satisfy the criterion of originality, para. 5 merely states what today is accepted as a general principle of copyright. Para. 5 names encyclopaedias and anthologies, but these are merely examples. However, it should be noted that para. 5 only mentions collections of literary and artistic works, but not collections of unprotected elements, such as facts. But it does not seem to be necessary that the works collected are still subject to copyright, i.e. their term of protection may well have come to an end. Also, it can be argued that the works collected do not necessarily have to be original, as long as they can properly be described as literary or artistic productions. Moreover, the fact that a collection contains, besides literary or artistic works, other non-copyrightable elements as well, does not deprive the collection of copyright protection, although the selection and arrangement of such unprotected elements can probably not contribute to the finding of an intellectual creation. However, it should be noted that unprotected elements such as data and facts are now explicitly covered by both arts. 10(2) TRIPS and 5 WCT and, furthermore, art. 1(2) of the Database Directive. **(b) Originality.** Although the BC does not explicitly identify originality as the condition for protection (see above, note 2(d)), para. 5 requires an 'intellectual creation' by reason of the 'selection and arrangement' of the contents of the collection as the prerequisite for copyright protection. Both arts. 10(2) TRIPS and 5 WCT as well as art. 3(1) of the Database Directive have now adopted a broader and more appropriate definition of originality with regard to compilations by requiring that the creativity must be reflected in the selection 'or' arrangement of the contents of a collection. **(c) Without prejudice to the copyright in each of the works forming part of such collections.** On the one hand, copyright in the compilation exists in addition to any copyright in the works which form part of the collection protected. On the other hand, copyright in the collection as a whole does not by itself extend protection to the – protected or unprotected – parts which make up the compilation.

7. Obligation to protect; beneficiaries of protection (para. 6). Para. 6 clarifies three important principles. **(a) Obligation to protect.** Firstly, works covered by the BC shall 'enjoy protection in all countries of the Union'. This means that each BC Member State has an international obligation iure conventionis to protect the works covered by the BC in its national legislation. Because the BC is not concerned with the protection which a BC Member State grants to its own nationals (see art. 1 note 2(b)), this obligation only exists with regard to foreign Union authors. Another question is whether foreign authors can directly invoke the provisions of the BC in cases where national law does not expressly provide for such protection, which is often the case if a Member State does not grant the protection to its own nationals. Although it is sometimes stated that the provisions of the BC can be directly invoked, this is only true to the extent that the BC Member State in question has incorporated the BC into its own national law according to its own national rules (e.g., in Germany, a law which accepts adherence to the international treaty is sufficient in order to adopt the provisions of the international treaty in national law, whereas in the UK, the norms of an international treaty only become part of national law if, and to the extent, the UK parliament has enacted a law which contains the same rules and rights as does the international treaty). It follows that absent such incorporation of the BC rules into national law, an individual foreign author cannot claim, in such a country, the benefits granted to him by the BC. Rather, this country is then in breach of its international obligations under the BC, which can be redressed only by another BC Member State bringing the dispute before the International Court of Justice (see art. 33 BC), or, amongst TRIPS Members, by way of a WTO-Dispute Settlement (see art. 64 TRIPS) for violation of the obligation to comply with arts. 1-21 BC contained in art. 9(1) TRIPS.

(b) For the benefit of the author. Second, the protection granted by the BC shall operate for the benefit 'of the author'. Historically, the BC is thus based on the continental European author's rights tradition, according to which the 'author' of a work is always the natural person who has created the work. This approach is also reflected in the language of the BC which also speaks of 'owner of copyright' (see, e.g., art. 14bis(1) BC). However, even droit d'auteur countries admit initial authorship by legal entities other than natural persons, albeit under limited circumstances (e.g., the 'collective work' in France). Similarly, the EU legislation has not harmonized authorship within the EU (see, e.g., art. 2(1) of Computer Programs Directive: the author is the legal person designated as the rightholder by national legislation, if national legislation so permits, and whoever is considered the author of a collective work, where collective works are recognized by the legislation of a Member State). Moreover, national conflict of law rules govern which law to apply in order to determine issues of authorship. Hence, although the BC is based on the concept of the author as a natural person, this does not exclude legal entities from benefiting from the protection granted by the BC, if such legal entities are recognized as initial authors by the national legislation of any BC Member State. It should be noted that it is not clear whether art. 8(1) of Regulation Rome II, according to which the law applicable to the infringement of an intellectual property right shall be the law of the country for which protection is claimed, only applies to issues of infringement or whether it likewise determines the issue of authorship as well. **(c) Successors in title.** Third, para. 6 makes it clear that the successors in title enjoy the same protection as the protection enjoyed by the author. If, for example, the author has been a non-Union author (for definition see art. 3 note 1(a)), protection cannot be claimed by a successor who is a national of a BC Member State. A successor in title is the one who subsequently becomes entitled to all or some of the author's rights, for example, by way of inheritance or as an assignee, donee, trustee in bankruptcy and so forth. The successor in title is determined by the country of protection. However, it should be noted that the BC is not concerned with entitlement to the protection originally granted to an author in the case where, for example, a licence has been granted.

8. Works of applied art and industrial designs (para. 7). (a) Reason for special treatment. Historically, works of applied art and industrial designs and models were treated rather differently in different States. For example, whereas France granted full copyright protection to such works at a relatively early stage, Germany refused full copyright protection even to works of visual arts, once such works were used in an industrial context. In addition, the relationship between design law and copyright law differed widely amongst Member States, ranging from total cumulative application to mutual exclusivity. Even within the EU, the relationship between design law and copyright law has not been harmonized until now (see art. 17 of the Designs Directive and *Flos* (ECJ)). **(b) Discretion of Member States.** The BC leaves its Member States free to determine the extent of the application of

Dreier

their laws to works of applied art and industrial designs and models, as well as the conditions under which such works, designs and models shall be protected (para. 7, sentence 1). Moreover, para. 7 allows Member States to adopt a registration requirement for works of applied art under a design protection scheme. The only derogation to the general freedom thus granted to Member States is art. 7(4) BC ('subject to …'), according to which Member States which protect works of applied art as artistic works have to grant a minimum term of protection of 25 years from the making of such a work. Para. 7 also has the consequence that what has to be considered a work of applied art and how it is to be qualified is determined according to the national law of the place of protection. **(c) Substantive reciprocity.** Moreover, as a corollary to the freedom to determine the scope of protection of works of applied art and industrial designs and models by their own national laws, the principle of national treatment (see art. 5(1) BC) is restricted (para. 7, sentence 2). As a rule, an author, who is a national of a country which protects works of applied art only as designs and models, can in another BC Member State only claim for his or her work of applied art the special design protection which this other BC Member State grants to designs. This is substantive reciprocity, which is, however, not mandatory so that a BC Member State can give better treatment to such a foreign author. Only if this other BC Member State does not recognize special design law protection is the author entitled to this other BC Member State's copyright protection. In practice, this involves difficult questions with regard to comparability of the systems, such as whether the granting and the absence of design protection have to be judged on an abstract (with regard to the legal system as such) or on a concrete (with regard to the object at issue) level (see, e.g., *IPEM* (France)). **(d) Non-discrimination within the EU.** Again, within the EU, according to art. 18 TFEU, the reciprocity prescribed in art. 2(7) BC is not to be applied in all cases in which the mandatory EU principle of non-discrimination prevails (*Tod's* (ECJ)).

9. News of the day; facts (para. 8). Finally, no Member State is required under the BC to protect 'news of the day' or 'miscellaneous facts having the character of mere items of press information'. This applies to writings which can under no circumstances qualify as copyrightable works. However, journalistic reporting of news can qualify for copyright protection. From the wording of this provision ('this Convention shall not apply') it may be deduced that even if Member States do grant copyright protection to their own nationals with regard to news and facts, they are not bound by the national treatment requirement of art. 5(1) BC with regard to foreign Union authors. Within the EU, however, the principle of non-discrimination applies (art. 18 TFEU).

[Possible limitation of protection of certain works]

Article 2bis

(1) It shall be a matter for legislation in the countries of the Union to exclude, wholly or in part, from the protection provided by the preceding Article political speeches and speeches delivered in the course of legal proceedings.

(2) It shall also be a matter for legislation in the countries of the Union to determine the conditions under which lectures, addresses and other works of the same nature which are delivered in public may be reproduced by the press, broadcast, communicated to the public by wire and made the subject of public communication as envisaged in Article 11bis(1) of this Convention, when such use is justified by the informatory purpose.

(3) Nevertheless, the author shall enjoy the exclusive right of making a collection of his works mentioned in the preceding paragraphs.

1. General. Art. 2bis allows Member States to limit copyright protection for political speeches and speeches delivered in the course of legal proceedings (para. 1) as well as for lectures, addresses and other works of the same nature which are delivered in public (para. 2). This faculty to limit copyright protection is justified by the informatory purpose of the distribution and public communication of the works mentioned. However, if a Member State makes use if this possibility, the authors must at least retain the exclusive right of making a collection of these works (para. 3). As always, the exact definitions of the terms used in art. 2bis such as 'political speeches and speeches delivered in the course of legal proceedings', 'lectures, addresses and other works of the same nature' and 'collections' are determined by the law of the country of protection. It should be noted that according to art. 2(8) BC, mere news of the day and items of press information are not subject to copyright protection at all.

2. Political speeches and speeches delivered in the course of legal proceedings (para. 1). (a) Scope. Since the authors of political speeches and speeches delivered in the course of legal proceedings retain their right to include these works in collections (see para. 3), para. 1 does not give Member States the freedom to exclude political speeches and speeches delivered in the course of legal proceedings from copyright protection altogether (see art. 2(1) BC). Rather, Member States may provide for the freedom of using political speeches and speeches delivered in the course of legal proceedings without authorization of their authors and without payment of any remuneration in all areas and for all purposes except in the publication of a collection. **(b) European legislation.** The European legislature has made use of art. 2bis(1) BC in art. 5(3)(f) of the Information Society Directive, according to which Member States may provide for exceptions or limitations to the reproduction right and the right of communication to the public in the case of use of political speeches as well as extracts of public lectures or similar works or subject-matter to the extent justified by the informatory purpose and provided that the source, including the author's name, is indicated, except where this turns out to be impossible.

3. Uses of lectures etc. delivered in public (para. 2). (a) Scope. *Permitted exceptions.* The informatory purpose also allows Member States to determine the conditions of use of lectures, addresses and other works of the same nature – but not sermons – which are delivered in public. This may be done either by way of compulsory licensing and a duty to pay adequate remuneration, or by providing for limitations and exceptions to the exclusive rights of the authors with regard to the works enumerated in art. 2bis(2) BC. However, copyright in lectures, addresses and other works of the same nature which are delivered in private is not affected. The possibility under para. 2 is not limited to reproduction by the press, but since the Stockholm Revision Conference in 1967 it also encompasses primary and secondary uses made by way of radio and television as well as distribution by wire. However, the remaining types of film reportage (newsreels) are not covered by art. 2bis(2) but only by the more restrictive art. 10bis(2) BC. *Informatory purpose.* The uses made according to para. 2 must be justified by the informatory purpose, that is, there must be a current purpose of informing the public. The actual use of the work in question must be made with the objective of informing the public. It is not, however, necessary that the subject dealt with in the lecture qualifies as 'news' or as a 'current event' as in art. 10bis(2) BC. *Moral rights.* Moreover, para. 2 does not limit moral rights. The authors of the works covered by para. 2 can thus claim name attribution (as explicitly provided for in arts. 10(3) and 10bis(1) sentence 2 BC). **(b) European legislation.** The European legislature has made use of art. 2bis(2) BC in art. 5(3)(c) of the Information Society Directive by allowing EU Member States to introduce limitations and exceptions with regard to the reproduction by the press, the communication to the public or the making available of published articles on current economic, political or religious topics or of broadcast works or other subject-matter of the same character, in cases where such use is not expressly reserved, and as long as the source, including the author's name, is indicated, or use of works or other subject-matter in connection with the reporting of current events, to the extent justified by the informatory purpose and as long as the source, including the author's name, is indicated, unless such indication is impossible.

4. Right to make collections of such works (para. 3). (a) Exclusive right retained. In any case, authors of the works mentioned in paras. 1 and 2 must retain the exclusive right of making a collection of these works, that is, to authorize the making of such collections and to prohibit the inclusion of their works in a collection in cases where the inclusion has not been authorized. **(b) Definition of collection.** For the definition of the term 'collection' see art.

2(5) BC. Although the wording of art. 2bis(3) BC suggests that the mandatory exclusive right only extends to collections which merely contain works of one author, protection of the authors would be incomplete if they could not prohibit – and also authorize – the inclusion of their works in collections which contain works of other authors as well. **(c) Moral rights.** In addition to retaining the right to make collections of the works mentioned in paras. 1 and 2, authors of such works retain their moral rights according to art. 6bis BC.

[Criteria of eligibility for protection]

Article 3

(1) The protection of this Convention shall apply to:
> **(a) authors who are nationals of one of the countries of the Union, for their works, whether published or not;**
> **(b) authors who are not nationals of one of the countries of the Union, for their works first published in one of those countries, or simultaneously in a country outside the Union and in a country of the Union.**

(2) Authors who are not nationals of one of the countries of the Union but who have their habitual residence in one of them shall, for the purposes of this Convention, be assimilated to nationals of that country.

(3) The expression 'published works' means works published with the consent of their authors, whatever may be the means of manufacture of the copies, provided that the availability of such copies has been such as to satisfy the reasonable requirements of the public, having regard to the nature of the work. The performance of a dramatic, dramatico-musical, cinematographic or musical work, the public recitation of a literary work, the communication by wire or the broadcasting of literary or artistic works, the exhibition of a work of art and the construction of a work of architecture shall not constitute publication.

(4) A work shall be considered as having been published simultaneously in several countries if it has been published in two or more countries within thirty days of its first publication.

1. General. (a) Criteria of eligibility of protection. Art. 3 BC defines the criteria of eligibility of protection of foreign authors under the BC. These criteria are also called points of attachment of protection. An author who fulfills any one of these points of attachment is called a Union author, i.e. an author who for all or part of his works is protected under the BC. With regard to the question what happens to works of authors of countries which newly accede to the BC, see art. 18. **(b) Nationality (para 1(a)).** The general and primordial rule is that the nationality of the author is decisive (para. 1(a)). According to this rule, authors who are nationals of a BC Member State enjoy protection within the other BC Member States for all their works, whether published within or without of the Union, and whether published or not. **(c) Habitual residence (para. 2).** To these authors are assimilated those authors who are not nationals of any one BC Member State, but who have their habitual residence in one of the BC Member States (para. 2). **(d) First or simultaneous publication (para. 1(b), 4).** Moreover, authors who are not nationals of, and do not have their habitual residence in, any BC Member State enjoy protection under the BC at least for those of their works that have been first published in a BC Member State, or simultaneously published in a country outside the Union and in a country of the Union (so called back-door protection). Publication need not necessarily be simultaneous in the strict sense. Rather, according to para. 4, it is sufficient that publication within a BC Member State occurs no later than 30 days after first publication in a non-BC Member State. A definition of what is to be understood by 'published works' is contained in para. 3. **(e) Additional points of attachment (art. 4 BC).** For additional points of attachment with regard to cinematographic works and works of architecture or of other artistic works incorporated in a building or other structure, see art. 4 BC. **(f) Burden of proof.** Any author who invokes art. 3 BC in order to obtain protection within a BC Member State as a national of a non-BC Member State must prove that the conditions of art. 3 BC are fulfilled.

2. Nationality of the author (para. 1(a)). (a) General rule. The primary point of attachment is the nationality of the author. Whether a given author is a national of a particular country or not is determined by those country's national laws. In exceptional cases, such as expatriation for political reasons, however, BC Member States are not bound to accept another State's decision, if doing so would be contrary to their own ordre public. In addition, the equal treatment of stateless persons and the nationals of one Member State does not make these stateless persons nationals of this Member State for the purposes of art. 3 BC. For nationals of a BC Member State, it does not make a difference whether their works are published or where they are published. This was different under the older Rome and Brussels versions of the BC. **(b) Change in nationality.** Although the issue of a change in nationality of an author is not explicitly addressed in the text of the BC, it is generally assumed that such a change is irrelevant once protection for a particular work has been established. In other words, the BC follows the rule that protection depends on the situation at the time at which the right to protection arose, and not at the time when protection is claimed (see also art. 4 note 2).

3. Habitual residence of the author (para. 2). Since nationals of a BC Member State are already protected for all their works by virtue of para. 1(a), protection because of residence is only of importance for authors who are not nationals of any BC Member State. The BC does not contain a definition of 'habitual residence', which is thus left to Member States. In essence, habitual residence means the country in which the author habitually stays, which is not altered by temporary absences. In case of two or more habitual residences one has to determine the residence to which the author has the greatest attachment. However, it is not required that the author stays at a particular place within a given country.

4. First or simultaneous publication (paras. 1(b), 3 and 4). (a) Principle. If an author does not qualify as a Union author under either para. 1(a) or 2, he or she can still obtain protection under the BC according to arts. 1(b), 3 and 4 BC for works that have first or simultaneously been published in a BC country. The same is true for anonymous or pseudonymous works where the identity and hence nationality of an author cannot be ascertained. Other than under the Rome and Brussels versions of the BC, which required publication at exactly the same day within and without the Union, according to para. 4 it is sufficient that publication within the Union takes place within thirty days of its first publication outside the Union. **(b) Exceptions.** It should be noted, however, that according to art. 6 BC, Member States can limit the protection granted to non-Union authors who obtain protection within the BC for some of their works under art. 3(1)(b), if the country of the non-Union author fails to protect the works of authors who are nationals of one of the countries of the Union adequately. **(c) The notion of publication (para. 3).** The definition of when works are to be considered 'published' in para. 3 is largely self-explanatory, although it raises several questions of interpretation and leaves some room for national interpretation with regard to the distinction between a fixation and a copy. Publication within the meaning of the BC always requires the consent of the author or the authors. Illegal copies can therefore not trigger the protection of the BC. Moreover, the definition of such copies 'as to satisfy the reasonable requirements of the public' makes clear that the few copies needed for the distribution of a motion picture are sufficient to constitute publication (see, for example, *Gold Rush* (Germany) and *The Gold Rush* (Switzerland)). However, it has been decided both in the UK and in Germany that the mere distribution of copies in private circles is not publication within the Berne Union, because the copies are not accessible to the general public (case of the so-called Samiszdat in the former Soviet Union; see *Bodley Head* v *Flegon* (UK); *August Fourteen* (Germany)). Also, if copies are only in the hands of intermediaries, such as movie theatre owners, publication only occurs once these copies have been made (indirectly) available to the public. Nevertheless, if copies are available, it does not matter that the public does not ask for them. The publication of a translation constitutes a publication of the work translated (case *Laras Tochter* (Germany)). Finally, in para. 3 sentence 2, it is explicitly stated that public performance, public recitation, broadcasting and cablecasting, where no copy is being made available to the public, do not constitute a 'publication' for the purposes of the BC, nor does the construction of a work of architecture. For online-publication under the WCT, see art. 3 WCT, note 4(b).

[Criteria of eligibility for protection of cinematographic works, works of architecture and certain artistic works]

Article 4

The protection of this Convention shall apply, even if the conditions of Article 3 are not fulfilled, to:

   (a) authors of cinematographic works the maker of which has his headquarters or habitual residence in one of the countries of the Union;

   (b) authors of works of architecture erected in a country of the Union or of other artistic works incorporated in a building or other structure located in a country of the Union.

1. General. For the general criteria for protection, see art. 3. Art. 4 BC contains two additional criteria for protection, one with regard to cinematographic works (art. 4(a) BC), and one for works of architecture and artistic works incorporated in a building or other structure. Because these conditions for protection apply 'even if the conditions of art. 3 are not fulfilled', they are to be taken as a subsidiary point of attachment. As under art. 3 BC, any author who invokes art. 4 BC in order to obtain protection within a BC Member State as a national of a non-BC Member State, must prove that the conditions of art. 4 BC are fulfilled.

2. Authors of cinematographic works (art. 4(a)). Since the Stockholm Version of 1967, protection of cinematographic works depends on the headquarters (in the case of a legal entity) or habitual residence (in the case of a natural person) of the film producer. It follows from the history of the drafting process that co-producers are to be treated as co-authors. Since art. 2(1) BC treats cinematographic works and works expressed by a process analogous to cinematography alike, art. 4(a) BC also applies to films produced for television. Similar to the effect of an author's change in nationality under art. 3 BC (see art. 3, note 2(b)), a change of the location of headquarters or of habitual residence of the film producer is only relevant if it is made before the publication of the cinematographic work in question. The BC follows the rule that protection depends on the situation at the time at which the right to protection arose, and not at the time when protection is claimed (see, for example, *Kandinsky III* (Germany)).

3. Authors of works of architecture and artistic works incorporated in a building (art. 4(b)). A separate provision dealing with the points of attachment was necessary for foreign authors of works of architecture and artistic works incorporated in a building (such as murals and reliefs inside or outside a building) or other artistic structure located in a country in the Union (such as monuments attached to real estate), since as a rule such works are not published within the meaning of art. 3(1)(b) BC. According to art. 4(b), which was inserted at the Stockholm Revision Conference, authors of such works who are not nationals of a BC Member State benefit from the protection of the BC if their works are situated within the territory of a BC Member State.

[Rights guaranteed]

Article 5

(1)   Authors shall enjoy, in respect of works for which they are protected under this Convention, in countries of the Union other than the country of origin, the rights which their respective laws do now or may hereafter grant to their nationals, as well as the rights specially granted by this Convention.

The enjoyment and the exercise of these rights shall not be subject to any formality; such enjoyment and such exercise shall be independent of the existence of protection in the country of origin of the work. Consequently, apart from the provisions of this Convention, the extent of protection, as well as the means of redress afforded to the author to protect his rights, shall be governed exclusively by the laws of the country where protection is claimed.

Protection in the country of origin is governed by domestic law. However, when the author is not a national of the country of origin of the work for which he is protected under this Convention, he shall enjoy in that country the same rights as national authors.

The country of origin shall be considered to be:

    (a) in the case of works first published in a country of the Union, that country; in the case of works published simultaneously in several countries of the Union which grant different terms of protection, the country whose legislation grants the shortest term of protection;

    (b) in the case of works published simultaneously in a country outside the Union and in a country of the Union, the latter country;

    (c) in the case of unpublished works or of works first published in a country outside the Union, without simultaneous publication in a country of the Union, the country of the Union of which the author is a national, provided that:

        (i) when these are cinematographic works the maker of which has his headquarters or his habitual residence in a country of the Union, the country of origin shall be that country, and

       (ii) when these are works of architecture erected in a country of the Union or other artistic works incorporated in a building or other structure located in a country of the Union, the country of origin shall be that country.

1. General. (a) Role. Together with arts. 3 and 4, art. 5 BC forms the central pillar of the BC. Art. 5 defines the scope of the protection granted under the BC with regard to each work of each individual author who is covered by the BC according to arts. 3 and 4. To this effect, art. 5 formulates the following principles. **(b) National treatment and minimum rights (para. 1).** According to the fundamental principle of national treatment, in countries other than the country of origin of a given work, an author who is covered by the BC enjoys the same rights as those which that foreign country grants to its own nationals. In addition, in countries other than the country of origin of the work, a Union author enjoys the rights specially granted by the BC (so-called minimum rights). **(c) No formalities (para. 2, sentence 1, first half-sentence).** Moreover, the protection as well as its exercise shall not be subject to any formalities in the country – other than the country of origin – where protection is sought. **(d) Independence of protection in country of origin (para. 2, sentence 1, second half-sentence).** Furthermore, the protection to be enjoyed in a country other than the country of origin of the work is independent of the existence of protection in the country of origin of the work. **(e) Extent of protection and means of redress to be determined by laws of the country of protection (para. 2, sentence 2).** Likewise, the laws of the country where protection is claimed govern both the extent of protection and the means of redress available to the author in order to protect his or her rights. **(f) Protection in the country of origin (para. 3).** It follows from the system of the BC that protection in the country of origin of the work is granted by national law. And if the author is not a national of the country of origin, then he or she shall nevertheless enjoy the same protection as national authors of this particular country. **(g) Definition of 'country of origin' (para. 4).** Finally, para. 4 contains the definition of what is to be understood by the 'country of origin' of a work. **(h) European law.** It should be noted, however, that within the EU, the principle of national treatment is superposed by the principle of non-discrimination (art. 18 TFEU) which is applicable to copyright (*Phil Collins* (ECJ), *Land Hessen* v *Ricordi* (ECJ) and *Tod's* (ECJ)). But it should likewise be noted that the non-discrimination principle is not infringed because the BC does not apply when the country of origin of the work is the author's home country (*Vredestein* and *Cassina* (Netherlands)). Moreover, some of the minimum rights have been harmonized either with regard to certain protected matter (Computer Programs Directive, Database Directive, and Resale Right Directive), or in a general way for all categories of works (Rental Directive, harmonizing rental and lending rights; Satellite and Cable Directive, harmonizing satellite broadcasting and cable retransmission; and the Information Society Directive harmonizing the rights of reproduction, public communication including making available, and distribution). In addition, the term of protection has been harmonized throughout the EU (Term Directive).

2. Principle of national treatment (para. 1, first half-sentence). (a) General rule. The principle of national treatment is the cornerstone of the BC protection system, because it abandons the principle of substantive reciprocity, according to which protection in a country of protection other than the country of origin is only granted if, and to the extent, the country of origin likewise protects works which originated in the country of protection. Historically, this benevolence towards works that originated in other states mirrors the strong belief in the internationalization of relationships between States at the time of the inception of the BC. National treatment may be better (see art. 19 BC), equal to or less than the level of protection granted by the BC. However, in the latter case, the principle of national treatment is accompanied by minimum rights to be granted in countries other than the country of origin of a work, if the national laws of that other country provide for a level of protection which falls short of the generally accepted BC standard. Moreover, in certain cases, the BC itself allows for substantive reciprocity. The most notable of these exceptions is the so-called comparison of terms laid down in art. 7(8) BC, according to which the term of protection in the country of protection shall not exceed the term fixed in the country of origin of the work, unless the legislation of the country of protection provides otherwise. Other exceptions to the principle of national treatment are the possibility to retaliate under art. 6 BC, and the limitation with regard to works of applied art (art. 2(7) BC). The rule of national treatment not only applies to the rights granted by the national laws of the country of protection at the time when the work in question was created, but it also extends to all rights that the country of protection might grant thereafter ('rights which their respective laws do now or may hereafter grant'). National treatment covers both statutory provisions and rights granted by the courts, and it applies to procedural rights as well (see *Sicherheitsanweisung für Flugpassagiere* (Austria)). **(b) Effect of national treatment together with the rule of no formalities.** Since art. 5(2) BC prohibits the requirement of any formalities for copyright to come into existence, the principle of national treatment leads to the result that once a work that is covered by the BC is protected in one Union Member State, it is automatically protected by copyright in all other Member States. Moreover, since authors who are nationals of one of the BC Member States are also protected for their unpublished works (art. 3(1)(a) BC), protection of Union authors comes into existence throughout the Union once a copyrightable work has been finished. **(c) Problem issues.** Clear-cut as this may seem to be, the principle of national treatment poses a number of problems in cases where it is not quite clear whether or not a particular work is covered by the BC, and where one may have doubts as to whether or not a particular right, in particular a claim for remuneration, is part of copyright. *Works.* For example, it is not clear whether or not computer programs are covered by the BC (for discussion see art. 2 note 2(c)). Consequently, if a country does not grant copyright protection to computer programs of its own nationals, national treatment results in no protection for computer programs from other countries of origin. The result is, however, much less clear if a country has decided to protect computer programs by its own national copyright law. On

Dreier

the one hand, one might argue that a country which is free to refuse copyright protection in such cases may also grant a reduced form of protection, i.e. protection without national treatment. On the other hand, it seems to be more in line at least with the spirit of the BC that once a BC Member State decides to grant copyright protection to a certain object of protection under its national copyright laws, it should not withhold this protection to works which originate in other BC Member States and therefore be under an obligation to grant national treatment. Of course, if an object does not qualify as an object of protection under art. 2 BC, then Member States are likewise not bound to grant national treatment. *Protection by copyright and related rights.* A similar problem arises if a particular object of protection is protected by copyright in one country, but only by a related right in another (as is the case, e.g. with regard to sound records, which are protected by copyright in the US, but only by a neighbouring right in the countries which adhere to the Rome Convention). Whereas according to the above discussion, the country granting copyright protection would be bound to grant the same protection, a country which only provides neighbouring rights' protection would not, but would only be bound to grant protection under the neighbouring rights Convention (see, e.g., case *Die Zauberflöte* (Germany)). *Rights.* Finally, the question of whether national treatment has to be granted may arise if the country of protection grants rights to authors that are not rights mentioned in the BC. This is notably the case with regard to statutory claims for remuneration, for example, the levies paid in some countries for activities like private copying, simultaneous cable retransmission and so on. Of course, if such moneys are collected under tax law and paid to the benefit of national authors, then the obligation to grant national treatment does not apply. However, it seems that whenever the claim for remuneration is based on, or if its reason is, the use made of copyrighted subject matter, then the BC Member State granting such a claim would have to apply national treatment. The same is true with regard to the distribution of moneys collected by collecting societies.

3. Minimum rights (para. 1, second half sentence). In addition to the protection which the laws of the country of protection grant to their own nationals, the author of a work enjoys, in the country of protection other than the country of origin (para. 3, first sentence) and other than his or her home country (because the BC does not interfere with relations between a BC Member State and its own nationals), the minimum rights granted by the BC. It should be noted that although it is often stated that authors covered by the BC can 'directly' – or iure conventions – invoke the minimum rights granted by the BC, this is only the case if the minimum rights granted by the BC have become part of the law in force in the country of protection (see already art. 2 note 7(a)). In practice, authors will opt for the minimum rights if these give them greater protection than the rights granted by national legislation of the country of protection to the nationals of this country. If, however, the protection granted by the legislation of the country of protection to its own nationals is more advantageous to the author in question, then he or she will invoke these national rights under the principle of national treatment (there are no maximum rights under the BC). In general, however, the protection granted by the national legislation of a Union country will in most cases not be lower than the protection granted by the minimum rights of the BC, since a lower national protection would give foreign authors a better protection and discriminate against this Union countries' own nationals. Historically, however, the raising of BC minimum rights by a Revision Conference above the level of protection actually granted in a BC Member State has prevented many Member States from timely accession to the latest version of the BC.

4. No formalities (para. 2, sentence 1, first half-sentence). Another important principle of the BC is that Member States may not make 'the enjoyment and the exercise' of copyright protection for works of another country of origin subject to any formality, such as deposit or registration (for the effect of this prohibition of formalities together with the principle of national treatment, see above, note 2(b)). An exception to this general rule is provided for in art. 2(7) BC, according to which Member States may determine the conditions for the protection of works of applied art as designs and models, which includes the possibility to adopt the formality of a registration requirement. The prohibition contained in para. 2, sentence 1, first half-sentence concerns the enjoyment, that is, the coming into existence, and the exercise of these rights. Therefore, when adhering to the BC in 1989, the US had to abolish the registration requirement as a condition for a published work not to fall into the public domain. Also, the previous requirement of copyright registration prior to the bringing of an infringement action had to be abolished. However, the US legislature maintained the requirement to deposit works for works first published in the US, though this is no longer a condition for copyright protection. In addition, the US legislature was of the opinion that advantages to the copyright notice with regard to a prima facie evidence of the validity of copyright (sec. 410(c) US Copyright Act) and damages (see secs. 401(d) and 402(d) US Copyright Act) do not offend the BC because they do not deny access to courts, but rather concern available remedies. The prohibition of formalities does not preclude, however, national requirements that questions of proof be decided upon notification, registration and the like (see also the presumption of authorship, art. 15 BC). Also, national copyright legislation may prescribe that certain dealings in copyright be in writing. Likewise, the mandatory exercise of rights by way of collecting societies (see, e.g., art. 9(1) of the Satellite and Cable Directive, for simultaneous cable retransmission rights) is not a formality within the meaning of art. 5(2) BC. It should be noted, however, that in view of the broad wording of art. 5(2) BC, each requirement of this kind has to be carefully scrutinized with regard to the burden it puts on the exercise of the rights granted to the authors.

5. Independence of protection in country of origin (para. 2, sentence 1, second half-sentence). It follows from the principle of territoriality that the protection granted in each country is independent of the protection granted in any other country. Moreover, the rule of national treatment would not be effective if protection outside of the country of origin were dependent on the protection granted in the country of origin, because this would mean reciprocity. Hence a work is protected in a Union country other than the country of origin even if the work does not enjoy protection in the country of origin, for example, for lack of originality according to the stricter standards of the country of origin. Exceptions to the independence from protection in the country of origin are the dependence of protection for works of applied arts on the design protection in the country of origin according to art. 2(7) BC, and the comparison of terms according to art. 7(8) BC, which provides that unless the legislation of the country of protection provides otherwise, the term of protection in the country of protection shall not exceed the term fixed in the country of origin of the work.

6. Extent of protection and redress governed by the law of the country where protection is claimed (para. 2, sentence 2). Para. 2, sentence 2 clarifies that both the extent of protection and the remedies available in the case of infringement are governed by the law of the country where protection is claimed. **(a) Issues.** However, this needs some additional explanation. *Procedural law.* Firstly, it follows from principles of international procedural law that the remedies granted by the courts in a given country can only be the remedies which the procedural law of this particular country provides for. However, due to the rules of international jurisdiction, the country 'where' protection is sought (the forum state) need not necessarily be the country 'for which' protection is sought (the country of protection). *Remedies.* Second, according to procedural rules, the courts in one country may well be in a position to grant remedies which have an affect in other countries as well. This is the case, since the conflict of laws rules of the forum country may call for the application of the substantive copyright law of another country. *Conflict of laws.* Third, it has been the subject of dispute whether para. 2 sentence 2 likewise contains a general rule of conflict of laws which would by definition make the law of the place for which protection is sought the law applicable to a particular infringement with regard to all issues that have to be decided (such as qualification as a copyrightable work, first ownership of rights, transfer of rights, scope of rights granted, exceptions and limitations, remedies and contractual issues). However, although a conflict of laws rule which declares the law of the country for which protection is sought is certainly in line with the principle of territoriality, on which the BC is also based, such a far-reaching conclusion is neither supported by the wording of art. 5(2) BC (which speaks only of the country where protection is sought), nor is it generally accepted by the BC Member States. Indeed, BC Member States' copyright conflict of laws rules differ widely with regard to the question of which law to apply to the individual issues named above. Whereas some countries, such as Germany, subject most of the issues to the law of the country for which protection is sought, others, including France, determine

at least issues of first ownership according to the law of the country of origin.
(b) European legislation. *Jurisdiction and enforcement.* The EU rules on jurisdiction and enforcement of judgements are contained in Regulation (EU) No 1215/2012 (formerly (EC) No 44/2001; within the European Economic Area, the same issues are dealt with by the Locarno Convention). Art. 7(2) of this Regulation provides jurisdiction in the courts for the place where the harmful event occurred or may occur, i.e. where the infringement took place (for details see *G* v *Cornelius Visser* (ECJ), *Hi Hotel HCF* (ECJ) and *Folien Fischer and Fofitec* (ECJ)). However, in contrast to cases of infringement of personality rights (*eDate Advertising and Martinez* (ECJ)), in IP cases jurisdiction based on art. 7(2) of Regulation No. 2015/2012 cannot be established where the centre of plaintiff's interest is based (*Wintersteiger* (ECJ)). With regard to remedies, the ECJ has decided that in case of transborder infringement, damages for all countries in which the infringement had its effects can only be granted by the court of the place of domicile of the defendant, whereas other courts, the jurisdiction of which is based on the place of infringement alone, may rule solely in respect of the harm caused in the state of the court seized (*Hejduk* (ECJ), *Pinckney* (ECJ), *Hi Hotel HCF* (ECJ) and earlier for personality rights infringement *Shevill* (ECJ)). *Conflict of laws.* The conflict of law rules with regard to copyright have been harmonized by Regulation Rome II. According to its art. 8(1), 'the law applicable to a non-contractual obligation arising from an infringement of an intellectual property right shall be the law of the country for which protection is claimed'. Whereas this provision undisputedly covers issues of infringement, it can be argued that it does not cover other copyright issues of copyright infringement actions, such as, most notably, the issue of first authorship. Moreover, it should be noted that art. 1(2)(b) of the Satellite and Cable Directive, which provides that transmission of a protected work via satellite only takes place in the country of uplink, does not contain a rule of applicable law but merely regulates where the act of communication to the public takes place in such cases (see also *Lagardère* (ECJ)). For the determination of the infringing act in the case of the sui generis database right according to art. 7 of the Database Directive, see *Football Dataco/Sports Radar* (ECJ) and in the case of several participants *Donner* (ECJ).

7. Protection in the country of origin (para. 3). As has been noted above (note 2), the BC is only concerned with the protection granted to authors in countries other than the country of origin of the work. From this it follows that protection in the country of origin is exclusively governed by the domestic laws of that country, that is, the author cannot claim the minimum rights granted by the BC in the country of origin. In order to prevent the laws of the country of origin from excluding foreigners from the benefits of their national laws, para. 3 second sentence ensures that authors who are not nationals of the country of origin are treated in the same way as authors who are nationals of that country. This rule was necessary because art. 5 BC is not based on the nationality of the author but rather on the country of origin of the work, which can differ. The requirement of national treatment in para. 1 first half-sentence BC does not deal with this situation since it only concerns protection outside the country of origin of the work.

8. Definition of the 'country of origin' (para. 4). According to para. 4, the country of origin is determined by reference to the place of first publication. For the definition of 'publication' see art. 3(3) and of 'simultaneous publication', that is, publication within thirty days of its first publication, art. 3(4) BC. Depending on where such first publication took place, the country of origin is as follows: **(a) Works first published in a country of the Union (para. 4(a), first half-sentence).** If a work is first published in a country of the Union, then this country is the country of origin, irrespective of the nationality of its author. **(b) Works published simultaneously in several countries of the Union (para. 4(a), second half-sentence).** If a work is simultaneously published in more than one country of the Union which grant different terms of protection, the country that grants the shortest term is to be considered the country of origin. The BC is silent, however, with regard to simultaneous publication in several countries of the BC which provide for an equal term of protection. It seems that in these cases a work can have more than one country of origin. **(c) Simultaneous publication outside and inside the Union (para. 4(b)).** If a work is simultaneously published in a country outside the Union and in a country of the Union, then the country of the Union is to be considered the country of origin. **(d) Works first published in a country outside the Union, without simultaneous publication in a country of the Union; unpublished works (para. 4(c)).** If a work has first been published in a country outside of the Union without being simultaneously published in a country of the Union, then the country of the Union of which the author is a national shall be considered the country of origin. The nationality of the author of the work is also decisive in the case of unpublished works. For these two cases (and for these two cases only), para. 4(c) contains two special provisions with regard to cinematographic works (para. 4(c)(i)) and works of architecture or other artistic works which are incorporated in a building or other structure (para. 4(c)(ii)). With regard to cinematographic works, the habitual residence of the film-maker within the Union shall determine the country of origin; with regard to works of architecture or other artistic works which are incorporated in a building or other structure, the country of origin is the country in which the said works have been erected or are located (a similar special rule with regard to cinematographic works and architectural as well as artistic works determining the applicability of the BC is contained in art. 4 BC). Finally, it should be noted that in the remaining two cases, that is, first publication of a work by a non-Union author in a country outside of the Union and unpublished works of a non-Union authors, the works in question are not covered by the BC at all (see art. 3 BC).

[Possible restriction of protection in respect of certain works of nationals of certain countries outside the Union]

Article 6

(1) Where any country outside the Union fails to protect in an adequate manner the works of authors who are nationals of one of the countries of the Union, the latter country may restrict the protection given to the works of authors who are, at the date of the first publication thereof, nationals of the other country and are not habitually resident in one of the countries of the Union. If the country of first publication avails itself of this right, the other countries of the Union shall not be required to grant to works thus subjected to special treatment a wider protection than that granted to them in the country of first publication.

(2) No restrictions introduced by virtue of the preceding paragraph shall affect the rights which an author may have acquired in respect of a work published in a country of the Union before such restrictions were put into force.

(3) The countries of the Union which restrict the grant of copyright in accordance with this Article shall give notice thereof to the Director General of the World Intellectual Property Organization (hereinafter designated as 'the Director General') by a written declaration specifying the countries in regard to which protection is restricted, and the restrictions to which rights of authors who are nationals of those countries are subjected. The Director General shall immediately communicate this declaration to all the countries of the Union.

1. General. This article, which is self-explanatory, allows Member States to restrict protection in respect of certain works of nationals of countries outside of the Berne Union which do not protect the works of authors who are nationals of one of the countries of the Union in an adequate manner. This is an element of limited, restricted reciprocity. Since works of authors that have been published outside the Union are not protected by the BC at all if the authors are neither nationals of nor have their habitual residence in one of the Union countries, art. 6 only applies to works of such authors that have first been published in a Berne Union country and therefore enjoy protection by virtue of art. 3(1)(b) BC. In addition, if a Member State has made use of the possibility of art. 6 BC, other Member States are likewise free to limit copyright protection in their national territory to the protection granted in the country of first publication. The notification required in para. 3 is said to have a merely declaratory character.

2. Practical importance. The only such declaration of retaliation as mentioned in para. 3 had been made by Canada with regard to the USA before the latter joined the Universal Copyright Convention. Today, since all TRIPS Members are automatically bound by the minimum protection of the BC (see art. 9(1) TRIPS), art. 6 BC is without practical significance.

[Moral rights]

Article 6bis

(1) Independently of the author's economic rights, and even after the transfer of the said rights, the author shall have the right to claim authorship of the work and to object to any distortion, mutilation or other modification of, or other derogatory action in relation to, the said work, which would be prejudicial to his honor or reputation.

(2) The rights granted to the author in accordance with the preceding paragraph shall, after his death, be maintained, at least until the expiry of the economic rights, and shall be exercisable by the persons or institutions authorized by the legislation of the country where protection is claimed. However, those countries whose legislation, at the moment of their ratification of or accession to this Act, does not provide for the protection after the death of the author of all the rights set out in the preceding paragraph may provide that some of these rights may, after his death, cease to be maintained.

(3) The means of redress for safeguarding the rights granted by this Article shall be governed by the legislation of the country where protection is claimed.

1. General. (a) Moral rights protection. Art. 6bis BC, which was introduced at the Rome Revision Conference in 1928, grants to authors of copyright works the minimum moral rights protection in the form of the paternity right and the right to integrity. These minimum rights can be directly invoked by authors protected by the BC in countries other than the country of origin of the work in question. While para. 1 deals with the rights as such, para. 2 regulates their duration. Para. 3 concerns remedies in case of infringement of moral rights. It should be noted, however, that the moral right of the author to decide whether and in what form to first publish his or her work is not mentioned in art. 6bis BC. Rather, this right derives from the exclusive rights granted to the authors in arts. 3(3), 10(1), 10bis, 11, 11ter and 14 BC, which reserve to the authors the publication in every type of exploitation. Also, the issue of (non-) transferability of moral rights is not dealt with in the BC. **(b) No EU harmonization of moral rights.** On the one hand, moral rights are a concept deeply enshrined in authors' rights' countries such as France and Germany, although there are remarkable differences between those countries with regard to the source of the rights (monistic versus dualistic theory and their respective impact on transferability of rights), scope and duration. On the other hand, the concept of moral rights is alien to copyright as initially granted by common law countries, such as the UK, where limited moral rights protection was introduced as late as 1988. However, this did not hinder the UK from being a BC Member, and no other BC Member State has ever accused the UK of being in violation of the BC before the International Court of Justice (see art. 33 BC).

Likewise, the issue of whether US law is in full compliance with art. 6bis BC has never officially been addressed. Until now, these differences in approach have prevented harmonization of moral rights within the EU. Moral rights do not have the same economic impact as exploitation rights, and their harmonization has never ranked high on the EU commission's harmonization agenda. It should be noted, however, that the EU has harmonized the economic adaptation right with regard to authors of computer programs (art. 4(1)(b) of the Computer Programs Directive) and databases (art. 5(b) of the Database Directive), which enables authors to prevent some acts done with respect to a protected work that could also be prevented on the basis of the moral right of integrity. **(c) No moral rights under TRIPS.** It should also be noted that upon the insistence of the US, which consider BC-style moral rights protection as a hindrance to the economic exploitation in particular of cinematographic works, the obligation of TRIPS Members to adhere to the minimum protection of the BC expressly excludes moral rights protection according to art. 6bis BC (see art. 9(1) TRIPS).

2. Paternity and integrity right (para. 1). Under art. 6bis BC, authors of protected works enjoy both the right to claim authorship of their works (paternity right) and the right to object to any distortion, mutilation or other modification of, or other derogatory action in relation to their works (integrity right). **(a) Paternity right.** The paternity right is the right of the author to have his or her authorship of his or her works recognized in a clear and unambiguous way. What exactly an author can claim in a given situation will be decided by the courts according to national standards. Moreover, the right to claim authorship enables the author to enjoin non-authors from usurping authorship. However, besides the positive right of an author to be named, art. 6bis(1) BC does not speak of the negative right of the author to remain anonymous. **(b) Integrity right.** Art. 6bis BC does not grant authors a right to absolute integrity of their works. Rather, protection is limited to distortions, mutilations or other modifications of, or other derogatory actions in relation to protected works, which would be prejudicial to the author's honour or reputation. Therefore, to find infringement of an author's moral integrity right is the result of balancing the author's integrity interests with opposing interests of users of the works in question, such as the interest of the owner of an architectural work who uses the building in an altered form. Member States are free to grant stronger protection, since art. 6bis is only a minimum right, and indeed, case law demonstrates that Member States use quite different standards in this respect. This also is true regarding the question of whether authors can only prevent actual or likewise potential distortions. The adaptation right, which in practice is closely linked to the integrity right, is granted in art. 12 BC.

3. Moral rights' protection after the author's death (para. 2). (a) Duration of moral rights. Since the Stockholm Revision Conference in 1967, the moral rights of authors continue to exist at least until the term of copyright protection (see art. 7 BC) runs out. This leaves Member States the freedom to provide for an eternal moral right, such as granted, for example, in France. In addition, the last sentence of para. 2 allows Member States who, at the time of ratification of or accession to the BC, provided that moral rights' protection comes to an end with the death of the author may continue to do so. **(b) Exercise of moral rights after the death of the author.** However, it is left to each Member State's legislation to decide who is entitled to exercise the moral rights of a deceased author.

4. Means of redress (para. 3). Para. 3 seems to be superfluous since remedies are always determined by the law of the country of protection.

[Term of protection]

Article 7

(1) The term of protection granted by this Convention shall be the life of the author and fifty years after his death.

(2) However, in the case of cinematographic works, the countries of the Union may provide that the term of protection shall expire fifty years after the work has been made available to the public with the consent of the author, or, failing such an event within fifty years from the making of such a work, fifty years after the making.

(3) In the case of anonymous or pseudonymous works, the term of protection granted by this Convention shall expire fifty years after the work has been lawfully made available to the public. However, when the pseudonym adopted by the author leaves no doubt as to his identity, the term of protection shall be that provided in paragraph (1). If the author of an anonymous or pseudonymous work discloses his identity during the above-mentioned period, the term of protection applicable shall be that provided in paragraph (1). The countries of the Union shall not be required to protect anonymous or pseudonymous works in respect of which it is reasonable to presume that their author has been dead for fifty years.

(4) It shall be a matter for legislation in the countries of the Union to determine the term of protection of photographic works and that of works of applied art in so far as they are protected as artistic works; however, this term shall last at least until the end of a period of twenty-five years from the making of such a work.

(5) The term of protection subsequent to the death of the author and the terms provided by paragraphs (2), (3) and (4) shall run from the date of death or of the event referred to in those paragraphs, but such terms shall always be deemed to begin on the first of January of the year following the death or such event.

(6) The countries of the Union may grant a term of protection in excess of those provided by the preceding paragraphs.

(7) Those countries of the Union bound by the Rome Act of this Convention which grant, in their national legislation in force at the time of signature of the present Act, shorter terms of protection than those provided for in the preceding paragraphs shall have the right to maintain such terms when ratifying or acceding to the present Act.

(8) In any case, the term shall be governed by the legislation of the country where protection is claimed; however, unless the legislation of that country otherwise provides, the term shall not exceed the term fixed in the country of origin of the work.

1. General. This article – which found its present form at the Stockholm Conference – contains the obligation of Berne Member States with regard to the duration of copyright protection (term of protection). *General rule*. The general rule of life plus fifty is contained in para. 1. The starting date of computation is contained in para. 5. *Special rules*. The other paras. contain special rules for cinematographic works (para. 2), for anonymous and pseudonymous works (para. 3), as well as for photographic works and works of applied art (para. 4). A special provision allowed Members who were bound by the Rome Act of the BC to maintain the shorter term of that Act when ratifying or acceding to the subsequent Stockholm Act (para. 7). *Minimum protection*. According to para. 6, the terms specified in this article are minimum, not maximum terms. For cinematographic works this follows also from para. 2 ('may provide'), for photographic works and works of applied arts from para. 4 ('at least'), and in general also from art. 19 BC. Indeed, Member States have repeatedly granted longer terms in national law, such as the life plus 70 years under art. 1(1) of the Term Directive harmonizing the term of protection of copyright and certain related rights. *Comparison of terms*. Para. 8 expressly states that the term of protection is determined by the country where protection is claimed (so-called lex loci protectionis), but deviates from the principle of national treatment (see art. 5(1) BC) in that unless the legislation of that country otherwise provides, the term shall not exceed the term fixed in the country of origin of the work (so-called comparison of terms). *Relationship to TRIPS*. Art. 7 BC has also been incorporated in the TRIPS Agreement (art. 9(1) TRIPS). Moreover, art. 12 TRIPS contains a special provision for works for which the term of protection is calculated in national law on a basis other than the life of a natural person (for the significance of this article in view of the incorporation of art. 7 in the TRIPS Agreement, see comment on art. 12 TRIPS). *Significance within the EU*. Within the EU, art. 7 BC has been superseded as the provision setting the minimum duration by the Term Directive harmonizing the term of protection of copyright and certain related rights. Since, within the EU, all national terms are now longer than the minimum terms required by art. 7 BC, an EU national no longer has to rely directly on art. 7 BC in any of the other EU Member States. Moreover, amongst EU nationals the principle of non-discrimination (art. 18 TFEU) excludes the comparison of terms prescribed by art. 7(8) BC.

2. General rule (para. 1). As a general rule, authors of copyright works are not only protected during their lifetime, but also a certain period thereafter ('life plus …'). Initially, the BC left the determination of the term of protection to the national legislation of its Member States. After many countries had prolonged their national terms, fifty-years after the death of the author (post mortem auctoris, p.m.a.) had first been retained at the revision Conference in Berlin 1908, and elevated to binding Convention law at the Conference in Brussels 1948, after Austria (1933) and Germany (1934) had also raised their national terms from 30 to 50 years, and after other countries such as the UK, Sweden and Switzerland had declared that they would follow this example. Although the general rule of life-plus-fifty has remained unchanged in the BC and in the TRIPS Agreement so far, at national level, the trend to increase the term of protection seems unstoppable. In view of the increases in Germany (1965: 70 years) and France (1985: 70 years for musical works), the EU term has finally also been raised in 1995 by the Term Directive (old version), now the consolidated Term Directive to 70 years post mortem auctoris (for the reasons Introductory remarks note 1). The US followed after fierce debate (see para. 102(b) and (d), Copyright Term Extension Act and the decision *Eldred* v *Ashcroft* (US)). Current bilateral trade negotiations by the US indicate a strong desire on the part of copyright industries to see the term of protection raised even further.

3. Cinematographic works (para. 2). With regard to cinematographic works, however, para. 2 allows Member States to deviate from the general life-plus-fifty year protection prescribed in para. 1. Rather, BC Members are free to provide a 50-year term after the work has been made available to the public with the consent of the author, or, failing such an event within fifty years from the making of such a work, fifty years after the making. In countries which have, in their internal legislation, made use of this possibility, in practice the maximum protection for a cinematographic work can be up to 100 years after the making (in cases where the cinematographic work has first been made available to the public shortly before the expiry of the 50-year period after the making, so that the making available to the public triggers another 50-year period). The notion of 'making available to the public' in this para. is not the same as the term 'publication' in art. 3(3) BC. However, in the EU, according to art. 2(2) of the Term Directive the term of protection of cinematographic or audiovisual works now expires 70 years after the death of the last of the following persons to survive, whether or not these persons are designated as co-authors: the principal director, the author of the screenplay, the author of the dialogue and the composer of music specifically created for use in the cinematographic or audiovisual work.

4. Anonymous and pseudonymous works (para. 3). In the case of anonymous or pseudonymous works, where the true identity of the author is not known and hence the computation of the term cannot be made according to the general rule contained in para. 1, para. 3 provides that the 50 years shall be calculated from the date the work has been lawfully made available to the public. However, the term of protection must be calculated in accordance with the general rule of para. 1 in two cases: firstly, if the pseudonym adopted by the author leaves no doubt as to his or her identity, and second, if the author of an anonymous or pseudonymous work discloses his or her identity during the 50-year period after the date the work has been lawfully made available to the public. Moreover, no BC Member State is required to protect anonymous or pseudonymous works in respect of which it is reasonable to presume that their author has been dead for fifty years. As in para. 3, the notion of 'lawfully made publication' is not the same as 'publication' in art. 3(3). In the EU, art. 1(3) of the Term Directive contains the same rule for anonymous and pseudonymous works as art. 7(3) sentences 1–3, with the exception of a term of 70 instead of 50 years.

5. Photographic works and works of applied art (para. 4). Para. 4 exempts photographic works as well as works of applied art from the general rule contained in para. 1 and prescribes only a minimum period of protection of 25 years calculated from the making of such a work. In the EU, however, art. 1(1) (for works of applied art) and art. 6 (for photographic works) of the Term Directive grant the general life-plus-seventy year protection also to photographic works and works of applied art.

6. Starting date of computation (para. 5). According to para. 5, all terms referred to in paras. 1 to 4 run from the date of the death of the author or the relevant dates referred to in paras. 2 to 4, but the 50 years are only computed from 1 January of the year following the death or such event. The same starting date of computation has been adopted by art. 8 of the EU Term Directive. In practice this means that the works of an author who has died on 2 January 2015 are protected after his or her death from 3 January 2015 onwards, but the 50 years (art. 7(1) BC) only start running on 1 January 2016 and will end on 31 December 2065, (with protection ending on 31 December 2085 under the EU Directive). In other words, all terms end at the end of the year which in its last digit corresponds with that of the death year of the author.

7. Longer terms (para. 6). The EU, with the Term Directive harmonizing the term of protection of copyright and certain related rights, has made use of the possibility granted to BC Members to provide for longer terms than those prescribed by paras. 1 to 4 of art. 7 (for the general rule see art. 1(1), for cinematographic works art. 2, for anonymous or pseudonymous works art. 1(3) and for photographic works art. 6 of the Term Directive; for the development of the term of protection in general see note 2).

8. Shorter terms (para. 7). The possibility to maintain, in national law, shorter terms was initially introduced in order to accommodate Bulgaria, Poland and Rumania. However, now all three States have by now signed the Paris Act. May 2015 the remaining States that are still not bound by the Paris Act are Lebanon, Malta, New Zealand, Pakistan and Zimbabwe.

9. Applicable law and comparison of terms (para. 8). (a) Applicable law. The first half-sentence of para. 8 makes it clear that the term of protection is determined by the country where protection is claimed. This is in line with the principle of lex loci protectionis generally deduced from the national treatment principle of art. 5(1) BC (see art. 5, note 6(a)). Since BC Members are not barred from adopting longer terms (see para. 6) and in some cases even maintain shorter terms (see para. 7), determining the term of protection according to the national law of the country where protection is claimed means that the same work is protected in different countries for different periods of time. **(b) Comparison of terms.** However, in order to mitigate this result, and also in order not to frustrate the efforts of countries which grant longer protection, the BC from its beginning allowed for the term of works of foreign authors not to exceed the term fixed in the country of origin of the work, unless the legislation of the country with the longer protection expressly provided to the contrary. This is an express deviation from the principle of national treatment contained in art. 5(1). **(c) Exclusion of the comparison of terms in the EU.** Due to the principle of non-discrimination laid down in art. 18 TFEU applicable also in the field of copyright (see joined cases *Phil Collins* (ECJ), *Land Hessen* v *Ricordi* (ECJ) and *Tod's* (ECJ)), no comparison of terms of art. 7(8) BC takes place in an EU Member State with regard to copyright works by other EU nationals. This is true with regard to works of living authors and to authors from other EU Member States who are already dead and this is irrespective of whether the author died after or before the EC Treaty entered into force in the Member State of which he or she was a national (see case *Land Hessen* v *Ricordi* (ECJ): the Italian composer Puccini died in 1924 and, under Italian Law, enjoyed 56 years of protection post mortem auctoris; consequently, in Italy the copyright in his opera 'La Bohème' ran out in 1980, whereas under German law, which at that time already granted life plus 70 years of protection, it only ran out at the end of 1994). The reason is that copyright may be relied upon not only by an author, but also by those claiming rights under him or her. However, it is still an open question whether the principle of non-discrimination likewise precludes the comparison of terms in cases in which the shorter term was no longer running at the time when the author's home State was becoming a Member of the EU. Such cases will arise with regard to authors who died before 1944 and were nationals of States that acceded to the EU in 2004. On the one hand, the principle of non-discrimination is part of the EU Treaty and hence did not oblige Member States not to discriminate against nationals of States before those States joined the EU. Hence, it might be argued that terms of protection which had come to an end within the EU because of the legitimate application of the comparison of terms before the particular author's home State entered the EU, did not revive after that home State has joined the EU. On the other hand, however, denying such a revival would mean that, at the time of the judgment, the holders of the deceased author's rights would be treated differently from the holders of rights going back to national authors. Since art. 10(2) of the Term Directive provides for a revival of already extinct copyright terms in order to achieve instant harmonization of all terms running with regard to a particular work in all Member States (see art. 10 Term Directive, note 2(b)), it seems more likely that the ECJ will apply the principle of non-discrimination to such cases as well, where the shorter term was no longer running at the time when the home State of the author became a Member of the EU.

[Term of protection for works of joint authorship]

Article 7bis

The provisions of the preceding Article shall also apply in the case of a work of joint authorship, provided that the terms measured from the death of the author shall be calculated from the death of the last surviving author.

1. General. The text of this provision is self-explanatory. It suffices to add that it also applies in cases where not all joint authors are Union authors. So, if only one of the joint authors is a Union author, the work is as such protected by the BC, and the term of protection is calculated according to the death of the last surviving author, even if this last surviving author is a non-Union author. Whether a work has been created in joint authorship or whether there is a mere juxtaposition of works is to be decided according to the country of protection (see art. 5(2) BC).

2. European legislation. The corresponding European rule is contained in art. 1(2) of the Term Directive. In addition, art. 2(2) of the same Directive contains a special rule with regard to co-authorship of cinematographic and audiovisual works. According to this provision, the term of protection of cinematographic or audiovisual works expires 70 years after the death of the last of the following persons to survive, whether or not designated as co-authors under national law: the principal director, the author of the screenplay, the author of the dialogue and the composer of music specifically created for use in the cinematographic or audiovisual work. This harmonizing rule was necessary because art. 2(1) of the Term Directive only prescribes that the principal director of a cinematographic or audiovisual work is to be considered its author or one of its authors, but leaves it to the EU Member States to designate other co-authors. According to art. 1(7) of the Term Directive, which was added by the Term Extension Directive, the term of protection of a musical composition with words is not calculated separately for the music and the words, but runs for 70 years after the death of the last of the following persons to survive, whether or not those persons are designated as co-authors: the author of the lyrics and the composer of the musical composition, provided that both contributions were specifically created for the respective musical composition with words.

[Right of translation]

Article 8

Authors of literary and artistic works protected by this Convention shall enjoy the exclusive right of making and of authorizing the translation of their works throughout the term of protection of their rights in the original works.

1. General. (a) Exclusive translation right. Art. 8 BC contains the exclusive translation right. In addition, arts. 11(2) and 11ter(2) BC grant rights to the author of the original work with regard to the exploitation of translations. **(b) Translation and adaptation.** A translation is any transfer of a work into another language. If the transfer requires additional changes, the exclusive right of authorizing adaptations, arrangements and other alterations granted in art. 12 BC is also touched upon. The separation of the translation and the adaptation right in the BC has mainly historic reasons. Some national copyright laws treat translations as a special case of alterations and grant protection by one and the same exclusive right. **(c) Limitations.** Although the BC does not provide for any limitations to the translation right, it is certainly subject to the minor exceptions (see art. 9, note 4(b)). **(d) Copyrightability of translations.** According to art. 2(3) BC, translations are themselves subject to copyright if they satisfy the criterion of originality. **(e) Reservations.** It should be noted, however, that the BC provides for two types of reservations to the translation right. Firstly, art. 30(2)(b) BC allows any newly acceding country to substitute, with regard to translations into a language in general use in the said country, for art. 8 BC the provisions of art. 5 of the Union Convention of 1886, as completed at Paris in 1896, which limited the translation right to ten years from the publication of the original work in one of the countries of the Union. Even if only few Member States have currently made such a reservation (Cyprus and the ex-Yugoslav states Bosnia-Herzegovina, Serbia and Montenegro, and Slovenia), theoretically this reservation can still be of importance, since according to art. 18(2) BC, once a translation right has been extinguished due to the time limit of the reservation, it does not revive upon abandonment of the reservation (see, for example, *Emil Zola* (Germany)). Second, according to arts. II and III(5) of the Appendix to the BC adopted at the Paris Revision Conference in 1971, developing countries may – in addition to compulsory reproduction rights – also provide for compulsory translation rights. Alternatively, they may make a declaration according to art. 30(2)(b) BC (art. V(1)(a)(ii) Appendix BC). It should be noted, however, that no developing country has so far made use of the possibilities offered by the Appendix.

2. European Legislation. In Europe, the translation right has only been harmonized with regard to computer programs (art. 4(1)(b) of the Computer Programs Directive) and databases (art. 5(b) of the Database Directive; as to the extent to which computer programs and databases are covered by the BC at all, see art. 2, note 2(c)). However, the translation right is found in all national copyright laws of the EU Member States.

[Right of reproduction]

Article 9

(1) Authors of literary and artistic works protected by this Convention shall have the exclusive right of authorizing the reproduction of these works, in any manner or form.

(2) It shall be a matter for legislation in the countries of the Union to permit the reproduction of such works in certain special cases, provided that such reproduction does not conflict with a normal exploitation of the work and does not unreasonably prejudice the legitimate interests of the author.

(3) Any sound or visual recording shall be considered as a reproduction for the purposes of this Convention.

1. **General. (a) Right of reproduction.** Art. 9 BC contains the reproduction right. Although a core right covering the oldest known type of exploitation, the right of reproduction was only expressly recognized as an all encompassing minimum right at the Stockholm Conference in 1967. The right is defined in para. 1. Para. 3 clarifies that sound and visual recordings are also to be considered reproductions. **(b) Limitations and exceptions.** Most important, para. 2 permits Member States to make exceptions to the exclusive reproduction right, but only within defined limits: the limitation must be limited to 'certain special cases', it may 'not conflict with normal exploitation' and it may 'not unreasonably prejudice the legitimate interests of the author'. This so-called 'three-step test' later found its way into art. 13 TRIPS. Under TRIPS, the three-step test applies to the additional rights granted by TRIPS, and, because of the incorporation of arts. 1-21 BC into TRIPS (see art. 9(1) TRIPS) also to all limitations and exceptions granted under the BC. According to art. 10(2) WCT, the same is true for Members of the WIPO Copyright Treaty. In other words, BC Members which have also adhered to the WCT are limited in granting national exceptions by the three-step test laid down in art. 10(2) WCT (see art. 10 WCT, note 2). Moreover, art. 10(1) WCT applies the three-step test to the rights granted under the WCT. Additional limitations are permitted according to arts. 2bis, 10 and 10bis BC, and for further restrictions on the exercise of the rights see arts. 11bis(2), 13 and 17 BC. Moreover, developing countries may declare reservations with regard to the reproduction right according to art. III Appendix BC. However, this does not mean that Member States are, by way of the operation of the three-step test, under an obligation to limit exceptions and limitations explicitly provided for under the BC even further than formulated in the text of the BC. It should be

noted that the Marrakesh Treaty, once it enters into force, will contain in its art. 4 a mandatory limitation or exception to the right of reproduction (as well as the right of distribution, and the right of making available to the public as provided by the WCT), to facilitate the availability of works in accessible format copies for beneficiary persons. The limitation or exception provided in national law should permit changes needed to make the work accessible in the alternative format.

2. Right of reproduction (para. 1). (a) Scope. The reproduction right is granted to literary and artistic works as defined in art. 2(1) BC, that is, to all works covered by the BC. Reproduction within the meaning of the BC is the reproduction in any manner or form. The right is an exclusive right, that is, that the author is the only person who has the right to reproduce the work and to prohibit others from reproducing it. A reproduction is each single additional copy of a work. The method of reproduction is irrelevant, as is the medium in which the reproduction is fixed. **(b) European legislation.** In Europe, the reproduction right granted to authors has been harmonized for computer programs (art. 4(1)(a) of the Computer Programs Directive), databases (art. 5(1) of the Database Directive) and for all other works (art. 2(a) of the Information Society Directive). The latter provision makes it clear that acts of direct or indirect, temporary or permanent reproduction constitute a copyright-relevant reproduction as well, which does not necessarily follow from the wording of art. 9(1) BC.

3. Sound and visual recordings (para. 3). Para. 3 clarifies that sound and visual recordings are also to be considered as reproductions for purposes of the BC including para. 1. Today, this is commonly accepted so that para. 3 now appears to be superfluous.

4. Limitations and exceptions (para. 2). (a) Function. Para. 2 permits BC Members to limit the exclusive reproduction right granted by para. 1, but they may do so only within the limits set forth in the so-called 'three-step test'. The three-step test works as a limitation on permitted limitations and exceptions. It sets the maximum of what Member States can exempt from the exclusive rights vis-à-vis foreign Convention authors. **(b) The 'three-step test'.** *General.* According to the drafting history, the three-step test is the result of a compromise formula which allows Member States to retain a variety of national exceptions which in economic terms infringe only little upon the authors' exclusive reproduction right, and which were therefore considered to be of minor nature. The language ultimately adopted leaves much room for interpretation. But since no dispute has ever been brought to the International Court of Justice (see art. 33 BC), there is no authoritative interpretation of the three-step test under the BC. However, it should be noted that the three-step test of art. 13 TRIPS – which for TRIPS Members also applies to limitations and exceptions granted under the BC because of the incorporation of the latter into TRIPS (see note 1) – has been interpreted at great length by a WTO Dispute settlement panel (see panel report United States – Section 110(5) of the US Copyright Act; see also

Canada – Term of Patent Protection on the comparable patent law provision in art. 30 TRIPS). Also, some national courts have applied, or at least referred to, the three-step test (see, e.g. cases *Kopienversanddienst, Elektronischer Pressespiegel* (both Germany)). The three-step test has been taken over by both art. 10 WCT and art. 5(5) of the Information Society Directive (for additional detail see the respective comments to these two provisions). *Relationship of the three steps.* The way in which the three-step test is formulated makes it clear that all three steps of the test are cumulative. A national limitation only passes the three-step test if it passes all three criteria. From this it follows that the first step ('certain special cases') is the broadest gate to pass, and the third ('not unreasonably prejudice the legitimate interests of the author') the narrowest. However, since a strict subsequent application of the three steps might not take into account all relevant interests at stake and, in particular, not those of users or the copyright system as a whole, it has been suggested that the three steps should be applied with a comprehensive overall assessment in which no single step is to be prioritized. *Certain special cases.* It can be assumed that the acts covered by the limitation or exception at issue must be sufficiently precise (although it should be noted that the 'fair-use doctrine' under US copyright law would pass that test in view of the precise and narrow interpretation given to it by the courts) and limited in scope with regard to the exclusive right (i.e. they may not take away too much of the exclusivity). However, it is an open question whether the limit in scope has to be evaluated in economic terms or on an abstract level, and whether, in the case of the latter, the exclusive rights granted by law have to be regarded individually or taken together. *Normal exploitation.* On the one hand, one can reasonably assume that normal exploitation encompasses both current exploitation and certain future ways of exploiting the protected work. On the other hand, normal exploitation cannot be interpreted to mean any imaginable future exploitation whatsoever, since in that case no limitation or exception would ever pass the test of the second step. However, it is rather difficult to draw the line between what is still part of normal exploitation and what is not. This is particularly true with regard to the different forms of digital exploitation, some of which may be part of normal practice, even though the complaining rightholder is not pursuing them for the time being, whereas others may only prove to be uses that will replace primary uses made of protected works in the more or less distant future. However, it appears to be an open question whether a claim for remuneration provided for in national law in order to adequately compensate the author for the economic loss incurred by the statutory limitation or exception can help this limitation or exception to pass the second step once a conflict with normal exploitation has been found. *Unreasonably prejudice the legitimate interests of the author.* This third step leaves the greatest flexibility. It certainly is the legitimate interest of the author to exploit his work and obtain remuneration for its use. But in order to judge the reasonableness or unreasonableness of a prejudice against the author's legitimate interests by a statutory limitation, it seems appropriate to balance these proprietary interests with regard to other interests of the general public, in particular such as the interest of access to information and of maintaining competition. Although much remains still unclear, there seems to be widespread agreement that a claim for remuneration due to authors for the use permitted without their authorization under a limitation or exception which passes the first two steps, may have as a result that the legitimate interests of the author are no longer unreasonably prejudiced. *Minor exceptions*. During the negotiations at the Brussels and the Stockholm Revision conferences, several national exceptions of minor economic importance were alluded to, such as uses made for religious ceremonies, military bands and the needs for child and adult education. Even if not expressly provided for in the text of the BC, these exceptions should still be permissible (see, e.g., case *Thermenhotel* (Austria): simple collective house antennas and even radio and television switching facilities as well as communal antenna facilities were seen as covered by the minor exceptions of national legislation). Since these exceptions were only mentioned in the conference materials, they can only serve as legitimate supplementary aid to the interpretation of both the three-step test in art. 9(2) BC and all other limitations and exceptions expressly or impliedly permitted under the BC. Moreover, the cases mentioned are not per se permissible, but have to pass the three-step test of art. 9(2) BC in order to be permitted. **(c) European legislation.** The European legislature has permitted the continued existence of already existing minor exceptions under art. 5(3) (o) and has taken over the three-step test in art. 5(5) of the Information Society Directive.

[Certain free uses of works]

Article 10

(1) It shall be permissible to make quotations from a work which has already been lawfully made available to the public, provided that their making is compatible with fair practice, and their extent does not exceed that justified by the purpose, including quotations from newspaper articles and periodicals in the form of press summaries.

(2) It shall be a matter for legislation in the countries of the Union, and for special agreements existing or to be concluded between them, to permit the utilization, to the extent justified by the purpose, of literary or artistic works by way of illustration in publications, broadcasts or sound or visual recordings for teaching, provided such utilization is compatible with fair practice.

(3) Where use is made of works in accordance with the preceding paragraphs of this Article, mention shall be made of the source, and of the name of the author if it appears thereon.

1. General. (a) Scope. Art. 10 BC contains further limitations to the exclusive rights of the authors of works protected by copyright under the

BC. Whereas limitations for purposes of quotations (para. 1) are mandatory, limitations for the purpose of teaching are optional (para. 2). In both cases, however, both the source and the name of the author have to be mentioned when use is made of a limitation or exception under art. 10 BC (para. 3). **(b) Other limitations.** Additional limitations are permitted according to arts. 2bis, 9(2) and 10bis BC. For further restrictions on the exercise of the rights see arts. 11bis(2), 13 and 17 BC, and for the so-called minor exceptions art. 9 BC, note 4(b). **(c) Application of the three-step test.** It should be noted that BC Members which are also Members to either the TRIPS Agreement or the WCT, have to apply the three-step test, that is, they have to confine any limitations of, or exceptions to, rights provided for in the BC to certain special cases that do not conflict with a normal exploitation of the work and do not unreasonably prejudice the legitimate interests of the author (see arts. 13 TRIPS; 9(2) WCT). As already stated above (art. 9 note 1(b)), this does not mean that Member States are, by way of the operation of the three-step test, under an obligation to limit exceptions and limitations explicitly provided for under the BC even further than formulated in the text of the BC.

2. Quotations (para. 1). (a) Scope. The permission to make quotations from a copyright work is mandatory. Quotations are not limited to the reproduction right. *A work.* Art. 10(1) BC does not distinguish between different kinds of works. Although, historically, mainly printed works may have been envisaged, quotations are thus also permitted from musical, pictorial and other artistic works. *Lawfully made available to the public.* A work has been lawfully made available to the public, if the public can access it and if this possibility of access has been either authorized by the rightholder, provided for under a permitted compulsory licence, or is permitted by a statutory limitation or exception. The term is therefore not the same as the notion of 'publication' in art. 3(3) BC (see also art. 7 BC, notes 3 and 4). *Compatible with fair practice.* Fair practice does not mean prior existing practice. Rather, the practice must be fair in and of itself, according to an objective appreciation. This is the case if the quotation is made in support of the ideas expressed by the person quoting, if it serves as an illustration of this person's views, if it encourages the seeking of more information, and if it does not merely substitute for the use of the work that has been quoted from. *To the extent justified by the purpose.* The extent of any quotation must be justified by its purpose. This means that no more may be quoted than is necessary in order to support or illustrate the ideas expressed by the person making the quotation for scientific, critical, informatory, educational or even artistic purposes. Although a quotation may usually not reproduce the whole work in question, a full quotation may sometimes be necessary, in particular with regard to paintings, graphical works and photographs. The justification requirement may also be seen as an element of fair practice. *Press summaries.* With regard to the press, art. 10(1) BC only allows for short summaries (the term 'quotations in the form of summaries' is a contradiction in itself). But see also arts. 2bis(1) and (2), 10bis(2) BC for limitations benefiting the press with regard to whole political speeches and speeches delivered in the course of legal proceedings as well as lectures, addresses and other works of the same nature which are delivered in public. **(b) European legislation.** The European legislature has implemented the freedom to make quotations in art. 5(3)(d) of the Information Society Directive, according to which Member States may provide for exceptions or limitations to the reproduction right and the right of communication to the public in the case of quotations for purposes such as criticism or review, provided that they relate to a work or other subject-matter which has already been lawfully made available to the public, and that their use is in accordance with fair practice, and to the extent required by the specific purpose. According to the ECJ, it is not necessary that the work in which the citation is made is itself protected by copyright (*Painer* (ECJ); see also for indication of source and name of the author).

    3. Illustrations for teaching (para. 2). (a) Scope. Contrary to limitations and exceptions for purposes of quotations under para. 1, limitations for purposes of teaching under para. 2 are not mandatory but left to the Member States. *Literary and artistic works.* The term literary and artistic works refers to art. 2(1) BC and includes not only the works expressly listed there, but also every production in the literary, scientific and artistic domain which falls under the BC. *Illustration for teaching.* The use made under a teaching exception must be for illustration of the subject matter taught, and it must relate to teaching activities. According to the materials of the BC, the only such teaching activities which benefit from art. 10(2) BC are those that take place within public and private schools. However, instruction outside of these institutions, such as in commercial courses or courses arranged by organizations for their members or employees do not fall under this category. *To the extent justified by the purpose.* Again, the extent of illustrations for teaching must be justified by the teaching purpose. This means that no more can be used than is necessary in order to illustrate the subject matter taught. This does not mean that the complete work may never be used. *In publications, broadcasts or sound or visual recordings.* Under the exception of para. 2, use may be made by way of illustration in publications, broadcasts or sound or visual recordings. There is no limitation to the number of copies to be made. However, the limited enumeration excludes the production of a film as well as communication to the public by wire. Moreover, it does not allow for adaptations. *Compatible with fair practice.* As with regard to quotations, the use made under a teaching limitation or exception must be fair in view of the balance between the teaching needs on the one hand, and the infringement upon the interests of authors in the control over and exploitation of the work on the other. Here also, fair practice is not the same thing as prior existing practice. **(b) European legislation.** The European legislature has made use of art. 10(2) BC in art. 5(3)(a) of the Information Society Directive, according to which Member States may provide for exceptions or limitations to the reproduction right and the right of communication to the public in the case of the use of the protected work for the sole purpose of illustration for teaching or scientific research.

4. Indication of source and author (para. 3). (a) Paternity right. Since the Brussels Revision Act, para. 3 expressly protects the paternity right of the author in respect of both exceptions permitted under art. 10bis BC. This duplicates the paternity right granted in art. 6bis BC, which can, however, be limited in time to come to an end with the death of the author (see art. 6bis(2) sentence 2 BC). The obligation to indicate the name of the author – including a pseudonym – is limited to cases where the name of the author appears on the work in question, and, consequently, it does not exist when the work has been published anonymously. Art. 10bis(3) BC does not, however, require the integrity right of art. 6bis BC to be respected. **(b) Indication of source.** In addition to the author's name, the name of the source must be indicated. The person who reads, sees or hears a quotation from a work for purposes of teaching must be able to locate the work in question. Examples of the information to be provided are the work's title, number, the year of publication, the page where a contribution and a quotation begins and, if necessary, volume and edition numbers. In the two provisions cited above, the Information Society Directive takes care of these requirements.

[Further possible free uses of works]

Article 10bis

(1) It shall be a matter for legislation in the countries of the Union to permit the reproduction by the press, the broadcasting or the communication to the public by wire of articles published in newspapers or periodicals on current economic, political or religious topics, and of broadcast works of the same character, in cases in which the reproduction, broadcasting or such communication thereof is not expressly reserved. Nevertheless, the source must always be clearly indicated; the legal consequences of a breach of this obligation shall be determined by the legislation of the country where protection is claimed.

(2) It shall also be a matter for legislation in the countries of the Union to determine the conditions under which, for the purpose of reporting current events by means of photography, cinematography, broadcasting or communication to the public by wire, literary or artistic works seen or heard in the course of the event may, to the extent justified by the informatory purpose, be reproduced and made available to the public.

1. General. (a) Scope. Art. 10bis BC contains two further limitations to the exclusive rights of authors of works protected by copyright under the BC. Both limitations are optional to Member States. The first of these limitations concerns the reproduction and public communication of articles published in newspapers or periodicals on current economic, political or religious topics, and of broadcast works of the same character (para. 1). The second limitation concerns the use of works seen or heard in connection with the reporting of current events (para. 2). **(b) Other limitations.** Additional limitations are permitted according to arts. 2bis, 9(2), 10 BC. For further restrictions on the exercise of the rights see arts. 11bis(2), 13 and 17 BC. **(c) Application of the three-step test.** It should be noted that BC Members which are also Members to either the TRIPS Agreement or the WCT, have to apply the three-step test, i.e. they have to confine any limitations of, or exceptions to, rights provided for in the BC to certain special cases that do not conflict with a normal exploitation of the work and do not unreasonably prejudice the legitimate interests of the author (see arts. 13 TRIPS; 9(2) WCT). As already stated above (art. 9 note 1(b)), this does not mean that Member States are, by way of the operation of the three-step test, under an obligation to limit exceptions and limitations explicitly provided for under the BC even further than formulated in the text of the BC.

2. Articles published in newspapers or periodicals and broadcasts on current economic, political or religious topics (para. 1). (a) Scope. *Articles published in newspapers or periodicals and broadcast works on current economic, political or religious topics*. Member States are free to decide that for the purpose of public discussion articles published in newspapers or periodicals and broadcasts (but not communications to the public by wire) on current economic, political or religious topics can be further disseminated. This includes a wide range of newspaper and periodical writing, such as literary and artistic reviews, sports reports, articles on scientific, technical and economic matters and so forth. 'Current' means of immediate importance, rather than topics discussed within a longer-term framework. Works broadcast 'of the same character' as articles are commentaries, reports, discussions, interviews and speeches. Para. 1 does not limit this exception to parts of the works, but permits the taking of whole articles and works broadcast. *Reproduction by the press and public communication*. Such further dissemination can be made both by way of reproduction and by way of public communication, including any act of subsequent further dissemination, with the exception of reporting by way of film (news-reels). A classic example is press reviews. *Expressly reserved*. The rightholders of the articles and works broadcast can prevent the effects of this limitation by expressly reserving the rights in question. Since such a reservation concerns individual works, it has to be made with regard to each individual article or each individual broadcast. *Indication of source*. The source refers to the publisher of the article or the broadcaster who has broadcast the work on current economic, political or religious topics. However, unlike art. 10(3) BC, art. 10bis(1) BC does not require that the author be named. The latter right derives directly from art. 6bis BC. *Legal consequences of breach*. The reference to the national law of the country of protection is superfluous, since it follows from the logic of the BC itself. **(b) European legislation.** The European legislature has made use of the optional limitation of para. 1 in art. 5(3)(c) of the Information Society Directive.

In addition to repeating the wording of art. 10bis(1) BC, the European provision expressly also mentions making available as a permitted means of use.

3. Use of works seen or heard in connection with the reporting of current events (para 2). (a) Scope. *Reporting current events.* The reporting must of a current event (see note 2). Therefore, for example, an interview which takes place on the occasion of a current event, is not itself a current event. *By means of …* The privileged acts of news reporting are photography, cinematography, broadcasting and communication to the public by wire. This covers all ways of reporting with the exception of reproduction, which can, however, be covered be arts. 10(1) and 9(2) BC. In addition, the making of recordings for subsequent broadcasting is covered by art. 1 1bis(3) BC. *Works seen or heard in the course of the event.* The limitation extends to all literary and artistic works within the meaning of art. 2(1) BC, that is, to all works covered by the BC. The work need not be the work that is reported on; rather, it can be any work that is heard or seen in the course of reporting, such as music or a sculpture in the background of the event reported. However, adding a work merely for purposes of embellishment of the report is not permissible. *To the extent justified by the informatory purpose.* The limitation under para. 2 permits the taking of protected works only to the extent that it is justified by the informatory purpose. The informatory purpose also determines how much of a protected work can be taken. Any reproduction or making available to the public which is not mandated by the informatory purpose therefore infringes the author's exclusive rights if it is not authorized or permitted by another limitation. A similar condition is also contained in arts. 10(1) and (2) BC. **(b) European legislation.** The European legislature has likewise made use of the optional limitation of para. 2 in art. 5(3)(c) of the Information Society Directive, which repeats the wording of art. 10bis(2) BC almost verbatim and which contains the additional requirement that in these cases the source, including the author's name, must be indicated, unless this is impossible.

[Certain rights in dramatical and musical works]

Article 11

(1) **Authors of dramatic, dramatico-musical and musical works shall enjoy the exclusive right of authorizing:**
- (i) **the public performance of their works, including such public performance by any means or process;**
- (ii) **any communication to the public of the performance of their works.**

(2) **Authors of dramatic or dramatico-musical works shall enjoy, during the full term of their rights in the original works, the same rights with respect to translations thereof.**

1. General. (a) The public communication rights in the BC. For historic reasons, the BC does not contain an all-encompassing right to public communication of protected works, as does art. 8 WCT. Rather, the right is granted in separate provisions to different groups of authors and, moreover, with regard to different forms of public communication: art. 11 (authors of dramatic, dramatico-musical and musical works/public performance and communication to the public of performances); art. 11bis (authors of literary and artistic works/broadcasting, communication to the public by wire or by rebroadcasting, and public communication by loudspeaker or any other analogous instrument transmitting the broadcast of the work); art. 11ter (authors of literary works/public recitation and any communication to the public of the recitation of their works); art. 14(1)(ii) (authors of literary or artistic works/public performance and communication to the public by wire of works adapted and reproduced in cinematographic works); and art. 14bis(1) BC (authors of cinematographic works/public performance, communication to the public, broadcasting, communication to the public by wire or by rebroadcasting, and public communication by loudspeaker or any other analogous instrument transmitting the broadcast of the cinematographic work). It should be noted that the BC distinguishes between the right of public performance (arts. 11(1)(i) and 11ter(1)(i) BC) on the one hand, and the right of communication to the public (arts. 11(1)(ii) and 11ter(1)(ii) BC) on the other. Similarly, both distinct terms are used in art. 14(1)(ii) BC. The difference is that a public performance situation is given when members of the public gather at a specific place to jointly attend a performance at a predetermined time, whereas if there is transmission to another place, the right of pubic communication is concerned. In this sense, the right of publicly playing or showing a work's broadcast granted in art. 11bis(1)(iii) BC is to be qualified as a public performance right as well, even though being labelled a right of 'public communication' in the provision itself. **(b) Rights granted by art. 11.** Art. 11 BC grants authors of dramatic, dramatico-musical and musical works the exclusive right to public performance of their works and to any communication to the public of the performance of their works (para. 1). In addition, it is made clear that authors of dramatic or dramatico-musical works also enjoy the exclusive translation right with regard to their works for the full term of copyright (para. 2). **(c) Exceptions.** Although the BC does not expressly provide for limitations to the exclusive right granted in art. 11 BC, there is general agreement that at least the so-called minor exceptions are permissible (for definition of minor exceptions see art. 9, note 4(b); for a strict view see, however, case *Musikwiedergabe* (Belgium)). The same has been considered as true by the states adopting a mandatory exception, amongst others, of the right of communication to the public in art. 4 of the Marrakesh Treaty for the benefit of the blind, visually impaired or otherwise print disabled. After the incorporation of arts. 1 to 21 BC into TRIPS, all limitations and exceptions have now also to be measured against the three-step test of art. 13 TRIPS as reiterated by art. 5(5) Information Society Directive (see also art. 9 BC, note 4(b)). **(d) European implementation.** Art. 3(1) of the Information Society Directive contains a general and broader public communication right that is horizontally harmonized for all authors and which encompasses the right of making protected works available to the public in such a way that members of the public may access them from a place and at a time individually chosen by them as laid down in art. 8 WCT, but which excludes public performances with the public being physically present at the time of the live performance (*Circul Globus Bucureşti* (ECJ)). The optional exceptions to the European public communication right are listed in art. 5(3) of the Information Society Directive.

2. Public communication right (para. 1). (a) Authors of dramatic, dramatico-musical and musical works. Dramatic works are theatrical works (the authors of non-dramatic literary works are protected by art. 11ter BC); dramatico-musical works are works which combine drama and music, such as operas and musicals, and musical works are works that consist of music alone. **(b) Public performance (para. 1(i)).** The public performance of para. 1(i) is the live-performance of dramatic, dramatico-musical and musical works. The work need not necessarily be performed by the human voice, but a performance by any means or process will be covered where it includes a performance by phonogram or film. **(c) Communication to the public (para. 1(ii)).** In addition, the authors covered by art. 11 BC also enjoy the exclusive right with regard to any indirect communication to the public of the performance of their works. This includes the communication by way of cable or wire to another location where it is presented to the audience by loudspeaker or on a screen. However, communication to the public by way of broadcasting and original cable casting as well as by any rebroadcasting or retransmission of a broadcast by cable are all covered by art. 11bis BC. **(d) Public.** What constitutes 'public' in either case will be determined by the national law of the country of protection.

3. Protection of translations (para. 2). Para. 2 makes it clear that the authors covered by art. 11 BC enjoy the public communication rights granted by para. 1 also with respect to translations thereof for the time of the copyright in the original work. For the definition of 'translation', see art. 8, note 1(b). If authors of musical works are not mentioned, this is due to the fact that musical works cannot be translated. However, since the rule of para. 2 only states what is obvious, it also applies to adaptations of musical works.

[Broadcasting and related rights]

Article 11bis

(1) **Authors of literary and artistic works shall enjoy the exclusive right of authorizing:**

(i) the broadcasting of their works or the communication thereof to the public by any other means of wireless diffusion of signs, sounds or images;

(ii) any communication to the public by wire or by rebroadcasting of the broadcast of the work, when this communication is made by an organization other than the original one;

(iii) the public communication by loudspeaker or any other analogous instrument transmitting, by signs, sounds or images, the broadcast of the work.

(2) It shall be a matter for legislation in the countries of the Union to determine the conditions under which the rights mentioned in the preceding paragraph may be exercised, but these conditions shall apply only in the countries where they have been prescribed. They shall not in any circumstances be prejudicial to the moral rights of the author, nor to his right to obtain equitable remuneration which, in the absence of agreement, shall be fixed by competent authority.

(3) In the absence of any contrary stipulation, permission granted in accordance with paragraph (1) of this Article shall not imply permission to record, by means of instruments recording sounds or images, the work broadcast. It shall, however, be a matter for legislation in the countries of the Union to determine the regulations for ephemeral recordings made by a broadcasting organization by means of its own facilities and used for its own broadcasts. The preservation of these recordings in official archives may, on the ground of their exceptional documentary character, be authorized by such legislation.

1. General. As stated in art. 11 note 1, for historic reasons, the BC does not contain an all-encompassing right to public communication of protected works, as this has now been formulated in art. 8 WCT. Rather, the right is granted in separate provisions to different groups of authors and, moreover, with regard to different forms of public communication, namely performances to a public present and communications to a public at a distance. **(a) Broadcasting, etc. (para. 1).** Art. 11bis BC, which was first introduced at the Rome Revision Conference in 1928 and then modified at Brussels in 1948, grants to all authors of literary and artistic works the right to broadcast the work (para. 1(i)), to re-cablecast and rebroadcast (para. 1(ii)), and to communicate a broadcast by loudspeaker or other technical means (para. 1(iii)). These rights complement the rights granted by art. 11 BC with regard to the public performance of dramatic and dramatico-musical works, and by art. 11ter BC with regard to the right of public recitation and of communication to the public of a recitation. **(b) Exercise of the rights (para. 2).** However, although the rights granted under para. 1 are exclusive rights, according to para. 2, BC Member States are free to regulate the exercise of these rights. **(c) Ephemeral recordings (para. 3).** Para. 3 makes it clear that, absent any contractual provision to the contrary, permission given by the author to use the protected work in a way as described under para. 1 only allows the broadcaster to make ephemeral recordings to be used for its own broadcasts. Also, Member States are free to allow the permanent preservation of recordings of broadcasts which have an exceptional documentary character. Para. 3 thus concerns the reproduction right of art. 9(1) rather than the rights granted in art. 11bis(1) BC. **(d) Exceptions.** For exceptions, see art. 11, note 1(c). **(e) European legislation.** In Europe, the rights granted to authors under art. 11bis BC have been harmonized under the relatively broadly defined right of communication of works in art. 3(1) of the Information Society Directive (see *Football Association Premier League* (ECJ)). For optional exceptions under European law see art. 5(3) of the Information Society Directive.

2. Broadcasting, etc. (para. 1). (a) Authors. Art. 11bis BC applies to authors of literary and artistic works, that is, to all authors covered by the BC. **(b) Broadcasting right (para. 1(i)).** According to the English understanding of the term, broadcasting within the sense of the BC is limited to wireless diffusion. Therefore, it includes terrestrial and satellite broadcasting. Also, broadcasting comprises both radio and television. However, original communication to the public by wire is granted to authors of dramatic, dramatico-musical and musical works by art. 11(1)(ii) BC, to authors of literary works by art. 11ter(1)(ii) BC, and to all authors with regard to the public communication by wire of their works that have been adapted for, or reproduced in, cinematographic works, by art. 14(1)(ii) BC, and for authors of cinematographic works in art. 14bis(1) BC. With regard to the original cablecasts, other authors (photographers, creators of works of fine art, map designers, choreographers) remain unprotected under the BC. As far as transborder satellite transmission is concerned, it is unclear whether from a legal perspective such a transmission takes place only in the country of origin or, in addition, in all countries in which the programme-carrying signals can be received (so-called Bogsch Theory, named after the former Director General of WIPO). It should be noted that in art. 1(2)(b) of the Satellite and Cable Directive, the EU has opted for the country-of-origin approach whenever the signals originate from a Member State or one of the places outside of the EU designated as subsidiary points of attachment in art. 1(2)(d)(i) and (ii) of this Directive. **(c) Broadcasting by wire and rebroadcasting (para. 1(ii)).** *Broadcasting by wire.* Art. 11bis BC also grants to authors of literary and artistic works the exclusive right to broadcast their works by cable. This is of particular importance with regard to the communication of works over the internet at the instigation of the rightholder (push-technology). In contrast, it is an open question whether this also covers works made available to members of the public in such a way that they may access the works from a place and at a time individually chosen by them (pull-technology). In view of this uncertainty, the right was explicitly laid down in art. 8 WCT. Another question is whether or not in this regard the Bogsch Theory should be applied or not. In the EU, the ECJ has refuted the country-of-origin approach and held that the making available takes place at least in those states in which the making available was targeted at the public (*Football Dataco/Sports Radar* (ECJ)). *Rebroadcasting.* Communication of – again only a wireless – broadcast of protected works by either wire or wireless rebroadcasting is reserved to authors as an exclusive right, provided this communication is made by an organization other than the original one. This latter restriction is due to the fact that the original broadcaster, who has acquired a broadcasting licence, shall likewise have the right to rebroadcast the work in question. The restriction has given rise to quite a number of national cases with regard to the question of whether cable retransmission in area networks infringes copyright and under what conditions community antenna systems have to be considered rebroadcasting by wire and not mere copyright-free reception (see *Gemeinschaftsantenne-Feldkirch* (Austria); *Kabelfernsehen in Abschattungsgebieten* and *Kabelfernsehen II* (Germany); *Amstelveen* and *Small Cable Networks* (Netherlands); *Coditel* (Belgium); see also *Gemeinschaftsantenne Altdorf* (Switzerland)). Similarly, the ECJ initially left it to the Member States to determine whether the reception by a hotel establishment of satellite or terrestrial television signals and their distribution by cable to the various rooms of that hotel is an act of communication to the public or reception by the public, since this question was not governed by the Satellite and Cable Directive (*Egeda* (ECJ); for national decisions see, e.g., *Le Printemps* (France), *Thermenhotel* (Austria)), but in a later decision it has given its own definition as to what constitutes a communication to the public when signals are rebroadcast in hotels (*SGAE* (ECJ) and *OSD-DTOE* (ECJ); see also *SCF* (ECJ) and the earlier cases *Mediakabel* (ECJ) and *Lagardère* (ECJ); concerning linking see *Svensson* (ECJ) and *BestWater* (ECJ)). **(d) Public communication by loudspeaker (para. 1(iii)).** Finally, para. 1(iii) grants the exclusive right of communication of the broadcast of a protected work publicly by loudspeaker or any other analogous instrument such as, in particular, television. Although this right is called a 'public communication right', according to the systematic of the BC it rather is a right of public performance (for the difference see art. 11, note 1(a), and for EU case law *Football Association Premier League* (ECJ)). **(e) Making available.** However, the right to make protected works available to the public in such a way that members of the public may access these works from a place and at a time individually chosen by them (making-available right) has only been granted explicitly by art. 8 WCT. Hence it can be argued that it has not yet been granted as a minimum right by art. 11bis BC. **(f) Public.** Under the BC, it is left to the Member States to decide what constitutes a communication to the 'public'. The same is, however, not true regarding art. 3(1) of the Information Society Directive which is interpreted uniformly for all EU Member States by the ECJ (for additional comment see comments to art. 3 of the Information Society Directive, note 2(a)).

3. Exercise of the rights (para. 2). (a) Compulsory licenses. According to para. 2, BC Member States are free to determine the conditions under which the rights granted under para. 1 may be exercised. Consequently, BC

Member States are free to subject the rights granted under para. 1 to mandatory exercise by collecting societies, or to introduce compulsory licensing for copyright works, as occurs with regard to the rights of performing artists and phonogram producers. The form and the extent of such licences are left to national legislation to determine. Historically, this possibility may be explained by the intent of many national legislatures to benefit broadcasting organizations. But para. 2 makes it clear that the effect of a compulsory licence granted under para. 2 is limited to the territory of the State which has granted the licence. Therefore, a national compulsory licence in state A cannot serve as the basis for broadcasting the work in, or into, country B. Also, it has been argued that the rule of the country of emission retained in art. 1(2)(b) of the Satellite and Cable Directive with regard to transborder satellite broadcasting would be incompatible with para. 2. However, this could only be true on the assumption that transborder satellite broadcasting interferes with the broadcasting rights of the receiving States, which is the very question at issue. **(b) Equitable remuneration.** According to the second sentence of para. 2, authors must at least remain entitled to an equitable remuneration if a Member State provides, in its national law, for a compulsory licence according to para. 2 first sentence. Ideally, such compensation should be freely negotiated amongst the parties. However, in the absence of such an agreement, an authority must be competent to fix an adequate remuneration. Since equitable remuneration is the minimum granted, it also follows that in a State which fails to protect one of the rights mentioned in para. 1, a foreign author cannot claim exclusivity, but rather is limited to equitable remuneration. What is to be considered 'equitable' should be decided with regard to what is usual in the countries of the BC which have no compulsory licensing scheme in place, since if what is equitable would be left fully at the Member States' discretion, mentioning remuneration should be equitable would be superfluous. **(c) Moral rights.** Finally, the second sentence of para. 2 makes it clear that any limitation of the exclusive rights granted under para. 1 by national legislation does not affect the author's moral rights, art. 6bis BC. **(d) European legislation.** The European legislature has made use of para. 2 only for simultaneous and unaltered cable retransmissions. Art. 9(1) of the Satellite and Cable Directive provides for mandatory exercise of the exclusive cable retransmission right by collecting societies, and art. 9(3) of the same Directive allows EU Member States to provide that when a rightholder authorizes the initial transmission within its territory of a work or other protected subject matter, he or she shall be deemed to have agreed not to exercise his or her cable retransmission rights on an individual basis but to exercise them in accordance with the provisions of this Directive. However, no such limitation exists with regard to the general exclusive public communication right granted in art. 3(1) of the Information Society Directive.

4. Ephemeral recordings (para. 3). (a) General rule. Broadcasting organizations which have to license the rights granted to authors under para. 1 may also wish, or even have to, make a recording of the broadcast. In this respect, para. 3 contains the clarification that absent a contractual provision to this effect, the grant of the rights described in para. 1 does not cover the right to reproduce the work broadcast. **(b) Exceptions.** However, para. 3 contains two possibilities to deviate from this principle. Firstly, Member States are free to deviate with regard to so-called ephemeral recordings, that is, recordings which are only kept for a short period and deleted thereafter, provided that such ephemeral recordings are made by the broadcaster's own facilities and exclusively used for its own broadcasts. The reason for this exception is that broadcasters should be able to make and use recorded material for their broadcasts. Second, Member States may provide, in their national legislation, that recordings thus made may be preserved in official archives, provided the recordings are of an exceptional documentary character. Again, it has to be decided by national courts how long recordings can be kept in order to be still considered 'ephemeral', and which record of a broadcast has an exceptional documentary character. It should be noted that these exceptions also apply where Member States have introduced compulsory licensing according to para. 2. **(c) European legislation.** The European legislature has made use of both possibilities in art. 5(2)(d) of the Information Society Directive. For the scope of this provision see *DR and TV2 Danmark* (ECJ)). Moreover, recital 41 of the said Directive states that when applying this exception it is understood that a broadcaster's own facilities include those of a person acting on behalf of and under the responsibility of the broadcasting organization.

[Certain rights in literary works]

Article 11ter

(1) Authors of literary works shall enjoy the exclusive right of authorizing:
- **(i)** the public recitation of their works, including such public recitation by any means or process;
- **(ii)** any communication to the public of the recitation of their works.

(2) Authors of literary works shall enjoy, during the full term of their rights in the original works, the same rights with respect to translations thereof.

1. General. As already stated, for historic reasons, the BC does not contain an all-encompassing right to public communication of protected works, as that has now been formulated in art. 8 WCT. Rather, the right is granted in separate provisions to different groups of authors and with regard to different forms of public communication (for details see art. 11, note 1). **(a) Para. 1.** Art. 11ter(1)(i) and (ii) BC grants to authors of literary works the right of public recitation and of communication to the public of a recitation. The provision mirrors art. 11 BC which regulates public performance of dramatic and dramatico-musical works. Both public performance and public recital are sub-categories of live presentations. For additional comment see notes to art. 11 BC. **(b) Para. 2.** Para. 2 makes it clear that authors also enjoy the same rights granted in para. 1 with regard to translations of their works. For the translation right itself see art. 8 BC. **(c) Exceptions.** For exceptions see art. 11, note 1(c).

2. European legislation. In Europe, the rights granted to authors under art. 11ter BC have been harmonized under the broadly defined right of communication of works in art. 3(1) of the Information Society Directive. For optional exceptions under European law see art. 5(3) of the Information Society Directive.

[Right of adaptation, arrangement and other alteration]
Article 12

Authors of literary or artistic works shall enjoy the exclusive right of authorizing adaptations, arrangements and other alterations of their works.

1. General. (a) Adaptation right. Art. 12 BC contains the exclusive adaptation right. The exclusive translation right is separately granted in art. 8 BC. **(b) Definition.** Art. 12 BC covers any alteration of a work protected by copyright, even if it is only of minor nature. The exact definition of what constitutes an adaptation for the purpose of copyright and when use of a protected work is free and therefore not subject to authorization, is left to the Member States. **(c) Limitations.** Although art. 12 BC does not itself provide for any limitations to the translation right, a limitation exists according to art. 10bis(2) BC (use made of works in the course of news reporting which does not exceed what is justified by the informatory purpose). Additional limitations are implicitly contained in art. 2bis BC (optional limitations to the protection of certain speeches and certain uses of lectures and addresses); art. 10bis(1) BC (limitation with regard to articles published in newspapers or periodicals on current economic, political or religious topics, and of broadcast works of the same character); and art. 9(2) (exceptions to the reproduction right). Moreover, any alterations necessary in the course of an authorized use are also permitted. However, alterations made under an exception may not exceed the limits set by the protection of moral rights in art. 6bis BC. **(d) Copyrightability of adaptations.** According to art. 2(3) BC, adaptations are themselves subject to copyright if they satisfy the criterion of originality.

2. European legislation. In Europe, the adaptation right has only been harmonized with regard to computer programs in art. 4(1)(b) of the Computer Programs Directive, and to databases in art. 5(b) of the Database Directive (as to the extent to which computer programs and databases are covered by the BC at all, see art. 2, note 2(c)). However, the adaptation right is found in all national copyright laws of the EU Member States.

[Possible limitation of the right of recording of musical works and any words pertaining thereto]

Article 13

(1) Each country of the Union may impose for itself reservations and conditions on the exclusive right granted to the author of a musical work and to the author of any words, the recording of which together with the musical work has already been authorized by the latter, to authorize the sound recording of that musical work, together with such words, if any; but all such reservations and conditions shall apply only in the countries which have imposed them and shall not, in any circumstances, be prejudicial to the rights of these authors to obtain equitable remuneration which, in the absence of agreement, shall be fixed by competent authority.

(2) Recordings of musical works made in a country of the Union in accordance with Article 13 (3) of the Conventions signed at Rome on June 2, 1928, and at Brussels on June 26, 1948, may be reproduced in that country without the permission of the author of the musical work until a date two years after that country becomes bound by this Act.

(3) Recordings made in accordance with paragraphs (1) and (2) of this Article and imported without permission from the parties concerned into a country where they are treated as infringing recordings shall be liable to seizure.

1. General. Art. 13 BC allows Member States to provide for a compulsory licence to make physical copies of musical works and accompanying lyrics once the respective authors have authorized a first recording of both the music and the accompanying words. However, the authors must obtain equitable remuneration which is to be agreed upon by the parties, or, in the absence of such agreement, determined by a competent authority (para. 1). Para. 2 contains a transitional provision, and para. 3 makes it clear that the effects of any compulsory licence granted according to art. 13(1) BC are limited to the territory of the country which has availed itself of the possibility of licences under art. 13 BC.

2. Compulsory licence (para. 1). (a) Restrictions on the exclusive rights. According to art. 13(1) BC, Member States are free to provide in their national copyright legislation for reservations and conditions limiting the exclusive right granted to the author of a musical work and to the author of any words, once these authors have authorized the recording. These restrictions apply to the 'authorization' of the sound recording, that is, to both the reproduction right and the distribution right with regard to copies of sound recordings produced under a restriction in accordance with art. 13(1) BC. The restriction does not, however, extend to the public communication right. Rather, any public performance of a sound recording made under art. 13(1) BC has to be separately licensed. One might ask whether national schemes according to art. 13 BC are still permitted for EU Member States after the EU has harmonized the exclusive reproduction right in art. 2(a) of the Information Society Directive, without expressly providing for an exception similar to art. 13 BC. However, it can be argued that the exclusive reproduction right remains intact, at least as long as national law only allows for the possibility of a compulsory licence rather than eliminating the exclusive rights altogether by the imposition of a statutory licence (it should be noted that, for example, the German legislature has expressly preserved its compulsory licensing scheme under art. 13 BC when implementing of the Information Society Directive). Another question is whether the three-step test of art. 13 TRIPS/art. 5(5) of the Information Society Directive will have to be applied to licensing schemes provided for in national law under art. 13 BC, since although such schemes are not limitations in the strict sense, they nevertheless conflict with normal exploitation and unreasonably prejudice the legitimate interests of rightholders in much the same way as true limitations. But TRIPS did not abolish art. 13 BC per se. **(b) Equitable remuneration.** In any case, the authors of protected music and protected words must obtain equitable remuneration which is to be agreed upon by the parties, or, in the absence of such agreement, determined by a competent authority. **(c) Effects limited to national territory.** In accordance with a general rule, the effects of any compulsory licence under a national scheme adopted by a BC Member State according to art. 13(1) BC are limited to the territory of that particular State. Therefore, as a rule, copies made under art. 13(1) BC that are imported into another BC Member State without the authorization of the authors of the music and the accompanying lyrics have to be treated as illegal copies in that other State (see para. 3) and can therefore not be imported into another BC Member State without the permission of the holders of the rights in both the music and the words embodied in the sound recording. Of course, this result conflicts with the principle of free movement of goods (art. 28 EC Treaty) and the question is whether within the EU the principle of exhaustion as formulated by the ECJ (see cases *Deutsche Grammophon* and *Musik-Vertrieb Membran)* applies in such cases, or whether the separation of territories resulting from art. 13 BC must be accepted as long as the EU legislator has not harmonized the matter. On the one hand, at least in cases where national law requires the consent of the authors under a compulsory licensing scheme, it can be argued that exhaustion does apply, in particular since authors have received a mandatory remuneration and hence have been duly compensated. On the other hand, different compulsory licensing schemes could be regarded as non-harmonized areas of copyright so that the negative effects on the free movement of goods have to be tolerated (see cases ECJ *Patricia* and *Christiansen)).*

3. Transitional measures (para. 2). The transitional measures contained in para. 2 only applied to those States which were bound to the Rome or Brussels version of the BC of 1928 and 1948 respectively. Once those States became bound by the Stockholm Act of the BC of 1967, they could allow recordings of musical works which had been made in a country of the Union in accordance with art. 13 (3) of the former versions of the BC be free to be reproduced for another two years after the respective country became bound by the Stockholm version of the BC. Now that all EU Members are bound by the Stockholm and the later Paris versions of the BC, the transitory provision has lost its significance.

4. Seizure on importation of copies made without the author's permission (para. 3). Since the effects of any restriction to the exclusive right according to paras. 1 and 2 are limited to the territory of the State which in its national law has made use of art. 13 BC, copies of recordings made under art. 13(1) BC in such a State will be regarded as infringing copies in other Member States which have not adopted similar restrictions (see note 2, also regarding the issue of EU-wide exhaustion). According to para. 3, such copies that are regarded as infringing in another State shall be liable to seizure. This is superfluous insofar as it refers to the remedies of the State of protection. Likewise, the prescription of seizure of infringing copies as a minimum remedy is provided for in art. 16(1) BC.

[Cinematographic and related rights]

Article 14

(1) Authors of literary or artistic works shall have the exclusive right of authorizing:
> (i) the cinematographic adaptation and reproduction of these works, and the distribution of the works thus adapted or reproduced;
> (ii) the public performance and communication to the public by wire of the works thus adapted or reproduced.

(2) The adaptation into any other artistic form of a cinematographic production derived from literary or artistic works shall, without prejudice to the authorization of the author of the cinematographic production, remain subject to the authorization of the authors of the original works.

(3) The provisions of Article 13 (1) shall not apply.

1. General. (a) Contents. Art. 14 BC contains the rights of authors of literary or artistic works, that is, of all authors protected by the BC, with regard to the cinematographic adaptation of their works, the reproduction of their pre-existing works in films, the distribution (para. 1(1)) and the public performance and communication to the public by wire of these films (para. 1(ii)). Also, authors enjoy a right to authorize further adaptations of their works contained in cinematographic productions (para. 2). The application of a compulsory mechanical licence to the music incorporated in a film is expressly excluded (para. 3). Today, the rights granted by art. 14 BC appear as sub-cases of the general adaptation (art. 12 BC) and reproduction rights (art. 9(1) BC). However, the historic presence of art. 14 BC may be explained by the fact that it dates from times when, because of the format change which the adaptation of copyright works in a film required, such adaptations were not necessarily regarded as adaptations within the traditional understanding. The protection of holders of copyright in the cinematographic work itself, as well as issues of authorship in cinematographic works, are dealt with in art. 14bis BC. **(b) Exceptions.** Since art. 14 BC is a mere clarification or sub-set of the rights already granted to authors by arts. 9(1) and 12 BC, Member States are free to subject the rights set out in art. 14 BC to the exceptions that are possible under those other articles.

2. Rights with regard to cinematographic reproductions (para. 1). (a) Authors of pre-existing works. Although it is not expressly mentioned in art. 14 BC, this provision is only concerned with authors of pre-existing works, that is, of works that were already in existence when the film was made and that were not created for use as part of the cinematographic production (for a definition see art. 14bis, note 3(b)). It does not make any difference whether the film for which the copyright works have been adapted or into which they have been incorporated qualifies for protection as a work (art. 14 speaks of cinematographic 'productions'). **(b) Para. 1(i).** This provision describes two rights: firstly, the right to adapt and reproduce pre-existing works – such as novels, music not expressly written for a film, stage design in the filming of a theatrical performance, or photographic works and pre-existing film sequences incorporated into a film – in cinematographic works; and second, the right to authorize distribution of these works adapted for, or incorporated in, cinematographic productions, thus granting a limited right of first release. **(c) Para. 1(ii).** This provision grants to authors of pre-existing works a right to public performance and a right to communicate these works to the public by wire. This is a mere repetition with regard to authors of dramatic, dramatico-musical and musical works who enjoy the exclusive right to authorize granted by art. 11(1)(ii) BC, and to authors of literary works who enjoy this right also by virtue of art. 11ter(1)(ii) BC. However, the broadcasting right is granted to all authors in art. 11bis BC (regarding the historically unsystematic regulation of the public communication rights in the BC, see art. 11, note 1), and can therefore be withheld from authors with regard to cinematographic reproductions and adaptations of their works, or made subject to compulsory licensing.

3. Adaptation of cinematographic productions (para. 2). Para. 2 clarifies that the adaptation right also covers the right of further adaptation of film productions which incorporate the pre-existing work. This right also is a sub-set of the general adaptation right of art. 12 BC.

4. No compulsory licenses (para. 3). By declaring art. 13(1) BC to be not applicable to the adaptation of protected works to films, the BC clarifies that music, including accompanying works the recording of which has already been authorized, cannot be used for the cinematographic work under a compulsory licensing scheme.

[Special provisions concerning cinematographic works]

Article 14bis

(1) Without prejudice to the copyright in any work which may have been adapted or reproduced, a cinematographic work shall be protected as an original work. The owner of copyright in a cinematographic work shall enjoy the same rights as the author of an original work, including the rights referred to in the preceding Article.

(2)

(a) Ownership of copyright in a cinematographic work shall be a matter for legislation in the country where protection is claimed.

(b) However, in the countries of the Union which, by legislation, include among the owners of copyright in a cinematographic work authors who have brought contributions to the making of the work, such authors, if they have undertaken to bring such contributions, may not, in the absence of any contrary or special stipulation, object to the reproduction, distribution, public performance, communication to the public by wire, broadcasting or any other communication to the public, or to the subtitling or dubbing of texts, of the work.

(c) The question whether or not the form of the undertaking referred to above should, for the application of the preceding subparagraph (b), be in a written agreement or a written act of the same effect shall be a matter for the legislation of the country where the maker of the cinematographic work has his headquarters or habitual residence. However, it shall be a matter for the legislation of the country of the Union where protection is claimed to provide that the said undertaking shall be in a written agreement or a written act of the same effect. The countries whose legislation so provides shall notify the Director General by means of a written declaration, which will be immediately communicated by him to all the other countries of the Union.

(d) By 'contrary or special stipulation' is meant any restrictive condition which is relevant to the aforesaid undertaking.

(3) Unless the national legislation provides to the contrary, the provisions of paragraph (2)(b) above shall not be applicable to authors of

scenarios, dialogues and musical works created for the making of the cinematographic work, or to the principal director thereof. However, those countries of the Union whose legislation does not contain rules providing for the application of the said paragraph (2)(b) to such director shall notify the Director General by means of a written declaration, which will be immediately communicated by him to all the other countries of the Union.

1. General. (a) Contents. Whereas the rights of authors of pre-existing works which are adapted to cinematographic works are regulated in art. 14 BC, art. 14bis BC contains additional special provisions concerning the rights relating to cinematographic works themselves. According to para. 1, the owners of copyright in a cinematographic work enjoy the same protection as authors of other works, including the rights granted in art. 14 BC. Because film authorship differed, and still differs, widely in national law (in essence, national laws provide for original authorship of the film producer, legal transfer of exploitation rights by way of a cessio legis to the film producer, rebuttable presumption of transfer of exploitation right, and general rules on authorship), paras. 2 and 3 neither grant minimum rights to film authors nor regulate copyright contract law with regard to cinematographic works. Rather, paras. 2 and 3 only contain certain minimum rights for film producers with regard to the exercise of the exclusive rights and to court actions with regard to rights in the cinematographic works. These rights apply irrespective of whether the film producer is considered an author of the cinematographic work under national law. However, despite their detail, the provisions are of relatively little practical importance. **(b) European legislation.** Even within the EU, authorship with regard to cinematographic works is harmonized only to a limited extent. Art. 2(1) of the Term Directive only prescribes that the principal director of a cinematographic or audiovisual work shall be considered to be its author or one of its authors. This entails that the EU Member States can no longer invoke art. 14bis BC in order to justifiy the exclusion of the principal director from film authorship (*Luksan* (ECJ), also to the entitlement and non-automatic transferability of the principal director to the claim for adequate remuneration). However, Member States are explicitly free to designate other co-authors. Moreover, with regard to calculating the term of protection of a cinematographic or audiovisual work, art. 2(2) of the Term Directive names the following persons, irrespective of whether these persons are designated co-authors by national law: the principal director, the author of the screenplay, the author of the dialogue and the composer of music specifically created for use in the cinematographic or audiovisual work.

2. Assimilation to other works (para. 1). (a) Sentence 1. According to para. 1 sentence 1, cinematographic works are to be protected as original works. This seems now superfluous in view of the fact that since the Brussels Revision Conference in 1948, cinematographic works are already explicitly covered by art. 2(1) BC. Also, it is only a clarification of a general copyright principle that copyright in a cinematographic work does in no way abridge copyright in any work which may have been adapted or reproduced by the cinematographic work. **(b) Sentence 2.** According to para. 1 sentence 2, the owners of copyright in a cinematographic work enjoy the same protection as authors of other works, including the rights granted in art. 14 BC. The BC purposely uses the term 'owners of copyright' rather than 'authors' because the rights granted under art. 14bis(1) BC are granted to the film producer irrespective of whether he or she has rights of his or her own or derivative rights. Enjoyment of the 'same rights' also means that the same exceptions and limitations apply, such as the possibility to provide for compulsory licensing for broadcasting according to art. 11bis(2)BC.

3. Ownership; limitation of certain rights of certain contributors (para. 2). (a) General. Para. 2, together with para. 3, seeks, on the one hand, to establish a balanced and rather complicated compromise between the interests of Member States in regulating authorship of cinematographic works, and, on the other hand, the needs of film producers to exploit the cinematographic works without being burdened by too many exclusive rights of persons who have contributed to the film. Although film producers are not explicitly mentioned in the text of para. 2, they are the intended beneficiaries of the paragraph. Art. 14bis BC does not contain a definition of who is to be considered a film producer, but art. 15(2) BC contains a rebuttable presumption in favour of the natural or legal person whose name appears on a cinematographic work in the usual manner. **(b) No harmonization of authorship.** Firstly, para. 2(a) BC explicitly leaves the regulation of authorship to the national law of the country where protection is claimed. Since the BC is not concerned with the protection which national law accords to its own nationals, the reference to regulation by national law means that foreign authors are subject to the national rules of authorship with regard to cinematographic works in the country where protection is claimed. **(c) Limitation of rights of contributors.** Second, however, in order to strengthen the position of the film producer, para. 2(b) then provides for certain limitations on the rights of authors who have undertaken to contribute to the making of the cinematographic work, in countries with national legislation that treats such contributors as owners of copyright in a cinematographic work, provided the relevant undertaking satisfies the requirements laid down in para. 2(c). Such authors may not object, on the basis of their legal status, to the reproduction, distribution, public performance, communication to the public by wire, broadcasting or any other communication to the public, or to the subtitling or dubbing of texts of the cinematographic work. Of course, the parties may always deviate from this general rule by way of 'contrary or special stipulation' as defined in para. 2(d). Moreover, according to para. 3, para. 2(b) does not apply at all to authors of scenarios, dialogues and musical works created for the making of the cinematographic work, or to the principal director thereof, unless national legislation provides to the contrary. This leaves, as authors who have brought 'contributions' to the cinematographic production, all authors whose contribution has been 'created for the making of the cinematographic work, as opposed to authors of pre-existing works who are covered by art. 14 BC. **(d) Form of undertaking.** Para. 2(c) regulates the form in which the undertaking of a contributor must have been made, in order to trigger the rule of para. 2(b) in favour of the producer. Para. 2(c) contains a deviation from the universal rule of international conflict of laws, according to which the form is governed by the law of the place where the legal transaction has been made. Rather, the question of form – 'a written agreement or a written act of the same effect' – is governed by the law of the country where the maker of the cinematographic work has his or her headquarters or habitual residence. But any Member State may stipulate in its own law that a written agreement or a written act of the same effect is required even in cases where the law of the country where the maker of the cinematographic work has his or her headquarters or habitual residence requires fewer formalities. However, the Director General of WIPO must be notified of such deviating legislation.

4. Exception to para. 2(b) (para. 3). According to para. 3, the rule of para. 2(b), which benefits film producers by limiting the rights of authors who contribute to the making of a film with regard to the exploitation of the cinematographic work, does not apply to authors of scenarios, dialogues and musical works created for the making of the cinematographic work, or to the principal director thereof, unless national legislation provides to the contrary. In the case of the director of a cinematographic work, however, the Director General of WIPO must be notified of the absence of a rule providing for the application of para. 2(b). It is unclear whether notification is a necessary condition for the legal rule to apply, or whether failure to notify is a mere violation of international law.

['Droit de suite' in works of arts and manuscripts]

Article 14ter

(1) The author, or after his death the persons or institutions authorized by national legislation, shall, with respect to original works of art and original manuscripts of writers and composers, enjoy the inalienable right to an interest in any sale of the work subsequent to the first transfer by the author of the work.

(2) The protection provided by the preceding paragraph may be claimed in a country of the Union only if legislation in the country to which the author belongs so permits, and to the extent permitted by the country where this protection is claimed.

(3) The procedure for collection and the amounts shall be matters for determination by national legislation.

1. General. (a) Droit de suite/resale royalty right. Art. 14ter BC, which was introduced at the Brussels Revision Conference of 1948, provides for the so-called droit de suite or resale royalty right. This right, which is limited to original works of art and original manuscripts of writers and composers, is not a right with regard to the use of a protected work, but a right to obtain a share of the proceeds of any sale of the original of the work after the initial sale. The idea is that authors can only sell these originals once and that at the first sale they often obtain a remuneration which does not properly reflect the inherent future value of the artwork or manuscript in question. **(b) Optional minimum right.** Contrary to most other minimum rights granted by the BC, the droit de suite/resale royalty right is not obligatory (para. 2, second part), and the conditions for collection and the amounts to be paid are to be determined by national legislation (para. 3). **(c) Material reciprocity.** Moreover, the droit de suite/resale royalty is subject to material reciprocity (para. 2, first part), that is, a BC author only has a claim to the granting of the droit de suite/resale royalty right which another BC country grants to its own nationals, if the author's home country also grants the droit de suite/resale royalty. **(d) European legislation.** In the EU, before its enlargement, 11 of the 15 Member States (including notably Belgium, France and Germany) had introduced in their national copyright legislation a droit de suite/resale royalty right, but other Member States (notably the United Kingdom and the Netherlands) had not. However, in spite of fears that the auction market for works of modern art might move to Switzerland or the USA, the EU has harmonized the droit de suite/resale royalty right by the Resale Right Directive. This Directive provides for the mandatory introduction of the droit de suite/resale royalty right and it harmonizes the works to be covered and the rates to be applied. The harmonization avoids the possibility that, based on the principle of non-discrimination (art. 18 TFEU), authors from countries without a droit de suite/resale royalty right could claim the benefits of the droit de suite/resale royalty right in a country that grants the right, whereas authors from the latter country could not claim a droit de suite/resale royalty right in the former country. Therefore, within the EU, art. 14ter BC will be limited in its application to non-EU BC authors and to non-BC authors whose countries are bound to arts. 1-21 BC by way of art. 9(1) TRIPS. For further details see the commentary on the Resale Right Directive.

2. Content (para. 1). (a) Persons entitled/works covered. Under art. 14bis BC, only the authors of original works of art and original manuscripts (whether created by writers or composers) benefit from the droit de suite/resale royalty right. Art. 14bis BC does not, however, mention photographs. But since art. 14ter BC is an optional minimum right, Member States are free to provide that the droit de suite/resale royalty right also covers additional works such as artistic photographs or photographic works in general. If granted, the right shall be transferable to the persons or institutions authorized by national law. These may be the heirs (for the EU see *Fundación Gala-Salvador Dalí and VEGAP* (ECJ): designation of the heirs left to the

Member States), but a Member State is also free to collect the droit de suite/ resale royalty right for the benefit of a public institution. **(b) Original work of art or manuscript.** The droit de suite/resale royalty right only applies to the original of an artwork or to original manuscripts of writers and composers, but not, however, to copies thereof. In the case of multiple originals (bronze casts, serial editions etc.) it is not always easy to distinguish originals from copies, but this is a matter for national legislation. **(c) Interest in any sale of the work subsequent to the first transfer.** The droit de suite/ resale royalty right does not apply to the first sale of the work in question, but only to any sale after the first sale, but then it applies even if these subsequent sales take place at short intervals. Moreover, the author also participates in the proceeds of the sale if the work in question is sold at no gain and even if it is sold at a loss. In order to give rise to a payment on the basis of the droit de suite/resale royalty right, the transaction must be a sale, that is, the former owner must part with all of his or her property interest in the original object. Therefore, rental, lending and leasing do not trigger the droit de suite/ resale royalty right. Finally, art. 14ter BC does not limit the droit de suite/ resale royalty right to the sale by professional art dealers and auction houses, but covers also private sales. However, since Member States are not bound to introduce the droit de suite/resale royalty right at all (see note 3), they are also free to exclude private sales.

3. Optional right and material reciprocity (para. 2). (a) Optional right. Para. 2 second part leaves Member States the entire freedom to introduce a droit de suite/resale royalty. It must then also be permissible for Member States to introduce a limited form of droit de suite/resale royalty right. Similarly, since the introduction of a droit de suite/resale royalty is optional, it is also permissible for national legislation to set a minimum resale price for the droit de suite to apply, thus excluding works of only little monetary value from the droit de suite/resale royalty right. Also, national law may require that the droit de suite/resale royalty right only applies if the sale takes place within the national territory, irrespective of the seller's nationality and the origin of the artwork (see, for example, *Folgerecht bei Auslandsbezug* (Germany)). **(b) Material reciprocity.** Para. 2 first part makes the droit de suite/ resale royalty right for foreigners dependent on the granting of a droit de suite/resale royalty right in the author's home country (material reciprocity). However, on the one hand it seems that the mere existence of such a right in principle would not be sufficient. Rather, the criterion of material reciprocity requires that the droit de suite/resale royalty right can be enforced and the sums be effectively claimed. On the other hand, it cannot be a requirement of national law that the droit de suite/resale royalty right in the home country of the author making the claim provides for exactly the same rates as the droit de suite/resale royalty right in the country where the money is claimed. Another question is whether, in the case of substantive reciprocity, the country where the droit de suite/resale royalty right is claimed by a foreign author can limit the scope of this right to the substantive protection granted by the author's home country, or whether it is then bound by the principle of national treatment to grant to the foreign author the droit de suite/resale royalty right in the same way as it does to its own nationals. The BC is silent on this point, but some courts (see, e.g., case *Jeannot* (Germany)) as well as some authors have suggested that in such cases the principle of national treatment should apply. Indeed, in view of the fact that the granting of additional rights outside of the BC upon material reciprocity is always possible, art. 14ter BC would otherwise be superfluous.

4. Procedure (para. 3). It is a matter for national legislation to regulate both the amounts due under the national droit de suite/resale royalty scheme and the procedure for their collection. It is thus permissible that national legislation fixes the amounts due. This includes the possibility that the amount to be paid can decrease as the resale price obtained becomes higher. Also, national legislation may provide for a cap on the highest amount to be paid. Moreover, mandatory collection by a collecting society, such as in Germany, is permissible under para. 3. For the freedom of Member States in the EU to regulate details of the payments due as well as for the freedom of the parties involved to decide who – seller or buyer – shall ultimately bear, in whole or in part, the cost of the royalty, see *Christie's France* (ECJ).

[Right to enforce protected rights]
Article 15

(1) In order that the author of a literary or artistic work protected by this Convention shall, in the absence of proof to the contrary, be regarded as such, and consequently be entitled to institute infringement proceedings in the countries of the Union, it shall be sufficient for his name to appear on the work in the usual manner. This paragraph shall be applicable even if this name is a pseudonym, where the pseudonym adopted by the author leaves no doubt as to his identity.

The person or body corporate whose name appears on a cinematographic work in the usual manner shall, in the absence of proof to the contrary, be presumed to be the maker of the said work.

In the case of anonymous and pseudonymous works, other than those referred to in paragraph (1) above, the publisher whose name appears on the work shall, in the absence of proof to the contrary, be deemed to represent the author, and in this capacity he shall be entitled to protect and enforce the author's rights. The provisions of this paragraph shall cease to apply when the author reveals his identity and establishes his claim to authorship of the work.

(4)

(a) In the case of unpublished works where the identity of the author is unknown, but where there is every ground to presume that he is a national of a country of the Union, it shall be a

matter for legislation in that country to designate the competent authority which shall represent the author and shall be
entitled to protect and enforce his rights in the countries of the
Union.

(b) Countries of the Union which make such designation under
the terms of this provision shall notify the Director General by
means of a written declaration giving full information concerning the authority thus designated. The Director General shall
at once communicate this declaration to all other countries of
the Union.

1. General. This provision obliges Member States to provide for certain
presumptions to the benefit of authors (para. 1), filmmakers (para. 2), publishers (para. 3) and national folklore authorities (para. 4). These presumptions
are of a procedural nature rather than being matters of substantive law. They
concern the presumption of authorship and the identity of the maker of a
film, and the presumption to be entitled to exercise the rights granted and
to institute infringement proceedings. If national law provides for more far-
reaching rules in favour of the beneficiaries named in art. 15 BC, then those
beneficiaries can rely on those more far-reaching national rules according to
art. 19 BC.

2. Contents. Art. 15 BC is mostly self-explanatory and needs little further
comment. **(a) Name.** A 'name' is any designation which clearly identifies
a certain person as author or maker of a cinematographic work. **(b) Usual
manner.** It is up to the court in the country of protection to determine what
is the 'usual manner' of the appearance of the name on the work (see, for
example, *Bora Bora* (Germany): the presumption does not require that the
copyright notice be affixed on a printed copy of the music and lyrics before
the first publication of the work). However, what is decisive is the practice in
the country of origin of the work, since it is the practices in this country which
will have led the author to affix his or her name to the work in a particular
way. **(c) Be regarded as; be presumed.** The presumptions contained in art.
15(1) and (2) BC only concern the initial authorship/identity as the maker of
a cinematographic work, not, however, any succession of title, originality or
other criterion for copyright protection. If several authors are named, it is to
be presumed that they are co-authors (see *Bora Bora* (Germany)). **(d) Proof
to the contrary.** It is a question for the law applicable at the place where
protection is sought (lex fori) to determine the conditions which must be
fulfilled in order to rebut the presumptions of art. 15 BC.

3. European legislation. In the EU, the presumptions of authorship and
of holding rights related to copyright have been harmonized by art. 5 of the
Enforcement Directive. However, at present no harmonization exists within
the EU regarding the representation of the authors of anonymous and pseudonymous works (art. 15(3) BC), nor has the EU regulated the exercise of

rights in the case of certain unpublished works of unknown authorship (art. 15(4) BC). Although it does not directly relate to art. 15 BC, it should be noted that the Orphan Works Directive allows for the digitization and making available of works where none of the rightholders is identified or, even if one or more of the rightholders is identified, none is located despite a diligent search.

[Infringing copies]

Article 16

(1) Infringing copies of a work shall be liable to seizure in any country of the Union where the work enjoys legal protection.

(2) The provisions of the preceding paragraph shall also apply to re-productions coming from a country where the work is not protected, or has ceased to be protected.

(3) The seizure shall take place in accordance with the legislation of each country.

1. General. Art. 16 BC is one of the rare provisions in the BC which mandates remedies in cases of copyright infringement. This provision obliges Member States to provide for the seizure of infringing copies of works which enjoy copyright protection in the particular Member State where protection is sought. This obligation extends to copies which have been produced in countries where the work in question does not enjoy copyright protection or where protection has already run out (principle of territoriality). Art. 16(2) BC thus partially recognizes a distribution right which is otherwise not granted by the BC. Moreover, art. 13(3) BC explicitly contains the right of seizure of recordings which have been manufactured abroad under a compulsory licensing scheme as described by arts. 13(1) and (2) BC and imported without permission from the parties concerned into a country where they are treated as infringing recordings. However, art. 16 BC does not deal with the question of exhaustion in cases of parallel importation, that is, where copies put on the market by the rightholder or with his or her consent in a foreign country are imported into the country where protection is sought. This much-debated question is not addressed by the BC, and it has deliberately been left open in art. 6 TRIPS. Regarding this issue, the ECJ has established the rule of Union-wide exhaustion of the distribution right once a work has been put into circulation within the European Union either by the rightholder him or herself or with his or her consent (see *Deutsche Grammophon* (ECJ) and *Musik-Vertrieb Membran* (ECJ)); however, no exhaustion takes place with regard to the right of public communication (see *Coditel I* (ECJ); see, however also *UsedSoft* (ECJ) for a case where the inline download of a computer program has not been considered by the ECJ as an immaterial communication, but rather as a material sale, and also art. 3(3) of the Information Society

Directive). But according to art. 4(2) of the Information Society Directive, no such exhaustion takes place when copies have first been put onto the market outside of the European Union.

2. Seizure. Seizure means preliminary sequestration by way of temporary injunction or order for receivership or a similar provisional remedy, not final confiscation. Member States are free to define the details of this remedy. The provision is a minimum provision. This means that Member States are free to adopt measures for final confiscation and destruction of illegal copies. In this respect, it should be noted that arts. 50 and 51 et seq. TRIPS contain more detailed minimum requirements regarding provisional measures and border measures.

3. Applicable law. According to para. 3, the seizure shall take place in accordance with the legislation of each country. This is in line with the rule laid down art. 5(2) BC, according to which the means of redress afforded to the author to protect his or her rights shall be governed exclusively by the laws of the country where protection is claimed.

4. European legislation. (a) EU legislation. In accordance with the requirements laid down in arts. 51 et seq. TRIPS, the EU has regulated border measures in its Regulation No. 608/2013 on Customs Enforcement (earlier versions were Regulation (EC) No. 1383/2003 and No. 3295/94, as amended by Regulation (EC) No. 241/1999,). Moreover, art. 9(1)(b) of the Enforcement Directive contains obligations with regard to provisional seizure. Aside from this, other Directives contained provisions aimed at harmonizing national law with regard to seizure, notably art. 7 of the Computer Programs Directive and art. 8(2) of the Information Society Directive. **(b) National legislation of EU Member States.** In addition, EU Member States have their own national rules governing border measures as well as national rules regarding seizure of infringing copies.

[Possibility of control of circulation, presentation and exhibition of works]

Article 17

The provisions of this Convention cannot in any way affect the right of the Government of each country of the Union to permit, to control, or to prohibit, by legislation or regulation, the circulation, presentation, or exhibition of any work or production in regard to which the competent authority may find it necessary to exercise that right.

1. General. This article expressly recognizes the right of each Member State to control or even prohibit the circulation, presentation, or exhibition of a work protected by copyright under the BC in cases where a Member State finds it necessary to do so. The provision dates back to the original version of

1886 and can be found in older bilateral treaties. On the one hand, it merely states the obvious principle that copyright does not prevent Member States from enforcing their national public policy and that authors of copyright works must abide by national laws regulating issues such as pornography, blasphemy, libel and slander, race-hatred speech, incitation to war and the like, including restrictions resulting from national tax, customs and currency control laws as well as antitrust legislation. On the other hand, the power in question is that of censorship. Although censorship is contrary to the principle of free speech and the exercise of both the author's moral rights and exploitation rights, the obligations of the BC can therefore not be used to force Member States to alleviate or even abandon such practices.

2. Acts covered. (a) Permission, control and prohibition of copyright works. According to art. 17 Member States remain free to regulate the details of the exploitation of copyright works. They also can subject the exploitation of copyright works to special permission or prohibit it altogether. However, such permission must not be a 'formality' within the meaning of art. 5(2) BC. It is another question whether art. 17 BC goes as far as allowing Member States to withhold copyright protection altogether from certain works which the Member State considers contrary to public policy, as some countries do with regard to works of a pornographic nature. **(b) By legislation or regulation.** Legislation means the laws made by the Member State's principle legislative body. Regulation refers to administrative decisions based on national legislation. **(c) Circulation, presentation, or exhibition.** The authors of copyright works cannot, on the basis of the BC, invoke their copyright against any restriction regarding the public dissemination of their work. However, other substantive rights such as the making of translations, adaptations, reproductions and recordings are not covered by art. 17 BC. **(d) Which national authorities may find necessary.** Member States have a far-reaching discretion in regulating their public policy. Even a complete ban on the exploitation of certain material (such as some or all pornographic material in many countries, or Hitler's 'Mein Kampf' in Germany, the copyright of which, however, runs out at the end of 2015) is not in violation of the BC.

3. Acts not covered. However, in spite of the term 'to permit', the provision does not allow Member States to cut back the mandatory minimum rights granted by the BC nor to remove authors' rights for reasons of public policy, since that would amount to a total withdrawal of the minimum protection to be granted under the BC. The same is true with regard to any partial removal of such rights, even in the form of compulsory licences, which goes beyond the scope of limitations and exceptions permitted under the BC. Art. 17 BC cannot serve as the basis to force authors to publish or use their works. But treaty obligations can temporarily be suspended in times of war with regard to authors from enemy countries.

[Works existing on Convention's entry into force]

Article 18

(1) This Convention shall apply to all works which, at the moment of its coming into force, have not yet fallen into the public domain in the country of origin through the expiry of the term of protection.

(2) If, however, through the expiry of the term of protection which was previously granted, a work has fallen into the public domain of the country where protection is claimed, that work shall not be protected anew.

(3) The application of this principle shall be subject to any provisions contained in special conventions to that effect existing or to be concluded between countries of the Union. In the absence of such provisions, the respective countries shall determine, each in so far as it is concerned, the conditions of application of this principle.

(4) The preceding provisions shall also apply in the case of new accessions to the Union and to cases in which protection is extended by the application of Article 7 or by the abandonment of reservations.

1. General. (a) Transitional rules. Art. 18 BC contains the transitional provisions for entry of the BC into force. The transitional provisions play a role in cases of new accessions to the BC (para. 4), or if a state becomes bound for the first time to arts. 1-21 BC by way of its accession to the WTO and hence the TRIPS Agreement (see arts. II(2) WTO-Agreement, 9(1) and 70(2) TRIPS), or, as the case may be, to the WCT (art. 1(4) WCT also requires compliance of WCT-Members with arts. 1-21 BC). Moreover, since each new Revision Conference ended with a version of the BC that contained the same transitional provisions, art. 18 BC is also of importance when Member States that were bound by an older version ratified, or acceded to, a newer version of the BC (para. 4). Another case, though of minor practical importance, where the transitional provisions come into play is the extension of protection by the application of art. 7 BC or when prior reservations are abandoned (also para. 4). The transitional provisions strike a balance between the expectations of authors with regard to the protection of their works created before the BC became binding on them on the one hand, and the legitimate exploitation interests of those persons who have begun to exploit such works before the BC became applicable. **(b) Contents of transition rules.** According to the general rule of para. 1, those works which have not yet fallen into the public domain in the country of origin benefit from the (new version of the) BC (so-called rule of retroactivity). However, a revival of protection does not take place if a work has already fallen in the public domain because of the expiry of its term as previously granted in the country where protection is sought (para. 2). What is much less clear, however, is the meaning of the rule that BC Members may deviate from these principles by way of special agreement, and that in the absence of such provisions the respective countries shall determine the conditions of application of this principle (para. 3).

2. Protection dependent on continuing protection in the country of origin (para. 1). Firstly, the rule that works created prior to the entry into force of the BC with regard to new accessions enjoy protection, provided their protection has not run out in the country of protection at the time of accession, is not self-evident. In contrast, art. VII UCC provides that the continuing protection in the country of protection is decisive. Under the BC, the rule is, however, not compulsory, but Member States are always free to grant more far-reaching protection (see also art. 19 BC, but for TRIPS see below note 4). Second, with regard to newly acceding States (para. 4), the rule as laid down in para. 1 has the following consequences: a work whose country of origin is a BC Member State becomes protected in the newly acceded Member State from the day on which the accession became effective, that is, three months after the date on which the Director General has notified the deposit of its instrument of accession, unless a subsequent date has been indicated in the instrument deposited (art. 29(2)(a) BC). At the same date, works whose country of origin is the newly acceding State, and whose term of protection has not yet run out in this new Member State, become protected in all of the BC Member States (see, for example, *Lepo Sumera* (Germany): protection of works of an Estonian author irrespective of the fact that Estonia had left the former Soviet Union, and hence was in the meantime no longer bound by the latter's international obligations). In the case of a State which was already bound by an earlier version of the BC, the 'moment of coming into force' of the later version is the date of accession of that State, if this date is later than the ratification.

3. No revival of protection (para. 2). However, when a work has fallen into the public domain by way of expiry of the term of protection in the country of protection, then copyright does not revive, if by way of accession to the BC or one of its versions that prolonged the term of protection the work would, in theory, still be within the newly granted longer period. However, today, where all problems among BC Member States which are due to differing terms of protection are regulated by art. 7(8) BC, there is scarcely anything left to regulate with regard to duration. An exception can be found in the possibility under art. 30(2)(b) BC to make a reservation with regard to the translation right of art. 8 BC. Such a reservation may extinguish the translation right with regard to translations in a language spoken in that particular country by art. 5 of the Union Convention of 1886, which limited the translation right to ten years from the publication of the original work in one of the countries of the Union. Once such a translation right has been extinguished due to the time limit of the reservation, according to art. 18(2) BC it does not revive upon abandonment of the reservation (see, for example, *Emil Zola* (Germany)). More importantly, however, art. 18(2) BC could possibly may be in conflict with sec. 12 of the US Berne Convention Implementation

Act, according to which the US Copyright Act does not provide copyright protection for any work that is in the public domain in the United States. Unless it is restrictively interpreted, this rule clearly contradicts art. 18(1) BC. But it may be argued that under US law prior to the adherence of the US to the BC, all unpublished works of foreign authors were protected by common law copyright, but lost statutory protection upon publication for failure to comply with the then existing US-formalities. This would then be a case where protection has come to an end, although it is still subject to doubt whether in these cases the works have fallen into the public domain 'through the expiry of the term of protection which was previously granted' as required by art. 18(2) BC in order for copyright protection not to revive.

4. Special Conventions; application of principles (para. 3). With regard to special Conventions, it should be noted that art. 18(3) BC has likewise been invoked in order to make sec. 12 US Berne Convention Implementation Act compatible with the BC. Under this interpretation, art. 18(3) BC would allow newly acceding and existing BC Member States to individually negotiate the transitional provisions. Moreover, according to art. 70(2) sentence 2 TRIPS, art. 18 BC also governs copyright obligations with respect to existing works under TRIPS. This extends the disputed issue of (non)-retroactivity under art. 18(1) and (2) BC (see above, note 3) to the area of TRIPS, and now also to the WCT (see art. 1(4) WCT). Furthermore, the reference to the freedom of Member States to decide the 'conditions of application' does not allow for a free decision on whether to apply the clause of retroactivity at all, but only on how to apply it. Therefore, para. 3 allows national provisions to regulate the extent of rights of authors with regard to the rights of those persons who legally exploited public domain works in the past. However, no such regulation can completely deny the principle of retroactivity for all or a certain category of works.

5. Additional application (para. 4). Regarding the application of the transitional rules to newly acceding States, see above, note 2. The application of the rules to both the application of art. 7 BC and the abandonment of reservations is self-explanatory. Whereas the first case (subsequent prolongation of the term of protection in between revision conferences) is no longer of importance, examples for the latter (withdrawal of a reservation with the effect of increasing protection for BC authors) are reservations made with regard to the translation right of art. 8 BC according to art. 30(2)(b) BC (see note 3) by developing countries under arts. II and III of the Appendix, and also several reservations that have been maintained, and later withdrawn, by countries from earlier versions of the BC (such as the abandonment by Japan beginning with 1 January 1981, of a reservation regarding the translation right with regard to works of Union authors that was possible until the Rome Convention).

Dreier

[Protection greater than resulting from Convention]

Article 19

The provisions of this Convention shall not preclude the making of a claim to the benefit of any greater protection which may be granted by legislation in a country of the Union.

No maximum protection. This article makes it clear that foreign authors, when claiming copyright protection in another country, are not limited to the substantive rights granted by the BC. Rather, any Member State is free to grant authors greater protection than that granted by the BC. The substantive rights of the BC are thus minimum and not maximum rights.

[Special agreements among countries of the Union]

Article 20

The Governments of the countries of the Union reserve the right to enter into special agreements among themselves, in so far as such agreements grant to authors more extensive rights than those granted by the Convention, or contain other provisions not contrary to this Convention. The provisions of existing agreements which satisfy these conditions shall remain applicable.

1. General. Similar to art. 19 BC, according to which Member States are free to grant to authors of foreign works greater protection than that granted by the BC, art. 20 BC allows Member States to enter into special agreements regulating copyright, provided such agreements grant to authors more extensive rights than those granted by the BC, or contain provisions which are at least not contrary to the BC.

2. Examples. (a) General. At the international level, both the TRIPS Agreement and the WCT are examples of agreements according to art. 20 BC (having the effect of giving more extensive rights granted to authors by way of special agreements from a TRIPS perspective and the most-favoured nation principle, see commentary of art. 4 TRIPS in the volume 'General and Procedural IP Law'). In contrast, the Marrakesh Treaty benefitting the visually impaired, does not provide for more rights than those to be granted under the BC, but rather provides for a mandatory exception to the reproduction right and an optional limitation to the public performance right. However, it may be argued that these and similar exceptions and limitations are not contrary to the provisions of the BC as long as they remain within the boundaries defined by the three-step test of art. 9(2) BC and the so-called minor exceptions. **(b) European level.** At the European level, the TFEU is another example of an agreement within the meaning of art. 20 BC. Although the TFEU itself does not grant rights to authors, it contains the principle of non-discrimination on grounds of nationality (art. 18 TFEU; for its application to copyright see joined cases *Phil Collins* (ECJ), *LandHessen* v *Ricordi* (ECJ) and *Tod's* (ECJ)). This principle has the effect that the comparison of terms under art. 7(8) BC can no longer be applied to works of EU nationals. Hence, EU nationals benefit, in other EU Member States, from a term of protection longer than that granted by the BC. In addition, the TFEU empowers the EU legislature to provide, by way of Directives harmonizing national copyright laws, for more extensive copyright protection than that granted to foreign authors under the BC. However, to the extent the rights granted in the Information Society Directive – such as the public communication right granted in art. 3(1) of this Directive – are both minimum and maximum rights, individual EU Member States can no longer invoke art. 20 BC in order to unilaterally adhere to an agreement which creates greater protection than that granted under the Information Society Directive (*Svensson* (ECJ)).

[Special provisions regarding developing countries]

Article 21

(1) Special provisions regarding developing countries are included in the Appendix.

(2) Subject to the provisions of Article 28 (1) (b), the Appendix forms an integral part of this Act.

1. General. (a) Purpose of the Appendix. In the era of decolonization, developing countries felt that in view of their economic situation and social or cultural needs, they might not consider themselves immediately in a position to make provision for the protection of all the rights as provided for in the BC. Also, they feared that they might not be in a position to obtain access to all foreign copyright material desirable for their cultural progress. Therefore, at the Paris Conference in 1971, an Appendix was added to the BC parallel to provisions already contained in the Universal Copyright Convention. The Appendix, which forms an integral part of the BC unless a Member has declared that it will not be bound by the substantive provisions of this act (art. 28(1)(b) BC), shall enable developing countries to access works in cases where no such copies are available in the developing country. **(b) Other benefits for developing countries.** In addition, developing countries do not have to make the same contribution to the budget of WIPO as industrialized countries. According to art. 25(4) BC, BC Members are free to place themselves in one out of seven contribution classes, with the highest class being 25 times as expensive as the lowest one. Also, it should be noted that TRIPS does not exclude the possibility of developing countries making use of the Appendix (see art. 9(1) TRIPS). Moreover, TRIPS provided for a special transitional period for developing countries (see art. 65 TRIPS and for least-developed countries art. 66 TRIPS).

2. Developing countries. A developing country is a country which is regarded as a developing country in conformity with the established practice of the General Assembly of the United Nations (Appendix, art. I(1)). An indicator of the established practice is whether the country in question receives assistance from the UN Development Program through the UN or one of its specialized agencies. Nevertheless the term remains somewhat vague.

3. Scope of the Appendix. The Appendix allows developing countries to claim the benefits of the Appendix by way of a special declaration (Appendix, art. I). In essence, these benefits consist in replacing the exclusive translation right of art. 8 BC with regard to printed works for the purpose of teaching, scholarship or research (Appendix, art. II) and/or the exclusive reproduction right (Appendix, art. III), by a system of non-exclusive and non-transferable licences under the conditions as further defined in Appendix, arts. II, III and IV. However, there are several conditions and restrictions. In general, a licence requires that the work in question is not available in the developing country and that the licensee has unsuccessfully tried to obtain a contractual licence from the original rightholder. Moreover, the rightholders are entitled to 'just compensation that is consistent with standards of royalties normally operating on licenses freely negotiated between persons in the two countries concerned' (Appendix, art. IV(6)). Finally, even any licence granted under the provisions of the Appendix is limited in time as well as with regard to the territory of the country in which it has been granted.

4. Practical effect. However, it is worth mentioning that only a few countries have claimed, at the time of accession to, or ratification of, the BC, the benefits of the Appendix. These countries are Algeria, Bahrain, Bangladesh, Cuba, North Korea, Jordan, Mongolia, the Philippines, and Singapore. But as it seems, even in these countries, no substantial use, if any, has been made of the provisions of the Appendix to the BC. This may be due to the fact that the procedure provided for under art. 21 and the Appendix is still rather complicated and burdensome. In addition, access to foreign books might not be too difficult in French and English-speaking former colonies. Another explanation is that in order to strengthen their own culture, developing countries are more inclined to encourage domestic cultural production rather than to reproduce or translate foreign works. Consequently, rightholders have little to fear regarding their exclusive rights because of the special treatment given to developing countries under art. 21 BC and the Appendix.

[Organizational and transitory provisions]

Articles 22-38

1. General. Arts. 22 to 38 BC contain the organizational and transitory provisions of the Convention. They deal with the institutional organization of the Berne Union constituted according to art. 1 BC (arts. 22 to 26 BC), the revision of the Convention (art. 27 BC), ratification and accession as well as duration and the possibility for denunciation on the part of Member States (arts. 28–31, 34 and 35 BC), the relationship of the Paris Act 1971 to older versions of the BC (art. 32 BC), disputes amongst Member States concerning the interpretation or application of the BC (competency of the International Court of Justice, art. 33 BC), the application of the BC in internal law (art. 36 BC), final clauses including official languages (art. 37 BC), and transitory provisions (art. 38 BC). To the extent that these provisions are of no interest for the application of substantive copyright law they are neither reprinted nor commented upon here. Rather, comments are limited to the following provisions.

2. Article 32 [Applicability of this Act and of earlier Acts]. (a) General rule. Art. 32(1) BC clarifies which of the different Acts of the BC are applicable as regards relations between the countries of the Union. In general, this is the 1971 Paris Act if, and to the extent to which, both parties are bound by it. **(b) Exception with regard to Union Member States.** However, the Acts previously in force continue to be applicable, in their entirety or to the extent that the Paris Act does not replace them, in relations with countries of the Union which are only bound, in total or in part, by older Acts of the BC. It should be noted that although art. 1(1) TRIPS requires TRIPS Members to comply with arts. 1 to 21 BC and the Appendix thereto of the Paris Act of 1971 (with the exception of its art. 6bis BC, the provision on moral rights), quite a number of States are still bound, in total or in part, by earlier Acts of the BC (according to art. 28(1)(b) BC Members can declare that they do not apply arts. 1 to 21 BC or the Appendix of the Paris Act; for details see the list at the WIPO-Website). **(c) Countries which have acceded to the BC after 1971.** According to art. 32(2) BC, countries which have acceded to the BC after 1971 shall nevertheless apply the Paris Act with respect to any country of the Union which is – in whole or in part – not bound by it. However, the said country of the Union only has to apply, to the newly acceded country, the provisions of the most recent Act by which it is bound.

3. Article 36 [Application of the Convention]. According to art. 36(1) BC, '[a]ny country party to this Convention undertakes to adopt, in accordance with its constitution, the measures necessary to ensure the application of this Convention'. According to art. 36(2) BC '[i]t is understood that, at the time a country becomes bound by this Convention, it will be in a position under its domestic law to give effect to the provisions of this Convention'. It should be noted, however, that the question of how, and to what extent, the substantive rules of the BC become an integral part of national law and enforceable within an individual Member State depends on the law of each individual Member State. This is also true with regard to the question of whether the rights granted by the BC may be considered as self-executing or not (the United States, for example, in its national accession legislation has expressly stated that it is not). In some States, transformation of international rights and obligations into national norms is required, in others mere incorporation by national legislation is needed. Moreover, in case of doubt whether a Member State's national law fully complies with the BC, the only recourse available is to the International Court of Justice in the Hague according to art. 33(1) BC, unless the countries concerned agree on some other method of settlement. However, in the long history of the BC this possibility has never been used. The weakness of appropriate mechanisms to enforce Member States' BC obligations has contributed to the strengthening and application of the Dispute Settlement Procedure to rights granted under the TRIPS Agreement.

4. Article 37(1) [Final clauses: languages]. According to art. 37(1)(a) BC, a single copy of the Paris Act of the BC, in French and English, has been signed. According to art. 37(1)(b) BC other official texts are in Arabic, German, Italian, Portuguese and Spanish. Also, additional language texts may be established in other languages designated by the Assembly. Thus the text of the BC also exists in Russian and in Chinese. However, in order to solve differences of opinion on the interpretation of the various texts, art. 37(1)(c) BC declares that in such cases the French text shall prevail.

Below, the provisions of the Appendix to the BC are reprinted without further comment.

APPENDIX. SPECIAL PROVISIONS REGARDING DEVELOPING COUNTRIES

[Faculties open to developing countries]

Article I

(1) **Any country regarded as a developing country in conformity with the established practice of the General Assembly of the United Nations which ratifies or accedes to this Act, of which this Appendix forms an integral part, and which, having regard to its economic situation and its social or cultural needs, does not consider itself immediately in a position to make provision for the protection of all the rights as provided for in this Act, may, by a notification deposited with the Director General at the time of depositing its instrument of ratification or accession or, subject to Article V(1)(c), at any time thereafter, declare that it will avail itself of the faculty provided for in Article II, or of the faculty provided for in Article III, or of both of those faculties. It may, instead of availing itself of the faculty provided for in Article II, make a declaration according to Article V(1)(a).**

(2)

    (a) **Any declaration under paragraph (1) notified before the expiration of the period often years from the entry into force of Articles 1 to 21 and this Appendix according to Article 28(2)** shall be effective until the expiration of the said period. Any such declaration may be renewed in whole or in part for periods of ten years each by a notification deposited with the Director General not more than fifteen months and not less than three months before the expiration of the ten-year period then running.

(b) Any declaration under paragraph (1) notified after the expiration of the period of ten years from the entry into force of Articles 1 to 21 and this Appendix according to Article 28(2) shall be effective until the expiration of the ten-year period then running. Any such declaration may be renewed as provided for in the second sentence of subparagraph (a).

Any country of the Union which has ceased to be regarded as a developing country as referred to in paragraph (1) shall no longer be entitled to renew its declaration as provided in paragraph (2), and, whether or not it formally withdraws its declaration, such country shall be precluded from availing itself of the faculties referred to in paragraph (1) from the expiration of the ten-year period then running or from the expiration of a period of three years after it has ceased to be regarded as a developing country, whichever period expires later.

Where, at the time when the declaration made under paragraph (1) or (2) ceases to be effective, there are copies in stock which were made under a license granted by virtue of this Appendix, such copies may continue to be distributed until their stock is exhausted.

(5) Any country which is bound by the provisions of this Act and which has deposited a declaration or a notification in accordance with Article 31(1) with respect to the application of this Act to a particular territory, the situation of which can be regarded as analogous to that of the countries referred to in paragraph (1), may, in respect of such territory, make the declaration referred to in paragraph (1) and the notification of renewal referred to in paragraph (2). As long as such declaration or notification remains in effect, the provisions of this Appendix shall be applicable to the territory in respect of which it was made.

(6)

(a) The fact that a country avails itself of any of the faculties referred to in paragraph (1) does not permit another country to give less protection to works of which the country of origin is the former country than it is obliged to grant under Articles 1 to 20.

(b) The right to apply reciprocal treatment provided for in Article 30(2)(b), second sentence, shall not, until the date on which the period applicable under Article I(3) expires, be exercised in respect of works the country of origin of which is a country which has made a declaration according to Article V(1)(a).

[Limitations on the right of translation]

Article II

(1) Any country which has declared that it will avail itself of the faculty provided for in this Article shall be entitled, so far as works published in printed or analogous forms of reproduction are concerned, to substitute for the exclusive right of translation provided for in Article 8 a system of non-exclusive and non-transferable licenses, granted by the competent authority under the following conditions and subject to Article IV.

(2)

(a) Subject to paragraph (3), if, after the expiration of a period of three years, or of any longer period determined by the national legislation of the said country, commencing on the date of the first publication of the work, a translation of such work has not been published in a language in general use in that country by the owner of the right of translation, or with his authorization, any national of such country may obtain a license to make a translation of the work in the said language and publish the translation in printed or analogous forms of reproduction.

(b) A license under the conditions provided for in this Article may also be granted if all the editions of the translation published in the language concerned are out of print.

(3)

(a) In the case of translations into a language which is not in general use in one or more developed countries which are members of the Union, a period of one year shall be substituted for the period of three years referred to in paragraph (2)(a).

(b) Any country referred to in paragraph (1) may, with the unanimous agreement of the developed countries which are members of the Union and in which the same language is in general use, substitute, in the case of translations into that language, for the period of three years referred to in paragraph (2)(a) a shorter period as determined by such agreement but not less than one year. However, the provisions of the foregoing sentence shall not apply where the language in question is English, French or Spanish. The Director General shall be notified of any such agreement by the Governments which have concluded it.

(4)

(a) No license obtainable after three years shall be granted under this Article until a further period of six months has elapsed, and no license obtainable after one year shall be granted under this Article until a further period of nine months has elapsed

      (i) from the date on which the applicant complies with the requirements mentioned in Article IV(1), or

     (ii) where the identity or the address of the owner of the right of translation is unknown, from the date on which the applicant sends, as provided for in Article IV(2), copies of his application submitted to the authority competent to grant the license.

  (b) If, during the said period of six or nine months, a translation in the language in respect of which the application was made is published by the owner of the right of translation or with his authorization, no license under this Article shall be granted.

(5) Any license under this Article shall be granted only for the purpose of teaching, scholarship or research.

(6) If a translation of a work is published by the owner of the right of translation or with his authorization at a price reasonably related to that normally charged in the country for comparable works, any license granted under this Article shall terminate if such translation is in the same language and with substantially the same content as the translation published under the license. Any copies already made before the license terminates may continue to be distributed until their stock is exhausted.

(7) For works which are composed mainly of illustrations, a license to make and publish a translation of the text and to reproduce and publish the illustrations may be granted only if the conditions of Article in are also fulfilled.

(8) No license shall be granted under this Article when the author has withdrawn from circulation all copies of his work.

(9)

  (a) A license to make a translation of a work which has been published in printed or analogous forms of reproduction may also be granted to any broadcasting organization having its headquarters in a country referred to in paragraph (1), upon an application made to the competent authority of that country by the said organization, provided that all of the following conditions are met:

      (i) the translation is made from a copy made and acquired in accordance with the laws of the said country;

     (ii) the translation is only for use in broadcasts intended exclusively for teaching or for the dissemination of the results of specialized technical or scientific research to experts in a particular profession;

    (iii) the translation is used exclusively for the purposes referred to in condition (ii) through broadcasts made lawfully and intended for recipients on the territory of the said country, including broadcasts made through the medium of sound or visual recordings lawfully and exclusively made for the purpose of such broadcasts;

    (iv) all uses made of the translation are without any commercial purpose.

(b) Sound or visual recordings of a translation which was made by a broadcasting organization under a license granted by virtue of this paragraph may, for the purposes and subject to the conditions referred to in subparagraph (a) and with the agreement of that organization, also be used by any other broadcasting organization having its headquarters in the country whose competent authority granted the license in question.

(c) Provided that all of the criteria and conditions set out in sub-paragraph (a) are met, a license may also be granted to a broadcasting organization to translate any text incorporated in an audio-visual fixation where such fixation was itself prepared and published for the sole purpose of being used in connection with systematic instructional activities.

(d) Subject to subparagraphs (a) to (c), the provisions of the preceding paragraphs shall apply to the grant and exercise of any license granted under this paragraph.

[Limitations on the right of reproduction]

Article III

(1) Any country which has declared that it will avail itself of the faculty provided for in this Article shall be entitled to substitute for the exclusive right of reproduction provided for in Article 9 a system of non-exclusive and non-transferable licenses, granted by the competent authority under the following conditions and subject to Article IV.

(2)

    (a) If, in relation to a work to which this Article applies by virtue of paragraph (7), after the expiration of

        (i) the relevant period specified in paragraph (3), commencing on the date of first publication of a particular edition of the work, or

       (ii) any longer period determined by national legislation of the country referred to in paragraph (1), commencing on the same date, copies of such edition have not been distributed in that country to the general public or in connection with systematic instructional activities, by the owner of the right of reproduction or with his authorization, at a price reasonably related to that normally charged in the country for comparable works, any national of such country may obtain a license to reproduce and publish such edition at that or a lower price for use in connection with systematic instructional activities.

(b) A license to reproduce and publish an edition which has been distributed as described in subparagraph (a) may also be granted under the conditions provided for in this Article if, after the expiration of the applicable period, no authorized copies of that edition have been on sale for a period of six months in the country concerned to the general public or in connection with systematic instructional activities at a price reasonably related to that normally charged in the country for comparable works.

(3) The period referred to in paragraph (2)(a)(i) shall be five years, except that

(i) for works of the natural and physical sciences, including mathematics, and of technology, the period shall be three years;

(ii) for works of fiction, poetry, drama and music, and for art books, the period shall be seven years.

(4)

(a) No license obtainable after three years shall be granted under this Article until a period of six months has elapsed

(i) from the date on which the applicant complies with the requirements mentioned in Article IV(1), or

(ii) where the identity or the address of the owner of the right of reproduction is unknown, from the date on which the applicant sends, as provided for in Article IV(2), copies of his application submitted to the authority competent to grant the license.

(b) Where licenses are obtainable after other periods and Article IV(2) is applicable, no license shall be granted until a period of three months has elapsed from the date of the dispatch of the copies of the application.

(c) If, during the period of six or three months referred to in sub-paragraphs (a) and (b), a distribution as described in paragraph (2)(a) has taken place, no license shall be granted under this Article.

(d) No license shall be granted if the author has withdrawn from circulation all copies of the edition for the reproduction and publication of which the license has been applied for.

(5) A license to reproduce and publish a translation of a work shall not be granted under this Article in the following cases:

(i) where the translation was not published by the owner of the right of translation or with his authorization, or

(ii) where the translation is not in a language in general use in the country in which the license is applied for.

Dreier

(6) If copies of an edition of a work are distributed in the country referred to in paragraph (1) to the general public or in connection with systematic instructional activities, by the owner of the right of reproduction or with his authorization, at a price reasonably related to that normally charged in the country for comparable works, any license granted under this Article shall terminate if such edition is in the same language and with substantially the same content as the edition which was published under the said license. Any copies already made before the license terminates may continue to be distributed until their stock is exhausted.

(7)

(a) Subject to subparagraph (b), the works to which this Article applies shall be limited to works published in printed or analogous forms of reproduction.

(b) This Article shall also apply to the reproduction in audio-visual form of lawfully made audio-visual fixations including any protected works incorporated therein and to the translation of any incorporated text into a language in general use in the country in which the license is applied for, always provided that the audiovisual fixations in question were prepared and published for the sole purpose of being used in connection with systematic instructional activities.

[Provisions common to licenses under article II and III]

Article IV

(1) A license under Article II or Article III may be granted only if the applicant, in accordance with the procedure of the country concerned, establishes either that he has requested, and has been denied, authorization by the owner of the right to make and publish the translation or to reproduce and publish the edition, as the case may be, or that, after due diligence on his part, he was unable to find the owner of the right. At the same time as making the request, the applicant shall inform any national or international information center referred to in paragraph (2).

If the owner of the right cannot be found, the applicant for a license shall send, by registered airmail, copies of his application, submitted to the authority competent to grant the license, to the publisher whose name appears on the work and to any national or international information center which may have been designated, in a notification to that effect deposited with the Director General, by the Government of the country in which the publisher is believed to have his principal place of business.

The name of the author shall be indicated on all copies of the translation or reproduction published under a license granted under Article II or Article III. The title of the work shall appear on all such copies. In the case of a translation, the original title of the work shall appear in any case on all the said copies.

(4)

    (a) No license granted under Article II or Article III shall extend to the export of copies, and any such license shall be valid only for publication of the translation or of the reproduction, as the case may be, in the territory of the country in which it has been applied for.

    (b) For the purposes of subparagraph (a), the notion of export shall include the sending of copies from any territory to the country which, in respect of that territory, has made a declaration under Article I (5).

    (c) Where a governmental or other public entity of a country which has granted a license to make a translation under Article II into a language other than English, French or Spanish sends copies of a translation published under such license to another country, such sending of copies shall not, for the purposes of subparagraph (a), be considered to constitute export if all of the following conditions are met:

      (i) the recipients are individuals who are nationals of the country whose competent authority has granted the license, or organizations grouping such individuals;

     (ii) the copies are to be used only for the purpose of teaching, scholarship or research;

    (iii) the sending of the copies and their subsequent distribution to recipients is without any commercial purpose; and

    (iv) the country to which the copies have been sent has agreed with the country whose competent authority has granted the license to allow the receipt, or distribution, or both, and the Director General has been notified of the agreement by the Government of the country in which the license has been granted.

(5) All copies published under a license granted by virtue of Article II or Article III shall bear a notice in the appropriate language stating that the copies are available for distribution only in the country or territory to which the said license applies.

(6)

    (a) Due provision shall be made at the national level to ensure

      (i) that the license provides, in favour of the owner of the right of translation or of reproduction, as the case may be, for just compensation that is consistent with standards of royalties normally operating on licenses freely negotiated between persons in the two countries concerned, and

     (ii) payment and transmittal of the compensation: should national currency regulations intervene, the competent authority shall make all efforts, by the use of international machinery, to ensure transmittal in internationally convertible currency or its equivalent.

(b) Due provision shall be made by national legislation to ensure a correct translation of the work, or an accurate reproduction of the particular edition, as the case may be.

[Alternative possibility for limitation of the right of translation]

Article V

(1)

(a) Any country entitled to make a declaration that it will avail itself of the faculty provided for in Article II may, instead, at the time of ratifying or acceding to this Act:

　(i) if it is a country to which Article 30 (2) (a) applies, make a declaration under that provision as far as the right of translation is concerned;

　(ii) if it is a country to which Article 30 (2) (a) does not apply, and even if it is not a country outside the Union, make a declaration as provided for in Article 30 (2) (b), first sentence.

(b) In the case of a country which ceases to be regarded as a developing country as referred to in Article I (1), a declaration made according to this paragraph shall be effective until the date on which the period applicable under Article I (3) expires.

(c) Any country which has made a declaration according to this paragraph may not subsequently avail itself of the faculty provided for in Article II even if it withdraws the said declaration.

(2) Subject to paragraph (3), any country which has availed itself of the faculty provided for in Article II may not subsequently make a declaration according to paragraph (1).

(3) Any country which has ceased to be regarded as a developing country as referred to in Article I (1) may, not later than two years prior to the expiration of the period applicable under Article I (3), make a declaration to the effect provided for in Article 30(2)(b), first sentence, notwithstanding the fact that it is not a country outside the Union. Such declaration shall take effect at the date on which the period applicable under Article I (3) expires.

[Possibilities of applying, or admitting the application of, certain provisions of the Appendix before becoming bound by it]

Article VI

(1) Any country of the Union may declare, as from the date of this Act, and at any time before becoming bound by Articles 1 to 21 and this Appendix:

    (i) if it is a country which, were it bound by Articles 1 to 21 and this Appendix, would be entitled to avail itself of the faculties referred to in Article I (1), that it will apply the provisions of Article II or of Article III or of both to works whose country of origin is a country which, pursuant to (ii) below, admits the application of those Articles to such works, or which is bound by Articles 1 to 21 and this Appendix; such declaration may, instead of referring to Article II, refer to Article V;

   (ii) that it admits the application of this Appendix to works of which it is the country of origin by countries which have made a declaration under (i) above or a notification under Article I.

(2) Any declaration made under paragraph (1) shall be in writing and shall be deposited with the Director General. The declaration shall become effective from the date of its deposit.

WIPO COPYRIGHT TREATY (WCT)

adopted in Geneva on 20 December 1996

[Introductory remarks]

1. General. Together with the WPPT, the WCT is the first international treaty that deals with the copyright issues raised by digital and networking technologies. The WCT contains rules on copyrightable subject matter (computer programs and databases), exclusive rights (distribution right, rental right and right of communication to the public, including the new right of making copyrighted works available to the public), the term of protection (for photographic works). It also provides for legal protection against the unauthorized circumvention of technical protection measures and the manipulation of rights management information. The WCT is an independent international treaty within the meaning of art. 20 BC (art. 1(1) WCT), open to all WIPO Members (art. 17(1) WCT).

2. History. After further revisions of the Berne Convention had become unlikely, and after the TRIPS Agreement had consolidated worldwide copyright protection, it was felt that the changes brought about by digital and networking technologies called for a new international instrument. Upon the initiative of WIPO, a series of meetings of a special Committee of Experts resulted in a text that was then submitted to a Diplomatic Conference in December 1996. Initially conceived as a protocol to the Berne Convention, the WCT was finally adopted as a separate international treaty within the meaning of art. 20 BC. The WCT entered into force on 6 March 2002, upon deposit of the thirtieth instrument of ratification or accession with the Director General of WIPO. In May 2015, there were 93 Contracting Parties (for details see the WIPO website).

3. Status of the European Union. The EU has not only taken part in the negotiation of the WCT, but can likewise become a Contracting Party (art. 17(3) WCT). In order to bring the national laws of EU Member States in conformity with the substantive provisions of the WCT, the EU has adopted, in 2001, the Information Society Directive. On 14 December 2009, the EU ratified the WCT to finally become a Contracting Party on 14 March 2010. As a Contracting Party, the EU can exercise as many votes as it has Member States (the exercise of a vote by a EU Member and by the EU itself being mutually exclusive; art. 15(3)(b) WCT).

4. Impact on ECJ jurisprudence. According to established case law of the ECJ, EU legislation must, so far as possible, be interpreted in a manner that is consistent with international law, in particular where its provisions are intended to give effect to an international agreement concluded by the EU, such as the WCT (*SGAE* (ECJ), *Peek & Cloppenburg* (ECJ) and *Football Association*

Premier League and Others (ECJ)). Therefore, the concepts underlying EU legislation in the field of copyright must be interpreted in the light of relevant international provisions. The WCT is particularly relevant to the interpretation of the Information Society Directive which, as reflected in recital 15 of its preamble, serves the purpose of bringing EU law in line with the international obligations following from the WCT (*Peek & Cloppenburg* (ECJ)).

[Bibliography]

J.E. Cohen, 'WIPO Copyright Treaty Implementation in the United States: Will Fair Use Survive?' (1999) EIPR 236-247

M. Ficsor, 'The Spring 1997 Horace S. Manges Lecture – Copyright for the Digital Era: The WIPO "Internet" Treaties' (1997) *Columbia-VLA Journal of Law & the Arts* 197-223

M. Ficsor, *The Law of Copyright and the Internet: The 1996 WIPO Treaties, their Interpretation and Implementation* (Oxford University Press 2002)

S. Fitzpatrick, 'Copyright Imbalance: U.S. and Australian Responses to the WIPO Digital Copyright Treaty' (2000) EIPR 214-228

C. Geiger, J. Griffiths and R. Hilty, 'Towards a Balanced Interpretation of the "Three-step test" in Copyright Law' (2008) EIPR 489-499

J. Ginsburg, 'From Having Copies to Experiencing Works: the Development of an Access Right in U.S. Copyright Law' (2003) *Journal of the Copyright Society of the USA* 113-131

J. Ginsburg, 'The (New?) Right of Making Available to the Public' in D.Vaver, L. Bently (eds.), *Intellectual Property in the New Millenium – Essays in Honour of William R. Cornish* (Cambridge University Press 2004) 234-247

P. Goldstein and P.B. Hugenholtz, *International Copyright: Principles, Law and Practice* (3rd edn., Oxford University Press 2012)

L. Guibault, *Copyright Limitations and Contracts – An Analysis of the Contractual Overridability of Limitations on Copyright* (Kluwer Law International 2002)

P.B. Hugenholtz (ed.), *The Future of Copyright in a Digital Environment* (Kluwer 1996)

P.B. Hugenholtz (ed.), *Copyright and Electronic Commerce – Legal Aspects of Electronic Copyright Management* (Kluwer 2000)

A. Kerever, 'The New WIPO Treaties: the WIPO Copyright Treaty and the WIPO Performances and Phonograms Treaty' (1998) 2 *UNESCO Copyright Bulletin* 3-17

K. Koelman, 'A Hard Nut to Crack: The Protection of Technological Measures' (2000) EIPR 272-288

M. Lemley, 'Dealing with Overlapping Copyrights on the Internet' (1997) *University of Dayton Law Review* 547-585

S. von Lewinski, *International Copyright Law and Policy* (Oxford University Press 2008)

J. Reinbothe and S. von Lewinski, *The WIPO Treaties 1996: Commentary and Legal Analysis* (Butterworths 2002)

S. Ricketson, 'The Boundaries of Copyright: Its Proper Limitations and Exceptions: International Conventions and Treaties' (1999) *Intellectual Property Quarterly* 56-94

S. Ricketson and J. Ginsburg, *International Copyright and Neighbouring Rights: The Berne Convention and Beyond* (Oxford University Press 2006)

P. Samuelson, 'Challenges for the World Intellectual Property Organization and the Trade-related Aspects of Intellectual Property Rights Council in Regulating Intellectual Property Rights in the Information Age' (1999) EIPR 578-591

M. Senftleben, *Copyright, Limitations and the Three-Step Test: An Analysis of the Three-Step Test in International and EC Copyright Law* (Kluwer Law International 2004)

M. Senftleben, 'Towards a Horizontal Standard for Limiting Intellectual Property Rights? WTO Panel Reports Shed Light on the Three-Step Test in Copyright Law and Related Tests in Patent and Trademark Law' (2006) IIC 407-438

WIPO (ed.), *WIPO Worldwide Symposium on the Future of Copyright and Neighboring Rights* (WIPO 1994)

[Preamble]

The Contracting Parties,

Desiring to develop and maintain the protection of the rights of authors in their literary and artistic works in a manner as effective and uniform as possible, Recognizing the need to introduce new international rules and clarify the interpretation of certain existing rules in order to provide adequate solutions to the questions raised by new economic, social, cultural and technological developments,

Recognizing the profound impact of the development and convergence of information and communication technologies on the creation and use of literary and artistic works,

Emphasizing the outstanding significance of copyright protection as an incentive for literary and artistic creation,

Recognizing the need to maintain a balance between the rights of authors and the larger public interest, particularly education, research and access to information, as reflected in the Berne Convention,

Have agreed as follows:

1. General. The preamble provides guidance for the interpretation of the Treaty. At the 1996 Diplomatic Conference, Main Committee I discussed and adopted the preamble after having dealt with the substantive provisions of the Treaty. The recitals thus summarize fundamental principles that formed the basis of the deliberations at the Conference and reflect the rationales for adopting the WCT.

2. Reference to the Berne Convention (first recital). The wording of the first recital was modelled on the first recital of the preamble of the 1971 Paris Act of the Berne Convention. The use of the language can even be traced back to the preamble of the original text of the Berne Convention adopted in 1886. The direct reference to this long-standing formulation in the preamble of the WCT heralds a cautious approach seeking to continue the tradition of the BC. A core element of this tradition is the aim to protect the rights of authors in a manner as effective and uniform as possible. The principle of effectiveness underlines the need to ensure that authors can profit from an adequate international minimum standard of protection. The principle of uniformity refers to the goal of establishing comparable, if not identical, protection regimes. The fact that these objectives are to be realized insofar 'as possible' makes it clear that the protection of authors' rights must be carefully weighed against legitimate competing interests reflecting economic, social and cultural conditions in the Contracting Parties.

3. Reasons for the new treaty (second recital). The second recital explains why it was deemed necessary to adopt a new copyright treaty. Rather than merely seeking to react to new technology, the WCT aims to respond adequately to the economic, social and cultural implications thereof. Both the introduction of new rules and the clarification of existing rules were considered appropriate ways of arriving at satisfactory solutions. In fact, an amalgam of both principles was applied when drafting the Treaty. Arts. 2, 4 and 5 WCT, for instance, clarify art. 2 BC. The Agreed Statement concerning art. 1(4) WCT clarifies the ambit of operation of the general right of reproduction laid down in art. 9(1) BC. Art. 10 WCT clarifies and broadens the scope of the three-step test known from arts. 9(2) BC and 13 TRIPS. Art. 8 WCT establishes a new general right of communication to the public on the basis of pre-existing Berne provisions. Arts. 11 and 12 WCT, finally, constitute new international rules.

4. Digital revolution (third recital). The third recital directly addresses the digital revolution, although not mentioning its most prominent exponent: the Internet. It shows that the WCT was negotiated in the light of the potential of digital technology to impact deeply on the framework in which works of the intellect are to be used and created. In fact, digital technology seems to offer two extreme solutions – the free flow of information on the one hand, and a new dimension of monitoring and controlling the use of copyrighted material on the other. It remains to be seen which position between these two poles will finally result from the application of the WCT.

5. Importance of copyright protection (fourth recital). The fourth recital was introduced as a countermove to the reference to the 'larger public interest' made in the following fifth recital. Its main objective, therefore, is an additional emphasis on the importance of adequate copyright protection. Interestingly, a utilitarian rationale of copyright protection was used to achieve this goal. Instead of invoking an author-centric natural law argument, it is underlined that copyright protection does not form an end in itself but is granted to give an incentive to create.

6. Importance of copyright limitations (fifth recital). The fifth recital refers directly to the delicate balance between rights and limitations to be struck in copyright law. It stresses in particular the public interest in education, research and access to information. The recital shows that, in line with the reference already made in the first recital, a resort to the BC was perceived as the most appropriate solution. By formally recognizing the need to maintain an appropriate balance in the preamble itself, the recital indicates that both elements – rights and limitations – are central to the copyright system and, for this reason, must be carefully weighed against each other. At the same time, the recital makes it clear that the rules of the BC should govern the weighing process. Hence, a balance of traditional shape was envisaged rather than a drastic re-orientation of the system.

[Relation to the Berne Convention]

Article 1

(1) **This Treaty is a special agreement within the meaning of Article 20 of the Berne Convention for the Protection of Literary and Artistic Works, as regards Contracting Parties that are countries of the Union established by that Convention. This Treaty shall not have any connection with treaties other than the Berne Convention, nor shall it prejudice any rights and obligations under any other treaties.**

(2) **Nothing in this Treaty shall derogate from existing obligations that Contracting Parties have to each other under the Berne Convention for the Protection of Literary and Artistic Works.**

(3) **Hereinafter, 'Berne Convention' shall refer to the Paris Act of July 24, 1971 of the Berne Convention for the Protection of Literary and Artistic Works.**

(4) **Contracting Parties shall comply with Articles 1 to 21 and the Appendix of the Berne Convention.**

Agreed Statement Concerning Article 1(4)

The reproduction right, as set out in Article 9 of the Berne Convention, and the exceptions permitted thereunder, fully apply in the digital environment, in particular to the use of works in digital form. It is understood that the storage of a protected work in digital form in an electronic medium constitutes a reproduction within the meaning of Article 9 of the Berne Convention.

1. Interface with other treaties (para. 1). (a) Legal connection with the Berne Convention (first sentence). The historical background to art. 20 BC shows that the provision was primarily devised to regulate bilateral agreements between countries party to the BC. The underlying objective is to safeguard the standard of protection reached in the Convention. It follows from this legal connection that WCT provisions may not be interpreted so as to fall short of the Berne standard of protection. **(b) No connection with other treaties (second sentence).** In fact, the TRIPS Agreement impacted deeply on certain provisions of the WCT (see arts. 4, 5, 7 and accompanying Agreed Statements). Nevertheless, the second sentence of para. 1 expressly denies any legal connection. This stipulation renders TRIPS provisions on law enforcement and, in particular, the WTO dispute settlement mechanism inapplicable to the WCT. Indirect repercussions on its interpretation, however, can hardly be avoided.

2. Berne safeguard clause (para. 2). This provision underlines the need for members of the Berne Union to reconcile the application of the WCT with the obligations they have under the BC. As para. 2 concerns only obligations, derogations from rights Berne Union members enjoy under the Convention are possible. Accordingly, it is permissible to derogate from the right to determine the term of protection of photographic works and works of applied art set forth in art. 7(4) BC by virtue of art. 9 WCT.

3. Specification of the relevant act of the Berne Convention (para. 3). It follows from the term 'hereinafter' that references to the BC in preceding provisions are not confined to a specific act. Consequently, the safeguard clause in para. 2 applies to any obligation a Berne Union member has under any act of the Berne Convention.

4. Incorporation of Berne provisions by reference (para. 4). The compliance clause enshrined in para. 4 goes beyond the parallel stipulation in art. 9(1) TRIPS in that it encompasses the moral rights laid down in art. 6bis BC. As arts. 1 to 21 and the Appendix of the BC are incorporated by reference, the provisions carry with them their drafting and negotiating history which may serve as a supplementary means of interpretation pursuant to art. 32 of the Vienna Convention (*see United States – Section 110(5) of the US Copyright Act* (WTO panel report)). By virtue of para. 4, the EU can assume the obligation to comply with the substantive Berne provisions without being obliged to accede to the BC. The latter is only open for accession by States but not by intergovernmental organizations, such as the EU (see art. 29(1) BC).

5. The Agreed Statement. (a) The first sentence. It already follows from art. 9(1) BC that the right of reproduction and relevant permissible limitations apply to reproductions of a work 'in any manner or form' and, therefore, also to reproductions in digital format. Accordingly, the first sentence of the Agreed Statement merely confirms the broad scope of the reproduction right recognized in art. 9(1) BC. **(b) The second sentence.** In contrast to the first sentence, the second sentence of the Agreed Statement was not adopted unanimously but only by a majority of votes at the 1996 Diplomatic Conference. It remained controversial because no agreement could be reached on the interpretation of the word 'storage'. At the core of the controversy lay acts of temporary, transient or incidental reproduction, such as browsing and caching. In this respect, two different models were discussed. On the one hand, there were delegations seeking to exclude temporary, transient and incidental acts from protection by denying their characterization as relevant acts of reproduction. Consequently, they would not fall within the scope of the right of reproduction from the outset ('exclusion model'). On the other hand, the view was expressed that acts of temporary, transient or incidental reproduction were covered by art. 9(1) BC. Proponents of this position held the view that the introduction of limitations was sufficient to exempt these acts from the control of the authors ('limitation model'). *The impact of the three-step test.* Under the exclusion model, it may be argued that the three-step tests of arts. 9(2) BC and 10(2) WCT are inapplicable because, by virtue of the outlined restrictive interpretation of the term 'reproduction', there is no reproduction which could be limited in the case of temporary acts (see art. 10, note 1(c), with regard to the notion of limitations and exceptions underlying the three-step test). Under the limitation model, the aforementioned three-step tests, by contrast, would have to be observed. An inquiry into a potential conflict with a normal exploitation or an unreasonable prejudice to legitimate economic interests (see art. 10, notes 4 and 5, as to the applicable test procedure), however, would give rise to the question of the economic significance of temporary reproductions. *Remaining ambiguity.* The Agreed Statement cannot be understood to reflect only one of the two outlined models under discussion. Rather, it seems that different interpretations of the term 'storage' and, correspondingly, both the broad as well as the more restrictive approach to the scope of the reproduction right may be followed. On the basis of the exclusion model, it may be argued that temporary, transient or incidental acts do not constitute relevant acts of storage in the sense of the Agreed Statement. Under the limitation model, temporary acts of this kind would be regarded as acts of storage. **(c) European legislation.** Arts. 2 and 5(1) in connection with art. 5(5) of the Information Society Directive follow the limitation model. Temporary acts of reproduction are brought within the scope of the harmonized right of reproduction granted in art. 2. The mandatory exemption in art. 5(1), then, limits this exclusive right with regard to temporary acts. This limitation, in turn, must keep within the limits following from the three-step test laid down in art. 5(5). **(d) ECJ jurisprudence.** In principle, the exemption of temporary acts of reproduction in art. 5(1) of the Information Society Directive must be interpreted strictly in light of the three-step test of art. 5(5) (*Infopaq International* (ECJ)). Formal adherence to this 'dogma' of strict interpretation, however, did not hinder the ECJ from also pointing out that the exemption had to be interpreted in a way that enabled its effectiveness and observed its purpose. In particular, the interpretation had to allow and ensure the development and operation of new technologies and safeguard a fair balance between the rights and interests of right holders and users (*Football Association Premier League and Others* (ECJ)). This further consideration can be placed in the context of the recognition of a need to maintain a balance between copyright and the larger public interest in the last recital of the WCT preamble. It is also in line with the Agreed Statement concerning art. 10 WCT which reflects the necessity to devise appropriate new limitations and exceptions in the digital environment. The ECJ also held that a temporary act of reproduction satisfying all conditions set forth in art. 5(1) of the Information Society Directive, such as computer screen copies and internet cache copies made by an end-user in the course of viewing a website, did not cause a conflict with a normal exploitation or unreasonably prejudice legitimate interests in the sense of the three-step test of art. 5(5) (*Football Association Premier League and Others* (ECJ), *Infopaq International 2* (ECJ), *Public Relations Consultants Association* (ECJ)). The three-step test of art. 5(5) is thus unlikely to further restrict the scope of the exemption of temporary acts of reproduction in art. 5(1). In sum, the ECJ developed several safeguards against an overly strict interpretation in the light of the three-step test that would erode the mandatory exemption of temporary acts of reproduction. Although EU legislation adopted the limitation model, the practical result may thus come close to the exclusion model which was discussed as an alternative at the 1996 Diplomatic Conference.

[Scope of copyright protection]

Article 2

Copyright protection extends to expressions and not to ideas, procedures, methods of operation or mathematical concepts as such.

1. Idea/expression dichotomy. This article reflects the fundamental copyright principle of the idea/expression dichotomy. As the Agreed Statements concerning arts. 4 and 5 WCT show, an express clarification in this respect was particularly sought in view of the protection of computer programs and databases. The wording of the provision leans heavily on art. 9(2) TRIPS. The four indications of subject matter ineligible for copyright protection are to be understood as mere examples.

2. European legislation. Art. 1(2) of the Computer Programs Directive contains a similar provision.

3. ECJ jurisprudence. Referring to the idea/expression dichotomy reflected in art. 2 WCT, the ECJ held that the functionality of a computer program was ineligible for protection as a computer program in the sense of the Computer Programs Directive. The grant of copyright protection for computer program functionality would amount to the monopolization of ideas and have a detrimental effect on technological progress and industrial development. Because of the need to keep the functionality of a computer program free, an authorized user also enjoys the freedom of observing, studying and testing the functioning of the program in order to determine the underlying ideas and principles (*SAS Institute* (ECJ)).

[Application of articles 2 to 6 of the Berne Convention]

Article 3

Contracting Parties shall apply mutatis mutandis the provisions of Articles 2 to 6 of the Berne Convention in respect of the protection provided for in this Treaty.

Agreed Statement Concerning Article 3

It is understood that in applying Article 3 of this Treaty, the expression 'country of the Union' in Articles 2 to 6 of the Berne Convention will be read as if it were a reference to a Contracting Party to this Treaty, in the application of those Berne Articles in respect of protection provided for in this Treaty. It is also understood that the expression 'country outside the Union' in those Articles in the Berne Convention will, in the same circumstances, be read as if it were a reference to a country that is not a Contracting Party to this Treaty, and that 'this Convention' in Articles 2(8), 2bis(2), 3, 4 and 5 of the Berne Convention will be read as if it were a reference to the Berne Convention and this Treaty. Finally, it is understood that a reference in Articles 3 to 6 of the Berne Convention to a 'national of one of the countries of the Union' will, when these Articles are applied to this Treaty, mean, in regard to an intergovernmental organization that is a Contracting Party to this Treaty, a national of one of the countries that is member of that organization.

1. General. By virtue of the reference made in this article, core principles of international copyright protection, laid down in arts. 2 to 6 BC, are incorporated into the WCT. Most importantly, the reference in art. 3 WCT introduces the principle of national treatment and establishes its interplay with minimum rights (see arts. 5 and 6 BC). In line with the BC system, WCT minimum rights give foreign authors a stronger position than the guarantee of national treatment if national legislation falls short of the minimum standard of protection set forth in the WCT. Moreover, not only are the Berne criteria for determining the eligibility for protection to be applied (see arts. 3 and 4 BC) but so are the definition of protected subject matter, and certain rules on exclusions from and limitations on protection (see arts. 2 and 2bis BC). The reference in art. 3 WCT also clarifies that the enjoyment and the exercise of the rights granted in the WCT may not be subjected to any formalities (see art. 5(2) BC). This prohibition of formalities concerns formal requirements as to the coming into being or the enforcement of the rights (so-called 'external conditions'). However, it leaves room for formalities regulating the extent, quality and contents of protection ('internal conditions'). As a result, opt-out formalities, such as the necessity to reserve rights (see art. 10bis(1) BC) or the option of putting an end to an exemption of certain privileged acts (see art. 5 Orphan Works Directive), remain permissible under art. 3 WCT and art. 5(2) BC.

2. Protected works. (a) Inclusion of Berne Convention concept. A reference to 'literary and artistic works' can be found in the preamble and arts. 6(1), 8 and 10(1) WCT. The term is defined in art. 2(1) BC as including 'every production in the literary, scientific and artistic domain, whatever may be the mode or form of its expression'. Art. 3 WCT renders this broad definition applicable in the framework of the WCT, as well as the more specific rules enshrined in arts. 2(2), (3) and (5) BC which concern the requirement of material fixation, and alterations and collections of works. In connection with art. 2(6) BC, art. 3 WCT clarifies that the protection granted in the WCT operates for the benefit of the author and his or her successors in title (as to further right holders, such as licensees, see art. 11, note 5). The WCT interface with works of applied art and industrial designs and models follows from the reference to art. 2(7) BC. In this context, the minimum term of protection of 25 years set forth in art. 7(4) BC must be observed. **(b) ECJ jurisprudence.** The ECJ used several sources to establish an originality test in EU copyright law, including the 'general scheme of the Berne Convention' and, more specifically, art. 2(5) and (8) BC. As this Berne concept, by virtue of the reference made in art. 3 WCT, also underlies the WCT, the use of these sources is consistent with the approach taken in the WCT. Considering the Berne concept, the ECJ arrived at the conclusion that for a literary or artistic creation to be eligible for copyright protection, it had to be original in the sense that it was its author's own intellectual creation (*Infopaq International* (ECJ)). The required level of originality can be achieved through the 'choice, sequence and combination' of elements constituting a work (*Infopaq International* (ECJ) and *SAS Institute* (ECJ)). In determining whether sufficient creative choices have been made, the various stages and circumstances of the production process must be taken into account (*Painer* (ECJ)). Where the expression underlying a work is dictated by its technical function, the originality test is not met (*BSA* (ECJ) and *Football Association Premier League and Others* (ECJ)).

3. Permissible exclusions and limitations. In connection with art. 2(8) BC, art. 3 WCT excludes from protection news of the day and miscellaneous facts having the character of mere press items (see art. 11, note 2(b), as to the mandatory nature of this exclusion). Official texts and translations, as well as political speeches and speeches delivered in the course of legal proceedings may be excluded pursuant to the reference to arts. 2(4) and 2bis(1) and (3) BC. The reference to arts. 2bis(2) and (3) BC enables limitations serving the reproduction by the press, as well as the broadcasting and public communication of lectures, addresses and similar works delivered in public. No guidelines are given as to the analogous application of this provision in the context of the WCT. Considering the underlying informatory purpose, it is likely to apply to the distribution of relevant works by the press (art. 6 WCT), and their communication and making available to the public (art. 8 WCT). The difference between an exclusion pursuant to arts. 2(4), 2(8) or 2bis(1) BC, and a limitation based on art. 2bis(2) BC, lies in the fact that only in the latter case of a limitation the further requirements of the three-step test (art. 10(2) WCT) must be met (see art. 10, note 1(c)).

4. Eligibility for protection. (a) General. The reference to arts. 3 and 4 BC brings the criteria of eligibility for protection into line with the system established in the BC. Accordingly, the nationality or habitual residence of the author in one of the Contracting Parties to the WCT are relevant factors (art. 3 BC). Film authors may furthermore assert headquarters or the habitual residence of the maker of the film. In the case of architectural works and other works incorporated in a building or other structure, the location in a Contracting Party may be decisive (see art. 4 BC). Also, first or simultaneous publication is decisive. Consequently, by way of reference, art. 3 WCT includes into the WCT the definition of 'published works' laid down in art. 3(3) BC. **(b) Online publication.** This raises the issue of whether, and under what circumstances, works that have exclusively been published online should be regarded as 'published' within the meaning of the WCT. Clearly, the act of making a work available to the public in the sense of the second part of art. 8 WCT constitutes neither a performance nor a broadcast or other traditional form of communication to the public within the meaning of the second sentence of art. 3(3) BC, and hence does not appear to be excluded per se from the notion of publication. In addition, online publication may result in a degree of constant availability that is comparable to the distribution of material copies. Therefore, it is not excluded to consider online publication as 'publication' within the meaning of arts. 3(3) BC and 3 WCT. On the one hand, it appears inappropriate to deny publication altogether because this would deprive authors publishing their works exclusively online of one of the factors from which the eligibility for protection may follow pursuant to art. 3(1)(b) BC. On the other hand, it would hardly make sense to apply the definition of 'published works' in the context of the WCT so as to lead to simultaneous publications in all countries in which the work can be accessed via the Internet. A solution could be to require a certain degree of availability in terms of language, permanence and ease of location, in order to find conditions 'such as to satisfy the reasonable requirements of the public'. If this is the case, the country of publication and thus of origin in the sense of art. 5(4) BC, would not be the country in which the server is located, but rather the country in which the arrangements for the adequate online publication fulfilling the aforementioned requirements have been made.

5. Country of origin. Besides the principle of national treatment and minimum rights, and the prohibition of formalities already mentioned above (see note 1), the reference to art. 5 BC also incorporates the Berne system for identifying a work's country of origin established in art. 5(4) BC. Accordingly, the first or simultaneous publication in a Contracting Party to the WCT is the main factor to be considered. In the Contracting Party of origin, protection is governed by domestic legislation (art. 5(3) BC). The principle of national treatment is to be applied to authors who are not nationals. Consequently, these authors enjoy the same rights as national authors, but may not invoke WCT minimum rights in the Contracting Party of origin. It is to be noted that the term of protection in the Contracting Party of origin may also be applied in other Contracting Parties pursuant to the comparison of terms following from arts. 1(4) WCT and 7(8) BC (see art. 7 BC, note 9), which is, however, excluded within the EU due to the principle of non-discrimination laid down in art. 18 TFEU (see joined cases *Phil Collins* (ECJ) and *Ricordi* (ECJ)).

6. Restriction of protection. By virtue of the reference to art. 6 BC, a Contracting Party to the WCT, under certain circumstances, may restrict the protection of works created by nationals of a country which is not party to the WCT if the latter country fails to offer adequate protection to works of nationals of the Contracting Party. This limited element of reciprocity only concerns works that have first or simultaneously been published in a Contracting Party to the WCT and therefore enjoy protection by virtue of the reference to art. 3(1)(b) BC (see art. 6 BC, note 1).

7. The Agreed Statement. The Agreed Statement issues guidelines for the analogous application of arts. 2 to 6 BC. The last rule concerning intergovernmental organizations was included to clarify the specific situation emerging in the EU.

[Computer programs]

Article 4

Computer programs are protected as literary works within the meaning of Article 2 of the Berne Convention. Such protection applies to computer programs, whatever may be the mode or form of their expression.

Agreed Statement Concerning Article 4

The scope of protection for computer programs under Article 4 of this Treaty, read with Article 2, is consistent with Article 2 of the Berne Convention and on a par with the relevant provisions of the TRIPS Agreement.

1. General. (a) Status in the copyright system. The protection of computer programs 'as literary works' set forth in art. 4 reflects case law and legislative developments in many States including the EU (see art. 1(1) Computer Programs Directive), and at the international level (see art. 10 TRIPS). The assimilation to literary works makes it clear, for instance, that protection in line with the international rules governing works of applied art would be insufficient (see arts. 2(7), 7(4) BC). **(b) European legislation.** For EU legislation on the protection of computer programs, see particularly the Computer Programs Directive.

2. Scope. (a) Computer program. The WCT does not define the term 'computer program'. As with other work categories enumerated in art. 2(1) BC, the issue is left to national legislators and courts. Art. 4 WCT, however, clarifies that it may not be made a condition that the computer program be expressed in a specific 'mode or form'. The corresponding formula at the end of the article stems from art. 2(1) BC. Against the background of art. 10(1) TRIPS, it can be understood to indicate in particular that protection is to be granted regardless of whether source code or object code is used. **(b) Other subject matter.** Copyright protection for computer programs does not extend to other subject matter that may be contained in a computer program, such as, for example, databases, photographs, or the design of the program's visual appearance on the screen. **(c) ECJ jurisprudence.** Only the forms of expression and the preparatory design work capable of leading to the reproduction or the subsequent creation of a computer program constitute relevant 'computer programs' in the sense of the Computer Programs Directive (*BSA* (ECJ)). It follows from this definition that the graphic user interface of a computer program is not eligible for protection as a computer program because it does not enable the reproduction of the program as such. However, ineligibility for protection as a computer program does not exclude the possibility of the graphic user interface enjoying 'ordinary' copyright protection under the Information Society Directive if it is original in the sense that it is its author's own intellectual creation (*BSA* (ECJ)). Besides the graphic user interface, the functionality of a computer program, as well as the programming language and the format of data files used in a computer program, are also ineligible for protection as a computer program. While the functionality underlying a computer program must be kept free to avoid the monopolization of ideas and the impediment of follow-on innovation in the software sector, the programming language and the format of data files may attract ordinary copyright protection under the Information Society Directive. Moreover, the source or object code in a computer program relating to the use of a specific programming language and data file format may constitute a protected part of that program (*SAS Institute* (ECJ)).

3. Decompilation. Art. 4 does not deal with the issue of decompilation. It is unclear whether a norm such as art. 6 of the Computer Programs Directive has to be measured against the three-step tests of arts. 9(2) BC and 10(2) WCT, or whether it is left to the discretion of Member States. If decompilation is seen as a means of deciphering the ideas, procedures, methods and concepts underlying a computer program, it is consistent to place the exemption of acts of decompilation in the context of the idea/expression dichotomy reflected in art. 2 WCT. As the idea/expression dichotomy does not constitute a limitation or exception in the sense of the three-step test, this approach leads to the conclusion that the three-step test need not be taken into account. If, by contrast, decompilation is qualified as a relevant act of reproduction, the exemption of acts of decompilation constitutes a limitation imposed on the right of reproduction recognized in art. 9(1) BC which, by virtue of art. 4 WCT, also applies to computer programs. Based on this approach, the three-step tests of arts. 9(2) BC and 10(2) WCT come into play. Art. 6(3) of the Computer Programs Directive indicates that the latter view prevailed during the drafting of the EU regime for the protection of computer programs.

4. Limitations. (a) Quotations. The only mandatory limitation to be found in the BC is art. 10(1) BC permitting quotations (see art. 11, note 3(b)). As literary works, obviously, form one of its main fields of operation, the question arises in which way this important limitation can be adapted appropriately to the field of computer programs. **(b) Illustrations for teaching.** The inclusion of parts of a computer program in teaching material may be exempted by virtue of art. 10(2) BC. **(c) Private copying.** Private copying of computer programs may be permitted on the basis of the three-step tests laid down in arts. 9(2) BC and 10(2) WCT. The scope of corresponding private use privileges need not necessarily be confined to the making of so-called 'back-up' copies (see art. 5(2) of the Computer Programs Directive, see art. 10, notes 1(c) and 4).

5. The Agreed Statement. The purpose of the Agreed Statement is twofold. Firstly, it creates a close link to arts. 10(1) and 9(2) TRIPS, thereby underlining the intention not to exceed the level of protection reached in the TRIPS Agreement ('on a par'). Second, it gives evidence of the understanding that the decision to add computer programs to the canon of work categories eligible for copyright protection does not run counter to art. 2 BC. With regard to the reference to art. 2 WCT, see the comments on this article made above.

[Compilations of data (databases)]

Article 5

Compilations of data or other material, in any form, which by reason of the selection or arrangement of their contents constitute intellectual creations, are protected as such. This protection does not extend to the data or the material itself and is without prejudice to any copyright subsisting in the data or material contained in the compilation.

Agreed Statement Concerning Article 5

The scope of protection for compilations of data (databases) under Article 5 of this Treaty, read with Article 2, is consistent with Article 2 of the Berne Convention and on a par with the relevant provisions of the TRIPS Agreement.

1. General. (a) Underlying provisions. To establish the text of this article, an amalgam of arts. 2(5) BC and 10(2) TRIPS was applied. The need for a separate norm dealing specifically with databases arose from the restriction of art. 2(5) BC to collections of 'literary or artistic works'. Although it was felt that collections containing material ineligible for copyright protection could enjoy copyright protection on the basis of the broad art. 2(1) BC by virtue of an original selection or arrangement (see art. 2 BC, note 2), an explicit confirmation of this understanding was deemed desirable. This goal could first be achieved in the framework of the TRIPS negotiations leading to the adoption of art. 10(2) TRIPS. At the 1996 Diplomatic Conference, it was decided not to go beyond the level of protection reached in the TRIPS Agreement. Accordingly, art. 10(2) TRIPS served as a point of reference for the drafting of art. 5 (see art. 4, note 1). **(b) European legislation.** See Database Directive for EU legislation on the protection of databases.

2. Scope. (a) Compilations of data; databases. Like other terms identifying a work category listed in art. 2(1) BC, the terms 'compilations of data' or 'database' are not defined. The word 'compilation' stems from art. 10(2) TRIPS. To ensure consistency with the Berne Convention (in line with the special agreement status expressed in art. 1(1) WCT), it should not be interpreted to deviate from the concept of collection in art. 2(5) BC. The expression 'data or other material' indicates that any material may be used irrespective of whether or not it enjoys copyright or some other kind of protection. The protection of the database as such solely depends on an original selection or arrangement (see note 3) but not on the material compiled. The clarification 'in any form' comprises particularly machine readable form which is mentioned explicitly in art. 10(2) TRIPS. It also covers traditional non-electronic compilations. **(b) Compiled material.** The protection of the compilation as a whole in no way affects the status of protection of single material used. Unprotected material remains unprotected. Material enjoying some kind of protection is not deprived of this protection. The explicit mention of copyrighted material at the end of art. 5 must be regarded as a mere example. In fact, other types of protection, such as patent, trademark or industrial design protection, and particularly protection evolving from neighbouring rights, are not prejudiced by the protection of a compilation containing relevant material.

3. Intellectual creations. (a) Originality standard. By requiring an intellectual creation, art. 5 confines the scope of protection to compilations of data or other material which meet a certain originality standard to be determined at the national level. Hence there is no international obligation to provide for the kind of sui generis protection of non-original databases granted in art. 7 of the Database Directive. In line with the prevailing French text of art. 2(5) BC (see art. 37(1)(c) BC), the necessary level of originality may be reached through a creative selection 'or' arrangement of the material compiled. If, for instance, all data concerning a specific issue is compiled so that a selection can no longer be made, protection may still be obtained by arranging the comprehensive material in a creative manner. The second authentic text of art. 2(5) BC, in the English language (see art. 37(1)(a) BC), may give rise to misunderstandings in this case because it refers to selection 'and' arrangement. **(b) ECJ jurisprudence.** In line with the international standard reflected in art. 5 WCT, the ECJ held that for a database to enjoy copyright protection, it had to constitute its author's own intellectual creation by reason of the selection or arrangement of the database contents. This originality test is fulfilled when the author expresses his creative ability in an original manner by making free and creative choices with regard to the selection or arrangement of data. The investment of significant skill and labour, by contrast, is not sufficient to justify copyright protection (*Football Dataco and Others* (ECJ)).

4. The Agreed Statement. In respect of the objectives underlying the Agreed Statement, the comments on the corresponding Agreed Statement concerning art. 4 may be consulted (see art. 4, note 5). The reference to the TRIPS Agreement concerns arts. 10(2) and 9(2) TRIPS.

[Right of distribution]

Article 6

(1) Authors of literary and artistic works shall enjoy the exclusive right of authorizing the making available to the public of the original and copies of their works through sale or other transfer of ownership.

(2) Nothing in this Treaty shall affect the freedom of Contracting Parties to determine the conditions, if any, under which the exhaustion of the right in paragraph (1) applies after the first sale or other transfer of ownership of the original or a copy of the work with the authorization of the author.

Agreed Statement Concerning Articles 6 and 7

As used in these Articles, the expressions 'copies' and 'original and copies', being subject to the right of distribution and the right of rental under the said Articles, refer exclusively to fixed copies that can be put into circulation as tangible objects.

1. General. (a) Formal recognition in international law. By virtue of this article, a general right of first distribution is formally recognized in international copyright law. Prior to the WCT, this right could only be inferred from the consideration that on its merits, it is a corollary of the right of reproduction. In the field of cinematographic works, however, specific distribution rights are laid down in arts. 14(1) and 14bis(1) BC. **(b) European legislation.** See art. 4 of the Information Society Directive, art. 4(c) of the Computer Programs Directive, art. 5(c) of the Database Directive and art. 9 of the Rental Right Directive as to the distribution right recognized in EU law. **(c) Impact on ECJ jurisprudence.** To clarify the meaning of the open concept of distribution set forth in art. 4(1) of the Information Society Directive ('distribution to the public by sale or otherwise'), the ECJ relied on the definition provided in art. 6(1) WCT. It inferred from this international source (and the corresponding definitions given in arts. 8 and 12 WPPT) that distribution in the sense of the Information Society Directive required a transfer of ownership. The term 'sale or otherwise' had to be understood in the light of art. 6(1) WCT as a requirement of 'sale or other transfer of ownership'. Hence, it is not sufficient to grant to the public a right of use of a copyrighted object, or exhibit such an object. These acts do not fall within the scope of the distribution right of art. 4(1) of the Information Society Directive (*Peek & Cloppenburg* (ECJ)).

2. Definition (para. 1). (a) Making available. The requirement of making available 'through sale or other transfer of ownership' could be misunderstood to indicate that the mere offer for sale or other transfer of ownership does not constitute a relevant act of distribution. The reference, however, was made to exclude temporary acts of distribution, such as public lending or commercial rental. It does not define the central act of 'making available' which, consequently, is not confined to the final transfer of ownership but includes preparatory acts, such as an offer for sale (see art. 8, note 5). **(b) Original and copies.** The reference to 'the original and copies of [authors'] works' does not establish a cumulative requirement but has an affirmative meaning: not only with regard to the original but also in respect of potential copies of their works, authors may assert the right of first distribution. Hence the right can be invoked if there is only an original, for instance, of a painting or a sculpture, but no copies. For exhaustion in the digital environment see below, note 3(d). **(c) The public.** The term 'public' is not defined in the WCT. National legislators and courts are called upon to fill the gap (for further detail see art. 8, note 3).

3. Exhaustion (para. 2). (a) Conditions. The WCT does not define the term 'exhaustion'. In general, exhaustion is meant to indicate that a right holder can no longer invoke his exclusive distribution right once he has exercised it. The exhaustion of the right of distribution depends on the fulfilment of two conditions: first, the original or a copy of the work must have been sold or the ownership must have been transferred in another way. Exhaustion therefore does not apply in a situation where a reproduction of a protected work, after having been marketed in the EU with the copyright holder's consent, has undergone an alteration of its medium, such as the transfer of that reproduction from a paper poster onto a canvas, and is placed on the market again in its new form (*Art & Allposters International* (ECJ)). Second, this change in ownership must have been carried out with the authorization of the author. **(b) Territorial effect.** Within this framework, the Contracting Parties to the WCT are free to adopt different models (see art. 6 TRIPS where the issue of exhaustion has been left open). They may provide for national or regional exhaustion, requiring the first sale or other transfer of ownership to take place on the territory of a State or intergovernmental organization (such as the EU) and, as a corollary, vesting authors with a right of importation (see art. 4(2) of the Information Society Directive as to the model adopted in the EU; see also *Deutsche Grammophon* (ECJ) and *Musik-Vertrieb Membran* (ECJ)). Alternatively, they may apply a concept of international exhaustion, considering any first sale or other transfer of ownership sufficient for exhausting the right of distribution – irrespective of the place where such transfer occurs. **(c) Safeguard clause.** Pursuant to the clause at the beginning of art. 6(2) ('Nothing in this Treaty shall…'), this freedom of Contracting Parties is not affected by other WCT provisions. Accordingly, the choice between national, regional or international exhaustion, for instance, is not subject to the three-step test enshrined in art. 10(1) WCT. **(d) Scope in the digital environment.** It is to be noted, however, that the scope of the safeguard clause itself seems to be confined to tangible copies due to the Agreed Statement concerning arts. 6 and 7 WCT. When read together with the Agreed Statement, the expression 'the original or a copy of the work' used in the safeguard clause must be understood to refer exclusively to fixed copies that can be put into circulation as tangible objects. The extension of the exhaustion principle to copies of a computer program that are put into circulation via downloads from the Internet instead of distribution on CD-ROM or DVD (*UsedSoft* (ECJ)) may thus fall outside the scope of the safeguard clause. As a result, this interpretation would give rise to the question of whether the application of the exhaustion principle to intangible copies offered on the Internet must be measured against the three-step test of art. 10(1) WCT. On the one hand, this conclusion is not inescapable. The download of a copy from the Internet onto a data carrier finally leads to a tangible copy on that carrier. From this perspective, the requirement of a 'fixed copy' in the Agreed Statement is fulfilled. The safeguard clause can thus be understood to cover the copy on the data carrier resulting from the download. On the other hand, the ECJ based its extension of the exhaustion principle to copies obtained via downloads from the Internet on the presumption that the right holder had been able to receive a remuneration corresponding to the economic use value of the program in question in cases where the first acquirer obtains a right to use the program copy for an unlimited period of time (*UsedSoft* (ECJ)). Even if the three-step test was applicable, this precondition could be seen as a sufficient safeguard against a conflict with a normal exploitation of the computer program (second step) and an unreasonable prejudice to legitimate interests (third step). Hence, the extension of the exhaustion principle need not give rise to concerns about non-compliance with the three-step test in art. 10(1) WCT. For the time being, it remains unclear whether or not the ECJ will come to the same conclusion, if the issue is not the exhaustion of the distribution right with regard to a computer program covered by the Computer Programs Directive, but a work covered by the Information Society Directive such as an e-book.

4. The Agreed Statement. (a) Requirement of fixed copies. According to the wording of the Agreed Statement to art. 6, the rules concerning the right of distribution set forth in art. 6(1) and (2) are only applicable to fixed copies in the sense of the Agreed Statement. This requirement of fixed copies clarifies the interplay between the right of distribution of art. 6 WCT and the right of communication to the public of art. 8 WCT. Whereas the making available of fixed copies and thus tangible objects is governed by art. 6, the making available of intangible copies through interactive on-demand communications falls within the scope of art. 8 (see art. 8, note 5). Domestic legislation need not necessarily follow the same route. The international obligation to grant the interactive making available right set forth in art. 8, for instance, may also be fulfilled by providing for a broader national right of distribution extending to on-demand Internet transmissions. **(b) Approach taken by the ECJ.** Whereas the international distinction between distribution on the one hand and communication to the public on the other hand thus depends on whether the work is disseminated in tangible or intangible form, the ECJ asks whether a transfer of ownership has taken place. According to the Court, the existence of a transfer of ownership changes an act of communication to the public (in the sense of art. 3 of the Information Society Directive) into an act of distribution (in the sense of art. 4 of the Information Society Directive) (*UsedSoft* (ECJ)). This incongruence with the international criterion is surprising as it is established case law of the ECJ that concepts of EU copyright law must be interpreted, so far as possible, in a manner that is consistent with international law (*Peek & Cloppenburg* (ECJ)). From an international perspective, EU copyright law need not follow the concepts underlying international law as long as it does not fall short of the international minimum standard of protection. In other words, domestic lawmakers are free to qualify an act of communication to the public in the sense of the WCT as an act of distribution in domestic law, provided that the protection granted under that different label is at least as favourable as the international minimum standard following from the right of communication to the public in the sense of the WCT. Hence, the problem that may arise from the application of the criterion of a transfer of ownership (instead of the criterion of a tangible/intangible copy) lies in a possibly overbroad application of the freedom to regulate exhaustion (following from art. 6(2) WCT) in situations which, from the perspective of the international criterion of a tangible/intangible copy, would have fallen under the right of communication to the public granted in art. 8 WCT. In the context of art. 8, this freedom to regulate exhaustion cannot be inferred from art. 6(2) WCT but, instead, must be derived from the three-step test set forth in art. 10(1) WCT. It seems that the ECJ has not yet disregarded the international minimum standard of protection in the area of communication to the public by applying the criterion of a transfer of ownership. The extension of the exhaustion principle to copies of computer programs obtained via downloads from the Internet (*UsedSoft* (ECJ)) can be understood to either lead to a 'fixed copy' in the sense of the Agreed Statement (and thus fall under the right of distribution in the sense of the WCT), or comply with the three-step test of art. 10(1) WCT because of the remuneration which the right holder was able to receive when transferring ownership (see note 3(d) above).

[Right of rental]

Article 7

(1) Authors of
    (i) computer programs;
    (ii) cinematographic works; and
    (iii) works embodied in phonograms, as determined in the national law of Contracting Parties,
shall enjoy the exclusive right of authorizing commercial rental to the public of the originals or copies of their works.
    (2)   Paragraph (1) shall not apply
      (i) in the case of computer programs, where the program itself is not the essential object of the rental; and
      (ii) in the case of cinematographic works, unless such commercial rental has led to widespread copying of such works materially impairing the exclusive right of reproduction.
    (3)   Notwithstanding the provisions of paragraph (1), a Contracting Party that, on April 15,1994, had and continues to have in force a system of equitable remuneration of authors for the rental of copies of their works embodied in phonograms may maintain that system provided that the commercial rental of works embodied in phonograms is not giving rise to the material impairment of the exclusive right of reproduction of authors.

Agreed Statement Concerning Articles 6 and 7

As used in these Articles, the expressions 'copies' and 'original and copies', being subject to the right of distribution and the right of rental under the said Articles, refer exclusively to fixed copies that can be put into circulation as tangible objects.

Agreed Statement Concerning Article 7

It is understood that the obligation under Article 7(1) does not require a Contracting Party to provide an exclusive right of commercial rental to authors who, under that Contracting Party's law, are not granted rights in respect of phonograms. It is understood that this obligation is consistent with Article 14(4) of the TRIPS Agreement.

1. General. (a) Influence of TRIPS provisions. Art. 7 WCT provides for a right of rental which does not exist in the BC. The complex framework established in art. 7 becomes understandable in the light of the rental rights granted in arts. 11 and 14(4) TRIPS. Although art. 9(1) of the Basic Proposal for the 1996 Diplomatic Conference reflected the aim to recognize a general right of rental covering all categories of works, it was finally decided not to go beyond the fragmentary compromise solution found in the TRIPS context. Accordingly, art. 7 WCT was carefully modelled on arts. 11 and 14(4) TRIPS and applies only to computer programs, cinematographic works and works embodied in phonograms. **(b) European legislation.** For EU legislation on rental rights, see the Rental Right Directive in which a broad approach relating to authors of all categories of works, as well as performers and producers of phonograms and films is taken. With regard to computer programs, see art. 4(c) of the Computer Programs Directive.

2. Relevant acts. (a) Commercial rental. By virtue of art. 7, authors may control commercial rental. Non-commercial activities are excluded to avoid interference with public lending serving the dissemination of information and educational purposes. While the specific line between commercial rental and non-profit lending is to be drawn by Contracting Parties, the term 'commercial' seems to indicate that the right of rental, in any case, can be asserted when a direct economic advantage accrues from business-like activities. If, on the other hand, a public library charges user fees only to recoup administrative costs, it appears safe to deny an act of commercial rental. What remains is the question of indirect economic advantages a company may derive from a non-profit public library which it runs, besides potential further objectives, to support its commercial activities. **(b) The public.** The term 'public' is not defined in the WCT. National legislators and courts are called upon to fill the gap (see art. 8, note 3, as to its likely meaning). **(c) Unaffected by exhaustion.** Unlike the right of distribution, the right of rental is not subject to the principle of exhaustion. It can thus be invoked after the first distribution of the original or a copy of the work through sale or other transfer of ownership (see art. 6, note 3).

3. Impairment test (paras. 2(ii) and 3). (a) Function. In line with arts. 11 and 14(4) TRIPS, the international obligation to provide for an exclusive right of rental may depend on material impairment of the right of reproduction, as recognized internationally in art. 9(1) BC. In the field of cinematographic works, the exclusive right of rental need not be granted in the absence of a material impairment (para. 2(ii)). In respect of works embodied in phonograms, the exclusive right may be replaced with a long-standing system of equitable remuneration unless a material impairment arises (para. 3). **(b) Comparison with the three-step test.** In the context of the right of reproduction, the second criterion of the three-step test, laid down in art. 9(2) BC, serves the same function of forming the threshold for entering the sphere of the exclusive right (see art. 9 BC, note 4(b) and comments on art. 10 WCT and 13 TRIPS). In sum, it can be posited that the right of reproduction is materially impaired if commercial rental activities come into conflict with a normal exploitation of the work in the field of the right of reproduction. In this particular case, the analysis (see art. 10, note 4) must necessarily focus on the specific situation in the field of the right of reproduction and not on the overall commercialization of cinematographic works or works embodied in phonograms.

4. Computer programs. (a) Beneficiaries (para. 1(i)). In line with art. 11 TRIPS, art. 7(1)(i) WCT confers on authors of computer programs an exclusive right of rental (see note 2 as to its scope). **(b) Limitation (para. 2(i)).** The international obligation to grant the right of rental does not arise if the computer program does not constitute the essential object of the rental, as in the case of renting cars, aircrafts or other machines equipped with computers and driven by specific software. In general, it may be stated that a computer program is not essential in the sense of art. 7(2)(i) if it merely allows another main object of rental to be used properly. To illustrate the distinction to be made, the rental of a computer may serve as an example. If only a regular operating system has been installed on the rented computer, the computer program is not essential. If, however, specific application software has been uploaded, the software forms a separate essential element of the rental, in respect of which the exclusive right following from art. 7(1)(i) would apply.

5. Cinematographic works. (a) Beneficiaries (para. 1(ii)). Pursuant to the reference to art. 14bis(2)(a) BC made in art. 1(4) WCT, the circle of authors of cinematographic works is to be drawn by national legislation. In line with art. 11 TRIPS, these authors enjoy the exclusive right of rental set forth in art. 7(1)(ii) (see note 2 as to its scope). **(b) Indirect impairment test (para. 2(ii)).** On account of art. 7(2)(ii), the obligation to grant the exclusive right of rental does not arise unless commercial acts of renting cinematographic works have led to widespread copying materially impairing the right of reproduction. Therefore, the starting point for carrying out the impairment test (see note 3) is not the rental of cinematographic works as such. Although a potential purchaser may no longer feel inclined to buy a copy of a film after renting and watching it, this potential direct impact on the sale of copies is irrelevant. **(c) Problem of private copying.** Instead, empirical evidence of the following complex indirect relationship is to be offered. First, it must be shown that private copying results from the rental of cinematographic works. Second, it is to be demonstrated that this specific form of private copying materially impairs the right of reproduction. Only then, must the right of rental be granted which, given the circumstances, appears as a specific kind of compensation for substantial losses in the field of the right of reproduction.

6. Works embodied in phonograms. (a) Beneficiaries (para. 1(iii)). In line with art. 14(4) TRIPS, it is a matter for national legislation to determine the authors enjoying the right of rental set forth in art. 7(1)(iii). Composers, the writers of song lyrics, and writers whose texts have been recorded are not unlikely to feature among the beneficiaries of the provision. **(b) Equitable remuneration (para. 3).** The exclusive right may be replaced with a system of equitable remuneration by virtue of art. 7(3). Meticulously following art. 14(4) TRIPS, it is made a condition that the continuous operation of the remuneration system can be traced back to the date of adopting the TRIPS Agreement. The provision thus reflects the aim not to deviate from the TRIPS compromise solution (see note 1). Like art. 14(4) TRIPS, it 'grandfathers' national remuneration systems which have been run continuously since 15 April 1994. **(c) Direct and indirect impairment test.** The maintenance of a system of equitable remuneration is no longer permissible once the commercial rental of works embodied in phonograms gives rise to the material impairment of the right of reproduction (see note 3). The use of the general term 'gives rise' seems to indicate that, unlike in the case of cinematographic works (see note 5(b)), both potential direct (people renting and listening to a work no longer want to purchase a copy) and indirect (people renting a work make their own private copy) effects on the right of reproduction are to be considered in this context.

7. The Agreed Statement concerning arts. 6 and 7. The rental rights recognized in art. 7 only apply to fixed copies in the sense of the Agreed Statement. The statement also clarifies the interplay with art. 8 WCT (see art. 6, note 4).

8. The Agreed Statement concerning art. 7. Art. 14(4) TRIPS confers rental rights on phonogram producers and 'any other right holders in phonograms as determined in a Member's law'. The latter passage reflects different views held with regard to the circle of beneficiaries. A restrictive approach to rights in phonograms would not go beyond the group of phonogram producers. Authors, such as composers and songwriters, as well as performers, only enter the picture if the reference to 'right holders in phonograms' is construed so as to include right holders in material embodied in phonograms. Art. 7(1)(iii) WCT seems to follow this latter interpretation.

Against this background, the Agreed Statement concerning art. 7 deals with the exclusion of authors on the grounds that they are not granted rights 'in respect of phonograms'. Virtually, the statement may be perceived as a means to uphold the ambiguity of art. 14(4) TRIPS. As Contracting Parties are free to determine the beneficiaries of the right of renting works embodied in phonograms pursuant to para. 1(iii) anyway, the Agreed Statement does not seem to add much.

[Right of communication to the public]

Article 8

Without prejudice to the provisions of Articles 11(1)(ii), 11bis(1)(i) and (ii), 11ter(1)(ii), 14(1)(ii) and 14bis(1) of the Berne Convention, authors of literary and artistic works shall enjoy the exclusive right of authorizing any communication to the public of their works, by wire or wireless means, including the making available to the public of their works in such a way that members of the public may access these works from a place and at a time individually chosen by them.

Agreed Statement Concerning Article 8

It is understood that the mere provision of physical facilities for enabling or making a communication does not in itself amount to communication within the meaning of this Treaty or the Berne Convention. It is further understood that nothing in Article 8 precludes a Contracting Party from applying Article 11bis(2).

1. General. (a) Trend towards broad exclusive rights. This article establishes a general right of communication to the public (first part of the provision) encompassing interactive on-demand acts (second part) but not extending to public performances (see note 2). It gives evidence of a trend towards broad exclusive rights in international copyright law. At the 1967 Stockholm Conference for the revision of the BC, a general right of reproduction was set forth in art. 9(1) BC. The BC, however, does not contain a general right of communication to the public (see art. 1 BC, note 1). **(b) Applicable law.** It should be noted that the WCT is silent on the question of which law, or which laws, to apply in the case of a transborder communication to the public. This question is of relevance both to transborder satellite transmission of protected works and to the making available of protected works over the Internet. In both cases the WCT does not seem to preclude any solution. **(c) European legislation.** As to the implementation of art. 8 WCT into EU legislation, see art. 3(1) of the Information Society Directive.

2. Concept of communication to the public. As the WCT is a special agreement within the meaning of art. 20 BC (art. 1(1) WCT), the notion of communication to the public underlying art. 8 must be seen in the context of the provisions of the BC. **(a) Relationship to Berne public performance rights.** In arts. 11 and 11ter BC, a distinction is drawn between the right of public performance (subpara. 1(i) of these provisions) and the right of communication to the public (subpara. 1(ii)). Similarly, both distinct terms are used in art. 14(1)(ii) BC. A public performance occurs when members of the public gather at a specific place to jointly attend a performance at a predetermined time. Hence there is no transmission to another place. In this sense, the right of publicly playing or showing a work's broadcast granted in art. 11bis(1)(iii) BC is to be qualified as a public performance right as well, even though being labelled a right of 'public communication' in the provision itself. The described distinction between public performance and communication to the public was maintained in the WCT. This can be inferred from the fact that the 'without prejudice' clause at the beginning of art. 8 does not refer to the aforementioned arts. 11(1)(i), 11bis(1)(iii), 11ter(1)(i) BC specifically dealing with a work's public performance. The concept of public communication underlying art. 8, consequently, does not extend to public performances. If members of the public enjoy the performance of a work at the same place and time, only the Berne public performance rights apply and art. 8 is inapplicable. **(b) Overlap with Berne public communication rights.** The general right of communication to the public set out in art. 8 covers all remaining situations (see note 4 on the general public communication right: different place/predetermined time, and note 5 on the making available right: different place/individually chosen time). It coexists with the public communication rights recognized in the BC. Their relationship to the general right of art. 8 is clarified through the 'without prejudice' clause at the beginning of the article (notes 4(b) and 5(b)). **(c) Boundary line drawn in European legislation.** A distinction between the right of public performance and the right of communication to the public is also drawn in European legislation. According to recital 23, the Information Society Directive only covers communication to the public not present at the place where the communication originates. Hence, the public performance situation where the public gathers at a specific place to jointly attend a performance, as in the case of live presentations or performances of a work, falls outside the scope of the Directive (*Circul Globus București* (ECJ)). However, the ECJ also made it clear that such an element of direct physical contact (excluding the application of the harmonized right of communication to the public) was absent where a television broadcast was presented to a public in a bar, hotel or restaurant via a television screen and speakers. In this case, it was not sufficient for denying the application of the harmonized right of communication to the public that the public was present at the place of transmission of the television signals. By contrast, the right was only inapplicable in cases where the public is present at the place where the communication originates, in the sense of presence at the place where the broadcast performance is actually performed (*Football Association Premier League and Others* (ECJ)). **(d) Departure from the international concept.** This concept of communication to the public developed by the ECJ is broader than the concept underlying international copyright law.

The 'without prejudice' clause at the beginning of art. 8 does not refer to art. 11bis(1)(iii) BC – the international right of communicating broadcasts to the public by loudspeaker or analogous instruments. This indicates that the right of communicating works to the public via a television screen and speakers is seen as a public performance right in international copyright law. The departure from this broader international concept of public performance does not make EU copyright law incompatible with the Berne Convention and the WCT. The EU need not follow the distinction between different kinds of exclusive rights drawn at the international level as long as the standard of protection in the EU does not fall short of the international minimum standard of protection. However, the departure from the international concept is relevant with regard to the relationship between harmonized EU law and national legislation of EU Member States. By broadening the international concept of communication to the public, the ECJ brings forms of public performance within the scope of the harmonized right of communication to the public which, according to the international concept, would have remained unaffected by the Information Society Directive. In other words, the ECJ curtails the freedom of EU Member States to regulate television screen and loudspeaker communications in bars, hotels and restaurants which constitute acts of public performance from the perspective of international law. It is to be conceded, however, that the international concept of communication to the public in the field of neighbouring rights also differs from the concept in international copyright law. The ECJ may thus find support for its broader approach in the international regulation of neighbouring rights.

3. The public. (a) No international definition. The WCT does not define the 'public' to which a work must be communicated or made available in order to invoke the rights granted in art. 8. In the absence of a treaty definition, national legislators and courts are called upon to fill the gap in the light of the preamble of the WCT. It appears safe to assume that a circle consisting of family members and close social acquaintances does not constitute a relevant 'public' in the sense of art. 8. A school, university or company intranet, on the other hand, is likely to fall within the province of the article. **(b) Approach taken by the ECJ.** The ECJ developed an elastic concept of the 'public', including the notion of a 'new public' in the sense of an audience that is larger than the direct users of a broadcast of a work, such as the clientele of a bar, hotel or restaurant (*SGAE* (ECJ), *Football Association Premier League and Others* (ECJ)), and the notion of a 'wider public' in the sense of a public going beyond the one targeted by the original broadcasting organization, such as subscribers to a satellite package (*Airfield and Canal Digitaal* (ECJ)). To identify a 'new' or 'wider' public, the ECJ takes as a starting point the public which was taken into account by the right holder when authorizing the broadcasting or other initial act of communication to the public. This public is then compared with the public reached through the intervention of other operators (*SGAE* (ECJ), *Football Association Premier League and Others* (ECJ), *Airfield and Canal Digitaal* (ECJ), *ITV Broadcasting* (ECJ), *Svensson* *and Others* (ECJ) and *BestWater International* (ECJ)). The ECJ requires an indeterminate number of potential users (*Mediakabel* (ECJ), *Lagardère Active Broadcast* (ECJ)) or at least a 'fairly large number of persons' who succeed each other quickly (*SGAE* (ECJ)). The Court thus considers the cumulative effects of making works available to potential audiences, including the effect on persons following each other in succession. The requirement of a fairly large number of persons, however, implies a de minimis threshold which excludes from the concept groups of persons which are too small or insignificant, such as patients in a private dental practice (*SCF* (ECJ)). Moreover, the ECJ only looks for a 'new public' if the communication is made by the same technical means as the initial communication, whereas a public will invariably be found if the communication is made by other technical means than those by which the first communication was made (*SGAE* (ECJ), *OSDDTOE* (ECJ), *ITV Broadcasting and Others* (ECJ), *Svensson and Others* (ECJ) and *BestWaterInternational* (ECJ)). For further discussion, see the commentary on art. 3 of the Information Society Directive.

4. The general public communication right (first part of the article). (a) General. The general right set forth in the first part of art. 8 overcomes the fragmentary nature of the public communication rights set forth in the BC. Firstly, it is applicable to all kinds of works including graphic and photographic works. Second, it covers both wired and wireless means of communication. Third, it is a technology-neutral right intended to respond to the challenges of the digital environment. In the context of the first part of art. 8, the expression 'communication to the public' particularly refers to situations in which a work is transmitted at a predetermined time so that members of the public can perceive it at different places (so-called 'push' concept; as to the corresponding 'pull' concept, see note 5). **(b) Interplay with Berne public communication rights.** The 'without prejudice' clause at the beginning of art. 8 indicates that the recognition of a general right of communication to the public is not intended to interfere with the operation of the enumerated specific provisions of the BC. Art. 8 WCT supplements the provisions of the BC, as far as the right of communication is not yet covered by the Berne Convention.

5. The making available right (second part of the article). (a) General. Pursuant to the second part of art. 8, the general right of communication to the public explicitly includes interactive on-demand communication to the public, in particular via the Internet. Like the general right established in the first part of art. 8, the right of making available is applicable to all kinds of works and extends to wired and wireless means of communication alike. The relevant act of making available lies in offering a work for individual access by users, for instance, when running a website. It is not necessary that any user take advantage of the service. Once a work is accessed, however, the right covers the entire transmission to the user. The making available right concerns situations in which members of the public are free to choose individually the place and time for perceiving a work. It is thus characterized by the individual choice of the user (interactive on-demand 'pull' concept; as to the corresponding 'push' concept, see note 4). To determine whether an element of individual choice prevails, the final act rendering the work perceivable is decisive. **(b) Interplay with Berne public communication rights.** It remains unclear whether or not making works available to the public can be seen as already covered by arts. 11(1)(ii), 11bis(1)(i) and (ii), 11ter(1)(ii), 14(1)(ii) and 14bis(1) BC. On the one hand, these provisions might not be construed to cover situations in which members of the public individually choose the time and place for perceiving a work (successive public), both for historic reasons and to avoid that making works available to the public over the Internet could be subjected to non-voluntary licensing pursuant to art. 11bis(2) BC. On the other hand, the territorial scope of such a non-voluntary license according to art. 11bis(2) BC is limited to the territory of the granting State and can therefore not be used to allow transborder communications via the Internet without the consent of the authors. **(c) New digital services.** Art. 8 is silent on the issue of how new digital services, such as push services, webcasting, simulcasting and near-on-demand will have to be treated, that fall 'in between' traditional broadcasting on the one hand and making available on the other. However, the question is of lesser importance under the WCT than it is under the WPPT, since art. 8 WCT grants authors of copyrighted works a broad public communication right, whereas the WPPT only grants an exclusive right of making available, but leaves both performers and producers of phonograms only with a claim for remuneration in the case of a public communication made on the basis of a commercial phonogram. **(d) Implementation in national law.** In line with the deliberations at the 1996 Diplomatic Conference, the right of making available need not necessarily be implemented in national legislation by applying a public communication right even though it is listed as such in art. 8. Other rights, such as the right of distribution, may come into play as well. The ECJ distinguishes between acts of communication to the public and acts of distribution on the basis of the criterion of a sale or other transfer of ownership (*UsedSoft* (ECJ)). As the distinction between these exclusive rights in the WCT depends on whether the work is made available to the public in tangible or intangible form, it cannot be excluded that certain acts qualifying as communication to the public under the WCT fall under the right of distribution in EU copyright law (see art. 6, note 4(b)).

6. The Agreed Statement. (a) The first sentence. *General.* Firstly, the Agreed Statement clarifies that the mere provision of the hardware infrastructure necessary to communicate a work does not constitute a relevant act of communication in its own right. This tribute paid to telecommunication companies and Internet service providers, however, does not impact on national liability rules. Although not an act of communication, the provision of physical facilities may nevertheless trigger contributory or vicarious liability. Furthermore, the question has yet to be answered whether the Agreed

Statement also influences the judgment of non-physical facilities, such as a computer program enabling file-sharing. *Hyperlinking*. The supply of links to sites making a work available has been held not to be an independent act of communication to the public in the sense of art. 8 (*Paperboy* (Germany), *Svensson and Others* (ECJ), *BestWater International* (ECJ)). To arrive at this conclusion, the ECJ assumes that, at least in the case of links to protected works made available by the copyright holder on the Internet without any access restriction, no new public in the sense of EU copyright law is reached (*Svensson and Others* (ECJ), *BestWater International* (ECJ)). This approach is compatible with art. 8 WCT. In the Basic Proposal for the WCT, it was expressed clearly that 'communication to the public' required an act of 'transmission'. It was found that, as communication always involved transmission, the term 'transmission' could have been chosen as the key term to describe the relevant act requiring authorization. Nonetheless, the term 'communication' was finally maintained to ensure consistency with the English text of the Berne Convention. In light of the interchangeability of the terms, however, the Basic Proposal pointed out that national legislation may opt for a right of 'transmission' instead of providing for a right of 'communication'. Linking technology does not involve a transmission or retransmission of protected works. It only provides users with the location of a protected work on the Internet (*Paperboy* (Germany)). Therefore, the use of links falls outside the scope of art. 8 WCT. By offering protection in cases where a new public is reached through a link (for instance, in case of a link circumventing access restrictions), the ECJ *de facto* offers WCT-plus protection. **(b) The second sentence.** Second, the Agreed Statement clarifies that the ambit of operation of art. 11bis(2) BC remains unaffected by art. 8 WCT. At the 1996 Diplomatic Conference, it was feared that, in the absence of this second sentence, art. 8 could encroach upon non-voluntary licences serving the retransmission of broadcasts. The statement solely reflects the status quo prior to the WCT. It must not be misunderstood to extend the scope of art. 11bis(2) BC to art. 8 WCT. Non-voluntary licences may be imposed on art. 8 on the basis of the three-step test enshrined in art. 10(1) WCT (see art. 10, note 5).

[Duration of the protection of photographic works]

Article 9

In respect of photographic works, the Contracting Parties shall not apply the provisions of Article 7(4) of the Berne Convention.

1. Assimilation of photographic works. The legal status of photographic works within the realm of protected literary and artistic works has been controversial since the adoption of the BC in 1886. Express mention of photographic works in the non-exhaustive list of art. 2(1) BC was not made before the 1948 Brussels Conference. Agreement on a minimum term of protection could not be reached prior to the 1967 Stockholm Conference. Since then, art. 7(4) BC has provided for a minimum period of protection of 25 years from the making of the photographic work. Against this background, art. 9 WCT appears as the last stage of the gradual assimilation of photographic works to 'classical' work categories, such as writings, musical compositions and paintings. By virtue of art. 9 WCT, the general rules (see notes on art. 7 BC) for determining the term of protection set forth in art. 7(1), (3) and (5) to (8) BC are also to be applied to photographic works instead of invoking the specific rules embodied in art. 7(4) BC. The general minimum term of protection is thus the life of the photographer and 50 years after his or her death (art. 7(1) BC), running from the first of January of the following year (art. 7(5) BC). Specific rules are to be observed in the case of anonymous or pseudonymous works (art. 7(3) BC). Deviations may moreover result from a comparison of terms under art. 7(8) BC or the privilege relating to certain national legislation based on the Rome Act of the BC (art. 7(7) BC). The application in time of the prolonged protection follows the rules laid down in arts. 13 WCT and 18 BC.

2. European legislation. In EU legislation, a term of protection of the life of the photographer and 70 years after his or her death is set forth in art. 6 of the Term Directive in respect of photographic works (see art. 7 BC, notes 1 and 5).

[Limitations and exceptions]

Article 10

(1) Contracting Parties may, in their national legislation, provide for limitations of or exceptions to the rights granted to authors of literary and artistic works under this Treaty in certain special cases that do not conflict with a normal exploitation of the work and do not unreasonably prejudice the legitimate interests of the author.

(2) Contracting Parties shall, when applying the Berne Convention, confine any limitations of or exceptions to rights provided for therein to certain special cases that do not conflict with a normal exploitation of the work and do not unreasonably prejudice the legitimate interests of the author.

Agreed Statement Concerning Article 10

It is understood that the provisions of Article 10 permit Contracting Parties to carry forward and appropriately extend into the digital environment limitations and exceptions in their national laws which have been considered acceptable under the Berne Convention. Similarly, these provisions should be understood to permit Contracting Parties to devise new exceptions and limitations that are appropriate in the digital network environment.

It is also understood that Article 10(2) neither reduces nor extends the scope of applicability of the limitations and exceptions permitted by the Berne Convention.

1. General. (a) Development in international copyright law. At the 1967 Stockholm Conference, the so-called three-step test of art. 9(2) BC was introduced in international copyright law to pave the way for the formal recognition of the general right of reproduction in art. 9(1) BC (see art. 9 BC, note 4(b)). In 1994, the three-step test reappeared in art. 13 TRIPS. Two years later, it was also included in art. 10 WCT. **(b) Structure and purpose.** The three steps of the three-step test are: first, limitations must be confined to special cases; second, they must not conflict with a normal exploitation of the work, and third, they must not unreasonably prejudice the legitimate interests of the author. These three tests apply cumulatively. A limitation must fulfil all of them to be permissible. Traditionally, the three-step test is moreover understood to require a step-by-step approach: a limitation must pass the first step before reaching the second step; and the second step before arriving at the third step. On the one hand, this traditional view can be defended on the basis of the drafting history underlying the first three-step test in art. 9(2) BC. At the 1967 Stockholm Conference, the drafting committee dealing with the three-step test reversed the order of the unreasonable prejudice test and the normal exploitation test to afford a more logical order for the interpretation of the test. On the other hand, modern interpretations of the three-step test underline inevitable overlaps between the contents of the different steps and the function of the three-step test to serve as a refined proportionality test. The three-step test sets limits to limitations on exclusive rights. However, its aim likewise is to allow national legislation a certain freedom to tailor limitations to domestic social, cultural and economic needs. The three-step test is thus both a limiting and an enabling clause. It is a proportionality test which enables the weighing of the different interests involved at the national level so as to strike a proper balance between rights and limitations. In this weighing process, the final, most flexible test concerning an unreasonable prejudice to legitimate interests (see note 5, below) can play a fundamental role. Against this background, a holistic understanding of the three-step test is preferable which sees the test as an indivisible whole and its individual steps as parts of a comprehensive overall assessment of a limitation in the light of the principle of proportionality. **(c) Notion of limitations and exceptions.** The three-step test of art. 10 WCT concerns 'limitations' and 'exceptions'. However, the provision is silent on the meaning of these terms. Considering the contents of the different steps of the three-step test, it makes little sense to follow an extensive interpretation qualifying forms of use that are permitted by law on the basis of an exemption as 'exceptions', and seeing as 'limitations' the idea/expression dichotomy (art. 2 WCT), exclusions from protection (arts. 2(4), 2(8) and 2bis(1) BC), the limitation of the term of protection (arts. 7 and 7bis BC) and the prohibition of works because of a conflict with principles of morality or public order, or an abuse of right (art. 17 BC). It can hardly have been the intention of Contracting Parties to confine the scope of these last-mentioned limitations to certain special cases which do not conflict with a work's normal exploitation and do not unreasonably prejudice the author's legitimate interests. Moreover, it seems difficult, if not impossible, to apply these criteria in any meaningful way to subject matter that is excluded from copyright protection altogether, or no longer enjoys protection after the expiry of protection. 'Limitations and exceptions' in the sense of the three-step test, therefore, only designate forms of use that are permitted by law on the basis of an exemption. The double reference to 'limitations' on the one hand, and 'exceptions' on the other hand, can be explained in different ways. First, the double reference seeks to cover both traditions of copyright law. Use of the term 'limitations' seems more appropriate in the Anglo-American copyright tradition where copyright is seen as a granted prerogative that need not go beyond what is necessary to achieve the underlying utilitarian objectives. The term 'exceptions', on the other hand, may be more appropriate in the continental European tradition where copyright is seen as a general rule following from the author's natural right to his work. Secondly, the term 'exceptions' can be understood to refer to exemptions not requiring the payment of equitable remuneration, whereas 'limitations' would mean exemptions for which equitable remuneration is paid. It should be noted in this respect that the distinction made by the ECJ between a complete exclusion of a right to authorize particular acts of use from the material scope of the right on the one hand, and a mere limitation of the right in question on the other hand (*VG Wort and Others* (ECJ)) is not very clear. **(d) European legislation.** An almost literal copy of the international three-step test has been incorporated into art. 5(5) of the Information Society Directive (see Information Society Directive, art. 5 note 6). Also, arts. 6(3) of the Computer Programs Directive, 10(3) of the Rental Right Directive and 6(3) of the Database Directive are modelled on the three-step test. It should be noted, however, that the functions of the three-step test in the WCT and in the EU directives differ substantially. Whereas within the framework of the WCT, the three-step test defines the limits of Member States' freedom to devise limitations and exceptions in their respective national laws, in the EU directives the three-step test further limits the limitations and exceptions already provided for in these same directives. The three-step test of art. 5(5) of the Information Society Directive, for instance, is not intended to extend the scope of exceptions or limitations listed in art. 5 of the Directive (*ACI Adam* (ECJ)). **(e) ECJ jurisprudence.** The ECJ expressed the view that copyright limitations had to be interpreted strictly in the light of the three-step test of art. 5(5) of the Information Society Directive (*Infopaq International* (ECJ), *ACI Adam* (ECJ)). As a general rule, this starting point for the interpretation of copyright limitations is questionable when considering the WCT. As expressly pointed out in the Agreed Statement concerning art. 10 WCT (see note 6, below), the three-step test laid down in art. 10 WCT is understood to allow Contracting Parties to carry forward and appropriately extend limitations into the digital environment. Contracting Parties also enjoy the freedom of devising new limitations. Given the fast evolution of new business models and services in the digital environment, this requires a flexible approach to traditional and new limitations instead of a strict interpretation that offers little room for the further development of limitations to reconcile copyright protection with competing social, cultural and economic needs. The EU and its Member States are free not to avail themselves of this flexibility reflected in the Agreed Statement concerning art. 10 WCT. However, it follows clearly from the Agreed Statement that the strict interpretation of copyright limitations is no international obligation. The ECJ, therefore, comes closer to the international acquis underlying the three-step test of art. 5(5) of the Information Society Directive where it recognized the need to strike a proper balance between copyright protection on the one hand, and the purposes served by a limitation on the other hand. Following this approach, the Court underlined the need to guarantee the proper functioning of limitations and ensure an interpretation that takes due account of underlying objectives and purposes. That interpretation had to safeguard a fair balance between the rights and interests of right holders on the one hand, and those of users on the other hand (*Football Association Premier League and Others* (ECJ), *Technische Universität Darmstadt* (ECJ)), in particular a fair balance between the right of freedom of expression of users and the exclusive rights of copyright holders (*Painer* (ECJ), *Deckmyn* (ECJ)).

2. Structure of the article. (a) Limitations on WCT rights (para. 1). Art. 10(1) concerns the rights newly granted in the WCT. It forms the only international rule to be observed when setting limits to the rights conferred in arts. 6, 7 and 8 WCT. As art. 9(2) BC, art. 10(1) WCT can therefore directly be invoked as a basis for national limitations. **(b) Limitations on Berne rights (para. 2).** By contrast, national limitations to rights granted under the BC cannot be based on art. 10(2) WCT. By virtue of art. 1(1) WCT, the WCT is a special agreement in the sense of art. 20 BC. This implies that Contracting Parties to the WCT are not in a position to weaken the exclusive rights granted in the BC by using art. 10(2) WCT as an independent basis for new limitations. The intention not to depart from the Berne standard of protection is also expressed in art. 1(2) WCT prohibiting derogations from existing obligations under the BC. Therefore, art. 10(2) WCT serves as an additional safeguard. For Contracting Parties to the WCT, it is not sufficient that a limitation based on arts. 2bis(2) BC (public lectures, addresses and other works), 9(2) BC (limitations on the right of reproduction), 10(1) BC (right of quotation), 10(2) BC (illustrations for teaching), 10bis(1) BC (newspaper articles on current economic, political or religious topics), 10bis(2) BC (reporting of current events), 11bis(2) BC (compulsory licensing in the area of broadcasting), 11bis(3) BC (ephemeral recordings) or 13(1) BC (compulsory licensing in the area of sound recordings), or on the implied limitations recognized under the BC, such as the so-called 'minor reservations doctrine' (see art. 9

BC, note 4), meets all requirements set forth in the Convention. In addition, it must comply with the three-step test of art. 10(2) WCT. However, the impact of art. 10(2) WCT on Berne limitations is reduced by the second Agreed Statement concerning art. 10 (see note 6(b), below). Moreover, permissible exclusions from protection (arts. 2(4) BC (official texts), 2(8) BC (news of the day) and 2bis(1) BC (political speeches and speeches delivered in court) are not subject to the three-step test (note 1(c), above).

3. First step: certain special cases. (a) Certainty. The term 'certain' has been interpreted to mean that copyright limitations must be clearly defined. This requirement of legal certainty, however, need not necessarily be seen in the light of the civil law approach with copyright limitations being precisely defined or even restrictively delineated. There is no need to identify explicitly each and every possible situation to which a limitation could apply, provided that its scope is known and particularized (*United States – Section 110(5) of the US Copyright Act* (WTO panel report)). Accordingly, it seems consistent to factor into the equation established case law when assessing open-ended common law limitations, such as the US fair use doctrine. **(b) Speciality.** Interpreting art. 13 TRIPS, a WTO Panel has put an emphasis on quantitative considerations, such as restrictions to the number of beneficiaries, on order to define the term 'special' (*United States – Section 110(5) of the US Copyright Act* (WTO panel report)). Some national courts, however, have interpreted the term 'special' in a normative sense. Interpreted in this way, a limitation must rest on a rational justificatory basis, such as, for example, education, research and access to information, which makes its adoption plausible (see *Kopienversanddienst* (Germany)). It can be argued that the latter approach distinguishes more clearly than the former between the first and the second criterion prohibiting a conflict with a normal exploitation. If the quantitative question of the number of beneficiaries (or other quantitative parameters) is already asked in the context of the first criterion, the certain special cases test is transformed into an economic analysis of the impact of the limitation on the market for the work. This economic analysis, however, anticipates and preempts the normal exploitation test which constitutes the second criterion of the three-step test.

4. Second step: conflict with a normal exploitation. (a) Central problem. The key problem posed by the second criterion is the market analysis to be conducted. *Actual markets*. First of all, it is clear that a conflict with a normal exploitation may arise with regard to the market actually exploited by the right holder. Second, if an empirical approach is taken, it may be argued that a limitation does not conflict with a normal exploitation because the author does not exploit his work in the area covered by the limitation. The reason for this, however, is the limitation itself. The result is thus a circular line of argument. In other words, the mere fact that the right holder does not exploit his work in the area of a limitation cannot be used as an argument to discard a conflict with a normal exploitation. Instead of asking whether the author exploits his work in the area covered by a limitation, it is thus necessary to examine whether the limitation kills demand for the work by providing users with substitutes for the copies marketed by the right holder. *Potential future markets.* If the relevant market considered in the analysis is extended to potential future sources of royalty revenue, it may be asserted that a normal exploitation encompasses each and every possibility of exploiting a work. In the digital environment, this may result in the erosion of almost all existing limitations once DRM systems open up new markets in areas previously covered by limitations. It could be argued that the protection of these new forms of 'a normal exploitation' requires the abolition of the limitations concerned. In consequence, the preceding certain special cases test and the following unreasonable prejudice test would be rendered more or less meaningless. Furthermore, there hardly would be any room left for the widening of existing or the introduction of new limitations. This, however, would contradict the second sentence of the first paragraph of the Agreed Statement concerning art. 10, which expressly permits Contracting Parties to devise new exceptions and limitations that are appropriate in the digital network environment. **(b) Solution.** As a way out, only actual or potential markets of considerable economic or practical importance should be considered (*United States – Section 110(5) of the US Copyright Act* (WTO panel report)). This formula limits the scope of the second criterion to the economic core of copyright if the overall commercialization of works affected by a limitation is chosen as a reference point for determining a conflict with a normal exploitation. Accordingly, the effects of the limitation on the exploitation of the copyrighted work as such would have to be considered. Limitations which do not erode major sources of royalty revenue would be unlikely to conflict with a normal exploitation, and could be dealt with in the framework of the more flexible third criterion prohibiting an unreasonable prejudice to legitimate interests. Following this approach considering the impact of a limitation on the overall commercialization of a work, the ECJ found an exemption of private copying including copies made from unlawful sources to adversely affect a work's normal exploitation in the sense of volume of sales and other lawful transactions (*ACI Adam* (ECJ)). More restrictive interpretations, however, focus on each individual exclusive right recognized in international copyright law (*United States – Section 110(5) of the US Copyright Act* (WTO panel report)). As a result, a limitation may come into conflict with a normal exploitation even though it affects only a small exclusive right which does not play a decisive role in a work's overall commercialization. **(c) Development of normal exploitation over time.** In the normal exploitation analysis, it is also to be considered that a work's normal commercialization does not necessarily cover the entire term of copyright protection. In many cases, a work's normal exploitation will already be completed after several months or years, whereas the term of protection is much longer. This implies that a dynamic temporal element must be included in the normal exploitation analysis: the normal exploitation test is no longer relevant to the assessment of a limitation once a work's normal exploitation has been completed. This dynamic temporal element is central, for instance, to the assessment of the Orphan Works Directive. Art. 6(1) of that Directive exempts the making available to the public and certain acts of reproduction of orphan works. However, this use privilege only becomes available if the right holder cannot be found through a diligent search (art. 3 of the Orphan Works Directive). This situation is unlikely to arise before the normal exploitation has been completed. As long as significant, tangible or considerable income accrues from the work's commercialization, it should not be difficult to find the right holder. Art. 6(5) of the Orphan Works Directive also provides for the payment of 'fair compensation' in case the right holder turns up and puts an end to the orphan work status. This can be seen as an additional safeguard against the remaining risk of an unreasonable prejudice to legitimate interests.

5. Third step: unreasonable prejudice to legitimate interests. (a) General. The third criterion comprises three elements. First, from all interests the author might have, only those interests will be considered that are 'legitimate'. Second, the prejudice to these interests caused by the limitation in question must reach an impermissible unreasonable level. Third, in answering the second question, the payment of equitable remuneration can be considered. At the 1967 Stockholm Conference, the principle was established that the payment of equitable remuneration could be taken into account in the context of the third criterion. Accordingly, an unreasonable prejudice to legitimate interests of the author can be reduced to a permissible reasonable level by providing for the payment of equitable remuneration. Following modern interpretations of the three-step test that understand the test's different steps as indivisible parts of an overall assessment of a limitation in the light of the principle of proportionality (note 1(b), above), it can be argued that the payment of equitable remuneration should also be taken into account in the context of the other steps. **(b) Legitimate interests.** An interest can be qualified as legitimate if it is justifiable in the sense that it is supported by relevant public policies or other social norms (*Canada – Term of Patent Protection* (WTO panel report) concerning art. 30 TRIPS which include third party interests). Also, it has been held that, in particular, the economic value of exclusive copyrights is to be taken into account (*United States – Section 110(5) of the US Copyright Act* (WTO panel report)). In the context of the WCT, it might seem appropriate to likewise consider the author's moral interests (see art. 1, note 4). As to the interests of other right holders, such as licensees, see art. 11, note 5. **(c) Unreasonable prejudice.** Inevitably, every copyright limitation prejudices an author's interests to some extent. For this reason, the third criterion does not prohibit a prejudice as such but only a prejudice which reaches an unreasonable level. The question of whether or not a limitation gives rise to an unreasonable prejudice can be answered in the light of the justification given for its existence (see note 3(b)). Moreover, the detriment to the authors must be reasonably related to the benefit of the users. Insofar as the objective underlying a limitation justifies the entailed prejudice to the author's legitimate interests, it can be approved. **(d) Payment of equitable remuneration.** If a limitation causes an unreasonable prejudice, it need not automatically be abolished. In the context of the third criterion, the payment of equitable remuneration is to be taken into account (see already note 5(a)). By providing for equitable remuneration, the unreasonable prejudice can be reduced to a permissible reasonable level. Accordingly, equitable remuneration must only be paid insofar as the limitation in question does not keep within reasonable limits. The amount of the remuneration should be measured in such a way that it appears fair and just under the given circumstances. In practice, the determination of the right amount of equitable remuneration can be a matter of considerable difficulty, for instance, in the area of private copying where levy systems may be used to generate extra income compensating right holders for losses suffered because of the use privilege. In the EU, the ECJ added further complexity to the task of ascertaining the right amount of equitable remuneration by establishing the unpractical criterion of harm flowing from the introduction of the private copying exception and drawing a distinction between reproduction equipment, devices and media made available to private users and those made available to professional parties (*Padawan* (ECJ); *VG Wort* (ECJ); *Amazon. com International Sales* (ECJ), *Copydan Båndkopi* (ECJ)). Moreover, the payment of equitable remuneration is not sufficient in all cases. Even if copyright holders are compensated for private copying, a private copying regime permitting the making of copies from unlawful sources goes too far and causes an unreasonable prejudice (*ACI Adam* (ECJ)).

6. The Agreed Statement. (a) The first paragraph. The first paragraph of the Agreed Statement underlines that the three-step test must not be misunderstood as an instrument serving solely the restriction of limitations. Rather, it makes clear that the test does not bar Contracting Parties from crafting appropriate national limitations in the digital environment (see note 1(b) and preamble, note 6). **(b) The second paragraph.** *Underlying objective*. At the 1996 Diplomatic Conference, it was feared that the application of the three-step test as an additional safeguard could curtail the scope of the limitations permitted under the Berne Convention (see note 2(b)). For this reason, the second paragraph of the Agreed Statement was adopted which makes it clear that their field of application should be neither reduced nor extended. *Impact on the additional review of Berne limitations*. It follows that the additional application of the three-step test to Berne limitations serves primarily the clarification of those provisions of the Berne Convention, the wording of which offers a gateway for the criteria of the three-step test, such as arts. 10(1) BC (right of quotation) and 10(2) BC (illustrations for teaching) referring to 'fair practice'. The implied limitations of the BC open a similar field of application (as to the 'minor reservations doctrine' (see *United States – Section 110(5) of the US Copyright Act* (WTO panel report)).

[Obligations concerning technological measures]

Article 11

Contracting Parties shall provide adequate legal protection and effective legal remedies against the circumvention of effective technological measures that are used by authors in connection with the exercise of their rights under this Treaty or the Berne Convention and that restrict acts, in respect of their works, which are not authorized by the authors concerned or permitted by law.

1. General. (a) New obligations. While other WCT provisions primarily reflect international copyright norms known from the BC and the TRIPS Agreement, and seek to clarify their operation in the digital environment, arts. 11 and 12 contain new international obligations. For the first time, attention is devoted to technological measures deployed to protect authors' rights. The deliberations at the 1996 Diplomatic Conference show that arts. 11 and 12 were not intended to broaden the scope of substantive copyright provisions. Instead, they parallel the substantive rules in the sense that they safeguard the effective operation of technological means affording the exercise of copyrights in the digital environment. Viewed from this perspective, they can be qualified as a specific form of enforcement provisions. **(b) European legislation.** See art. 6 of the Information Society Directive as to the implementation of art. 11 WCT into EU legislation.

2. Connection with the exercise of rights. The requirement of a connection with the exercise of WCT or Berne rights reflects the principle expressed at the 1996 Diplomatic Conference that the protection of technological measures should complement the grant of exclusive rights so as to allow their effective enforcement in the digital environment. Accordingly, the international obligation to protect against acts of circumvention does not arise if the use of technological measures goes beyond the scope of the rights granted in the WCT or the BC. **(a) Term of protection.** For this reason, technological measures do not enjoy protection pursuant to art. 11 once the term of protection of the work to which they are applied has expired (see art. 7 BC). **(b) Mandatory exclusions from protection.** Similarly, art. 11 is inapplicable in cases where Contracting Parties are obliged not to grant protection. Pursuant to art. 1(2) WCT, nothing in the WCT shall derogate from the obligations under the BC. One of these obligations concerns an exclusion from protection. It follows from arts. 3 WCT and 2(8) BC that Contracting Parties shall not protect news of the day or miscellaneous facts having the character of mere items of press information. It would therefore be inconsistent to extend the protection of technological measures to cases in which they are applied to subject matter falling within the scope of art. 2(8) BC. **(c) Other exclusions from protection.** To the extent to which Contracting Parties are free to provide for other exclusions from protection, art. 11

WCT is also inapplicable because the use of technological measures then no longer serves the exercise of rights. An example of relevant exclusions might be the exclusion from copyright protection of official texts as well as political speeches and speeches delivered in the course of legal proceedings, on the basis of arts. 3 WCT, 2(4) and 2bis(1) BC.

3. Authorized use and copyright limitations. (a) General. Art. 11 does not cover technological measures which are used to restrict acts authorized by the author or permitted by law. The latter ('not permitted by law') refers to limitations and exceptions to copyright. In other words, Contracting Parties are not required to grant legal anti-circumvention protection if the use made is one that the right holder cannot control by an exclusive right because it is permitted by a copyright limitation. **(b) Anti-circumvention protection and limitations.** It is, however, another question to what extent Contracting Parties are free to protect technical protection measures even in cases where the act of use which is prevented by such measures is permitted under a copyright limitation. According to art. 1(2) WCT, nothing in the WCT may derogate from existing obligations under the BC. As art. 1(2) WCT equally safeguards Berne obligations in the field of limitations, it might be concluded that Contracting Parties are only free to give preference to technical protection measures if the affected limitation is not mandatory. Accordingly, anti-circumvention protection for technical measures must not override the mandatory right of quotation in art. 10(1) BC. A further international obligation to safeguard limitations against the corrosive effect of technical protection measures will follow from the 2013 Marrakesh Treaty to Facilitate Access to Published Works for Persons who are Blind, Visually Impaired, or Otherwise Print Disabled, once the EU and its Member States adhere to this Treaty. Art. 7 of the Marrakesh Treaty obliges Contracting Parties to take appropriate measures to ensure that the legal protection of technical measures does not prevent blind, visually impaired or print-disabled persons from enjoying the limitations set forth in the Treaty. The present regulation of the interface between technical measures and copyright limitations in art. 6(4) of the Information Society Directive offers some room to let limitations for the benefit of people with a disability (art. 5(3)(b) of the Information Society Directive) prevail over the protection of technical measures. This safeguard for limitations falling within the province of the Marrakesh Treaty, however, is incomplete because art. 6(4) of the Information Society Directive generally exempts from the obligation to ensure the effectiveness of limitations works made available on the Internet on the basis of contractual agreements. If blind, visually impaired or print-disabled persons conclude an online contract to download a work in an appropriate format from the Internet, technical measures may thus still impede the enjoyment of the limitations reflected in the Marrakesh Treaty. Moreover, art. 6(4) does not cover the right of quotation laid down in art. 5(3)(d) of the Information Society Directive. The compliance of EU copyright law with international obligations concerning the relation between technical measures and limitations is thus doubtful.

4. Effective technological measures. Art. 11 only protects technological measures that are effective. This requirement must not be misunderstood to indicate that a technological measure is to be qualified as ineffective if it can be circumvented. Such circular reasoning would obviously render the provision pointless. **(a) Capacity to protect.** Nevertheless, the requirement of effectiveness makes clear that a certain minimum standard must be met. It is not sufficient that a specific device is labelled a technological protection measure. By contrast, it must be capable of controlling the use of a work in practice (see art. 6(3) of the Information Society Directive). If the process of bypassing a device is or becomes widely known among regular users and can easily be applied, doubt may be cast upon its effectiveness (see the Information Society Directive, art. 6, note 2(b)). Technological protection measures are not limited to those applied to the housing system containing the protected work, but can also be embedded in portable equipment or consoles intended to ensure access to protected works and control their use, such as videogame consoles (*Nintendo and Others* (ECJ)). **(b) No technology mandate.** Besides establishing this minimum requirement, the term 'effective' points towards the potential conflict of interest between copyright holders and other industries, such as manufacturers of equipment allowing the enjoyment of intellectual works. A technological measure does not function properly and may thus be regarded as ineffective if it interferes with the operation of such equipment or the rendering of corresponding services. In other words, technology and service providers need not align their activities with technological measures used by copyright holders.

5. Use by the author. The reference to 'the author' corresponds to the general use of the term 'author' in the WCT and the BC. Pursuant to arts. 3 WCT, 2(6) BC, it includes successors in title. With regard to licensees, such as publishers, record companies or film distributors, the situation appears less clear. As in the case of exclusive rights, however, it would not make sense to exclude them. The requirement of use 'by the author' thus means use by any right holder.

6. Circumvention. (a) Preparatory Acts. Art. 13(1) of the Basic Proposal sought to prohibit 'the importation, manufacture or distribution of protection-defeating devices, or the offer or performance of any service having the same effect'. Hence, the provision focused on preparatory acts enabling the circumvention of technological measures. The final text of art. 11, however, was limited to the acts of circumvention as such. Ultimately, it is the implementation of the provision into national laws that must show whether adequate legal protection can also be achieved without prohibiting preparatory acts. **(b) European legislation.** Art. 6(2) of the Information Society Directive explicitly includes preparatory acts and seeks to draw a line between multipurpose devices and services and those solely or primarily serving the objective to circumvent technological measures (see the Information Society Directive, art. 6, note 4).

7. Adequate legal protection. The use of the term 'adequate' leaves Contracting Parties some room to manoeuvre. In particular, it permits a careful balancing of interests along the lines of the principle of proportionality. The balancing exercise may result in the establishment of additional subjective criteria. For instance, it seems consistent to make it a condition that the person circumventing an effective technological measure knows, or has reasonable grounds to know, that he or she is pursuing that objective (see arts. 12 WCT, 6(1) of the Information Society Directive).

8. Effective legal remedies. At the 1996 Diplomatic Conference, the view was held that the remedies to be provided in respect of circumvention activities needed not necessarily be criminal in nature but could also consist of civil or administrative remedies. The broad reference to 'effective legal remedies' in art. 11 seems to reflect this understanding. It must be seen in the context of art. 14(2) WCT, which was modelled on the first sentence of art. 41(1) TRIPS. Against this background, 'effective legal remedies' can be understood to require particularly fair and equitable procedures (see art. 41(2) TRIPS). As regards civil remedies, injunctive relief, payment of damages and seizure, disposal and destruction of circumvention devices might be deemed standard procedures (see arts. 44 to 46 TRIPS, 13(3) and 16 BC). Resort may be had to arts. 41 to 61 TRIPS to concretize the requirement of effective legal remedies (see art. 14 WPT, note 2). In domestic law, the concrete shape of effective remedies is not unlikely to depend on whether or not the protection against circumvention is extended to preparatory acts (see note 5). This is particularly true as regards provisional measures and border measures (see arts. 50 to 60 TRIPS).

[Obligations concerning rights management information]

Article 12

(1) Contracting Parties shall provide adequate and effective legal remedies against any person knowingly performing any of the following acts knowing, or with respect to civil remedies having reasonable grounds to know, that it will induce, enable, facilitate or conceal an infringement of any right covered by this Treaty or the Berne Convention:

    (i) to remove or alter any electronic rights management information without authority;

    (ii) to distribute, import for distribution, broadcast or communicate to the public, without authority, works or copies of works knowing that electronic rights management information has been removed or altered without authority.

(2) As used in this Article, 'rights management information' means information which identifies the work, the author of the work, the owner of any right in the work, or information about the terms and conditions of use of the work, and any numbers or codes that represent such

information, when any of these items of information is attached to a copy of a work or appears in connection with the communication of a work to the public.

Agreed Statement Concerning Article 12

It is understood that the reference to 'infringement of any right covered by this Treaty or the Berne Convention' includes both exclusive rights and rights of remuneration.

It is further understood that Contracting Parties will not rely on this Article to devise or implement rights management systems that would have the effect of imposing formalities which are not permitted under the Berne Convention or this Treaty, prohibiting the free movement of goods or impeding the enjoyment of rights under this Treaty.

1. General. (a) Overview. The protection of technological measures would be incomplete without corresponding obligations concerning rights management information. DRM systems afford right holders the opportunity to monitor precisely the particulars of individual uses. Besides the mere protection against unauthorized copying, they serve as a means to control and manage the circumstances under which a work may be accessed and enjoyed. Specific use parameters can be set relating to individual consumers or consumer groups (see the Information Society Directive, art. 7, note 1). The proper functioning of DRM systems, however, depends on the integrity of the rights management information determined by the right holder. Accordingly, art. 12 complements art. 11 by safeguarding electronic rights management information from manipulation, and prohibiting the making available of manipulated copies. The obligations set forth in art. 12 were newly introduced at the international level in the context of the WCT (see art. 11, note 1). **(b) European legislation.** See art. 7 of the Information Society Directive as to the implementation of art. 12 WCT into EU legislation.

2. Prohibited acts. (a) Removal or alteration (para. 1(i)). The prohibition laid down in para. 1(i) concerns only the elimination or modification of existing electronic rights management information. It does not cover situations in which electronic rights management information is attached to a copy in relation to which no such information is used. Moreover, preparatory acts, such as manufacturing devices for removing or altering information or offering corresponding services, are not covered (see art. 11, note 6). **(b) Making available (para. 1(ii)).** The enumeration of prohibited subsequent acts in para. 1(ii) may be interpreted broadly. The reference to distribution includes rental and lending. Communication to the public encompasses interactive on-demand acts of making available to the public in the sense of the second part of art. 8 (see art. 8, note 5). The person carrying out relevant acts must not only have knowledge of the removal or alteration of the rights management information, but also of the fact that the removal or alteration was undertaken without authority. Private activities are beyond the scope of para. 1(ii). The distribution of a manipulated copy in the family circle or its importation for personal use as part of one's personal luggage are therefore not affected by the provision (see art. 8, note 3). **(c) Without authority.** The discussions at the 1996 Diplomatic Conference give evidence of the intention not to subject lawful acts to art. 12. Correspondingly, the acts delineated in para. 1(i) and (ii) are not performed 'without authority' if they are permitted by law.

3. Knowledge requirements. Besides the specific knowledge requirement set forth in para. 1(ii), a person carrying out any prohibited act must have the following knowledge: **(a) With regard to the acts delineated in para. 1(i) and (ii).** On the one hand, the person must know that he or she is performing an act falling under para. 1(i) or (ii). It would be insufficient, for instance, if a removal of electronic rights management information resulted from an unintended error in a computer system. On the other hand, the person must have knowledge of the facts which qualify his or her act as an act performed without authority. **(b) With regard to a future infringement of WCT or Berne rights.** Art. 12(1) makes it a prerequisite that an act falling under para. 1(i) or (ii) has a certain connection with an infringement of a right granted in the WCT or the BC. For the knowledge requirement applicable to this consequential infringement it is sufficient, with respect to civil remedies, that the person has reasonable grounds to know that the act he or she performed (para. 1(i) or (ii)) will induce, enable, facilitate or conceal an infringement. In this respect, the notion of negligence may serve as a point of reference. The implementation of this lower knowledge standard into national laws is likely to differ in accordance with existing differences between national legal systems.

4. Infringement of any right. The infringement of 'any right covered by this Treaty or the Berne Convention' need not necessarily concern an economic right of the author. On account of art. 6bis(1) BC, moral rights also come into play. The right to claim authorship, for instance, is affected if rights management information identifying the author is removed or altered. As long as the manipulation of electronic rights management information does not impact on the appearance, performance or functioning of a work, however, a 'distortion, mutilation or other modification' in the sense of art. 6bis BC should not be assumed. With regard to the inclusion of rights of remuneration, see note 7.

5. Adequate and effective legal remedies. See art. 11, note 8, and art. 14, note 2, as to this international obligation laid down in art. 12(1).

6. Definition of 'rights management information' (para. 2). The definition offered in para. 2 avoids any reference to specific DRM systems. It is confined to the items of information such a system may contain. The reference to communication of a work to the public at the end of the provision covers not only interactive on-demand acts of making available but also broadcasting (see art. 8, note 4).

7. The Agreed Statement. (a) The first sentence. At the 1996 Diplomatic Conference, it was feared that the reference to 'an infringement of any right' in para. 1 could be interpreted restrictively to exclude rights to equitable remuneration. It was thus deemed advisable to clarify the matter by way of an Agreed Statement. **(b) The second sentence.** Moreover, there was agreement that no obligation should be imposed on right holders to use electronic rights management information. The objective to reflect this understanding lies at the core of the second sentence. The prohibition of formalities follows from arts. 3 WCT, 5(2) BC. With regard to the free movement of goods, the Agreed Statement clarifies that art. 12 cannot be invoked as a justification for prohibitions.

[Application in time]

Article 13

Contracting Parties shall apply the provisions of Article 18 of the Berne Convention to all protection provided for in this Treaty.

Application mutatis mutandis. Two main principles follow from the reference to arts. 18(1) and (2) BC. **(a) Country of origin.** Firstly, the WCT applies to all works which, at the moment of its coming into force, have not yet fallen into the public domain in the Contracting Party of origin (see arts. 3 WCT, 5(4) BC) through the expiry of the term of protection. The latter criterion is not fulfilled if a work is in the public domain on the grounds that it does not comply with formality requirements, the prohibition of which results from arts. 3 WCT and 5(2) BC, or belongs to a work category not yet enjoying protection – a situation which might arise, for instance, in respect of computer programs or databases (see arts. 4 and 5 WCT). In these cases, protection must be granted. **(b) Country of protection.** Second, however, if the work is no longer protected in the Contracting Party for which protection is sought because of the expiry of the term of protection previously granted in that Contracting Party (the forum where protection is claimed is irrelevant), it shall not be protected anew. **(c) Scope.** Art. 18(4) BC extends the ambit of operation of these rules to certain further situations, in particular later accessions to the WCT (see art. 18 BC, note 5). Modifications may follow from special conventions or domestic legislation (art. 18(3) BC).

[Provisions on enforcement of rights]

Article 14

(1) Contracting Parties undertake to adopt, in accordance with their legal systems, the measures necessary to ensure the application of this Treaty.

(2) Contracting Parties shall ensure that enforcement procedures are available under their law so as to permit effective action against any act of infringement of rights covered by this Treaty, including expeditious remedies to prevent infringements and remedies which constitute a deterrent to further infringements.

1. Implementation in national law (para. 1). (a) Reference to national legal systems. Art. 14(1) was modelled on art. 36(1) BC. The application of the WCT, firstly, depends on whether international norms can be applied directly at the national level or become applicable only after the enactment of domestic legislation giving effect to them (see arts. 22-38 BC, note 3). Second, it is to be considered that, in practice, implementation measures may consist of legislative as well as administrative acts. Contracting Parties thus enjoy a certain degree of discretion. **(b) European legislation.** See the Enforcement Directive as to the enforcement of intellectual property rights in the EU.

2. Enforcement obligations (para. 2). With regard to law enforcement, art. 16 of the Basic Proposal sought to ensure the application of arts. 41 to 61 TRIPS. At the Diplomatic Conference, this proposal was not approved. Instead, art. 14(2) was adopted which contains the same global obligation which is set forth in the first sentence of art. 41(1) TRIPS. Although the direct inclusion of arts. 41 to 61 TRIPS would have contributed to more clarity, it seems that this solution, virtually, leads to the same result. 'Effective action' against infringing acts certainly requires fair and equitable procedures. This objective can hardly be realized as long as procedures are unnecessarily complicated or costly, or entail unreasonable time limits or unwarranted delays (see art. 41(2) TRIPS). Similarly, 'expeditious remedies' can hardly be ensured without providing for injunctive relief, payment of damages and the seizure, disposal and destruction of infringing material (see arts. 44 to 46 TRIPS, 13(3) and 16 BC). The abstract rule of art. 14(2) WCT is therefore to be concretized along the lines of arts. 41 to 61 TRIPS. It goes beyond the TRIPS provisions particularly in that the rights 'covered by this Treaty' comprise the moral rights recognized in art. 6bis BC by virtue of the reference made in art. 1(4) WCT. Art. 9(1) TRIPS excludes these rights. Similarly, art. 8 of the Information Society Directive does not extend sanctions and remedies to the field of moral rights. They remain outside the scope of the Directive pursuant to recital 19 thereof.

[Final and administrative clauses]

Articles 15-25 (*omitted*)

1. General. The final and administrative clauses of the WCT are laid down in arts. 15 to 25. They concern the work in the Assembly of Contracting

Parties (art. 15), the administrative tasks to be accomplished by the International Bureau of WIPO (art. 16), the eligibility for, the effective date of, and the rights and obligations resulting from becoming party to the WCT (arts. 17, 18 and 21), the signature, entry into force and denunciation of the WCT (arts. 19, 20 and 23), the exclusion of any reservations (art. 22), the official languages of the WCT (art. 24), and its deposition with the Director General of WIPO (art. 25). To the extent that these provisions are not of interest in the context of EU legislation, they are neither reprinted nor commented upon in the present context.

2. Status of the EU. (a) Eligibility for becoming party. By virtue of art. 17(2), the Assembly of Contracting Parties (art. 15) may decide to admit any intergovernmental organization to become party to the WCT. However, it is made a condition that the intergovernmental organization declare that it is competent in respect of the WCT in the sense that it has its own legislation on matters covered by the WCT and the potential to bind all its Member States in this regard. Moreover, the intergovernmental organization must declare that it has been duly authorized, in accordance with its internal procedures, to become party to the WCT. In art. 17(3), it is clarified that the EU has already made the aforementioned declaration in the 1996 Diplomatic Conference. Accordingly, it is stated that the EU may become party to the WCT. **(b) Participation in the Assembly.** The EU, as any other Contracting Party, may be represented by one delegate in the Assembly of Contracting Parties. The delegate may be assisted by alternate delegates, advisors and experts (art. 15(1)(b)). The Assembly deals with matters concerning the maintenance and development, as well as the application and operation of the WCT (art. 15(2)(a)). In particular, it decides the convocation of any diplomatic conference for the revision of the WCT (art. 15(2)(c)). Pursuant to art. 15(3)(b), the EU may participate in any vote in the Assembly, in place of its Member States, with a number of votes equal to the number of its Member States which are party to the WCT. However, it may not participate in the vote if any one of its Member States exercises its right to vote and vice versa.

3. Languages of the WCT (art. 24). (a) Authentic texts (para. 1). Pursuant to art. 24(1), the WCT has been signed in a single original in the English, Arabic, Chinese, French, Russian and Spanish languages. It is clarified that the versions in all these languages are equally authentic. Accordingly, no language version is to prevail in case there arise differences of opinion on the interpretation of the various texts. Hence, the interpretation should follow the different language versions to the greatest extent possible, having regard to the object and purpose of the treaty (see art. 33(4) of the Vienna Convention). **(b) Official texts (para. 2).** It follows from art. 24(2), that an official text of the WCT in any language other than the six UN languages referred to in para. 1 shall be established by the Director General of WIPO on the request of an interested party, after consultation with all the interested parties. With regard to the expression 'interested party', it is clarified that this refers to any

Member State of WIPO whose official language, or one of whose official languages, is involved. In this context, it is pointed out that the same rule applies in the case of the EU, if one of its official languages is involved.

INTERNATIONAL CONVENTION FOR THE PROTECTION OF PERFORMERS, PRODUCERS OF PHONOGRAMS AND BROADCASTING ORGANIZATIONS

done at Rome on 26 October 1961

[Introductory remarks]

1. General. The 1961 Rome Convention (RC) is the first major international convention in the field of so-called neighbouring rights. The performers, phonogram producers and broadcasting organizations it protects are often considered the 'traditional' holders of neighbouring rights. There are other international conventions in the field of neighbouring rights, such as the Convention for the Protection of Producers of Phonograms Against Unauthorized Duplication of Their Phonograms of 1971 and the WIPO performances and Phonograms Treaty (WPPT) of 1996, which are both commented upon in this volume. Other Conventions are, for example, the European Agreement on the Protection of Television Broadcasts of 1960 and the Convention Relating to the Distribution of Programme-Carrying Signals Transmitted by Satellite of 1974. However, these Conventions are not dealt with in this volume due to their limited practical importance. Finally, there is the Beijing Treaty on Audiovisual Performances which was adopted on 24 June 2012, but has not entered into force yet.

2. Background. Since the technological developments of the late nineteenth and the early twentieth century, in particular the emergence of the phonogram industry and the advent of radio, performers have been confronted with the problem of unemployment. After two unsuccessful attempts to have performers considered adaptors of underlying musical works at the Diplomatic Conferences held to revise the Berne Convention in Rome (1928) and Brussels (1948), delegates to the final conference expressed the wish for performers to be considered for protection through neighbouring rights outside the framework of the Berne Convention, but together with protection afforded to producers of phonograms and even broadcasting organizations. Then, the International Bureaux for the Protection of Intellectual Property (BIRPI, predecessor of WIPO) started to work with the International Labour Organization (ILO) to elaborate such international protection and the effort was later joined by UNESCO. The collaboration between these three international organizations led to a proposal for the international protection of performers, phonogram producers and broadcasting organizations, which was submitted to and – after amendment – accepted by the Diplomatic Conference held in Rome from 10 to 26 October 1961.

3. EU legislation. Most Member States of the EU have ratified the Rome Convention. While the EU is not a contracting party, and the Convention therefore not part of the legal order of the EU (*SCF* (ECJ)), the protection granted by the Rome Convention has been harmonized by way of the Rental Right Directive. Also, the Information Society Directive has made some changes and additions to neighbouring rights protection in the EU. The provisions of these directives must therefore be interpreted in the light of the equivalent concepts in the Convention (*SCF* (ECJ)).

[Bibliography]

J. Blomqvist, *Primer on International Copyright and Related Rights* (Elgar 2014)

G. Davies, 'The 50th Anniversary of the Rome Convention for the Protection of Performers, Producers of Phonograms and Broadcasting Organisations: Reflections on the Background and Importance of the Convention' (2012) 2 *Queen Mary Journal of Intellectual Property* 206–224

M. Ficsor, *Guide to the Copyright and Related Rights Treaties Administered by WIPO And Glossary Of Copyright And Related Rights Terms* (WIPO 2003) <http://www.wipo.int/edocs/pubdocs/en/copyright/891/wipo_pub_891.pdf>

P. Goldstein and P.B. Hugenholtz, *International Copyright* (3rd edn., Oxford University Press 2012)

C. Masouyé, *Guide to the Rome Convention and to the Phonograms Convention* (WIPO 1981)

W. Nordemann, K. Vinck, P. Hertin and G. Meyer, *International Copyright and Neighboring Right Law: Commentary* (Weinheim 1990)

S. Ricketson and J. Ginsburg, *International Copyright and Neighbouring Rights: The Berne Convention and Beyond* (2nd edn., Oxford University Press 2006)

S. Stewart, *International Copyright and Neighbouring Rights* (2nd edn., Butterworths 1989)

E. Ulmer, 'The Rome Convention for the Protection of Performers, Producers of Phonograms and Broadcasting Organizations' (1962-1963) 10 *Bull. Copyright Soc'y U.S.A.* 90-101, 165-178, 219-248

[Preamble]

The Contracting States, moved by the desire to protect the rights of performers, producers of phonograms, and broadcasting organizations, Have agreed as follows:

[Safeguard of copyright protection]

Article 1

Protection granted under this Convention shall leave intact and shall in no way affect the protection of copyright in literary and artistic works. Consequently, no provision of this Convention may be interpreted as prejudicing such protection.

1. General. This provision is a legal guarantee that the introduction of protection for performers, phonogram producers and broadcasters will not prejudice the copyright protection of literary or artistic works. Several provisions were introduced in the Rome Convention to enforce this guarantee, notably arts. 15(2), 23, 24(2), 27 and 28(4) and (5) RC.

2. Scope. This provision goes no further, however, and does not provide for the primacy of copyright over the protection afforded performers, phonogram producers and broadcasters. Such a hierarchy was clearly rejected by the 1961 Rome diplomatic conference. Some delegates submitted a proposal to amend this provision by introducing the word 'exercise', so that the provision would have read: 'Protection granted under this Convention shall leave intact and shall in no way affect the protection and the exercise of copyright in literary and artistic works'. However, after it became clear that such an amendment would effectively block the exercise of any protection under the Rome Convention (because any refusal by a performer, phonogram producer or broadcaster to use their protected material would hinder the exercise by a copyright holder who authorizes such use), it was immediately rejected (RC Conference Proceedings). In some countries, e.g. France, it has been argued that this rejection of the primacy of copyright over the protection of performers, phonogram producers and broadcasters only concerns the protection expressly provided by the Rome Convention and does not apply to the protection granted by national law above the conventional minimum, for example regarding moral rights of performers.

3. No guarantee against financial harm. This provision does not guarantee that recognition of the protection of performers, phonogram producers and broadcasters does not harm the financial interests of copyright holders. Indeed, copyright collection societies tend to believe that such recognition harms the collection of royalties on behalf of their members as broadcasters' budgets, for instance, are limited and the arrival of 'newcomers' only further restricts that share of the budget allocated to the copyright holder (the so-called 'cake theory'). However, the Intergovernmental Committee which examined this issue, in 1979, was unable to find any such difficulties or consequences that would have arisen since the entry into force of the Rome Convention.

[National treatment]

Article 2

(1) For the purposes of this Convention, national treatment shall mean the treatment accorded by the domestic law of the Contracting State in which protection is claimed:

    (a) to performers who are its nationals, as regards performances taking place, broadcast, or first fixed, on its territory;

    (b) to producers of phonograms who are its nationals, as regards phonograms first fixed or first published on its territory;

    (c) to broadcasting organisations which have their headquarters on its territory, as regards broadcasts transmitted from transmitters situated on its territory.

(2) National treatment shall be subject to the protection specifically guaranteed, and the limitations specifically provided for, in this Convention.

1. General. This provision defines what should be considered 'national treatment', an obligation of the Contracting States under the Rome Convention. Like the requirements of national treatment in other international conventions, national treatment in the RC is not concerned with the protection of nationals of the Contracting States on their own territory but with the protection of foreign persons or entities aspiring for neighbouring rights protection in other Contracting States than their own.

2. National treatment (para. 1). (a) General. According to this definition, national treatment is the treatment accorded by the national laws of the Contracting State in which protection is sought to its 'own national' performers, phonogram producers and broadcasting organizations, to foreign performers, phonogram producers and broadcasting organizations, provided the latter meet certain well-defined points of attachment, as defined in arts. 4, 5 and 6 of the Rome Convention. **(b) (para. 1(a)-(c)).** *Performers who are its nationals (para. 1(a)).* 'Performers who are its own nationals' are performers who are nationals of and whose performance took place, was broadcast or first fixed on the territory of the Contracting State in which protection is sought. *Producers of phonograms who are its nationals (para. 1(b)).* 'Producers of phonograms who are its nationals' are producers who are the nationals of and whose phonograms were first fixed or first published on the territory of the Contracting State in which protection is sought. *Broadcasting organizations (para. 1(c)).* Finally, national broadcasting organizations are broadcasters whose headquarters are located on the territory of the Contracting State in which protection is sought, as regards broadcasts transmitted from transmitters situated on this territory. It suffices that one of these criteria be met in order to trigger the obligation to accord 'national treatment' to foreign performers, phonogram producers and/or broadcasters.

3. Conventional minimum (para. 2). The obligation for the Contracting States to provide national treatment is without prejudice to the so-called 'conventional minimum' of the Rome Convention, including the limitations on that conventional minimum provided therein (see, for example, arts. 15, 16 and 19 RC). This provision arguably does not allow the Contracting States where protection is sought to limit their 'national treatment' to the conventional minimum as expressly provided in the 1961 Rome Convention (RC Conference Proceedings), provided, of course, national law is in the domain of the Rome Convention at all.

[Definitions]

Article 3

For the purposes of this Convention:
- (a) 'performers' means actors, singers, musicians, dancers, and other persons who act, sing, deliver, declaim, play in, or otherwise perform literary or artistic works;
- (b) 'phonogram' means any exclusively aural fixation of sounds of a performance or of other sounds;
- (c) 'producer of phonograms' means the person who, or the legal entity which, first fixes the sounds of a performance or other sounds;
- (d) 'publication' means the offering of copies of a phonogram to the public in reasonable quantity;
- (e) 'reproduction' means the making of a copy or copies of a fixation;
- (f) 'broadcasting' means the transmission by wireless means for public reception of sounds or of images and sounds;
- (g) 'rebroadcasting' means the simultaneous broadcasting by one broadcasting organisation of the broadcast of another broadcasting organisation.

1. General. This provision contains important definitions of certain terms used throughout the Rome Convention which are important in order to determine the scope of international protection under the Rome Convention.

2. Definition of a performer (art. 3(a)). (a) Performer. The definition of 'performer' begins with a non-exhaustive list of persons considered to be performers – actors, singers, musicians and dancers – and ends with an open description of who can be considered a performer, namely anyone who performs a literary or artistic work, such as by acting, singing, delivering, reciting, playing or otherwise. Two examples of persons considered to perform a literary or artistic work who are mentioned in the documents of the 1961 Rome Diplomatic Conference are an orchestra conductor and a choir director (RC Conference Proceedings). Moreover, scholars generally agree that theatre directors should also be considered performers. However, technical and sports performances are generally considered excluded from the scope of this protection. **(b) Literary or artistic work.** With respect to the condition of performing a 'literary or artistic work', reference should be made to the notion of a 'literary or artistic work' as used in art. 2(1) of the Berne Convention (BC) and art. I of the Universal Copyright Convention (UCC). More particularly, this reference is intended to cover musical, dramatic and musical-dramatic (such as opera) works covered by copyright (RC Conference Proceedings). Most likely, the notion of a 'literary or artistic work' should not be restricted to those intended to be performed in public (such as the musical and dramatic works mentioned above) but should be construed in broader terms as referring to any kind of work that is capable of being performed in public (such as poetry, which can be recited in public even if it is not specifically intended to be performed publicly). The performance should not concern a 'protected' work, in that the performed work can also be a work that has already fallen into the public domain. **(c) Other performances.** However, according to art. 9 of the Rome Convention, Contracting States of the Rome Convention remain free to extend, in their national law, the protection provided for in this Convention to artists who do not perform literary or artistic works, such as such as variety and circus numbers (see art. 9, note 2).

3. Definition of a phonogram (art. 3(b)). A 'phonogram' is defined as any exclusively aural fixation of sounds of a performance or of other sounds, thus clearly excluding any audiovisual fixation. A fixation can concern sounds of a given performance as well as other sounds, such as a bird call or any other natural noise (RC Conference Proceedings). This definition has been modernized in art. 2(b) WPPT.

4. Definition of a producer (art. 3(c)). A 'producer' is a natural person or legal entity that first fixes the sounds of a performance or other sounds. Anyone who reproduces former fixations is not considered a producer within the meaning of the Rome Convention and thus is not eligible to claim protection. The use of the verb to 'fix' is probably not intended to include in the scope of protection someone who materially fixes sounds but rather to protect one who invests in such fixation. Also this definition has been adjusted in art. 2(d) WPPT.

5. Definition of publication (art. 3(d)). A phonogram is considered 'published' when copies are offered to the public in a reasonable quantity. This is of particular importance for the claim of remuneration granted by art. 12 of the Rome Convention. This definition has been amended in art. 2(c) WPPT.

6. Definition of reproduction (art. 3(e)). 'Reproduction' means the making of a copy or copies of a fixation and, therefore, must be interpreted narrowly. It does not encompass all acts relating to the material copies of a fixation, such as the distribution of copies.

7. Definition of broadcasting (art. 3(f)). 'Broadcasting' means the transmission for public reception of sounds or of images and sounds by wireless means. A broadcast can involve sounds or images, or a combination of the two, and therefore covers both radio and television broadcasts. The Rome Convention does not require that the sounds and/or images originate from a performance (of an underlying literary or artistic work). The term 'broadcasting' only concerns the transmission of a signal, not the production of an underlying program. The transmission must be made for reception by the general public. According to the Conference documents, reception by a well-defined group, such as taxi drivers, is not covered by this definition (RC Conference Proceedings). This definition has been broadened by art. 2(f) WPPT to transmission by satellite; transmission by wire still not being covered. See also art. 7 RC, note 4(a), and art. 13 RC, note 1(a).

8. Definition of rebroadcasting (art. 3(g)). 'Rebroadcasting' means the simultaneous transmission by one broadcasting organization of a broadcast of another broadcasting organization. It does not mean a delayed transmission.

[Performances protected. Points of attachment for performers]

Article 4

Each Contracting State shall grant national treatment to performers if any of the following conditions is met:
- **(a) the performance takes place in another Contracting State;**
- **(b) the performance is incorporated in a phonogram which is protected under Article 5 of this Convention;**
- **(c) the performance, not being fixed on a phonogram, is carried by a broadcast which is protected by Article 6 of this Convention.**

1. General. (a) Nationality not a criterion. This provision identifies three alternative points of attachment for performers to claim national treatment (and the conventional minimum). Unlike for phonogram producers and broadcasters, the 'nationality' of the performer is not a point of attachment used by the Rome Convention. This can be explained by the practical difficulties that would otherwise result in the case of collective performances. **(b) Principle of non-discrimination within the EU.** This rule has as a consequence that a foreign performer cannot claim national treatment and hence protection if his performance took place in a non-Rome Convention country. This is the case even if the country for which protection is sought does grant protection for performances which took place in a non-Rome country to its own nationals. However, within the EU, according to the principle of non-discrimination laid down in art. 12 EC Treaty, such discrimination against nationals of other Member States is not permitted (*Phil Collins* (ECJ)).

2. Place of performance (art. 4(a)). The performance need not be in public. For example, studio musicians are also entitled to protection.

3. Place of fixation in a protected phonogram (art. 4(b)). This point of attachment refers to the point of attachment for protected phonograms as defined in art. 5 RC. In other words, according to this alternative, performers are entitled to national treatment (and the Convention minimum), if their performance is fixed in a phonogram the producer of which is a national of another Contracting State, or if the first fixation of the sound was made in another Contracting State, or if the phonogram was first published in another Contracting State, which includes simultaneous publication no longer than thirty days after first publication in a non-contracting State.

4. Performance carried in a broadcast (art. 4(c)). This last alternative point of attachment, which is only applicable if no fixation in a protected phonogram has occurred, refers to the point of attachment for protected broadcasts as defined in art. 6 RC. In other words, according to this alternative, performers are entitled to national treatment (and the Convention minimum), if their performance that is not fixed in a phonogram has been broadcast by an organization that has its headquarters in another Contracting State, or if the broadcast was transmitted from a transmitter situated in another Contracting State (for a possible reservation with regard to this latter alternative, see art. 6(2) RC).

[Protected phonograms]

Article 5

(1) Each Contracting State shall grant national treatment to producers of phonograms if any of the following conditions is met:
  (a) the producer of the phonogram is a national of another Contracting State (criterion of nationality);
  (b) the first fixation of the sound was made in another Contracting State (criterion of fixation);
  (c) the phonogram was first published in another Contracting State (criterion of publication).

If a phonogram was first published in a non-contracting State but if it was also published, within thirty days of its first publication, in a Contracting State (simultaneous publication), it shall be considered as first published in the Contracting State.

By means of a notification deposited with the Secretary-General of the United Nations, any Contracting State may declare that it will not apply the criterion of publication or, alternatively, the criterion of fixation. Such notification may be deposited at the time of ratification, acceptance or accession, or at any time thereafter; in the last case, it shall become effective six months after it has been deposited.

1. General. This provision identifies three alternative points of attachment for phonogram producers in order to claim national treatment (and the conventional minimum).

2. Nationality (para. 1(a)). The first criterion of nationality does not require further explanation. However, it should be noted that art. 17 RC allows Contracting States to apply the criterion of fixation alone and, thus, to exclude both the criterion of nationality (para. 1(a) and of first publication (para. 1(c)).

3. Place of fixation (para. 1(b)). The second criterion is the place of the first fixation of sounds, extended to the place of presumed 'simultaneous' publication as defined in para. 2. However, according to para. 3, sentence 2, Contracting States can exclude the application of this criterion as a point of attachment by way of a notification (see note 6).

4. Place of publication (para. 1(c)). The third criterion is the place of the first publication of the phonogram, as defined in art. 3(d) RC. However, like the second criterion of the place of fixation, this third criterion of application can also be excluded by Contracting States as a point of attachment by way of a notification. Again, such a reservation can be made on the date of the deposit of the instrument of ratification, acceptance or accession. In these cases it becomes effective on the corresponding date. It can also be made later, in which case it becomes effective only six months after its filing date. Moreover, it should be noted that art. 17 RC allows Contracting States to apply the criterion of fixation alone, thus excluding both the criteria of first publication (para. 1(c)) and of nationality (para. 1(a)).

5. Simultaneous publication (para. 2). For the purposes of the Rome Convention, the first publication of a phonogram need not necessarily have been made in a Contracting State. Rather, if the first publication was made in a non-contracting State, and a subsequent publication took place in a Contracting State within 30 days of its first publication in a non-contracting State, then the publication is still considered first publication within that Contracting State (the so-called 'back-door' protection, similar to art. 3(4) BC).

6. Reservations (para. 3). (a) Non-application of first fixation and/or first publication. As already stated in notes 2 and 4, Contracting States can exclude, by way of a notification, both the second criterion (first fixation) and the third criterion (first publication) of application either immediately on the date of the deposit of the instrument of ratification, acceptance or accession, or at any time later, in which case the reservation becomes effective only six months after its filing date. **(b) First fixation only.** Alternatively, art. 17 RC allows Contracting States to apply only the criterion of first fixation, thus excluding both the criterion of first publication (para. 1(c)) and of nationality (para. 1(a)). **(c) Territorial scope.** For the territorial scope of such reservations, see art. 27(2) RC.

[Protected broadcasts]

Article 6

(1) Each Contracting State shall grant national treatment to broadcasting organisations if either of the following conditions is met:
  (a) the headquarters of the broadcasting organisation is situated in another Contracting State;
  (b) the broadcast was transmitted from a transmitter situated in another Contracting State.

(2) By means of a notification deposited with the Secretary-General of the United Nations, any Contracting State may declare that it will protect broadcasts only if the headquarters of the broadcasting organisation is situated in another Contracting State and the broadcast was transmitted from a transmitter situated in the same Contracting State. Such notification may be deposited at the time of ratification, acceptance or accession, or at any time thereafter; in the last case, it shall become effective six months after it has been deposited.

1. General. This provision identifies two alternative points of attachment for broadcasting organizations in order to claim national treatment (and the conventional minimum). It should be noted that since the WPPT only protects performers and producers of phonograms, art. 6 RC is the only international treaty protecting broadcasting organizations until a special treaty to protect broadcasting organizations has been adopted (see WPPT Introductory remarks note 2(b)).

2. Nationality (para. 1(a)). The first criterion is the location of the headquarters of the broadcasting organization. If this criterion is combined by a Contracting State with the criterion of transmission to become two cumulative points of attachment, this has to be done by means of a special notification according to para. 2 (see note 4).

3. Place of transmission (para. 1(b)). The second criterion is the location of the transmitter which transmits the broadcast. Again, this criterion can be combined by a Contracting State with the criterion of nationality to become two cumulative points of attachment. This has to be done by means of a special notification according to para. 2 (see note 4).

4. Reservations (para. 2). (a) Cumulation of the two criteria. As already stated in notes 2 and 3, Contracting States can combine both criteria of application to the effect that they will protect broadcasts only if the headquarters of the broadcasting organization is situated in another Contracting State and the broadcast was transmitted from a transmitter situated in the same Contracting State. **(b) Notification.** This has to be done by way of a notification, either immediately on the date of the deposit of the instrument of ratification, acceptance or accession, or at any time later, in which case the reservation becomes effective only six months after its filing date. **(c) Territorial scope.** For the territorial scope of such reservations see art. 27(2) RC.

[Minimum protection for performers]

Article 7

(1) The protection provided for performers by this Convention shall include the possibility of preventing:

    (a) the broadcasting and the communication to the public, without their consent, of their performance, except where the performance used in the broadcasting or the public communication is itself already a broadcast performance or is made from a fixation;

    (b) the fixation, without their consent, of their unfixed performance;

    (c) the reproduction, without their consent, of a fixation of their performance:

        (i) if the original fixation itself was made without their consent;

       (ii) if the reproduction is made for purposes different from those for which the performers gave their consent;

      (iii) if the original fixation was made in accordance with the provisions of Article 15, and the reproduction is made for purposes different from those referred to in those provisions.

(2)

    (1) If broadcasting was consented to by the performers, it shall be a matter for the domestic law of the Contracting State where protection is claimed to regulate the protection against rebroadcasting, fixation for broadcasting purposes and the reproduction of such fixation for broadcasting purposes.

    (2) The terms and conditions governing the use by broadcasting organisations of fixations made for broadcasting purposes shall be determined in accordance with the domestic law of the Contracting State where protection is claimed.

    (3) However, the domestic law referred to in sub-paragraphs (1) and (2) of this paragraph shall not operate to deprive performers of the ability to control, by contract, their relations with broadcasting organisations.

1. (a) General. This provision sets forth the minimum protection for performers, as defined in art. 3(a), who fulfil the (maximum) formal conditions set forth in art. 11 RC in relation to phonograms. See art. 11, note 1(b). **(b) EU legislation.** In the EU, the rights of performers are harmonized by arts. 7-9 of the Rental Right Directive and arts. 2-3 of the Information Society Directive.

2. No exclusive rights. The Rome Convention does not oblige Contracting States to grant the protection to performers as exclusive rights. Rather, the obligation only concerns the possibility of performers to prevent certain acts without their consent. This less than far-reaching protection can be explained by reference to the protection existing at the time when the Rome Convention was adopted for performers in the United Kingdom, where the 1925 Dramatic and Musical Performers Protection Act only provided for criminal sanctions once certain acts had occurred without the performers' consent. In other words, in the UK, performers at that time could only be protected a posteriori and could not prevent the conclusion of certain acts without their consent a priori. Since the UK was an important negotiator at the 1961 Rome Diplomatic Conference, the delegates decided to limit the protection afforded by the Convention to the 'possibility to prevent'. This also allows other modes of protection to continue to exist, such as recourse to, for example, personality rights, fair trade practices, tort law, and so forth, provided that such other modes of protection require the performer's 'consent'.

3. Broadcasting (paras. 1(a) and 2). (a) Right to prevent. The Rome Convention provides performers protection against the broadcasting of a live, that is an unfixed and unbroadcast performance without the performers' consent. As is made explicit in the Documents of the Diplomatic Conference, this right covers broadcasting of a performance both in whole or in part. The notion of 'broadcasting' is defined in art. 3(f) RC (see art. 3, note 7). According to para. 2(2), the terms and conditions governing the use by broadcasting organizations of fixations made for broadcasting purposes are determined in accordance with the national law of the Contracting State where protection is sought, without the possibility to deprive performers of the ability to control, by contract, their relations with broadcasting organizations (para. 2(3)). **(b) No right to prevent rebroadcasting.** However, the Rome Convention does not provide protection for performers against the rebroadcasting, as defined in art. 3(g) RC, of their performances without their consent. **(c) Claim for remuneration.** The restriction of this provision to unfixed and unbroadcast performances is compensated to a certain extent by the claim for remuneration for the use of phonograms that have been commercially published for broadcasting according to art. 12 RC (see note 4(b)).

4. Communication to the public (para. 1(a)). (a) Right to prevent. Similarly, the Rome Convention provides protection to performers against communication to the public of a live, that is unfixed and unbroadcast performance without the performers' consent. This right also covers communication to the public of a performance in whole or in part. However, neither the term 'communication' nor the term 'public' is defined in the Rome Convention. **(b) Claim for remuneration.** The restriction of this provision to unfixed and unbroadcast performances is compensated to a certain extent by the claim for remuneration for the use of phonograms that have been commercially published communications to the public according to art. 12 RC.

This remuneration right has been maintained by art. 15 WPPT. However, according to art. 10 WPPT, performers have obtained an exclusive right at least for the making available of their fixed performances to the public. See art. 12, notes 1 and 4.

5. First fixation (paras. 1(b) and 2(1)). (a) Protection. The Rome Convention provides an obvious form of protection for performers, namely protection against the first fixation of a performance without the performers' consent, in whole or in part (see also note 6). Such protection is useful against fixations of performances of which the artist is unaware. **(b) Exception.** However, according to para. 2(1), the protection against the fixation for broadcasting purposes can be excluded in the national law of the Contracting State where protection is sought, once the performer has consented to the broadcast.

6. Reproduction (paras. 1(c) and 2(1)). (a) Protection. The Rome Convention also provides limited protection against reproduction of the fixation of a performance without the performer's consent. The notion of 'reproduction' is defined in art. 3(e) RC. As the Conference documents state, this right covers reproduction of a performance in whole or in part (RC Conference Proceedings). However, the protection against reproduction of a fixation only exists in three cases: firstly, the original fixation was made without the performer's consent (para. 1(c)(i)); second, the reproduction is made for purposes different from those for which the performer consented to the original fixation (para. 1(c)(ii)); and, third, the original fixation was made in accordance with the provisions of art. 15 RC (listing the exceptions to the protection of performers in the Rome Convention), and the reproduction is made for purposes different from those referred to in those provisions (para. 1(c)(iii)). **(b) Exception.** However, according to para. 2(1), if the reproduction is made for purposes different from those for which the performer consented to the original fixation, the protection against reproduction can be excluded in the national law of the Contracting State where protection is sought, once the performer has consented to the broadcast.

7. No distribution right. The Diplomatic Conference of 1961 did not recognize a distribution right for performers (RC Conference Proceedings). Since the reproduction right for performers clearly does not have a broad application (see note 6), no distribution right can be based on this right.

8. No moral rights. Likewise, the Rome Convention does not protect the moral rights of performers, although some scholars (Nordemann/Vinck/Hertin) have tried to defend the embryonic existence of a moral right based on art. 11 RC, which mentions the identification of the identities of performers on phonograms. However, art. 11 RC is not part of the so-called conventional minimum, and it allows modes of identification other than the performer's name, such as trademarks or other appropriate designations. However, performers do enjoy moral rights protection under art. 5 WPPT.

9. Ownership and transfer. It can be deduced from art. 3 (a) RC that the rights inure initially to the benefit of the physical performer. Since the Rome Convention does not contain any clear mention in respect of the assignability or transferability of these rights to a third party, it is up to the Contracting States to decide these issues. Indeed, many national States do allow for the assignability and/or transferability of these rights.

10. Limitations. For permitted exceptions to the rights to prevent the acts listed in art. 7 RC, see arts. 15 and 19 RC (which contain exceptions to this protection) and 14 RC (concerning the term of protection).

[Performers acting jointly]

Article 8

Any Contracting State may, by its domestic laws and regulations, specify the manner in which performers will be represented in connection with the exercise of their rights if several of them participate in the same performance.

1. General. This provision deals with the effect of the protection afforded by the Rome Convention on performers who perform collectively, such as in a symphony orchestra or a choir. This provision does not curtail the protection given to these performers, nor does it submit the exercise of this right to certain conditions (such as a statutory license, see RC Conference Proceedings). Rather, it helps users of a collective performance to obtain the necessary authorization by allowing the Contracting States to specify in their national laws how performers of collective performances shall be represented to exercise their rights.

2. Modes of representation. The Contracting States can take certain measures, like limiting the persons whom users have to ask for authorization and/or the appointment of a representative for performers of collective performances, by law or on a voluntary basis. The threshold for the application of the Rome Convention in this respect is not clear, but it seems that it shall suffice if 'several', which means two or more performers participate in the same performance.

[Variety and circus artists]

Article 9

Any Contracting State may, by its domestic laws and regulations, extend the protection provided for in this Convention to artists who do not perform literary or artistic works.

1. General. This provision has to be read in conjunction with art. 3(a) RC, which contains the definition of who is a 'performer' for purposes of the Rome Convention.

2. Possible extension. According to art. 9 RC, Contracting States are free to grant protection, under their national laws, to those artists who, like acrobats, magicians and the like, present, for example, variety and circus performances. It has been debated whether professional athletes can also qualify for neighbouring rights protection. Such artists are not covered by the definition of 'performers' of art. 3(a) RC, since what they perform is not a literary or artistic work. The WPPT, in its art. 2(a) extended the protection to the performance of 'expression of folklore'.

[Right of reproduction for phonogram producers]

Article 10

Producers of phonograms shall enjoy the right to authorise or prohibit the direct or indirect reproduction of their phonograms.

1. (a) General. This provision grants a right of reproduction to phonogram producers, as defined in art. 3(c) RC. According to art. 11 RC (see art. 11, note 1(b) however), Contracting States may subject this protection to the formalities described in this article. Protection to phonogram producers is also granted under the Convention for the Protection of Producers of Phonograms Against Unauthorized Duplication of Their Phonograms (Geneva Convention) of 1971, which is also commented upon in this volume. **(b) EU legislation.** In the EU the rights of phonogram producers are harmonized by arts. 7-9 of the Rental Right Directive and arts. 2-3 of the Information Society Directive.

2. Exclusive rights. Unlike performers (see art. 7, note 2), phonogram producers enjoy exclusive rights under the Rome Convention ('the right to authorize or prohibit').

3. Reproduction. Art. 10 RC provides phonogram producers an exclusive right to reproduce their phonograms. The term 'reproduction' is defined in art. 3 (e) RC. As the Conference Documents state, this right covers both direct and indirect reproduction of phonograms. This right covers the reproduction in whole or in part (RC Conference Proceedings).

4. No distribution right. However, as stated above for performers, the Rome Convention does not recognize a distribution right and therefore no importation right for phonogram producers (RC Conference Proceedings).

5. No right to communicate to the public or broadcast. (a) General. Nor does the Rome Convention provide for phonogram producers an exclusive right to communicate to the public or broadcast their phonograms. In contrast, art. 14 WPPT now grants to phonogram producers an exclusive right at least with regard to the making available of their phonograms to the public. **(b) Claim for remuneration.** However, this lack of protection against acts of communication to the public and broadcasting is made up for to some extent by the claim for remuneration for the use of phonograms that have been commercially published for broadcasting and public performances according to art. 12 RC. This remuneration right has been maintained by art. 15 WPPT.

6. No moral rights. The Rome Convention does not protect the moral rights of phonogram producers. However, for name attribution in connection with formalities under national law, see art. 11 RC.

7. Ownership and transfer. Since the Rome Convention does not contain any clear mention of the assignability or transferability of these rights to a third party, it is up to the Contracting States to decide these issues. Indeed, many national States do allow for the assignability and/or transferability of these rights.

8. Limitations. For permitted exceptions to the rights to prevent the acts listed in art. 10 RC, see arts. 15 (exceptions to this form of protection) and 14 RC (term of protection).

[Formalities for phonograms]

Article 11

If, as a condition of protecting the rights of producers of phonograms, or of performers, or both, in relation to phonograms, a Contracting State, under its domestic law, requires compliance with formalities, these shall be considered as fulfilled if all the copies in commerce of the published phonogram or their containers bear a notice consisting of the symbol (P), accompanied by the year date of the first publication, placed in such a manner as to give reasonable notice of claim of protection; and if the copies or their containers do not identify the producer or the licensee of the producer (by carrying his name, trade mark or other appropriate designation), the notice shall also include the name of the owner of the rights of the producer; and, furthermore, if the copies or their containers do not identify the principal performers, the notice shall also include the name of the person who, in the country in which the fixation was effected, owns the rights of such performers.

1. (a) General. This provision does not require that performers or phonogram producers fulfil certain formalities in order to claim protection under the Rome Convention, but does not forbid the Contracting States from enacting such provisions in their national laws. This provision harmonizes, however, the formalities that can be required from performers and/or phonogram producers by the Contracting States such as the US which still provides for such formalities, and states the maximum formalities that can be required in order to obtain protection. **(b) WPPT.** Art. 20 WPPT abolished formalities for performers and phonogram producers.

2. Maximum formalities. The maximum formalities that can be required from performers and/or phonogram producers in accordance with the Rome Convention are twofold. **(a) Indication of the producer.** If the national law of a Contracting State requires formalities and if the copies or their packaging do not identify the producer or the licensee by name, trademark or other appropriate designation, these formalities shall be fulfilled by the placement of the symbol (P), the year of the first publication of the phonogram on all copies in trade of the published phonogram or their packaging. The notice must be placed in such a manner so as to give reasonable notice of protection, and include the names of the principal performers or, if the copies or their packaging do not identify the principal performers, the name of the person who holds the performers' rights in the country in which the fixation was effected. **(b) Producer not indicated.** If the copies or their packaging do not identify the producer or the licensee by name, trademark or other appropriate designation, then the notice shall indicate the name of the holder of the producer's rights.

[Secondary uses of phonograms]

Article 12
If a phonogram published for commercial purposes, or a reproduction of such phonogram, is used directly for broadcasting or for any communication to the public, a single equitable remuneration shall be paid by the user to the performers, or to the producers of the phonograms, or to both. Domestic law may, in the absence of agreement between these parties, lay down the conditions as to the sharing of this remuneration.

1. (a) General. This provision strives to encourage the Contracting States to compensate to a certain extent for the lack of protection of performers and phonogram producers against communication to the public of commercial phonograms (see arts. 7 and 10 RC). This provision seeks to strike a balance between the interests of broadcasters, who may not be required to obtain authorization from performers and phonogram producers (and thus be confronted with a possible refusal to broadcast these phonograms), on the one hand, and the necessary financial compensation for performers and phonogram producers for such use on the other. **(b) WPPT.** This remuneration right has been maintained in art. 15 WPPT, but in certain circumstances changed into an exclusive right in arts. 10 and 14 WPPT.

2. Conditions for application. The conditions for application for this right can be divided into those relating to the object and those dealing with the use of that object. First, the remuneration right of art. 12 RC only applies to phonograms, as defined in art. 3(b) RC, which have been made public, as defined in art. 3(d) RC, for commercial purposes. Second, the remuneration right of art. 12 RC only applies to broadcasting, as defined in art. 3(f) RC and/ or to communication to the public of these phonograms, insofar as these uses can be considered 'direct'. This excludes, for instance, rebroadcasting (RC Conference Proceedings).

3. Remuneration right. (a) 'Single' remuneration. Performers and/or phonogram producers can claim a right to equitable remuneration for this so-called 'secondary use' of commercial phonograms. In order to avoid payments to two groups of rightholders, which would in all likelihood subject the broadcasting organization to a higher overall payment, and to present broadcasting organizations with only one negotiator, the remuneration must be a single one. However, it is left to the Contracting States who should be considered as holder of such remuneration right, whether it is the performers, the phonogram producers or both. Even if there are two categories of rightholders (performers and phonogram producers), 'single' remuneration should be understood to mean that the users of commercial phonograms shall be deemed to have fulfilled their obligation to pay equitable remuneration if they pay one category of rightholder. **(b) 'Equitable' remuneration.** The Rome Convention does not define what should be considered 'equitable' remuneration. Rather, the determination of an equitable remuneration is left to the Contracting States. **(c) Distribution.** Moreover, if both performers and phonogram producers are entitled to remuneration under the national law of a Contracting State, they must then decide on the proper distribution of the monies collected. In the absence of an agreement between the rightholders concerned, distribution modalities shall be determined by the national laws of the Contracting States.

4. Reservations. It should be noted, however, that because national law varies greatly with regard to the legal regime of the use of commercial phonograms by broadcasting organizations, the Rome Convention permits Contracting States to make several reservations to the right of art. 12 RC. According to art. 16(1)(a) RC, Contracting States may declare that they either do not apply the provisions of art. 12 at all; that they restrict them to certain uses mentioned in art. 12 RC; that they exclude remuneration for the use of phonograms produced by persons who are not nationals of a Contracting State; and/or that they subject the right with regard to phonograms produced by producers of other Contracting States to certain conditions of reciprocity. Such reservations can either be made with immediate effect when the instrument of ratification, acceptance or accession is deposited, or at any time thereafter with effect six months after the date of deposit.

[Minimum rights for broadcasting organizations]

Article 13

Broadcasting organisations shall enjoy the right to authorise or prohibit:

- (a) **the rebroadcasting of their broadcasts;**
- (b) **the fixation of their broadcasts;**
- (c) **the reproduction:**
    - (i) **of fixations, made without their consent, of their broadcasts;**
    - (ii) **of fixations, made in accordance with the provisions of Article 15, of their broadcasts, if the reproduction is made for purposes different from those referred to in those provisions;**
- (d) **the communication to the public of their television broadcasts if such communication is made in places accessible to the public against payment of an entrance fee; it shall be a matter for the domestic law of the State where protection of this right is claimed to determine the conditions under which it may be exercised.**

1. (a) General. This provision provides protection for broadcasters. Although the term 'broadcaster' is not defined by the Rome Convention, the protected act of 'broadcasting' is defined in art. 3(f) RC. Given the technology-narrow definition of 'broadcasting' in this article, only wireless broadcasters can claim protection, thus excluding cable broadcasters as well as webcasters. **(b) EU legislation.** In the EU the rights of broadcasting organizations are harmonized by arts. 7-9 of the Rental Right Directive and arts. 2-3 of the Information Society Directive.

2. Exclusive rights. Like phonogram producers, but contrary to performers, broadcasting organizations enjoy exclusive rights under the Rome Convention ('the right to authorize or prohibit').

3. Fixation (art. 13(b)). The Rome Convention provides an exclusive right for broadcasters for the fixation of their broadcasts. Again, this right covers fixation both in whole or in part.

4. Reproduction (art. 13(c)). The Rome Convention provides a limited exclusive right for broadcasters for the reproduction of their broadcasts. This right covers reproduction of a broadcast both in whole or in part (RC Conference Proceedings). The notion of 'reproduction' is defined in art. 3(e) RC. This protection only exists in two cases: firstly, if the original fixation was made without the broadcaster's consent and, second, if the original fixation was made under a limitation as described in art. 15 RC (exceptions to the protection granted by the Rome Convention), for purposes different from those referred to in those provisions.

5. Communication to the public (art. 13(d)). The Rome Convention provides a limited exclusive right for broadcasters to communicate their broadcasts to the public, namely if they fulfil two cumulative conditions. Firstly, if such communication is made in a place accessible to the public and second, if these places are only accessible to the public against payment of an entrance fee. This right covers communication to the public of a broadcast both in whole or in part. Furthermore, it is left to the discretion of the Contracting State where protection is sought to determine the conditions under which this right may be exercised. However, according to art. 16(1)(b) RC Contracting States can make a reservation with regard to this broadcasters' right of communication to the public (see note 9).

6. No protection of moral rights. The Rome Convention does not grant moral rights' protection to broadcasting organizations.

7. Ownership and transfer. Since the Rome Convention does not contain any clear mention in respect of the assignability or transferability of these rights to a third party, it is up to the Contracting States to decide these issues. Indeed, many national States do allow for the assignability and/or transferability of these rights.

8. Limitations. Exceptions to the rights of broadcasters are to be found in art. 15 RC. The term of protection is defined in art. 14 RC.

9. Reservations. Art. 16(1)(b) RC allows Contracting States to make a reservation with regard to this broadcasters' right of communication to the public granted in art. 13(d), by declaring that they do not apply the protection granted by art. 13(d). In such a case, art. 16(1)(b) RC opens up the possibility of reciprocity. The other Contracting State is then no longer under the obligation to grant the right referred to in art. 13(d), to broadcasting organizations whose headquarters are in that State. Again, such reservation can either be made with immediate effect when the instrument of ratification, acceptance or accession is deposited, or at any time thereafter with effect six months after the date of deposit.

[Minimum duration of protection]

Article 14

The term of protection to be granted under this Convention shall last at least until the end of a period of twenty years computed from the end of the year in which:

    (a) the fixation was made for phonograms and for performances incorporated therein;

    (b) the performance took place for performances not incorporated in phonograms;

    (c) the broadcast took place for broadcasts.

1. General. (a) Term of protection under the Rome Convention. This provision describes in general terms the minimum term of protection for performers, phonogram producers, and broadcasters and defines for each rightholder the starting point to calculate this term of protection. **(b) TRIPS; WPPT.** It should be noted, however, that art. 14(5) TRIPS has raised the minimum protection for performers and phonogram producers to 50 years to be calculated from the end of the year in which the fixation was made or the performance took place. Similarly, art. 17 WPPT provides for 50 years for performers (from the end of the year in which the performance was fixed in a phonogram) and for producers of phonograms (from the end of the year in which the phonogram was published, or failing such publication within 50 years from fixation of the phonogram, 50 years from the end of the year in which the fixation was made). However, the 20-year term of protection granted to broadcasters from the end of the year in which the broadcast took place, remained unaffected by TRIPS. **(c) EU legislation.** In the EU, the terms for holders of neighbouring rights were initially harmonized by art. 12 of the Rental Right Directive. They are currently harmonized by art. 3 of the Term Directive as amended by the Term Extension Directive, which extended, under conditions, the term of protection of fixations of performances on phonograms from 50 to 70 years.

2. Minimum term of protection. Under the Rome Convention, the minimum term of protection is twenty years for all rightholders, to be calculated as indicated in notes 3-6.

3. Performers (art. 14(a) and (b)). For performers, the term of protection starts to run from one of two points in time: either from the time the (presumably first) fixation is made (for performances incorporated in phonograms), or from the time the performance takes place (for performances not incorporated in phonograms but, for example, in audiovisual fixations, even though according to art. 19 RC, the protection for performers of art. 7 RC does not apply in this case).

4. Phonogram producers (art. 14(a)). The term of protection for phonogram producers starts to run at the time the fixation is made.

5. Broadcasters (art. 14(c)). The term of protection for broadcasters starts to run when the broadcast occurs.

6. Calculation of the term of protection. In all cases, the term of protection is calculated from the end of the year in which the preceding facts occurred.

[Permitted Exceptions]

Article 15

(1) Any Contracting State may, in its domestic laws and regulations, provide for exceptions to the protection guaranteed by this Convention as regards:
  (a) **private use;**
  (b) **use of short excerpts in connection with the reporting of current events;**

    (c) **ephemeral fixation by a broadcasting organisation by means of its own facilities and for its own broadcasts;**

    (d) **use solely for the purposes of teaching or scientific research.**

(2) Irrespective of paragraph 1 of this Article, any Contracting State may, in its domestic laws and regulations, provide for the same kinds of limitations with regard to the protection of performers, producers of phonograms and broadcasting organisations, as it provides for, in its domestic laws and regulations, in connection with the protection of copyright in literary and artistic works. However, compulsory licences may be provided for only to the extent to which they are compatible with this Convention.

1. General. (a) Permitted exceptions. This provision contains optional exceptions to the protection afforded by the Rome Convention, that is only when protection is granted to foreigners. There are four specific exceptions in para. 1 of this article. In addition, para. 2 contains a general clause referring to the exceptions permitted under copyright law. It should be noted that art. 15 RC prescribes the maximum exceptions which Contracting States are allowed to introduce with regard to the minimum protection granted by the Rome Convention. As a consequence, Contracting States enjoy a complete freedom to provide for less far-reaching exceptions and limitations in their respective national laws. Also, they may decide not to grant them at all. **(b) Other limitations to protection.** It should be noted, however, that art. 19 RC automatically excludes the protection granted to performers if a performer has consented to the incorporation of his performance in a visual or audio-visual fixation. Moreover, according to arts. 5(3), 6(2), 16(1) and 17 RC, Contracting States may make quite a number of reservations to the rights granted under the Rome Convention. These reservations remained unaffected by TRIPS (art. 14(6) TRIPS), but are no longer permitted under the WPPT. **(c) EU legislation.** In the EU the exceptions to the rights of performers, phonogram producers and broadcasting organizations are harmonized by art. 10 of the Rental Right Directive and art. 5 of the Information Society Directive.

2. Private use (para. 1(a)). This first exception deals with the private use of protected materials, without defining what should be considered 'private' and without specifying certain additional conditions such as 'non-commercial purposes'. Also, the RC does not limit the granting of exceptions by Contracting States in the same way as does the so-called three-step test, according to which limitations are confined to certain special cases which do not conflict with the normal exploitation and do not unreasonably prejudice the legitimate interests of rightholders (see art. 9(2) BC and arts. 10 WCT and 16 WPPT). Rather, as stated in note 1(a), Contracting States have discretion to impose such additional conditions or not to grant them at all.

3. Reporting of current events (para. 1(b)). This exception concerns the reporting of current events, insofar as only short excerpts of protected materials are used. This exception probably covers all acts against which the 1961 Rome Convention provides any form of protection, that is, fixation, reproduction, communication to the public and broadcasting. However, it is not further defined what should be considered 'reporting', 'current events', and 'short excerpts'. As stated in note 1(a), Contracting States have discretion to impose additional conditions, to limit the scope of this exception, or not to grant it at all.

4. Ephemeral fixations (para. 1(c)). This exception concerns ephemeral fixations of protected materials insofar as they are done by a broadcasting organization using its own facilities and for its own broadcasts. The terms 'ephemeral' and 'own facilities' are not clearly defined, but it seems appropriate to assume that 'ephemeral' fixations are intended to be destroyed after being broadcast and thus do not include fixations for archival purposes. The term 'fixation' will have to be interpreted narrowly in order to exclude subsequent reproductions of fixations. As regards the term 'own facilities', the Diplomatic Conference specified that it could cover financial, organizational or other means (RC Conference Proceedings). As stated in note 1(a), Contracting States have discretion to impose such additional conditions, to limit the scope of this exception or not to grant it at all.

5. Teaching and scientific research (para. 1(d)). This exception, which can be assumed to cover all acts against which the Rome Protection provides any protection, that is, fixation, reproduction, communication to the public and broadcasting, concerns the use of protected materials for teaching and scientific research. Here again, the terms such as 'teaching' and 'scientific research' are not defined, nor are certain additional conditions specified, but, as stated in note 1(a), Contracting States have discretion to impose such additional conditions, to limit the scope of this exception or not to grant it at all.

6. Analogy to copyright (para. 2). Finally, the general exception contained in para. 2 allows a Contacting Party to provide any other exception with regard to the protection of performers, phonogram producers, and broadcasters that it provides in its national laws regarding copyright of literary and artistic works. This general exception can be explained by the desire to avoid inconsistence with copyright and to giving preferential treatment to performers, phonogram producers and broadcasters over copyright holders. However, the Rome Convention expressly states that compulsory licenses may only be granted to the extent they are compatible with the Rome Convention, thus prohibiting the application mutatis mutandis of, for instance, exceptions in accordance with the Berne Convention, such as legal licenses in favour of developing countries.

[Reservations]

Article 16

(1) Any State, upon becoming party to this Convention, shall be bound by all the obligations and shall enjoy all the benefits thereof. However, a State may at any time, in a notification deposited with the Secretary-General of the United Nations, declare that:

(a) as regards Article 12:
  (i) it will not apply the provisions of that Article;
  (ii) it will not apply the provisions of that Article in respect of certain uses;
  (iii) as regards phonograms the producer of which is not a national of another Contracting State, it will not apply that Article;
  (iv) as regards phonograms the producer of which is a national of another Contracting State, it will limit the protection provided for by that Article to the extent to which, and to the term for which, the latter State grants protection to phonograms first fixed by a national of the State making the declaration; however, the fact that the Contracting State of which the producer is a national does not grant the protection to the same beneficiary or beneficiaries as the State making the declaration shall not be considered as a difference in the extent of the protection;

(b) as regards Article 13, it will not apply item 13(d); if a Contracting State makes such a declaration, the other Contracting States shall not be obliged to grant the right referred to in Article 13(d), to broadcasting organisations whose headquarters are in that State.

(2) If the notification referred to in paragraph 1 of this Article is made after the date of the deposit of the instrument of ratification, acceptance or accession, the declaration will become effective six months after it has been deposited.

1. General. This provision allows the Contacting States to make reservations at any time with regard to both arts. 12 and 13 of the Rome Convention. For the territorial scope of reservations made pursuant to art. 16 RC, see art. 27(2) RC.

2. Reservations to art. 12 (para. 1(a)). The remuneration right provided in art. 12 RC to performers and/or to producers of phonograms is subject to several possible reservations. A Contracting State can exclude the application of this article either in whole or in part. Partial exclusions can concern the points of attachment to claim remuneration (for additional reservations with regard to the criterion of 'fixation' see art. 17 RC), uses that give rise to a right to remuneration, and the scope of the right or its duration.

3. Reservations to art. 13 (para 1(b)). Contracting States can make reservations with regard to the application of art. 13(d) RC, which confers an exclusive right to communicate a television broadcast to the public at places where the public only has access against payment of an entrance fee. However, no reservations can be made with regard to the other exclusive rights granted to broadcasting organizations under art. 13(a)-(c) RC.

[Certain countries applying only the 'fixation' criterion]

Article 17

Any State which, on October 26,1961, grants protection to producers of phonograms solely on the basis of the criterion of fixation may, by a notification deposited with the Secretary-General of the United Nations at the time of ratification, acceptance or accession, declare that it will apply, for the purposes of Article 5, the criterion of fixation alone and, for the purposes of paragraph 16.1(a)(iii) and 16.1(a)(iv), the criterion of fixation instead of the criterion of nationality.

1. General. This provision has to be read in conjunction with arts. 5 (points of attachment for national treatment of phonogram producers) and 16 RC (reservations to the right to remuneration for 'secondary' use of commercial phonograms). For the territorial scope of reservations made pursuant to art. 17 RC, see art. 27(2) RC.

2. Reservations to art. 5. A Contracting State which, on 26 October 1961, granted protection to phonogram producers solely on the basis of the criterion of fixation as defined in art. 5(1)(b) may continue to apply this sole criterion by filing a notice to this effect upon ratification of the Rome Convention.

3. Reservations to art. 16. Such a Contracting State may apply the fixation criterion rather than the criterion of nationality, as used in art. 16(1)(a) (iii) and (iv) RC.

[Withdrawal of reservations]

Article 18

Any State which has deposited a notification under Article 5.3, Article 6.2, Article 16.1 or Article 17, may, by a further notification deposited with the Secretary-General of the United Nations, reduce its scope or withdraw it.

1. General. This provision is self-explanatory. For the territorial scope of any reservation and withdrawal see also art. 27(2) RC.

[Performers' rights in films]

Article 19

Notwithstanding anything in this Convention, once a performer has consented to the incorporation of his performance in a visual or audio-visual fixation, Article 7 shall have no further application.

1. General. Apart from the general exceptions to the legal protection granted to performers under art. 15 RC, art. 19 RC contains another exception to the protection of performers which applies automatically and does not require the Contracting Parties to opt for an exception to the minimum of the Rome Convention. This provision expresses the general fear of film producers that performers who enjoy rights to prevent certain acts with regard to audiovisual works might use these rights in order to hinder the exploitation of cinemato-graphic works. More than 40 years after the adoption of the Rome Convention, these fears still persist. They have led to the failure of the proposed new Treaty for the protection of audiovisual performances (WIPO Audiovisual Performances Treaty) at the Diplomatic Conference in 2000. Today a compromise has been found and built into the Beijing Treaty on Audiovisual Performances (see RC, Introductory Remarks, note 1), more particularly in its art. 12.

2. Scope of application. Once a performer has consented to the incorporation of his performance in an (audio-)visual fixation, that performer loses, vis-à-vis the film producer, protection under art. 7 RC.

3. EU legislation. In the EU, this issue has been dealt with in art. 3 of the Rental Right Directive.

[Non-retroactivity]

Article 20

(1) This Convention shall not prejudice rights acquired in any Contracting State before the date of coming into force of this Convention for that State.

(2) No Contracting State shall be bound to apply the provisions of this Convention to performances or broadcasts which took place, or to phonograms which were fixed, before the date of coming into force of this Convention for that State.

1. General (para. 2). The Rome Convention only applies to performances, fixations or broadcasts from the date of its entry into force and, thus, does not apply to pre-existing materials.

2. Acquired rights (para. 1). Rights acquired prior to the entry into force of the Rome Convention shall not be affected.

[Protection by other means]

Article 21

The protection provided for in this Convention shall not prejudice any protection otherwise secured to performers, producers of phonograms and broadcasting organisations.

1. General. The international protection for performers, phonogram producers, and broadcasters granted by the Rome Convention is a minimum protection. It follows that additional protection for these rightholders, such as by copyright, personality rights, fair trade practices, tort law and the like, is not prejudiced by this Convention.

[Special agreements]

Article 22

Contracting States reserve the right to enter into special agreements among themselves in so far as such agreements grant to performers, producers of phonograms or broadcasting organisations more extensive rights than those granted by this Convention or contain other provisions not contrary to this Convention.

1. General. This provision makes clear that the international protection provided to performers, phonogram producers and broadcasters is only a minimum standard. It is possible for the Contracting States to conclude other agreements insofar as these arrangements grant more extensive rights than this Convention or at least do not contain provisions that run contrary to this Convention. The provisions in art. 14 TRIPS as well as the WPPT are both special agreements within the meaning of art. 22 RC.

[Signature and deposit]

Article 23

This Convention shall be deposited with the Secretary-General of the United Nations. It shall be open until June 30, 1962, for signature by any State invited to the Diplomatic Conference on the International Protection of Performers, Producers of Phonograms and Broadcasting Organisations which is a party to the Universal Copyright Convention or a member of the International Union for the Protection of Literary and Artistic Works.

1. General. Only States which were already members of the International Union for the Protection of Literary and Artistic Works (Berne Union) and hence the Berne Convention (see art. 1 BC) and/or party to the Universal Copyright Convention (UCC) were invited to sign the Rome Convention. The link between the Rome Convention and the two conventions on copyright is also present in art. 28(4) RC, according to which a State automatically ceases to be a Contracting State of the Rome Convention from the time that it is no longer party to the UCC nor a member of the Berne Union. This provision should safeguard and encourage copyright protection (see art. 1 RC). For ratification and acceptance, see also art. 24(2) RC.

[Becoming party to the Convention]

Article 24

(1) This Convention shall be subject to ratification or acceptance by the signatory States.

(2) This Convention shall be open for accession by any State invited to the Conference referred to in Article 23, and by any State Member of the United Nations, provided that in either case such State is a party to the Universal Copyright Convention or a member of the International Union for the Protection of Literary and Artistic Works.

(3) Ratification, acceptance or accession shall be effected by the deposit of an instrument to that effect with the Secretary-General of the United Nations.

1. General. This provision determines who can become a Contracting State of the Rome Convention and the modalities for ratification, acceptance or accession. Again, only States which were already members of the International Union for the Protection of Literary and Artistic Works (Berne Union) and hence the Berne Convention (see art. 1 BC) and/or party to the Universal Copyright Convention (UCC) were invited to become Contracting States of the Rome Convention. This provision should safeguard and encourage copyright protection. See also comment to art. 23 RC.

[Entry into force]

Article 25

(1) This Convention shall come into force three months after the date of deposit of the sixth instrument of ratification, acceptance or accession.

(2) Subsequently, this Convention shall come into force in respect of each State three months after the date of deposit of its instrument of ratification, acceptance or accession.

1. General. (a) Entry into force. The Rome Convention entered into force on 18 May 1964. The initial Contracting States were the Democratic

Republic of Congo, Ecuador, Mexico, Niger, Sweden, and the United Kingdom. **(b) Current Members.** Since then, membership has steadily increased. However, it should be noted that the US is still not a Contracting State to the Rome Convention. This explains why the Convention for the Protection of Producers of Phonograms Against Unauthorized Duplication of Their Phonograms (Geneva Convention) was considered necessary, and also why the TRIPS Agreement does not incorporate the RC as such. On 1 January 2015, there were 92 Contracting States to the Rome Convention, of which 27 were EU Member States. For the current status see the WIPO website.

2. Entry into force for States subsequently adhering. For newly adhering States, the Rome Convention enters into force three months after the filing date of the instrument of ratification, acceptance or accession.

[Implementation of the Convention by the provision of domestic law]

Article 26

(1) Each Contracting State undertakes to adopt, in accordance with its Constitution, the measures necessary to ensure the application of this Convention.

(2) At the time of deposit of its instrument of ratification, acceptance or accession, each State must be in a position under its domestic law to give effect to the terms of this Convention.

1. General. It should be noted that if a Contracting State fails to properly give effect to the terms of the Rome Convention in its domestic law, according to art. 30 RC, other Contracting Parties may refer the issue to the International Court of Justice (ICJ) for decision, or solve it by another mode of settlement. However, no case has been brought before the ICJ to date.

[Applicability of the Convention to certain territories]

Article 27

(1) Any State may, at the time of ratification, acceptance or accession, or at any time thereafter, declare by notification addressed to the Secretary-General of the United Nations that this Convention shall extend to all or any of the territories for whose international relations it is responsible, provided that the Universal Copyright Convention or the International Convention for the Protection of Literary and Artistic Works applies to the territory or territories concerned. This notification shall take effect three months after the date of its receipt.

(2) The notifications referred to in Article 5.3, Article 6.2, Article 16.1 and Articles 17 and 18, may be extended to cover all or any of the territories referred to in paragraph 1 of this Article.

1. General. This technical provision also has certain effects on arts. 23, 24(2) and 28(5) RC.

[Denunciation of the Convention]

Article 28

(1) Any Contracting State may denounce this Convention, on its own behalf or on behalf of all or any of the territories referred to in Article 27.

(2) The denunciation shall be effected by a notification addressed to the Secretary-General of the United Nations and shall take effect twelve months after the date of receipt of the notification.

(3) The right of denunciation shall not be exercised by a Contracting State before the expiry of a period of five years from the date on which the Convention came into force with respect to that State.

(4) A Contracting State shall cease to be a party to this Convention from that time when it is neither a party to the Universal Copyright Convention nor a member of the International Union for the Protection of Literary and Artistic Works.

(5) This Convention shall cease to apply to any territory referred to in Article 27 from that time when neither the Universal Copyright Convention nor the International Convention for the Protection of Literary and Artistic Works applies to that territory.

1. Denunciation (paras. 1 and 2). Notwithstanding the minimum period of adherence specified in para. 3, any Contracting State may denounce this Convention by giving notice as provided in the Convention.

2. Minimum period of adherence (para. 3). However, the minimum term of ratification, acceptance or accession to the Rome Convention is five years from its entry into force in a given Contracting State.

3. Termination (paras. 4 and 5). The Rome Convention shall cease to apply when a Contracting State is no longer a party to the International Union for the Protection of Literary and Artistic Works and hence neither to the Berne Convention (see art. 1 BC) nor to the Universal Copyright Convention (UCC).

[Revision of the Convention]

Article 29

(1) After this Convention has been in force for five years, any Contracting State may, by notification addressed to the Secretary-General of the United Nations, request that a conference be convened for the purpose of revising the Convention. The Secretary-General shall notify

all Contracting States of this request. If, within a period of six months following the date of notification by the Secretary-General of the United Nations, not less than one half of the Contracting States notify him of their concurrence with the request, the Secretary-General shall inform the Director-General of the International Labour Office, the Director-General of the United Nations Educational, Scientific and Cultural Organization and the Director of the Bureau of the International Union for the Protection of Literary and Artistic Works, who shall convene a revision conference in co-operation with the Intergovernmental Committee provided for in Article 32.

(2) The adoption of any revision of this Convention shall require an affirmative vote by two-thirds of the States attending the revision conference, provided that this majority includes two-thirds of the States which, at the time of the revision conference, are parties to the Convention.

(3) In the event of adoption of a Convention revising this Convention in whole or in part, and unless the revising Convention provides otherwise:

(a) this Convention shall cease to be open to ratification, acceptance or accession as from the date of entry into force of the revising Convention;

(b) this Convention shall remain in force as regards relations between or with Contracting States which have not become parties to the revising Convention.

1. General. (a) Procedure. This provision sets out the rules for possible revision of the Rome Convention. **(b) WPPT.** However, instead of revising the Rome Convention, the WPPT has been concluded as a special and separate agreement within the meaning of art. 22 RC.

[Settlement of disputes]

Article 30

Any dispute which may arise between two or more Contracting States concerning the interpretation or application of this Convention and which is not settled by negotiation shall, at the request of any one of the parties to the dispute, be referred to the International Court of Justice for decision, unless they agree to another mode of settlement.

1. General. (a) Rome Convention. As a rule, the International Court of Justice (ICJ) has jurisdiction to settle disputes between Contracting States concerning the Rome Convention. However, no such dispute has ever been brought before the ICJ. **(b) TRIPS.** However, due to the incorporation of some of the rights of the neighbouring rightholders covered by the Rome Convention into the TRIPS Agreement (art. 14 TRIPS), the WTO dispute settlement mechanism is now open to all violation complaints against countries that are also WTO Member States.

[Limits on Reservations]

Article 31

Without prejudice to the provisions of Article 5.3, Article 6.2, Article 16.1 and Article 17, no reservation may be made to this Convention.

1. General. The provision merely restates that no other reservations may be made by Contracting Parties, neither on the date of deposit of the instrument of ratification, acceptance or accession, nor at any time thereafter. However, this does not apply to the reservations offered to Contracting States under arts. 5(3), 6(3) and 16(1) RC, regarding the claim for remuneration of performers and producers of phonograms under art. 12 RC and broadcasting organizations under art. 13 RC, and art. 17 RC with regard to points of attachment of protection.

[Intergovernmental Committee]

Article 32

(1) An Intergovernmental Committee is hereby established with the following duties:

  (a) to study questions concerning the application and operation of this Convention; and

  (b) to collect proposals and to prepare documentation for possible revision of this Convention.

(2) The Committee shall consist of representatives of the Contracting States, chosen with due regard to equitable geographical distribution. The number of members shall be six if there are twelve Contracting States or less, nine if there are thirteen to eighteen Contracting States and twelve if there are more than eighteen Contracting States.

(3) The Committee shall be constituted twelve months after the Convention comes into force by an election organised among the Contracting States, each of which shall have one vote, by the Director-General of the International Labour Office, the Director-General of the United Nations Educational, Scientific and Cultural Organization and the Director of the Bureau of the International Union for the Protection of Literary and Artistic Works, in accordance with rules previously approved by a majority of all Contracting States.

(4) The Committee shall elect its Chairman and officers. It shall establish its own rules of procedure. These rules shall in particular provide for the future operation of the Committee and for a method of selecting

its members for the future in such a way as to ensure rotation among the various Contracting States.

(5) Officials of the International Labour Office, the United Nations Educational, Scientific and Cultural Organization and the Bureau of the International Union for the Protection of Literary and Artistic Works, designated by the Directors-General and the Director thereof, shall constitute the Secretariat of the Committee.

(6) Meetings of the Committee, which shall be convened whenever a majority of its members deems it necessary, shall be held successively at the headquarters of the International Labour Office, the United Nations Educational, Scientific and Cultural Organization and the Bureau of the International Union for the Protection of Literary and Artistic Works.

(7) Expenses of members of the Committee shall be borne by their respective Governments.

1. General. Following the rules established by art. 32 RC, the Rome Convention established an Intergovernmental Committee which consists of representatives of the Contracting States (para. 2). The Secretariat is of the Committee is composed by members of WIPO, ILO and UNESCO (paras. 3 and 5). These three organizations jointly administer the Rome Convention.

[Languages]

Article 33

(1) The present Convention is drawn up in English, French and Spanish, the three texts being equally authentic.

(2) In addition, official texts of the present Convention shall be drawn up in German, Italian and Portuguese.

1. General. There are three authentic texts (English, French and Spanish) and three official texts (German, Italian and Portuguese) of the Rome Convention.

[Notifications]

Article 34

(1) The Secretary-General of the United Nations shall notify the States invited to the Conference referred to in Article 23 and every State Member of the United Nations, as well as the Director-General of the International Labour Office, the Director-General of the United Nations Educational, Scientific and Cultural Organization and the Director of the Bureau of the International Union for the Protection of Literary and Artistic Works:

   (a) **of the deposit of each instrument of ratification, acceptance or accession;**

   (b) **of the date of entry into force of the Convention;**

   (c) **of all notifications, declarations or communications provided for in this Convention;**

   (d) **if any of the situations referred to in paragraphs 28.4 and 28.5 arise.**

(2) The Secretary-General of the United Nations shall also notify the Director-General of the International Labour Office, the Director-General of the United Nations Educational, Scientific and Cultural Organization and the Director of the Bureau of the International Union for the Protection of Literary and Artistic Works of the requests communicated to him in accordance with Article 29, as well as of any communication received from the Contracting States concerning the revision of the Convention.

1. General. Whenever a notification has been made, the Secretary-General of the UN shall notify all UN Member States as well as the Directors of WIPO, ILO and UNESCO. For the joint administration of the Rome Convention by WIPO, ILO and UNESCO, see also art. 32 RC.

CONVENTION FOR THE PROTECTION OF PRODUCERS OF PHONOGRAMS AGAINST UNAUTHORIZED DUPLICATION OF THEIR PHONOGRAMS

done at Geneva 29 October 1971

[Preamble]

The Contracting States,

concerned at the widespread and increasing unauthorized duplication of phonograms and the damage this is occasioning to the interests of authors, performers and producers of phonograms;

convinced that the protection of producers of phonograms against such acts will also benefit the performers whose performances, and the authors whose works, are recorded on the said phonograms;

recognizing the value of the work undertaken in this field by the United Nations Educational, Scientific and Cultural Organization and the World Intellectual Property Organization;

anxious not to impair in any way international agreements already in force and in particular in no way to prejudice wider acceptance of the Rome Convention of October 26, 1961, which affords protection to performers and to broadcasting organizations as well as to producers of phonograms;

have agreed as follows:

[Introductory remarks]

1. General. The Geneva Convention (GC), which was concluded in 1971, has as its sole aim to protect phonogram producers against record piracy ('unauthorized duplication of phonograms'). Compared to the Berne and Rome Conventions, it is a simple international instrument. It merely prescribes certain minimum standards of protection, but does not determine the legal means by which Contracting States must achieve this goal, nor does it require national treatment. States may opt for (special) rules of unfair competition law, criminal law provisions, neighbouring rights or even copyright protection, as in the United States where neighbouring rights do not exist and sound recordings are protected by copyright. Indeed, the Geneva Convention was initiated primarily because the United States were unwilling to adhere to the Rome Convention, which required protection of phonogram producers by neighbouring rights. Nevertheless, the Geneva Convention does reproduce parts of the Rome Convention, and is without prejudice to the latter.

[Bibliography]

G. Davies, *Piracy of Phonograms* (2nd edn., ESC Publishing 1986)

E. Ulmer, 'The Convention for the Protection of Producers of Phonograms Against Unauthorized Duplication of Their Phonograms' (1972) 3 IIC 317

A. Kaminstein, 'The Phonograms Convention' (1972) 19 *Bull. Copr. Soc'y* 175

M. Ficsor, *Guide to the Copyright and Related Rights Treaties Administered by WIPO And Glossary Of Copyright And Related Rights Terms* (WIPO 2003) <http://www.wipo.int/edocs/pubdocs/en/copyright/891/wipo_pub_891.pdf>

C. Masouyé, *Guide to the Rome Convention and to the Phonograms Convention* (WIPO 1981)

W. Nordemann, K. Vinck, P. Hertin and G. Meyer, *International Copyright and Neighboring Right Law: Commentary* (Weinheim 1990)

S. Ricketson and J. Ginsburg, *International Copyright and Neighbouring Rights: The Berne Convention and Beyond* (2nd edn., Oxford University Press 2006)

S. Stewart, *International Copyright and Neighbouring Rights* (2nd edn., Butterworths 1989)

[Definitions]

Article 1

> **For the purposes of this Convention:**
> (a) **'phonogram' means any exclusively aural fixation of sounds of a performance or of other sounds;**
> (b) **'producer of phonograms' means the person who, or the legal entity which, first fixes the sounds of a performance or other sounds;**
> (c) **'duplicate' means an article which contains sounds taken directly or indirectly from a phonogram and which embodies all or a substantial part of the sounds fixed in that phonogram;**
> (d) **'distribution to the public' means any act by which duplicates of a phonogram are offered, directly or indirectly, to the general public or any section thereof.**

1. General. Art. 1 GC contains definitions of four terms used throughout the Geneva Convention, namely 'phonogram', 'producer of phonograms', 'duplicate' and 'distribution to the public'. The first two terms correspond to those used in the Rome Convention (art. 3(b) and (c)), while the last two are new definitions introduced by the Geneva Convention.

2. Phonogram. A 'phonogram' is defined as any exclusively aural fixation of sounds of a performance or of other sounds, thus clearly excluding any audiovisual fixation. Note that the definition is not limited to recordings of performances of musical works. Any fixation of 'sounds' will qualify as a phonogram.

3. Producer of phonograms. A 'producer of phonograms' is the person or legal entity that first fixes the sounds of a performance or other sounds (see art. 3 RC, note 4). This will usually be the record company that invests in the sound recording. However, art. 1(b) GC does not contain the criteria of 'initiative' and 'responsibility' that will later introduced in art. 2(d) of the WPPT.

4. Duplicate. A duplicate is a material copy ('article') of a phonogram, which reproduces in whole or substantial part the sounds fixed on the phonogram. The Geneva Convention does not define or describe what should be considered 'substantial'. It may be argued that the term substantial has both a quantitative and a qualitative meaning. The copy can be made 'directly' (i.e. by direct reproduction) or 'indirectly' (i.e. by copying from a source that is itself a copy of the initial phonogram). An indirect duplicate would be, for instance, a copy made from a copy of a phonogram or from a broadcast phonogram.

5. Distribution to the public. The term distribution to the public refers to any act of physical distribution. It does not include immaterial acts of communication to the public, such as broadcasting or online transmission. Distribution to the public covers both direct and indirect offers to the public. The act of distribution must be directed to the public in general or to a portion thereof. The term 'general public' is not defined, and left to the discretion of the Contracting States.

[Obligations of Contracting States]
Article 2

Each Contracting State shall protect producers of phonograms who are nationals of other Contracting States against the making of duplicates without the consent of the producer and against the importation of such duplicates, provided that any such making or importation is for the purpose of distribution to the public, and against the distribution of such duplicates to the public.

1. General. Art. 2 GC contains the main substantive provision of the Geneva Convention. Contracting States must basically protect phonogram producers against the unauthorized making of duplicates, and the importation of such duplicates (see note 5). Art. 2 GC also designates which producers require protection by the Geneva Convention (see note 2).

2. Points of attachment. The primary point of attachment for protection under the Geneva Convention is the nationality of the producer. Contracting

States must protect phonogram producers who are nationals of other Contracting States. However, art. 7(4) GC permits a Contracting State to opt for 'the place of first fixation' of the phonogram as an alternative point of attachment, provided this State applied this criterion, and this criterion alone, in its domestic law on October 29, 1971, the date the Geneva Convention was concluded. A Contracting States opting for this alternative point of attachment must do so by way of a formal reservation (see art. 7, note 3).

3. International protection. The word 'other' in the phrase 'producers of phonograms who are nationals of other Contracting States' makes clear that the protection conferred by the Geneva Convention extends only to foreign producers, and does not cover national producers on the territory of a given Contracting State. In other words, the Geneva Convention guarantees only international protection.

4. Conventional minimum. The Geneva Convention does not require national treatment, as do other treaties in the field of copyright and neighbouring rights (notably art. 2(1) Rome Convention and art. 4 WPPT), but merely establishes a minimum level of protection. Differences in the protection afforded to national producers of phonograms and producers of phonograms located in other Contracting States remain possible, without prejudice to the minimum protection conferred by the Geneva Convention. Of course, Contracting States may always offer to foreign phonogram producers protection in excess of the minimum standards of the Geneva Convention.

5. Prohibited acts. The Convention offers international protection against piracy of phonograms. The acts prohibited by art. 2 GC are threefold: the making of duplicates, the importation of such duplicates, and the distribution thereof to the public. Art. 1 defines the relevant terms. **(a) Duplication.** First, the Geneva Convention prohibits duplication of a phonogram (i.e. the making of duplicates) without the consent of the phonogram producer, insofar as the phonogram is duplicated for the purpose of distribution to the public. According to art. 1(c) GC a duplicate is an article that embodies all or a substantial part of the sounds fixed in an initial phonogram. The Geneva Convention does not protect phonogram producers against the making of articles that reproduce only an insubstantial part of the phonogram (see art. 1, note 4). Nor does the Geneva Convention prohibit duplication for private use; its protection is limited to the making of duplicates for the purpose of distribution to the public. **(b) Importation.** Second, the Geneva Convention prohibits the importation of duplicates of a phonogram without the consent of the producer of the initial phonogram, insofar as the phonogram is imported for the purpose of distribution to the public. The Geneva Convention does not prohibit importing duplicates of phonograms for private use (see note 5(a)). **(c) Distribution to the public.** In the third place, the Geneva Convention prohibits the distribution to the public of duplicates without the consent of the producer of the initial phonogram. Note that the Geneva Convention does not prohibit the distribution of phonograms as such. Its scope is limited to the distribution to the public of duplicates which were made without the consent of the initial phonogram producer (i.e. illegal copies). The Geneva Convention does not offer protection against parallel imports. The term 'distribution to the public is defined in art. 1(d) GC, which refers to physical act's of distribution. Immaterial acts of communication to the public, such as broadcasting or online transmission, are not covered. The act of distribution must be directed to the public in general or to a portion thereof. The notion of 'public' is not defined, leaving its interpretation to the Contracting States. Distribution within the private sphere is not prohibited.

[Means of implementation by Contracting States]

Article 3

The means by which this Convention is implemented shall be a matter for the domestic law of each Contracting State and shall include one or more of the following: protection by means of the grant of a copyright or other specific right; protection by means of the law relating to unfair competition; protection by means of penal sanctions.

1. General. The Geneva Convention does not have direct effect within the jurisdictions of the Contracting States, and therefore must be transposed into the national laws of the Contracting States to become effective.

2. Possible means of protection. Contracting States may choose the legal means by which to transpose the obligations under the Geneva Convention. They may either grant producers of phonograms exclusive private rights (copyright or neighbouring rights for phonogram producers) or provide ex post legal protection for phonogram producers by way of unfair competition law or criminal sanctions, or any combination of the above.

[Term of protection]

Article 4

The duration of the protection given shall be a matter for the domestic law of each Contracting State. However, if the domestic law prescribes a specific duration for the protection, that duration shall not be less than twenty years from the end either of the year in which the sounds embodied in the phonogram were first fixed or of the year in which the phonogram was first published.

1. General. The term of protection is determined by the national law of the Contracting States. If a state provides for a specific term, for instance under a regime of copyright or neighbouring rights, the duration may not be less than twenty years. This term is to be calculated either from the end of the year in which the sounds embodied in the phonogram were first fixed or from the end of the year in which the phonogram was first published.

2. Commencement of term. The minimum term of protection may be calculated from either the end of the year in which the sounds embodied in the phonogram are first fixed or the end of the year in which the phonogram is first published. The term 'published' is not defined or described in the Convention, as it is in art. 3(d) of the Rome Convention. The term 'fixation' has not been defined either, but art. 2(c) of the WPPT does offer a definition. The Geneva Convention does not specify whether the first fixation or publication must take place within the territory of a Contracting State. Therefore, the minimum term of protection will apply irrespective of the territory within which the acts of fixation or publication has occurred.

3. Minimum term only for right of specific duration. The twenty-year minimum term is required only 'if the domestic law prescribes a specific duration for the protection'. This will normally be the case if the protection takes the form of a copyright or neighbouring right. Protection under unfair competition law usually does not come with a specific duration. Thus a Contracting State electing to protect phonograms under unfair competition law need not comply with the twenty-year minimum term. However, it was assumed by the framers of the Geneva Convention that such protection would not come to an end before twenty years from the first fixation or publication of the phonogram.

[Formalities]

Article 5

If, as a condition of protecting the producers of phonograms, a Contracting State, under its domestic law, requires compliance with formalities, these shall be considered as fulfilled if all the authorized duplicates of the phonogram distributed to the public or their containers bear a notice consisting of the symbol (P), accompanied by the year date of the first publication, placed in such manner as to give reasonable notice of claim of protection; and, if the duplicates or their containers do not identify the producer, his successor in title or the exclusive licensee (by carrying his name, trademark or other appropriate designation), the notice shall also include the name of the producer, his successor in title or the exclusive licensee.

1. General. As a rule, Contracting States are under no obligation to require compliance with formalities for phonogram producers to enjoy the protection conferred by the Convention. However, the Convention does allow Contracting States, such as the United States, to require the fulfilment of certain formalities, as described in this provision. The formalities permitted by art. 5 GC are similar but not identical to those allowed under art. 11 of the Rome Convention. Art. 5 GC also allows mentioning the phonogram producer's successor in title or exclusive licensee.

[Limitations on protection]

Article 6

Any Contracting State which affords protection by means of copyright or other specific right, or protection by means of penal sanctions, may in its domestic law provide, with regard to the protection of producers of phonograms, the same kinds of limitations as are permitted with respect to the protection of authors of literary and artistic works. However, no compulsory licenses may be permitted unless all of the following conditions are met:

(a) the duplication is for use solely for the purpose of teaching or scientific research;

(b) the license shall be valid for duplication only within the territory of the Contracting State whose competent authority has granted the license and shall not extend to the export of duplicates;

(c) the duplication made under the license gives rise to an equitable remuneration fixed by the said authority taking into account, inter alia, the number of duplicates which will be made.

1. General. The Geneva Convention does not provide for specific limitations on the protection of phonogram producers. But a Contracting State may declare all or some of its domestic limitations on the protection by copyright of literary and artistic works applicable to the phonogram producers. Art. 15(2) of the Rome Convention contains a similar rule (see art. 15 RC, note 6). In contrast to the Rome Convention, art. 6 GC allows compulsory licenses under three cumulative conditions (see note 2).

2. Compulsory licences. The Convention allows compulsory licences for the duplication of phonograms under three cumulative conditions: the duplication must be for the sole purpose of teaching or scientific research; the duplication must take place only in the territory of the Contracting State that provides for such a compulsory licence and will not cover the exportation of such duplicates; and the duplication must be compensated by equitable remuneration fixed under the domestic law of the Contracting State and taking into account the number of duplicates.

3. Field of application. Art. 6 GC refers only to situations where a Contracting State grants a 'copyright or other specific right' to phonogram producers, or provides for criminal sanctions. The rules on limitations and compulsory licenses do not apply whenever a state offers protection under the law of unfair competition. This is because a system of precisely circumscribed limitations is difficult to apply to the usually vague and case-specific norms of unfair competition law. Of course, when interpreting such norm, national courts may draw inspiration from the statutory limitations of copyright.

[Savings]

Article 7

(1) This Convention shall in no way be interpreted to limit or prejudice the protection otherwise secured to authors, to performers, to producers of phonograms or to broadcasting organizations under any domestic law or international agreement.

(2) It shall be a matter for the domestic law of each Contracting State to determine the extent, if any, to which performers whose performances are fixed in a phonogram are entitled to enjoy protection and the conditions for enjoying any such protection.

(3) No Contracting State shall be required to apply the provisions of this Convention to any phonogram fixed before this Convention entered into force with respect to that State.

(4) Any Contracting State which, on October 29, 1971, affords protection to producers of phonograms solely on the basis of the place of first fixation may, by a notification deposited with the Director General of the World Intellectual Property Organization, declare that it will apply this criterion instead of the criterion of the nationality of the producer.

1. Safeguard clause (paras. 1 and 2). In accordance with the preamble, art. 7(1) GC clarifies that the Convention shall in no way be interpreted to limit or prejudice the protection otherwise secured to authors, to performers, to producers of phonograms or to broadcasting organizations under any domestic law or international agreement. Art. 1 of the Rome Convention contains similar language. Art. 7(2) GC also notes the possibility of similar protection for performers, but leaves this the Contracting States.

2. Temporal scope (para. 3). The Convention does not require Contracting States to grant protection retroactively to phonograms that were fixed before the Convention's entry into force in that State. Contracting States remain free to decide whether or not the Convention should have retroactive effect. In any case the Convention must apply to all phonograms fixed from the date of its entry into force in a given territory.

3. Alternative point of attachment (para. 4). By derogation from art. 2 GC, a Contracting State may make the place of first fixation of a phonogram the point of attachment, provided this State applied this criterion, and this criterion alone, in its domestic law on October 29, 1971, the date on which the Geneva Convention was concluded (see art. 2, note 2). A Contracting State availing itself of this possibility, must notify the Director General of WIPO. Art. 17 of the Rome Convention allows for a similar reservation.

[Secretariat]

Article 8

(1) **The International Bureau of the World Intellectual Property Organization shall assemble and publish information concerning the protection of phonograms. Each Contracting State shall promptly communicate to the International Bureau all new laws and official texts on this subject.**

(2) **The International Bureau shall, on request, furnish information to any Contracting State on matters concerning this Convention, and shall conduct studies and provide services designed to facilitate the protection provided for therein.**

(3) **The International Bureau shall exercise the functions enumerated in paragraph (1) and paragraph (2) above in cooperation, for matters within their respective competence, with the United Nations Educational, Scientific and Cultural Organization and the International Labour Office.**

1. General. The task of providing the secretariat of the Convention is imposed on WIPO, which performs similar duties for the Berne and Paris Conventions. This task shall be performed in cooperation with UNESCO and the ILO 'for matters within their respective competence'. The same three organizations are jointly entrusted with the administration of the Rome Convention (art. 32 RC).

[Joining the Convention]

Article 9

(1) **This Convention shall be deposited with the Secretary-General of the United Nations. It shall be open until April 30, 1972, for signature by any State that is a member of the United Nations, any of the Specialized Agencies brought into relationship with the United Nations, or the International Atomic Energy Agency, or is a party to the Statute of the International Court of Justice.**

(2) **This Convention shall be subject to ratification or acceptance by the signatory States. It shall be open for accession by any State referred to in paragraph (1) of this Article.**

(3) **Instruments of ratification, acceptance or accession shall be deposited with the Secretary-General of the United Nations.**

(4) It is understood that, at the time a State becomes bound by this Convention, it will be in a position in accordance with its domestic law to give effect to the provisions of the Convention.

1. General. The Convention can be ratified or accepted by any State that is a member of the United Nations, any of its Specialized Agencies or the International Atomic Energy Agency (IAEA) or is a party to the Statute of the International Court of Justice. The Convention does not require adherence to the Berne Convention or any other international copyright treaty, as does the Rome Convention (arts. 23 and 24 RC). Instruments of ratification, acceptance or accession to the Geneva Convention must be notified to the Secretary-General of the United Nations.

[Reservations]

Article 10

No reservations to this Convention are permitted.

1. General. Apart from the reservation expressly mentioned in art. 7(4) GC, which allows Contracting States to deviate from the point of attachment prescribed in art. 2, the Geneva Convention does not permit the Contracting States to make reservations.

[Entry into force and applicability]

Article 11

(1) This Convention shall enter into force three months after deposit of the fifth instrument of ratification, acceptance or accession.

(2) For each State ratifying, accepting or acceding to this Convention after the deposit of the fifth instrument of ratification, acceptance or accession, the Convention shall enter into force three months after the date on which the Director General of the World Intellectual Property Organization informs the States, in accordance with Article 13, paragraph (4), of the deposit of its instrument.

(3) Any State may, at the time of ratification, acceptance or accession or at any later date, declare by notification addressed to the Secretary-General of the United Nations that this Convention shall apply to all or any one of the territories for whose international affairs it is responsible. This notification will take effect three months after the date on which it is received.

(4) However, the preceding paragraph may in no way be understood as implying the recognition or tacit acceptance by a Contracting State of the factual situation concerning a territory to which this Convention

is made applicable by another Contracting State by virtue of the said paragraph.

1. General. The Geneva Convention entered into force on 18 April 1973. At that time, the Contracting States were Fiji, Finland, France, Sweden and United Kingdom. Since that time, on 1 January 2015, the Convention has been ratified by 78 Contracting States, of which 23 are EU Member States.

2. Entry into force (Art. 11(2)). For each Contracting State the Convention shall enter into force three months after deposit of its instrument of ratification, acceptance or accession by the Contracting State concerned, provided it enters into force as a whole. Contracting States are not obliged to apply the norms of the Convention retroactively (see art. 7(3) GC).

[Denunciation of the Convention]

Article 12

(1) Any Contracting State may denounce this Convention, on its own behalf or on behalf of any of the territories referred to in Article 11, paragraph (3), by written notification addressed to the Secretary-General of the United Nations.

(2) Denunciation shall take effect twelve months after the date on which the Secretary-General of the United Nations has received the notification.

1. General. A Contracting State can denounce the Convention. This provision concerns the means of denunciation, by notification to the Secretary-General of the United Nations, and the entry into force of a denunciation (twelve months after the date of receipt of the notice) of the Convention.

[Languages and notifications]

Article 13

(1) This Convention shall be signed in a single copy in English, French, Russian and Spanish, the four texts being equally authentic.

(2) Official texts shall be established by the Director General of the World Intellectual Property Organization, after consultation with the interested Governments, in the Arabic, Dutch, German, Italian and Portuguese languages.

(3) The Secretary-General of the United Nations shall notify the Director General of the World Intellectual Property Organization, the Director-General of the United Nations Educational, Scientific and

Cultural Organization and the Director-General of the International Labour Office of:

    (a)   signatures to this Convention;

    (b)   the deposit of instruments of ratification, acceptance or accession;

    (c)   the date of entry into force of this Convention;

    (d)   any declaration notified pursuant to Article 11, paragraph (3);

    (e)   the receipt of notifications of denunciation.

(4) The Director General of the World Intellectual Property Organization shall inform the States referred to in Article 9, paragraph (1), of the notifications received pursuant to the preceding paragraph and of any declarations made under Article 7, paragraph (4). He shall also notify the Director-General of the United Nations Educational, Scientific and Cultural Organization and the Director-General of the International Labour Office of such declarations.

(5) The Secretary-General of the United Nations shall transmit two certified copies of this Convention to the States referred to in Article 9, paragraph (1).

1. General. The four official languages of the Convention are English, French, Russian and Spanish. All are equally authentic. The official texts are established by the Director General of WIPO. The Secretary-General of the United Nations must notify the Director-General, UNESCO and the ILO of any signature, ratification (or acceptance or accession), entry into force or denunciation of the Convention. The Director-General in turn informs the Contracting States of any such notification, as well as of any declaration regarding the points of attachment of phonogram producers (see art. 7(4) GC).

WIPO PERFORMANCES AND PHONOGRAMS TREATY (WPPT)

adopted in Geneva on 20 December 1996

[Introductory remarks]

1. General. Similar to the WIPO Copyright Treaty (WCT), the WIPO Performances and Phonograms Treaty (WPPT) is the first international treaty that deals with the neighbouring rights issues raised by digital and networking technologies. The WPPT confers protection only on performers in respect of their aural performances, and on phonogram producers. The 2012 Beijing Treaty on Audiovisual Performances (not yet in force) accords to performers protection of their audiovisual performances. Likewise, broadcasting organizations, film producers and other holders of so-called 'neighbouring rights' are not covered by the WPPT.

2. History and further development. (a) History. The Rome Convention (RC) was the first international convention in the field of neighbouring rights. Although by now a considerable number of states have become Contracting States of the Rome Convention, the US never adhered to this convention. Later on, the TRIPS Agreement limited the level of protection to the acquis of the RC, rather than adopting a RC-plus approach similar to the Berne-plus approach taken by the copyright provisions of TRIPS. Hence, it was felt that there should be a new instrument of international neighbouring rights protection. A 1991 proposal to include protection of phonogram producers in the Berne Convention (BC) by means of a protocol to the latter, which would have extended the protection potentially available to phonogram producers by copyright, met with substantial opposition and was finally rejected. Rather, the distinction between authors rights on the one hand, and neighbouring rights on the other, has been maintained at the international level by adopting a separate convention for performing artists and phonogram producers. Negotiations took place in parallel to the drafting of the WIPO Copyright Treaty (see WCT Introductory remarks note 2). Finally, the WPPT was signed, together with the WCT on 20 December 1996 at the conclusion of a Diplomatic Conference held in Geneva. The WPPT entered into force on 20 May 2002, upon deposit of the thirtieth instrument of ratification or accession with the Director General of WIPO. On 1 January 2015 there were 94 Contracting Parties, including the EU and all of its Member States. For the current state of accession see the WIPO website. **(b) Further development.** The WPPT does not protect performers for their audiovisual performances. Following a failed attempt to reach agreement at a Diplomatic Conference in Geneva in December 2000, a treaty on audiovisual performances was finally signed in Beijing on 24 June 2012 (Beijing Treaty on Audiovisual Performances, not yet in force). A further proposal for a treaty to protect broadcasting organizations is currently under discussion at WIPO.

3. Relation to EU legislation. Quite like the WCT, the WPPT is open for membership by the EU. Arts. 24(3)(b), 26(3) WPPT contain provisions identical to arts. 15(3)(b), 17(3) WCT; for commentary see WCT Introductory remarks, note 3. In order to bring the national laws of the Member States in conformity with the substantive provisions of the WPPT, the EU has amended the Rental Right Directive and raised the level of protection of performers and phonogram producers by way of the Information Society Directive (see Information Society Directive, recital 15). On 14 December 2009 the EU ratified the WPPT to become a Contracting Party on 14 March 2010, following the ratification of the WPPT by all its Member States **(b) No direct application.** According to the ECJ, the provisions of the WPPT are binding upon the EU and its Member States, and are therefore part of the legal order of the EU, but do not have direct effect in that individual citizens may rely upon these provision directly. Nevertheless, the courts must interpret the provisions of the directives that harmonize norms covered by the WPPT, notably the Rental Rights Directive and the Information Society Directive, as far as possible in the light of the equivalent concepts in the WPPT (*Peek & Cloppenburg, SCF*).

[Bibliography]

J. Blomqvist, *Primer on International Copyright and Related Rights* (Elgar 2014)

R. Brauneis, 'National Treatment in Copyright and Related Rights: How Much Work Does it Do?' (2013) GW Law Faculty Publications & Other Works, Paper 810 <http://scholarship.law.gwu.edu/faculty_publications/810>

M. Ficsor, 'Copyright for the Digital Era: The WIPO "Internet" Treaties' (1997) 21 *Columbia-VLA Journal of Law & the Arts* 197

M. Ficsor, *The Law of Copyright and the Internet the WIPO Treaties and Their Implementation* (Oxford University Press, 2002)

M. Ficsor, *Guide to the Copyright and Related Rights Treaties Administered by WIPO And Glossary Of Copyright And Related Rights Terms* (WIPO 2003) <http://www.wipo.int/edocs/pubdocs/en/copyright/891/wipo_pub_891.pdf>

P. Goldstein and P.B. Hugenholtz, *International Copyright* (3rd edn., Oxford University Press 2012)

A. Kerever, 'The new WIPO Treaties: the WIPO Copyright Treaty and the WIPO Performances and Phonograms Treaty' (1998) 32 *UNESCO Copyright Bulletin* 3

D. Nimmer, 'A Tale of Two Treaties' (1997) 22 *Columbia-VLA Journal of Law & the Arts* 1

J. Reinbothe, 'The New WIPO Treaties: A First Resume' (1997) EIPR 171-184.

J. Reinbothe and S. von Lewinski, *The WIPO Treaties 1996: The WIPO Copyright Treaty and the WIPO Performances and Phonograms Treaty: Commentary and Legal Analysis* (Butterworths 2002)

S. Ricketson and J. Ginsburg, *International Copyright and Neighbouring Rights: The Berne Convention and Beyond* (2nd edn., Oxford University Press 2006)

J. Sterling, *World Copyright Law* (3rd edn., Thomson/Sweet & Maxwell 2008)

[Preamble]

The Contracting Parties,

Desiring to develop and maintain the protection of the rights of performers and producers of phonograms in a manner as effective and uniform as possible,

Recognizing the need to introduce new international rules in order to provide adequate solutions to the questions raised by economic, social, cultural and technological developments,

Recognizing the profound impact of the development and convergence of information and communication technologies on the production and use of performances and phonograms,

Recognizing the need to maintain a balance between the rights of performers and producers of phonograms and the larger public interest, particularly education, research and access to information,

Have agreed as follows:

1. General. The preamble to the WPPT is based on, and copied mutatis mutandis from, the preamble to the WCT (for discussion, see WCT Preamble notes 2-6). However, there are two notable exceptions. First, in the preamble to the WPPT there is no reference to the need for clarification of the interpretation of certain rules (see second sentence of the preamble to the WCT). Second, there is no emphasis on the significance of such protection as an incentive to performers and phonogram producers (see the fourth sentence of the preamble to the WCT).

CHAPTER I. GENERAL PROVISIONS

[Relation to other Conventions]

Article 1

(1) Nothing in this Treaty shall derogate from existing obligations that Contracting Parties have to each other under the International Convention for the Protection of Performers, Producers of Phonograms and Broadcasting Organizations done in Rome, October 26, 1961 (hereinafter the 'Rome Convention').

(2) Protection granted under this Treaty shall leave intact and shall in no way affect the protection of copyright in literary and artistic works. Consequently, no provision of this Treaty may be interpreted as prejudicing such protection.

(3) This Treaty shall not have any connection with, nor shall it prejudice any rights and obligations under, any other treaties.

Agreed Statement Concerning Article 1(2)

It is understood that Article 1(2) clarifies the relationship between rights in phonograms under this Treaty and copyright in works embodied in the phonograms. In cases where authorization is needed from both the author of a work embodied in the phonogram and a performer or producer owning rights in the phonogram, the need for the authorization of the author does not cease to exist because the authorization of the performer or producer is also required, and vice versa.

It is further understood that nothing in Article 1(2) precludes a Contracting Party from providing exclusive rights to a performer or producer of phonograms beyond those required to be provided under this Treaty.

1. **General remarks.** This provision concerns the relationship of the WPPT with other international treaties, in particular the Rome Convention for the Protection of Performers, Producers of Phonograms and Broadcasting Organizations of 1961 (RC), as well as the relationship of the rights of performers and phonogram producers to those of authors.

2. **Relationship to the Rome Convention (para. 1).** The WPPT is not to be considered a revision of the Rome Convention but rather a special agreement within the meaning of art. 22 of the Rome Convention. Therefore, the Rome Convention need not be ratified before ratifying the WPPT. However, ratification of the WPPT cannot derogate from existing obligations between Contracting Parties of the Rome Convention.

3. **Relationship to the protection of authors (para. 2). (a) General rule.** Art. 1(2) WPPT, according to which the WPPT leaves intact and does in no way affect or prejudice the protection of authors copies art. 1 RC. Consequently, based on the Diplomatic Conference and the Agreed Statement

concerning art. 1(2) of the WPPT, this provision should be interpreted in accordance with art. 1 RC. Like art. 1 RC, art. 1(2) WPPT rejects the existence of any hierarchy between authors' rights, on the one hand, and the rights of performers and phonogram producers, on the other. In particular, art. 1(2) WPPT rejects the prevalence of authors' rights over performers' and phonogram producers' rights. Moreover, the inclusion of this provision in the WPPT, which protects the moral rights of performers of aural performances, must likewise result in the rejection of the primacy of the moral rights of authors over the moral rights of performers. This is not contradicted by the fact that the Agreed Statement concerning art. 1(2) WPPT might be construed to refer solely to the economic rights of performers and phonogram producers. **(b) Agreed Statement Concerning Article 1(2), first paragraph.** In practical terms, a conflict of interest between authors' right and performers' and phonogram producers' rights may arise with regard to the exploitation of a phonogram which embodies copyrighted works, such as musical compositions and the accompanying lyrics. The Agreed Statement makes clear that whenever the authorization for exploiting the phonogram is needed from both the author of a work embodied in a phonogram and a performer or producer owning rights in the phonogram, then the fact that one of the rightholders has given his consent does not make the authorization of the other rightholder or rightholders obsolete. In other words, even if the author of the music embodied in a phonogram has given his consent to the exploitation of the phonogram in question, the need to obtain authorization from the performer and the phonogram producer persists. Similarly, an authorization given by the performer and the phonogram producer does not render authorization by the author of the music embodied in the phonogram obsolete. **(c) Agreed Statement Concerning Article 2(b).** In addition, the Agreed Statement concerning art. 2(b) WPPT makes it clear that that rights in a phonogram are in no way affected through their incorporation into a cinematographic or other audiovisual work.

4. Relationship to other treaties (para. 3). With the exception of the reference to the BC, art. 1(3) WPPT is identical in wording to art. 1(1) second sentence WCT. As stated in the commentary to the WCT (art. 1 WCT note 1(b)), this is of particular importance with regard to the TRIPS Agreement. Art. 14 TRIPS also provides for some – albeit limited – legal protection for performers, producers of phonograms (sound recordings) and broadcasting organizations. Consequently, the stipulation contained in art. 1(3) WPPT, which expressly denies any legal connection, renders TRIPS provisions on law enforcement and, in particular, the WTO dispute settlement mechanism inapplicable to the WPPT.

5. Agreed Statement Concerning Article 1(2), second paragraph. The second paragraph of the Agreed Statement concerning art. 1(2) WPPT clarifies that the legal protection granted to performers and producers of phonograms under the WPPT is only a minimum protection. Hence, States that have adhered to the WPPT are free to grant to performers and/or phonogram producers exclusive protection which goes beyond the minimum provided for under the WPPT.

[Definitions]

Article 2

For the purposes of this Treaty:

(a) 'performers' are actors, singers, musicians, dancers, and other persons who act, sing, deliver, declaim, play in, interpret, or otherwise perform literary or artistic works or expressions of folklore;

(b) 'phonogram' means the fixation of the sounds of a performance or of other sounds, or of a representation of sounds, other than in the form of a fixation incorporated in a cinematographic or other audiovisual work;

(c) 'fixation' means the embodiment of sounds, or of the representations thereof, from which they can be perceived, reproduced or communicated through a device;

(d) 'producer of a phonogram' means the person, or the legal entity, who or which takes the initiative and has the responsibility for the first fixation of the sounds of a performance or other sounds, or the representations of sounds;

(e) 'publication' of a fixed performance or a phonogram means the offering of copies of the fixed performance or the phonogram to the public, with the consent of the rightholder, and provided that copies are offered to the public in reasonable quantity;

(f) 'broadcasting' means the transmission by wireless means for public reception of sounds or of images and sounds or of the representations thereof; such transmission by satellite is also 'broadcasting'; transmission of encrypted signals is 'broadcasting' where the means for decrypting are provided to the public by the broadcasting organization or with its consent;

(g) 'communication to the public' of a performance or a phonogram means the transmission to the public by any medium, otherwise than by broadcasting, of sounds of a performance or the sounds or the representations of sounds fixed in a phonogram. For the purposes of Article 15, 'communication to the public' includes making the sounds or representations of sounds fixed in a phonogram audible to the public.

Agreed Statement Concerning Article 2(b)

It is understood that the definition of phonogram provided in Article 2(b) does not suggest that rights in the phonogram are in any way affected through their incorporation into a cinematographic or other audiovisual work.

Agreed Statement Concerning Article 2(e) and Articles 8, 9, 12 and 13

As used in these Articles, the expressions 'copies' and 'original and copies', being subject to the right of distribution and the right of rental under the said Articles, refer exclusively to fixed copies that can be put into circulation as tangible objects.

1. General remarks. This article contains a number of definitions of terms that are used throughout the WPPT. Most of these definitions are taken directly or at least based on the respective definitions contained in art. 2 RC ('performer', 'phonogram', 'producer of a phonogram', 'publication', and 'broadcasting'). The others were introduced by the WPPT ('fixation' and 'communication to the public').

2. Performer (art. 2(a)). (a) Performance of works. The WPPT retains the traditional definition according to which performers within the meaning of the WPPT are only those persons who perform literary or artistic works. It appears to be sufficient that the work performed qualifies as a work, irrespective of the fact that it might already have fallen into the public domain. Another question is whether the work performed also has to meet the criterion of originality. However, other 'performers', such as soccer players and those practicing other sports, do not fall within the ambit of the WPPT, unless their sportive activity involves choreography (such as dancers, ice dancers and the like). The Diplomatic Conference could not agree upon an extension to variety show and circus performers (for optional protection to the latter see art. 9 RC). **(b) Expressions of folklore.** But in addition to the definition contained in art. 3(a) RC, art. 2(a) WPPT also mentions 'expressions of folklore'. For a definition of the term 'folklore' one might refer to definition contained in the UNESCO-WIPO Model Provisions of 1982, which define folklore as 'productions consisting of characteristic elements of the traditional cultural heritage developed and maintained by a community of a particular country or by individuals reflecting the traditional artistic expectations of such a community, in particular, verbal expressions, such as folktales, folk poetry and riddles; musical expressions, such as folk songs and instrumental music; expressions by action, such as folk dances, plays and artistic forms or rituals, whether or not reduced to material form' (see also the ongoing efforts of WIPO to provide for international protection to traditional cultural expressions).

3. Phonogram (art. 2(b)). Rather than stating that the fixation must be 'exclusively aural' as in art. 3(b) RC, the WPPT states that the fixation must be 'other than in the form of a fixation incorporated in a cinematographic or other audiovisual work'. However, the Agreed Statement concerning art. 2(b) makes clear that that rights in a phonogram are in no way affected through their incorporation into a cinematographic or other audiovisual work.

Moreover, the general notion of 'representations' also covers digital forms of representation.

4. Fixation (art. 2(c)). This definition is new. By generally referring to the 'representation' of sounds, it also encompasses new digital technologies. However, by stating that the term 'fixation' only covers 'sounds', any audio-visual fixation is excluded from its scope. The embodiment of a sound need not meet any other criteria, such as durability. Whether or not the definition also includes temporary fixations seems unclear in view of the Agreed Statement concerning art. 7 (see art. 7, note 3, and art. 1 WCT, note 5, mutatis mutandis).

5. Producers of phonograms (art. 2(d)). The definition of 'producer of a phonogram' introduces two new criteria with regard to the older definition of art. 3(c) RC. The criteria that must be met are 'initiative' and 'responsibility' for the first fixation. It is now clear that producers' rights are not granted to those who actually make the first material fixation of a sound. In accordance with art. 2(b) and (c) WPPT, this definition also includes digital representations of sounds.

6. Publication (art. 2(e)). This definition adds to the older definition of publication in art. 3(d) RC that the offering of copies must be with the consent of the rightholder.

7. Broadcasting (art. 2(f)). This definition adds to the older definition of publication in art. 3(f) RC that transmission by satellite is also to be considered 'broadcasting' under the WPPT, as is transmission of encrypted signals, provided the means for decryption are provided to the public by the broadcasting organization or with its consent. However, broadcasting by wire is still not considered 'broadcasting' within the meaning of art. 2(f) WPPT, but rather 'communication to the public' in the sense of its art. 2(g). The reference to 'representations' that are used as the source for broadcasting means that not only live transmissions but also transmissions of recordings are covered. This would also include digital representations.

8. Communication to the public (art. 2(g)). This is a new definition which covers communication to the public 'by any medium'. However, it should be noted that for the purposes of the WPPT, in view of the special regime for broadcasting in art. 15 the definition of 'communication to the public' does not include broadcasting. Similarly, the notion of 'communication to the public' in art. 15 WPPT does not include 'making available', since the making available to the public of performances fixed in phonograms and of phonograms, by wire or wireless means, in such a way that members of the public may access them from a place and at a time individually chosen by them, gives rise to the exclusive right defined in arts. 10 and 14 WPPT. Thus, the concept of 'communication to the public' under the WPPT is not the same as the broader 'communication to the public' of art. 8 WCT, which covers both broadcasting and making available (see art. 8 WCT). According to the

ECJ, the concept of 'communication to the public' in art. 8(2) of the Rental Right Directive must be interpreted in the light of the equivalent concept in the WPPT (*SCF*, *Phonographic Performance (Ireland)*).

[Beneficiaries of protection under this Treaty]

Article 3

(1) Contracting Parties shall accord the protection provided under this Treaty to the performers and producers of phonograms who are nationals of other Contracting Parties.

(2) The nationals of other Contracting Parties shall be understood to be those performers or producers of phonograms who would meet the criteria for eligibility for protection provided under the Rome Convention, were all the Contracting Parties to this Treaty Contracting States of that Convention. In respect of these criteria of eligibility, Contracting Parties shall apply the relevant definitions in Article 2 of this Treaty.

(3) Any Contracting Party availing itself of the possibilities provided in Article 5(3) of the Rome Convention or, for the purposes of Article 5 of the same Convention, Article 17 thereof shall make a notification as foreseen in those provisions to the Director General of the World Intellectual Property Organization (WIPO).

Agreed Statement Concerning Article 3

It is understood that the reference in Articles 5(a) and 16(a)(iv) of the Rome Convention to 'national of another Contracting State' will, when applied to this Treaty, mean, in regard to an intergovernmental organization that is a Contracting Party to this Treaty, a national of one of the countries that is a member of that organization.

Agreed Statement Concerning Article 3(2)

For the application of Article 3(2), it is understood that fixation means the finalization of the master tape ('bande-mère').

1. General remarks. (a) Beneficiaries of protection (para. 1). Art. 3 WPPT defines the beneficiaries of protection under the WPPT, who can invoke national treatment and the rights granted there under (arts. 5 et seq. WPPT for performers, 11 et seq. for producers of phonograms, and 15 for both of them) as minimum rights. Whereas art. 5(1)(a) RC only mentions the nationality of producers of phonograms but not of performers as a connecting factor, art. 3(1) WPPT defines the nationality of performers and producers of phonograms alike as the sole connecting factor. **(b) Definition of 'nationals' (para. 2).** Moreover, para. 2 defines who shall be considered a 'national' of a Contracting Party and who can thus invoke, in another Contracting Party, national treatment (art. 4 WPPT) and the minimum level of protection (art.

3(1) WPPT together with arts. 5 et seq. WPPT for performers, 11 et seq. for producers of phonograms, and 15 for both of them).

2. Minimum protection (para. 1). The WPPT provides a minimum level of protection for nationals of other Contracting Parties. Such protection only extends to 'foreign' performers and phonogram producers ('nationals of other Contracting Parties'), whereas nationals of the Contracting Party where protection is sought, have to rely on the national law of that Contracting Party. Clearly, the Contracting Parties can provide greater protection for performers and phonogram producers than that granted under the WPPT, as is expressly stated in the Agreed Statement concerning its art. 1(2).

3. Definition of 'national' (paras. 2 and 3). (a) General. Para. 2 defines 'nationals' of the Contracting Parties with reference to the Rome Convention, that is with respect to arts. 2(1)(a) and 4 RC for performers and arts. 2(1)(b) and 5 RC for phonogram producers, and includes the reservations for phonogram producers foreseen in arts. 5(3) and 17 RC. At the same time, it takes into account the new definitions contained in art. 2 WPPT and the Agreed Statements concerning art. 3 WPPT. **(b) Performers, art. 4 RC.** According to art. 4(a)-(c) RC, performers are protected with regard to their performances that take place in another Contracting State that are incorporated in a phonogram which is protected under art. 5 RC, and performances that are not fixed on a phonogram, but carried by a broadcast which is protected by art. 6 RC. **(c) Producers of phonograms, art. 5 RC.** According to art. 5(1)(b)-(c) RC, producers of phonograms are protected when the first fixation of the sound was made in another Contracting State (criterion of fixation), and when the phonogram was first published in another Contracting State (criterion of publication). In addition, according to art. 5(2) RC, a phonogram that was first published in a non-contracting State but was also published, within 30 days of its first publication, in a Contracting State (simultaneous publication), is also considered as having been first published in the Contracting State. According to art. 3(3) WPPT, any Contracting Party which avails itself of the possibilities provided in art. 5(3) RC not to apply the criterion of publication or, alternatively, the criterion of fixation, or the criterion of fixation alone in line with art. 17 RC, shall make a notification to this effect to the Director General of the World Intellectual Property Organization (WIPO).

4. Agreed Statement Concerning Article 3(2). An Agreed Statement concerning art. 3(2) WPPT makes clear that for the application of art. 3(2), fixation means the finalization of the master tape ('bande-mère').

[National treatment]

Article 4

(1) Each Contracting Party shall accord to nationals of other Contracting Parties, as defined in Article 3(2), the treatment it accords to its

own nationals with regard to the exclusive rights specifically granted in this Treaty, and to the right to equitable remuneration provided for in Article 15 of this Treaty.

(2) The obligation provided for in paragraph (1) does not apply to the extent that another Contracting Party makes use of the reservations permitted by Article 15(3) of this Treaty.

1. General. (a) Principle of national treatment (para. 1). Art. 4(1) WPPT contains the national treatment obligation applicable to the nationals of other Contracting Parties (as defined in art. 3(2) WPPT). Together with the shift in the definition of the beneficiaries of protection by their nationality as defined by art. 3 RC – and the abandonment of the selective points of attachment defined in arts. 4 and 5 RC – it aligns the international protection of performers and producers of phonograms with the international protection of authors, for whom nationality also is the decisive factor according to art. 3(1)(a) BC. **(b) Exceptions (para. 2).** However, the principle of reciprocity may apply whenever a Contracting State avails itself of a reservation permitted by art. 15(3) WPPT with regard to the claim for remuneration in cases of secondary uses of phonograms as circumscribed in art. 15(1) thereof.

2. Scope of the national treatment principle (para. 1). Similar to art. 2(2) RC, national treatment as prescribed in para. 1 concerns exclusive rights 'specifically granted in this Treaty', and thus coincides with the minimum degree of protection afforded under the WPPT. 'Exclusive rights' should be construed to refer to both the moral and economic rights of performers and the economic rights of phonogram producers. National treatment is also to be applied to the right to equitable remuneration for so-called 'secondary use' of commercial phonograms (see note 3 and art. 15 WPPT, note 1 (b)). However, arguably no obligation to grant national treatment exists with regard to – both exclusive and remuneration – rights which a Contracting Party decides to grant to its own nationals in addition to the rights mentioned in the WPPT.

3. Exception to the principle of national treatment (para. 2). As para. 1 makes clear, the principle of national treatment also applies to the claim for remuneration for the broadcast and other public performance of a commercially published phonograph that is granted according to art. 15 WPPT. However, according to para. 2, a Contracting Party is under no obligation to grant the remuneration right according to art. 15 WPPT to nationals that make use of a reservation permitted by art. 15(3) of the WPPT, according to which a Contracting State may limit the claim for remuneration to certain uses or in any other way, or exclude it altogether. Hence, in such cases, the principle of reciprocity may prevail.

CHAPTER II. RIGHTS OF PERFORMERS
[Moral rights of performers]

Article 5

(1) Independently of a performer's economic rights, and even after the transfer of those rights, the performer shall, as regards his live aural performances or performances fixed in phonograms, have the right to claim to be identified as the performer of his performances, except where omission is dictated by the manner of the use of the performance, and to object to any distortion, mutilation or other modification of his performances that would be prejudicial to his reputation.

(2) The rights granted to a performer in accordance with paragraph (1) shall, after his death, be maintained, at least until the expiry of the economic rights, and shall be exercisable by the persons or institutions authorized by the legislation of the Contracting Party where protection is claimed. However, those Contracting Parties whose legislation, at the moment of their ratification of or accession to this Treaty, does not provide for protection after the death of the performer of all rights set out in the preceding paragraph may provide that some of these rights will, after his death, cease to be maintained.

(3) The means of redress for safeguarding the rights granted under this Article shall be governed by the legislation of the Contracting Party where protection is claimed.

1. General. (a) Moral rights protection (para. 1). One of the major innovations achieved by the WPPT is that for the first time in history moral rights of performers have been recognized on the international level. The first moral right is the right to claim authorship or to be identified as the performer of a work. The second moral right is the right of integrity or the right to object to modifications to the performance. These rights are not absolute, however. The right to claim authorship is limited by the manner in which the performance is used. Likewise, the right of integrity is limited to modifications that would be prejudicial to the performers' reputation. However, according to art. 22(2) WPPT, a Contracting Party may limit the application of art. 5 WPPT to performances which occurred after the entry into force of the WPPT for that Party. Para. 2 defines the duration of moral rights protection, yet leaves great freedom to Contracting Parties. Para. 3 points to national law as governing the means of redress in case of a violation of the moral rights. **(b) EU legislation.** In the EU moral rights have not been harmonized.

2. Independence of moral rights. Moral rights are independent from economic rights and remain with performers following transfer of their economic rights. However, this does not preclude the existence of contractual rules concerning the moral rights of performers.

3. Right to name attribution (para. 1, first part). The right of the performer to name attribution granted by art. 5(1), first part, WPPT is closely modeled after art. 6bis(1) BC, first alternative. It extends to both his live aural performances and his performances fixed in phonograms. However, as opposed to the provision in the BC, art. 5(1) WPPT expressly restricts the right of the performer to name attribution to cases where the omission is not dictated by the manner of the use of the performance. Thus, if, for example, a collective performance is communicated to the public by television, depending on the circumstances of the case, the method of use might justify the omission of the names of all the individual performers.

4. Right to integrity (para. 1, second part). The integrity right granted to performers in art. 5(1), second part, WPPT with regard to both his live aural performances and his performances fixed in phonograms, is a verbatim copy of the right of integrity granted to authors in art. 6bis(1) BC, second alternative. For comment, see art. 6bis BC, note 2(b).

5. Duration (para. 2). As a rule, the duration of moral rights is limited to the term of economic rights, as provided in art. 17 WPPT. Following the death of a performer, these rights can be exercised by the persons or entities authorized to do so by the legislation of the Contracting Party where protection is sought. However, Contracting Parties whose national laws, at the time of their ratification of or accession to the WPPT, do not provide for moral rights following the death of a performer, may stipulate that moral rights shall not endure posthumously. The duration provision is an almost verbatim copy of art. 6bis(2) BC regulating the duration of moral rights of authors. For additional comment, see art. 6bis BC, note 3.

6. Means of redress (para. 3). Finally, according to para. 3, the means of redress for safeguarding the rights granted under art. 5 WPPT shall exclusively be governed by the legislation of the Contracting Party where protection is claimed. Art. 5(3) WPPT copies art. 6bis(3) BC, but both appear to be superfluous since remedies are always determined by the law of the country of protection.

[Economic rights of performers in their unfixed performances]

Article 6

Performers shall enjoy the exclusive right of authorizing, as regards their performances:
> (i) **the broadcasting and communication to the public of their unfixed performances except where the performance is already a broadcast performance; and**
> (ii) **the fixation of their unfixed performances.**

1. General. (a) Rights granted. Following arts. 7(1)(a) and (b) RC and 14(1) TRIPS, art. 6 WPPT gives performers an exclusive right of fixation, as well as an exclusive right to communicate their performance to the public and to broadcast their unfixed performances. In addition, under the WPPT, performers enjoy an exclusive right to make their performances publicly available as defined in art. 10 WPPT. However, with regard to broadcasting and any communication to the public of performances incorporated in phonograms published for commercial purposes, performers only enjoy a claim to remuneration (art. 15(1) WPPT), jointly with producers of phonograms (art. 15(2) and (3) WPPT). **(b) EU legislation.** In the EU the protection regarding fixation provided for in art. 6(1) WPPT is granted to performers by art. 6(1), and the protection regarding broadcasting of unfixed performances in art. 8(1) of the Rental Right Directive.

2. Broadcasting (art. 6(i), first part). Broadcasting is defined in art. 2(f) WPPT. The definition excludes broadcasting by wire which could, however, be considered a communication to the public. The exclusive right to broadcast concerns unfixed and unbroadcast performances.

3. Communication to the public (art. 6(i), second part). Communication to the public is defined in art. 2(g) WPPT, but excludes making available as defined in art. 10 WPPT (making available to the public of performances fixed in phonograms and of phonograms, by wire or wireless means, in such a way that members of the public may access them from a place and at a time individually chosen by them). The WPPT thus adopts a different definition of communication to the public than the general definition used in art. 8 WCT. The exclusive right to broadcast unfixed ('live') performances concerns both unfixed and unbroadcast performances.

4. Fixation (art. 6(ii)). Moreover, performers have an exclusive right of fixation, as defined in art. 2(c) WPPT. This excludes the audiovisual fixation now covered by the Beijing Treaty on Audiovisual Performances (see Preamble, note 2(b)). The exclusive right of reproduction concerns the first fixation of a performance ('fixation of unfixed performances'), whereas subsequent fixations fall within the scope of the reproduction right granted by art. 7 WPPT.

[Right of reproduction]

Article 7

Performers shall enjoy the exclusive right of authorizing the direct or indirect reproduction of their performances fixed in phonograms, in any manner or form.

Agreed Statement Concerning Articles 7, 11 and 16

The reproduction right, as set out in Articles 7 and 11, and the exceptions permitted thereunder through Article 16, fully apply in the digital environment, in particular to the use of performances and phonograms in digital form. It is understood that the storage of a protected performance

or phonogram in digital form in an electronic medium constitutes a reproduction within the meaning of these Articles.

1. General. (a) Exclusive reproduction right. Parallel to the exclusive reproduction right granted to producers of phonograms in art. 11 WPPT, art. 7 WPPT also grants an exclusive reproduction right to performers, as art. 14(1) TRIPS already had done. **(b) EU legislation.** In the EU the reproduction right had initially been granted to performers and to producers of phonograms by art. 7(1) of the Rental Right Directive, and is now granted to performers by art. 2(b) of the Information Society Directive.

2. Reproduction. 'Reproduction' is not defined in the WPPT. A reproduction can be direct or indirect (for example, a reproduction of an original performance through a communications network) and can take any manner or form. The WPPT does not contain any criteria regarding the durability of reproductions (see art. 2(c) WPPT). Therefore, in principle, temporary reproductions may also be regarded as being covered. But the text and history of art. 7 WPPT and the Agreed Statement concerning this art. 7 may lead to a more cautious interpretation. In view of this uncertainty, however, it appears that the application of a right of reproduction to temporary reproductions is left to the discretion of the Contracting Parties (see also arts. 1 WCT, note 5, and 9 BC, note 2(a)).

3. Agreed Statement. The Agreed Statement concerning art. 7 WPPT and digital reproduction, which also applies to the reproduction right of producers of phonograms granted in art. 11 WPPT, is identical to the Agreed Statement concerning art. 1(4) WCT (see art. 1 WCT, note 5).

[Right of distribution]

Article 8

(1) Performers shall enjoy the exclusive right of authorizing the making available to the public of the original and copies of their performances fixed in phonograms through sale or other transfer of ownership.

(2) Nothing in this Treaty shall affect the freedom of Contracting Parties to determine the conditions, if any, under which the exhaustion of the right in paragraph (1) applies after the first sale or other transfer of ownership of the original or a copy of the fixed performance with the authorization of the performer.

Agreed Statement Concerning Article 2(e) and Articles 8, 9, 12 and 13

As used in these Articles, the expressions 'copies' and 'original and copies', being subject to the right of distribution and the right of rental under the said Articles, refer exclusively to fixed copies that can be put into circulation as tangible objects.

1. General. (a) Distribution right. Parallel to the exclusive distribution right granted to producers of phonograms in art. 12(1) WPPT, and to authors in art. 6(1) WCT, art. 8(1) WPPT grants an exclusive distribution right to performers, which does not have a precursor in the TRIPS Agreement. Although the general recognition of an exclusive distribution right is an important step forward, the conditions, if any, under which the distribution right is exhausted after the first sale or other transfer of ownership of the original or a copy of the fixed performance, provided such act has been done with the authorization of the performer, is left to the discretion of Contracting States (para. 2, which is parallel to arts. 12(2) WPPT and 6(2) WCT). **(b) EU legislation.** In the EU the distribution right is granted to performers by art. 9(1) of the Rental Right Directive. The corresponding provision on exhaustion is found in art. 9(2) of the Rental Right Directive. According to the ECJ, the distribution right in that Directive is to be interpreted in accordance with the WPPT and the WCT, meaning that exhaustion of the distribution right will occur only through the sale or other transfer of ownership (*Peek & Cloppenburg*).

2. Exclusive distribution right (para. 1). 'Distribution' is not defined in the WPPT. It is thought to concern the making available to the public of copies through sale or any other means of 'transfer of ownership' and refers solely to 'physical' distribution, that is the distribution of phonograms, originals or copies, incorporating a protected performance. For further comment regarding the distribution right of performers granted by art. 8(1) WPPT, see art. 6 WCT, note 2.

3. (Non)exhaustion of the distribution right (para. 2). Para. 2 leaves it up to the Contracting States if, and under what conditions, exhaustion of the distribution right takes place (see art. 6 WCT, note 3).

4. Agreed Statement. The Agreed Statement concerning art. 8 WPPT, which also applies to the rental right granted to producers of phonograms in art. 12 WPPT, is identical to the Agreed Statement concerning arts. 6 and 7 WCT (see art. 6 WCT, note 4).

[Right of rental]

Article 9

(1) Performers shall enjoy the exclusive right of authorizing the commercial rental to the public of the original and copies of their performances fixed in phonograms as determined in the national law of Contracting Parties, even after distribution of them by, or pursuant to, authorization by the performer.

(2) Notwithstanding the provisions of paragraph (1), a Contracting Party that, on April 15, 1994, had and continues to have in force a system of equitable remuneration of performers for the rental of copies of their performances fixed in phonograms, may maintain that system provided

that the commercial rental of phonograms is not giving rise to the material impairment of the exclusive right of reproduction of performers.

Agreed Statement Concerning Article 2(e) and Articles 8, 9, 12 and 13

As used in these Articles, the expressions 'copies' and 'original and copies', being subject to the right of distribution and the right of rental under the said Articles, refer exclusively to fixed copies that can be put into circulation as tangible objects.

1. General. (a) Exclusive rental right (para. 1). Parallel to art. 13 WPPT, which grants a rental right to producers of phonograms, art. 9(1) WPPT gives performers an exclusive right of commercial rental of the original and copies of their performances fixed in phonograms. For the rental right of authors see art. 7(1) WCT. **(b) No exhaustion.** In contrast to the distribution right (see art. 8(2) WPPT), the rental right granted in art. 9(1) WPPT is not exhausted after the first sale or distribution of tangible objects incorporating the protected performance with, or pursuant to, the performers' authorization. **(c) 'Grandfather clause' for systems of equitable remunerations (para. 2).** However, parallel to arts. 13(2) WPPT, 7(3) WCT and 14(4) TRIPS, art. 14(2) WPPT contains a 'grandfather clause' for systems of equitable remuneration that a Contracting Party had in existence prior to or on 15 April 1994, provided that the commercial rental of phonograms does not materially impair the exclusive rights of reproduction of performers. This possibility is not limited in time. **(d) EU legislation.** In the EU the rental right is granted to performers by art. 2(1) of the Rental Directive.

2. Exclusive rental right and exhaustion (para. 1). 'Rental' is not defined in the WPPT. However, the term only concerns 'commercial' rental to the public, and thus does not cover a private exchange between two individuals. Moreover, as is made clear by the Agreed Statement, rental refers only to the 'physical' rental of tangible objects. For further details see art. 7 WCT, notes 2 and 3.

3. Grandfathered remuneration systems (para. 2). For comments on the details regarding 'grandfathered' remuneration systems and the impairment test of art. 9(2) WPPT, see art. 7 WCT, note 3, mutatis mutandis.

4. Agreed Statement. The Agreed Statement concerning art. 9 WPPT, which also applies to the rental right granted to producers of phonograms in art. 13 WPPT, is identical to the Agreed Statements concerning arts. 6 and 7 WCT (see art. 6 WCT, note 4). However, the other Agreed Statement to art. 7 WCT only concerns certain authors' rights and thus is not applicable to art. 9 WPPT.

[Right of making available of fixed performances]

Article 10

Performers shall enjoy the exclusive right of authorizing the making available to the public of their performances fixed in phonograms, by wire or wireless means, in such a way that members of the public may access them from a place and at a time individually chosen by them.

1. General. (a) Exclusive right of making available. Art. 10 WPPT gives performers an exclusive right of making available to the public. The same right is granted to producers of phonograms in art. 14 WPPT, and to authors in art. 8 WCT. **(b) Claim for remuneration with regard to broadcasting and communication to the public.** It should be noted, however, that according to art. 15(1) WPPT, performers, like producers of phonograms, only enjoy a claim for remuneration with regard to the direct or indirect use of phonograms published for commercial purposes for broadcasting, or for any communication to the public which does not consist in making the phonogram publicly available under the particular circumstances mentioned in art. 10 WPPT. It follows that the concept of 'communication to the public' under the WPPT is narrower than the same concept under the WCT, where art. 8 WCT defines the right of making available as a sub-category of a broad and general right of communication to the public (including') (see art. 2, note 8). **(c) EU legislation.** In the EU the making available right is granted to performers by art. 3(2)(a) of the Information Society Directive.

2. Making available to the public. Art. 10 WPPT, like arts. 14 WPPT and 8 WCT, defines the concept of 'making available to the public' as making the protected subject matter available to the public, by wire or wireless means, in such a way that members of the public may access it from a place and at a time individually chosen by them. In particular, this refers, to the availability 'on demand' via the Internet. It also covers the making available in other networks such as WLANs and LANs, provided the users who can access the protected material in question can be considered to form a 'public'. As is expressed in the Agreed Statement concerning art. 15 WPPT, no agreement could be reached with regard to where exactly to draw the line between traditional broadcasting and activities of communication to the public other than making available to the public on the one hand, and making available to the public on the other (see art. 15, note 4(a)). For additional commentary regarding the right of making available see art. 8 WCT, note 5(a) and (c).

3. No Agreed Statement. Although no Agreed Statement concerning art. 10 WPPT was adopted at the Diplomatic Conference adopting the WPPT, it appears that the Agreed Statement concerning art. 8 WCT, first sentence, according to which it is understood that the mere provision of physical facilities for enabling or making a communication does not in itself amount to communication within the meaning of that Treaty, can also be applied to the right granted by art. 10 WPPT.

CHAPTER III. RIGHTS OF PRODUCERS OF PHONOGRAMS

[Right of Reproduction]

Article 11

Producers of phonograms shall enjoy the exclusive right of authorizing the direct or indirect reproduction of their phonograms, in any manner or form.

Agreed Statement Concerning Articles 7, 11 and 16

The reproduction right, as set out in Articles 7 and 11, and the exceptions permitted thereunder through Article 16, fully apply in the digital environment, in particular to the use of performances and phonograms in digital form. It is understood that the storage of a protected performance or phonogram in digital form in an electronic medium constitutes a reproduction within the meaning of these Articles.

1. General. (a) Exclusive reproduction right. Parallel to the exclusive reproduction right granted to performers in art. 7 WPPT, art. 11 WPPT grants an exclusive reproduction right to producers of phonograms, as art. 14(2) TRIPS already had. **(b) EU legislation.** In the EU the reproduction right had initially been granted to performers and to producers of phonograms by art. 7(1) of the Rental Directive, and is now granted to producers of phonograms by art. 2(c) of the Information Society Directive.

2. Details. For commentary on the details of the reproduction right granted to producers of phonograms by art. 11 WPPT, which covers the direct as well as indirect reproduction of their phonograms, in any manner or form, see comments in arts. 1 WCT, note 5, and 9 BC, note 2(a).

3. Agreed Statement. The Agreed Statement concerning art. 11 and digital reproduction, which also applies to the performers' reproduction right granted in art. 7 WPPT, is identical to the Agreed Statement concerning art. 1(4) WCT. For comment see art. 1 WCT, note 5.

[Right of distribution]

Article 12

(1) Producers of phonograms shall enjoy the exclusive right of authorizing the making available to the public of the original and copies of their phonograms through sale or other transfer of ownership.

(2) Nothing in this Treaty shall affect the freedom of Contracting Parties to determine the conditions, if any, under which the exhaustion of the right in paragraph (1) applies after the first sale or other transfer of ownership of the original or a copy of the phonogram with the authorization of the producer of the phonogram.

Agreed Statement Concerning Article 2(e) and Articles 8, 9, 12 and 13

As used in these Articles, the expressions 'copies' and 'original and copies', being subject to the right of distribution and the right of rental under the said Articles, refer exclusively to fixed copies that can be put into circulation as tangible objects.

1. General. (a) Exclusive distribution right (para. 1). Parallel to the exclusive distribution right granted to performers in art. 8(1) WPPT, and to authors in art. 6(1) WCT, art. 12(1) WPPT grants an exclusive distribution right to producers of phonograms, which does not have a precursor in the TRIPS Agreement. **(b) (Non)exhaustion of the distribution right (para. 2).** Although the general recognition of an exclusive distribution right is an important step forward, the conditions, if any, under which the distribution right is exhausted after the first sale or other transfer of ownership of the original or a copy of the phonogram, provided such act has been done with the authorization of the producer of the phonogram, is left to the discretion of Contracting States (para. 2, which is parallel to arts. 8(2) WPPT and 6(2) WCT). **(c) EU legislation.** In the EU the distribution right is granted to producers of phonograms by art. 9(1) of the Rental Right Directive. The corresponding provision on exhaustion can be found in art. 9(2) of the Rental Right Directive. According to the ECJ, the distribution right in that Directive is to be interpreted in accordance with the WPPT and the WCT, meaning that exhaustion of the distribution right will occur only through the sale or other transfer of ownership (*Peek & Cloppenburg*).

2. Details. (a) Para. 1. For commentary on the details of the distribution right of producers of phonograms granted by art. 12(1) WPPT, see comments on arts. 8 WPPT and 6 WCT, note 2. **(b) Para. 2.** For commentary on exhaustion, see comments on art. 6 WCT, note 3.

3. Agreed Statement. The Agreed Statement concerning art. 12 WPPT, which also applies to the rental right of performers granted in art. 8 WPPT, is identical to the Agreed Statement concerning arts. 6 and 7 WCT. For comment see art. 6 WCT, note 4.

[Right of Rental]

Article 13

(1) Producers of phonograms shall enjoy the exclusive right of authorizing the commercial rental to the public of the original and copies of their phonograms, even after distribution of them, by or pursuant to, authorization by the producer.

(2) Notwithstanding the provisions of paragraph (1), a Contracting Party that, on April 15, 1994, had and continues to have in force a system of equitable remuneration of producers of phonograms for the rental

of copies of their phonograms, may maintain that system provided that the commercial rental of phonograms is not giving rise to the material impairment of the exclusive rights of reproduction of producers of phonograms.

Agreed Statement Concerning Article 2(e) and Articles 8, 9, 12 and 13

As used in these Articles, the expressions 'copies' and 'original and copies', being subject to the right of distribution and the right of rental under the said Articles, refer exclusively to fixed copies that can be put into circulation as tangible objects.

1. General. (a) Exclusive rental right (para. 1). Parallel to art. 9(1) WPPT, which grants a rental right to performers, and following art. 14(4) TRIPS, art. 13 WPPT gives producers of phonograms an exclusive right of commercial rental of the original and copies of their phonograms. Performers and producers of phonograms are thus on equal footing with authors of computer programs, cinematographic works, and works embodied in phonograms (see art. 7(1) WCT). **(b) No exhaustion.** Other than the distribution right (see art. 12(2) WPPT), the rental right granted in art. 13(1) WPPT is not exhausted after the first sale or distribution of tangible phonograms with, or pursuant to, the performers' authorization. **(c) 'Grandfather clause' for systems of equitable remunerations (para. 2).** However, parallel to arts. 9(2) WPPT, 7(3) WCT and 14(4) TRIPS, art. 14(2) WPPT contains a 'grandfather clause' for systems of equitable remuneration that a Contracting Party had in existence prior to or on 15 April 1994, provided that the commercial rental of phonograms does not materially impair the exclusive rights of reproduction granted to producers of phonograms. This possibility is not limited in time. **(d) EU legislation.** In the EU the rental right is granted to producers of phonograms by art. 2(1) of the Rental Right Directive.

2. Details. (a) Para. 1. For commentary on the details of the rental right of producers of phonograms granted by art. 13(1) WPPT, see comments on arts. 9 WPPT and 7 WCT, notes 2 and 3. **(b) Para. 2.** For commentary on the details regarding 'grandfathered' remuneration systems and the impairment test of art. 13(2) WPPT, see comments on art. 7 WCT, note 3.

3. Agreed Statement. The Agreed Statement concerning art. 13 WPPT, which also applies to the rental right of performers granted in art. 9 WPPT, is identical to the Agreed Statements concerning arts. 6 and 7 WCT. For commentary see art. 6 WCT, note 4. However, the other Agreed Statement to art. 7 WCT only concerns certain authors' rights and thus is not applicable to art. 13 WPPT.

[Right of making available of phonograms]

Article 14

Producers of phonograms shall enjoy the exclusive right of authorizing the making available to the public of their phonograms, by wire
or wireless means, in such a way that members of the public may access
them from a place and at a time individually chosen by them.

1. General. (a) Exclusive right of making available. Art. 14 WPPT gives
producers of phonograms an exclusive right of making available to the public. The same right is granted to performers in art. 10 WPPT, and to authors
in art. 8 WCT. **(b) Claim for remuneration with regard to broadcasting
and communication to the public.** It should be noted, however, that according to art. 15(1) WPPT, producers of phonograms, like performers, enjoy
only a claim for remuneration with regard to the direct or indirect use of
phonograms published for commercial purposes, for broadcasting or for any
communication to the public that does not consist in making the phonogram
publicly available under the particular circumstances mentioned in art. 14
WPPT. As already stated with regard to arts. 2 and 10 WPPT, it follows that
the concept of 'communication to the public' under the WPPT is narrower
than the same concept under the WCT, where art. 8 WCT defines the right
of making available as a sub-category of a broad and general right of communication to the public. **(c) EU legislation.** In the EU the making available
right is granted to producers of phonograms by art. 3(2)(b) of the Information
Society Directive.

2. Details. For commentary on the details of the right of making available
granted by art. 14 WPPT, see art. 8 WCT, note 5(a) and (c).

3. No Agreed Statement. Although no Agreed Statement concerning
art. 14 WPPT has been adopted at the Diplomatic Conference adopting the
WPPT, it appears that the Agreed Statement concerning art. 8 WCT, first sentence, according to which it is understood that the mere provision of physical
facilities for enabling or making a communication does not in itself amount
to communication within the meaning of that Treaty, can also be applied to
the right granted by art. 14 WPPT.

CHAPTER IV. COMMON PROVISIONS

[Right to remuneration for broadcasting and communication to the public]

Article 15

(1) Performers and producers of phonograms shall enjoy the right to
a single equitable remuneration for the direct or indirect use of phonograms published for commercial purposes for broadcasting or for any
communication to the public.

Brison

(2) Contracting Parties may establish in their national legislation that the single equitable remuneration shall be claimed from the user by the performer or by the producer of a phonogram or by both. Contracting Parties may enact national legislation that, in the absence of an agreement between the performer and the producer of a phonogram, sets the terms according to which performers and producers of phonograms shall share the single equitable remuneration.

(3) Any Contracting Party may, in a notification deposited with the Director General of WIPO, declare that it will apply the provisions of paragraph (1) only in respect of certain uses, or that it will limit their application in some other way, or that it will not apply these provisions at all.

(4) For the purposes of this Article, phonograms made available to the public by wire or wireless means in such a way that members of the public may access them from a place and at a time individually chosen by them shall be considered as if they had been published for commercial purposes.

Agreed Statement Concerning Article 15

It is understood that Article 15 does not represent a complete resolution of the level of rights of broadcasting and communication to the public that should be enjoyed by performers and phonogram producers in the digital age. Delegations were unable to achieve consensus on differing proposals for aspects of exclusivity to be provided in certain circumstances or for rights to be provided without the possibility of reservations, and have therefore left the issue to future resolution.

Agreed Statement Concerning Article 15

It is understood that Article 15 does not prevent the granting of the right conferred by this Article to performers of folklore and producers of phonograms recording folklore where such phonograms have not been published for commercial gain.

1. General. (a) Claim to remuneration under the Rome Convention and TRIPS. Under the Rome Convention, performing artists and producers of phonograms only enjoy a right to remuneration, if a phonogram published for commercial purposes, or a reproduction of such phonogram, is used directly for broadcasting or for any communication to the public (so-called 'secondary uses'); see art. 12 RC, and, for possible reservations to this remuneration right, art. 16 RC. Due to the differences in national legislation in this respect, the TRIPS Agreement does not contain any comparable regulation. **(b) Claim to remuneration under the WPPT.** Under the WPPT, this special regime has been maintained, with the exception of the making available of – both unfixed and fixed – performances and – both non-commercial and commercial – phonograms according to arts. 6, 10 and 14 WPPT. Consequently, even under the WPPT, performers and producers of phonograms, as a rule, only enjoy a claim for a single remuneration as a minimum right for the direct or indirect use of phonograms published for commercial purposes for broadcasting or for any communication to the public (para. 1). Contracting Parties are free to determine who – performer and/or phonogram producer – shall be entitled to claim the remuneration from the user and how the remuneration shall be distributed amongst performers and producers of phonograms (para. 2). In addition, para. 3 still allows Contracting Parties to make far-reaching reservations with regard to this right to remuneration. However, as pointed out in the second Agreed Statement concerning art. 15 WPPT, the right to remuneration may not be an ideal and/or final solution in the digital age. **(c) EU legislation.** In the EU art. 8(2) of the Rental Directive ensures a right of equitable remuneration with regard to 'secondary uses'. According to the ECJ, the concept of 'communication to the public' in art. 8(2) of the Rental Right Directive must be interpreted in the light of the equivalent concept in the WPPT (*SCF*, *Phonographic Performance (Ireland)*).

2. Conditions. (a) Phonograms covered. Only phonograms as defined in art. 2(b) WPPT that have been published for commercial purposes will give rise to the claim to remuneration of para. 1. The condition of 'publication' is defined in art. 2(e) WPPT and specified in art. 15(4) WPPT as encompassing phonograms that have been made available to the public 'on demand'. In addition, as is made clear by the Agreed Statement concerning art. 15 WPPT, Contracting Parties may also provide for a claim for remuneration to performers of folklore and producers of phonograms of folklore where such phonograms have not been published for commercial gain. **(b) Acts covered.** The remuneration right applies to the direct or indirect use for broadcasting or any other communication to the public of a phonogram published for commercial purposes. For the notion of 'indirect' use, see art. 7 WPPT and accompanying note 3. According to the WPPT, the term 'communication to the public' includes broadcasting, as defined in art. 2(f) WPPT, and any other communication to the public, as defined in art. 2(g) WPPT, with the exception of making available on demand, which is an exclusive right of both performers and producers of phonograms (arts. 10 and 14 WPPT) (see art. 2, note 8).

3. Remuneration regime. Performers and phonogram producers shall have the right to a single equitable remuneration. The reason is that users who have to pay the remuneration have only one interlocutory, and that they know what to pay without having to make their calculations on the basis of several claims for remuneration. **(a) 'Single' remuneration.** According to art. 15(2) WPPT, Contracting Parties are free to decide whether the single remuneration can be claimed from the user either by the performers, or by the phonogram producers or by both categories of rightholders. **(b) 'Equitable' remuneration.** Art. 15 WPPT does not specify what should be considered to be an 'equitable' remuneration. However, it can be presumed that it should be a remuneration the amount of which somehow is in relation to the intensity of use or the market value. In other words, the intensity of the use and the market value should somehow be reflected in the amount of the remuneration to be paid. **(c) Distribution of the remuneration amongst rightholders.** Regarding the distribution of this remuneration between both categories of rightholders, art. 15(2) WPPT states that, in the absence of an agreement between performers and phonogram producers, the Contracting Parties may determine the share of both rightholders in the distribution of the collected remunerations.

4. Agreed Statements Concerning Article 15. (a) First Agreed Statement. The first of the two Agreed Statements concerning art. 15 WPPT express the uncertainties that the parties to the Diplomatic Conference of 1996 had with regard to exploitation of performances and phonograms by digital means. In view of the exclusive right of making available already granted to both performers and phonogram producers by arts. 10 and 14 WPPT, the uncertainty mainly related to such forms of digital exploitation as digital broadcasting, webcasting and near-on-demand services. **(b) Second Agreed Statement.** The second Agreed Statement deals with the special situation of recordings of folklore which are not always published for commercial gain.

[Limitations and exceptions]

Article 16

(1) Contracting Parties may, in their national legislation, provide for the same kinds of limitations or exceptions with regard to the protection of performers and producers of phonograms as they provide for, in their national legislation, in connection with the protection of copyright in literary and artistic works.

(2) Contracting Parties shall confine any limitations of or exceptions to rights provided for in this Treaty to certain special cases which do not conflict with a normal exploitation of the performance or phonogram and do not unreasonably prejudice the legitimate interests of the performer or of the producer of the phonogram.

Agreed Statement Concerning Articles 7, 11 and 16

The reproduction right, as set out in Articles 7 and 11, and the exceptions permitted thereunder through Article 16, fully apply in the digital environment, in particular to the use of performances and phonograms in digital form. It is understood that the storage of a protected performance or phonogram in digital form in an electronic medium constitutes a reproduction within the meaning of these Articles.

Agreed Statement Concerning Article 16

The Agreed Statement concerning Article 10 (on Limitations and Exceptions) of the WIPO Copyright Treaty is applicable *mutatis mutandis*

also to Article 16 (on Limitations and Exceptions) of the WIPO Performances and Phonograms Treaty.

1. General. (a) Overview. This article provides for possible limitations on the minimum protection for performers and phonogram producers under the WPPT (para. 1) and, in addition, contains the three-step test that limits the scope of the limitations made possible under para. 1 (para. 2). **(b) EU legislation.** In the EU limitations to the rights of performers and producers of phonograms are laid down in art. 10 of the Rental Right Directive and art. 5(2) and (3) of the Information Society Directive, subject to the three-step test (art. 10(3) of the Rental Right Directive and art. 5(5) of the Information Society Directive).

2. Possible limitations (para. 1). The Rome Convention, in addition to an illustrative enumeration of possible limitations on the minimum protection provided by art. 15(1) RC, had already left it to the discretion of its Member States to provide for the same kinds of limitations with regard to the protection of performers, producers of phonograms and broadcasting organizations, as they provide for, in their domestic laws and regulations, in connection with the protection of copyright in literary and artistic works (15(2) RC). This rule has been copied into the WPPT, dispensing both with the additional enumerative list and the reference to compulsory licensing as allowed under the RC but no longer under the WPPT.

3. Three-step test (para. 2). However, like art. 10(1) WCT for limitations and exceptions to the exclusive rights of authors, art. 16(2) WPPT now subjects possible limitations and exceptions to the exclusive rights of performers and phonogram producers to the so-called three-step test. Therefore, limitations and exceptions must be limited to certain special cases that do not conflict with a normal exploitation of the performance or phonogram and that do not unreasonably prejudice the legitimate interests of the performer or of the producer of the phonogram. Since the wording of art. 16(2) WPPT corresponds to the wording of art. 10(1) WCT, for commentary see art. 10 WCT, notes 1 and 3-5).

4. Agreed Statements Concerning Article 16. (a) First Agreed Statement. The first Agreed Statement concerning arts. 7, 11 and 16 WPPT, is identical in its substance with the Agreed Statement concerning art. 1(4) WCT. In its first sentence, it confirms the scope of the reproduction right, which also covers reproductions in digital format. Moreover, its second sentence clarifies that the storage of a protected performance or phonogram in digital form in an electronic medium constitutes a reproduction within the meaning of these articles. However, at the Diplomatic Conference, no consensus could be reached with regard to the meaning of the term 'storage'. Consequently, both a broad as well as a more restrictive approach to the scope of the reproduction right may be followed (for further details see art. 1 WCT, note 5). **(b) Second Agreed Statement.** The second Agreed Statement to art. 16 WPPT declares the Agreed Statement to art. 10 WCT applicable mutatis mutandis. It follows that the provisions of art. 16 WPPT permit Contracting Parties to carry forward and appropriately extend into the digital environment limitations and exceptions in their national laws which have been considered acceptable under the Berne Convention. Similarly, these provisions should be understood to permit Contracting Parties to devise new exceptions and limitations that are appropriate in the digital network environment (for further details see art. 10 WCT, note 6).

[Term of protection]

Article 17

(1) **The term of protection to be granted to performers under this Treaty shall last, at least, until the end of a period of 50 years computed from the end of the year in which the performance was fixed in a phonogram.**

(2) **The term of protection to be granted to producers of phonograms under this Treaty shall last, at least, until the end of a period of 50 years computed from the end of the year in which the phonogram was published, or failing such publication within 50 years from fixation of the phonogram, 50 years from the end of the year in which the fixation was made.**

1. General. Art. 17 WPPT sets the minimum term of protection for the exploitation rights of both performers (para. 1) and producers of phonograms (para. 2). The term of protection for performers' moral rights, however, is regulated by art. 5(2) WPPT. **(a) Term of protection prior to the WPPT.** Whereas the Rome Convention (art. 14(a) and (b) RC) prescribed a minimum term of protection for the economic rights of performers and producers of phonograms of only 20 years, computed from the end of the year in which either the fixation was made (for phonograms and for performances incorporated therein) or the performance took place (for performances not incorporated in phonograms), the TRIPS Agreement (art. 14(5) TRIPS) had already provided a minimum 50-year protection period to performers and producers of phonograms computed from the end of the calendar year in which the fixation was made or the performance took place. **(b) Term of protection of economic rights under the WPPT.** Under the WPPT, the term of protection for both performers and phonogram producers also is a minimum of 50 years. For performers, the term is now uniformly computed from the end of the year in which the fixation was made (art. 17(1) WPPT), whereas for producers of phonograms the period of 50 years is computed from the end of the year in which the phonogram was published, or failing such publication within 50 years from fixation of the phonogram, from the end of the year in which the fixation was made. **(c) Term of protection for moral rights of performers (art. 5(2)).** According to art. 5(2) WPPT, the term of protection for moral rights runs at least until the expiry of the economic rights. However, Contracting Parties whose legislation, at the moment of their ratification of or accession to this Treaty, does not provide for protection after the death of the performer of all moral rights granted by art. 5(1) WPPT, may provide that some of these rights will, after his death, cease to be maintained. **(d) EU legislation.** In the EU the terms of protection for performers are harmonized in art. 3(1), and for producers of phonograms in art. 3(2) of the Term Directive, as modified by the Term Extension Directive.

2. Commencement for performers. The term of protection for performers starts to run from the fixation of a performance on a phonogram. What constitutes a fixation is defined in art. 2(c) WPPT.

3. Commencement for phonogram producers. The term of protection for phonogram producers starts, as a rule, from publication of the phonogram as defined in art. 2(e) WPPT. However, if the phonogram is not published within 50 years from its fixation as defined in art. 2(c) WPPT, the term of protection runs from the date of its fixation. In practical terms this means that all phonograms enjoy a minimum protection of 50 years after their fixation, and that whenever a phonogram is published before these 50 years have expired, such a phonogram enjoys an additional 50-year protection period from that date of publication. In theory, this allows for a maximum of 100 years of protection, if a phonogram is published just before the end of the 50 years after its first fixation.

4. Calculation. For both performers and phonogram producers, the term of protection is calculated from the end of the year in which the act occurred that makes the term of protection start.

[Obligations concerning technological measures]

Article 18

Contracting Parties shall provide adequate legal protection and effective legal remedies against the circumvention of effective technological measures that are used by performers or producers of phonograms in connection with the exercise of their rights under this Treaty and that restrict acts, in respect of their performances or phonograms, which are not authorized by the performers or the producers of phonograms concerned or permitted by law.

1. General. (a) Principle. Art. 18 WPPT is an almost verbatim copy of art. 11 WCT, except that art. 18 WPPT does not refer to technological measures that are used by authors in connection with the exercise of their rights with respect to works, but to technological measures that are used by performers or producers of phonograms in connection with the exercise of their rights in respect of their performances or phonograms. **(b) EU legislation.** European rules regarding the legal protection of technological protection measures can be found in art. 6 of the Information Society Directive.

2. Comment. For commentary, see art. 11 WCT.

[Obligations concerning rights management information]

Article 19

(1) **Contracting Parties shall provide adequate and effective legal remedies against any person knowingly performing any of the following acts knowing, or with respect to civil remedies having reasonable grounds to know, that it will induce, enable, facilitate or conceal an infringement of any right covered by this Treaty:**
>   (i)   **to remove or alter any electronic rights management information without authority;**
>   (ii)   **to distribute, import for distribution, broadcast, communicate or make available to the public, without authority, performances, copies of fixed performances or phonograms knowing that electronic rights management information has been removed or altered without authority.**

(2) **As used in this Article, 'rights management information' means information which identifies the performer, the performance of the performer, the producer of the phonogram, the phonogram, the owner of any right in the performance or phonogram, or information about the terms and conditions of use of the performance or phonogram, and any numbers or codes that represent such information, when any of these items of information is attached to a copy of a fixed performance or a phonogram or appears in connection with the communication or making available of a fixed performance or a phonogram to the public.**

Agreed Statement Concerning Article 19

The Agreed Statement concerning Article 12 (on Obligations concerning Rights Management Information) of the WIPO Copyright Treaty is applicable mutatis mutandis also to Article 19 (on Obligations concerning Rights Management Information) of the WIPO Performances and Phonograms Treaty.

1. General. (a) Principle. Art. 19 WPPT is an almost verbatim copy of art. 12 WCT, except that art. 19 WPPT does not refer to works but to performances, copies of fixed performances, or phonograms. Differences exist with regard to 'other Treaties', which is not mentioned in the first sentence of art. 19(1) WPPT, and 'mak[ing] available to the public', which is expressly mentioned in art. 19(1)(ii) WPPT and in the Agreed Statement concerning art. 12 of the WPPT. The latter is due to the split treatment in the WPPT of communication to the public, on the one hand, and making available to the public, on the other hand (see arts. 15 and 10, 14). For details, see art. 12 WCT, notes 1-6. **(b) EU legislation.** European rules regarding the legal obligations concerning rights management information are found in art. 7 of the Information Society Directive.

2. Agreed Statement Concerning Article 19. The Agreed Statement concerning art. 19 WPPT declares the Agreed Statement concerning art. 12 WCT (for comment see art. 12 WCT, note 7) applicable mutatis mutandis. This means that the reference to 'infringement of any right covered by this Treaty' includes both exclusive rights and rights of remuneration. It is further understood that Contracting Parties will not rely on this article to devise or implement rights management systems that would have the effect of imposing formalities which are not permitted under the WPPT, prohibiting the free movement of goods, or impeding the enjoyment of rights under the WPPT.

[Formalities]
Article 20
The enjoyment and exercise of the rights provided for in this Treaty shall not be subject to any formality.

1. General. The possibility for Contracting States to make protection dependent on the compliance with formalities that were foreseen in the Rome Convention (art. 11 RC) has been abolished by the WPPT. Hence, neither the moral and economic rights of performers (arts. 5-10 WPPT) and of phonogram producers (arts. 11-14 WPPT), nor their right to equitable remuneration (art. 15 WPPT) can be made subject to the fulfilment of certain formalities, such as registration or the notice consisting of the symbol (P), accompanied by the year date of the first publication as described in art. 11 RC.

[Reservations]
Article 21
Subject to the provisions of Article 15(3), no reservations to this Treaty shall be permitted.

1. General. Other than the WCT, which does not allow for any reservations whatsoever (see art. 22 WCT), the WPPT allows its Contracting States to make a reservation with regard to the right to equitable remuneration for so-called 'secondary uses' of commercial phonograms for broadcasting or for any communication to the public. According to art. 15(3) WPPT, Contracting

Parties may apply this right of remuneration only in respect of certain uses, or limit its application in some other way, or not grant it at all.

2. Reservation with regard to application in time (art. 22(2)). Moreover, according to art. 22(2) WPPT, a Contracting Party may limit moral rights protection for performers (art. 5 WPPT) to performances that occurred after the entry into force of this Treaty for that Party.

[Application in time]

Article 22

(1) Contracting Parties shall apply the provisions of Article 18 of the Berne Convention, mutatis mutandis, to the rights of performers and producers of phonograms provided for in this Treaty.

(2) Notwithstanding paragraph (1), a Contracting Party may limit the application of Article 5 of this Treaty to performances which occurred after the entry into force of this Treaty for that Party.

1. General. Like art. 13 WCT, art. 22(1) WPPT declares the provisions of art. 18 BC with regard to the application in time of the WPPT applicable mutatis mutandis to the rights of performers and producers of phonograms provided for in the WPPT. However, as an exception – and in derogation from the WCT – Contracting Parties to the WPPT may limit moral rights protection of performers granted by art. 5 WPPT to performances which occurred after the entry into force of this Treaty for that Party.

2. Application of art. 18 BC (para. 1). It follows from the application of art. 18 BC mutatis mutandis that, as a rule, the provisions of the WPPT are immediately applicable to existing performances and phonograms which have not yet entered the public domain in their country of origin through the expiry of the term of protection, at the date of its entry into force in the Contracting State concerned. However, there seems to be no retroactivity if rights were lost for other – formal – reasons, such as, for example, publication without notice. For further comment see comments on arts. 13 WCT and 18 BC.

3. Exception for performers' moral rights protection (para. 2). However, as an exception to this rule, the application in time of the moral rights of performers is left to the Contracting States. Since art. 22(2) WPPT allows a Contracting State to limit moral rights protection to those performances that occurred after the entry into force of the WPPT for that particular Contracting State, Contracting States are probably also free to grant moral rights protection to performances that occurred before the entry into force of the WPPT for that particular Contracting State, but limit this protection to acts done after the entry into force of the WPPT.

[Provisions on enforcement of rights]

Article 23

(1) **Contracting Parties undertake to adopt, in accordance with their legal systems, the measures necessary to ensure the application of this Treaty.**

(2) **Contracting Parties shall ensure that enforcement procedures are available under their law so as to permit effective action against any act of infringement of rights covered by this Treaty, including expeditious remedies to prevent infringements and remedies which constitute a deterrent to further infringements.**

1. General. Art. 23 WPPT is identical in wording to art. 14 WCT. Art. 23(1) of the WPPT provides that the Contracting Parties undertake to adopt, in accordance with their legal systems, the measures necessary to ensure the application of that Treaty. It follows that the application of the provisions of the WPPT, in their implementation or effects, is subject to the adoption of subsequent measures. Therefore, such provisions have no direct effect in the law of the European Union and are not such as to create rights for individuals which they may rely on before the courts by virtue of that law (*SCF* (ECJ)).

CHAPTER V. ADMINISTRATIVE AND FINAL CLAUSES

Articles 24-33 [omitted]

1. General. The final and administrative clauses of the WPPT are laid down in arts. 24 to 33 WPPT, and not reproduced in this volume. They are identical in wording to arts. 15-25 WCT (with the exception of art. 22 WCT on the express exclusion of reservations to the WCT, a variant of which is found in art. 21 WPPT). These final and administrative clauses concern the work in the Assembly of Contracting Parties (art. 24 WPPT), the administrative tasks to be accomplished by the International Bureau of WIPO (art. 25 WPPT), the eligibility for, the effective date of, and the rights and obligations resulting from becoming party to the WPPT (arts. 26, 27 and 30 WPPT), the signature, entry into force and denunciation of the WPPT (arts. 28, 29 and 31 WPPT), the official languages of the WPPT (art. 32 WPPT), and its deposition with the Director General of WIPO (art. 33 WPPT).

2. Status of the European Union. (a) General. Art. 26(3) and art. 28 WPPT expressly state that the European Community (now the European Union) may become party to the WPPT and sign the Treaty. On 14 December 2009 the EU indeed ratified the WPPT to become a Contracting Party on 14 March 2010, following the ratification of the WPPT by all its Member States. After becoming party to the WPPT, the EU, like any other Contracting Party, may be represented by one delegate in the Assembly of Contracting Parties (art. 24 WPPT). Pursuant to art. 24(3)(b) WPPT, the EU may participate in any vote in the Assembly, in place of its Member States, with a number of votes equal to the number of its Member States which are party to the WPPT. However, it may not participate in the vote if any one of its Member States exercises its right to vote and vice versa. **(b) Details.** For further details see the commentary to arts. 15-25 WCT, note 2.

3. Languages of the WPPT (art. 32). (a) Authentic texts (para. 1). Like the WCT, the WPPT has been signed, pursuant to art. 32(1) WPPT, in a single original in the English, Arabic, Chinese, French, Russian and Spanish languages. The versions in all these languages are equally authentic. Accordingly, no language version is to prevail in case there arise differences of opinion on the interpretation of the various texts. Hence, the interpretation should follow the different language versions to the greatest extent possible, having regard to the object and purpose of the treaty (see art. 33(4) of the Vienna Convention). **(b) Official texts (para. 2).** Other official texts of the WPPT can be established by the Director General of WIPO on the request of an interested party, after consultation with all the interested parties (see also art. 24 WCT, note 3).

AGREEMENT ON TRADE-RELATED ASPECTS
OF INTELLECTUAL PROPERTY RIGHTS (TRIPS)
(WTO AGREEMENT, ANNEX 1C)

adopted in Marrakesh, 15 April 1994 articles 9-14[1]

[Introductory remarks]

1. General. The Agreement on Trade-Related Aspects of Intellectual Property Rights (TRIPS) was adopted in Marrakesh on 15 April 1994 as Annex 1C of the WTO Agreement. Since the TRIPS Agreement forms an integral part of the WTO Agreement, all WTO Members, including the European Union and its Member States, are bound by it. As part of the WTO framework, international compliance with the norms of the TRIPS Agreement is subject to mandatory WTO dispute resolution. Ultimately, Members found in contravention of the Agreement may be subjected to retaliatory measures. The TRIPS Agreement covers a broad spectrum of intellectual property rights, not only copyright and related rights, but also trademarks, geographical indications, industrial designs, patents, topographies of integrated circuits, and trade secrets; see art. 1(2) TRIPS. Like the Paris Convention and the Berne Convention, the TRIPS Agreement prescribes national treatment and sets minimum standards for the protection of intellectual property of qualified rights holders from WTO Members. Unlike these older treaties, the TRIPS Agreement also prescribes most favoured nation treatment, and establishes minimum standards for the enforcement of intellectual property rights. The TRIPS Agreement contains general provisions and basic principles (part I), standards concerning the availability, scope and use of intellectual property rights (part II), provisions on the enforcement of intellectual property rights, including general obligations, civil and administrative procedures and remedies, provisional measures, border measures and criminal procedures (part III), acquisition and maintenance of intellectual property rights and related inter-partes procedures (part IV), provisions concerning dispute prevention and settlement (part V), transitional arrangements (part VI), as well as institutional arrangements and final provisions (Part VII).

2. Basic principles. (a) No derogation from Berne and Rome Conventions. According to art. 2(2) TRIPS, nothing in Parts I to IV of the TRIPS Agreement shall derogate from existing obligations that Members may have to each other the Berne Convention and the Rome Convention. The TRIPS Agreement qualifies as a special agreements between states within the meaning of art. 20 of the Berne Convention. **(b) National treatment.** Art. 3 TRIPS

---

1. Only the provisions most relevant to copyright and neighbouring rights have been reprinted and commented upon here. For full commentary on the TRIPS Agreement see the volume *Concise General and Procedural IP Law*.

prescribes national treatment, which in respect of performers, producers of phonograms and broadcasting organizations, however, only applies in respect of the rights provided under the TRIPS Agreement. **(c) Most-favoured-nation treatment.** Art. 4 TRIPS lays down the traditional GATT principle of most-favoured-nation treatment, according to which any advantage, favour, privilege or immunity granted by a WTO Member to the nationals of any other country shall be accorded immediately and unconditionally to the nationals of all other Members. However, according to art. 4(b) TRIPS, are exempted from this obligation any advantage, favour, privilege or immunity accorded by a Member granted in accordance with the provisions of the Berne Convention or the Rome Convention authorizing that the treatment accorded be a function not of national treatment but of the treatment accorded in another country (that is, reciprocity). Therefore, most notably, both the reciprocity with regard to the protection of works of applied art (art. 2(7) BC) and the comparison of terms of protection (art. 7(8) BC) survive under TRIPS. It should be noted, however, that within the EU, because of the principle of non-discrimination (art. 18 TFEU) applicable to copyright (*Phil Collins* (ECJ)), the comparison of terms is excluded vis-à-vis nationals of EU and EEA Member States. Moreover, since according to art. 10(2) of the Term Directive the 70-year protection p.m.a. applies throughout the EU if a work was protected on 1 July 1995 in at least one Member State, the application of the comparison of terms is excluded even vis-à-vis non-nationals whenever one Member State does not apply the comparison of terms (*Sony Music Entertainment* (ECJ). According to art. 4(c), Members are likewise under no obligation to extend to other Members any advantage, favour, privilege or immunity accorded to another Member in respect of any rights of performers, producers of phonograms and broadcasting organizations that are not provided under the TRIPS Agreement. In addition, according to art. 4(d) are also exempted from the most-favoured-nation principle any advantage, favour, privilege or immunity accorded by a Member which derives from international agreements related to the protection of intellectual property which entered into force prior to the entry into force of the WTO Agreement, provided that such agreements are notified to the Council for TRIPS and do not constitute an arbitrary or unjustifiable discrimination against nationals of other Members. It remains an open issue to what extent the EU Treaty qualifies as such an international agreement. The question is of particular importance with regard to the non-discrimination of nationals of EU Member States (art. 12 EC Treaty), the limitation of the exhaustion of the exclusive distribution right to cases in which the first sale or other transfer of ownership has taken place, by the right holder or with his consent, within the Community (art. 4(2) of the Information Society Directive), and the reciprocity requirement of the Database Directive (art. 11 of the Database Directive). **(d) Other principles.** TRIPS leaves the issue of national or international exhaustion expressly to the Members (art. 6 TRIPS). Art. 7 TRIPS lays down the general objectives of the TRIPS Agreement, including contributing 'to a balance of rights and obligations'. Art. 8 TRIPS confirms that Members may

Dreier/Hugenholtz

adopt measures to promote, inter alia, 'the public interest in sectors of vital importance to their socio-economic and technological development, provided that such measures are consistent with the provisions of this Agreement', and to prevent abuses of intellectual property rights. **(e) No direct application in EU.** According to the ECJ, the provisions of the TRIPS Agreement are binding upon the EU and its Member States, and are therefore part of the legal order of the EU, but do not have direct effect in that individual citizens may rely upon these provision directly. Nevertheless, the courts must interpret the provisions of the directives that harmonize norms covered by the TRIPS Agreement, such as the Rental Right Directive and the Information Society Directive, in the light of the equivalent concepts in TRIPS (*SCF*).

3. Substantive rights. Part II of the TRIPS Agreement sets substantive minimum standards concerning the following categories of intellectual property rights: copyright and related rights; trademarks, geographical indications; industrial designs; patents, layout-designs (topographies) of integrated circuits, protection of undisclosed information and control of anti-competitive practices in contractual licences. The copyright provisions are found in part II(1) of the TRIPS Agreement. They incorporate by reference most of the norms of the Berne Convention (art. 9) and add several 'Berne-plus' elements, such as the protection of computer programs and compilations of data (art. 10) and rental rights (art. 11). In addition, this part deals with the term of copyright protection (art. 12), the three-step test that restricts the Members' freedom to provide for copyright exceptions and limitations (art. 13), and, finally, the protection of performers, producers of phonograms and broadcasting organizations.

4. Enforcement of rights. In the EU, the minimum standards on civil enforcement of intellectual property rights provided by part III of the TRIPS Agreement have been transposed, and enhanced, by the Enforcement Directive. The TRIPS rules on border measures are reflected in the Regulation on Customs Enforcement. The TRIPS provisions on criminal enforcement, however, have as yet not led to EU law. A 2005 proposal for a Directive on Criminal Measures has so far not been adopted.

[Bibliography]

C. Correa, *Trade Related Aspects of Intellectual Property Rights: A Commentary on the TRIPS Agreement* (Oxford University Press 2007)

C. Correa and A. Yusuf, *Intellectual Property and International Trade: The TRIPS Agreement* (2nd edn., Kluwer Law International 2008)

T. Cottier and P. Verron, *International and European IP Law* (3rd edn., Kluwer 2014)

G. Dinwoodie and R. Dreyfuss, *A Neofederalist Vision of TRIPS* (Oxford University Press 2012)

D. Gervais, *The TRIPS Agreement: Drafting History and Analysis* (4th edn., Kluwer 2012)

J. Malbon, Ch. Lawson and M. Davison, *The WTO Agreement On Trade-Related Aspects Of Intellectual Property Rights: A Commentary* (Elgar 2014)

A. Taubman, H. Wager and J. Watal, *A Handbook on the WTO TRIPS Agreement* (WTO 2012)

J. Watal, 'From Punta del Este to Doha and Beyond: Lessons from the TRIPS Negotiating Process' (2011) *WIPO Journal* 24-35

PART II. STANDARDS CONCERNING THE AVAILABILITY, SCOPE AND USE OF INTELLECTUAL PROPERTY RIGHTS

Section 1. Copyright and Related Rights [Relation to the Berne Convention]

Article 9

(1) Members shall comply with Articles 1 through 21 of the Berne Convention (1971) and the Appendix thereto. However, Members shall not have rights or obligations under this Agreement in respect of the rights conferred under Article 6bis of that Convention or of the rights derived therefrom.

(2) Copyright protection shall extend to expressions and not to ideas, procedures, methods of operation or mathematical concepts as such.

1. General. Art. 9(1) TRIPS incorporates all but one of the substantive provisions of the Berne Convention into TRIPS. Members are under an obligation to comply with arts. 1-21 BC (Paris Act), including the Appendix thereto which contains special provisions for developing countries, with the exception of the moral rights protected under art. 6bis BC. Since arts. 10-12 TRIPS go beyond the minimum standards of the BC (notably copyright protection for computer programs and compilations of data, rental rights and a partially prolonged term of protection), the minimum standards set by TRIPS in the field of copyright are commonly referred to as 'Berne-plus'. In addition, art. 9(2) TRIPS explicitly reformulates the principle that copyright protects a work's expression and not its underlying ideas.

2. Compliance with arts. 1-21 BC (para. 1). (a) Substantive provisions of the Berne Convention. The incorporation by reference of the substantive provisions of the Berne Convention into the TRIPS Agreement extends the obligations under the Paris Act of the Berne Convention to those WTO Members that are either only bound by earlier versions of the Berne Convention, or are not a Contracting State of the Berne Convention at all (see, for example, *Football Association Premiere League and others* (ECJ)). Para. 1 thus substantially enlarges the scope of application of the Berne Convention.

In addition, the incorporation by reference of the Berne norms not only avoids a lengthy duplication of the rights and exceptions as laid down in the Berne Convention, it also has substantive effects. On the one hand, the reference to the substantive provisions of the Berne Convention brings most of the Berne Convention under the WTO dispute settlement mechanism. On the other hand, a State which takes advantage of the Appendix to the BC, is not in violation of TRIPS, although the Appendix derogates from core exclusive rights of the BC and hence also of TRIPS. **(b) Exclusion of moral rights.** Members' obligation to adhere to the substantive provisions of the Berne Convention does not extend to moral rights protection according to art. 6bis BC. Presumably, moral rights are not sufficiently 'trade-related' to warrant inclusion in TRIPS. The underlying reason for this exception is the reluctance of the US to adhere to an internationally binding regime of authors' moral rights, in spite of the fact that it has repeatedly been stated that US law taken as a whole is in compliance with the obligations under the Berne Convention, including its moral rights protection. It follows, that no complaint can be brought before the WTO Dispute Settlement Body for the lack of moral rights protection in a particular WTO Member.

3. Protection of expression, not of ideas, procedures, methods of operation or mathematical concepts (para. 2). (a) Expression and ideas. It is a generally accepted principle of copyright law, both in continental European droit d'auteur and Anglo-American copyright, that copyright protects only the expression of a work and not the underlying idea (see *SAS Institute* (ECJ)). It is another matter to draw the exact line between what is and what is not protected in a particular work. This question can only be answered after careful examination in each individual case, and this often involves examination by experts. Moreover, it is left to Members to formulate the test for distinguishing protected expression from unprotected ideas. Thus, for example, under German and Dutch copyright law the distinction is not between expression and ideas, but between form and contents. Moreover, when it comes to analyzing whether a subsequent creation infringes the copyright in a preceding creation, para. 2 also seems to allow both for a one-step examination of infringement and for a two-step examination of, first, copyrightability and, second, infringement. **(b) Methods of operation or mathematical concepts.** Besides 'ideas', para. 2 also excludes from protection 'methods of operation' and 'mathematical concepts'. However, this exclusion only concerns methods of operation and mathematical concepts 'as such'. This implies that an original description of methods of operation and of mathematical concepts may well enjoy copyright protection, provided its expression shows sufficient originality. Therefore, the exclusion simply aligns 'methods of operation' and 'mathematical concepts' to unprotected ideas. Art. 2 WCT contains almost identical language. See also art. 1(2) of the Computer Programs Directive ('ideas and principles which underlie any element of a computer program, including those which underlie its interfaces').

[Computer programs and compilations of data]

Article 10

(1) Computer programs, whether in source or object code, shall be protected as literary works under the Berne Convention (1971).

(2) Compilations of data or other material, whether in machine readable or other form, which by reason of the selection or arrangement of their contents constitute intellectual creations shall be protected as such. Such protection, which shall not extend to the data or material itself, shall be without prejudice to any copyright subsisting in the data or material itself.

1. **General.** Under the Berne Convention, the argument could be made that original computer programs and databases were not covered by the notion of 'literary and artistic works', since the catalogue of works in art. 2(1) BC does not expressly mention them and 'collections of literary or artistic works' do not encompass collections of unprotected elements such as data (see art. 2 BC, notes 2(c) and 6(a)). Therefore art. 10 TRIPS explicitly mentions both 'computer programs' (para. 1) and 'compilations of data or other material' (para. 2) as copyright-protected subject matter. Art. 10 is thus an important element of the Berne-plus approach of the TRIPS Agreement (see art. 9, note 1). Similar provisions are found in arts. 4 and 5 WCT.

2. **Computer programs (para. 1). (a) General.** Art. 10(1) TRIPS does not define the term 'computer program'. However, the express reference to both 'source code' and 'object code' makes clear that a program is not only protected in its human-readable but also in its machine-readable form (see *BSA* (ECJ) and *SAS Institute* (ECJ)). The fact that computer programs have to be protected as works 'under the Berne Convention', makes all provisions of the Berne Convention, such as, for example, the reproduction right (art. 9 BC) and the translation right (art. 8 BC), applicable to computer programs. Moreover, since computer programs have to be protected 'as literary works', Members may not elect to protect computer programs by any other form of copyright protection instead. In particular, Members are barred from protecting computer programs as a special work category or limit their term of protection to that of, for instance, works of applied arts (see art. 2(7) BC). **(b) European legislation.** Already prior to the adoption of TRIPS, the EU had harmonized the legal protection of computer programs by way of the Computer Programs Directive, largely along the lines of TRIPS. According to art. 1(1) of the Computer Programs Directive, Member States shall protect computer programs by copyright as literary works within the meaning of the Berne Convention. The reference to protection of both source code and object code can be found in art. 1(2) of the Computer Programs Directive, according to which protection in accordance with this Directive shall apply to 'the expression in any form of a computer program'. The Computer

Programs Directive further specifies the conditions and the scope of copyright protection for computer programs, including the limitations and exceptions thereto. The initial term of 50 years p.m.a., which was in accordance with the minimum term of the Berne Convention (art. 7(1) BC), has subsequently been prolonged to 70 years p.m.a. by the Term Directive (arts. 1(1) and 11(1) Term Directive).

3. Compilations of data (para. 2). (a) General. Art. 10(2) TRIPS deals with databases, without using the term as such (see *Football Dataco and others* (ECJ)). The language of para. 2 closely resembles, but is not identical to, the definition of 'database' in art. 1 of the Database Directive (see note 3 (b)). In particular it does not include collections of works, since these fall within the ambit of art. 2(5) BC, which is incorporated by reference in art. 9 into the TRIPS Agreement. As a 'Berne-plus' element, para. 2 requires copyright protection of compilations of data 'or other material' that fall outside the scope of art. 2(5) BC (see art. 2 BC, notes 2(c) and 6(a)). Even so, the wording of para. 2 is clearly inspired by art. 2(5), in particular the criterion of 'selection or arrangement', and suggests a similar standard of originality. Note however that art. 2(5) BC requires originality qua selection 'and' arrangement of the contents, whereas under art. 10(2) TRIPS selection 'or' arrangement would apparently suffice. Art. 10(2) requires a test of 'intellectual creation' (that is, originality). The investment of human, technical, financial or other resources in the act of compilation does not in itself meet this standard (see *Football Dataco and others* (ECJ)). The required level of originality is not further specified, but left to the Member States. Copyright protection must be guaranteed for compilations 'whether in machine readable or other form', indicating that both electronic and paper-based compilations require protection. Note that TRIPS does not mandate sui generis protection of databases, as does the Database Directive. Indeed, because TRIPS is silent on sui generis protection of databases, that regime remains outside the definition of 'intellectual property' of art. 1(2) TRIPS, thus excluding it from the scope of the national treatment and most-favoured-nation treatment. **(b) European legislation.** The obligation of art. 10(2) to protect 'compilations of data or other material, whether in machine readable or other form, which by reason of the selection or arrangement of their contents constitute intellectual creations' is reflected in art. 3(1) of the Database Directive. The requirement to protect compilations 'whether in machine readable or other form' is satisfied by art. 1(2) of the Directive, which defines 'databases' in a very broad way (see art. 1 Database Directive, note 2). Similarly, art. 5 of the WIPO Copyright Treaty calls for copyright protection of compilations of data or other material 'in any form'. Like para. 2, second sentence, art. 3(2) of the Database Directive confirms that copyright protection of databases shall not extend to their contents (that is, to the data contained therein), and shall be without prejudice to any rights subsisting in those contents themselves.

[Rental rights]

Article 11

In respect of at least computer programs and cinematographic works, a Member shall provide authors and their successors in title the right to authorize or to prohibit the commercial rental to the public of originals or copies of their copyright works. A Member shall be excepted from this obligation in respect of cinematographic works unless such rental has led to widespread copying of such works which is materially impairing the exclusive right of reproduction conferred in that Member on authors and their successors in title. In respect of computer programs, this obligation does not apply to rentals where the program itself is not the essential object of the rental.

1. General. Art. 11 obliges WTO Members to provide for rights of commercial rental in respect of computer programs and, in principle, also for cinematographic works. In addition, art. 14(4) guarantees rental rights to producers of phonograms and any other right holders in phonograms (see art. 14, note 5). Rental rights are not among the minimum rights guaranteed by the Berne Convention. Art. 11 therefore constitutes a typical 'Berne-plus' element of TRIPS. The words 'at least' confirm that art. 11 sets a minimum standard, as do the other substantive norms of TRIPS. Members may choose to offer more protection, such as rental rights that apply to the entire spectrum of works or rights of (non-commercial) public lending. Members are not obliged to apply arts. 11 and 14(4) with respect to originals or copies purchased prior to the date of application of the WTO Agreement for that Member (art. 70(5) TRIPS). The TRIPS regime of rental rights, as set out in arts. 11 and 14(4), has served as the template for art. 7 WCT, which sets almost identical minimum standards.

2. Rental. The TRIPS Agreement does not define the terms 'rental' or 'public', and neither does the WCT. The wording 'originals or copies' indicate that the right encompasses only the transfer, by way of rental, of originals or physical copies of the work (see Agreed Statement concerning art. 6 and 7 WCT). The right therefore does not apply to acts of electronic transmission of works. The rental right concerns only 'commercial rental'. Non-commercial activities, such as public lending by libraries, remain outside the scope of the rental right (see art. 7 WCT, note 2).

3. Computer programs. Art. 11 guarantees to authors of computer programs and their successors in title an exclusive right of commercial rental. No such obligation however arises if the computer program does not constitute the essential object of the rental, as in the case of automobile rental or rental of equipment containing computers software. See art. 7 WCT, note 4(b).

4. Cinematographic works. The exclusive rental right in cinematographic works is subject to the so-called impairment exception. A Member is exempt from the obligation to offer a rental right, 'unless such rental has led to widespread copying of such works which is materially impairing the exclusive right of reproduction conferred in that Member on authors and their successors in title'. The impairment exception reflects the law of the United States that at the time of conclusion of the WTO Treaty did (and still does) not provide for a rental right in cinematographic works. The 'widespread copying' obviously refers to private copying resulting from acts of rental. Whether such copying is 'materially impairing' the right of reproduction may be assessed in the light of the three-step test. See art. 7 WCT, notes 3 and 5.

5. European legislation. The Rental Right Directive (old version), which was adopted in 1992, as well as its codified version of 2006 offers protection of rental rights that goes well beyond the substance and scope of arts. 11 and 14(4) TRIPS. In the EU the rental right is granted to authors of all categories of works, as well as to performers and producers of phonograms and films. Art. 1(2) of the Rental Right Directive broadly defines rental as the act of 'making available for use, for a limited period of time and for direct or indirect economic or commercial advantage'. The Directive does not allow for an impairment exception (see note 4), and does not deal with computer programs. Art. 4(c) of the Computer Programs Directive offers a special rental right possibly of more limited proportions (see art. 4 Computer Programs Directive, note 4(f), and art. 4 Rental Right Directive, note 1). The Computer Programs Directive however does not exclude acts of rental if the computer program does not constitute the essential object of the rental, as does art. 11 TRIPS (last sentence).

[Term of protection]

Article 12

Whenever the term of protection of a work, other than a photographic work or a work of applied art, is calculated on a basis other than the life of a natural person, such term shall be no less than 50 years from the end of the calendar year of authorized publication, or, failing such authorized publication within 50 years from the making of the work, 50 years from the end of the calendar year of making.

1. General. The minimum terms of copyright protection set by art. 7 of the Berne Convention are incorporated by reference into TRIPS by art. 9(1). As a general rule, the term shall expire 50 years after the author's death, but art. 7(2)-7(4) BC allows shorter terms in special cases. Art. 12 sets an additional minimum standard for terms that are not calculated on the basis of the life of a natural person. This will typically apply to situations where a legal person, such as a corporation, is deemed to be the author of a work. Such situations will arise, for instance, in countries such as France where legal persons are deemed to be authors of 'collective works' or in the US under the work for hire rule. Art. 12 may also apply to terms of works published anonymously, albeit that many Members will apply the normal post mortem auctoris term if the author's identity is eventually revealed (see art. 7(3) BC). The minimum term guaranteed by art. 12 TRIPS is either 50 years from publication, or absent publication within 50 years from creation of the work, 50 years after creation.

2. Publication. TRIPS does not define the term 'publication'. The likely meaning can be inferred from art. 3(3) of the Berne Convention, that describes publication in terms of the 'manufacture of copies', and clarifies that the 'performance of a dramatic, dramatico-musical, cinematographic or musical work, the public recitation of a literary work, the communication by wire or the broadcasting of literary or artistic works, the exhibition of a work of art and the construction of a work of architecture shall not constitute publication.' Arguably, posting a work on the Internet would not amount to 'publication' within the meaning of art. 12 TRIPS (but see also art. 3 WCT note 4(b)). Consequently, a work first posted on the Internet and published in print only at a later stage, would benefit from a longer term of protection.

3. Exceptions. The exclusion of photographic works and works of applied art in art. 12 reflects art. 7(4) BC that provides for a significantly shorter term of protection for these categories of works (25 years). Art. 9 WCT in turn overrules this exception in respect of photographic works.

4. European legislation. The terms of protection of authors, performing artists, producers of phonograms, broadcasting organizations and film producers have been harmonized by the Term Directive. The term of copyright has been set at the high level of 70 years after the death of the author, while neighbouring (related) rights generally expire after 50 years. However, the Term Extension Directive prolongs the protection of performing artists and producers of phonograms to 70 years if the performance is fixed in a phonogram that was lawfully published or lawfully communicated to the public. **(a) Anonymous or pseudonymous works.** Art. 1(3) of the Term Directive gives a special rule for anonymous or pseudonymous works. Here 'the term of protection shall run for 70 years after the work is lawfully made available to the public'. Note that the Directive uses the words 'made available to the public', which is a broader term than 'publication' (see note 2) and probably also encompasses posting a work on the Internet. In line with art. 7(3), art. 1(3) of the Directive provides that the normal term of 70 years post mortem auctoris will apply when the pseudonym leaves no doubt as to the author's identity, or if the author discloses his identity during the term of publication plus 70 years (see art. 1 Term Directive, note 3). **(b) Legal persons.** Art. 1(4) of the Term Directive leaves Member States the freedom to provide for special rules in respect of collective works or other cases where legal persons are designated as authors. If according to national law the copyright is vested in a collective or in a legal person, the term of protection will be 70 years after the work is lawfully made available to the public (see art. 1 Term Directive, note 4).

Dreier/Hugenholtz

[Limitations and exceptions]

Article 13

Members shall confine limitations or exceptions to exclusive rights to certain special cases which do not conflict with a normal exploitation of the work and do not unreasonably prejudice the legitimate interests of the right holder.

1. General. (a) Three-step test. While art. 7 TRIPS expressly recognizes achieving 'a balance of rights and obligations' as one of the main objectives of the TRIPS Agreement, art. 13 sets limits to the freedom of Members to enact or maintain statutory limitations or exceptions to exclusive rights. Such limitations must be subjected to the so-called 'three-step test': (1) they shall be confined to 'certain special cases', (2) 'do not conflict with a normal exploitation of the work', and (3) 'do not unreasonably prejudice the legitimate interests of the right holder'. The three steps of the test apply cumulatively. Art. 13 is substantially similar to art. 10 WCT (see extensive comments to art. 10 WCT, notes 1-6). **(b) Relation to Berne Convention.** The three-step test has its origin in art. 9(2) BC. In contrast to art. 9(2) BC, which only concerns the right of reproduction, art. 13 has a broader scope and covers limitations or exceptions 'to exclusive rights'. Moreover, art. 13 TRIPS refers to the interests of the 'right holder', whereas the three-step test of art. 9(2) BC concentrates on the interests of the author. Art. 13 applies not only to the rights that are expressly guaranteed by TRIPS, but also to the minimum rights and exceptions of the BC, that are incorporated into TRIPS by reference, including the so-called 'minor reservations' (art. 9 BC, note 4(b)). See *United States – Section 110(5) of the US Copyright Act* (WTO). **(c) Growing importance of three-step test.** The three-step test has long remained a rather vague and abstract norm in the law of international copyright that was primarily directed at national legislatures and of limited practical importance. Its incorporation in the TRIPS Agreement has given it an acute importance and relevance, both in international and national law. The three-step test has become a solid benchmark for copyright limitations, subject to WTO dispute settlement (see *United States – Section 110(5) of the US Copyright Act* (WTO)) and ultimately sanctions.

2. The three steps. Each of the three steps of art. 13 has been interpreted in intricate detail in *United States – Section 110(5) of the US Copyright Act* (WTO). For additional commentary, see art. 9 BC, note 4, as well as commentary on WCT art. 10. **(a) Certain special cases.** Limitations and exceptions must be 'certain', that is well defined and narrowly circumscribed. However, this does not rule out open norms, such as fair use in US copyright law. According to the WTO Panel 'there is no need to identify explicitly each and every possible situation to which the exception could apply, provided that the scope of the exception is known and particularised'. Limitations and exceptions must apply to 'special cases', that is pursue a specific public policy objective. But art. 13 does not require that this policy objective be legitimate in an objective normative sense. In other words, art. 13 leaves Members free to implement limitations and exceptions according to local needs and circumstances. **(b) No conflict with normal exploitation.** A limitation or exception may not conflict with the normal exploitation of the work. This should be tested for each exclusive right that is guaranteed by the BC or TRIPS separately. Obviously, 'normal' exploitation cannot be equated to full use of the exclusive right, or else limitations would never pass the test and become virtually meaningless (see art. 10 WCT, note 4). According to the WTO Panel, 'normal exploitation' has an empirical and a normative meaning. When applying the second step, both actual and potential effects of a limitation or exception should be taken into account, in particular 'those forms of exploitation which, with a certain degree of likelihood and plausibility, could acquire considerable economic or practical importance'. **(c) No unreasonable prejudice to right holder.** A limitation or exception may not cause unreasonable prejudice to the legitimate interests of the right holder. Both the words 'unreasonable' and 'legitimate' point to the interests of the users, or of society at large, which the limitation or exception supposedly serves. A certain amount of prejudice (harm) to the right holder is permitted, and indeed inevitable. To avoid unreasonable prejudice, legislatures may prefer not to create outright limitations, but resort to statutory licenses that provide for some form of remuneration of the affected right holders (see art. 10 WCT, note 5). **European legislation.** The three-step test has been incorporated in art. 5(5) of the Information Society Directive (see, for example, *ACI Adam and others* (ECJ)), and serves as a safeguard for the rights of reproduction and communication to the public that are covered by that Directive. Earlier versions can be found in art. 6(3) Computer Programs Directive, art. 10(3) Rental Right Directive and art. 6(3) Database Directive (see art. 5 Information Society Directive, note 6). Through its codification in the Information Society Directive the three-step test has become part of EU law, and therefore capable of being applied and interpreted by the ECJ and the national courts of the Member States (see, for example, *De Nederlandse Dagbladpers* (Netherlands)).

[Protection of performers, producers of phonograms (sound recordings) and broadcasting organizations]

Article 14

(1) In respect of a fixation of their performance on a phonogram, performers shall have the possibility of preventing the following acts when undertaken without their authorization: the fixation of their unfixed performance and the reproduction of such fixation. Performers shall also have the possibility of preventing the following acts when undertaken

without their authorization: the broadcasting by wireless means and the communication to the public of their live performance.

(2) Producers of phonograms shall enjoy the right to authorize or prohibit the direct or indirect reproduction of their phonograms.

(3) Broadcasting organizations shall have the right to prohibit the following acts when undertaken without their authorization: the fixation, the reproduction of fixations, and the rebroadcasting by wireless means of broadcasts, as well as the communication to the public of television broadcasts of the same. Where Members do not grant such rights to broadcasting organizations, they shall provide owners of copyright in the subject matter of broadcasts with the possibility of preventing the above acts, subject to the provisions of the Berne Convention (1971).

(4) The provisions of Article 11 in respect of computer programs shall apply mutatis mutandis to producers of phonograms and any other right holders in phonograms as determined in a Member's law. If on 15 April 1994 a Member has in force a system of equitable remuneration of right holders in respect of the rental of phonograms, it may maintain such system provided that the commercial rental of phonograms is not giving rise to the material impairment of the exclusive rights of reproduction of right holders.

(5) The term of the protection available under this Agreement to performers and producers of phonograms shall last at least until the end of a period of 50 years computed from the end of the calendar year in which the fixation was made or the performance took place. The term of protection granted pursuant to paragraph 3 shall last for at least 20 years from the end of the calendar year in which the broadcast took place.

(6) Any Member may, in relation to the rights conferred under paragraphs 1, 2 and 3, provide for conditions, limitations, exceptions and reservations to the extent permitted by the Rome Convention. However, the provisions of Article 18 of the Berne Convention (1971) shall also apply, mutatis mutandis, to the rights of performers and producers of phonograms in phonograms.

1. General. (a) Performers, producers of phonograms and broadcasting organizations. Art. 14 sets out the minimum protection which Members have to grant to performers, producers of phonograms and broadcasting organizations. Although these three categories are the same as those traditionally protected under the Rome Convention, the TRIPS Agreement does not adopt a 'Rome-plus approach' similar to the Berne-plus approach for copyrighted works (see art. 9, note 1). The reason is that the US was, and still is, not a Contracting State to the Rome Convention and, hence, did not want to become bound by all of its provisions. Therefore, the rights to be granted to performers, producers of phonograms and broadcasting organizations are formulated in full in art. 14. In substance, art. 14 hardly goes beyond the substantive rights of the Rome Convention. However, it is formulated in a neutral way so as to cover national regimes which protect, for example, sound recordings as copyrighted works on the one hand, and phonograms as objects of neighbouring rights protection on the other. The neutrality in formulation also explains the juxtaposition of 'phonograms' and 'sound recordings'. These terms may have a different meaning in different national laws, but TRIPS treats them as synonymous without prejudicing against the one or the other. **(b) Other neighbouring rights holders.** The express enumeration of performers, producers of phonograms and broadcasting organizations has the additional effect that holders of other neighbouring rights are not within the ambit of TRIPS. Therefore, Members remain free to grant neighbouring rights protection to other subject matter, such as scientific editions, posthumous works, non-original photographs or films, and databases. Moreover, the TRIPS dispute settlement mechanism cannot be invoked to claim national treatment or most-favoured-nation treatment, because such neighbouring rights do not qualify as 'intellectual property' within the meaning of art. 1(2), and therefore remain outside the reach of the TRIPS Agreement (see art. 10, note 3(a)). **(c) Relation to other neighbouring rights conventions.** Except for the reference in para. 6, there is no special relationship between TRIPS and other international conventions in the field of neighbouring rights, such as the Rome Convention, the Geneva Convention, the WIPO Performers and Phonograms Treaty and the Beijing Treaty on Audiovisual Performances.

2. Rights of performers (para. 1). (a) General. Art. 14(1) lists the minimum rights to be granted to performers. The provision mirrors arts. 7(1) RC, but without the limitations of art. 7(c)(i)-(iii) RC. More importantly, the protection required by TRIPS is limited to performances 'on a phonogram', thus excluding the application of TRIPS to audiovisual performances. This reflects the demands of the American film industry that for a long time did not want to see rights of performers protected in an international instrument that would become binding upon the US, but in 2012 consented to the Beijing Treaty on Audiovisual Performances. Similar to the Rome Convention, the protection granted to performers has not been formulated in terms of absolute, exclusive rights, but as rights to prevent acts that are done without authorization (see art. 7 RC, note 2). In this respect TRIPS does not impose greater obligations upon the Members than those might already have under the Rome Convention, but this has been changed under the WPPT (see arts. 7 et seq. WPPT). Contrary to the Rome Convention (art. 3(a) RC), art. 14 does not define the term 'performer'. **(b) European legislation.** In the EU the rights mentioned in art. 14(1) are granted to performers by arts. 6(1) and 8(1) of the Rental Right Directive and art. 2(b) of the Information Society Directive.

3. Rights of phonogram producers (para. 2). (a) General. Art. 14(2) grants producers of phonograms an exclusive right. It thus duplicates art. 10 RC. Whereas TRIPS does not provide for rights of distribution and importation, such as those mentioned in art. 2 of the Geneva Convention, art. 14(4) does grant to phonogram producers a rental right. **(b) European legislation.** In the EU the exclusive reproduction right was initially granted to producers of phonograms by art. 7(1) of the Rental Right Directive, but this provision was later superseded by art. 2(c) of the Information Society Directive.

4. Rights of broadcasting organizations (para. 3). (a) General. Art. 14(3) lays down the minimum rights to be granted to broadcasting organizations. The first sentence closely mirrors art. 13 RC by granting a right to prohibit the fixation, the reproduction of fixations, and the rebroadcasting by wireless means of broadcasts, as well as the communication to the public of television broadcasts of the same. However, art. 14(3) does not come with the restrictions to the reproduction right mentioned in art. 13(c)(i) and (ii) RC, nor does it limit the relevant communication of broadcasts to the public to places accessible to the public against payment of an entrance fee. Note that according to the second sentence the protection of broadcasting organizations is only optional. Members are free not to protect broadcasting organizations by rights of their own. Rather, it is sufficient that copyright owners in the subject matter of broadcasts (that is, the broadcast films and other programmes) can prevent the acts listed in art. 14(3) TRIPS. **(b) European legislation.** In the EU broadcasting organizations enjoy neighbouring rights of their own pursuant to arts. 6(2) and 8(3) of the Rental Right Directive and art. 2(e) of the Information Society Directive.

5. Rental right for phonograms (para. 4). (a) General. Parallel to art. 11 TRIPS, which grants a rental right for computer programs, art. 14(4) sentence 1 grants a rental right for phonograms to the benefit of both the producers of phonograms and any other person holding a right in a phonogram as determined by a Member's law. Arguably, the latter include the authors of the underlying music and text as well as performers. The reference 'mutatis mutandis' to art. 11 as far as computer programs, but not cinematographic works, are concerned has two consequences. First, Members are not exempt from their obligation to grant a rental right in phonograms if no material impairment of the reproduction right occurs. Second, the rental right with regard to phonograms does not apply where the phonogram is not the essential object of the rental. Moreover, according to art. 70(5), Members are not obliged to grant the rental right with respect to originals or copies purchased prior to the date of application of this Agreement for that Member. Moreover, para. 4 sentence 2 enables States such as Japan to grandfather equitable remuneration schemes that existed at the time of the conclusion of TRIPS, provided this does not materially impair the exclusive reproduction rights of the phonogram producers (see art. 11, note 4). **(b) European legislation.** In the EU, the rental right to phonogram producers is granted by art. 2(1) of the Rental Right Directive.

6. Term of protection (para. 5). (a) General. Para. 5 exceeds the minimum standard of the Rome Convention in that it raises the 20-year term of protection (art. 14 RC) for both performers and producers of phonograms to

50 years. However, no such longer term is required with regard to broadcasting organizations. Like in the Rome Convention, the dates are calculated from the end of the calendar year in which the event triggering the term of protection occurred. However, whereas art. 14(a) and (b) of the Rome Convention differentiates for performers according to whether or not the performance has been incorporated in a phonogram, art. 14 TRIPS merely refers to the 'year in which the fixation was made or the performance took place'. Arguably, Members that protect phonograms under copyright, will have to observe the minimum terms of copyright protection, since TRIPS does not derogate from existing obligations of Members pursuant to the Berne Convention (arts. 2(2) and 9 TRIPS). **(b) European legislation.** In the EU the terms of protection for performers, producers of phonograms and broadcasting organizations initially followed the minimum standard set by the Rome Convention (art. 12 of the Rental Right Directive), but were raised to 50 years by art. 3(1), (2) and (4) of the Term Directive.

7. Conditions, limitations, exceptions and reservations (para. 6). (a) Reference to the Rome Convention (sentence 1). With regard to performers, phonogram producers and broadcasting organizations, TRIPS allows for the same conditions as the Rome Convention with regard to the rights conferred in arts. 7 and 13 RC. It also permits the same reservations as arts. 15 and 16 RC, as well as compulsory licensing for broadcasts similar to art. 13(d) RC. Since other compulsory licenses, such as those allowed under arts. 11bis(2) and 13(2) BC, are not permitted under the Rome Convention, they should likewise be deemed excluded under TRIPS. **(b) Reference to the Berne Convention (sentence 2).** Para. 6 sentence 2 declares the retroactivity provision of art. 18 BC applicable also to the protection granted under art. 14 TRIPS (reiterated in art. 70(2) TRIPS). This rule affects performances and phonograms for which art. 14(5) TRIPS requires prolongation of the term of protection as compared to the shorter term to be granted under the Rome Convention. The reference to art. 18 BC means that performances and phonograms that already existed at the time of entry into force of TRIPS (1 January 1995) will benefit from the longer term, if they have not yet fallen into the public domain in the country of origin through the expiry of the term of protection. However, if the protection previously granted had already expired in the country where protection is claimed, the rights in the performance or phonogram shall not be revived.

DIRECTIVE 2009/24/EC OF THE EUROPEAN PARLIAMENT AND OF THE COUNCIL

(Computer Programs Directive)

of 23 April 2009 on the legal protection of computer programs

[Introductory remarks]

1. Legislative history. (a) Original Directive. Directive 91/250/EEC of 14 May 1991 on the legal protection of computer programs (Computer Programs Directive (old version)) was the first harmonizing legislation in the field of European copyright law. Its origins are to be found in the 1985 Commission White Paper on Completing the Internal Market and in the 1988 Green Paper on Copyright and the Challenge of Technology. Adopted under the co-operation procedure of what was then art. 149 of the EEC Treaty (now art. 294 TFEU), the Directive derived from an Initial Proposal submitted by the Commission on 5 January 1989. This was subject to substantial criticism in Parliament, and extensive lobbying took place, focusing particularly on the extent to which copyright protection of computer programs should be limited to enable access to and use of code for the purposes of enabling the creation of new programs that can be used with existing ones (so-called 'interoperability'). In the light of these criticisms, the Commission introduced an Amended Proposal on 18 October 1990. Following adoption of a common position between the Council and Commission on 13 December 1990, the Amended Proposal was referred back to the Parliament who gave it a second reading. Thereafter, Council adopted the Directive on 14 May 1991. The Directive was to be implemented by Member States by 1 January 1993. **(b) Report.** In April 2000, the Commission published a report on the implementation and effects of the Computer Programs Directive, thereby fulfilling an undertaking it had made at the time of the adoption of the common position to report on the working of the Directive by the end of 1996 (Report on the Computer Programs Directive). **(c) Codified version.** Council Directive 91/250/EEC was subsequently repealed and replaced by Directive 2009/24/EC of the European Parliament and of the Council of 23 April 2009 on the legal protection of computer programs (Computer Programs Directive), which consolidates the amendments made to the earlier version of the Directive, and retains the same substantive provisions. However, many of the recitals are consolidated: recitals 10-12 of Directive 91/250 in recital 10 of Directive 2009/24; recitals 13-15 in recital 11; recitals 17-18 in recital 13; recitals 20-24 in recital 15. Moreover, some provisions are relocated and others are differently subdivided (e.g., art. 9(2) of Directive 91/250 is now re-positioned in art. 1(4)). For details see Annex II to the Computer Programs Directive.

2. Objective of harmonization (recitals 2-5). The Directive is intended to remove differences between the laws of Member States to the extent that the differences 'have direct and negative effects on the functioning of the internal market' (recital 4). Recital 1 to the earlier version of the Directive indicates that the differences with which it is chiefly concerned are those that determine when a computer program will be protected and, where such protection exists, the attributes of such protection. Recital 5 acknowledges that differences which do not adversely affect the functioning of the internal market 'to a substantial degree' need not be removed or prevented from arising.

3. Amendments; relationship to other Directives. In its present version, the Directive comprises 12 articles and 20 recitals. Of these, the most controversial are arts. 5 and 6, which confer exceptions for certain uses of copyright protected programs, in particular permitting decompilation required to enable interoperability. The Computer Programs Directive (old version) had previously been amended by the Council's Term Directive which repealed the previously existing art. 8, replacing the term of copyright with the 70-year post mortem auctoris period. This amendment has since been incorporated into the present version of the Directive. Other, later Directives have purported to operate 'without prejudice' to the Computer Programs Directive. These Directives are the Rental Right Directive (art. 3), the Database Directive (art. 2(a)), the Information Society Directive (art. 1(2)(a)), and the Enforcement Directive (art. 2(2)). The Court of Justice has described the Directive as a 'lex specialis', so that its provisions need not necessarily precisely correspond to those applicable to other works under the Information Society Directive (*UsedSoft* (ECJ)). This piecemeal approach means there are inconsistencies in levels of protection between different subject matters, with practical implications where various subject matters are combined in the same artefact (such as a computer video game, comprising software and artistic works, see also *BSA* (ECJ)). The Commission is in the process of deciding whether further legislation is desirable to remove such inconsistencies (see Staff Working Paper on Copyright Review).

[Bibliography]

General

B. Czarnota and R. Hart, *Legal Protection of Computer Programs in Europe: A Guide to the EC Directive* (Butterworths 1991)

T. Dreier, 'The Council Directive of 14 May 1991 on the Legal Protection of Computer Programs' (1991) EIPR 319-330

A. Lucas, 'Copyright in the European Community: The Green Paper and the Proposal for a Directive Concerning Legal Protection of Computer Programs' (1991) *Columbia Journal of Transnational Law* 145-167

A. Palmer and T. Vinje, 'The EC Directive on the Legal Protection of Computer Software: New Law Governing Software Development' (1992) *Duke Journal of Comparative and International Law* 65-87

J. Huet and J. Ginsburg, 'Computer Programs in Europe: A Comparative Analysis of the 1991 EC Software Directive' (1992) *Columbia Journal of Transnational Law* 327-373

L. Raskind, 'Protecting Computer Software in the European Economic Community: The Innovative New Directive' (1992) *Brooklyn Journal of International Law* 729-750

J. Spoor, 'Copyright Protection and Reverse Engineering of Software: Implementation and Effects of the EC Directive' (1994) *University of Dayton Law Review* 1063-1086

J. Bing, 'Copyright Protection of Computer Programs' in Estelle Derclaye (ed.), *Research Handbook on the Future of EU Copyright* (Edward Elgar, 2009) 401-426

Scope of protection (SAS Institute)

P. Akester, 'SAS Institute Inc v World Programming Ltd, Case C-406/10: Exploratory Answers' (2012) EIPR 145-157

P. Samuelson, T. Vinje and W. Cornish, 'Does Copyright Protection under the EU Software Directive Extend to Computer Program Behaviour, Languages and Interfaces?' (2012) EIPR 158-166

D. Gervais and E. Derclaye, 'The Scope of Computer Program Protection after *SAS*: Are We Closer to Answers?' (2012) EIPR 565-572

Exhaustion (UsedSoft)

R. Hilty and K. Köklü, 'Software Agreements: Stocktaking and Outlook – Lessons from the *UsedSoft v Oracle* Case From a Comparative Law Perspective' (2013) IIC 263-292

Interoperability

S. Anderman, '*Microsoft v Commission* and the Interoperability Issue' (2008) EIPR 395-399

M. Dizon, 'Decompiling the Software Directive, the *Microsoft* CFI Case and the i2010 Strategy: How to Reverse Engineer an International Interoperability Regime' (2008) *Computer and Telecommunications Law Review* 213-219

A. van Rooijen, *The Software Interface Between Copyright and Competition Law: A Legal Analysis of Interoperability in Computer Programs* (Kluwer Law International 2010)

P. Samuelson, 'The Past, Present and Future of Software Copyright: Interoperability Rules in the European Union and United States' (2012) EIPR 229-236

S. Weston, 'Software Interfaces – Stuck in the Middle: The Relationship Between Law and Software Interfaces in Regulating and Encouraging Interoperability' (2012) IIC 427-450

[Preamble]

The European Parliament and the Council of the European Union,

Having regard to the Treaty establishing the European Community and in particular Article 95 thereof, Having regard to the proposal from the Commission, Having regard to the opinion of the European Economic and Social Committee,[1] Acting in accordance with the procedure laid down in Article 251 of the Treaty,[2]

Whereas:

(1) The content of Council Directive 91/250/EEC of 14 May 1991 on the legal protection of computer programs[3] has been amended.[4] In the interests of clarity and rationality the said Directive should be codified.

(2) The development of computer programs requires the investment of considerable human, technical and financial resources while computer programs can be copied at a fraction of the cost needed to develop them independently.

(3) Computer programs are playing an increasingly important role in a broad range of industries and computer program technology can accordingly be considered as being of fundamental importance for the Community's industrial development.

(4) Certain differences in the legal protection offered by the laws of the Member States have direct and negative effects on the functioning of the internal market as regards computer programs.

(5) Existing differences having such effects need to be removed and new ones prevented from arising, while differences not adversely affecting the functioning of the internal market to a substantial degree need not be removed or prevented from arising.

(6) The Community's legal framework on the protection of computer programs can accordingly in the first instance be limited to establishing that Member States should accord protection to computer programs under copyright law as literary works and, further, to establishing who and what should be protected, the exclusive rights on which protected persons should be able to rely in order to authorise or prohibit certain acts and for how long the protection should apply.

(7) For the purpose of this Directive, the term 'computer program' shall include programs in any form, including those which are incorporated into hardware. This term also includes preparatory design work leading to the development of a computer program provided that the

---

1. OJ No. C 204, 9 August 2008, p. 24.
2. OJ No. C 286E, 27 November 2009, p. 61 and Council Decision of 23 March 2009.
3. OJ No. L 122, 17 May 1991, p. 42.
4. See Annex I, Part A.

nature of the preparatory work is such that a computer program can result from it at a later stage.

(8) In respect of the criteria to be applied in determining whether or not a computer program is an original work, no tests as to the qualitative or aesthetic merit of the program should be applied.

(9) The Community is fully committed to the promotion of international standardisation.

(10) The function of a computer program is to communicate and work together with other components of a computer system and with users and, for this purpose, a logical and, where appropriate, physical interconnection and interaction is required to permit all elements of software and hardware to work with other software and hardware and with users in all the ways in which they are intended to function. The parts of the program which provide for such interconnection and interaction between elements of software and hardware are generally known as 'interfaces'. This functional interconnection and interaction is generally known as 'interoperability'; such interoperability can be defined as the ability to exchange information and mutually to use the information which has been exchanged.

(11) For the avoidance of doubt, it has to be made clear that only the expression of a computer program is protected and that ideas and principles which underlie any element of a program, including those which underlie its interfaces, are not protected by copyright under this Directive. In accordance with this principle of copyright, to the extent that logic, algorithms and programming languages comprise ideas and principles, those ideas and principles are not protected under this Directive. In accordance with the legislation and case-law of the Member States and the international copyright conventions, the expression of those ideas and principles is to be protected by copyright.

(12) For the purposes of this Directive, the term 'rental' means the making available for use, for a limited period of time and for profit-making purposes, of a computer program or a copy thereof. This term does not include public lending, which, accordingly, remains outside the scope of this Directive.

(13) The exclusive rights of the author to prevent the unauthorised reproduction of his work should be subject to a limited exception in the case of a computer program to allow the reproduction technically necessary for the use of that program by the lawful acquirer. This means that the acts of loading and running necessary for the use of a copy of a program which has been lawfully acquired, and the act of correction of its errors, may not be prohibited by contract. In the absence of specific contractual provisions, including when a copy of the program has been sold, any other act necessary for the use of the copy of a program may be performed in accordance with its intended purpose by a lawful acquirer of that copy.

(14) A person having a right to use a computer program should not be prevented from performing acts necessary to observe, study or test the functioning of the program, provided that those acts do not infringe the copyright in the program.

(15) The unauthorised reproduction, translation, adaptation or transformation of the form of the code in which a copy of a computer program has been made available constitutes an infringement of the exclusive rights of the author. Nevertheless, circumstances may exist when such a reproduction of the code and translation of its form are indispensable to obtain the necessary information to achieve the interoperability of an independently created program with other programs. It has therefore to be considered that, in these limited circumstances only, performance of the acts of reproduction and translation by or on behalf of a person having a right to use a copy of the program is legitimate and compatible with fair practice and must therefore be deemed not to require the authorisation of the rightholder. An objective of this exception is to make it possible to connect all components of a computer system, including those of different manufacturers, so that they can work together. Such an exception to the author's exclusive rights may not be used in a way which prejudices the legitimate interests of the rightholder or which conflicts with a normal exploitation of the program.

(16) Protection of computer programs under copyright laws should be without prejudice to the application, in appropriate cases, of other forms of protection. However, any contractual provisions contrary to the provisions of this Directive laid down in respect of decompilation or to the exceptions provided for by this Directive with regard to the making of a back-up copy or to observation, study or testing of the functioning of a program should be null and void.

(17) The provisions of this Directive are without prejudice to the application of the competition rules under Articles 81 and 82 of the Treaty if a dominant supplier refuses to make information available which is necessary for interoperability as defined in this Directive.

(18) The provisions of this Directive should be without prejudice to specific requirements of Community law already enacted in respect of the publication of interfaces in the telecommunications sector or Council Decisions relating to standardisation in the field of information technology and telecommunication.

(19) This Directive does not affect derogations provided for under national legislation in accordance with the Berne Convention on points not covered by this Directive.

(20) This Directive should be without prejudice to the obligations of the Member States relating to the time-limits for transposition into national law of the Directives set out in Annex I, Part B,

Have adopted this Directive:

[Object of protection]

Article 1

(1) In accordance with the provisions of this Directive, Member States shall protect computer programs, by copyright, as literary works within the meaning of the Berne Convention for the Protection of Literary and Artistic Works. For the purposes of this Directive, the term 'computer programs' shall include their preparatory design material.

(2) Protection in accordance with this Directive shall apply to the expression in any form of a computer program. Ideas and principles which underlie any element of a computer program, including those which underlie its interfaces, are not protected by copyright under this Directive.

(3) A computer program shall be protected if it is original in the sense that it is the author's own intellectual creation. No other criteria shall be applied to determine its eligibility for protection.

(4) The provisions of this Directive shall apply also to programs created before 1 January 1993, without prejudice to any acts concluded and rights acquired before that date.

1. Obligation to protect computer programs as literary works within the meaning of the Berne Convention (para. 1). Art. 1(1) imposes an obligation on Member States to protect computer programs, which has three elements. Firstly, Member States must protect computer programs by copyright, as opposed to using a sui generis system of protection, or any other regime, such as unfair competition. As art. 8 makes clear, however, the Directive is without prejudice to any such alternative system of legal protection of computer programs. Second, Member States must protect these as 'literary works', as opposed to any other category of copyright work. Nevertheless, subsequent legislative developments in the Community have made it clear that the rules relating to copyright in computer programs may, and in some cases of harmonization must, be differentiated from those relating to other literary works. Third, Member States must protect such subject matter as literary works 'within the Berne Convention'. It seems implicit in this that Member States must confer such protection without formality (art. 5(2) BC), according to the principle of national treatment (art. 5(1) BC), where such works have suitable connecting factors (art. 3 BC); that authors should benefit from moral rights (art. 6 BC), and that the term should be governed by the Berne minimum (art. 7 BC); and that the copyright owners should be able to control the reproduction of the copyright-protected program, as well as its translation, adaptation and communication by wireless means (arts. 8, 9, 11bis(1) and 12 BC). This obligation has subsequently been adopted internationally in art. 10 TRIPS and art. 4 WCT.

2. Computer program. (a) Definition. There is no definition of 'computer program' in the Directive. The Explanatory Memorandum to the Computer

Programs Directive had indicated that a 'computer program' meant 'a set of instructions the purpose of which is to cause an information processing device, a computer, to perform its functions', but that it was inadvisable to include this in the Directive lest it become outdated (see Explanatory Memorandum to the Computer Programs Directive). The Commission has subsequently indicated that it maintains this position (see Staff Working Paper on Copyright Review). However, recital 7 of the Directive indicates that 'the term "computer program" shall include programs in any form, including those which are incorporated into hardware', and it is clear that this definition covers programs whether in source code, assembly code, or object code and whatever their embodiment, whether on floppy disk, CD-ROM, or in hardware. The term 'computer program' has been held by various national courts to include hypertext mark-up language (.html) files (*Website Layout* (Austria)), and 'microcodes', or machine instruction sets used in microcontrollers (*Microchip* (Germany)). The ECJ has held that videogames are not to be regarded solely as computer programs, but should be treated as complex multimedia works that include graphical and sound elements as well as technical elements; accordingly, videogames may be protected as works under the Information Society Directive (*Nintendo and others* (ECJ)).

(b) Preparatory design material. Art. 1 does, however, state that the term 'computer programs' shall include their preparatory design material. Recital 7 suggests that this is confined to 'work leading to the development of a computer program provided that the nature of the preparatory work is such that a computer program can result from it at a later stage'. Preparatory design material thus covers 'flow charts or descriptions of sequences of steps in plain language' but does not cover 'user manuals' (Explanatory Memorandum to the Computer Programs Directive). This has been confirmed by the ECJ, which held that preparatory design work that is capable of leading to the subsequent creation of a computer program falls within the scope of protection conferred by the Directive (*BSA* (ECJ)).

3. Protection of expression but not ideas (para. 2). (a) General rule. Art. 1(2) clarifies that the general principle that copyright protects 'expression' rather than 'ideas' is to be adhered to in relation to computer programs. Recital 11 states that this provision was included 'for the avoidance of doubt'. The ECJ has interpreted this provision to mean that the protection conferred by the Directive applies to the expression in any form of a computer program and preparatory design work capable of leading, respectively, to the reproduction or subsequent creation of such a program (*BSA* (ECJ)). For this reason, it has been held that the functionality of a computer program, the programming language and format of data files used in a computer program, and the graphic user interface of a computer program do not constitute a form of expression of that computer program, and consequently cannot be protected under the Directive. However, it remains possible that programming languages, the formats of data files and graphic user interfaces may be protected, as works, by copyright under the Information Society Directive, provided they fulfil the criterion of 'author's own intellectual creation' (*BSA* (ECJ); *SAS Institute* (ECJ)). **(b) Logic, algorithms and programming languages.** Recital 11 adds that 'in accordance with this principle of copyright, to the extent that logic, algorithms and programming languages comprise ideas and principles, those ideas and principles are not protected under this Directive.' As indicated earlier, while programming languages are not protected as computer programs under the Directive, the ECJ has not excluded the possibility that they may still be protected as works under the ordinary law of copyright (*SAS Institute* (ECJ)). However, the English High Court has held that an ad hoc computer language in the form of a defined user command interface and a programming language designed for use with a specific suite of programs, respectively, were not protected by copyright (*Navitaire* (UK); *SAS Institute* (UK, High Court, 2013)). **(c) Interfaces.** The effect of the general principle on the protection of 'interfaces' was a topic of heated debate during the passage of the Directive, but, despite calls for clarification, art. 1(2) provides little additional assistance, simply restating that ideas and principles which underlie interfaces are not protected. The Explanatory Memorandum to the Computer Programs Directive had suggested that where 'idea' and 'expression' were inextricably linked so that someone using the 'idea' would inevitably reproduce the 'expression', then no infringement would occur. Some clarification has since been provided by the ECJ, which has defined 'interfaces' as 'parts of a computer program which provide for interconnection and interaction of elements of software and hardware with other software and hardware and with users in all the ways in which they are intended to function'. This includes, in particular, a graphic user interface, being an interaction interface which enables communication between the computer program and its user (*BSA* (ECJ)). As a graphic user interface does not enable the reproduction of the computer program to which it relates, but is merely an element by means of which users make use of the features of that program, it was held not to constitute a form of expression of that computer program and therefore not protected under the Directive, though it might still be protected, as a work, by copyright under the Information Society Directive, provided it is the author's own intellectual creation. Prior to this, the Paris Court of Appeal had held that an identification sequence that enabled a memory to communicate with a reader was an unprotectable interface (*Société Nomai* (France)). This can be contrasted with the approach taken in the US, where the Court of Appeals for the Federal Circuit has held that application programming interfaces, which enable communication between two or more computer programs, are capable of being protected by copyright (*Oracle/Google* (USA, 2014).

4. Criteria of protection (para. 3). (a) History. The Initial Proposal of the Computer Programs Directive contained no indication that the threshold of protection should be harmonized, and merely referred Member States to the originality criteria applicable to literary works generally. This led to concerns that such an approach would perpetuate existing divergences between the thresholds for eligibility for protection applied to computer programs in different Member States. In particular, Germany operated a high threshold, and the United Kingdom a low one. The German Supreme Court prior to the Directive had required that the arrangement of a program significantly surpass the average ability of the programmer (*Inkasso-Programm* (Germany)), whereas the United Kingdom required merely an exercise of 'labour, skill and judgment'. Consequently, the Commission in its Amended Proposal accepted Parliament's recommendation that the threshold for eligibility should be clarified. **(b) Meaning.** Art. 1(3) harmonizes the threshold that a program must meet to be protected. It indicates that a program is to be protected if it is original in the sense that it is 'the author's own intellectual creation'. Recital 8 adds that 'in respect of the criteria to be applied in determining whether or not a computer program is an original work, no tests as to the qualitative or aesthetic merits of the program should be applied'. The 'author's own intellectual creation' is the only criterion that may be applied by a Member State, so operates as both a maximum and a minimum. It is now clear from the decisions of the ECJ that there is to be a single standard applicable to all works of authorship (*Infopaq International* (ECJ)). The ECJ has held, in the context of art. 6 of the Term Directive relating to copyright protection for photographs, that an intellectual creation is the author's own if the author was able to express his or her creative abilities in the production of the work by making free and creative choices (*Painer* (ECJ)). The ECJ has also stated that features of a work that are dictated by the function it performs lack originality (*BSA* (ECJ), [48]-[50]).This appears consistent with the approach taken by the Austrian court in holding that, for a computer program to be protected by copyright, it should have a certain degree of complexity, in the sense that it permits a number of solutions and the programmer has sufficient intellectual scope for the development of individual features; another decisive factor was whether the program had been created as new or whether the programmer essentially had recourse to existing program modules (*TerraCAD* (Austria)). **(c) Impact.** In its Report on the Computer Programs Directive, the Commission has stated that the Directive required 12 Member States to lower their threshold, and three to 'lift the bar'. The Federal Supreme Court (*Buchhaltungsprogramm* (Germany)) has recognized that the standard is lower. While the Commission has criticized the United Kingdom for its failure to implement art. 1(3) expressly (Report on the Computer Programs Directive), it seems clear that the courts apply the test from the Directive (*SAS Institute* (UK, High Court, 2010; UK, High Court, 2013; UK, Court of Appeal, 2013)).

5. Transitional provision (para. 4). (a) General. As with the other Directives on copyright, being informed by the goal of harmonization, this Directive applies to existing works. Were it otherwise, there would be no harmonization for many decades. Consequently, the implementation of the Directive might alter rights and obligations that existed prior to the implementation of the Directive. Art. 1(4) clarifies that the Directive should not prejudice 'any acts concluded' before the date on which it should have been implemented. Moreover, it adds that the Directive should not affect 'rights acquired' before that date. The Database Directive and Information Society Directive use the same formula (art. 14(4) of the Database Directive, art. 10(2) of the Information Society Directive). **(b) 'Acts concluded'.** The phrase 'acts concluded' can be contrasted with the phrases 'acts of exploitation performed' and 'any contracts concluded' used in arts. 11(2) and (5) of the Rental Right Directive. The Computer Programs Directive is unclear as to whether 'acts concluded' includes contracts agreed before the relevant date but intended to remain applicable thereafter. It is thus unclear whether or not, for example, a contract made before 1 January 1993 forbidding the making of a back-up copy, remains unaffected by the prohibition on such contracts in art. 5(2) because the contract was an 'act concluded'. **(c) 'Rights acquired'.** The second saving is for 'rights acquired'. One situation where this might be relevant is where a program would not constitute an 'intellectual creation' under art. 1(3) but might have been protected by copyright in some Member States (such as the UK). In principle, such national copyrights are 'rights acquired' which should survive implementation of the Directive. Another situation where 'rights acquired' may be significant is where a program would not have been protected in a Member State prior to harmonization (as was thought to be the case with many programs under German law), but would be protected once art. 1(3) was implemented. In such cases of 'springing copyrights', the 'rights acquired' by parties relying on the absence of copyright (such as rights in stock of copies of the program) should be safeguarded.

[Authorship of computer programs]

Article 2

(1) **The author of a computer program shall be the natural person or group of natural persons who has created the program or, where the legislation of the Member State permits, the legal person designated as the rightholder by that legislation.**

Where collective works are recognised by the legislation of a Member State, the person considered by the legislation of the Member State to have created the work shall be deemed to be its author.

(2) **In respect of a computer program created by a group of natural persons jointly, the exclusive rights shall be owned jointly.**

(3) **Where a computer program is created by an employee in the execution of his duties or following the instructions given by his employer, the employer exclusively shall be entitled to exercise all economic rights in the program so created, unless otherwise provided by contract.**

1. Authorship (para. 1). (a) Importance of concept of authorship. The concept of 'authorship' plays a central part in copyright law, in particular, defining when a work is eligible for protection (art. 3 BC), the term of protection (art. 7 BC), as well as initial ownership of economic rights (art. 5(1) BC) and moral rights (art. 6bis BC). **(b) General rule for determining authorship.** The Directive establishes a general principle by which authorship of computer programs is to be determined (art. 2(1)), but gives Member States considerable flexibility to deviate from this in their legislation (art. 2(1), 2(2)). The general principle is that the author shall be the natural person, that is, the human being, who has 'created' the program. No further elaboration is provided of what is meant by 'create' in this context, but it almost certainly indicates the person who is responsible for the manner in which a program is expressed, rather than a person who suggests the ideas and principles which underlie it (recital 11). Two variations of this general principle are permitted. **(c) Permissible recognition of legal persons as authors.** Firstly, Member States may alternatively, or additionally, allow for a 'legal person', such as a company, to be treated as the 'author' (art. 2(1) first subparagraph). One situation where this could be relevant is where, according to UK law, copyright in a program 'which is computer-generated' vests in the person by whom the arrangements necessary for the creation of the work are undertaken. **(d) Permissible application of rules as to authorship of collective works.** The second permitted variation of the general rule is that Member States may apply their provisions on collective works to computer programs (art. 2(1) second subparagraph). No definition of 'collective work' is provided, and it appears this is to be left to national law. Where national legislative rules exist relating to authorship of collective works, they typically allow for the natural person or legal entity who initiated or organized the creation of the collective work, or under whose name it was published, to be treated as the author of that work. Collective works are recognized by the laws of, for example, France, as well as of some other Member States.

2. Ownership (paras. 2 and 3). (a) Implicit general rule that author is initial owner of copyright. Although the Directive does not expressly say so, arts. 2(2) and 2(3) (as well as recital 15) implicitly indicate that Member States should treat the 'author' of a computer program as the initial owner of 'exclusive rights' therein. **(b) Joint authorship.** Art. 2(1) indicates how this principle is to be applied to cases of joint authorship, a matter which is likely to be commonplace in the creation of computer programs. The article indicates that where 'a group of natural persons' creates a computer program jointly, the 'exclusive rights' shall be owned jointly. In stating that the rights are 'owned jointly', the article implies that all joint owners must consent to any person doing any of the acts encompassed by the exclusive rights. There is no harmonization as to how the relative shares of contributors are to be calculated, nor as to how disputes between co-authors as to the exploitation of the program are to be resolved. These remain matters for national law. **(c) Employees.** Art. 2(3) creates a special rule on the initial allocation of the right to exercise 'economic rights'. This specifies that where a computer program is created by an employee in the execution of his or her duties or following instructions given by the employer, the employer shall be exclusively entitled to exercise all economic rights in the program, unless the parties provide otherwise in a contract. Five elements of this article merit comment. Firstly, it should be observed that this rule only applies to 'employees', and the meaning of this is to be regarded as a matter for Member States (see Directives 80/987/EEC on the approximation of the laws of the Member States relating to the protection of employees in the event of the insolvency of their employer, now codified as Directive 2008/94/EC, and 91/533/EEC on an employer's obligation to inform employees of the conditions applicable to the contract or employment relationship). Second, the special rule only operates when the program is made by the employee when carrying out his obligations as an employee, or when carrying out instructions. In applying this rule, it will be necessary to determine the scope of the employee's obligations from the terms of the employment contract. Third, the rule requires that the employer shall be entitled to exercise the 'economic rights' (or 'patrimonial rights') in the computer program, rather than the 'exclusive rights' (see art. 2(2)), although there seems to be no difference between these two terms. 'Moral rights', however, are unaffected and remain a matter for national law (see Explanatory Memorandum to the Amended Proposal of the Computer Programs Directive). Fourth, the Directive only requires that the employer be exclusively 'entitled to exercise' the rights. The Directive does not require the Member State to make the employer the 'owner' of copyright (or 'author' of the work). In this way, the Directive avoids disrupting the principles of those systems which treat authors' rights as non-transferable. For example, in Germany this transfer is by way of a statutory exclusive licence (*Wetterführungspläne* (Germany)). Fifth, the rule on initial allocation of rights may be varied, but only 'by contract' rather than through some less formal agreement or practice. **(d) Commissioned works.** The Initial Proposal of the Computer Programs Directive contained a provision stating that the person who commissions a computer program shall be entitled to exercise 'all rights' in respect of that program, unless otherwise provided by contract. This was rejected by the Parliament and Council, and the Directive contains no special provisions relating to commissioned works. Thus, under the general rules on authorship set out in the Directive, where the creation of a computer program results from a commission, the exclusive rights will initially belong to the author; however, the parties to such an arrangement may provide for the transfer of economic rights to the commissioner in so far as this is possible, and in accordance with the provisions of national law.

[Beneficiaries of protection]

Article 3

Protection shall be granted to all natural or legal persons eligible under national copyright legislation as applied to literary works.

Eligibility. Art. 3 requires each Member State to grant protection in respect of computer programs to all persons eligible under that Member State's law applicable to literary works. Member States, as adherents to the Berne Convention, are under an obligation to confer protection on programs the authors of which are nationals of one of the countries of the Berne Union, or (if not) where the program is 'first published' in a country of the Union (art. 3 BC). In cases of joint authorship, where one joint author is 'eligible' for protection, the extent to which rights are conferred on other ('ineligible') authors is left as a matter for national law (see Initial Proposal of the Computer Programs Directive).

[Restricted acts]

Article 4

(1) Subject to the provisions of Articles 5 and 6, the exclusive rights of the rightholder within the meaning of Article 2 shall include the right to do or to authorise:

    (a) the permanent or temporary reproduction of a computer program by any means and in any form, in part or in whole; in so far as loading, displaying, running, transmission or storage of the computer program necessitate such reproduction, such acts shall be subject to authorisation by the rightholder;

    (b) the translation, adaptation, arrangement and any other alteration of a computer program and the reproduction of the results thereof, without prejudice to the rights of the person who alters the program;

    (c) any form of distribution to the public, including the rental, of the original computer program or of copies thereof.

(2) The first sale in the Community of a copy of a program by the rightholder or with his consent shall exhaust the distribution right within the Community of that copy, with the exception of the right to control further rental of the program or a copy thereof.

1. Exclusive rights. This article specifies the nature of some of the rights to be conferred on the 'rightholder' (see recitals 13 and 15 which refer to the exclusive rights of 'the author'). The article is non-exhaustive, leaving other rights to be determined by national law, in accordance with international and other EU obligations, such as, in particular, the right to communicate a work to the public. The exclusive rights specified are referred to as the rights 'to do or to authorise' particular acts. Despite the difference in the linguistic form from that adopted in subsequent Directives, which tend to describe exclusive rights in terms of the right 'to authorise or prohibit' (arts. 1(1), 7 and 8 of the Rental Right Directive; arts. 2, 3 and 4 of the Information Society Directive), an owner of copyright in computer programs is not freed by the Directive from the need to respect the rights of others, and the general law, before carrying out the specified acts.

2. Reproduction (para. 1(a)). (a) General. The rightholder is given the right to control the reproduction of the computer program, whether permanent or temporary, by whatever means and in whatever form, and whether in whole or in part. This provision goes beyond the definition of the reproduction right in the Berne Convention (art. 9(1) BC), which requires that authors be granted the right of authorizing reproduction 'in any manner or form'. However, the definition of 'reproduction' in the Computer Programs Directive does not go as far as the express reference to '*direct or indirect*' acts of reproduction in art. 2 of the Information Society Directive. This failure to refer to 'indirect' reproduction in the Computer Programs Directive should not be regarded as a matter of concern, for the principle that copyright can be infringed 'indirectly' as well as 'directly' is well-established within copyright laws. Nevertheless, the Staff Working Paper on Copyright Review suggested alignment of the terminology of the Computer Programs Directive so as to remove this inconsistency, but the wording was not changed in the consolidation process. **(b) The meaning of reproduction.** While art. 4(1) (a) provides various activities that might amount to 'reproduction', nothing is said about the criteria that apply when deciding whether something is a 'reproduction.' In particular, the Directive fails to indicate whether the test of finding a reproduction in law turns on technical or economic assessment or, in other words, whether any act which can be treated from a technical perspective as duplicating a program amounts to a reproduction, or whether the act must have some economic significance. The Information Society Directive (arts. 2 and 5, recital 21) has been held to require a broad construction of the acts covered by the right of reproduction (*Infopaq International* (ECJ)), which might suggest that any technical reproduction would suffice. However, it may be doubted whether an inference as to the meaning of 're-production' in the Computer Programs Directive can legitimately be drawn from this later Information Society Directive, which operates explicitly 'without prejudice to the provisions' of the Directive. A further reason to doubt the legitimacy of such an inference is the absence of any equivalent to art. 5(1) of the Information Society Directive in the Directive (exception for certain temporary acts of reproduction). **(c) Reproduction 'by whatever means and in whatever form'.** This clarifies that reproduction need not be in the same medium as the original program. For example, conversion of a protected program comprising source code into object code is generally regarded as a reproduction. Reproduction of a computer program can take place by photocopying source code, by duplicating a program in electronic form in hardware, on a floppy disc, or by downloading a copy from an Internet site (for the reverse case of the reproduction, in a computer program or a user manual for that program, of certain elements described in a user manual, see *SAS Institute* (ECJ)). **(d) Reproduction 'whether permanent or temporary'.** Art. 4(1)(a) clarifies that the concept of reproduction includes 'temporary' reproductions. Therefore it is possible for storage of a computer program to be 'reproduction' even where the electronic copy is later deleted (see Explanatory Memorandum to the Initial Proposal of the Computer Programs Directive). 'Reproduction' therefore might in principle include temporary copies made in a computer's Random Access Memory (RAM) when any program is run, or temporary copies made in the process of 'caching'. As stated above, it should be noted that there is no exception for certain transient or incidental copies such as contained in art. 5(1) of the Information Society Directive. **(e) Reproduction 'in whole or in part'.** Art. 4(1)(a) indicates that the reproduction right can be infringed where a person copies or uses part rather than the whole of the program. The reproduction of insubstantial parts is non-infringing. Moreover, reproduction of ideas or principles, rather than expression, is not reproduction of 'part' of a protected computer program (art. 1(2)). The reproduction of a part of a protected work has been held to constitute reproduction within the meaning of art. 2 of the Information Society Directive, provided that part contains an element of the work which expresses the author's own intellectual creation (*Infopaq International* (ECJ)), and there seems no reason why the same logic would not apply in relation to computer programs. This reasoning has been adopted by the English courts (*SAS Institute* (UK, Court of Appeal, 2013)). **(f) Loading, display, running, transmission or storage.** Loading, display, running, transmission or storage are not treated per se as requiring authorization, but will do so in any situation where the particular act involves reproduction of the program (according to the Explanatory Memorandum to the Amended Proposal of the Computer Programs Directive, as of 1990 it was understood that all these acts did in fact involve reproduction). While accepting that the installation of a program amounts to reproduction, the German courts do not see the Directive as providing any clear indication as to when these acts will be a reproduction (see *Holzhandelsprogramm* (Germany)). The English High Court has on at least one occasion considered the act of loading a computer program to be an act of reproduction (*Sony/Owen* (UK)).

3. Alterations (including translation) (para. 1(b)). (a) General. The Directive requires Member States to treat the translation, adaptation, arrangement and any other alteration of a computer program as acts which require the consent of the rightholder. This does not seem to go beyond what is required under the Berne Convention (arts. 8 and 12 BC). The Initial Proposal of the Computer Programs Directive refers only to the act of adaptation, though the Explanatory Memorandum makes it clear that 'adaptation' should be taken to include 'translation'. The wording was subsequently amended to bring the text more into conformity with arts. 8 and 12 of the Berne Convention (see Explanatory Memorandum to the Amended Proposal of the Computer Programs Directive). **(b) Translation.** The concept would cover translation of a computer program from one computer language to another (for example, from COBOL to BASIC). The concept of adaptation or translation might also cover transformation of a work from source code to object code, or object code back into source code or, through decompilation, into 'pseudo source code', see art. 6(1). In such a situation, the single act might constitute both a reproduction and a translation. **(c) Adaptation, arrangement and alteration.** There is no definition of what constitutes an adaptation, arrangement or alteration of a protected computer program. The legislative text uses the term 'alteration' as the general notion and considers adaptations and arrangements as forms of alterations. The Austrian Supreme Court has held that an adaptation occurs when a computer program is given a new external form which can be regarded as the adaptor's own intellectual creation, while retaining the essential individual features of the original work. 'Adaptation' thus includes adjusting or further developing a computer program to meet the particular conditions of the user, such as the creation of an update, but does not include minor adjustments or rearrangements, pure error correction, adjustments to changed hardware or updates resulting from changes in the user's enterprise or statutory requirements (*TerraCAD* (Austria)). However, it should be noted that Austria has not implemented expressly the 'any other alteration' phrase set out in the Directive. Consequently, the scope of this right under Austrian law may be narrower (see Report on the Computer Programs Directive). The notion of 'alteration' can be understood broadly. For example, national case law has considered the removal of a 'dongle check' from a program so that it could run on unauthorized hardware to be a prohibited alteration (*Dongle* (Germany)). As far as infringement is concerned, the Directive gives no guidance as to whether a claimant's program should be subjected to a process of 'abstraction', with ideas and non-original elements 'filtered out' before any comparison is made with an alleged infringing program (such as under US copyright law, see *Computer Associates* (USA)). Although in one case, the English High Court rejected any direct application of the US abstraction-filtration-comparison test to cases decided under UK copyright law (*IBCOS v Barclays* (UK)), in another the court accepted that 'filtration' of unprotected components of a program was appropriate prior to comparing the defendant's program with it (*SAS Institute* (UK, High Court, 2013, [46])). **(d) Exploitation of the derived work.** Art. 4(1)(b) also requires that the reproduction of a translated, arranged, adapted or altered program is to be regarded as an act requiring the authorization of the rightholder. In contrast to the Database Directive (art. 5(e)), there is no explicit indication that other acts, such as distribution, rental, communication to the public or translation of an altered or translated work, are to be regarded as within the exclusive rights of the rightholder. **(e) Rights of creators of derivative works.** Art. 4(1)(b) states that the rightholder's exclusive right to control the reproduction of an altered computer program should operate without prejudice to the rights of the person who alters the program. Translations, adaptations and arrangements seem here to be encompassed within the concept of 'alteration'. Member States should therefore confer copyright protection upon the creator of the derivative work as long as it meets the relevant standards of originality and eligibility. Member States thus may not apply to computer programs a rule that there can be no copyright protection for works which infringe copyright in other works to such situations.

4. Distribution (para. 1(c)). (a) General. Art. 4(1)(c) requires that Member States confer on rightholders a right to control distribution of computer programs, and copies, including the rental thereof. The provision requires Member States to treat this right as exhausted by the first sale of each copy. Subsequent Directives have required Member States to give similar rights to rightholders in other copyright works, though the provisions differ in detail (arts. 1, 3 and 9 of the Rental Right Directive; art. 5 of the Database Directive; art. 4 of the Information Society Directive). **(b) Distribution.** Art. 4(1) (c) refers to 'any form of distribution to the public, including the rental, of the original computer program or of copies thereof'. An uncontroversial example of distribution to the public would be the sale of a copy of the program through a shop. The text of the Directive makes it clear that 'distribution' includes rental, and from the legislative history it seems that 'distribution' also includes licensing, lease and importation (Initial Proposal, art. 4(c), Amended Proposal, art. 4(c)). **(c) To the public.** There is no definition of 'the public' in the context of the Computer Programs Directive. However, the transfer of copies by a manufacturer to a wholesaler for re-sale should be regarded as a 'distribution to the public'. The ECJ has, in interpreting the right of communication of a work to the public under art. 3 of the Information Society Directive, referred to its own statement in a previous decision under the Satellite and Cable Directive to the effect that 'the public' refers to an indeterminate number of potential listeners (or television viewers) (*SGAE* (ECJ); *Lagardère* (ECJ)). In this context, the ECJ rejected the submission that the definition of 'the public' should be left to the Member States, although the Commission had earlier expressed its preference for such an approach (see Staff Working Paper on Copyright Review). However, it remains unclear to what extent the definition of what constitutes a 'public' as defined by the ECJ under the Information Society Directive (*SCF*, *ITV Broadcasting and others*, *Svensson*, *BestWater* (ECJ)) also applies under the Computer Programs Directive. **(d) Of the original or of copies.** Although the distribution right enables the copyright owner to control the 'release date' of a program to the public, the distribution right is not merely a right of divulgation, but requires the copyright owner's consent to the release of every single copy (for trade mark law, see *Sebago* (ECJ)). **(e) Electronic distribution.** The legislative history of the Directive suggests that the phrase 'any form' was intended to simplify the draft proposal's language (which referred to distribution by 'sale, licensing, lease, rental and importation') rather than to extend the notion to cover distribution of pure electronic copies which are not embodied in any tangible medium. However, the ECJ has since taken the contrary approach, holding that under certain circumstances the right of distribution of a copy of a computer program is exhausted even where the copy in question is distributed electronically and is not embodied in a tangible medium. To limit the application of the principle of exhaustion to copies that are embodied in a tangible medium would enable the copyright holder to control the resale of electronic copies and to demand further remuneration for each new sale, thus going beyond what is necessary to safeguard the specific subject matter of the intellectual property concerned (*UsedSoft* (ECJ)). However, in such a case, the first acquirer of the copy of the computer program in question must take steps to render his copy unusable at the time of its resale, and the copyright holder is entitled to make use of technical measures in order to ensure that this is done. **(f) Rental.** The rightholder is to be granted the right to rent copies of the program. The Directive defines 'rental' as the making available for use, for a limited period of time and for profit-making purposes, of a computer program or a copy thereof (recital 12). This would cover the activities of any entity which allows customers, on making a payment, to take home computer games for a limited period of time. It would not cover a situation where the entity sold the game to a customer and provided favourable terms for the repurchase of the game from the customer (see *Yapon* (Sweden)). Since rental is a form of distribution, and distribution relates to both copies that are not embodied in a tangible medium as well as copies that are, it appears that the Directive now covers so-called 'electronic rental'. Rental is confined to making available of copies 'for profit-making purposes'. In the Rental Right Directive, a broader notion 'not for direct or indirect economic or commercial advantage' was preferred. **(g) Incidental rental.** Although the Computer Programs Directive does not contain an explicit exemption from liability for persons who rent articles where the essential object of the rental is not the program (see, however, art. 11 TRIPS and art. 7(2)(i) WCT; see also art. 2(3) of the Rental Right Directive: exception for rental and lending rights in relation to buildings and to works of applied art), it is a reasonable interpretation to conclude that, for example, the rental of automobiles is not subject to the rental right provided under the Computer Programs Directive. **(h) Lending not covered.** According to recital 12, the act of 'lending', that is making available for use for a limited period of time gratuitously, is not within the concept of rental, and accordingly remains outside the scope of the Directive. However, the Rental Right Directive requires Member States give a public lending right with respect to copyright-protected works, which would include computer programs.

5. Exhaustion (para. 2). (a) Community exhaustion. The first sale in the Community (or EEA) of a copy of a program by the rightholder owner or with his or her consent exhausts the distribution right in relation to that copy within the Community. This means that thereafter the rightholder cannot object to further distribution of that copy, through resale or further transfer of the same copy. A rightholder may, however, object to rental of any copy which has been distributed, that aspect of the 'distribution right' being expressly saved from exhaustion. Other rights, such as communication to the public, are, on general principles, not exhausted by first sale of a copy (*Coditel I* and *II* (ECJ); recital 33 of the Database Directive; recital 29 of the Information Society Directive; *Laserdisken* (ECJ)). **(b) Sale.** Exhaustion only occurs where there is 'sale … by the rightholder or with his consent'. The restriction of exhaustion to sale contrasts with other EC Directives which refer to the sale 'or other transfer of ownership' (see art. 4(2) of the Information Society Directive). The Austrian Supreme Court has held that exhaustion will occur through transfer in the EEA which is in substance a sale even if the transaction is described in other terms, for example, as a licence (*HWP WIN* (Austria)). To determine whether there has been a sale, the tribunal should examine whether the transfer is permanent, whether the period of use is limited and whether a one-time payment was involved (see *Adobe Systems* (Finland)). This approach has since been confirmed by the ECJ, which has adopted a broad definition of 'sale' as meaning an agreement by which a person, in return for payment, transfers to another person his rights of ownership in an item of tangible or intangible property belonging to him. 'Sale' thus is not limited to the transfer of ownership in a physical program copy, but includes a transaction in which the copyright holder has authorized the downloading of a copy of a computer program from the internet onto a data carrier, and has conferred on the purchaser, whether through a so-called 'user licence agreement' or otherwise, the right to use that copy for an unlimited period, in return for the payment of a fee intended to enable the copyright owner to obtain a remuneration corresponding to the economic value of the copy of the work. This means that exhaustion also applies in those cases of online transmission in which the transfer of use rights has to be regarded as a first sale of a copy of a program. However, in these cases a sale only leads to exhaustion if the first acquirer makes his own copy unusable at the time of its resale, which is not the case when a licence which relates to a greater number of users is unbundled (*UsedSoft* (ECJ); it is unclear whether this only applies to programs of a client-server architecture or to the unbundling of licences with regard to all sorts of computer programs). In addition, whenever there is a 'sale' within the meaning just described, any subsequent acquirer is to be regarded as a lawful acquirer of a copy of a computer program within the meaning of art. 5(1) and hence benefits from the right of reproduction provided for in that provision. Moreover, the German Supreme Court has held that the principle of exhaustion is not affected if the rightholder markets a computer program on DVD in such a way that it can only be used after online attribution of an individual ID, where it is a term of the contract that this ID may not be transferred to third parties, even if the ability of the first purchaser to resell the DVD containing the program is restricted or cannot de facto be exercised because of the limited use possibilities without the ID. The principle of exhaustion does not require the rightholder to grant to the subsequent purchaser a use possibility (*Half-Life 2* (Germany)). However, this position may now have to be re-examined in the light of *UsedSoft*, given the ECJ's insistence in that case that the copyright holder ought not to be allowed to render ineffective the principle of exhaustion by relying on his other exclusive rights. **(c) Legitimate reasons for opposing further commercialization.** In contrast with provisions in the Trademark Directive, the

Community Patent Convention and the Agreement on the Unitary Patent, the Computer Programs Directive makes no reference to the right of a copyright owner to prevent further circulation of goods which have been placed on the market where there are 'legitimate reasons' for opposing such further circulation. The German Supreme Court has held that a copyright owner who disposes of copies to an original equipment manufacturer for sale only with such equipment, exhausts its rights and thus cannot object to further distribution of the software separately from the equipment (*OEM-Version* (Germany)). In *Adobe Systems* (Finland), the Supreme Court of Finland indicated that the principle of exhaustion meant that the copyright owner could not object to further sales of a program by a purchaser who had itself amended the program before resale. **(d) No international exhaustion.** Exhaustion only occurs where the first sale takes place in the 'Community'. Given the harmonizing intent of the Directive, it can be assumed that the inference can be drawn that there is to be no exhaustion from the sale of copies of a program outside the EEA. That is, Member States are not free to apply the principle of international exhaustion, and must give the rightholder the ability to consent to importation into the Community of copies which have only been placed on the market outside the Community (see art. 4(2) of the Information Society Directive; see also *Silhouette* (ECJ); *Micro Leader* (CFI)). However, refusal to permit importation of copies might, in an exceptional case, breach art. 102 of the TFEU (see *Micro Leader* (CFI)).

[Exceptions to the restricted acts]

Article 5

(1) In the absence of specific contractual provisions, the acts referred to in points (a) and (b) of Article 4(1) shall not require authorisation by the rightholder where they are necessary for the use of the computer program by the lawful acquirer in accordance with its intended purpose, including for error correction.

(2) The making of a back-up copy by a person having a right to use the computer program may not be prevented by contract in so far as it is necessary for that use.

(3) The person having a right to use a copy of a computer program shall be entitled, without the authorisation of the rightholder, to observe, study or test the functioning of the program in order to determine the ideas and principles which underlie any element of the program if he does so while performing any of the acts of loading, displaying, running, transmitting or storing the program which he is entitled to do.

1. Exceptions. The Directive requires Member States to recognize that certain specified persons may use computer programs in particular ways without infringing copyright. The exact relationship between these exceptions and those provided for in national law is left unclear. Recital 19 states that the Directive does not affect derogations provided for under national legislation in accordance with the Berne Convention 'on points not covered by this Directive.' Consequently, where the limits of legitimate uses have been carefully defined in the Directive, Member States should not maintain broader exemptions. For example, since art. 5(2) refers to the making of back-up copies in certain circumstances, Member States should not apply private use defences from national law to cover the making of back-up copies in other cases (see Report on the Computer Programs Directive; Explanatory Memorandum to the Amended Proposal of the Computer Programs Directive; *Mars/Teknowledge* (UK)).

2. Act necessary to execute intended use of program (para. 1). (a) General. Member States are required to provide that a user does not infringe where he reproduces or alters a program where this is necessary to use the program for its intended purpose (see art. 6(1) of the Database Directive). In the absence of such a provision, a purchaser of a program would have to rely on an 'implied licence' to avoid infringing copyright when they simply load or run the program. As well as permitting reproduction, the exception also enables the user (or their nominee) to alter the program, for example to remove so-called 'bugs', but not to 'maintain' the program in any manner. Moreover, the exception is limited in four ways: firstly, it only justifies acts which are 'necessary' for the use of the computer program for its intended purpose; second, it is only available where the acts are necessary to achieve the program's 'intended purpose'; third, it is only available to facilitate the intended purposes of a 'lawful acquirer'; and, finally, the exception subject to express contractual restriction. **(b) Necessity of act.** The act must be 'necessary' to enable the achievement of the 'intended purpose'. The use of the term 'necessary' can be contrasted with the term 'indispensable' used in relation to art. 6 and, also, the terms of art. 5(1) of the Information Society Directive, permitting reproductions 'whose sole purpose is to enable … lawful use'. From this, it can be inferred that 'necessity' is an objective requirement (in contrast to 'sole purpose'), but that it does not require that the intended purpose can only be effected by doing a restricted act (as 'indispensable' might). The requirement seems thus to require that reproduction or alteration be practically necessary, as opposed to absolutely essential or merely convenient. This view is consistent with recital 13 which indicates that the exception covers reproductions which are 'technically necessary' (as opposed to absolutely essential) for the use of the program. **(c) Intended purpose of program.** Although the English version of the Directive is not totally clear as to whose 'intention' is relevant (the referent of the 'it' in the phrase 'its intended purpose' could be the acquirer), recital 13 refers to the 'intended purpose' of the program itself. Consequently, German courts have taken the view that the Directive's 'intended purpose' was meant to be defined so as to take account of the interests of both author and user (*Dongle* (Germany)). During the legislative process, it was decided that the exact scope of determination of the 'intended purpose' would be left to be decided by the courts of the Member States in individual cases. Assuming that the intended purpose of a program is to be determined objectively, rather than solely from the viewpoint of the acquirer, relevant factors appear to be: any agreement between rightholder and acquirer (see recital 34 of the Database Directive, allowing uses 'for the purposes and in the way set out in the agreement with the rightholder'); the inherent character and structure of the program; how the product is advertised or presented to the purchaser or licensee by the copyright owner or authorized manufacturer or distributor; how the product has historically been used by consumers; whether the acquirer has made clear to the seller or copyright owner any specific purposes that the acquirer has in mind; the cost of the program, and any contractual obligations relating to the provision of services. In the case of a mass-marketed program, the intended purpose is thus likely to be determined primarily by the copyright owner when it decides the manner in which the program is presented as an article of commerce. For example, if a computer program is sold with a dongle, a tribunal is unlikely to infer that the intended purpose of the program includes use without the dongle (*Dongle* (Germany)). Similarly, if a program is sold in 'versions' then it is unlikely that a tribunal would regard it as acceptable for the acquirer to modify one version to achieve the effects of a later one. In contrast, where software is created for a specific user, the 'intended purpose' is likely to be determined by reference to what the parties expressly agreed or what a reasonable bystander considers both parties to understand. If the program is very expensive, this intended purpose might include the adaptation of the program so that it works with different hardware or other applications, or so that it works more efficiently. Where copies of a computer program are sold and distributed electronically, the downloading of a copy by a purchaser onto his computer constitutes an act of reproduction that is necessary for the use of the program in accordance with its intended purpose (*UsedSoft* (ECJ)). **(d) Lawful acquirer.** The relevant acts must be done with a view to enabling the lawful acquirer to effect the intended purpose. Importantly, the relevant acts may be carried out by a third party, without any specific authorization but the lawful acquirer's (see. art. 6(1)(a)) as long as they are necessary for the lawful acquirer to use the computer program as was intended. The concept of 'lawful acquirer' seems to cover a purchaser, renter, licensee from the rightholder, as well as persons who purchase copies legitimately in circulation (in accordance with art. 4(1)(c); see also Report on the Computer Programs Directive). Other provisions of the Directive (arts. 5(2), (3), 6(1)(a)) use different terminology, that is, a person having 'a right to use'; and other Directives, such as art. 6(1) of the Database Directive, the term 'lawful user.' The notion of 'lawful acquirer' may be broader in some important respects than these other provisions, since legality is only assessed in relation to acquisition rather than conditions of use. Moreover, a person who has legally purchased a copy of a computer program for which the distribution right is exhausted (i.e. 'used' software) falls within the ambit of 'lawful acquirer' (see *UsedSoft* (ECJ)). A purchaser of a computer program in Japan will be a lawful acquirer under UK law even if the licence accompanying the sale purports only to permit use of the program in Japan (see *Sony/Owen* (UK)). **(e) Contrary stipulation.** Art. 5(1) states that the exception operates in 'the absence of specific contractual provisions'. Recital 13 (recital 17 of the Computer Programs Directive (old version)), in contrast, states that 'the acts of loading and running necessary for the use of a copy of a program which has been lawfully acquired, and the act of correction of its errors, may not be prohibited by contract'. Consequently, the owner of the copyright in a computer program may not prevent, by relying on the licensing agreement, the person who has obtained that licence from performing the acts of loading and running necessary for the use of the computer program (*SAS Institute* (ECJ)). This is in line with the recital that allows contractual stipulations in other situations, so that loading, running and error correction may not be prohibited by contract, but other acts may be (see Report on the Computer Programs Directive). The recital states that contractual stipulations include those made 'when a copy of the program has been sold', but the question of whether conditions encountered by a purchaser in documentation accompanying a program that is only learned of after sale has occurred are contractually binding must remain one of national law. **(f) Error correction.** Art. 5(1) refers to 'error correction' as an act within the scope of the article. During the legislative process, it was suggested that acts necessary for 'maintenance' be expressly permitted, but concerns existed that such a broad term might imply that acquirers were to be regarded generally as entitled to perform acts to improve the program.

3. Back-up copies (para. 2). This article requires Member States to prohibit the use of contract to prevent the making of a 'back-up copy' where the making of such a copy is necessary for the use of the program. **(a) Making the copy.** The making of the copy itself would constitute a restricted act under art. 4(1)(a) but fall within the exception mandated by art. 5(1) if it was necessary for the use of the program. The Commission has stated that the notion of back-up is intended to mean 'for security reasons' (see Report on the Computer Programs Directive). It seems that making such a copy will always be necessary to ensure continued use of a program unless either (i) there is no risk of corruption of, damage to, or loss of a program or (ii) the provider undertakes to supply replacement copies should the original become damaged. The English courts have held that it will rarely be necessary to make a back-up copy of a program sold on CD-ROM (see *Sony/Owen* (UK); *Sony/Ball* (UK)). The Commission has emphasized that only one copy is permitted for this purpose (see Report on the Computer Programs Directive). Where a program is widely available commercially, there seems no reason why the back-up copy should be made from the specific original copy supplied to the user if it is more convenient to make the copy from another source. Although the necessity to make a copy must relate to the lawful acquirer, there also seems to be no reason why a third party should not be authorized by that person to make the copy for them. **(b) Contractual variation invalid.** Art. 5(2) merely ensures that this right cannot be restricted further by contract. A contractual provision limiting the right to make a back-up copy is null and void (art. 8).

4. Observation, study and testing of program (para. 3). (a) General. Together with art. 6, art. 5(3) contains exceptions designed to enable computer program users to gain access to the unprotected ideas underlying the program (*SAS Institute* (ECJ, AG [92]). According to art. 5(3) of the Directive, Member States must provide an exception entitling a person to observe, study or test the functioning of the program in order to determine the ideas and principles which underlie any element of the program. This has been referred to as the 'black box' reverse-analysis provision. The exception is subject to three conditions: first, it only applies to a person having 'a right to use' a copy of a computer program; secondly, it only covers acts of observation, study or testing the functioning of the program in order to determine the ideas or principles which underlie any element; and thirdly, it only applies where the acts occur 'while performing' acts of loading, displaying, running, transmitting or storing the program which the user is entitled to be doing. **(b) Observe, study or test.** The exemption permits observation, study and testing of a program. The reason why these purposes might, absent this exception, render acts such as running the program infringing acts is because the user may only be permitted to carry out those acts in order to achieve the intended purpose of the program (art. 5(1)). Thus, as soon as the user has another purpose, the act of loading or running the program to achieve that purpose may become a restricted act of reproduction under art. 4(1)(a). Effectively, this exemption allows the user to adopt a secondary purpose. **(c) In order to determine the ideas or principles which underlie any element.** The exemption is confined to observation, studying and testing a program to determine ideas and principles which underlie any element of it. Ideas and principles are themselves unprotected (art. 1(2), recital 11). The exemption would not appear to justify the accessing of source code: *SAS Institute* (ECJ)). **(d) By a person having 'a right to use'.** The exception is only available to a person having a 'right to use' the program. A company that has purchased copies of a computer program can be regarded as the licensee having 'the right to use' the program, even though the party who indicated assent to the click-wrap agreement preceding the installation of the program was an individual human employee (*SAS Institute* (UK, Court of Appeal, 2013)). **(e) While performing specified acts which he is entitled to do.** The exemption only applies when the observation and so on takes place while performing any of the acts of loading, displaying, running, transmitting or storing the program which he is entitled to do. The ECJ has drawn a distinction between the 'acts' that are permitted, explicitly or by virtue of art. 5(1), and the 'purpose' for which those acts are done: as long as the 'acts' (reproduction, translation, etc.) are permitted by the licence (or art. 5(1)), then a user can claim the benefit of the art. 5(3) exception even if the purpose of undertaking the acts goes beyond what is formally permitted by the licence terms (*SAS Institute* (ECJ)). Where a licence allowed the loading and running of a program but purported to limit such acts to those carried out for 'non-production purposes', the exemption applied such that the licensee could run the program with a view to making and testing the operation of a program which achieved the same ends (*SAS Institute* (UK, High Court, 2013; UK, Court of Appeal, 2013)). **(f) Contrary stipulation.** Art. 8 states that any contractual provision contrary to art. 5(3) shall be null and void. Although contractual restrictions determine when a person has a right to use the software, and the acts they may undertake, conditions as to the purpose or use of a program that purport (explicitly or implicitly) to prevent the study and observation of the program are unenforceable.

[Decompilation]

Article 6

(1) The authorisation of the rightholder shall not be required where reproduction of the code and translation of its form within the meaning of points (a) and (b) of Article 4(1) are indispensable to obtain the information necessary to achieve the interoperability of an independently created computer program with other programs, provided that the following conditions are met:

    (a) those acts are performed by the licensee or by another person having a right to use a copy of a program, or on their behalf by a person authorised to do so;

    (b) the information necessary to achieve interoperability has not previously been readily available to the persons referred to in point (a); and

    (c) those acts are confined to the parts of the original program which are necessary in order to achieve interoperability.

(2) The provisions of paragraph 1 shall not permit the information obtained through its application:

    (a) to be used for goals other than to achieve the interoperability of the independently created computer program;

    (b) to be given to others, except when necessary for the interoperability of the independently created computer program; or

    (c) to be used for the development, production or marketing of a computer program substantially similar in its expression, or for any other act which infringes copyright.

(3) In accordance with the provisions of the Berne Convention for the protection of Literary and Artistic Works, the provisions of this Article may not be interpreted in such a way as to allow its application to be used in a manner which unreasonably prejudices the rightholder's legitimate interests or conflicts with a normal exploitation of the computer program.

1. Decompilation. (a) General. Art. 6 permits a person, in specified circumstances and subject to a number of conditions, to reproduce and translate the code of a program in order to obtain information necessary to achieve interoperability, and to use the information thus obtained for this purpose. The aim of the provision is to prevent the exclusive rights conferred on the copyright holder in accordance with art. 4 from inhibiting other persons from creating programs that are technically compatible with, inter alia, the computer program in question. No such provision was made in the Initial Proposal of the Computer Programs Directive, and the debate over what form, if any, such a provision should take occupied most of those involved in the legislative process. **(b) History.** Those who opposed such a provision feared that it might offer competitors opportunities to investigate and appropriate ideas underlying a program, and the limited form of the exception is explicable by a desire to meet some of those concerns. In its Report on the Computer Programs Directive, the Commission has claimed that 'the balance found then appears to be still valid today'. The Staff Working Paper on Copyright Review, however, recognizes that the provision may be insufficient and states that 'there is a need to reflect on this issue in the light of the evolution of computing networks'. But so far, no attempts have been made to this effect. Moreover, it seems worth noting that there is hardly any case law relating to the boundaries of permissible decompilation.

2. Conditions (para. 1). (a) Decompilation. It should be noted from the outset that the acts permitted are limited to 'reproduction of the code and translation of its form'. The aim is to facilitate copying of the object code of the computer program and its 'decompilation' into 'pseudo source code'. Some national laws go beyond this, while others are narrower in scope; the Commission was particularly critical of the latter (see Report on the Computer Programs Directive). **(b) 'Interoperability'.** The defence only applies where the acts are indispensable to obtain information necessary to achieve 'interoperability'. Recital 10 defines 'interoperability' as 'the ability to exchange information and mutually to use the information which has been exchanged', and indicates that the particular form of interoperability of relevance is the functional interconnection and interaction between software and hardware that permit such software and hardware to work with other software and hardware. Although art. 6(1) itself only refers to interoperability of an independently created computer program with other programs, the context suggests that this includes interoperability between software and hardware (see Staff Working Paper on Copyright Review). In *Microsoft* (CFI), the concept of 'two-way' interoperability used by the Commission was held to be consistent with that envisaged in the Directive, being a degree of interoperability which would enable competing software products to exchange information with and make use of information from Microsoft's corresponding products; Microsoft's contention that the requirement of interoperability under the Directive was limited to 'one-way' interoperability, which would be achieved if all the functionality of the competing software product could be accessed from Microsoft's own products, was rejected. **(c) Of an independently created program with other programs.** The exemption only applies where decompilation takes place in order to achieve interoperability of an 'independently created computer program' with other programs. It appears implicit that the program for which interoperability is being sought must pre-exist or at the very least have been conceived sufficiently to comprise preparatory design material before the user begins to decompile the target program (see Report on Computer Programs Directive). Most importantly, however, the defence is not confined to decompilation in order to gain information necessary to achieve interoperability with the decompiled program itself, but extends also to actions necessary to achieve interoperability with 'other programs'. Thus the defence might permit decompilation of parts of a rightholder's copyright program (such as an operating system) as part of a process of creating a program to compete with that of the rightholder (e.g. another operating system) and which was compatible technically with other programs (such as applications) which hitherto had interfaced with the rightholder's program. **(d) The information must be necessary to achieve interoperability.** Decompilation is only permitted to obtain the information 'necessary' to achieve the interoperability required. According to art. 6(1) (c), the only information which is necessary for interoperability relates to the parts of the original program which are necessary to achieve interoperability, and thus the exemption is confined to acts of decompilation (or more specifically, reproduction and translation) of these parts. In *Microsoft* (CFI), the interoperability information which Microsoft was ordered by the Commission to disclose to its competitors took the form of detailed specifications for all the protocols implemented in Windows work-group server operating systems and used by Windows work-group servers to deliver file and print services and group and user administration without, however, including Microsoft's own implementation of those specifications, in particular the internal structure or source code of its products. **(e) Decompilation must be indispensable.** Decompilation is only permitted where it is 'indispensable' to obtain the relevant information. In effect, decompilation must be the only way of obtaining the information. This requirement effectively requires the user to exhaust other avenues for achieving interoperability (or that it be obviously pointless to pursue such alternative avenues). If the relevant information has been made available, for example in manuals, or can be accessed without decompilation, then decompilation is not to be regarded as 'indispensable'. If a contract provides that the copyright holder will supply such information on reasonable terms, decompilation may well be regarded as not being 'indispensable' to obtain the information. This is again expressed in the limiting condition of para. 1(b). However, there is no consensus amongst commentators as to whether it is always necessary to apply to the copyright owner for the information before decompilation can be regarded as indispensable. Such a requirement might place the user at a commercial disadvantage, as well as introduce undesirable delays. **(f) Persons entitled to decompile (para.**

1(a)). Moreover, decompilation is only permitted if the three conditions of paras. 1(a)-(c) are met. First, according to para. 1(a), the exception conferred by art. 6 is limited to acts which are performed by the licensee or by another person having a right to use a copy of a program, or on their behalf by a person authorized to do so. **(g) Information necessary is not readily available (para. 1(b))**. Secondly, para. (1)(b) further states that decompilation is only permissible if the information necessary to achieve interoperability has not previously been 'readily available' (in the French version 'facilement et rapidement accessibles'). This additional condition seems superfluous, given the general limitation of the decompilation provision. If the relevant information is 'readily available', it then likewise appears not to be 'indispensable' to decompile in order to obtain the information. Moreover, even if the information was not previously readily available, that does not mean that the user can legitimately decompile to obtain the information. Rather, for this to be permitted under the exemption, this act must still be 'indispensable'. However, in its reference to the information 'previously' having been made available, the article may suggest that the user is not required to approach the rightholder and negotiate. **(h) Acts confined to the parts of the original program which are necessary to achieve interoperability (para. 1(c))**. Rightholders feared that users might take advantage of art. 6 in order to decompile the whole code of the protected program while searching for interface information. Therefore, para. 1(c) limits the acts of decompilation permitted by art. 6 to those parts of the original program which are necessary to achieve interoperability. While in most cases, this clearly does not allow the user to decompile the whole program on the one hand, on the other hand, it can be argued that the user may decompile more than just the program code which implements a particular interface. The reason is that in order to achieve the interoperability desired, the user who decompiles another computer program must first of all find the relevant parts of the program code that implement the relevant interface information.

3. Conditions on the use of the information obtained by decompilation (para. 2). (a) General. While decompilation is permitted only where it is necessary to achieve interoperability, and this only if the three additional conditions as laid down in paras. 1(a)-(c) are met, users are subject to three conditions on how they can use and deal with the information so obtained. Thus while copyright law does not normally prevent use or dissemination of information, this Directive requires Member States to treat information obtained through this statutory permission as usable only for that limited purpose. **(b) Restrictions.** The relevant restrictions on use of the information are: first, that it should not be used for goals other than to achieve the interoperability of the independently created computer program; secondly, that it should not to be given to others, except when necessary for the interoperability of the independently created computer program; and thirdly, the information should not be used for the development, production or marketing of a computer program substantially similar in its expression, or for any other act which infringes copyright (see *Société Nomai* (France)). The Directive does not, however, explain the nature of the obligation thus imposed on the decompiler. Most Member States have merely duplicated the article, thus providing no insight into how they understand the nature of the obligation. Of those that have attempted to deal with the issue, some jurisdictions, such as the UK and Spain, appear to treat the obligations as regards use of the information as conditions for the operation of the defence, so that legitimate acts of decompilation retrospectively become illegitimate if the information is later used for a forbidden purpose. The Czech Republic in contrast, implements art. 6(2) as requiring the imposition of a distinct legal obligation on the acquirer of information under the exception.

4. The 'three-step' test (para. 3). Although the decompilation exception is limited by a number of conditions (and thus applies only 'in certain special cases' in accordance with art. 9(2) BC), art. 6(3) also indicates that the provisions of art. 6 are not to be interpreted in such a way as to allow the exception to be used in a way which 'unreasonably prejudices the rightholder's legitimate interests or conflicts with a normal exploitation of the computer program'. Although this purports to implement the Berne Convention, the use of the term 'rightholder' rather than 'author' anticipates art. 13 TRIPS. While the article may seem somewhat superfluous (and recital 15 suggests that acts that comply with art. 6(1) are legitimate and fair), the Commission's Report on the Computer Programs Directive criticizes those countries which have failed to implement the limitation explicitly, observing that this 'could lead to unreasonable detriment to the rightholder'.

5. Contractual variation invalid. Art. 8 specifies that any contractual provision contrary to art. 6 shall be null and void. A contract which states that the user must not decompile would therefore not be enforced. It is unclear how a court should treat a contract which supplies relevant information for interoperability but states that it is confidential and must not be used without prior authorization, or which requires a payment of a fee for use of such information.

6. Competition law. The provisions are supplemented by the general rules on competition in the Treaty and national law (see recital 17), in particular art. 102 TFEU. Given that the copyright owner's rights are limited in favour of interoperability by art. 6, whether the copyright owner is dominant or not, it has been held that the refusal by an undertaking in a dominant position to supply interoperability information may constitute an abuse of its dominant position where exceptional circumstances exist. This occurs particularly where (a) the refusal relates to information indispensable to the exercise of a particular activity on a neighbouring market; (b) the refusal is of such a kind as to exclude any effective competition on the neighbouring market; (c) the refusal prevents the appearance of a new product for which there is potential consumer demand; and (d) where the refusal is not objectively justified (*Microsoft* (CFI); *IMS Health* (ECJ)).

[Special measures of protection]

Article 7

(1) Without prejudice to the provisions of Article 4, 5 and 6, Member States shall provide, in accordance with their national legislation, appropriate remedies against a person committing any of the following acts:

(a) any act of putting into circulation a copy of a computer program knowing, or having reason to believe, that it is an infringing copy;

(b) the possession, for commercial purposes, of a copy of a computer program knowing, or having reason to believe, that it is an infringing copy;

(c) any act of putting into circulation, or the possession for commercial purposes of, any means the sole intended purpose of which is to facilitate the unauthorised removal of circumvention of any technical device which may have been applied to protect a computer program.

(2) Any infringing copy of a computer program shall be liable to seizure in accordance with the legislation of the Member State concerned.

(3) Member States may provide for the seizure of any means referred to in point (c) of paragraph 1.

1. General. Art. 7(1) requires Member States to provide appropriate remedies against a person committing specified acts 'in accordance with their national legislation'. Given that Directives are a form of European legislation designed to give freedom to Member States as to the means of implementation (art. 288 TFEU) this qualification may seem redundant. Nevertheless, the article recognizes that Member States have hitherto treated those involved in dealing in infringing works through different provisions, some civil, some administrative and some criminal, and art. 7 effectively clarifies that the choice of such avenues remains a matter for Member States. The general provision gives little indication as to when such measures will be regarded as 'appropriate' (see also art. 12 of the Database Directive). In contrast, art. 8 of the Information Society Directive requires 'effective, proportionate and dissuasive' remedies. More specific remedies are now prescribed by the Enforcement Directive, but these only apply to works protected under the Information Society Directive but not to computer programs protected under the Computer Programs Directive. This is clearly an existing lack of harmonization.

2. Putting into circulation; possession (secondary infringement, paras. 1(a) and (b)). Member States are required to provide appropriate remedies against persons who execute certain acts with 'infringing copies', knowing that the copies are infringing. Nothing is said about what amounts to an 'infringing copy' but the term must be taken, at the very least, to encompass any copy made in breach of art. 4(1)(a). In both cases, the remedies need only be available against persons who 'know, or have reason to believe' the copy is infringing (see art. 6 of the Information Society Directive, which refers to persons carrying out acts 'in the knowledge, or with reasonable grounds to know'). The relevant acts are any act of putting into circulation a copy (art. 7(1)(a)) and the possession, for commercial purposes, of a copy (art. 7(1)(b)). 'Putting into circulation' would certainly cover sale, importation and distribution, and may possibly also encompass rental. It is not obvious what this adds to the obligation under art. 4(1)(c), but perhaps an infringing copy of a computer program might be put into circulation by acts of making available or communication to the public that might not count as 'distribution'. 'Possession, for commercial purposes' would cover possession with a view to sale or rental for profit, but also possession with a view to using the program as part of a business enterprise. Although the primary targets of such provisions are commercial pirates, that is, persons who participate knowingly in trade in infringing copies, it should be noted that the provisions are not limited to such cases, and could cover, for example, businesses which are aware that employees are working with illicit copies of copyright-protected software on their computers.

3. Technological protection measures (para. 1(c)). (a) General. In recognition of the fact that many developers of computer programs use technical measures, such as dongles, to protect the work from being copied or used for unauthorized purposes, Member States are also required to provide appropriate remedies against trade in mechanisms intended to circumvent such measures. More specifically, art. 7(1)(c) requires Member States to provide remedies against any act of putting into circulation, or the possession for commercial purposes of, any means the sole intended purpose of which is to facilitate the unauthorized removal or circumvention of any technical device which may have been applied to protect a computer program. Anti-circumvention protection according to art. 7 of the Computer Programs Directive is a special law with regard to, and remains unaffected by, the general anti-circumvention protection contained in art. 6 of the Information Society Directive. The latter does therefore not apply to computer programs. In the case of videogames, however, it seems that the general anti-circumvention provisions under art. 6 of the Information Society Directive, rather than specific provisions found in art. 7 of the Computer Programs Directive, will be applicable, as videogames are to be treated as complex multimedia works protected under the Information Society Directive, rather than solely as computer programs (*Nintendo and Others* (ECJ)). **(b) Any technical device.** The provision only applies where a 'technical device' has been applied to protect a computer program. The undefined concept of 'technical device' should be contrasted with the much more elaborate concept and definition of 'technological measure' in art. 6(3) of the Information Society Directive. Under art. 7(1)(c), it is only required that the technical device in issue 'protects' a program. It is not required that the device be applied to the program. It might equally be incorporated in the hardware with which the program interacts (*Sony/Ball* (UK)). **(c) The prohibited acts.** The remedies need only relate to the act of putting into circulation, or to the possession for commercial purposes of, circumvention means (and the scope of these acts can be assumed to be equivalent to those under art. 7(1)(a) and (b)). Art. 7(1)(c) does not provide explicitly for protection against the act of circumvention itself. In this respect it is to be contrasted with art. 6(1) of the Information Society Directive, which does cover acts of circumvention when done knowingly. It might also be questioned whether a Member State that merely implements art. 7(1)(c) complies with WCT art. 11, which requires effective remedies 'against the circumvention'. **(d) Circumvention means.** Member States need only provide remedies against possession or dealing with circumvention means, that is, 'any means the sole intended purpose of which is to facilitate the unauthorised removal or circumvention' of the device. The term 'any means' is clearly intended to be broad and would cover 'devices, products or components' (the phrase used in art. 6(2) of the Information Society Directive), but would not appear to cover the provision of services. In *Adobe Systems* (Finland), the Supreme Court of Finland held that the distribution of written instructions which enabled a purchaser to install program updates did not amount to distribution of a device for circumventing the protection of a program contrary to the terms of the Finnish Copyright Act. As the Directive refers to 'means' to circumvent a device, this decision should not be regarded as an authoritative application of art. 7(1)(c) of the Directive. **(e) Sole intended purpose.** The provision only applies to means 'the sole intended purpose' of which is circumvention. If the relevant means has a second intended purpose, other than one that is so insignificant as to be regarded as 'de minimis', the prohibition is not engaged. Nor, where there is a secondary purpose, is the article engaged even if the device is promoted or marketed as suitable as a circumvention device (see art. 6(2) of the Information Society Directive). **(f) Permitted uses.** The prohibition on possession and distribution of 'circumvention means' seems to apply to any means intended to circumvent a device irrespective of whether such acts of circumvention may themselves be done in order to carry out acts that do not require authorization, such as the making of a back-up copy (where that is necessary). In such circumstances the 'sole intended purpose' of the device remains circumvention, and circumvention is 'unauthorised'. The provision is not limited to situations where the person 'knows or has reason to believe that the means will be used to make infringing copies' (see *Sony/Ball* (UK)).

4. Seizure (paras. 2 and 3). Member States are required to provide for seizure of any infringing copy of a computer program. The person from whom the infringing copy is seized need not necessarily be an infringer. This seems justified since it is hardly possible to use a copy of a protected computer program without committing one of the acts reserved to the rightholder in art. 4. However, the procedure by which seizure is effected, and circumstances in which it is to be available, are in other respects left to the legislation of the Member State concerned. The Directive also permits Member States to provide for seizure of circumvention means within the meaning of art. 7(1) (c). This might, perhaps, be regarded as an attempt to prompt Member States to apply seizure provisions to such circumvention means. These remedial provisions should now be seen in the light of the much more far-reaching Enforcement Directive, which, though expressed to be 'without prejudice' to the particular provisions in the Computer Programs Directive relating to the enforcement of rights, requires Member States to provide for seizure of articles infringing intellectual property rights both for the preservation of evidence and as preliminary measures pending trial (see arts. 7 and 9 of the Enforcement Directive).

[Continued application of other legal provisions]

Article 8

(1) The provisions of this Directive shall be without prejudice to any other legal provisions such as those concerning patent rights, trademarks, unfair competition, trade secrets, protection of semi-conductor products or the law of contract.

(2) Any contractual provisions contrary to Article 6 or to the exceptions provided for in Article 5(2) and (3) shall be null and void.

1. Other legal provisions (para. 1). The Directive is intended to leave intact other legal forms of protection for computer programs, and provides a non-exhaustive list of some of those mechanisms: patents, trade marks, unfair competition, trade secrets, protection of semi-conductor products or the law of contract. The most important of these is probably the patent system of Member States that are all parties to the European Patent Convention. While art. 52 of the Convention excludes computer programs 'as such' from being patented, patents are available for inventions which are implemented by computers and embodied in computer programs, as long as such inventions meet the relevant criteria of novelty and inventiveness.

2. Mandatory provisions (para. 2). In derogation from the general position, namely that the Directive does not prejudice the law of contract, art. 8 requires Member States to treat as null and void any contractual provisions contrary to art. 6 or to the exceptions provided for in art. 5(2) and (3). However, it is not quite clear to what extent the mandatory nature of the provisions of art. 5(2) and (3) and art. 6 of the Computer Programs Directive can be avoided by contractual agreement amongst the parties that the contract should be governed by a law of a non-EU state. The answer to this question might be different depending on whether or not the contract in question has a substantive connection with one or more of the EU Member States. See also art. 3(3), (4) and art. 9 of Regulation Rome II.

Bently/Yin-Harn

[Communication]

Article 9

Member States shall communicate to the Commission the provisions of national law adopted in the field governed by the Directive.

1. General. The communication of national legislation adopted by the Member States helps the Commission to monitor if, and to what extent, each individual Member State has fulfilled its obligations in implementing the Directive into its respective national law.

[Repeal]

Article 10

(1) Directive 91/250/EEC, as amended by the Directive indicated in Annex I, Part A, is repealed, without prejudice to the obligations of the Member States relating to the time-limits for transposition into national law of the Directives set out in Annex I, Part B.

(2) References to the repealed Directive shall be construed as references to this Directive and shall be read in accordance with the correlation table in Annex II.

1. General. The present Directive repeals and replaces Directive 91/250/EEC as amended by the Term Directive. It is a straightforward codification of the text of Directive 91/250/EEC, and its substantive provisions remain unchanged. For the small changes regarding both the articles and the regrouping of the recitals see the Introductory remarks, note 1.

[Entry into force]

Article 11

This Directive shall enter into force on the 20th day following its publication in the *Official Journal of the European Union*.

1. General. The Directive was published in the Official Journal on 5 May 2009 and entered into force on the 20th day following that date.

[Addressees]

Article 12

This Directive is addressed to the Member States.

1. General. According to art. 288 TFEU, Directives are binding, as to the result to be achieved, upon each Member State to which it is addressed, but shall leave to the national authorities the choice of form and methods.

ANNEX I

PART A

Repealed Directive with its amendment
(referred to in Article 10)

Council Directive 91/250/EEC (OJ L 122, 17.5.1991, p. 42)

Council Directive 93/98/EEC (OJ L 290, 24.11.1993, p. 9) Article 11(1) only

PART B

List of time-limits for transposition into national law
(referred to in Article 10)

Directive	Time-limit for transposition
91/250/EEC	31 December 1992
93/98/EEC	30 June 1995

ANNEX II

Correlation table

Directive 91/250/EEC	This Directive
Article 1(1), (2) and (3)	Article 1(1), (2) and (3)
Article 2(1), first sentence	Article 2(1), first subparagraph
Article 2(1), second sentence	Article 2(1) second subparagraph
Article 2(2) and (3)	Article 2(2) and (3)
Article 3	Article 3
Article 4, introductory words	Article 4(1), introductory words
Article 4(a)	Article 4(1), point (a)
Article 4(b)	Article 4(1), point (b)
Article 4(c), first sentence	Article 4(1), point (c)
Article 4(c), second sentence	Article 4(2)
Articles 5, 6 and 7	Articles 5, 6 and 7
Article 9(1), first sentence	Article 8, first paragraph
Article 9(1), second sentence	Article 8, second paragraph
Article 9(2)	Article 1(4)
Article 10(1)	—
Article 10(2)	Article 9
—	Article 10
—	Article 11
Article 11	Article 12
—	Annex I
—	Annex II

ANNEX II
Correlation table

DIRECTIVE 2006/115/EC OF THE EUROPEAN PARLIAMENT AND OF THE COUNCIL

(Rental and Lending Right Directive)

of 12 December 2006 on rental right and

lending right and on certain rights related

to copyright in the field of intellectual property (codified version)

[Introductory remarks]

1. Legislative history. (a) Original Directive. The original Rental and Lending Right Directive of 19 November 1992 was the second European directive in the field of copyright (Rental Right Directive (old version)), following the Computer Programs Directive of 1991. The basis for the Directive was the European Commission's Green Paper on Copyright and the Challenge of Technology (1988), in particular its chapters 2 (piracy) and 4 (distribution right, exhaustion and rental right). After a consultation round the European Commission decided to also include a public lending right and certain rights related to copyright. The original proposal for a Directive was published by the Commission on 5 December 1990 (Initial Proposal of the Rental Right Directive). An amended proposal followed on 29 April 1992 (Amended Proposal of the Rental Right Directive). The Directive was adopted on 19 November 1992 and was to be implemented by Member States by 1 July 1994. A report on public lending right in the Community, as required by art. 5(4), was published by the Commission in the course of 2002 (Report on Public Lending Right). **(b) Codified version.** The Rental Right Directive (old version) was amended several times to reflect changes following from developments in copyright, in particular from directives in the field of copyright from a later date, such as the Information Society Directive. These amendments have been consolidated in a 'codified version' of the Directive that was adopted on 12 December 2006 (Rental Right Directive). The codified version supersedes and replaces the Rental Right Directive (old version). The codified version preserves the content of the acts incorporated in it and nothing more is intended than to bring the amendments together with only such formal amendments as are required by the codification exercise itself (see Explanatory Memorandum, Proposal of the Rental Right Directive (codified version)). In the codified version, the first three recitals of the original Directive have been deleted and the articles have been renumbered.

2. Aim of harmonization. Like the other directives in the field of copyright and related rights, the Directive has its legal basis in arts. 57(2), 66 and 100A of the EC Treaty (now arts. 53, 62 and 114 TFEU). The differences in legal protection between the Member States in respect of rental rights and neighbouring rights were considered to have a negative impact on intra-Community trade and on the functioning of the internal market, in particular in relation to the free movement of goods and services (see recital 5). In reaching this conclusion, the Commission referred to *Christiansen* (ECJ). In that decision, the ECJ held that the varying legislation in the Member States with respect to rental rights was likely to affect intra-Community trade in products such as videocassettes.

3. Scope of Directive. The Directive not only deals with rental and lending rights, as its informal title suggests, but also with neighbouring ('related') rights of performing artists, phonogram producers, film producers and broadcasting organizations. These neighbouring rights are different subject matter, unrelated to rental and lending. The European Commission decided to harmonize these rights in the Rental Right Directive because the rights of lending and rental covered by the Directive would otherwise have created rights with respect to subject matter (e.g. phonograms) not yet protected in all Member States. As such, combining these matters in a single Directive made sense. The Directive covers subject matter that was – and to a certain extent remains – far from harmonized. With respect to public lending for instance, the Directive intended to harmonize national legislation, recognizing that certain Member States had already introduced national arrangements many years before, such as Denmark, Norway, Finland and Sweden, later joined by the United Kingdom, Austria and Germany, while others had not yet codified any national arrangement.

4. Duration of rights. The Rental Right Directive (old version) included a chapter on the duration of the rights granted under the Directive. The chapter was repealed by the Term Directive. In 2011 the Term Directive was amended to extend the duration of certain related rights (see Term Directive, Introductory remarks). The terms of the rights covered by the Rental Right Directive follow the general rules on the duration of copyright and related rights set by the Term Directive.

5. International context. (a) Treaties. Three of the four categories of neighbouring rightholders covered by the Directive (performing artists, phonogram producers and broadcasting organizations) derive international protection from the Rome Convention, and from art. 13 of the TRIPS Agreement. Performers and phonogram producers are also protected by the WPPT. A decision of the Council and representatives of the governments of the Member States authorizing the Council to negotiate a future Convention of the Council of Europe on the protection of neighbouring rights of broadcasting organizations (Recommendation Rec(2002)7) was annulled by the ECJ on the ground that such negotiations fall within the exclusive competence of the European Union (*Commission/Council* (ECJ)). **(b) National treatment.** The Directive does not deal with the application of rights to rightholders outside the European Union. For non-Member States that are a party to the Berne Convention or to a treaty providing a broad rule of national treatment

Krikke

similar to art. 5(1) BC, the rental rights shall automatically be covered. Member States will have to grant rightholders from such countries the rental rights as provided for in the Directive as implemented in the national laws of that Member State, even if such third countries do not provide for a rental right, or not in the form of an exclusive right. The scope of national treatment under the Rome Convention is controversial and the rental right, which is not a minimum right under the Rome Convention, is therefore not clearly covered by national treatment. With respect to neighbouring rights, national treatment is restricted in art. 3(1) TRIPS and art. 4 WPPT to the minimum rights as described in those articles.

[Bibliography]

E. Bonadio and M. Belleza, 'Exceptions to Public Lending Rights and Authors' Remuneration' (2012) JIPL 768-770

H. Comte, 'A Step Towards a Copyright Europe: The EEC Directive of 19 November 1992 on Lending and Rental' (1993) 158 RIDA 2-72

P. Geller, 'The Proposed EC Rental Right: Avoiding Some Berne Incompatibilities' (1992) EIPR 4

S. von Lewinski, 'Rental Right, Lending Right and Certain Neighbouring Rights: The EC Commission's Proposal for a Council Directive' (1991) EIPR 117

S. von Lewinski, 'Public Lending Right: General and Comparative Survey of the Existing Systems in Law and Practice' (1992) 154 RIDA 3-79

S. von Lewinski, 'Rental and Lending Rights Directive' in M. Walter and S. von Lewinski (eds.), *European Copyright Law. A Commentary* (Oxford University Press 2010)

J. Reinbothe, 'The EC Directive on Rental and Lending Rights Related to Copyrights' in H. Cohen Jehoram, *Audiovisual Media and Copyright in Europe* (Kluwer 1994)

J. Reinbothe and S. von Lewinski, 'The EC Rental Directive One Year after its Adoption: Some Selected Issues' (1993) EntLR 169

J. Reinbothe and S. von Lewinski, *The EC Directive on Rental and Lending Rights and on Piracy* (Sweet & Maxwell 1993)

[Preamble]

The European Parliament and the Council of the European Union,

Having regard to the Treaty establishing the European Community, and in particular Articles 47(2), 55 and 95 thereof,

Having regard to the proposal from the Commission,

Having regard to the opinion of the Economic and Social Committee,

Acting in accordance with the procedure laid down in Article 251 of the Treaty,[1]

Whereas:

(1) Council Directive 92/100/EEC of 19 November 1992 on rental right and lending right and on certain rights related to copyright in the field of intellectual property[2] has been substantially amended several times.[3] In the interests of clarity and rationality the said Directive should be codified.

(2) Rental and lending of copyright works and the subject matter of related rights protection is playing an increasingly important role in particular for authors, performers and producers of phonograms and films. Piracy is becoming an increasing threat.

(3) The adequate protection of copyright works and subject matter of related rights protection by rental and lending rights as well as the protection of the subject matter of related rights protection by the fixation right, distribution right, right to broadcast and communication to the public can accordingly be considered as being of fundamental importance for the economic and cultural development of the Community.

(4) Copyright and related rights protection must adapt to new economic developments such as new forms of exploitation;

(5) The creative and artistic work of authors and performers necessitates an adequate income as a basis for further creative and artistic work, and the investments required particularly for the production of phonograms and films are especially high and risky. The possibility of securing that income and recouping that investment can be effectively guaranteed only through adequate legal protection of the rightholders concerned.

(6) These creative, artistic and entrepreneurial activities are, to a large extent, activities of self-employed persons. The pursuit of such activities must be made easier by providing a harmonized legal protection within the Community.

To the extent that these activities principally constitute services, their provision should equally be facilitated by a harmonized legal framework in the Community.

---

1. Opinion of the European Parliament delivered on 12 October 2006 (not yet published in the Official Journal).
2. OJ L 346, 27.11.1992, p. 61. Directive as last amended by Directive 2001/29/EC of the European Parliament and of the Council (OJ L 167, 22.6.2001, p. 10).
3. See Annex I, Part A.

Krikke

(7) The legislation of the Member States should be approximated in such a way as not to conflict with the international conventions on which the copyright and related rights laws of many Member States are based.

(8) The legal framework of the Community on the rental right and lending right and on certain rights related to copyright can be limited to establishing that Member States provide rights with respect to rental and lending for certain groups of rightholders and further to establishing the rights of fixation, distribution, broadcasting and communication to the public for certain groups of rightholders in the field of related rights protection.

(9) It is necessary to define the concepts of rental and lending for the purposes of this Directive.

(10) It is desirable, with a view to clarity, to exclude from rental and lending within the meaning of this Directive certain forms of making available, as for instance making available phonograms or films for the purpose of public performance or broadcasting, making available for the purpose of exhibition, or making available for on-the-spot reference use. Lending within the meaning of this Directive does not include making available between establishments which are accessible to the public.

(11) Where lending by an establishment accessible to the public gives rise to a payment the amount of which does not go beyond what is necessary to cover the operating costs of the establishment, there is no direct or indirect economic or commercial advantage within the meaning of this Directive.

(12) It is necessary to introduce arrangements ensuring that an unwaivable equitable remuneration is obtained by authors and performers who must remain able to entrust the administration of this right to collecting societies representing them.

(13) The equitable remuneration may be paid on the basis of one or several payments an any time on or after the conclusion of the contract.

It should take account of the importance of the contribution of the authors and performers concerned to the phonogram or film.

(14) It is also necessary to protect the rights at least of authors as regards public lending by providing for specific arrangements, However, any measures taken by way of derogation from the exclusive public lending right should comply in particular with Article 12 of the Treaty.

(15) The provisions laid down in this Directive as to rights related to copyright should not prevent Member States from extending to those exclusive rights the presumption provided for in this Directive with regard to contracts concerning film production concluded individually or collectively by performers with a film producer. Furthermore, those provisions should not prevent Member States from providing for a rebuttable presumption of the authorization of exploitation in respect of the exclusive rights of performers provided for in the relevant provisions of this Directive, in so far as such presumption is compatible with the

International Convention for the Protection of Performers, Producers of Phonograms and Broadcasting Organizations (hereinafter referred to as the Rome Convention).

(16) Member States should be able to provide for more far reaching protection for owners of rights related to copyright than that required by the provisions laid down in this Directive in respect of broadcasting and communication to the public.

(17) The harmonized rental and lending rights and the harmonized protection in the field of rights related to copyright should not be exercised in a way which constitutes a disguised restriction on trade between Member States or in a way which is contrary to the rule of media exploitation chronology, as recognized in the Judgment handed down in Société Cinéthèque v. FNCF.[4]

(18) This Directive should be without prejudice to the obligations of the Member States relating to the time-limits for transposition into national law of the Directives as set out in Part B of Annex I,

Have adopted this Directive:

CHAPTER I. RENTAL AND LENDING RIGHT

[Object of harmonization]

Article 1

(1) In accordance with the provisions of this Chapter, Member States shall provide, subject to Article 6, a right to authorize or prohibit the rental and lending of originals and copies of copyright works, and other subject matter as set out in Article 3(1).

(2) The rights referred to in paragraph 1 shall not be exhausted by any sale or other act of distribution of originals and copies of copyright works and other subject matter as set out in Article 3(1).

1. General. The article requires the Member States to provide for exclusive rights to authorize or prohibit the rental or lending of copyrighted works or related subject matter. Although exclusivity is the general rule for both rental and lending, art. 6 allows Member States to derogate from the exclusive nature of the lending right by granting a right to remuneration instead. In addition, art. 1 clarifies that rental and lending rights shall not be exhausted by any sale or other act of distribution.

2. Exclusive rights (para. 1). Para. 1 sets forth the nature of rental and lending rights as exclusive rights and prescribes for which subject matter rental and lending rights shall be provided. **(a) Exclusive nature.** The rental and lending rights are rights to authorize or to prohibit which rights shall

---

4.   Joined cases 60/84 and 61/84, [1985] ECR, 2 605.

belong exclusively to the rightholders. Although art. 1(1) does not explicitly mention exclusivity, a right to authorize or prohibit is by definition an exclusive right. The use of the words 'to authorize or prohibit' was not intended to express a meaning other than the term 'exclusive' used in other articles of the Directive. Both terms express that the rights granted are not mere remuneration rights. The Directive does not set forth how rental and lending rights should be fitted into the system of copyright and neighbouring rights, for example whether the rights should be considered as a distribution right or be granted as separate rights. **(b) Protected subject matter.** Rental and lending rights shall be provided for all originals and copies of copyrighted works and for other subject matter as set forth in art. 3(1), namely, fixations of performances, phonograms and (the original and copies of) first fixations of films. Excluded from the domain of copyrighted works, however, are buildings and works of applied art (see art. 3(2) and art. 3, note 3(a)). The Directive is also without prejudice to the rules on rental of computer programs of the Computer Programs Directive (see art. 4(c) Computer Programs Directive). **(c) Electronic rental or lending.** The making available of protected material by way of electronic data transmission is not dealt with in the framework of this Directive. Art. 1(1) provides that rights should be granted for rental and lending of 'originals' and 'copies' of copyrighted works and other subject matter. This wording suggests the area of application to be that of physical objects. This is in line with the subject matter of the lending right described by the Commission as 'objects ... which incorporate protected works or performances' (Explanatory Memorandum, Initial Proposal of the Rental Right Directive (old version)). This was confirmed by the Commission in its 2002 review of the Directive (Report on Public Lending Right). The electronic domain was considered to be the exclusive domain of the rights owners, as had been clarified in 2001 in art. 3(1) of the Information Society Directive. Nevertheless, the question of whether the Directive covers electronic rental or lending, in particular lending of e-books by public libraries, has resurfaced. In its *UsedSoft* decision, the ECJ ruled in the light of the Computer Programs Directive that downloading of computer programs can be so substantially similar to distribution of physical copies that the exhaustion rule applies. This decision inspired prejudicial questions regarding the lending of e-books by public libraries being posed to the ECJ (*VOB* (Netherlands)).

3. No exhaustion (para. 2). Para. 2 sets forth that the exclusive rental and lending rights shall not be affected by the sale or any other form of distribution of the relevant material. The term 'exhaustion' means that a rightholder can no longer control the further distribution of a copy or original of protected material once it has been brought onto the market with the rightholder's consent (see art. 4 Information Society Directive, note 3). Para. 2 clarifies that rental and lending rights explicitly deviate from this principle. Rental and lending shall remain under the control of the rightholder with respect to all originals and copies of protected material, irrespective of the sale or any further distribution thereof. This also means that when a rightholder has allowed rental in one Member State, he can still prevent the rental of the same material in other Member States (*Laserdisken* (ECJ)). In *Christiansen* and again in *Metronome Musik* the ECJ held that the deviation from the principle of exhaustion with respect to rental and lending is in accordance with EC law.

[Definitions]

Article 2

(1) **For the purposes of this Directive the following definitions shall apply:**

    (a) **'rental' means making available for use, for a limited period of time and for direct or indirect economic or commercial advantage;**

    (b) **'lending' means making available for use, for a limited period of time and not for direct or indirect economic or commercial advantage, when it is made through establishments which are accessible to the public;**

    (c) **'film' means a cinematographic or audiovisual work or moving images, whether or not accompanied by sound.**

(1) **The principal director of a cinematographic or audiovisual work shall be considered as its author or one of its authors. Member States may provide for others to be considered as its co-authors.**

1. General. Para. 1 provides for definitions of the essential terms 'rental' and 'lending'. The definitions are to be read in conjunction with art. 1(1), which reads that such rights of lending and rental are to be provided for originals and copies of copyrighted works and other covered subject matter. Para. 1 also defines the notion of 'film'. Para. 2 sets forth who is to be considered as the author of a cinematographic or audiovisual work.

2. Rental (para. 1). A definition of rental is given in art. 2(1)(a). The definition consists of three criteria that need to be fulfilled in order for an activity to qualify as a rental: the material has to be (i) made available for use; (ii) for a limited period of time; and (iii) for direct or indirect economic or commercial advantage. While the first two criteria also apply to lending, the third criterion distinguishes rental from lending. **(a) Making available for use.** The words 'making available for use' in this article do not refer to the 'right of making available to the public' mentioned in art. 3(1) of the Information Society Directive, which is part of the general right of communication to the public. In the initial phase of the original Directive, it was debated whether lending and rental should be limited to the making available for private use by end users only, or whether use for public purposes should also be covered. Some Member States wanted to explicitly exclude certain forms of making available outside the scope of private use. A specific example was the rental of a film to a film theatre for the public performance of that film to the theatre audience. Other examples were inter library loans, the rental of sheet music for the purpose of broadcasting or public performance and loans of art works between museums for the purpose of an exhibition. However, proposed amendments which either excluded use 'for public presentation and performance' or limited the term 'making available for use' to 'making available for use by an end user' were rejected. Consensus was also not reached on a specification of the examples that should be excluded. The matter was solved by the introduction of recital 10 of the Directive, which sets forth that it is desirable that Member States exclude from the definition of rental and lending certain forms of making available, such as the making available of films or phonograms for public performance or broadcasting, making available for the purpose of exhibition, or making available for on-the-spot reference use. Given the use of the term 'desirable' and the lack of consensus about the examples given, the Member States are not obliged to allow all the types of use mentioned. As the list of examples is not exhaustive, Member States may also exclude similar forms of use from the rental and lending regimes. **(b) For a limited period of time.** The making available should be 'for a limited period of time', as opposed to the use for an unlimited period of time such as in the case of a sale. The duration of the period is therefore irrelevant for the qualification as 'rental' or 'lending', as long as it cannot be considered to be permanent or unlimited. This raises the question of how to qualify a situation that either may or may not be permanent, such as a sale with a right to retransfer or a purchase on approval. According to the German Supreme Court, a purchase on approval is to be qualified as the making available for a limited period of time because the buyer still has the option to return the object within a specified period of time (*Kauf auf Probe* (Germany)). **(c) Commercial nature.** In order to qualify as rental, the making available has to be 'for direct or indirect economic or commercial advantage'. This third criterion is meant to distinguish rental from lending. Lending should not have a commercial purpose. The classic example to show the difference between having or not having a commercial advantage is the rental of CDs or videos by rental shops as opposed to the lending of the same materials by public libraries. There is no further guidance in the Directive as to what is to be considered as direct or indirect advantage, economic or commercial advantage. In the initial proposal, the wording 'for profit making purposes' was used, which was, however, found to be inadequate (Initial Proposal of the Rental Right Directive). In general, any intended economic or commercial gain or advantage will qualify the activity as rental rather than lending. According to the German Supreme Court, the seller in a purchase on approval obviously intends a commercial gain and hence the conditional sale is for an indirect commercial advantage, thus qualifying as rental under the Directive. In a similar case relating to rental of a computer program governed by the Computer Programs Directive, the sale of a computer game with favourable conditions for repurchase was not qualified as rental (*Yapon* (Sweden)). Whether or not an act is or is for economic or commercial gain can be a delicate matter, as follows from *SCF* (ECJ), see art. 8, note 3(b).

3. Lending (para. 1). The definition of lending in art. 2(1)(b) consists of four criteria, each of which needs to be fulfilled. Lending is: (i) the making available for use; (ii) for a limited period of time; (iii) not for direct or indirect economic or commercial advantage; and (iv) made through establishments that are accessible to the public. The first two criteria are also found in the definition of rental, while the last two are meant to distinguish rental from lending. Any activity that meets the first two criteria and also aims at a commercial gain of some sort will be qualified as rental. If there is no such commercial purpose, the activity will be qualified as lending, provided that it is carried out by an establishment that is accessible to the public. **(a) Making available for use.** The definitions do not clarify whether rental and lending is limited to rental and lending to end users for private purposes only. However, according to recital 10 of the Directive it is desirable that certain forms of making available are excluded from rental and lending. One of the specific and non-exhaustive list of examples given is on-the-spot reference use. This example was inserted to accommodate the desire of certain Member States to exempt from the definition of lending the reference use by library visitors on the premises of a public library. Although there is no certainty whether Member States are allowed to ignore these suggested exemptions that are phrased as 'desirable', the legislative history would suggest so (see art. 2, note 2(a)). Recital 10 adds one example that does not leave the Member States any room to manoeuvre: the making available of works between establishments that are accessible to the public does not qualify as 'lending'. Examples may be the lending of materials between libraries, so-called inter library loans and the lending of works of art between museums for the purpose of an exhibition. **(b) For a limited period of time.** See note 2(b). According to the Supreme Court of the Netherlands, an extension of a loan term in a public library loan (for which the user does not pay an additional fee) does not qualify as a new act of lending and does not trigger an additional right to remuneration under art. 6 of the Directive (*Stichting Leenrecht* (the Netherlands)). **(c) Non-commercial nature.** The payment of a fee for lending, either a general library membership fee or a specific fee for the lending of certain material or for late return thereof, does not automatically qualify the activity as rental. Recital 11 of the Directive clarifies that no commercial advantage is deemed to exist where libraries request payment of an amount that does not exceed the operating costs of the lending institution. **(d) Accessible to the public.** In order to qualify as lending, the making available should not only lack a profit-making purpose, it also has to be undertaken by establishments that are accessible to the public. The Directive does not provide guidance as to which establishments are considered to be 'accessible to the public'. The original proposal contained a list of examples of institutions that would qualify, including public libraries, research libraries and school libraries (Initial Proposal of the Rental Right

Directive). This list was not included in the Directive and the Member States did not agree on a definition of 'public'. Art. 5(3), allowing Member States to exempt certain categories of establishments from payment of remuneration, suggests that a rather large number of categories of establishments qualify as being 'accessible to the public'.

4. Film (para. 1). Art. 2(1)(c) contains a definition of the term 'film'. This was felt to be appropriate as the term was much debated and as no international treaties were in place defining such term. For the purposes of the Directive, 'film' is defined as a 'cinematographic or audiovisual work or moving images, whether or not accompanied by sound'. This definition is broad and will in principle govern any film material, whether made for cinema or television or for any other media, and whether or not qualifying as a copyright work and fixed on whichever medium. In practice, the rental and lending rights so far have proven to be relevant mainly for film rental on video, DVD or CD-ROM or similar media, particularly given the fact that rental or lending for the purposes of public performance and broadcasting are generally excluded (see recital 10).

5. Principal director (para. 2). The term 'author' is not defined in the Directive. Art. 2(2) however provides with respect to cinematographic and audiovisual works that for the purposes of this Directive the principal director thereof shall be considered as its author or one of its authors (see art. 2(1) Term Directive). It was thus clarified that, apart from the rights granted to the producer of a film, at least the principal director should be granted rental and lending rights with respect to film works, irrespective of any (further) choices made in national law. Any provision in national legislation which directly allocates these rights by operation of law to the producer of the work violates this rule (*Luksan* (ECJ)). The application in time with respect to this right for principal directors may, however, be limited in time to works created after 1 July 1994 (see art. 11(4)).

[Rightholders and subject matter of rental and lending right]

Article 3

(1) **The exclusive right to authorize or prohibit rental and lending shall belong to the following:**
  (a) **the author in respect of the original and copies of his work;**
  (b) **the performer in respect of fixations of his performance;**
  (c) **the phonogram producer in respect of his phonograms;**
  (d) **the producer of the first fixation of a film in respect of the original and copies of his film.**
(2) **This Directive does not cover rental and lending rights in relation to buildings and to works of applied art.**
(3) **The rights referred to in paragraph 1 may be transferred, assigned or subject to the granting of contractual licences.**

(4) Without prejudice to paragraph 6, when a contract concerning film production is concluded, individually or collectively, by performers with a film producer, the performer covered by this contract shall be presumed, subject to contractual clauses to the contrary, to have transferred his rental right, subject to Article 5.

(5) Member States may provide for a similar presumption as set out in paragraph 4 with respect to authors.

(6) Member States may provide that the signing of a contract concluded between a performer and a film producer concerning the production of a film has the effect of authorizing rental, provided that such contract provides for an equitable remuneration within the meaning of Article 5. Member States may also provide that this paragraph shall apply mutatis mutandis to the rights included in Chapter II.

1. General. Art. 3 designates the rightholders and subject matter of rental and lending rights. Paragraph 1 specifies to which first owners of which subject matter the rights shall be granted, while transfer, assignment and licensing of the rights are addressed in paras. 3 to 6. In para. 2, certain subject matter is specifically excluded from the scope of the Directive.

2. Rightholders (para. 1). Para. 1 provides an exhaustive list of persons to whom exclusive rental and lending rights shall be granted: authors, performers, phonogram producers and film producers. In principle, other persons shall not be granted lending or rental rights, as was confirmed by the ECJ in respect of video producers (*Commission/Portugal II* (ECJ)). This means that a broadcasting organization for instance shall not be granted lending or rental rights unless such organization also qualifies as a film producer or phonogram producer. In art. 2, the Directive provides little guidance for the interpretation of the terms used to describe rightholders and subject matter covered by the Directive. This was a deliberate choice, so as not to interfere with concepts already governed by national laws and international treaties. Only the terms 'film' and 'film producers' are defined in the Directive, as these terms were not yet defined in international treaties. Thus, any other interpretation issue regarding in whom the rental and lending rights shall vest or for which materials such rights should apply, will have to be interpreted in accordance with national laws and in the light of the applicable international treaties, in particular the Berne and Rome Conventions. **(a) Author.** The term 'author' is not defined in the Directive, nor is the term 'works'. However, art. 2(2) does provide that the principal director of a cinematographic audiovisual work shall be considered as its author for the purpose of the Directive (see art. 2, note 5). **(b) Performer.** The term 'performer' is not defined in the Directive. Art. 3(a) of the Rome Convention contains a definition that may aid interpretation: '"performers" means actors, singers, musicians, dancers, and other persons who act, sing, deliver, declaim, play in, or otherwise perform literary or artistic works'. According to art. 9 Rome Convention, Contracting States may extend the protection provided for in this Convention to 'artists who do not perform literary or artistic works'. One of such categories can be found in art. 2(a) WPPT, which adds 'expressions of folklore' to the definition. Apart from the guidance in the international treaties, issues with respect to the terms will have to be settled based on the national laws of the Member States. In a British case (*Experience Hendrix* (UK)), it was argued that the Rental and Lending Directive does not create obligations with respect to dead performers. The argument was that recital 7 (now 5) of the Directive limits the extent of the performing right by identifying the purpose to secure an adequate income as a basis for further creative work, hence no rights would need to be created for already dead performers who are no longer capable of further creative work. This argument was rejected. The court ruled that recital 7 (now 5) of the Directive is to be read as no more than a general justification for conferring rights on performers and not as restricting the group of persons eligible for protection. **(c) Phonogram producer.** The Directive does not define the term 'phonogram producer'. Guidance may be found in art. 3(b) of the Rome Convention, where a 'producer of phonograms' is defined as 'the person who, or the legal entity which, first fixes the sounds of a performance or other sounds' and in art 2(d) WPPT as 'the person, or the legal entity, who or which takes the initiative and has the responsibility for the first fixation of the sounds of a performance or other sounds, or the representations of sounds'. The term 'phonogram' is defined in art. 3(b) of the Rome Convention as: 'any exclusively aural fixation of sounds of a performance or of other sounds'. Art. 2(b) WPPT defines a phonogram as: 'the fixation of the sounds of a performance or of other sounds, or of a representation of sounds, other than in the form of a fixation incorporated in a cinematographic or other audiovisual work'. The term 'representations of sounds' refers in particular to computer recordings based on sound databases as opposed to actual sounds being recorded. A fixation refers to the material object on which the sounds are fixed. There is no limitation of material objects on which a fixation may be made, thus including in principle any kind of object, such as music cassettes, CDs, memory cards or computer hard disks. **(d) Film producer.** Art. 3(1)(d) specifies that rental and lending rights shall be granted to producers of the first fixation of a film in respect of the original and all copies thereof. A clarification is envisaged as to whom shall be regarded as a film producer entitled to rental and lending rights: the wording means to exclude producers of rather simple copies or adaptations of a film, such as copies of cinema film as adapted for video or DVD. With respect to producers of videograms this was confirmed by the ECJ in *Commission/Portugal II*. The ECJ held that Portugal had not correctly implemented art. 2(1) of the Rental Right Directive (old version) (now art. 3(1)) by creating a rental right also in favour of producers of videograms. **(e) No other rightholders or subject matter.** The list of rightholders and subject matter is exhaustive. Hence, in principle no persons other than authors, performers, phonogram producers and film producers shall be entitled to rental or lending rights and only with respect to the described subject matter.

3. Subject matter (paras. 1 and 2). Art. 3(1) specifies four categories of protected subject matter, namely (copyright) works, fixations of performances, phonograms and films. **(a) Excluded subject matter.** Art. 3(2) excludes buildings and works of applied art from the scope of the Directive. The situation where an architect might prohibit the rental of (parts of) a building by the owner is thus avoided, as is a claim in respect of car rental by the designer of the car. The aim of the excluded categories was to not interfere with the regimes for rental of property. As no other purpose was intended, it is argued that the lending and rental regimes do apply when buildings or works of applied art are included in film, photographs or drawings, i.e. in a two-dimensional form.

4. Transfer, assignment and licensing (para. 3). Art. 3(3) provides that rental and lending rights may be transferred, assigned or licensed. The article clarifies that the rights owners to whom rental and lending rights are granted pursuant to art. 3(1) are free to dispose of their rights by way of transfer, assignment or license. It is left up to the Member States to implement these possibilities into their national laws in a way that fits the respective legal systems.

5. Parallel rights (paras. 4, 5 and 6). It may occur that various persons or entities can concurrently exercise exclusive rental and lending rights with respect to the same material. For instance, the composer of a song, the performing artist(s) and the producer of a phonogram containing a fixation of such song will each have the right to authorize or prohibit rental and lending of such fixations. The same may apply to the film producer, screenplay writer, music composer, actors and other rightholders with respect to a film. Paras. 4, 5 and 6 address a few situations where parallel rights exist. **(a) Presumed transfer.** Art. 3(4) provides for a presumed transfer of rental rights to the film producer by performers who have entered into a contract with the film producer concerning the production of a film. Thus, when an actor enters into an agreement with a film producer to play a role in a film, the actor will be presumed to have transferred his rental rights with respect to the film to the producer, even if the contract does not explicitly provide for such transfer. If the actor wishes to retain the rental right, this should be explicitly specified in the agreement. Contracts to which this rule applies may be entered into between individual performers and film producers, or collectively, for instance between unions of performers and a producer or an association of producers. Pursuant to art. 3(5), the Member States may provide for a similar presumed transfer of rights with respect to authors entering into agreements with film producers. While a presumption of transfer is mandatory with respect to performers in a film production, it is left to the Member States to include in their national copyright laws a similar rule of presumption of transfer of authors' rights in a film. In *Luksan* the ECJ considered that the legal instrument of a presumption of transfer to the film producer was devised in order to acquire a balance between the rights and interests of the authors and those of the film producer so as to guarantee that the film producer acquires the rental right in the cinematographic work, while providing that the principal director may freely dispose of the rights which he holds in his capacity as author in order to safeguard his interests. The ECJ held that a presumption of transfer by operation of law is allowed as long as such presumption is not irrebuttable, thus allowing the principal director to agree otherwise. Art. 3(6) allows the Member States to provide (again, without obligation to do so) that a presumption of transfer shall only be effective if the contract between the performer(s) and the film producer(s) provide for an equitable remuneration within the meaning of art. 5 of the Directive. In such case, the presumed transfer of rights shall not have any effect unless the performer is granted a right to remuneration with respect to the rental of the film.

[Rental of computer programs]

Article 4

This Directive shall be without prejudice to Article 4 (c) of Council Directive 91/250/EEC of 14 May 1991 on the legal protection of computer programs.[5]

1. General. The Directive does not affect the rights of rightholders of computer programs granted in art. 4(c) of the Computer Programs Directive. That article provides that the rights owner of a computer program has the right of distribution to the public, including rental, of originals and copies of computer programs. The reference to the Computer Programs Directive seeks to ensure that the Directive does not change or undo the rental right as already provided for in the Computer Programs Directive, which preceded this Directive. Note that Directive 91/250/EEC (Computer Programs Directive (old version)) was repealed and replaced by Directive 2009/25/EC. References to the repealed Directive shall however be construed as references to the current Directive (art. 10 Computer Programs Directive).

2. Rental. One might question whether another regime for rental of computer programs was contemplated, in the Computer Programs Directive, as this Directive uses the wording 'for profit making purposes' (see recital 16) instead of the term 'for direct or indirect economic or commercial advantage'. The definition as used in the Computer Programs Directive was also introduced in the original proposal for the Rental Right Directive (old version), but it was adapted in the course of the legislative process with the

---

5. OJ L 122, 17.5.1991, p. 42. Directive as amended by Directive 93/98/EEC (OJ L 290, 24.11.1993, p. 9).

intention to bring more clarity. A difference in meaning was not intended. If through time the terms should nevertheless develop a different meaning, the interpretation of the term 'rental' under the Directive should not affect the rental rights in respect of computer programs as granted under the Computer Programs Directive. A notable difference between regimes is that the Directive contains certain exceptions to the notion of rental that the Computer Programs Directive does not include, such as the exception of buildings and works of applied art (art. 3(2)) and the possible exclusion of certain forms of making available, such as for public performance or on-the-spot reference use (recital 10). With a view to art. 4, these exceptions cannot automatically apply to the rental of computer programs and works containing computer programs.

3. Rental only. Art. 4 provides that the Directive is without prejudice only to art. 4(c) of the Computer Programs Directive. Thus, while the rental of computer programs needs to be considered in the light of art. 4(c) of the Computer Programs Directive, any other matters covered by the Directive must be deemed to apply also to computer programs, such as the provisions in respect of public lending. Recital 16 of the Computer Programs Directive brings public lending of computer programs outside the scope of that Directive. This does not mean however that there is no public lending right for computer programs, as follows from art. 6(2) of the Directive. This article allows Member States to derogate from the exclusive lending rights with respect to certain works if a remuneration for authors is introduced instead. Computer programs are explicitly mentioned here as a category of works for which Member States may deviate from the exclusive lending right. In other words, an exclusive lending right with respect to computer programs was intended.

[Unwaivable right to equitable remuneration]

Article 5

(1) **Where an author or performer has transferred or assigned his rental right concerning a phonogram or an original or copy of a film to a phonogram or film producer, that author or performer shall retain the right to obtain an equitable remuneration for the rental.**

(2) **The right to obtain an equitable remuneration for rental cannot be waived by authors or performers.**

(3) **The administration of this right to obtain an equitable remuneration may be entrusted to collecting societies representing authors or performers.**

(4) **Member States may regulate whether and to what extent administration by collecting societies of the right to obtain an equitable remuneration may be imposed, as well as the question from whom this remuneration may be claimed or collected.**

Krikke

1. General. Art. 5 seeks to ensure that authors and performers will benefit from their rental rights, taking into account their generally weak bargaining positions in relation to producers. Art. 5 therefore provides for an unwaivable right to remuneration to which authors and performers will remain entitled even after having transferred their rental rights to a producer. The construct of a right to equitable remuneration that cannot be waived is unique to this Directive. The logic of having an assignable exclusive right on the one hand and a right to remuneration that cannot be waived on the other is to guarantee to authors and performers a fair share of the proceeds while ensuring that producers remain able to freely exploit productions. Guidance as to the interpretation of the article can be found in recitals 12 and 13.

2. Scope (para. 1). There are several limitations to the scope of the remuneration right granted to authors and performers. In the first place, art. 5 limits the remuneration right to rental, thus apparently excluding lending. It has however been argued that lending was not meant to be excluded and that it would therefore be correct to apply art. 5 also with respect to lending. In other words, the right to remuneration for public lending would also be unwaivable. Secondly, the right is granted only with respect to phonograms and films, thus excluding (other) copyrighted works and fixations of performances. Apparently, the need to grant to authors and performers an unwaivable right to remuneration was felt to be acute only in the film and phonographic industry. Thirdly, a remuneration right will be retained only if the rental right is transferred to a phonogram or film producer, not in case of a transfer to another party involved in the exploitation.

3. Equitable remuneration. Whether a right to equitable remuneration can indeed offer authors and performers the benefit of their rental right will depend on what is considered to be 'equitable'. The original proposal provided for a right 'to obtain an adequate part of the said payment', referring to the payment for the authorization of the rental. According to recital 13, second sentence, account must be taken of the importance of the contribution of the authors and performers to the phonogram or film. Thus, there should be a connection between the relevance of the contribution and the amount of the remuneration. The term 'remuneration' deviates from the term 'compensation' used in the Information Society Directive. However, in *Luksan* the ECJ held, with reference to its *VEWA* decision, that the notion of 'remuneration' is also designed to compensate authors.

4. Payment methods. Recital 13 of the Directive sets forth that the remuneration may be paid on the basis of one or several payments at any time on or after the conclusion of the contract between author or performer and producer. Thus, it was contemplated that a producer may pay the author or performer an up-front flat fee or several repeated payments.

5. Unwaivable right (para. 2). Para. 2 provides that the right to an equitable remuneration for rental cannot be waived. This provision limits the contractual freedom of parties for the benefit of authors and performers. The ECJ ruled in *Luksan* that Member States may not provide for a presumption of transfer by law in favour of the producer of a cinematographic work, of the right to fair compensation vesting in the principal director of that work, whether that presumption is in irrebuttable terms or may be departed from.

6. Collecting societies (para. 3). Para. 3 stipulates that the administration of the remuneration right may be entrusted to collecting societies (see recital 12). The wording is broad and would seem to allow any construction by which the administration of the right is carried out by any organization that collects revenues on behalf of authors and/or performers. Para. 4 sets forth that the Member States may, without having the obligation to do so, impose the administration of the remuneration right by collecting societies. See art. 1(4) of the Satellite and Cable Directive for a definition of 'collecting society'.

7. Freedom to regulate (para. 4). Member States have the freedom to regulate if and to what extent collecting societies shall administer the equitable remuneration right and who shall be responsible for the payment of the remuneration. This freedom to regulate should however not undermine the purpose of art. 4 to ensure an equitable remuneration, as the ECJ pointed out in *Commission/Portugal II*. The Portuguese legislation was ambiguous as to who would be responsible for paying the remuneration owed to performers on assignment of the rental right, either the film producer or the videogram producer. The effect, according to the ECJ, was a situation which might prevent performers from collecting the remuneration to which they are entitled. Thus, the ECJ held that Portugal had not correctly implemented art. 4 of the Rental Right Directive (old version), in conjunction with art. 2(5) and (7) thereof.

[Derogation from the exclusive public lending right]

Article 6

(1) Member States may derogate from the exclusive right provided for in Article 1 in respect of public lending, provided that at least authors obtain a remuneration for such lending. Member States shall be free to determine this remuneration taking account of their cultural promotion objectives.

(2) Where Member States do not apply the exclusive lending right provided for in Article 1 as regards phonograms, films and computer programs, they shall introduce, at least for authors, a remuneration.

(3) Member States may exempt certain categories of establishments from the payment of the remuneration referred to in paragraphs 1 and 2.

1. General. In order to facilitate public lending, art. 6 offers the Member States broad opportunities to deviate from the lending right and provide, at least for authors, for remuneration instead. The term 'public lending right' in the title of art. 6 is not considered to add meaning to the article. In fact, the term 'public lending right' tends to be seen as the right of libraries to lend out their collections without having to acquire the consent of the rightholders. Given the broad options to deviate from the exclusive lending right, the Directive was not expected to lead to a high level of harmonization with respect to lending. Historically, Member States have deployed various systems to compensate authors for public lending by libraries, either through their copyright acts or, through other regulations, like for instance in Denmark, Sweden and (until 1995) the Netherlands. The Directive allows such national compensation rules and only intends to define the circumstances that trigger remuneration – i.e. public lending.

2. Right to remuneration. (a) Categories of works. The exclusive right may be set aside in respect of all types of material in the collection of a library, or in respect of certain categories of material only. Member States may, for example, grant an exclusive lending right with respect to phonograms and a remuneration right with respect to books. Member States may also chose to replace the exclusive right by a right to remuneration after a certain period; for example, by providing that the exclusive lending right with respect to phonograms shall be replaced by a right to remuneration six months after the release of the phonogram. **(b) Categories of rightholders.** The Directive demands a remuneration at least for authors. Member States may thus decide to grant remuneration for public lending to all rightholders concerned, to various categories of rightholders (including authors), or to authors only. Some Member States remunerate a broader category, for example including publishers (e.g. the Netherlands). The Directive does not stipulate whether payment of the remuneration may be limited to national authors, only. Because the Directive does not require that the remuneration be implemented in the framework of copyright, the principle of national treatment under the Berne Convention does not necessarily apply. Guidance may be found in recital 14, setting forth that any measures based on art. 6 have to comply with EU law, in particular with art. 18 TFEU, the principle of non-discrimination on the grounds of nationality. **(c) Remuneration.** Member States are free to determine the amount of remuneration, the party or parties that shall be responsible for payment, and the method of administration of the remuneration. The wide margin of appreciation of the Member States was confirmed by the ECJ in *VEWA*. In establishing the amount of the remuneration, the cultural promotion objectives of the Member State may be taken into account. In other words, the Member States may reduce the remuneration that would otherwise be paid, for the benefit of their general cultural promotion objectives. In practice, different systems are used to define the amount of remuneration. While in some countries the number of lending acts is decisive (e.g. in Belgium and the Netherlands), other Member States deploy a lump sum model irrespective of actual lending (e.g. Germany, the United Kingdom, Austria and Finland). Contrary to art. 5, which governs the remuneration for rental, art. 6 does not stipulate that remuneration for lending should be equitable. This word was deleted from the original proposal, addressing the concern of certain Member States about the financial impact of the remuneration right. The ECJ considered in *VEWA* that this difference in drafting implies that the two concepts must not be interpreted in the same way. The ECJ held that, given that lending does not have an economic or commercial character, the amount of remuneration cannot be quantified in light of the commercial value of the use and will necessarily be less than an equitable remuneration and may even be fixed on a flat-rate basis. However, its amount cannot be purely symbolic. The wording of art. 5(1) reserves a wide margin of discretion to the Member States, which may determine the amount of the remuneration due to authors in the event of public lending in accordance with their own cultural promotion objectives. The determination of the amount of that remuneration, as the ECJ continues, cannot be completely dissociated from the elements that constitute the harm caused to the authors by the lending. The remuneration due should thus take account of the extent to which the works are made available. The ECJ mentions the number of works made available by a library and the number of borrowers registered as relevant qualifiers. Merely taking into account the number of borrowers, as in the Belgian *VEWA* case, was held to be insufficient. In its consideration of the harm caused to the authors, the ECJ refers to its *Padawan* decision with respect to fair compensation under the Information Society Directive. Taking the *VEWA* (ECJ) decision into consideration, the Netherlands Supreme Court held that an extension of a public library loan term does not qualify as a new loan and therefore does not create an additional right to remuneration (*Stichting Leenrecht* (the Netherlands)).

3. Phonograms, films and computer programs (para. 2). Para. 2 confirms the principle set forth in para. 1 with respect to phonograms, films and computer programs. The paragraph does not seem to add much to para. 1, merely repeating the same principle for these three categories of works. Para. 2 was inserted as a compromise between two Member States who disagreed whether an exclusive right or a remuneration right should be granted in respect of these types of works. Unlike para. 1, para. 2 does not contain the provision that the remuneration may be reduced for the benefit of cultural promotion objectives. Arguably, one may conclude that such reduction was not contemplated with respect to categories of works addressed in para. 2.

4. No remuneration (para. 3). Para. 3 allows Member States to exempt 'certain categories of establishments' from payment of the remuneration altogether. It provides for an exemption to the exception: the exclusive right may be set aside for the benefit of public lending on the condition that a remuneration is paid, but some institutions do not have to pay a remuneration either. Public libraries, universities and educational establishments were envisaged as categories of establishments that could be exempted under art. 6(3). In practice, art. 6(3) is applied on a large scale throughout the Member States. Most

Member States have exempted certain categories of libraries, such as school libraries, university libraries or public libraries. In some Member States, all categories were exempted and thus no remuneration was paid whatsoever. The ECJ held in infringement proceedings against Ireland, Italy, Portugal and Spain that Member States that exempt from the public lending right almost all or all categories of lending establishments accessible to the public have not correctly implemented arts. 1 and 6 of the Directive (*Commission/Ireland*, *Commission/Italy*, *Commission/Portugal I* and *Commission/Spain*). A payment system that leads to a de facto exemption of many establishments also violates art. 6(1) (*VEWA*). In that case, the ECJ ruled that art. 6(1) precludes legislation that establishes a system under which the remuneration payable to authors in the event of public lending is calculated exclusively according to the number of borrowers registered with public establishments, on the basis of a flat-rate amount fixed per borrower and per year.

CHAPTER II. RIGHTS RELATED TO COPYRIGHT

[Fixation right]

Article 7

(1) **Member States shall provide for performers the exclusive right to authorize or prohibit the fixation of their performances.**

(2) **Member States shall provide for broadcasting organizations the exclusive right to authorize or prohibit the fixation of their broadcasts, whether these broadcasts are transmitted by wire or over the air, including by cable or satellite.**

(3) **A cable distributor shall not have the right provided for in paragraph 2 where it merely retransmits by cable the broadcasts of broadcasting organizations.**

1. General. The article provides for exclusive rights for performers and broadcasting organizations (including cable distributors) to authorize or prohibit the fixation of their performances and broadcasts. Fixation is the first reproduction of a performance or broadcast on a tangible medium, and is as such a prerequisite for any further exploitation of the original performance or broadcast. Art. 7 does not cover any further reproduction of the initial fixation. Further reproduction was originally addressed in art. 7 of Rental Right Directive (old version), which article was abolished under the Information Society Directive and is now covered by the general reproduction right in art. 2 of that Directive. The exclusive nature of the fixation right corresponds with the exclusivity of rental and lending rights (see art. 1, note 2).

2. Performers (para. 1). Para. 1 provides for an exclusive right for performers to authorize or prohibit the first fixations of their performances. As such, it offers performers a stronger right than art. 7 of the Rome Convention, which contemplates a more general 'possibility of preventing'. The terms 'performer' and 'performance' are not defined, so as not to interfere with the interpretation of these terms in a broader scope under national laws and international treaties, in particular the Rome Convention (see art. 3, notes 2 and 3).

3. Broadcasting organizations (para. 2). Para. 2 provides for an exclusive right for broadcasting organizations to authorize or prohibit the fixation of their previously unfixed broadcasts. What is considered as a broadcasting organization can be deduced from art. 7(2) and 7(3), namely traditional broadcasting organizations, satellite broadcasters and cable distributors. The rights granted thus apply to broadcasts transmitted by wire or over the air, including broadcasts made via satellites and transmission by cable services, but not to mere acts of simultaneous retransmission (see para. 3).

4. Cable distributors (para. 3). Cable distributors who make their own programmes fully enjoy the fixation right. They do not have a fixation right in respect of unaltered or simultaneous retransmission by cable of broadcasts received from another broadcasting organization.

[Broadcasting and communication to the public]

Article 8

(1) Member States shall provide for performers the exclusive right to authorize or prohibit the broadcasting by wireless means and the communication to the public of their performances, except where the performance is itself already a broadcast performance or is made from a fixation.

(2) Member States shall provide a right in order to ensure that a single equitable remuneration is paid by the user, if a phonogram published for commercial purposes, or a reproduction of such phonogram, is used for broadcasting by wireless means or for any communication to the public, and to ensure that this remuneration is shared between the relevant performers and phonogram producers. Member States may, in the absence of agreement between the performers and phonogram producers, lay down the conditions as to the sharing of this remuneration between them.

(3) Member States shall provide for broadcasting organizations the exclusive right to authorize or prohibit the rebroadcasting of their broadcasts by wireless means, as well as the communication to the public of their broadcasts if such communication is made in places accessible to the public against payment of an entrance fee.

1. General. Art. 8 aims at harmonization of certain rights for performers, phonogram producers and broadcasting organizations with regard to broadcasting and other forms of communication to the public. Recital 16 of the Directive clarifies that minimum harmonization is sought, allowing Member States to provide for broader protection under national law. Art. 8 is based on art. 7(1) and 13(a) and (d) of the Rome Convention, but offers more protection on several aspects. Art. 8 is explicitly without prejudice to the corresponding provisions of the Satellite and Cable Directive, which governs the definition of 'communication to the public by satellite'. Unlike art. 9, art. 8 does not stipulate that the rights can be transferred. Hence it will be a matter of national law whether, and how, the rights can be transferred.

2. Broadcasting by wireless means (para. 1). In order to avoid conflicts with the Satellite and Cable Directive, the right to authorize or prohibit broadcasting was limited to broadcasting by wireless means. This includes broadcasting by satellite, as is set forth explicitly in art. 4 of that Directive. As art. 8 aims at minimum harmonization, Member States may grant performers exclusive rights with respect to cable broadcasts as well, as long as the provisions of the Satellite and Cable Directive are respected. The rights granted under para. 1 cover 'live' performances only: performances which have already been broadcast or broadcasts from earlier fixations are explicitly excluded. Hence, a performer cannot prevent the repeated broadcasting or rebroadcasting of a first broadcast made from his personal performance. Again, Member States are free to grant performers broader protection. The WPPT provides for similar protection (see art. 6 WPPT, note 1).

3. Remuneration (para. 2). Para. 2 provides for a right to remuneration for performers and phonogram producers for broadcasts made on the basis of commercial phonograms and other communication to the public of such phonograms, for example, the playing of a phonogram in a public area. **(a) Phonograms published for commercial purposes.** Any sound recordings produced for commercial gain and any reproductions of such recordings may qualify as phonograms published for commercial purposes, including private recordings from pre-recorded sound recordings. The remuneration right was not intended for recordings which are not meant to be released onto the market, such as recordings which are used for the sole purpose of repeated broadcasts, or unpublished phonograms and recordings. **(b) Use for broadcasting and public communication.** The original proposal of the Directive stipulated that both direct and indirect use of phonograms would lead to a payment obligation. Direct use was meant to refer to the situation in which a broadcast is made directly on the basis of a phonogram or where a phonogram is played in a public place. Indirect use referred to, for instance, the use of a phonogram for a broadcast which is subsequently rebroadcast by another broadcasting station, or a broadcast (made on the basis of a phonogram) that is shown on television or played on the radio in a public place. Both types of use were meant to be covered. Although the final text does not contain explicit reference to direct and indirect use, no limitation in interpretation was intended. According to the ECJ, a hotel operator that provides television or radio sets in hotel rooms to which it transmits broadcast program signals is making a communication to the public of the broadcast (*Phonographic Performance (Ireland)* (ECJ)); see also *SGAE* (ECJ). The ECJ also held that a hotel operator providing guests in hotel rooms with CD players and CDs is making a communication to the public of a phonogram (*Phonographic Performance (Ireland)* (ECJ)). Live streaming of television broadcasts at substantially the same time as the original broadcast also qualifies as communication to the public under art. 8(2) (*ITV Broadcasting and others*). In *SCF* the ECJ however found that the playing of phonograms in a private dentist's waiting room does not constitute a communication to the public for the purposes of the equitable remuneration right. The ECJ took into consideration the small and limited number of people in the dentist's waiting room at any one time, coupled with the fact that the patients cannot choose which records are listened to and the Court also assumed that the dentist had no commercial motive to play records in the waiting room. The ECJ however noted that the concept of communication to the public in this Directive is not necessarily the same as in the Information Society Directive, given the fact that the objectives pursued by these directives, while similar, are none the less different. The Court thus opened the door to a different interpretation of the same term. **(c) Single equitable remuneration.** Art. 8 (2) sets forth that the user has to pay a single equitable remuneration, which remuneration is to be shared between the relevant beneficiaries. Member States are free to provide that the payment shall be made to performers and producers jointly, or to either group of beneficiaries, who will then be obliged to pay a share to the other beneficiaries. The Member States must however ensure that whoever receives the remuneration is fully accountable to the other. As per art. 12 of the Rome Convention, para. 2 also allows Member States to set the conditions for the sharing of remunerations between performers and producers when there is no explicit agreement between those two groups of beneficiaries. The article does not provide further guidance on what is to be considered 'equitable', leaving the interpretation thereof up to the Member States. According to the ECJ, art. 8(2) does not preclude a model for the calculation of an equitable remuneration that takes variable and fixed factors into account, provided that such a model enables a proper balance between the interests of performing artists and producers in obtaining remuneration for the broadcast of a particular phonogram, and the interest of third parties in being able to broadcast the phonogram on terms that are reasonable (*Sena* (ECJ)). Factors in the calculation model were the number of hours of phonograms broadcast, the viewing and listening volumes achieved by the radio and television broadcasters represented by the broadcast organization, the tariffs fixed by agreement in the field of performance rights and broadcast rights in respect of musical works protected by copyright, the tariffs set by the public broadcast organizations in the Member States bordering on the Member State concerned, and the amounts paid by commercial stations. The ECJ ruled in *Lagardère* that the broadcasting company is not entitled to unilaterally deduct from the amount of the royalty for phonogram use payable in the Member State in which it is established, the amount of the royalty paid or claimed in the Member State in whose territory the terrestrial transmitter broadcasting to the first State is located.

4. Rebroadcasting (para. 3). Para. 3 provides for the exclusive rights of rebroadcasting and communication to the public for broadcasting organizations. The rights were modelled on arts. 13(a) and 3(d) of the Rome Convention. **(a) Rebroadcasting.** The term rebroadcasting refers to the simultaneous broadcasting by a broadcasting organization of the broadcast of another organization. Deferred retransmission is meant to be governed by art. 7(2), as a broadcast must be fixed before such a retransmission can take place. Rebroadcasting under this paragraph is restricted to rebroadcasting by wireless means. **(b) Communication to the public.** Broadcasting organizations have the exclusive right to authorize or prohibit the communication to the public of their broadcasts if such communication is made in places accessible to the public against payment of an entrance fee. The Member States explicitly decided not to grant broadcasting organizations a broad exclusive right to prohibit the public showing or playing their broadcasts in general. However, as minimum harmonization was aimed at, Member States are allowed to extend the rights of broadcasting organizations, for example, to include showing or playing television or radio broadcasts in cafés, restaurants and shops. According to the ECJ, this principle implies that the Member States may grant broadcasting organizations an exclusive right to authorize or prohibit acts of communication to the public of their transmissions on conditions different from those laid down in art. 8(3), in particular transmissions to which members of the public may obtain access from a place individually chosen by them, on the condition that such a right does not affect the protection of copyright in any way, as provided for in art. 12 of the Directive (*C More Entertainment* (ECJ)).

[Distribution right]

Article 9

(1) Member States shall provide the exclusive right to make available to the public, by sale or otherwise, the objects indicated in points a) to d), including copies thereof, hereinafter 'the distribution right':

(a) **for performers, in respect of fixations of their performances;**

(b) **for phonogram producers, in respect of their phonograms;**

(c) **for producers of the first fixations of films, in respect of the original and copies of their films;**

(d) **for broadcasting organizations, in respect of fixations of their broadcast as set out in Article 7 (2).**

(2) The distribution right shall not be exhausted within the Community in respect of an object as referred to in paragraph 1, except where the first sale in the Community of that object is made by the rightholder or with his consent.

(3) The distribution right shall be without prejudice to the specific provisions of Chapter I, in particular Article 1 (2).

(4) The distribution right may be transferred, assigned or subject to the granting of contractual licences.

1. General. This article provides for an exclusive distribution right for performers, phonogram and film producers and broadcasting organizations, and also for the exhaustion and transferability of said right. The right is granted with respect to phonograms and first fixations of performances, films and broadcasts and to any copies of such objects. Cable distributors who merely retransmit broadcasts of other broadcasting organizations do not enjoy a distribution right with respect to fixations of such retransmitted broadcasts. This can be deduced from the reference to art. 7(2). This reference should be understood to refer to art. 7(2) and 7(3) jointly, as art. 7(2) was split in two at a very late stage. For comments on the rightholders and the protected subject matter, see art. 3, notes 2 and 3, and art. 7, notes 2 and 3. **(a) Exclusive right.** Art. 9 provides for 'an exclusive right to reproduction', rather than an exclusive right 'to authorize or prohibit reproduction.' This difference is considered to be unimportant and does not indicate a conceptual difference. **(b) Public.** The term 'public' is not defined. It is therefore left to the Member States to determine the scope of this term.

2. Exhaustion (para 2). This provision lays down the established theory of exhaustion as created by the jurisprudence of the European Court of Justice. The distribution right shall be exhausted within the Community when protected material (or copies thereof) has been put onto the market in the Community by the rightholder or with his consent. This Community-wide exhaustion principle has now been adopted in respect of distribution of any material protected by copyright or neighbouring rights (see art. 4 Information Society Directive).

3. Rental and lending rights (para. 3). Art. 9(3) was added in order to clarify that the rules of art. 9 regarding the distribution right do not in any way affect the specific provisions for rental and lending in Chapter I of the Directive. This was felt to be particularly necessary with a view to art. 1(2), which addresses the non-exhaustion of rental and lending rights.

4. Transfer (para. 4). Art. 9(4) is similar to art. 3(3), in that it provides that distribution rights may be transferred, assigned or licensed. It is left to the Member States to implement this provision into their national laws in a way that fits their respective law systems.

[Limitations to rights]

Article 10

(1)   Member States may provide for limitations to the rights referred to in this Chapter in respect of:

(a) private use;
(b) use of short excerpts in connection with the reporting of current events;
(c) ephemeral fixation by a broadcasting organization by means of its own facilities and for its own broadcasts;
(d) use solely for the purposes of teaching or scientific research.

(2) Irrespective of paragraph 1, any Member State may provide for the same kinds of limitations with regard to the protection of performers, producers of phonograms, broadcasting organizations and of producers of the first fixations of films, as it provides for in connection with the protection of copyright in literary and artistic works. However, compulsory licences may be provided for only to the extent to which they are compatible with the Rome Convention.

(3) The limitations referred to in paragraphs 1 and 2 shall be applied only in certain special cases which do not conflict with a normal exploitation of the subject matter and do not unreasonably prejudice the legitimate interests of the rightholder.

1. General. Art. 10 is the equivalent of art. 15 of the Rome Convention and lists the possible limitations which Member States may choose to apply with respect to the rights provided for in Chapter II. The Member States are free to apply, or not to apply, any of the limitations provided for. However, they cannot apply any limitations other than those allowed under art. 10. Harmonization of limitations was later addressed in the Information Society Directive. Although the Information Society Directive does not affect the rights granted under this Directive, the provisions with respect to limitations therein will have an impact on the interpretation of art. 10 of this Directive, as well.

2. Limitations (para. 1). Private use. Art. 10(1)(a) allows Member States to provide for limitations for the purpose of private use, leaving this to the discretion of the Member States. Note that home copying of audiovisual material, which originally fell within the scope of this article, is now harmonized in art. 5(2)(b) of the Information Society Directive. According to the ECJ this limitation cannot be invoked to exempt hotel operators who communicate to the public phonograms from the obligation to pay remuneration (*Phonographic Performance (Ireland)* (ECJ)). **(a) Short excerpts.** Art. 10(1)(b) refers, for example, to the broadcasting of a short excerpt from a performance or a fragment of a movie included in a television programme on current events, such as a programme about recently released movies. **(b) Ephemeral fixation.** Broadcasting organizations mostly broadcast from tapes which they produce for the purpose of broadcasting. Art. 10(1)(c) enables Member States to allow such fixations, provided they are made using a broadcasting organization's own facilities, and exist for a limited period of time only. It is understood that a broadcaster's own facilities include those of a person acting on behalf of and under the auspices of the broadcasting organization. **(c) Educational purposes.** Art. 10(1)(d) refers to a limitation of the exclusive rights in order to facilitate the use for purposes of teaching or scientific research. This includes the right to reproduce a performance in order to replace an old copy in an archive collection.

3. Copyright in literary and artistic works (para. 2). Art. 10(2) sets forth that the Member States are allowed to provide for the same kind of limitations on neighbouring rights as they provide for in respect of the rights of authors in their national laws. The last sentence refers to art. 15(2) of the Rome Convention, which states that 'compulsory licences may be provided for only to the extent to which they are compatible with this Convention'. With respect to limitation of author's rights, reference is made to art. 5 of the Information Society Directive.

4. Legitimate interests of the rightholder (para. 3). The original art. 10(3) was replaced by art. 11(1)(b) of the Information Society Directive. The text refers to a careful and well-balanced use of limitations by the Member States and should be interpreted in the light of the similarly worded 'three-step test' of art. 5(5) of the Information Society Directive (see also recital 44 of that Directive).

CHAPTER III. COMMON PROVISIONS

[Application in time]

Article 11

(1) This Directive shall apply in respect of all copyright works, performances, phonograms, broadcasts and first fixations of films referred to in this Directive which were, on 1 July 1994, still protected by the legislation of the Member States in the field of copyright and related rights or which met the criteria for protection under this Directive on that date.

(2) This Directive shall apply without prejudice to any acts of exploitation performed before 1 July 1994.

(3) Member States may provide that the rightholders are deemed to have given their authorization to the rental or lending of an object referred to in points a) to d) of Article 3(1) which is proven to have been made available to third parties for this purpose or to have been acquired before 1 July 1994. However, in particular where such an object is a digital recording, Member States may provide that rightholders shall have a right to obtain an adequate remuneration for the rental or lending of that object.

(4) Member States need not apply the provisions of Article 2(2) to cinematographic or audiovisual works created before 1 July 1994.

(5) This Directive shall, without prejudice to paragraph 3 and subject to paragraph 7, not affect any contracts concluded before 19 November 1992.

(6) **Member States may provide, subject to the provisions of paragraph 7, that when rightholders who acquire new rights under the national provisions adopted in implementation of this Directive have, before 1 July 1994, given their consent for exploitation, they shall be presumed to have transferred the new exclusive rights.**

(7) **For contracts concluded before 1 July 1994, the unwaivable right to an equitable remuneration provided for in Article 5 shall apply only where authors or performers or those representing them have submitted a request to that effect before 1 January 1997. In the absence of agreement between rightholders concerning the level of remuneration, Member States may fix the level of equitable remuneration.**

1. General. Art. 11 addresses the application in time of the rights to be granted pursuant to the Directive. The article was much debated. If the Commission had proposed that the Directive should apply to new works and productions only, the effect of harmonization would have been delayed far into the future. Instead, it was proposed that the Directive should also apply to existing works, performances and productions which had not yet fallen in the public domain. In general, the rights must now be applied to all activities having taken place after the implementation date of 1 July 1994. However, art. 11 allows various transitional arrangements in order to facilitate the transposition of the Directive.

2. Implementation date (para. 1). Art. 11(1) sets forth that the Directive shall apply in respect of all protected materials covered by the Directive that (i) were protected under copyright or neighbouring rights in the relevant Member State on 1 July 1994, or (ii) met the criteria for protection according to the provisions of this Directive on that date. The first criterion implies that a copyrighted work that enjoyed protection until 1 July 1994 would benefit from the rights granted under the Directive, while a work for which the term of protection had lapsed on 30 June 1994 would not. Equally, a work that still enjoyed copyright in one Member State but not in another would only enjoy the Directive rights in the first state mentioned. The second criterion means that materials that never enjoyed protection under copyright or neighbouring rights under national law, would nevertheless benefit from the rights granted under the Directive if such work was eligible for protection under the Directive on 1 July 1994. This second criterion was inserted to cover materials protected by neighbouring rights in those Member States which did not have neighbouring rights protection in place. A British court confirmed that, under the Directive as implemented in British law, a 1969 performance by Jimi Hendrix in Stockholm was a qualifying performance for the purposes of performer's rights, notwithstanding that Sweden did not join the Community until 1995 and was not designated a qualifying country until 1989 (*Experience Hendrix* (UK)). In other words, if a performance took place in a qualifying country, the date on which such country became a qualifying country is not relevant. See also art. 10 Term Directive, note 2, and particularly *Ricordi* (ECJ).

3. Exploitation before 1 July 1994 (para. 2). Art. 11(2) clarifies that the Directive does not apply to acts of exploitation that have taken place before the implementation date of 1 July 1994.

4. Pre-existing collection (para. 3). Art. 11(3) seeks to safeguard the position of rental shops and lending institutions with respect to their existing collections of books, CDs and other material. Member States could provide that such establishments might continue to rent and lend the materials collected before 1 July 1994, as if the rightholders in respect of those materials had authorized the rental and lending activities. The rental shops and lending institutions would have to prove that the materials had already been rented or lent, or had been acquired, before 1 July 1994. **(a) Remuneration.** Where continued rental and lending was allowed, the payment of an adequate remuneration to be paid to the rightholders should be imposed, particularly if the object of rental in lending is a digital recording. Member States might provide for a remuneration right with respect to digital recordings only, or with respect to any protected material. Member States could also decide that no remuneration shall be payable for any material.

5. Film directors (para. 4). Art. 11(4) sets forth that film directors need not be considered as film authors in respect of films created before 1 July 1994. Accordingly, such pre-existing films may be exempted from rental and lending rights altogether, also with respect to future exploitation.

6. Exclusive right (paras. 5 and 6). Paras. 5 and 6 address pre-existing contractual arrangements. Art. 11(5) stipulates that any contracts concluded before the Directive's adoption date on 19 November 1992 shall not be affected by the Directive. This provision is mandatory. Art 11(6) provides that Member States shall be allowed to provide that rightholders who acquire new rights pursuant to implementation of the Directive and who have given their consent to exploitation before, shall be presumed to have transferred the newly acquired rights. Accordingly, an actor in a film who is granted lending and rental rights as a consequence of the implementation of the Directive, shall be presumed to have transferred those rights to the film producer with whom a contract was entered into before the implementation date of the Directive. This provision is optional.

7. Remuneration rights (para. 7). Para. 7 provides for transitional arrangements with respect to the remuneration right for rental. Para. 7 provides that with respect to contracts concluded before 1 July 1994, the remuneration right for rental shall only apply if a request to that effect has been made before 1 January 1997. This provision is mandatory. The purpose of this provision was to prevent a situation where producers or other parties exploiting protected works were obliged to go through the time-consuming task of tracing all those authors and performers who contributed to a film or phonogram under 'old' contracts in order to pay them the newly introduced remuneration for rental. Member States were thus allowed to grant a remuneration right with respect to acts of exploitation as of 1 July 1997. The request for payment of a remuneration may be made by the authors or performers of those representing them, generally collecting societies. The Directive does not specify to whom the request should be made.

[Relation between copyright and related rights]

Article 12

Protection of copyright-related rights under this Directive shall leave intact and shall in no way affect the protection of copyright.

1. General. The article clarifies that the protection of copyright is not affected by the rights granted in the Directive. The exercise of copyrights may however be affected by this Directive. After all, a film director as a (co-)author will no longer be able to rent out copies of the film on video without the film producer's consent.

[Communication]

Article 13

Member States shall communicate to the Commission the main provisions of domestic law adopted in the field covered by this Directive.

1. General. The Rental Right Directive (old version) provided that Member States were to transpose the Directive by 1 July 1994. A number of Member States failed to accomplish the time limit, resulting in various actions by the Commission against such Member States. The time limits for implementation are now included in Annex I part B.

[Repeal]

Article 14

Directive 92/100/EEC is hereby repealed, without prejudice to the obligations of the Member States relating to the time-limits for transposition into national law of the Directives as set out in Part B of Annex I.

References made to the repealed Directive shall be construed as being made to this Directive and should be read in accordance with the correlation table in Annex II.

[Entry into force]

Article 15

This Directive shall enter into force on the twentieth day following that of its publication in the Official Journal of the European Union.

1. General. This Directive was published on 27 December 2006. (OJ L 376, 27.12.2006, p. 28–35). Therefore it entered into force on 16 January 2007.

[Addressees]

Article 16

This Directive is addressed to the Member States.

1. General. According to art. 288 TFEU, Directives are binding, as to the result to be achieved, upon each Member State to which it is addressed, but shall leave to the national authorities the choice of form and methods.

ANNEX I

PART A

Repealed Directive with its successive amendments

Council Directive 92/100/EEC (OJ L 346, 27.11.1992, p. 61)

Council Directive 93/98/EEC (OJ L 290, 24.11.1993, p. 9) Article 11(2) only

Directive 2001/29/EC of the European Parliament and of the Council (OJ L 167, 22.6.2001, p. 10) Article 11(1) only

PART B

List of time-limits for transposition into national law
(referred to in Article 14)

Directive	Time-limit for transposition
92/100/EEC	1 July 1994
93/98/EEC	30 June 1995
2001/29/EC	21 December 2002

ANNEX II

CORRELATION TABLE

Directive 92/100/EEC	This Directive
Article 1(1)	Article 1(1)
Article 1(2)	Article 2(1), introductory words and point (a)
Article 1(3)	Article 2(1), point (b)
Article 1(4)	Article 1(2)
Article 2(1), introductory words	Article 3(1), introductory words
Article 2(1), first indent	Article 3(1)(a)
Article 2(1), second indent	Article 3(1)(b)
Article 2(1), third indent	Article 3(1)(c)
Article 2(1), fourth indent first sentence	Article 3(1)(d)
Article 2(1), fourth indent second sentence	Article 2(1), point (c)
Article 2(2)	Article 2 (2)
Article 2(3)	Article 3(2)
Article 2(4)	Article 3(3)
Article 2(5)	Article 3(4)
Article 2(6)	Article 3(5)
Article 2(7)	Article 3(6)
Article 3	Article 4
Article 4	Article 5
Article 5(1) to (3)	Article 6(1) to (3)
Article 5(4)	—
Article 6	Article 7
Article 8	Article 8
Article 9(1), introductory words and final words	Article 9(1), introductory words
Article 9(1), first indent	Article 9(1)(a)
Article 9(1), second indent	Article 9(1)(b)

Directive 92/100/EEC	This Directive
Article 9(1), third indent	Article 9(1)(c)
Article 9(1), fourth indent	Article 9(1)(d)
Article 9(2), (3) and (4)	Article 9(2), (3) and (4)
Article 10(1)	Article 10(1)
Article 10(2), first sentence	Article 10(2), first subparagraph
Article 10(2), second sentence	Article 10(2), second subparagraph
Article 10(3)	Article 10(3)
Article 13(1) and (2)	Article 11(1) and (2)
Article 13(3), first sentence	Article 11(3), first subparagraph
Article 13(3), second sentence	Article 11(3), second subparagraph
Article 13(4)	Article 11(4)
Article 13(5)	—
Article 13(6)	Article 11(5)
Article 13(7)	Article 11(6)
Article 13(8)	—
Article 13(9)	Article 11(7)
Article 14	Article 12
Article 15(1)	—
Article 15(2)	Article 13
—	Article 14
—	Article 15
Article 16	Article 16
—	Annex I
—	Annex II

COUNCIL DIRECTIVE 93/83/EC

(Satellite and Cable Directive)

of 27 September 1993 on the coordination of certain rules concerning copyright and rights related to copyright applicable to satellite broadcasting and cable retransmission

[Introductory remarks]

1. Legislative history. The Satellite and Cable Directive has its roots in the Green Paper on Television without Frontiers that was published by the European Commission in 1984. The Green Paper proposed to eliminate legal barriers to trans-frontier television services within the European Community (now the European Union), especially in the area of broadcasting regulation and copyright law. The Green Paper eventually led to the Television without Frontiers Directive of 1989 which however did not contain any rules on copyright. The current Directive is the direct result of a Discussion Paper on Broadcasting and Copyright in the Internal Market that was issued by the European Commission in November 1990. This led to a proposal for a directive in 1991 which after discussion in the European Parliament was amended and subsequently adopted in the course of 1993. The Member States were obliged to implement the provisions of the Directive by 1 January 1995. Pursuant to art. 14(3) an evaluation report was published by the European Commission on 26 July 2002 (Report on the Satellite and Cable Directive).

2. Aim and scope of Directive. The Directive's main purpose is to eliminate copyright-related barriers to trans-frontier broadcasting services within the European Union. The Directive is the counterpart of the Television without Frontiers Directive of 1989 (replaced in 2010 by the Audiovisual Media Services Directive), which has the same objective with respect to barriers in the field of broadcasting and advertising law. In contrast to its 'sister' Directive, the Satellite and Cable Directive deals both with broadcast television and radio services. In contrast to other directives in the field of copyright law, the Directive does not however provide many norms of substantive law. Instead it has introduced two legal instruments that are designed to facilitate the licensing of satellite broadcasting and cable retransmission of radio and television programmes. Firstly, the Directive has established a Union-wide right of communication to the public by satellite, which is a restricted (protected) act only in the country of origin ('uplink') of the satellite transmission. This instrument was felt necessary because in some Member States courts had determined that a satellite broadcast is a restricted act in all States within the footprint of the satellite, meaning that rightholders in one Member State would be able to block a satellite broadcast intended for the whole of Europe. Secondly, the Directive has created a system of compulsory collective management of cable retransmission rights, in order to facilitate and promote collective licensing. This instrument was felt necessary because cable operators are unable to negotiate licenses with all rightholders concerned prior to the broadcasting and simultaneous retransmission of the programme. It was feared that individual rightholders might exercise their exclusive rights of retransmission, and thus create 'black-outs' in programmes retransmitted by cable operators.

[Bibliography]

T. Dreier, 'The Satellite and Cable Directive' in M. Walter, S. von Lewinski (eds.), *European Copyright Law: A Commentary* (Oxford University Press 2010) 391-498

P.B. Hugenholtz, 'Copyright without Frontiers' in A. Roßnagel (ed.), *Die Zukunft der Fernsehrichtlinie/The Future of the 'Television without Frontiers' Directive* (Nomos 2005) 65-73

P.B. Hugenholtz, 'SatCab Revisited: The Past, Present and Future of the Satellite and Cable Directive' (2009) 8 *IRIS plus* 7-19

E. McKnight, 'Exclusive Licensing of Television Programmes: The Cable and Satellite Directive' (1995) *Ent. L. Rev.* 287

Ph. Kern, 'The EC Common Position on Copyright Applicable to Satellite Broadcasting and Cable Retransmission' (1993) 8 EIPR 281

W. Rumphorst, 'The EC Directive on Satellite and Cable' (Autumn 1993) Diffusion (EBU) 30

[Preamble]

The Council of the European Communities,

Having regard to the Treaty establishing the European Economic Community,

and in particular Articles 57 (2) and 66 thereof,

Having regard to the proposal from the Commission,[1]

In cooperation with the European Parliament,[2]

Having regard to the opinion of the Economic and Social Committee,[3]

(1) Whereas the objectives of the Community as laid down in the Treaty include establishing an ever closer union among the peoples of

---

1. OJ No. C 255, 1 October 1991, p. 3 and OJ No. C 25, 28 January 1993, p. 43.
2. OJ No. C 305, 23 November 1992, p. 129 and OJ No. C 255, 20 September 1993.
3. OJ No. C 98, 21 April 1992, p. 44.

Europe, fostering closer relations between the States belonging to the Community and ensuring the economic and social progress of the Community countries by common action to eliminate the barriers which divide Europe;

(2) Whereas, to that end, the Treaty provides for the establishment of a common market and an area without internal frontiers; whereas measures to achieve this include the abolition of obstacles to the free movement of services and the institution of a system ensuring that competition in the common market is not distorted; whereas, to that end, the Council may adopt directives for the coordination of the provisions laid down by law, regulation or administrative action in Member States concerning the taking up and pursuit of activities as self-employed persons;

(3) Whereas broadcasts transmitted across frontiers within the Community, in particular by satellite and cable, are one of the most important ways of pursuing these Community objectives, which are at the same time political, economic, social, cultural and legal;

(4) Whereas the Council has already adopted Directive 89/552/EEC of 3 October 1989 on the coordination of certain provisions laid down by law, regulation or administrative action in Member States concerning the pursuit of television broadcasting activities,[4] which makes provision for the promotion of the distribution and production of European television programmes and for advertising and sponsorship, the protection of minors and the right of reply;

(5) Whereas, however, the achievement of these objectives in respect of cross-border satellite broadcasting and the cable retransmission of programmes from other Member States is currently still obstructed by a series of differences between national rules of copyright and some degree of legal uncertainty; whereas this means that holders of rights are exposed to the threat of seeing their works exploited without payment of remuneration or that the individual holders of exclusive rights in various Member States block the exploitation of their rights; whereas the legal uncertainty in particular constitutes a direct obstacle in the free circulation of programmes within the Community;

(6) Whereas a distinction is currently drawn for copyright purposes between communication to the public by direct satellite and communication to the public by communications satellite; whereas, since individual reception is possible and affordable nowadays with both types of satellite, there is no longer any justification for this differing legal treatment;

(7) Whereas the free broadcasting of programmes is further impeded by the current legal uncertainty over whether broadcasting by a satellite whose signals can be received directly affects the rights in the country of transmission only or in all countries of reception together; whereas, since communications satellites and direct satellites are treated alike for

---

4. OJ No. L 298, 17 October 1989, p. 23.

copyright purposes, this legal uncertainty now affects almost all programmes broadcast in the Community by satellite;

(8) Whereas, furthermore, legal certainty, which is a prerequisite for the free movement of broadcasts within the Community, is missing where programmes transmitted across frontiers are fed into and retransmitted through cable networks;

(9) Whereas the development of the acquisition of rights on a contractual basis by authorization is already making a vigorous contribution to the creation of the desired European audiovisual area; whereas the continuation of such contractual agreements should be ensured and their smooth application in practice should be promoted wherever possible;

(10) Whereas at present cable operators in particular cannot be sure that they have actually acquired all the programme rights covered by such an agreement;

(11) Whereas, lastly, parties in different Member States are not all similarly bound by obligations which prevent them from refusing without valid reason to negotiate on the acquisition of the rights necessary for cable distribution or allowing such negotiations to fail;

(12) Whereas the legal framework for the creation of a single audiovisual area laid down in Directive 89/552/EEC must, therefore, be supplemented with reference to copyright;

(13) Whereas, therefore, an end should be put to the differences of treatment of the transmission of programmes by communications satellite which exist in the Member States, so that the vital distinction throughout the Community becomes whether works and other protected subject matter are communicated to the public; whereas this will also ensure equal treatment of the suppliers of cross-border broadcasts, regardless of whether they use a direct broadcasting satellite or a communications satellite;

(14) Whereas the legal uncertainty regarding the rights to be acquired which impedes cross-border satellite broadcasting should be overcome by defining the notion of communication to the public by satellite at a Community level; whereas this definition should at the same time specify where the act of communication takes place; whereas such a definition is necessary to avoid the cumulative application of several national laws to one single act of broadcasting; whereas communication to the public by satellite occurs only when, and in the Member State where, the programme-carrying signals are introduced under the control and responsibility of the broadcasting organization into an uninterrupted chain of communication leading to the satellite and down towards the earth; whereas normal technical procedures relating to the programme-carrying signals should not be considered as interruptions to the chain of broadcasting;

(15) Whereas the acquisition on a contractual basis of exclusive broadcasting rights should comply with any legislation on copyright and rights

related to copyright in the Member State in which communication to the public by satellite occurs;

(16) Whereas the principle of contractual freedom on which this Directive is based will make it possible to continue limiting the exploitation of these rights, especially as far as certain technical means of transmission or certain language versions are concerned;

(17) Whereas, in arriving at the amount of the payment to be made for the rights acquired, the parties should take account of all aspects of the broadcast, such as the actual audience, the potential audience and the language version;

(18) Whereas the application of the country-of-origin principle contained in this Directive could pose a problem with regard to existing contracts; whereas this Directive should provide for a period of five years for existing contracts to be adapted, where necessary, in the light of the Directive; whereas the said country-of-origin principle should not, therefore, apply to existing contracts which expire before 1 January 2000; whereas if by that date parties still have an interest in the contract, the same parties should be entitled to renegotiate the conditions of the contract;

(19) Whereas existing international co-production agreements must be interpreted in the light of the economic purpose and scope envisaged by the parties upon signature; whereas in the past international co-production agreements have often not expressly and specifically addressed communication to the public by satellite within the meaning of this Directive a particular form of exploitation; whereas the underlying philosophy of many existing international co-production agreements is that the rights in the co-production are exercised separately and independently by each co-producer, by dividing the exploitation rights between them along territorial lines; whereas, as a general rule, in the situation where a communication to the public by satellite authorized by one co-producer would prejudice the value of the exploitation rights of another co-producer, the interpretation of such an existing agreement would normally suggest that the latter co-producer would have to give his consent to the authorization, by the former co-producer, of the communication to the public by satellite; whereas the language exclusivity of the latter co-producer will be prejudiced where the language version or versions of the communication to the public, including where the version is dubbed or subtitled, coincide(s) with the language or the languages widely understood in the territory allotted by the agreement to the latter co-producer; whereas the notion of exclusivity should be understood in a wider sense where the communication to the public by satellite concerns a work which consists merely of images and contains no dialogue or subtitles; whereas a clear rule is necessary in cases where the international co-production agreement does not expressly regulate the division of rights in the specific case of communication to the public by satellite within the meaning of this Directive;

(20) Whereas communications to the public by satellite from non-member countries will under certain conditions be deemed to occur within a Member State of the Community;

(21) Whereas it is necessary to ensure that protection for authors, performers, producers of phonograms and broadcasting organizations is accorded in all Member States and that this protection is not subject to a statutory licence system; whereas only in this way is it possible to ensure that any difference in the level of protection within the common market will not create distortions of competition;

(22) Whereas the advent of new technologies is likely to have an impact on both the quality and the quantity of the exploitation of works and other subject matter;

(23) Whereas in the light of these developments the level of protection granted pursuant to this Directive to all rightholders in the areas covered by this Directive should remain under consideration;

(24) Whereas the harmonization of legislation envisaged in this Directive entails the harmonization of the provisions ensuring a high level of protection of authors, performers, phonogram producers and broadcasting organizations; whereas this harmonization should not allow a broadcasting organization to take advantage of differences in levels of protection by relocating activities, to the detriment of audiovisual productions;

(25) Whereas the protection provided for rights related to copyright should be aligned on that contained in Council Directive 92/100/EEC of 19 November 1992 on rental right and lending right and on certain rights related to copyright in the field of intellectual property[5] for the purposes of communication to the public by satellite; whereas, in particular, this will ensure that performers and phonogram producers are guaranteed an appropriate remuneration for the communication to the public by satellite of their performances or phonograms;

(26) Whereas the provisions of Article 4 do not prevent Member States from extending the presumption set out in Article 2 (5) of Directive 92/100/EEC to the exclusive rights referred to in Article 4; whereas, furthermore, the provisions of Article 4 do not prevent Member States from providing for a rebuttable presumption of the authorization of exploitation in respect of the exclusive rights of performers referred to in that Article, in so far as such presumption is compatible with the International Convention for the Protection of Performers, Producers of Phonograms and Broadcasting Organizations;

(27) Whereas the cable retransmission of programmes from other Member States is an act subject to copyright and, as the case may be, rights related to copyright; whereas the cable operator must, therefore, obtain the authorization from every holder of rights in each part of

---

5. OJ No. L 346, 27 November 1992, p. 61.

Hugenholtz

the programme retransmitted; whereas, pursuant to this Directive, the authorizations should be granted contractually unless a temporary exception is provided for in the case of existing legal licence schemes;

(28) Whereas, in order to ensure that the smooth operation of contractual arrangements is not called into question by the intervention of outsiders holding rights in individual parts of the programme, provision should be made, through the obligation to have recourse to a collecting society, for the exclusive collective exercise of the authorization right to the extent that this is required by the special features of cable retransmission; whereas the authorization right as such remains intact and only the exercise of this right is regulated to some extent, so that the right to authorize a cable retransmission can still be assigned; whereas this Directive does not affect the exercise of moral rights;

(29) Whereas the exemption provided for in Article 10 should not limit the choice of holders of rights to transfer their rights to a collecting society and thereby have a direct share in the remuneration paid by the cable distributor for cable retransmission;

(30) Whereas contractual arrangements regarding the authorization of cable retransmission should be promoted by additional measures; whereas a party seeking the conclusion of a general contract should, for its part, be obliged to submit collective proposals for an agreement; whereas, furthermore, any party shall be entitled, at any moment, to call upon the assistance of impartial mediators whose task is to assist negotiations and who may submit proposals; whereas any such proposals and any opposition thereto should be served on the parties concerned in accordance with the applicable rules concerning the service of legal documents, in particular as set out in existing international conventions; whereas, finally, it is necessary to ensure that the negotiations are not blocked without valid justification or that individual holders are not prevented without valid justification from taking part in the negotiations; whereas none of these measures for the promotion of the acquisition of rights calls into question the contractual nature of the acquisition of cable retransmission rights;

(31) Whereas for a transitional period Member States should be allowed to retain existing bodies with jurisdiction in their territory over cases where the right to retransmit a programme by cable to the public has been unreasonably refused or offered on unreasonable terms by a broadcasting organization; whereas it is understood that the right of parties concerned to be heard by the body should be guaranteed and that the existence of the body should not prevent the parties concerned from having normal access to the courts;

(32) Whereas, however, Community rules are not needed to deal with all of those matters, the effects of which perhaps with some commercially insignificant exceptions, are felt only inside the borders of a single Member State;

(33) Whereas minimum rules should be laid down in order to establish and guarantee free and uninterrupted cross-border broadcasting by satellite and simultaneous, unaltered cable retransmission of programmes broadcast from other Member States, on an essentially contractual basis;

(34) Whereas this Directive should not prejudice further harmonization in the field of copyright and rights related to copyright and the collective administration of such rights; whereas the possibility for Member States to regulate the activities of collecting societies should not prejudice the freedom of contractual negotiation of the rights provided for in this Directive, on the understanding that such negotiation takes place within the framework of general or specific national rules with regard to competition law or the prevention of abuse of monopolies;

(35) Whereas it should, therefore, be for the Member States to supplement the general provisions needed to achieve the objectives of this Directive by taking legislative and administrative measures in their domestic law, provided that these do not run counter to the objectives of this Directive and are compatible with Community law;

(36) Whereas this Directive does not affect the applicability of the competition rules in Articles 85 and 86 of the Treaty,

Has adopted this Directive:

CHAPTER I. DEFINITIONS

[Definitions]

Article 1

(1) For the purpose of this Directive, 'satellite' means any satellite operating on frequency bands which, under telecommunications law, are reserved for the broadcast of signals for reception by the public or which are reserved for closed, point-to-point communication. In the latter case, however, the circumstances in which individual reception of the signals takes place must be comparable to those which apply in the first case.

(2)(a) For the purpose of this Directive, 'communication to the public by satellite' means the act of introducing, under the control and responsibility of the broadcasting organization, the programme-carrying signals intended for reception by the public into an uninterrupted chain of communication leading to the satellite and down towards the earth.

(b) The act of communication to the public by satellite occurs solely in the Member State where, under the control and responsibility of the broadcasting organization, the programme-carrying signals are introduced into an uninterrupted chain of communication leading to the satellite and down towards the earth.

(c) If the programme-carrying signals are encrypted, then there is communication to the public by satellite on condition that the means for decrypting the broadcast are provided to the public by the broadcasting organization or with its consent.

(d) Where an act of communication to the public by satellite occurs in a non-Community State which does not provide the level of protection provided for under Chapter II,

   (i) if the programme-carrying signals are transmitted to the satellite from an uplink situation situated in a Member State, that act of communication to the public by satellite shall be deemed to have occurred in that Member State and the rights provided for under Chapter II shall be exercisable against the person operating the uplink station; or

   (ii) if there is no use of an uplink station situated in a Member State but a broadcasting organization established in a Member State has commissioned the act of communication to the public by satellite, that act shall be deemed to have occurred in the Member State in which the broadcasting organization has its principal establishment in the Community and the rights provided for under Chapter II shall be exercisable against the broadcasting organization.

(3) For the purposes of this Directive, 'cable retransmission' means the simultaneous, unaltered and unabridged retransmission by a cable or microwave system for reception by the public of an initial transmission from another Member State, by wire or over the air, including that by satellite, of television or radio programmes intended for reception by the public.

(4) For the purposes of this Directive 'collecting society' means any organization which manages or administers copyright or rights related to copyright as its sole purpose or as one of its main purposes.

(5) For the purposes of this Directive, the principal director of a cinematographic or audiovisual work shall be considered as its author or one of its authors. Member States may provide for others to be considered as its co-authors.

1. Definition of satellite (para. 1). Art. 1(1) defines the term 'satellite' in a broad and technology-neutral way. The term encompasses both satellites broadcasting on frequencies intended for satellite broadcasting (Direct Broadcasting Satellites), and communications satellites using other frequencies (Fixed Services Satellites), but serving as broadcasting satellites nonetheless. From a copyright perspective, these technical distinctions, which derive from the law of telecommunications, are basically irrelevant (recital 6). What is relevant is whether the signals transmitted by satellite can be received by the general public. If a communications satellite is used to transmit encoded signals that can be received only by using equipment that is available solely to professionals, and not to the general public, the satellite does not qualify as a 'satellite' within the meaning of Art. 1(1), and the provisions of the Directive do not apply (*Lagardère* (ECJ)).

2. Communication to the public by satellite (para. 2(a)). (a) General. Satellite broadcasting is perceived as a unitary act committed by a broadcasting organization, which begins by the introduction of signals by or under the control and responsibility of the broadcasting organization. This will usually precede the actual (technical) 'uplink' to the satellite. The communication to the public is completed by the transmission from the satellite back towards the earth ('downlink'). **(b) Control and responsibility of the broadcasting organization.** The broadcasting organization need not actually transmit the signals, as long as the signals are introduced under its control and responsibility. For example, the broadcasting of live sports events or other content produced by third parties may occur without any actual (technical) intervention of a broadcasting organization. On the other hand, an organization that merely technically transmits the signals, is not considered a broadcaster for the purposes of this Directive. **(c) Intended for reception by the public.** The signals must be intended for reception by the public. Whether they are actually received by members of the public is irrelevant. Moreover, it is the signals that must be intended for reception by the public, not the programmes that they carry (see *Airfield and Canal Digitaal* (ECJ)). Therefore, the transmission by satellite of encoded signals solely intended for reception by a terrestrial transmitter that subsequently broadcasts them to the general public does not qualify as communication to the public (*Lagardère* (ECJ)). **(d) Public.** The notion of 'public' is not defined, and therefore left to interpretation by the courts. According to the ECJ a limited circle of persons who can receive the signals from the satellite only if they use professional equipment cannot be regarded as 'public', given that the latter must be made up of an indeterminate number of potential listeners (*Lagardère* (ECJ)). Similarly, the transmission by satellite of encoded programme-carrying signals that are intended solely for reception by cable operators was held by the Dutch Supreme Court not to constitute communication to the public (*BUMA/Chellomedia* (Netherlands)). **(e) Uninterrupted chain.** This criterion serves to allocate liability for acts of satellite broadcasting at the broadcasting organization that is responsible for the transmission, not at the operator of the satellite or other facilitator. The chain of communication from studio to transmitter to satellite (transponder) to earth may not be interrupted, for instance by adding content (e.g. advertisements) to the signals, or by storing the signals and retransmitting them after a certain delay. Normal technical procedures relating to programme-carrying signals are not considered as interruptions (recital 14), nor is the use of a series of satellites, or even the intermediate reception, encoding and subsequent uplinking of broadcast television signals by a satellite package provider (*Airfield and Canal Digitaal* (ECJ)). Nevertheless, according to the ECJ, retransmission by a satellite package provider does require authorization if he makes the protected works accessible to a new public, that is to say, a public which was not taken into account by the rightholders when granting permission to broadcast the works by satellite (*Airfield and Canal Digitaal* (ECJ)). The Directive presupposes a closed communications system of which the satellite forms the central, essential and irreplaceable element. Its rules do not apply to a system of terrestrial broadcasting of which the satellite is a non-essential component. (*Lagardère* (ECJ)).

3. Place of act of communication to the public by satellite (para. 2(b)). (a) General. Art. 1(2)(b) provides the main rule of the satellite part of the Directive. Communication to the public by satellite is a relevant act only in the Member State where the signals originate, as set out in art. 1(2)(a). Therefore, Member States are barred from applying the so-called Bogsch (or reception) theory, which held that satellite broadcasting is a relevant act in all countries within the footprint of the satellite. A broadcasting organization will need to acquire licenses only from rightholders in the Member State of origin of the signal. However, art. 1(2)(b) does not rule out that license fees and other contractual conditions take into account the size of the footprint (i.e. number countries reached) of the satellite broadcast. On the contrary, recital 17 instructs the parties concerned to 'take account of all aspects of the broadcast, such as the actual audience, the potential audience and the language version'. **(b) No territorial exclusivity.** Art. 1(2)(b) precludes that right owners divide the right of communication to the public by satellite into territorially defined parts. However, parties remain free to contractually agree on obligations to apply encryption or other technical means so as to avoid reception by the general public of programme-carrying signals in countries for which the broadcast is not intended. By limiting the making available of decoders, territorial exclusivity can still be achieved, notwithstanding the aim of the Directive to create an internal market for trans-frontier satellite broadcasting (see Report on the Satellite and Cable Directive). **(c) Conflicts of law.** The country of origin rule art. 1(2)(b) is a provision of substantive law, not a conflicts rule. It does not designate the national law that applies to an act of satellite broadcasting, but simply clarifies, as a matter of EU law, that acts of satellite broadcasting only occur in the country of origin of the signal. It leaves it to the courts of the Member States to apply its national rules of private international law to such acts.

4. Encrypted signals (para. 2(c)). Art. 1(2)(c) confirms that communication to the public takes place even if the programme-carrying signals are encrypted. Therefore, transmitting copyright protected works over satellite-based pay television services is a restricted act. However, in these cases, communication to the public occurs only if the means for decrypting the broadcast are provided to the public by the broadcasting organization or with its consent. This condition is intended to prevent the sale of illegal decoders from resulting in the unjustified application of the Directive's country of origin rule.

5. Satellite broadcasting from outside the EU (para. 2(d)). Art. 1(2) (d) extends the definition of communication to the public by satellite (art. 1(2)(b)) to cover two situations where the communication in reality occurs outside the European Union. The provision seeks to discourage broadcasting organizations from relocating their operations outside the European Union to avoid the application of the Directive (recital 24). If an act of communication to the public occurs outside the European Union, but either the signal is up-linked from within the EU or a broadcasting organization established in the EU has commissioned the transmission, the communication shall be deemed to have occurred in the Member State where the uplink has taken place or where the broadcasting organization is established. This legal fiction, however, applies only if the non-EU State where the communication actually occurs does not offer the level of protection provided under Chapter II (most importantly, an exclusive right of communication to the public by satellite). For example, if a broadcaster established in Luxembourg were to use a satellite network owned and operated by an African state, to broadcast to European audiences, the broadcast would be deemed to occur in Luxembourg, unless the copyright law of that state provided for an exclusive right of communication to the public by satellite. With respect to satellite broadcasts from outside the EU not covered by art. 1(2)(d), Member States remain free to apply the Bogsch (or reception) theory.

6. Definition of cable retransmission (para. 3). (a) General. Art. 1(3) defines the act of 'cable retransmission', a notion that is central to Chapter III (articles 8–12) of the Directive. Retransmission does not comprise acts of cablecasting, i.e. initial broadcasting over cable networks. The definition limits the scope of application of the Directive's rules on cable retransmission in several ways. In line with the Directive's purpose to facilitate the freedom of trans-border broadcasting services across the EU, the Directive applies only to cable retransmission of 'an initial transmission' from another Member State. Thus, the Directive leaves the Member States' autonomy to deal with cases of purely national retransmission, or of retransmission of programmes originating outside the European Union, intact. Such 'initial transmissions' must be 'intended for reception by the public', and can occur either over the air (broadcasting) or by wire (cablecasting). **(b) Simultaneous, unaltered and unabridged.** Retransmission of broadcast programmes must be 'simultaneous, unaltered and unabridged' to qualify. Delayed retransmissions are outside the scope of the Directive, as are incomplete transmissions, e.g. in cases where advertisements contained in the original broadcast programme are replaced by 'local' advertisements. Arguably, the application of mere technical procedures, such as analogue-to-digital conversion, remains within the ambit of the definition. **(c) Cable or microwave system.** The Directive applies to retransmission not only by cable networks, but also by microwave systems. Acts of secondary over-the air broadcasting, however, remain outside the scope of the Directive. **(d) Intended for reception by the public.** The definition applies only to cases of cable retransmission of initial transmissions of television or radio programmes 'intended for reception by the public'. In light of art. 1(2)(c) this includes initial transmissions in encrypted form, insofar as the means for decrypting the signal are provided to the public by the broadcasting organization or with its consent (see *Lagardère* (ECJ)). According to the Dutch Supreme Court an encoded satellite transmission of television programmes receivable only by cable head stations is not 'intended for reception by the public' (*BUMA/Chellomedia* (Netherlands)). According to the same court, the same applies in the case of programme-carrying signals being injected through a 'media gateway' directly into the cable networks. Absent an initial transmission that is 'intended for the public', retransmission by cable qualifies as an act of primary communication to the public not subject to the Directive's special rules on cable retransmission in art. 9 (*Norma/NLKabel* (Netherlands)). **(e) Transmission over the internet.** The Directive could not take into account the use of the Internet as a programme-carrying medium. Whether retransmission of radio or television programs by way of Internet streaming can be qualified as retransmission by a 'cable system' is a matter of speculation. If so, the simulcasting of radio or television programmes over the Internet would be subject to the Directive's rules on mandatory collective exercise of retransmission rights (see art. 9).

7. Definition of collecting society (para. 4). The definition of collecting society is relevant mainly to Chapter III of the Directive, which provides for a system of mandatory collective management of cable retransmission rights. In addition, the term collecting society is used in art. 3(2) that allows Member States to apply a system of 'extended' collective licensing to satellite broadcasting. The definition of collecting society is very broad, encompassing 'any organization which manages or administers copyright or rights related to copyright as its sole purpose or as one of its main purposes'. It includes collecting societies of all sorts, whether unregulated or operating under a statutory licence or monopoly. In addition, it includes other organizations, such as trade unions, that engage in collective rights management of their members. The definition is certainly much broader than the more precise definition of art. 3(a) of the Collective Rights Management Directive.

8. Authorship of audiovisual works (para. 5). Art. 1(5) designates as the author of a cinematographic (i.e. film) work or other audiovisual work its principal director, but only for the purpose of this Directive. The provision repeats similar provisions in other directives, notably art. 2(1) of the Term Directive and art. 2(2) of the Rental Right Directive. It is relevant only in connection with art. 2 that guarantees to authors an exclusive right of communication to the public by satellite. Member States, therefore, must grant this minimum right to the main director of a film, even if under national copyright law authorship in films is attributed to other creators, such as screen writers, as well. Therefore, according to the ECJ, art. 1(5) precludes Member

States from vesting sole authorship of cinematographic works in film producers. Member States may nevertheless provide for a statutory presumption of transfer of the right of communication to the public by satellite in favour of film producers, as long as this presumption is rebuttable (*Luksan*).

CHAPTER II. BROADCASTING OF PROGRAMMES BY SATELLITE

[Broadcasting right]

Article 2

Member States shall provide an exclusive right for the author to authorize the communication to the public by satellite of copyright works, subject to the provisions set out in this chapter.

1. (a) General. Art. 2 instructs Member States to provide for an exclusive right, under copyright law, to communicate to the public by satellite. This provision is the necessary counterpart to the country-of-origin rule of art. 1(2)(b). If in the country of origin of the satellite broadcast no such right existed, rightholders across the European Union would have no right to authorize or prevent it. The act and place of communication to the public by satellite are defined in art. 1(1) and 1(2). Art. 2 has been largely superseded by art. 3 of the Information Society Directive that provides for a more generally phrased right of communication to the public that includes acts of satellite broadcasting. **(b) Retransmission by satellite.** Retransmission by satellite of broadcast programmes also qualifies as communication to the public by satellite (see *ITV Broadcasting and others* (ECJ), and art. 8, note 2). According to the ECJ, this is also the case for a satellite package provider that intervenes in the transmission of television programmes, unless the rightholders have consented to rebroadcasting through that provider, on condition, in the latter situation, that the provider's intervention does not make those works accessible to a new public (*Airfield and Canal Digitaal*).

2. Author. Art. 1(5) designates the principal director of a cinematographic or audiovisual work as one its authors, but leaves it to the Member States to designate other co-authors as well. According to the ECJ, art. 2 read in conjunction with art. 1(5) must be interpreted as meaning that the satellite broadcasting right vests by operation of law, directly and originally, in the principal director – precluding Member States, notably Austria, from allocating this right directly and exclusively to the film producer. Member States may however provide for a statutory presumption of transfer of the right of communication to the public by satellite in favour of film producers, as long as this presumption is rebuttable (*Luksan*).

[Acquisition of broadcasting rights]

Article 3

(1) Member States shall ensure that the authorization referred to in Article 2 may be acquired only be agreement.

(2) A Member State may provide that a collective agreement between a collecting society and a broadcasting organization concerning a given category of works may be extended to rightholders of the same category who are not represented by the collecting society, provided that:

- the communication to the public by satellite simulcasts a terrestrial broadcast by the same broadcaster, and
- the unrepresented rightholder shall, at any time, have the possibility of excluding the extension of the collective agreement to his works and of exercising his rights either individually or collectively.

(3) Paragraph 2 shall not apply to cinematographic works, including works created by a process analogous to cinematography.

(4) Where the law of a Member State provides for the extension of a collective agreement in accordance with the provisions of paragraph 2, that Member States shall inform the Commission which broadcasting organizations are entitled to avail themselves of that law. The Commission shall publish this information in the Official Journal of the European Communities (C series).

1. No statutory licensing (para. 1). The exclusive right of satellite broadcasting (art. 2) may not be made subject to a system of statutory licensing, even if art. 11bis (2) of the Berne Convention would allow this. Due to the immediate Union-wide effect of a communication to the public by satellite by virtue of the country of origin rule of art. 1(2)(b), a statutory licence in one Member State would effectively eliminate the exclusive right for the entire European Union. Art. 3(1) has been largely superseded by the Information Society Directive, which does not permit any exceptions or limitations to right of communication to the public except those expressly listed in art. 5(3) of that Directive.

2. Extended collective agreements permitted (paras. 2, 3 and 4). Notwithstanding para. 1, the system of 'extended' collective licensing, which already existed in the Nordic countries prior to the adoption of the Directive, may be applied to the right of communication to the public by satellite, but only in case of simulcasting by satellite of a terrestrial broadcast. According to para. 2 unrepresented rightholders (so-called outsiders) may withdraw their works from the extended license at any time. Rights in cinematographic works are excluded from extended licensing altogether. Member States concerned must inform the European Commission to which broadcasting organizations the extended licence applies.

[Rights of performers, phonogram producers and broadcasting organizations]

Article 4

(1) **For the purposes of communication to the public by satellite, the rights of performers, phonogram producers and broadcasting organizations shall be protected in accordance with the provisions of Articles 6, 7, 8 and 10 of Directive 92/100/EEC.**

(2) **For the purposes of paragraph 1, 'broadcasting by wireless means' in Directive 92/100/EEC shall be understood as including communication to the public by satellite.**

(3) **With regard to the exercise of the rights referred to in paragraph 1, Articles 2 (7) and 12 of Directive 92/100/EEC shall apply.**

1. General. Art. 4 concerns neighbouring rights of performing artists, phonogram producers and broadcasting organizations. These are rights related to copyright, which are primarily dealt with by the Rental Right Directive. Art. 4 does not increase the minimum rights conferred by that Directive, but simply clarifies (in para. 2) that 'broadcasting by wireless means' under the Rental Right Directive encompasses acts of communication to the public by satellite. Consequently, performers and phonogram producers' exclusive rights and rights to remuneration provided under that Directive will also relate to acts of satellite broadcasting.

2. Presumption of transfer (para. 3). The reference to art. 2(7), currently art. 3(6), of the Rental Right Directive is somewhat confusing. Art. 3(6) of that Directive allows for a rule of presumed transfer of rental rights, and does not refer to the act of broadcasting. Presumably, art. 4(3) is meant to allow Member States to provide for a similar rule, mutatis mutandis, in respect of the rights of satellite broadcasting of performers, phonogram producers and broadcasting organizations, as is confirmed by recital 26.

[Relation between copyright and related rights]

Article 5

Protection of copyright-related rights under this Directive shall leave intact and shall in no way affect the protection of copyright.

1. General. This provision is not a substantive norm. It simply confirms that copyrights and neighbouring (related) rights exist independently of each other. Similar statements appear previously in art. 1 of the Rome Convention, art. 12 of the Rental Right Directive, and art. 1(2) of the WIPO Performers and Phonograms Treaty (WPPT).

[Minimum protection]

Article 6

(1) Member States may provide for more far-reaching protection for holders of rights related to copyright than that required by Article 8 of Directive 92/100/EEC.

(2) In applying paragraph 1 Member States shall observe the definitions contained in Article 1 (1) and (2).

1. General. Art. 6 clarifies that Member States may go further in protecting holders of neighbouring rights than the minimum norms of the Rental Right Directive, as confirmed by art. 4. For instance, a Member State may grant to phonogram producers an exclusive right of satellite broadcasting. However, in granting such extra protection Member States may not deviate from the country-of-origin rule of satellite broadcasting, as set out in art. 1(1) and (2).

[Transitional provisions]

Article 7

(1) With regard to the application in time of the rights referred to in Article 4 (1) of this Directive, Article 13 (1), (2), (6) and (7) of Directive 92/100/EEC shall apply. Article 13 (4) and (5) of Directive 92/100/EEC shall apply mutatis mutandis.

(2) Agreements concerning the exploitation of works and other protected subject matter which are in force on the date mentioned in Article 14 (1) shall be subject to the provisions of Articles 1 (2), 2 and 3 as from 1 January 2000 if they expire after that date.

(3) When an international co-production agreement concluded before the date mentioned in Article 14 (1) between a co-producer from a Member State and one or more co-producers from other Member States or third countries expressly provides for a system of division of exploitation rights between the co-producers by geographical areas for all means of communication to the public, without distinguishing the arrangement applicable to communication to the public by satellite from the provisions applicable to the other means of communication, and where communication to the public by satellite of the co-production would prejudice the exclusivity, in particular the language exclusivity, of one of the co-producers or his assignees in a given territory, the authorization by one of the co-producers or his assignees for a communication to the public by satellite shall require the prior consent of the holder of that exclusivity, whether co-producer or assignee.

1. Neighbouring rights (para. 1). The reference to the transitional provisions of the Rental Right Directive is of little practical meaning, since the

Directive has not raised the standard of neighbouring rights protection set by that directive.

2. Pre-1995 broadcasting licenses (para. 2). For broadcasting licences that were effective before 1 January 1995, application of the Directive's country of origin rule is postponed until 1 January 2000. The broad language of the provision suggests that this is true even for agreements that do not mention acts of satellite broadcasting specifically.

3. Pre-1995 international co-production agreements (para. 3). Prior to the implementation of the Directive, international co-production agreements regularly provided for the division of exploitation (economic) rights along national borders. The Directive no longer supports such a 'splitting up' of rights, since the underlying copyrights in the countries of reception have disappeared. Nonetheless, such provisions in international co-production agreement concluded before 1 January 1995 have remained intact, subject to the detailed and complicated conditions set out in para. 3. Note however that the Directive does not actually prohibit territorial licensing, it merely does away with the underlying territorial copyrights. As the European Commission readily admits in its report, interested parties have remained free to persist in these age-old practices (Report on the Satellite and Cable Directive; see art. 14, note 2). Although para. 3 is limited to international co-production agreements, the German Federal Supreme Court has applied the provision to purely national co-production agreements as well (*Man spricht deutsh* (Germany)).

CHAPTER III. CABLE RETRANSMISSION

[Cable retransmission right]

Article 8

(1) Member States shall ensure that when programmes from other Member States are retransmitted by cable in their territory the applicable copyright and related rights are observed and that such retransmission takes place on the basis of individual or collective contractual agreements between copyright owners, holders of related rights and cable operators.

(2) Notwithstanding paragraph 1, Member States may retain until 31 December 1997 such statutory licence systems which are in operation or expressly provided for by national law on 31 July 1991.

1. General. (a) No statutory licensing. Art. 8(1) requires Member States to ensure that cable retransmission of programmes from other Member States is governed by contractual arrangements between rightholders and cable operators. Indeed, prior to the adoption of the Directive, such arrangements were already in place in an increasing number of Member States. The provision applies both to holders of copyrights and related rights in retransmitted programs, as do the other provisions of Chapter III. Statutory licences, such as existed in Austria and Denmark prior to the implementation of the Directive, are no longer permitted. The central notion of 'cable retransmission' is defined in art. 1(3). It follows from this definition that art. 8(1) applies only to cable retransmission of programmes originating in another Member State. Member States may therefore preserve and apply statutory licences in purely national situations. **(b) Relationship to art. 56 TFEU (freedom of services).** Art. 8 essentially confirms *Coditel I* (ECJ), in which the ECJ had left intact the copyright holder's exclusive right of cable retransmission under national Belgian law with regard to a cinematographic work that had been broadcast from a neighbouring Member State (Germany). According to the ECJ the cable retransmission right, being part of the 'specific object' (or essential function) of copyright, prevailed over the freedom to provide services across national boundaries, as enshrined in art. 56 TFEU (ex art. 49 EC Treaty).

2. Legal status of cable retransmission. Art. 8(1) does not expressly mandate an exclusive right of cable retransmission. Member States are merely obliged to ensure that 'the applicable copyright and related rights are observed' (see *Egeda* (ECJ)). Art. 8(1) only recognizes implicitly that cable retransmission is a restricted act under the laws of copyright of the Member States. This is confirmed by recital 27, in line with art. 11bis (1) (ii) of the Berne Convention. Substantive harmonization of the right of cable retransmission, as part of the general right to communication to the public, was achieved only much later in the Information Society Directive. Cable retransmission falls squarely within the terms of the right of communication to the public prescribed by art. 3(1), as clarified in recital 23, of that Directive (see *Uradex* (ECJ)). Whether the programmes retransmitted by cable are directly receivable over the air is irrelevant. According to the ECJ, arts. 2 and 8 of the Satellite and Cable Directive 'require fresh authorization for a simultaneous, unaltered and unabridged retransmission by satellite or cable of an initial transmission of television or radio programmes containing protected works, even though those programmes may already be received in their catchment area by other technical means, such as by wireless means or terrestrial networks' (*ITV Broadcasting and others*). In respect of neighbouring rights, however, things are different. Pursuant to the Rome Convention, national laws on neighbouring rights often do not recognize cable retransmission as a restricted act, nor does the Rental Right Directive (see art. 8 Rental Right Directive, note 4) or the Information Society Directive (see art. 3 Information Society Directive, note 3).

3. Contractual agreements (para. 1). Art. 8(1) requires that cable retransmission take place 'on the basis of individual or collective contractual agreements'. This language is somewhat surprising in view of the mandatory collective management of rights that the Directive prescribes in art. 9. However, art. 10 does allow broadcasting organizations to exercise cable retransmission rights individually; hence, the reference to 'individual' agreements.

4. Transitional rule (para. 2). Para. 2 permitted statutory licence systems existing in the Member States prior to 31 July 1991, just before the Directive was first proposed, to survive until 31 December 1997.

[Exercise of the cable retransmission right]

Article 9

(1) Member States shall ensure that the right of copyright owners and holders or related rights to grant or refuse authorization to a cable operator for a cable retransmission may be exercised only through a collecting society.

(2) Where a rightholder has not transferred the management of his rights to a collecting society, the collecting society which manages rights of the same category shall be deemed to be mandated to manage his rights. Where more than one collecting society manages rights of that category, the rightholder shall be free to choose which of those collecting societies is deemed to be mandated to manage his rights. A rightholder referred to in this paragraph shall have the same rights and obligations resulting from the agreement between the cable operator and the collecting society which is deemed to be mandated to manage his rights as the rightholders who have mandated that collecting society and he shall be able to claim those rights within a period, to be fixed by the Member State concerned, which shall not be shorter than three years from the date of the cable retransmission which includes his work or other protected subject matter.

(3) A Member State may provide that, when a rightholder authorizes the initial transmission within its territory of a work or other protected subject matter, he shall be deemed to have agreed not to exercise his cable retransmission rights on an individual basis but to exercise them in accordance with the provisions of this Directive.

1. General. Art. 9(1) is the centrepiece of the Directive's rules on cable retransmission. The right of cable retransmission may not be exercised by right owners individually, but only by way of a collecting society. In practice, even before the Directive was adopted, collective management of cable rights had become normal practice in many Member States of the European Union. The Directive's regime of mandatory collective rights management, which does not exist elsewhere in European copyright law, seeks to ensure that cable operators are in a position to acquire all rights necessary to allow cable retransmission of broadcast programmes. Its particular aim is to avoid a situation in which rightholders, in parts of broadcast programmes that are not represented by a collecting society, enforce their exclusive rights individually vis-à-vis cable operators, thereby causing 'black-outs' in retransmitted pro-grammes. Note that art. 9(1) applies only in cases of cable retransmission. In cases where cable operators do not retransmit initial transmissions 'intended for reception by the public' (art. 1(3)), collective management of retransmission rights is not mandatory. See art. 1, note 6(d).

2. Exclusive right left intact. Art. 9(1) replaces the statutory licence scheme that was originally envisaged by the European Commission in the Green Paper on Television without Frontiers. Art. 9(1) leaves the authorization right intact, and therefore does not qualify as a statutory or compulsory licence, which art. 8 expressly prohibits. A collecting society may still deny permission to cable operators to retransmit certain works represented by the society, albeit that art. 12 prohibits bad faith refusals to licence. Black-outs, therefore, may still occur in practice. However, viewed from the perspective of the individual right owner, the mandatory collective exercise of rights does closely resemble a compulsory licence. An individual film producer, for instance, will not be able to control cable retransmission in a foreign market, once he has licensed the film for television broadcasting.

3. Transfer of cable retransmission rights. Art. 9(1) does not prevent rightholders from individually assigning (transferring) their cable retransmission rights to other parties (see recital 28 and *Uradex* (ECJ)), for instance, to film producers or to broadcasting organizations wishing to clear cable rights up-front, so they can offer their programs to cable operators as 'clean products'. Exceptionally, art. 10 allows broadcasters to exercise retransmission rights on an individual basis.

4. Remuneration rights. Art. 9(1) refers to the right 'to grant or refuse authorization'. In cases where right owners, notably holders of neighbouring rights, do not enjoy exclusive rights, but merely a right to remuneration, the rule of mandatory collective exercise of rights does not apply.

5. Equal treatment of outsiders (para. 2). Whereas art. 9(1) prevents outsiders (i.e. right owners not represented by collecting societies) from enforcing their retransmission rights against cable operators, art. 9(2) deals with the relationship between such rightholders and the collecting societies. As follows logically from art 9(1), and as the ECJ has clarified in *Uradex*, the management by the collecting society of the rights of the outsider concerns not only the right to claim remuneration from cable operators, but also the exclusive right to prohibit retransmission. In other words, collecting societies may actually enforce the rights of non-represented authors or other right-holders. Art. 9(2) grants equal treatment to represented and unrepresented right owners. According to the first sentence of para. 2 'the collecting society which manages rights of the same category shall be deemed to be mandated to manage his rights'. If, for example, in a certain Member State a special collecting society exists for the management of cable rights of performing artists, cable rights of non-member performers will be deemed, by legal fiction, to be managed by that society as well. If more than one collecting society manages rights of the same category, the outsider concerned may designate the society that is deemed to be mandated by him. The elected society, consequently, has an obligation to treat the outsider as a normal member or associate of the society. Outsiders will be able to claim from the societies their share of the revenues received from the cable operators. Member States remain free to limit the period within which right owners must claim remuneration from collecting societies, with a minimum period of three years from the date of the cable retransmission concerned.

6. Legal presumption permitted (para. 3). Art. 9(3) was inserted at a late stage in view of the objections of certain Member States who believed that art. 9(1) would infringe upon constitutionally guaranteed rights of ownerships. Accordingly, such States are free to introduce a rule of collective cable rights management by way of legal presumption.

[Exercise of the cable retransmission right by broadcasting organizations]

Article 10

Member States shall ensure that Article 9 does not apply to the rights exercised by a broadcasting organization in respect of its own transmission, irrespective of whether the rights concerned are its own or have been transferred to it by other copyright owners and/or holders of related rights.

1. General. Art. 10 excepts broadcasting organizations from the obligation of art. 9(1) to manage cable retransmission rights collectively. This exception is justified by the purpose of art. 9(1), which is to simplify the acquisition of rights by cable operators. Whereas right owners in broadcast programme may be difficult to trace prior to transmission, the identity of the broadcasting organizations is usually well known to the cable operators. Therefore, no real need for collective rights management of broadcasters' rights exists.

2. Rights of broadcasters excepted from mandatory collective management. Excepted cable retransmission rights are such rights as are initially owned by the broadcasters themselves, such as neighbouring rights in the broadcasts or copyrights in Member States where the law recognizes broadcasters as initial copyright owners or where copyright in works made under employment is allocated directly to the employer. Excepted rights also include rights that have been 'transferred' to the broadcaster. The term 'transfer' obviously refers to the assignment of rights, but is perhaps broad enough to encompass exclusive licences as well.

[Mediators]

Article 11

(1) Where no agreement is concluded regarding authorization of the cable retransmission of a broadcast. Member States shall ensure that either party may call upon the assistance of one or more mediators.

(2) The task of the mediators shall be to provide assistance with negotiation. They may also submit proposals to the parties.

(3) It shall be assumed that all the parties accept a proposal as referred to in paragraph 2 if none of them expresses its opposition within a period of three months. Notice of the proposal and of any opposition thereto shall be served on the parties concerned in accordance with the applicable rules concerning the service of legal documents.

(4) The mediators shall be so selected that their independence and impartiality are beyond reasonable doubt.

1. General. Art. 11 requires Member States to establish a system of mediation when an agreement between right owners and cable operators cannot be concluded. This provision is intended as a flanking measure to further facilitate contractual solutions, and to avoid stalemates between broadcasters, collecting societies and cable operators. Member States are left with considerable discretion as to how this mediation will be structured and carried out. Prior to the Directive, various systems of mediation in the area of collective rights management already existed in some Member States, such as Germany. The mediation system prescribed by Art. 11, however, remains voluntary. If no party seeks recourse to mediation, prolonged stalemates may still occur, as has been, and still is, the case in several Member States. This may explain why the mediation systems set up in the Member States have been put to little use in practice (Report on the Satellite and Cable Directive).

2. Mediation process. Mediation can be initiated by either party (para. 1). Mediators may help the negotiating process by submitting a proposal (para. 2), which is deemed to be accepted if a party does not object to it within three months (para. 3). Note however, that the solutions offered by the mediators are not compulsory; a party remains free to reject any proposal. Finally, mediators must be independent and impartial (para. 4).

[Prevention of the abuse of negotiating positions]

Article 12

(1) Member States shall ensure by means of civil or administrative law, as appropriate, that the parties enter and conduct negotiations regarding authorization for cable retransmission in good faith and do not prevent or hinder negotiation without valid justification.

(2) A Member State which, on the date mentioned in Article 14 (1), has a body with jurisdiction in its territory over cases where the right to retransmit a programme by cable to the public in that Member State has been unreasonably refused or offered on unreasonable terms by a broadcasting organization may retain that body.

(3) Paragraph 2 shall apply for a transitional period of eight years from the date mentioned in Article 14 (1).

1. General. (a) Obligation to negotiate. Art. 12(1) provides yet another flanking measure aimed at facilitating contractual solutions. Member States must see to it that parties concerned (broadcasters, collecting societies and cable operators) conduct negotiations in good faith, and may not obstruct negotiations without justification. Since all parties concerned are monopolists in their own right, the chances of such abusive behaviour are real. Art. 12(1) leaves a broad measure of discretion to the Member States. States may provide remedies against abusive behaviour in civil or administrative law. Indeed, many countries already provided for remedies under general contract law or competition law, or the law of collective rights management. However, Member States cannot satisfy art. 12(1) by simple reference to general competition law, since a refusal to license retransmission rights does not, by itself, amount to anticompetitive behaviour. **(b) No obligation to grant license.** Art. 12(1) does not affect 'the contractual acquisition of cable retransmission rights' (recital 30). In other words, collecting societies cannot be forced into agreements with cable operators if conditions proposed by cable operators are unsatisfactory. A 'valid justification' to refuse a retransmission licence might also be found in the protection of the moral rights of authors. For instance, the author of a film may have a legitimate interest in preventing the retransmission of a broadcast version of his film ridden with commercial interruptions.

2. Transitional provisions (paras. 2 and 3). Paras. 2 and 3 contain transitional rules allowing Member States having special bodies with competence to deal with refusals to license cable retransmission rights, to retain such bodies until 1 January 2003.

CHAPTER IV. GENERAL PROVISIONS

[Collective administration of rights]

Article 13

This Directive shall be without prejudice to the regulation of the activities of collecting societies by the Member States.

1. National rules on collective rights management not affected. According to art. 13, the Directive shall be without prejudice to national rules on collective management. While the Directive keeps the collecting societies' freedom of contract largely intact, such national rules may go further and, for example, obligate a society to enter into contracts with users, or provide for the setting of license fees by courts or administrative bodies. Note that the 2004 Collective Rights Management Directive has partially harmonized the law on collecting societies in the EU.

2. Field of application. As a general provision, art. 13 applies not only to the rules on collective management of cable retransmission rights but also to the provisions on satellite broadcasting.

[Final provisions]

Article 14

(1) Member States shall bring into force the laws, regulations and administrative provisions necessary to comply with this Directive before 1 January 1995. They shall immediately inform the Commission thereof. When Member States adopt these measures, the latter shall contain a reference to this Directive or shall be accompanied by such reference at the time of their official publication. The methods of making such a reference shall be laid down by the Member States.

(2) Member States shall communicate to the Commission the provisions of national law which they adopt in the field covered by this Directive.

(3) Not later than 1 January 2000, the Commission shall submit to the European Parliament, the Council and the Economic and Social Committee a report on the application of this Directive and, if necessary, make further proposals to adapt it to developments in the audio and audiovisual sector.

1. Implementation deadline (para. 1). The implementation deadline expired on 1 January 1995.

2. Report (para. 3). The report mentioned in para. 3 was published by the Commission on 26 July 2002 (Report on Satellite and Cable Directive). In it the European Commission readily admits that the Directive has, at best, been a partial success. Market fragmentation along national borders persists, no longer on the basis of national copyrights, but through a combination of encryption technology and territorial licensing, a practice that the Directive does not prohibit.

[Addressees]

Article 15

This Directive is addressed to the Member States.

1. General. According to art. 288 TFEU (ex art. 249 EC Treaty), Directives are binding, as to the result to be achieved, upon each Member State to which it is addressed, but shall leave to the national authorities the choice of form and methods.

DIRECTIVE 2006/116/EC

(Term Directive)

**of the European Parliament and of the Council of 12 December 2006
on the term of protection of copyright and certain related rights
(codified version)**

as amended by

DIRECTIVE 2011/77/EU

(Term Extension Directive)

**of the European Parliament and of the Council of 27 September 2011
amending Directive 2006/116/EC on the term of protection of copyright
and certain related rights**

[Bibliography]

ALAI Study Days 2010 Vienna, *The Duration of Copyright and Related Rights* (Medien und Recht Publishing 2012)

C. Angelopoulos, 'The Myth of European Term Harmonisation: 27 Public Domains for the 27 Member States' (2012) 5 IIC 567

C. Angelopoulos, 'Determining the Term of Protection for Films: When Does a Film Fall into the Public Domain in Europe?' (2012) 2 IRIS Plus 7-21

R. Arnold, 'Joy: A Reply' (2001) 1 IPQ 10

L. Bently & B. Sherman, *Intellectual Property Law* (3rd edn., OUP 2009)

S. Dusollier, 'Scoping Study on Copyright and Related Rights and the Public Domain' (7 May 2010) WIPO Study, CDIP/4/3/REV./STUDY/INF/1

G. Dworkin, 'The EC Directive on the Term of Protection of Copyright and Related Rights' in H. Cohen Jehoram, et al. (eds.), *Audiovisual Media and Copyright in Europe* (Kluwer 1994) 33

Y. Gaubiac, B. Lindner & J. N. Adams, 'Duration of Copyright' in E. Derclaye, *Research Handbook on the Future of EU Copyright* (Edward Elgar 2009) 148

S. von Lewinski & M. Walter, 'Chapter 8 – Term Directive' in *European Copyright Law – A Commentary* (OUP 2010) 499-677

M. van Eechoud, P.B. Hugenholtz, et al., 'Chapter 2: Object, Subject, and Duration of Protection', 'Chapter 5: Term Extension for Sound Recordings' and 'Chapter 6: Term Calculation for Co-Written Musical Works' in

Harmonizing European Copyright Law – The Challenges of Better Lawmaking (Kluwer Law International 2009) 65-66

N. Helberger, P.B. Hugenholtz, et al., 'Never Forever: Why Extending the Term of Protection for Sound Recordings is a Bad Idea' (2008) 5 European Intellectual Property Review 174

P. Kamina, *Film Copyright in the European Union* (Cambridge University Press 2002)

G. Minero, 'The Term Directive' in I. Stamatoudi & P. Torremans (eds.), *EU Copyright Law: A Commentary* (Edward Elgar Publishing 2014) 248-297

T. Padfield, *Copyright for Archivists and Users of Archives* (2nd edn., Facet Publishing 2004)

S. Ricketson, 'The Copyright Term' (1992) 23 IIC 753

I. Stamatoudi, '"Joy" for the Claimant: Can A Film Also Be Protected as a Dramatic Work?' (2000) 1 IPQ 117

COMMUNIA Final Report, 'The Value of the Public Domain for Europe' (31 March 2011) Deliverable S.1.11

'Creativity Stifled? A Joint Academic Statement on the Proposed Copyright Term Extension for Sound Recordings' (2008) EIPR 341

[Introductory remarks]

1. Legislative history. The Term Directive harmonizes the term of protection of copyright and certain related rights. The initial Directive (Directive 93/98/EEC) was introduced in 1993. Following amendments made in 2001 by the Information Society Directive in 2006 a consolidated version (Directive 2006/116/EC) was adopted. Further changes followed in 2011 with Directive 2011/77/EU (Term Extension Directive). The Term Directive harmonizes the term of copyright at the relatively high level of 70 years after the death of the author. For neighbouring (related) rights the term is set at 50 years. All terms of protection in the Directive run from 1 January of the year following that in which the event that triggered the beginning of the term of protection took place (see art. 8). Surprisingly, the Directive sparked very little political controversy from its initial proposal, published by the European Commission on 23 March 1992, till its eventual adoption on 29 October 1993. This is particularly noteworthy given that this was one of the first issues in the area of copyright and related rights to be harmonized at the European level. By contrast, the 2011 Term Extension Directive, which introduced important alterations to the EU rules on the term of protection of performers' and phonogram producers' rights over sound recordings, as well as that of co-written musical works, proved much more controversial, its proposal in July 2008 sparking heated public debate. After a two-year stay before a divided Council, the Term Extension Directive was only adopted after Denmark removed itself from the blocking minority in April 2011. The original Directive was to be implemented by Member States by 1 July 1995. The 2011 amending Directive was due for full transposition by 1 November 2013.

2. Need for harmonization. (a) Situation before the Directive. Before the adoption of the Term Directive the term of protection for copyright varied considerably between the EU Member States. Most Member States provided a term of protection of 50 years after the death of the author (hereinafter: post mortem auctoris or pma), in accordance with the Berne Convention minimum. However, Germany (70 years pma), Greece (70 years pma), Austria, Belgium, France (70 years pma for musical works, 50 years pma for all other works) and Spain (60 years pma) all provided for longer terms of protection. **(b) Reason for harmonization.** These divergences were seen as impeding the free movement of copyright-protected goods and services and thereby distorting competition in the internal market (recital 3). This became apparent in *Patricia* (ECJ). In this case, the European Court found that, at the time, because of the longer term of protection in Germany, recorder producer EMI was allowed to prevent the resale in that country of Cliff Richard records that had been lawfully brought on the market in Denmark, where the rights in the recordings had already expired. It was felt that it was necessary to harmonize the terms of protection in order to avoid such trade barriers (see recital 3). **(c) Reason for harmonization at 70 years post mortem auctoris.** It is worth noting that because of the general agreement across the Community on 50 years, the Economic and Social Committee, consulted in 1992 under art. 114 TFEU had suggested that that term may provide a more useful base for facilitating international agreement on the term of protection. However the Commission opted to harmonize upwards in order to avoid the postponement of harmonization for 70 years that would otherwise result from the lengthy transitional provisions that would be necessary to maintain established rights in those countries that had a longer term (see recital 10). This would have hampered the completion of the internal market which was planned for the end of 1992. The extension was also justified by the increase in life expectancy within Europe which rendered a 50-year term insufficient to cover two generations (recital 6). It was also suggested that lengthening the term of protection would strengthen the position of the author during his lifetime when negotiating the assignment of his rights. **(d) Total harmonization.** The Term Directive provides for total harmonization: it imposes both an upper and lower limit for the permissible term of protection, leaving no room for national deviations from the European norm. Member States are not allowed to provide either shorter or longer terms of protection than those prescribed by the Directive (see recital 3). The rule of art. 7(6) BC, which allows Contracting Parties to grant terms of protection in excess of those provided by the treaty is thus not repeated in the Term Directive. If this were not the case, the Directive would not be able to achieve the desired harmonizing effect.

[Preamble to the Term Directive]

The European Parliament and the Council of the European Union,

Having regard to the Treaty establishing the European Community, and in particular Articles 47(2), 55 and 95 thereof,

Having regard to the proposal from the Commission,

Having regard to the opinion of the European Economic and Social Committee,[1]

Acting in accordance with the procedure laid down in Article 251 of the Treaty,[2]

Whereas:

(1) Council Directive 93/98/EEC of 29 October 1993 harmonising the term of protection of copyright and certain related rights[3] has been substantially amended.[4] In the interests of clarity and rationality the said Directive should be codified.

(2) The Berne Convention for the protection of literary and artistic works and the International Convention for the protection of performers, producers of phonograms and broadcasting organisations (Rome Convention) lay down only minimum terms of protection of the rights they refer to, leaving the Contracting States free to grant longer terms. Certain Member States have exercised this entitlement. In addition, some Member States have not yet become party to the Rome Convention.

(3) There are consequently differences between the national laws governing the terms of protection of copyright and related rights, which are liable to impede the free movement of goods and freedom to provide services and to distort competition in the common market. Therefore, with a view to the smooth operation of the internal market, the laws of the Member States should be harmonised so as to make terms of protection identical throughout the Community.

(4) It is important to lay down not only the terms of protection as such, but also certain implementing arrangements, such as the date from which each term of protection is calculated.

(5) The provisions of this Directive should not affect the application by the Member States of the provisions of Article 14 bis (2)(b), (c) and (d) and (3) of the Berne Convention.

---

1. OJ No. C 324, 30 December 2006, p 1.
2. Opinion of the European Parliament of 12 October 2006 (not yet published in the Official Journal) and Council Decision of 30 November 2006.
3. OJ L 290, 24.11.1993, p. 9. Directive as amended by Directive 2001/29/EC of the European Parliament and of the Council (OJ L 167, 22.6.2001, p. 10).
4. See Annex I, Part A.

(6) The minimum term of protection laid down by the Berne Convention, namely the life of the author and 50 years after his death, was intended to provide protection for the author and the first two generations of his descendants. The average lifespan in the Community has grown longer, to the point where this term is no longer sufficient to cover two generations.

(7) Certain Member States have granted a term longer than 50 years after the death of the author in order to offset the effects of the world wars on the exploitation of authors' works.

(8) For the protection of related rights certain Member States have introduced a term of 50 years after lawful publication or lawful communication to the public.

(9) The Diplomatic Conference held in December 1996, under the auspices of the World Intellectual Property Organization (WIPO), led to the adoption of the WIPO Performances and Phonograms Treaty, which deals with the protection of performers and producers of phonograms. This Treaty took the form of a substantial up-date of the international protection of related rights.

(10) Due regard for established rights is one of the general principles of law protected by the Community legal order. Therefore, the terms of protection of copyright and related rights established by Community law cannot have the effect of reducing the protection enjoyed by rightholders in the Community before the entry into force of Directive 93/98/EEC. In order to keep the effects of transitional measures to a minimum and to allow the internal market to function smoothly, those terms of protection should be applied for long periods.

(11) The level of protection of copyright and related rights should be high, since those rights are fundamental to intellectual creation. Their protection ensures the maintenance and development of creativity in the interest of authors, cultural industries, consumers and society as a whole.

(12) In order to establish a high level of protection which at the same time meets the requirements of the internal market and the need to establish a legal environment conducive to the harmonious development of literary and artistic creation in the Community, the term of protection for copyright should be harmonised at 70 years after the death of the author or 70 years after the work is lawfully made available to the public, and for related rights at 50 years after the event which sets the term running.

(13) Collections are protected according to Article 2(5) of the Berne Convention when, by reason of the selection and arrangement of their content, they constitute intellectual creations. Those works are protected as such, without prejudice to the copyright in each of the works forming part of such collections. Consequently, specific terms of protection may apply to works included in collections.

(14) In all cases where one or more physical persons are identified as authors, the term of protection should be calculated after their death. The question of authorship of the whole or a part of a work is a question of fact which the national courts may have to decide.

(15) Terms of protection should be calculated from the first day of January of the year following the relevant event, as they are in the Berne and Rome Conventions.

(16) The protection of photographs in the Member States is the subject of varying regimes. A photographic work within the meaning of the Berne Convention is to be considered original if it is the author's own intellectual creation reflecting his personality, no other criteria such as merit or purpose being taken into account. The protection of other photographs should be left to national law.

(17) In order to avoid differences in the term of protection as regards related rights it is necessary to provide the same starting point for the calculation of the term throughout the Community. The performance, fixation, transmission, lawful publication, and lawful communication to the public, that is to say the means of making a subject of a related right perceptible in all appropriate ways to persons in general, should be taken into account for the calculation of the term of protection regardless of the country where this performance, fixation, transmission, lawful publication, or lawful communication to the public takes place.

(18) The rights of broadcasting organisations in their broadcasts, whether these broadcasts are transmitted by wire or over the air, including by cable or satellite, should not be perpetual. It is therefore necessary to have the term of protection running from the first transmission of a particular broadcast only. This provision is understood to avoid a new term running in cases where a broadcast is identical to a previous one.

(19) The Member States should remain free to maintain or introduce other rights related to copyright in particular in relation to the protection of critical and scientific publications. In order to ensure transparency at Community level, it is however necessary for Member States which introduce new related rights to notify the Commission.

(20) It should be made clear that this Directive does not apply to moral rights.

(21) For works whose country of origin within the meaning of the Berne Convention is a third country and whose author is not a Community national, comparison of terms of protection should be applied, provided that the term accorded in the Community does not exceed the term laid down in this Directive.

(22) Where a rightholder who is not a Community national qualifies for protection under an international agreement, the term of protection of related rights should be the same as that laid down in this Directive. However, this term should not exceed that fixed in the third country of which the rightholder is a national.

Angelopoulos

(23) Comparison of terms should not result in Member States being brought into conflict with their international obligations.

(24) Member States should remain free to adopt provisions on the interpretation, adaptation and further execution of contracts on the exploitation of protected works and other subject matter which were concluded before the extension of the term of protection resulting from this Directive.

(25) Respect of acquired rights and legitimate expectations is part of the Community legal order. Member States may provide in particular that in certain circumstances the copyright and related rights which are revived pursuant to this Directive may not give rise to payments by persons who undertook in good faith the exploitation of the works at the time when such works lay within the public domain.

(26) This Directive should be without prejudice to the obligations of the Member States relating to the time-limits for transposition into national law and application of the Directives, as set out in Part B of Annex I,

[Preamble to the Term Extension Directive]

The European Parliament and the Council of the European Union,

Having regard to the Treaty on the Functioning of the European Union, and in particular Articles 53(1), 62 and 114 thereof,

Having regard to the proposal from the European Commission,

Having regard to the opinion of the European Economic and Social Committee,[5]

Acting in accordance with the ordinary legislative procedure,[6]

Whereas:

(1) Under Directive 2006/116/EC of the European Parliament and of the Council,[7] the term of protection for performers and producers of phonograms is 50 years.

(2) In the case of performers this period starts with the performance or, when the fixation of the performance is lawfully published or lawfully communicated to the public within 50 years after the performance is made, with the first such publication or the first such communication to the public, whichever is the earliest.

(3) For phonogram producers the period starts with the fixation of the phonogram or its lawful publication within 50 years after fixation, or, if

---

5. OJ C 182, 4.8.2009, p. 36.
6. Position of the European Parliament of 23 April 2009 (OJ C 184 E, 8.7.2010, p. 331) and Decision of the Council of 12 September 2011.
7. OJ L 372, 27.12.2006, p. 12.

it is not so published, its lawful communication to the public within 50 years after fixation.

(4) The socially recognised importance of the creative contribution of performers should be reflected in a level of protection that acknowledges their creative and artistic contribution.

(5) Performers generally start their careers young and the current term of protection of 50 years applicable to fixations of performances often does not protect their performances for their entire lifetime. There-fore, some performers face an income gap at the end of their lifetime. In addition, performers are often unable to rely on their rights to prevent or restrict an objectionable use of their performances that may occur during their lifetime.

(6) The revenue derived from the exclusive rights of reproduction and making available, as provided for in Directive 2001/29/EC of the Euro-pean Parliament and of the Council of 22 May 2001 on the harmonisation of certain aspects of copyright and related rights in the information society,[8] as well as fair compensation for reproductions for private use within the meaning of that Directive, and from the exclusive rights of distribution and rental within the meaning of Directive 2006/115/EC of the European Parliament and of the Council of 12 December 2006 on rental right and lending right and on certain rights related to copyright in the field of intellectual property,[9] should be available to performers for at least their lifetime.

(7) The term of protection for fixations of performances and for phonograms should therefore be extended to 70 years after the relevant event.

(8) The rights in the fixation of the performance should revert to the performer if a phonogram producer refrains from offering for sale in sufficient quantity, within the meaning of the International Convention on the Protection of Performers, Producers of Phonograms and Broad-casting Organisations, copies of a phonogram which, but for the term extension, would be in the public domain, or refrains from making such a phonogram available to the public. That option should be available on expiry of a reasonable period of time for the phonogram producer to carry out both of these acts of exploitation. The rights of the phonogram producer in the phonogram should therefore expire, in order to avoid a situation in which these rights would coexist with those of the performer in the fixation of the performance while the latter rights are no longer transferred or assigned to the phonogram producer.

(9) Upon entering into a contractual relationship with a phonogram producer, performers normally have to transfer or assign to the pho-nogram producer their exclusive rights of reproduction, distribution,

---

8.   OJ L 167, 22.6.2001, p. 10.
9.   OJ L 376, 27.12.2006, p. 28.

rental and making available of fixations of their performances. In exchange, some performers are paid an advance on royalties and enjoy payments only once the phonogram producer has recouped the initial advance and made any contractually defined deductions. Other performers transfer or assign their exclusive rights in return for a one-off payment (non-recurring remuneration). This is particularly the case for performers who play in the background and do not appear in the credits (non-featured performers) but sometimes also for performers who appear in the credits (featured performers).

(10) In order to ensure that performers who have transferred or assigned their exclusive rights to phonogram producers actually benefit from the term extension, a series of accompanying measures should be introduced.

(11) A first accompanying measure should be the imposition on phonogram producers of an obligation to set aside, at least once a year, a sum corresponding to 20 % of the revenue from the exclusive rights of distribution, reproduction and making available of phonograms. 'Revenue' means the revenue derived by the phonogram producer before deducting costs.

(12) Payment of those sums should be reserved solely for the benefit of performers whose performances are fixed in a phonogram and who have transferred or assigned their rights to the phonogram producer in return for a one-off payment. The sums set aside in this manner should be distributed to non-featured performers at least once a year on an individual basis. Such distribution should be entrusted to collecting societies and national rules on non-distributable revenue may be applied. In order to avoid the imposition of a disproportionate burden in the collection and administration of that revenue, Member States should be able to regulate the extent to which micro-enterprises are subject to the obligation to contribute where such payments would appear unreasonable in relation to the costs of collecting and administering such revenue.

(13) However, Article 5 of Directive 2006/115/EC already grants performers an unwaivable right to equitable remuneration for the rental of, inter alia, phonograms. Likewise, in contractual practice performers do not usually transfer or assign to phonogram producers their rights to claim a single equitable remuneration for broadcasting and communication to the public under Article 8(2) of Directive 2006/115/EC and to fair compensation for reproductions for private use under point (b) of Article 5(2) of Directive 2001/29/EC. Therefore, in the calculation of the overall amount to be dedicated by a phonogram producer to payments of the supplementary remuneration, no account should be taken of revenue which the phonogram producer has derived from the rental of phonograms, of the single equitable remuneration received for broadcasting and communication to the public or of the fair compensation received for private copying.

(14) A second accompanying measure designed to rebalance contracts whereby performers transfer their exclusive rights on a royalty basis to a phonogram producer, should be a 'clean slate' for those performers who have assigned their above-mentioned exclusive rights to phonogram producers in return for royalties or remuneration. In order for performers to benefit fully from the extended term of protection, Member States should ensure that, under agreements between phonogram producers and performers, a royalty or remuneration rate unencumbered by advance payments or contractually defined deductions is paid to performers during the extended period.

(15) For the sake of legal certainty it should be provided that, in the absence of clear indications to the contrary in the contract, a contractual transfer or assignment of rights in the fixation of the performance concluded before the date by which Member States are to adopt measures implementing this Directive shall continue to produce its effects for the extended term.

(16) Member States should be able to provide that certain terms in those contracts which provide for recurring payments can be renegotiated for the benefit of performers. Member States should have procedures in place to cover the eventuality that the renegotiation fails.

(17) This Directive should not affect national rules and agreements which are compatible with its provisions, such as collective agreements concluded in Member States between organisations representing performers and organisations representing producers.

(18) In some Member States, musical compositions with words are given a single term of protection, calculated from the death of the last surviving author, while in other Member States separate terms of protection apply for music and lyrics. Musical compositions with words are overwhelmingly co-written. For example, an opera is often the work of a librettist and a composer. Moreover, in musical genres such as jazz, rock and pop music, the creative process is often collaborative in nature.

(19) Consequently, the harmonisation of the term of protection in respect of musical compositions with words the lyrics and music of which were created in order to be used together is incomplete, giving rise to obstacles to the free movement of goods and services, such as cross-border collective management services. In order to ensure the removal of such obstacles, all such works in protection at the date by which the Member States are required to transpose this Directive should have the same harmonised term of protection in all Member States.

(20) Directive 2006/116/EC should therefore be amended accordingly.

(21) Since the objectives of the accompanying measures cannot be sufficiently achieved by the Member States, inasmuch as national measures in that field would either lead to distortion of competition or affect the scope of exclusive rights of the phonogram producer which are defined by Union legislation, and can therefore be better achieved at Union

level, the Union may adopt measures, in accordance with the principle of subsidiarity as set out in Article 5 of the Treaty on European Union. In accordance with the principle of proportionality, as set out in that Article, this Directive does not go beyond what is necessary in order to achieve those objectives.

(22) In accordance with point 34 of the interinstitutional agreement on better law-making,[10] Member States are encouraged to draw up, for themselves and in the interests of the Union, their own tables which will, as far as possible, illustrate the correlation between this Directive and their transposition measures, and to make them public,

Have adopted this Directive:

[Duration of authors' rights]

Article 1

(1) The rights of an author of a literary or artistic work within the meaning of Article 2 of the Berne Convention shall run for the life of the author and for 70 years after his death, irrespective of the date when the work is lawfully made available to the public.

(2) In the case of a work of joint authorship, the term referred to in paragraph 1 shall be calculated from the death of the last surviving author.

(3) In the case of anonymous or pseudonymous works, the term of protection shall run for 70 years after the work is lawfully made available to the public. However, when the pseudonym adopted by the author leaves no doubt as to his identity, or if the author discloses his identity during the period referred to in the first sentence, the term of protection applicable shall be that laid down in paragraph 1.

(4) Where a Member State provides for particular provisions on copyright in respect of collective works or for a legal person to be designated as the rightholder, the term of protection shall be calculated according to the provisions of paragraph 3, except if the natural persons who have created the work are identified as such in the versions of the work which are made available to the public. This paragraph is without prejudice to the rights of identified authors whose identifiable contributions are included in such works, to which contributions paragraph 1 or 2 shall apply.

(5) Where a work is published in volumes, parts, instalments, issues or episodes and the term of protection runs from the time when the work was lawfully made available to the public, the term of protection shall run for each such item separately.

---

10. OJ C 321, 31.12.2003, p. 1.

(6) In the case of works for which the term of protection is not calculated from the death of the author or authors and which have not been lawfully made available to the public within 70 years from their creation, the protection shall terminate.

(7) The term of protection of a musical composition with words shall expire 70 years after the death of the last of the following persons to survive, whether or not those persons are designated as co-authors: the author of the lyrics and the composer of the musical composition, provided that both contributions were specifically created for the respective musical composition with words.

1. General rule: 70 years post mortem auctoris (para. 1). The general rule and the most important provision of the Directive sets the term of protection for works of copyright at 70 years after the death of the author. The term of 70 years is to be calculated from the first day of January of the year following the death of the author (see art. 8). The determination of the date of the death of the author is left to the national legislatures and courts of the Member States. **(a) Literary or artistic work.** The term of 70 years post mortem auctoris applies to all categories of literary and artistic works within the meaning of art. 2 of the Berne Convention. There are no exceptions for works of applied art or photographic works (compare art. 7(4) BC), computer software, original databases or any other category of works: any work that is protected by copyright according to the applicable national law is protected for 70 years post mortem auctoris, subject to the exceptions laid out in other provisions of the Directive. It should be noted however that one of the basic conditions for protection as a literary or artistic work is that of originality. This, although increasingly convergent in the EU following the ECJ's decisions in *Infopaq International* and *BSA*, cannot yet be said to be completely harmonized and national divergences may still persist. **(b) Author.** The Directive likewise does not define the concept of authorship. The question of authorship of the whole or of a part of a work is a question of fact left to the national courts (see recital 14). **(c) Irrespective of the date when the work is lawfully made available to the public.** If the author is an identifiable individual, the date at which the work is lawfully made available to the public is irrelevant for the term of protection (compare art. 1(4)). Works that are made available for the first time after the death of the author do not receive special treatment, as was the case in the laws of several Member States prior to the adoption of the Directive. It should be noted that in all cases where the Term Directive refers to the publication, making available to the public or communication to the public of a work for the sake of clarification it explicitly mentions that such acts should take place 'lawfully' (see also art. 1(3), (5) and (6), art. 3(1), (2), (2a), (2b), (2c), (2e) and (3), art. 6 and art. 10a(2)). The likely meaning of 'lawfully' in this context is with the permission of the rightholder. It is unclear whether the word also covers situations where a work is made available to the public by a third party invoking an exception or limitation to copyright.

2. Joint authorship (para. 2). The term of protection of a work of joint authorship is calculated from the first day of January of the year following the death of the last surviving author (see art. 8). The Directive does not define or harmonize the concept of joint authorship. It is for the national laws and courts to decide under what circumstances a work is of joint authorship. It should be noted that this can result in drastic differences in the term of protection within the EU in cases where a work manages to qualify as a work of joint authorship in one Member State, but is treated as multiple separate works each of which abides by its own independent term in another. The Directive has attempted to address this issue with regard to cinematographic and audiovisual works (see art. 2) and co-written musical works (see art. 1(7)).

3. Anonymous or pseudonymous works (para. 3). A work is an anonymous or pseudonymous work if the author cannot be identified with a reasonable degree of certainty. Obviously, the term of protection of works of which the author is not known cannot be calculated on the basis of the date of the death of the author. **(a) Lawfully made available to the public.** Instead, the term of protection of anonymous or pseudonymous works is calculated from the first day of January of the year following the date on which the work was lawfully made available to the public. The rule follows the lead of art. 7(3) BC and, according to the proposal for the Term Directive, the term 'making available to the public' should be understood in the same way. The expression should not be confused with the exclusive right of 'making available to the public in such a way that members of the public may access them from a place and at a time individually chosen by them' of art. 3(2) Information Society Directive. 'Making available to the public' in the sense of the Term Directive is an older and broader term that encompasses the distribution of copies, public performance, broadcasting, communication to the public by wire, the interactive making available or any other method of dissemination. **(b) No doubt about the identity of the author.** When the pseudonym adopted by the author leaves no doubt as to his identity the normal term of protection of 70 years post mortem auctoris (art. 1(1)) applies. **(c) Disclosure of identity.** Likewise, if the author discloses his identity within 70 years after his work was lawfully made available to the public, the normal rule of 70 years post mortem auctoris (art. 1(1)) applies. So, for example, when JK Rowling revealed herself in July 2013 as the true author of the crime fiction novel *The Cuckoo's Calling* published under the pseudonym 'John Galbraith', the work's term of protection jumped from 1 January 2084, 70 years after its publication in April 2013, to 70 years after Rowling's death, whenever that might occur. Disclosure of identity has to be done by the author himself. It has no effect if it is done after his death by a third party, for instance successors in title hoping for a prolongation of the term of protection. Disclosure likely also lacks effect once the term of 70 years after the creation of an unpublished anonymous or pseudonymous work (see art. 1(6)) has lapsed and the work has fallen into the public domain.

4. Collective works/legal persons as rightholders (para. 4). If according to national law the work is classified as a collective work or the copyright is vested in a legal person, the term of protection is 70 years after the work is lawfully made available to the public (as in para. 3). This rule does not apply to cinematographic and audiovisual works (see art. 2). (a) Collective works. What constitutes a collective work is determined on the basis of national law. For example, art. L113-2 of the French Intellectual Property Code describes a collective work as a work created at the initiative of a natural or legal person who edits it, publishes it and discloses it under his direction and name and the personal contributions of the various authors who participated in its production are merged in the overall work for which they were conceived, without it being possible to attribute to each author a separate right in the work as created. Thus, as opposed to joint authorship, collective works under this definition will not require that concerted effort and common execution be exerted by the contributors. Instead, the work must be created at the initiative and under the direction of a '*maître*', whether a legal or natural person, who controls the creative process through the issue of instructions and harmonizes the different contributions. The concept is generally understood to cover dictionaries, encyclopaedias and periodical works, such as newspapers or magazines. Other countries have opted for different approaches. For example, the Czech Republic emphasizes economic rather than intellectual indivisibility: here although a collective work must still be created with the participation of more than one author at the initiative and under the management of a natural person or of a legal entity and made available to the public under that person's or entity's name, it will only qualify if the contributions involved are not capable of independent use. The recognition of the concept of collective works in the jurisdictions of the Member States is not obligatory under the Directive. Numerous Member States, including the UK, the Netherlands, Germany, Latvia, Cyprus, Ireland and the Nordic countries, know no special concept of collective works. Here the term of protection of works that would qualify as collective ones in other jurisdictions will only be 70 years after the work is lawfully made available to the public if the rightholder is a legal person. For example, the Dutch Copyright Act makes it clear that a public institution, association, foundation or company may be the author of a work if it lawfully communicates a work to the public as its own, without naming any natural person as the author. The UK's Copyright, Designs and Patents Act 1988 states that, where a literary, musical or artistic work is made by an employee in the course of his employment, the employer will be the first owner of the copyright in the work, subject to any agreement to the contrary. However, authorship of the work will remain with the person who created it. Accordingly, given that the term of protection is calculated on the basis of the death of the author, as opposed to the first owner, the term of protection remains unaffected by the corporate nature of the work. Whether this provision is compatible with art. 1(4) of the Term Directive, which speaks of the term of protection for works for which a legal person is the rightholder, and not the author, is open to examination. If the relevant jurisdiction neither knows a concept of collective works nor recognizes legal persons as authors, the term of protection will be calculated according to the regular rules at 70 years after the death of the (last surviving) compiler. (b) Natural persons. As an exception to the general rule for collective works or works of corporate authorship, if the natural persons having created the work are identified as such in the versions of the work that are made available to the public, the rules revert back to the main principle of paras. 1 and 2 and the term of protection of the collective work is 70 years after the death of the (last surviving co-)author. (c) Identified contributions of identified authors. The duration of the protection of a collective work as a whole is not intended to prejudice the rights of identified authors whose identifiable contributions are included in the collective work. In such cases, the term of protection of the collective work as a whole remains 70 years after it has been made available to the public, but the term of protection of each individual contribution will be 70 years after the death of (the last surviving co-)author.

5. Work published in parts (para. 5). If a work is published in volumes, parts, instalments, issues or episodes, and the term of protection runs from the time when the work was lawfully made available to the public the term of protection shall run for each part separately. Examples of such works might include an encyclopaedia or a multi-volume historical work.

6. Not lawfully made available within 70 years (para. 6). If a work, for which the term of protection is not calculated from the death of the author, has not been lawfully made available to the public within 70 years after creation, it loses protection. For example, if an anonymous work has remained undisclosed for over 70 years after its creation, the making available of such work will not revive copyright protection. In cases of works of joint authorship, co-written musical works or cinematographic or audiovisual works, the general rules apply even if only one of the joint authors is known.

7. Co-written musical works (para. 7). With the Term Extension Directive a new subparagraph to art. 1 was added governing the term of protection of 'musical compositions with words', i.e. works the lyricist and composer of which are different persons. Under the new provisions, copyright in such works shall last for 70 years after the death of the last of the following persons to survive, regardless of whether they are designated as co-authors under national law: the author of the lyrics and the composer of the musical composition, provided that both contributions were specifically created for the co-written musical work. The provision was introduced to counteract the absence of a definition of 'works of joint authorship' of art. 1(2) on the EU level, which has led to a lack of conceptual alignment of the notion between the different national EU jurisdictions. This can in turn lead to cases of the same work being protected for different lengths of time in different Member States, depending on whether it will qualify as a work of joint authorship or not in the relevant jurisdiction. The result is difficulties in administering copyright in works of joint authorship across the Union, as well as in the cross-border distribution of royalties for exploitation that occurs in different Member States. The joint authorship problem was found to be particularly acute in the case of co-written musical works (recitals 18 and 19 of the Term Extension Directive). In some jurisdictions, such as France or Spain, a co-written musical work would be classified as a single work of joint authorship with a unitary term of protection, to be calculated in accordance with the Directive's rule, from the death of the last surviving co-author. In others, such as the Netherlands or the UK, the lyrics and music would have been viewed as constituting two separate works, each with its own individual term of protection running from the death of its own author. Finally, specialized national provisions may apply. In Italy, for example, under the old, national rules, the separable parts of co-written musical works would be understood as being independent creations attracting their own individual term of protection. An exception covered dramatico-musical works (such as operas), works of dumb show and choreographic works, which, although not in fact understood as constituting works of joint authorship under Italian law, were nevertheless granted a term of protection starting from the date of death of the last contributing author to survive. With the new provision the same solution is applied to musical compositions with words as had been previously introduced under art. 2 for cinematographic and audiovisual works, by disentangling their term of protection from their nature as works of joint authorship. The new provisions apply to co-written musical works of which at least the musical composition or the lyrics were protected in at least one Member State on 1 November 2013 or which are created after that date (see art. 10(6)).

[Cinematographic or audiovisual works]

Article 2

(1) The principal director of a cinematographic or audiovisual work shall be considered as its author or one of its authors. Member States shall be free to designate other co-authors.

(2) The term of protection of cinematographic or audiovisual works shall expire 70 years after the death of the last of the following persons to survive, whether or not these persons are designated as co-authors: the principal director, the author of the screenplay, the author of the dialogue and the composer of music specifically created for use in the cinematographic or audiovisual work.

1. General: Before the Directive. Art. 7(2) BC allows Contracting Parties to deviate from the general rule of 50 years pma in the case of cinematographic works and instead provide a term of protection of 50 years after the work has been made available to the public with the consent of the author, or, failing such an event within 50 years from the making of the work, 50 years after the making. Before the adoption of the Term Directive, this was the approach taken in Ireland, Italy, Luxembourg, Portugal and the UK. For states that did not choose this route, the default rule would apply, giving cinematographic works protection until 50 years after the death of the author or most likely, given multiple persons usually involved in the production of a cinematographic work, 50 years after the death of the last-surviving of all the joint authors. This was the rule in force in the remaining EU Member States, with the exception of Spain (60 years after the death of the last-surviving joint author), Germany (70 years after the death of the last-surviving joint author) and, in respect of the music used in the sound track, France (70 years after the death of the last-surviving joint author). As a result, two factions regarding the mode of calculation of the term of protection for cinematographic and audiovisual works split the Community. In addition, even among those states that took the joint authorship approach, the similar rule did not result in a similar term of protection, as different countries recognized different persons as legitimate authors. Disparities in national rules on the initial attribution of authorship therefore translated into deeper divisions on the term of protection. The result was a wide diversity across the EU as to the term of protection of cinematographic and audiovisual works that would not have been remedied simply by the harmonized rule on the term of protection of works of joint authorship of art. 1(2). It was on the European Parliament's suggestion that a provision specific to cinematographic and audiovisual works was included to deal with this discrepancy. The initial proposal suggested providing for an irrefutable presumption vesting initial authorship with four designated authors. That was eventually watered down to the provision as it currently stands.

2. Cinematographic or audiovisual work (para. 1). The Directive does not define cinematographic or audiovisual works (see art. 14bis of the Berne Convention). The term must be understood in a broad way, applying to all kinds of films protected by copyright, such as feature films, documentaries, music videos and commercials. The exact determination will be dependent on national law. Multimedia works are not considered to be cinematographic or audiovisual works. **(a) Principal director.** The expression 'principal director' has been taken from art. 14bis BC and should be understood in the sense of that provision. If there is no 'principal director' in the traditional meaning, the leading person in the creative process should be regarded as the principal director. The Term Directive goes beyond the harmonization of the term of protection in explicitly designating the principal director as an obligate author of the work. This harmonization applies horizontally, even outside the context of this Directive, but it does not necessarily mean that the principal director is also a rightholder. According to recital 5, the provisions of the Directive do not affect the application by the Member States of art. 14bis (2)(b), (c) and (d), and (3) BC. However, according to the

ECJ, Member States can no longer rely on the power granted by art. 14bis BC to adopt provisions that compromise the principal director's status as author or to deny the author exploitation rights over the cinematographic or audiovisual work: in *Luksan* (ECJ) the ECJ confirmed that the rights to exploit a cinematographic or audiovisual work vest by operation of law, directly and originally, in the principal director. However, although Member States may not allocate such rights exclusively to the producer of the work, a presumption of transfer in favour of the producer of the exploitation rights is permissible, provided such a presumption is not an irrebuttable one that precludes the principal director of that work from agreeing otherwise. **(b) Other co-authors.** Only the principal director is required under the Directive to be recognized as an author of the work by national law. Pursuant to art. 14bis(2) BC, Member States are free to designate other co-authors, including the film producer. The rule of para. 2 on the term of protection of cinematographic and audiovisual works however will remain unaffected by national rules on authorship. All persons recognized by national law as authors of a cinematographic or audiovisual work will enjoy protection for the term provided in art. 2, regardless of whether they are considered in the calculation of the term of protection.

2. Last survivor (para. 2). The term of protection of a film is 70 years after 1 January of the year following the death of last survivor of the following four: **(a) Principal director.** Only the principal director is relevant for the determination of the term of protection. Other (assisting) directors will not be taken into account for the calculation of the term of protection. They can, however, be rightholders. **(b) Author of the screenplay.** There might be more than one author of the screenplay. Probably the last surviving of those authors should be taken into account, analogous to the rule of art. 1(2). **(c) Author of the dialogue.** There might also be multiple authors of the dialogue. Probably the last surviving of those authors should be taken into account, analogous to the rule of art. 1(2). **(d) Composer of music.** There might also be several composers of the film music. Again, the last surviving one should be taken into account, analogous to the rule of art. 1(2). The composer of any pre-existing music used in the work is not relevant and will not be taken into consideration in the calculation of the term. Whether or not the listed persons are designated as co-authors for other purposes is a separate question to be determined by national law; the rules of this paragraph deal exclusively with the calculation of the term of protection. It has been suggested that art. 2 of the Term Directive conflicts with the rules of the Berne Convention on the term of protection of cinematographic and audiovisual works. The more correct interpretation would probably be that the freedom Contracting States enjoy to designate the author(s) of cinematographic and audiovisual works includes the right to determine the authors who are deemed relevant for the term of protection. In any case, art. 7(2) BC permits calculation from the date of creation or of the making available of the work, which would most commonly result in a much shorter term than under the Term Directive.

3. Transitional measures. According to art. 10(4), Member States need not apply the provisions of art. 2(1) to cinematographic or audiovisual works created before 1 July 1994. This was to accommodate the countries in which the term of protection of cinematographic and audiovisual works was calculated as of the making available or creation of the work, which generally resulted in much shorter terms of copyright protection. According to art. 10(5) of Directive 93/98/EEC, which was removed from the consolidated version, Member States could determine the date as of which art. 2(1) shall apply, provided that date is no later than 1 July 1997.

[Duration of related rights]

Article 3

(1) The rights of performers shall expire 50 years after the date of the performance. However,
- if a fixation of the performance otherwise than in a phonogram is lawfully published or lawfully communicated to the public within this period, the rights shall expire 50 years from the date of the first such publication or the first such communication to the public, whichever is the earlier,
- if a fixation of the performance in a phonogram is lawfully published or lawfully communicated to the public within this period, the rights shall expire 70 years from the date of the first such publication or the first such communication to the public, whichever is the earlier.

(2) The rights of producers of phonograms shall expire 50 years after the fixation is made. However, if the phonogram has been lawfully published within this period, the said rights shall expire 70 years from the date of the first lawful publication. If no lawful publication has taken place within the period mentioned in the first sentence, and if the phonogram has been lawfully communicated to the public within this period, the said rights shall expire 70 years from the date of the first lawful communication to the public.

However, this paragraph shall not have the effect of protecting anew the rights of producers of phonograms where, through the expiry of the term of protection granted them pursuant to Article 3(2) of Directive 93/98/EEC in its version before amendment by Directive 2001/29/EEC, they were no longer protected on 22 December 2002.

(2a) If, 50 years after the phonogram was lawfully published or, failing such publication, 50 years after it was lawfully communicated to the public, the phonogram producer does not offer copies of the phonogram for sale in sufficient quantity or does not make it available to the public, by wire or wireless means, in such a way that members of the public may access it from a place and at a time individually chosen by them, the performer may terminate the contract by which the performer has transferred or assigned his rights in the fixation of his performance to a phonogram producer (hereinafter a 'contract on transfer or assignment'). The right to terminate the contract on transfer or assignment may be exercised if the producer, within a year from the notification by the performer of his intention to terminate the contract on transfer or assignment pursuant to the previous sentence, fails to carry out both of the acts of exploitation referred to in that sentence. This right to terminate may not be waived by the performer. Where a phonogram contains the fixation of the performances of a plurality of performers, they may terminate their contracts on transfer or assignment in accordance with applicable national law. If the contract on transfer or assignment is terminated pursuant to this paragraph, the rights of the phonogram producer in the phonogram shall expire.

(2b) Where a contract on transfer or assignment gives the performer a right to claim a non-recurring remuneration, the performer shall have the right to obtain an annual supplementary remuneration from the phonogram producer for each full year immediately following the 50th year after the phonogram was lawfully published or, failing such publication, the 50th year after it was lawfully communicated to the public. The right to obtain such annual supplementary remuneration may not be waived by the performer.

(2c) The overall amount to be set aside by a phonogram producer for payment of the annual supplementary remuneration referred to in paragraph 2b shall correspond to 20 % of the revenue which the phonogram producer has derived, during the year preceding that for which the said remuneration is paid, from the reproduction, distribution and making available of the phonogram in question, following the 50th year after it was lawfully published or, failing such publication, the 50th year after it was lawfully communicated to the public.

Member States shall ensure that phonogram producers are required on request to provide to performers who are entitled to the annual supplementary remuneration referred to in paragraph 2b any information which may be necessary in order to secure payment of that remuneration.

(2d) Member States shall ensure that the right to obtain an annual supplementary remuneration as referred to in paragraph 2b is administered by collecting societies.

(2e) Where a performer is entitled to recurring payments, neither advance payments nor any contractually defined deductions shall be deducted from the payments made to the performer following the 50th year after the phonogram was lawfully published or, failing such publication, the 50th year after it was lawfully communicated to the public.

(3) The rights of producers of the first fixation of a film shall expire 50 years after the fixation is made. However, if the film is lawfully published or lawfully communicated to the public during this period, the rights

shall expire 50 years from the date of the first such publication or the first such communication to the public, whichever is the earlier. The term 'film' shall designate a cinematographic or audiovisual work or moving images, whether or not accompanied by sound.

(4) The rights of broadcasting organisations shall expire 50 years after the first transmission of a broadcast, whether this broadcast is transmitted by wire or over the air, including by cable or satellite.

1. General comment. Art 3. handles four categories of related or neighbouring rights protected under the Rental Right Directive. The reason for harmonizing the term of protection of these rights was the same as for copyright (see introductory remarks). All terms of protection in the Directive run from 1 January following the year in which the event that triggered the beginning of the term of protection took place (see art. 8). The term of protection for the sui generis database right is dealt with in art. 10 of the Database Directive. Art. 11(1) and recital 19 make clear that Member States may introduce further related rights other than those listed in art. 3, on the sole condition that they notify the European Commission. Specific provisions governing the modalities of such additional rights as regards critical and scientific publications and non-original photographs are set out in arts. 5 and 6.

2. Performers (para. 1). The Directive does not define performers, and neither does the Rental Right Directive. Definitions can be found in arts. 3(a) and 9 of the Rome Convention and in art. 2(a) of the WPPT. The term of protection prescribed in the Directive applies to all performers protected according to national law. **(a) 50 years after the date of the performance.** The term of protection for performances is 50 years after 1 January following the year in which the performance took place, unless the performance is lawfully published or lawfully communicated to the public within this period. In practice the term of 50 years after the performance will be the exception rather than the rule, because most performances are lawfully published or lawfully communicated to the public within 50 years. **(b) Lawfully published or lawfully communicated to the public.** *Definitions.* Most performances are either published or communicated to the public within a few months or years after the performance. No definition of either 'publication' or 'communication to the public' is given in the Directive. However, an indicative interpretation can be inferred from the international treaties, as well as from later EU directives. Publication should accordingly be taken as meaning distribution of material copies of a fixation of the performance in reasonable quantity. Communication to the public refers to any way of making the performance accessible to the public, whether through public performance, broadcasting, making available over the internet or otherwise. The date on the distributed copies of the performance will usually suffice to determine the date of publication. In case of broadcasting, the date of the broadcast will be decisive. *Fixation otherwise than in a phonogram.* If a fixation of the performance otherwise than in a phonogram is lawfully published or lawfully communicated to the public within this period, the rights shall expire 50 years from the date of the first such publication or the first such communication to the public, whichever is earlier. In this way the 2011 prolongation to 70 years is avoided for the rights of performers in areas other than the music industry. *Fixation in a phonogram.* By contrast, if a fixation of the performance in a phonogram is lawfully published or lawfully communicated to the public within this period, the rights shall expire 70 years from the date of the first such publication or the first such communication to the public, whichever is earlier. This later provision was introduced with the Term Extension Directive to replace the older text that set a 50-year term regardless of the medium in which the performance was fixed (recital 7 of the Term Extension Directive). The new 70-year rule was significantly scaled back by the European Parliament from the Commission's initial proposal for an extension of 95 years from the triggering event. *Reasoning behind the extension.* The change is intended to accommodate the rise in life expectancy, as well as bring the protection of neighbouring rights further into line with that offered to copyright, which already lasts (as a general rule) for 70 years after the death of the author (recitals 5 and 6 of the Term Extension Directive). It thus aims to improve the insecure social situation and unrewarding financial landscape that the average performer, among the poorest earners in Europe according to the Explanatory Memorandum to the Term Extension Directive, typically faces. The extension is targeted in particular at session musicians, i.e. musicians that are hired on an ad hoc basis to play for a recording session, who, as opposed to featured artists, relinquish their exclusive rights to record companies in favour of a flat fee and rely exclusively on their statutory secondary remuneration claims for future revenue from their performances (recital 9 of the Term Extension Directive). As stated in the Explanatory Memorandum, the amendment was triggered by the imminent fall into the public domain of performances recorded and released in the 1950s and 1960s, the performers of which were approaching retirement at its adoption. It is worth noting that the extension of the term of protection of the rights of performers and phonogram producers was extremely controversial. Opponents of the extension contended that, despite the rhetoric, small artists stood to gain very little from the amendment, with the majority of the extra cash flow benefiting record labels instead. Moreover, the additional revenue for producers is likely to come from the most popular recordings, thus providing small relief to little-known performers, while depriving the public domain of high cultural value material. *Scope of the extension.* The extended term of protection for performers does not have retroactive effect, but instead only applies to fixations of performances and phonograms which, under the old rules, would still be protected on 1 November 2013, as well as any created after that date (see art. 10(5)).

3. Producers of phonograms (para. 2). The Directive does not define producers of phonograms, and neither does the Rental Right Directive. Definitions can be found in art. 3(c) of the Rome Convention, art. 1(c) of the Geneva Convention and in art. 2(b) and (d) of the WPPT. The term of protection prescribed in the Directive applies to all phonograms protected according to national law. (a) 50 years after fixation. The term of protection for phonograms is 50 years after 1 January following the year in which the fixation took place, unless the fixation is lawfully published or lawfully communicated to the public within this period. In practice the term of 50 years after the fixation will be the exception rather than the rule, because most phonograms are lawfully published or lawfully communicated to the public within 50 years. (b) Lawfully published or lawfully communicated to the public. Like performances, most phonograms are either published or communicated to the public, for instance by being broadcast, within a few months or years after the fixation (see art. 3, note 2(b)). Here too, as with performances, the term of protection was extended in 2011. In the case of phonogram producers, no difference in term exists depending on whether the fixation was in a phonogram or not. If the recording is lawfully published within the 50 year period post-fixation, phonogram producers' rights shall last until 70 years from that date. If the recording is not published, but is communicated to the public within the same period, the rights persist till 70 years after the date of the first lawful communication to the public. It should be noted that the new rules retain the lack of alignment that existed already under the 2006 Directive between the term of protection of performers' and that of phonogram producers' rights. This could prove significant in the context of the exploitation of phonograms in the internal market. For example, practical difficulties could result for the collection and distribution of the single equitable remuneration for the broadcasting or communication to the public of commercial sound recordings, which according to art. 8(2) of the Rental Right Directive is to be shared between performers and phonogram producers. The new term of protection applies to phonograms the producer of which was still protected under the old provisions on 1 November 2013, as well as any created after that date (see art. 10(5)). (c) Previous rules and transitional law. This is not the first time the term of protection of phonogram producers' rights was changed at the European level. Under Directive 93/98/EEC, if the phonogram was lawfully published or lawfully communicated to the public during the 50-year period after the fixation was made, the rights of producers of phonograms expired 50 years from the date of the first such publication or the first such communication to the public, whichever was the earlier. The provision was changed by the Information Society Directive. According to the second subparagraph of art. 3(2), the amended rule does not have the effect of reviving the rights of producers who were no longer protected under the older provision on 22 December 2002.

4. 'Use it or lose it' (para. 2a). In addition to extended terms, a set of new accompanying measures intended to benefit performers were introduced in paragraphs 2a-2e by the amending Directive (recital 10 of the Term Extension Directive). Under the new 'use it or lose it' clause (para. 2a), if, after 50 years from when the phonogram was lawfully published or, failing publication, after 50 years from when it was lawfully communicated to the public, a record producer does not market a sound recording, the performer may opt to reclaim his rights (recital 8 of the Term Extension Directive). The clause is intended to increase performers' bargaining power and enable them to find alternate ways to exploit the sound recording, e.g. by finding another producer or exploiting the sound recording independently. In this way phonogram producers are prevented from 'locking up' phonograms they do not find commercially interesting. The performer has to give one year's notification of his intention to terminate the contract on transfer or assignment of rights. If the producer fails to both offer copies of the sound recording for sale in sufficient quantify and make it available to the public within that year, their rights expire. Member States cannot permit waiver of the right to terminate on the part of the performer. In cases of multiple performers contributing to a single performance, the national rules on the termination of contracts apply. The 'use it or lose it' clause applies to fixations of performances and phonograms in regard to which the performer and producer are still protected under the old provisions on 1 November 2013, as well as any created after that date (see art. 10(5)).

5. Annual supplementary remuneration (para. 2b-2e). Under the new rules, record companies are obliged to set up compensation funds intended for payment of annual supplementary remuneration to performers (recitals 11-13 of the Term Extension Directive). The sums set aside into such funds shall amount to 20% of the revenues earned from the reproduction, distribution and making available of the sound recording in question during the year preceding that for which the said remuneration is paid, not however from the rental of the recording or from the equitable remuneration received for secondary uses (para. 2b). Payment of this annual supplementary remuneration is only reserved for performers who have transferred or assigned their rights in exchange for a one-off payment and will be due for each full year following the 50th year after the publication or, failing publication, the communication to the public of the phonogram (para. 2a). Phonogram producers are obliged to provide entitled performers with any information which may be necessary in order to secure payment of that remuneration on request. As with the 'use it or lose it' clause, this right too cannot be waived by the performer, although micro-enterprises for which the costs of collecting and administering such revenue would impose a disproportionate burden may be exempted by national rules (recital 12 of the Term Extension Directive). Member States are instructed to entrust the distribution of the sums set aside in this manner to collecting societies (para. 2d). To ensure that the appropriate percentage of the royalties arising during the extended term will go to them, performers are granted a 'clean slate' from advance payments or contractually defined deductions (para. 2e and recital 14 of the Term Extension Directive). This is intended to prevent record producers from making deductions on the royalties due for the extended 20-year period after the initial 50 years of protection are over. As with the other new provisions, the annual supplementary remuneration due to performers applies to fixations of performances and phonograms in regard to which the performer and producer are still protected under the old provisions on 1 November 2013, as well as any created after that date (see art. 10(5)).

6. Producers of the first fixation of a film (para. 3). Neither the Term Directive nor the Rental Right Directive define the producers of the first fixation of a film nor is a definition found in the broader European acquis. It is generally understood that the term refers to the producers of both cinematographic and audiovisual works protected by copyright and moving images without any originality. The term of protection prescribed in the Directive applies to all films protected according to national law. **(a) 50 years after the fixation.** The term of protection for the producers of the first fixation of a film is 50 years after 1 January following the year in which the fixation took place, unless the fixation is lawfully published or lawfully communicated to the public within this period, in which case the producers' rights expire 50 years after the publication or communication to the public, whichever comes earlier. **(b) First fixation of a film.** Art. 3(3) specifies that the term 'film' should be understood as designating 'a cinematographic or audiovisual work or moving images, whether or not accompanied by sound'. The definition is borrowed from the Rental Right Directive, where it was included in view of the lack of international specifications. This description suggests a very broad concept covering all moving images. Significantly, no originality is required. For example, moving images from closed circuit security cameras, news videos, amateur videos or films made by observation satellite are all likely protected (see art. 2(1)(c) Rental Right Directive, note 4). Silent pictures are also explicitly included. The mere duplication of a film however will not attract protection, as protection is limited only to the 'first fixation'. It should be noted that EU countries that do not have a tradition of a clear distinction between copyright over an original cinematographic work of authorship and the neighbouring protection for the producer of the first fixation of an (original or non-original) film have had difficulty incorporating this provision into their legislation. So, for example, the UK Copyright, Designs and Patents Act amalgamates the copyright and related rights protection provided by continental jurisdictions into a single system of copyright for 'films' as entrepreneurial works. No requirement of originality is imposed, protection instead being afforded to any film which is not a copy of a previous film. S. 5B of the CDPA defines the term 'film' as 'a recording on any medium from which a moving image may by any means be produced'. The producer of a film and its principal director are considered to be joint authors of the film. UK law grants protection to 'films' for 70 years after the death of the last to die from among the principal director, the author of the screenplay, the authors of the dialogue and the composer of music specifically created for and used in the film whose identity is known. Further provisions elaborate on the situation where these persons are unknown, identical to the provisions of the Term Directive on anonymous or pseudonymous works (70 years from making available to the public or, if the work is not made available within 70 years after its creation, 70 years from creation). When there is no person falling in the four listed categories copyright in films expires 50 years from the end of the calendar year in which the film was created. It could be argued that this final provision corresponds to art. 3(3) of the Term Directive, although opinions on whether this approach is compatible with EU law differ. Certainly, producers of cinematographic and audiovisual works in the UK will not benefit from the double protection the European Directives clearly intended. According to UK case law (*Norowzian/ArksII* (United Kingdom)), a film, which is 'a work of action [that] is capable of being performed before an audience' will also benefit from protection as a dramatic work, although the term of protection in this case will be 70 years after the death of the dramatist. In this way a second layer of protection is added, although the relevant terms of protection do not correspond to those set out in arts. 2(2) and 3(3). Similar problems are encountered in Ireland, where a film, defined as 'a fixation on any medium from which a moving image may, by any means, be produced, perceived or communicated through a device', is protected for 70 years after the death of the last of the following persons: principal director, author of the screenplay, author of the dialogue, author of music specially composed for use in the film. Strangely, where a film is first published during the period of 70 years following the death of the last of these, the term is 70 years after such publication. In Cyprus the term of protection for films is also 70 years from the death of the last to survive of the four Term Directive designated contributors, but no provision equivalent to that of art. 3(3) Term Directive giving a 50-year term of protection to films lacking originality is made. It is questionable whether these provisions are sufficiently in line with the Directive.

7. Broadcasting organizations (para. 4). The Directive does not contain a definition of broadcasting organizations, and neither does the Rental Right Directive. From the provisions of the two Directives however we can conclude that both broadcasts transmitted by wire and over the air are protected, including by cable or satellite. However, cable distributors do not qualify as broadcasting organizations where they merely retransmit broadcasts by cable. The term of protection for broadcasts is 50 years after 1 January following the year in which the transmission took place.

[Protection of previously unpublished works]

Article 4

Any person who, after the expiry of copyright protection, for the first time lawfully publishes or lawfully communicates to the public a previously unpublished work, shall benefit from a protection equivalent to the economic rights of the author. The term of protection of such rights shall be 25 years from the time when the work was first lawfully published or lawfully communicated to the public.

1. General. This article relates to a right separate from copyright for the owner or 'honest finder' of an unpublished work, which would have qualified for copyright protection as an original work of authorship, but of which the term of protection has lapsed. It is comparable to the right that already existed in Germany before the Directive. It was decided to introduce such a right as compensation for the fact that the Directive abolished the terms of protection for copyright calculated from the date of first publication after the death of the author.

2. Previously unpublished works. The right applies to any kind of unpublished work of authorship that would have qualified for copyright protection, but of which the term of protection has lapsed. Whether or not the subject matter qualifies as a work is to be determined according to current standards. It is not relevant whether the work qualified for copyright protection according to the standards of the time in which it was created or whether any kind of copyright protection existed at all at the time. 'Unpublished' should be interpreted by reference to art. 3(3) BC ('editio princeps'). It accordingly means that no tangible copies of the work have been made available to the public through distribution in reasonable quantities. It should be noted that the terms 'publication' and 'communication to the public' in European copyright law are not synonymous, creating an interesting discrepancy: art. 4 thus seems to be inconsistent with itself in that, although it grants protection to the person who either lawfully communicates a work to the public or publishes it for the first time, whether the unpublished work had at any time in the past been communicated to the public is apparently irrelevant. It would therefore seem that the person who publishes or lawfully communicates to the public a work that, although previously unpublished, had in the past been already communicated to the public, will nonetheless be eligible for protection. So, for example, works of visual art which were only previously publicly displayed (and therefore 'communicated to the public'), but had never before been 'published', may attract protection if subsequently published for the first time after they have fallen into the public domain. A contrary interpretation would face difficulties in its practical application, as the communication to the public of a work in the distant past would be hard to track or prove. Other authors have however suggested adjusted interpretations that would only benefit works which have previously been neither published nor communicated to the public or only previously unpublished works that are published for the first time.

3. After the expiry of copyright protection. The phrase 'after the expiry of copyright' does not imply that the previously unpublished work must at any time actually have been protected by copyright. Arguably, works that were never protected under copyright because such protection did not exist at the time of their creation, for example a Roman sculpture, would also qualify. Indeed, some Member States have explicitly extended the right to works in which copyright never subsisted. This is the case in Spain, as well as in the

Netherlands, in the latter case under the condition that the author died more than 70 years ago. Even if this interpretation were not to be accepted as the meaning intended by the provision, these overextended rights would probably be covered by Member States' freedom to introduce new related rights not foreseen in the Directive (recital 19).

4. First lawful publication or communication to the public. The right is triggered by the first lawful publication or communication to the public. It is not clear what the term lawful means in this context. Obviously, it cannot mean with permission of the owner of the copyright, because copyright in the work has expired. But there may exist a property right in the physical copy of the work. The likely meaning of lawful, therefore, is with permission of the owner of this physical copy. However, it can also be argued that lawful implies that the publication or communication to the public not be in breach of some other obligation, for instance a confidentiality clause or perpetual moral rights of making available to the public. Nothing in the Directive, however, expressly supports either of these interpretations.

5. Protection equivalent to the economic rights of the author. The scope of protection of this right must be equivalent to the exclusive rights that copyright owners enjoy under their national copyright laws, for example, right of reproduction, right of distribution, right of communication to the public, and so forth. The protection of moral rights is neither required nor prohibited by the Directive, although it would be peculiar to afford it to the person who merely published or communicated to the public a work, but is not its author.

6. Term of protection. The term of protection is 25 years from 1 January following the date of the first lawful publication or communication to the public (see art. 8). Providing protection for previously unpublished works is mandatory for the Member States.

[Critical and scientific publications]

Article 5

Member States may protect critical and scientific publications of works which have come into the public domain. The maximum term of protection of such rights shall be 30 years from the time when the publication was first lawfully published.

1. General. This article is not a mandatory provision. It simply permits Member States to retain or introduce special protection for critical and scientific publications of works which have fallen into the public domain. Such special protection can be seen as a related or neighbouring right. If a critical or scientific publication qualifies as an original work of authorship normal copyright protection applies. Whether the work edited in a critical or scientific way was ever protected in the country in which protection is sought is not relevant. However, the parallel protection of critical or scientific editions of works still under copyright is not permitted. As with the previous articles, 'published' should be understood in the sense of art. 3(3) BC, while 'lawfully' likely means with permission of the owner of the physical copy. Art. 5 is inspired by a similar provision in Germany. According to art. 11(1) and recital 19, Member States that introduce such a related right have to notify the European Commission ('in order to ensure transparency at Community level'). However, as this is an optional protection that only sets a maximum limit on the term of protection (30 years) this part of the Directive has little harmonizing effect. So, while in Germany the protection lasts for 25 years from publication or, failing publication, from the creation of the publication, Italy recognizes only 20 years after the first lawful publication by any means or in any form. Since art. 5 provides little guidance, Member States that choose to grant this right will have to determine the modalities of the right, including a definition of 'critical and scientific publications', at the national level. It follows from the words 'in particular' in recital 19 that Member States remain free to maintain or introduce other rights related to copyright.

[Protection of photographs]

Article 6

Photographs which are original in the sense that they are the author's own intellectual creation shall be protected in accordance with Article 1. No other criteria shall be applied to determine their eligibility for protection. Member States may provide for the protection of other photographs.

1. General. (a) Standards. This provision seeks to harmonize the term and conditions of copyright protection for photographic works. Art. 7(4) of the Berne Convention allows Contracting States to deviate from the normal Berne Convention term of 50 years post mortem auctoris, as long as a minimum term of 25 years from the making of such works is guaranteed. Indeed, prior to the adoption of the Directive different terms of protection existed within the EU. Moreover, different Member States applied varying standards of originality to photographic works. Art. 6 aligns the copyright regime – term and originality standard – for such works with other literary or artistic works within the meaning of art. 1. **(b) Originality standard.** According to recital 17 of the original Term Directive, defining the level of originality required of photographic works was necessary in order to achieve a sufficient harmonization of their term of protection, in particular as concerns those which, due to their artistic or professional character, are of importance within the internal market. Art. 6 therefore requires copyright protection of photographs that are original in the sense that they are the author's own intellectual creation. According to recital 16 a photographic work within the meaning of the Berne Convention is to be considered original if it is the author's own intellectual creation reflecting his personality, no other criteria such as merit or purpose being taken into account. An indication of what would qualify is given by *Painer* (ECJ), in which the Court confirmed that a portrait photograph may pass the originality test, providing the photographer has, by his free and creative choices made at various points in the production of the photograph, stamped the work with his 'personal touch'. The judgement also established that, in contrast to non-original photographs, the protection afforded to original portrait photographs should not in any way be construed as 'inferior' to other types of photographs or other original works. A similar standard is to be found in art. 1(3) of the Computer Programs Directive (for computer software) and in art. 3(1) of the Database Directive (for databases). **(c) No shorter term.** Art. 6 rules out granting a shorter term to original photographs, such as would be allowed under art. 7(4) BC. The term of protection for original photographs is thus 70 years after the death of the author. **(d) Neighbouring rights protection not affected.** Art. 6 explicitly allows Member States to introduce neighbouring rights for the protection of non-original photographs, but does not harmonize the term of protection of such rights. As a result, the terms of protection for non-original photographs vary wildly across the EU. In Italy, for example, non-original photographs receive a term of protection of 20 years after their creation, while in Spain, protection endures for 25 years after creation. In Germany and Austria the term of protection for non-original photographs is 50 years from their publication or, if they remain unpublished, 50 years from their creation. Finland, Sweden and Denmark all recognize a term of protection of 50 years from the end of the year in which the photograph was taken.

[Protection vis-à-vis third countries]

Article 7

(1) **Where the country of origin of a work, within the meaning of the Berne Convention, is a third country, and the author of the work is not a Community national, the term of protection granted by the Member States shall expire on the date of expiry of the protection granted in the country of origin of the work, but may not exceed the term laid down in Article 1.**

(2) **The terms of protection laid down in Article 3 shall also apply in the case of rightholders who are not Community nationals, provided Member States grant them protection. However, without prejudice to the international obligations of the Member States, the term of protection granted by Member States shall expire no later than the date of expiry of the protection granted in the country of which the rightholder is a national and may not exceed the term laid down in Article 3.**

(3) Member States which, on 29 October 1993, in particular pursuant to their international obligations, granted a longer term of protection than that which would result from the provisions of paragraphs 1 and 2 may maintain this protection until the conclusion of international agreements on the term of protection of copyright or related rights.

1. Comparison of terms; reciprocity (para. 1). The Directive prescribes reciprocity towards authors from non-EU countries for works for which the country of origin is not a Member State and whose author is not a 'Community national' (see recital 21). In such cases works are not protected any longer than they are protected in their country of origin, but protection may not exceed the term of the Directive (rule of shorter term). So, for example, if a work is protected for 50 years pma in its (non-EU) country of origin, as is the case in Canada or Japan, that will be the term of protection in all EU Member States as well. If however the country of origin is Mexico, where works are granted protection for 100 years after their author's death, the term of protection within the EU will be limited to 70 years pma. This is in conformity with the general rule of comparison of terms of art. 7(8) BC, the only difference being that the Directive does not allow Member States to deviate and give precedence to the longer term in their national law. It is most likely for this reason that after the adoption of the Term Directive in the EU several third countries, such as the United States, extended their own term of protection to 70 years pma. The rule of shorter term does not apply within the EU (*Patricia* and *Ricordi* (ECJ), see art. 10, note 2). **(a) Country of origin.** The country of origin is to be determined on the basis of arts. 3(4) and 5(4) BC. **(b) Community national.** If the country or origin of a work is not a Member State, the work may still enjoy the protection of the Directive if the author is a 'Community national', i.e. a national of a Member State. A national of an EEA contracting state should be considered a Community national. It is unclear if a mere resident should be assimilated to a national for the purposes of the Directive. It is also unclear which rule applies if the country of origin and the country of nationality of the author was not a Member State when the author died and the term of protection had already lapsed in all Member States due to the comparison of terms, if that country then accedes to the EU while the EU term of 70 years pma is still running. Questionable situations might also arise in the case of joint authors who are nationals of different countries, in cases of an author with dual nationality or if an author changes his nationality. The most convincing solution should be that that grants the longest of all available terms of protection. **(c) Application in time.** The rules of the Directive apply only if the criteria set out in the transitional provisions of art. 10(2) are met.

2. Neighbouring rights (para. 2). The Directive also prescribes reciprocity towards performers, producers and broadcasters from non-EU countries (see recital 22). As with copyright, nationals from EEA states outside the EU should be assimilated with nationals of EU states. As opposed to copyright however, this rule only applies if the Member States grant foreigners protection in their national law. The Term Directive's reticence regarding related rights is due to the relatively undeveloped condition of international coordination in this area. In contrast to the widely accepted international norms that govern copyright, in the area of related rights the existing multilateral treaties have only been signed by a relatively small number of countries. Since the adoption of the Term Directive, the TRIPS Agreement and WPPT have led to increased international harmonization. The EEA Agreement also includes an obligation that contracting states ratify the Rome Convention. The rule of shorter term is only applied if it doesn't cause Member States to act contrary to their international obligations. **(a) Community national.** Contrary to copyright, in the area of related rights the rule of shorter term applies with reference to the nationality of the rightholder and not the country of origin on the subject matter. **(b) Application in time.** Art. 7(2) should be read in conjunction with art. 10(2): according to *Sony Music Entertainment* (ECJ), the first is intended to outline the Directive's scope with regard to the persons to whom it grants protection, as opposed to the second, which concerns the material protected. As a consequence, art. 7(2) cannot govern situations were either of the two alternative conditions of art. 10(2) are met. It is instead intended to bring into play the bilateral and multilateral international treaties that bind Member States. As recital 22 states: '[w]here a rightholder who is not a Community national qualifies for protection under an international agreement, the term of protection of related rights should be the same as that laid down in this Directive'. If an international treaty requires that a Member State grant protection over certain subject matter on 1 July 1995, that protection under art. 10(2) will extend to all other Member States as well. This is indicated by the use of the plural 'Member States', as opposed to a more circumspect construction such as 'each Member State'. Commenters have disagreed with this interpretation suggesting instead that even if the Term Directive applies pursuant to art. 10(2), whether the holders of related rights who are not EEA nationals will enjoy protection in the Member State where protection is claimed will be decided according to the rule laid down in art. 7(2) by the national legislation of that Member State. Under this interpretation, the Directive did not intend full harmonization and leaves the individual Member States to decide on the treatment of nationals of third countries, with reference to their international obligations. **(c) Other related rights.** Art. 7 of the Term Directive limits itself to those related rights dealt with in art. 3, i.e. those of performers, producers of phonograms, broadcasting organizations and producers of first fixations of films. The protection of the third country owners of other related rights will thus depend exclusively on the domestic rules of the Member States and their international obligations. No international treaty currently regulates questions of recognition of term of the first fixation of films, so the harmonizing effect of art. 7(2) is limited in that area as well. With regard to the sui generis protection of databases, the special rule laid down in art. 11 of the Database Directive applies.

3. Existing international obligations (para. 3). Comparison of terms should not result in Member States being brought into conflict with their international obligations (see recital 23). Member States may therefore respect existing international obligations towards non-EU countries, such as bilateral treaties, entered into before the adoption of the original Directive on 29 October 1993. If, for instance, a Member State, on the basis of a bilateral agreement, instead of applying reciprocity towards a non-Community state the country of origin of which provides for a term of 50 years, grants it 70 years post mortem auctoris protection, the Member State in question may continue to do so, as long as no international harmonization of terms of protection has come about.

[Calculation of terms]

Article 8

The terms laid down in this Directive shall be calculated from the first day of January of the year following the event which gives rise to them.

1. Comment. As in most existing copyright and neighbouring rights treaties, all terms in the Directive are calculated from 1 January of the year following the event which gives rise to them.

[Moral rights]

Article 9

This Directive shall be without prejudice to the provisions of the Member States regulating moral rights.

1. General. Under the initial proposal for the Term Directive a harmonized minimum term of protection for moral rights would maintain them at least until the expiry of the economic rights. This suggestion proved contentious however and was withdrawn. The Directive thus does not harmonize the term of protection of moral rights (see recital 20), whether with regard to copyright or neighbouring rights. Longer terms of protection of moral rights exist in some countries, such as in France or Denmark, where the moral right is perpetual. Shorter terms of protection also exist, such as in the Netherlands, where the continuation of moral rights after the death of the author is dependent on whether or not the author has named in writing a successor to exercise his moral right, failing which, the morals rights cease to exist at the death of the author. In the UK, moral rights (the right to be identified as author or director, the right to object to derogatory treatment of the work and the right to privacy of certain photographs and films) endure as long as copyright subsists in the work. The right to object to false attribution however lasts only for 20 years after the death of the person to whom the work is falsely attributed. Art. 6bis(2) of the Berne Convention requires Contracting Parties to protect moral rights at least as long as economic rights, but also allows countries whose legislation at the moment of their ratification of or accession to the treaty did not provide for moral rights protection after the death of the author to maintain such rules.

[Application in time]

Article 10

(1) Where a term of protection which is longer than the corresponding term provided for by this Directive was already running in a Member State on 1 July 1995, this Directive shall not have the effect of shortening that term of protection in that Member State.

(2) The terms of protection provided for in this Directive shall apply to all works and subject matter which were protected in at least one Member State on the date referred to in paragraph 1, pursuant to national provisions on copyright or related rights, or which meet the criteria for protection under [Council Directive 92/100/EEC of 19 November 1992 on rental right and lending right and on certain rights related to copyright in the field of intellectual property].[11]

(3) This Directive shall be without prejudice to any acts of exploitation performed before the date referred to in paragraph 1. Member States shall adopt the necessary provisions to protect in particular acquired rights of third parties.

(4) Member States need not apply the provisions of Article 2(1) to cinematographic or audiovisual works created before 1 July 1994.

(5) Article 3(1) to (2e) in the version thereof in force on 31 October 2011 shall apply to fixations of performances and phonograms in regard to which the performer and the phonogram producer are still protected, by virtue of those provisions in the version thereof in force on 30 October 2011, as at 1 November 2013 and to fixations of performances and phonograms which come into being after that date.

(6) Article 1(7) shall apply to musical compositions with words of which at least the musical composition or the lyrics are protected in at least one Member State on 1 November 2013, and to musical compositions with words which come into being after that date.

The first subparagraph of this paragraph shall be without prejudice to any acts of exploitation performed before 1 November 2013. Member

---

11. OJ L 346, 27.11.1992, p. 61. Directive as last amended by Directive 2001/29/EC.

States shall adopt the necessary provisions to protect, in particular, acquired rights of third parties.

1. No shortening (para. 1). If a term of protection longer than the one provided for by the Directive was already running on 1 July 1995, the Directive does not have the effect of shortening that term of protection in that Member State. As a term of protection of a work protected by copyright usually starts with the creation of the work, works created before 1 July 1995 for which a longer term of protection applied, might remain protected under the old, longer term of protection until well into the 22nd century. However, the old, longer term of protection applies only in the Member State in which this term of protection formerly existed. **(a) Examples: longer national terms.** In the UK, for example, the perpetual copyright bestowed on the authors of unpublished literary, dramatic and musical works was replaced in 1988 with a term of 50 years after the death of the author, whether published or not. Literary, dramatic and musical works and engravings which were unpublished at the time of the author's death and remained that way until 1 August 1989, as well as unpublished photographs taken on or after 1 June 1957, were granted copyright protection for 50 years from 1 January 1990, i.e. until 31 December 2039. If a work in these categories was published after the death of the author, but before 1 August 1989, then the longer term of protection available will prevail. These longer terms are preserved even after amendment in compliance with the EU rules. Likewise, Spain, where the term of protection was 80 years pma until a legislative curtailment to 60 years in 1987, retains the 80-year protection period for works the authors of which died before 7 December 1987. **(b) Delayed harmonizing effect.** The result of art. 10(1) is a delay, in some cases by decades, in the onset of the application of the harmonized rules until the expiry of the longer domestic term. **(c) Which term is longer?** It is worth noting that it is not always self-evident whether an already running term of protection is longer than the term granted by the Term Directive. For example, in countries such as the Netherlands and Germany, in which cinematographic and audiovisual works prior to the transposition of the Term Directive were protected from the death of the last-surviving author and which allowed for a wider class of term-relevant authors than those persons listed in art. 2, the term of protection under the old national rules may have been longer than that granted under the rule of art. 2 Term Directive. This will be impossible to calculate however prior to the demise of either a) all the specified contributors of art. 2; or b) all remaining authors. It has been suggested that the phrase 'already running' should be interpreted as meaning that triggering events, such as the death of an author, should only be considered if they occurred before 1 July 1995. Another example comes from France, where a certain amount of confusion surrounds the war-related term extensions. According to the Intellectual Property Code, authors whose works were published before the end of WWI and which had not fallen into the public domain by 3 February 1919 were granted an additional 6 years and 152 days of protection. The rights of authors whose works were published before the end of WWII and which had not fallen into the public domain on 13 August 1941 were similarly extended for 8 years and 120 days. These provisions were not repealed by the French Parliament when it implemented the Term Directive into national law. However, in two decisions of 27 February 2007 concerning a portrait of Verdi painted by Boldini, who died in 1931, the French Court of Cassation rejected the rightholders' claims that protection lasted till 2016 and excluded the application of the extensions (*Boldini* (France)). Given that prior to the adoption of the Directive, in France non-musical works were protected only for 50 years pma, the Court ruled that the new harmonized term absorbed the 'extensions due to wars'. Commentators have concluded that musical works, which enjoyed a term of protection of 70 years pma all along, will logically continue to benefit from the extensions. French law also contains an additional 30-year extension in favour of authors who died fighting for France. The fate of this provision has not yet been decided by the courts. Italy, Belgium, Norway and Austria also contained war-related term extensions in their legislation prior to the adoption of the Term Directive, but these are all assumed to be fully absorbed with its implementation into national law.

2. Application of new terms (para. 2). The Directive's terms of protection apply to all works and subject matter that were protected in at least one Member State on 1 July 1995 according to the national law on copyright or related rights. Additionally, the terms of the Directive apply to subject matter which meets the criteria for protection under the Rental Right Directive. Art. 10(2) of the Term Directive makes reference to Directive 92/100/EEC (Rental Right Directive (old version)), but it should be noted that that Directive has since been replaced by Directive 2006/115/EC. **(a) EU citizens.** The ECJ has held that art. 18 (formerly 12) of the TFEU forbids discrimination on the basis of nationality within the EU and that the terms of copyright and neighbouring rights for all EU citizens should therefore be the same (*Collins and Patricia* (ECJ), confirmed by *Ricordi* (ECJ) and *Tod's* (ECJ)). In *Ricordi* the ECJ also made clear that the prohibition of discrimination also applies to cases where the author had died before the EC Treaty entered into force. In *Tod's* the ECJ furthermore held that art. 18 (formerly art. 12) of the EC Treaty also rules out discrimination on the basis of the country of origin of a work. In *Sony Music Entertainment* (ECJ) the ECJ confirmed that the terms of protection provided for in the Directive also apply if the subject matter at issue was at no time protected in the Member State in which protection is sought. As a consequence of the non-discrimination rule, a work that received protection in a country with a longer term of protection prior to the adoption of the Term Directive, such as Germany, which had a 70-year pma rule, will under the new rules also be protected in Member States which granted only 50 years pma, even if that protection had already expired in those Member States. Domestic courts are therefore obliged to investigate foreign law to determine the scope of protection within their own borders. Thus, in principle, all works of all EU authors who died less than 70 years before 1 July 1995 are (or were) protected in all Member States for the term laid out in the Directive. It is unclear whether the same is true if a copyright term had already run out in the country of origin of the work before that country acceded to the EU, due to the comparison of terms that would have been permitted up until then. It should probably be assumed that the general principle applies, with the 1 July 1995 being substituted for the date of accession of the country in question. With regard to the second part of art. 10(2), the right to rely on the Rental Right Directive arises only when its provisions have not been incorporated into national law by the appropriate date. The court in the Member State in which protection is sought must assess whether its own law or the law of another Member State protects these rights, and if not, whether it is appropriate to extend protection in light of the Rental Right Directive. **(b) Photographs.** Photographs are particularly interesting with regard to their qualification for the terms of protection of art. 6 of the Directive, as prior to the adoption of the Directive they were often granted only very short terms of protection in national law, even if they were recognized as original works. For example, in Germany until 1985 photographic works were protected by copyright for a mere 25 years upon publication. The introduction of the normal copyright term of 70 years pma in 1985 did not revive the copyright in photographs that were published before 1960. In Spain however, on 1 July 1995 all categories of works, including works of photography, were protected for the much longer term of 70 or 80 years pma (depending on the date of death of the author). Applying the EC Treaty's prohibition of discrimination, photographs made by EU nationals who died less than 80 years before 1 July 1995 were protected in Spain on that date, making them eligible for the harmonized term of protection of 70 years pma and revival of copyright throughout the EU, as long as they qualify according to the originality requirements of art. 6 (*U-Boot photo* (Germany)). **(c) Ownership of revived rights.** Art. 10(2) has led to a large-scale revival of copyrights in those Member States that formerly granted a term of 50 years pma. Unfortunately, art. 10 does not indicate whose rights are being revived, the heirs of the author (as is now the rule in Ireland), or the last rightholder who had acquired the copyright prior to its original termination through assignment or other transfer of rights (as is the rule in the Netherlands and the UK). Some national laws address this issue, many others do not (see art. 10(3) and *Butterfly* (ECJ)). **(d) Non-EU citizens.** Art. 10(2) also applies to authors from non-EU countries that were protected on 1 July 1995 in any Member State, either directly on the basis of the Member State's copyright law or (arguably also) on the basis of bilateral or multilateral treaty obligations. This is however a disputed issue. Art. 10(2) should not be understood as ruling out the solution of art. 7(2) in cases where its two alternative conditions are not met. Instead, art. 10(2) should be interpreted as meaning that the terms of protection provided for in the Directive, including those of art. 7(2), will apply in any situation where the work or subject matter at issue was, on 1 July 1995, protected as such in at least one

Member State under that Member State's national legislation on copyright and related rights and where the holder of such rights in respect of that work or subject matter, who is a national of a non-Member State, benefited, at that date, from the protection provided for by those national provisions (*Sony Music Entertainment* (ECJ)).

3. Acquired rights (para. 3). The Directive has no influence on acts of exploitation performed before 1 July 1995. Member States have to adopt provisions to protect acquired rights of third parties, but have considerable freedom in implementing this paragraph (see recital 25 and *Butterfly* (ECJ)). Details of such provisions are left to the discretion of the Member States, provided that they do not have the overall effect of preventing the application of the new terms of protection on the date laid down by the Directive. The ECJ ruled in *Butterfly* that a particular provision in Italian law which allowed for a limited period in which sound-recording media may be distributed by persons who, by reason of the expiry of the rights relating to those media under the previous legislation, had been able to reproduce and market them before that law entered into force, remained within the limits of art. 10(3) of the Directive. In the UK the revived copyright is treated as 'licensed by the copyright owner, subject only to the payment of such reasonable royalty or other remuneration as may be agreed or determined in default of agreement by the Copyright Tribunal'.

4. Transitional measures for cinematographic and audiovisual works (para. 4). In some countries films enjoyed much shorter terms of copyright protection before the transposition of the Directive (see art. 2). In order to achieve a smoother transition, according to art. 10(4), Member States need not apply the provisions of art. 2(1) to cinematographic or audiovisual works created before 1 July 1994. According to art. 10(5) of the initial version of the Directive Member States could determine the date as from which art. 2(1) would apply, provided that date was no later than 1 July 1997. The provision was not carried over to the codified version, as the deadline had lapsed years earlier.

5. Transitional measures for performers' and phonogram producers' right (para. 5). The new terms of protection for performers' and phonogram producers' rights apply to fixations of performances and phonograms the performers and producers of which were still protected under the old provisions on 1 November 2013, as well as any created after that date (see art. 3(1) and (2)). The same is true of the 'use it or lose it' clause, as well as the annual supplementary remuneration due to performers (art. 3(2a)-(2e)).

6. Transitional measures for co-written musical works (para. 6). The new provisions on co-written musical works apply to works at least the musical composition or the lyrics of which were already protected in at least one Member State on 1 November 2013 or which are created after that date (see art. 1(7)). In order to ensure a smoother transposition in cases of rights revived under this provision, the Directive states that it does not have any influence on acts of exploitation performed before 1 November 2013, while Member States are obliged to adopt measures protecting the acquired rights of third parties.

[Transitional Measures]

Article 10a

(1) In the absence of clear contractual indications to the contrary, a contract on transfer or assignment concluded before 1 November 2013 shall be deemed to continue to produce its effects beyond the moment at which, by virtue of Article 3(1) in the version thereof in force on 30 October 2011, the performer would no longer be protected.

(2) Member States may provide that contracts on transfer or assignment which entitle a performer to recurring payments and which are concluded before 1 November 2013 can be modified following the 50th year after the phonogram was lawfully published or, failing such publication, the 50th year after it was lawfully communicated to the public.

1. General. According to art. 10a, inserted with the Term Extension Directive, any contracts by which a performer transferred and assigned their rights in the fixation of their performance to a phonogram producer concluded before the adoption of the new rules is automatically extended along with the term of protection of performers' rights (recital 15 of the Term Extension Directive). The contract may of course still be terminated in case of activation of the 'use it or lose it' right (art. 2a). Exceptionally the extension does not apply if there were pre-arranged contractual indications to the contrary. In addition, such contracts may be modified ex post during the 20 added years of protection if Member States explicitly provide so in their legislation.

[Notification and communication]

Article 11

(1) Member States shall immediately notify the Commission of any governmental plan to grant new related rights, including the basic reasons for their introduction and the term of protection envisaged.

(2) Member States shall communicate to the Commission the texts of the provisions of internal law which they adopt in the field governed by this Directive.

1. Obligation to notify new related rights. To avoid new disparities that might affect the internal market, Member States must notify the European Commission of any initiatives to create new related rights (see also recital 19). For example, the United Kingdom has retained a related right in typographical arrangements of published editions which lasts for 25 years after publication. In Greece and Ireland the same right lasts for 50 years after the publication is made available to the public. In Spain, a similar right is granted to the publishers of public domain works over the reproduction, distribution and communication to the public of their editions, provided that these can be distinguished by their typographical composition, layout and other editorial characteristics. Protection is conferred for a period of 25 years following publication. The UK further grants special sui generis protection for computer-generated works, that is to say works created by a computer in circumstances such that there is no human author of the work. This lasts for 50 years after creation. The reference to 'related rights' should be interpreted broadly to include all rights related to copyright whether construed as exclusive rights or mere claims for equitable remuneration. The obligation to communicate applies equally to new states acceding to the European Union. Under art. 13(2) of the initial version of the Directive a deadline of 19 November 1993 (the date of notification of this Directive) was imposed. The provision was omitted in the codified version as it had long lost relevance. An additional obligation to forestall the introduction of related rights by three months, thereby enabling the Commission to initiate a subsequent directive, as was envisaged in the original proposal of the Directive, was not included in the final Term Directive.

[Repeal]

Article 12

Directive 93/98/EEC is hereby repealed, without prejudice to the obligations of the Member States relating to the time-limits for transposition into national law, as set out in Part B of Annex I, of the Directives, and their application.

References made to the repealed Directive shall be construed as being made to this Directive and should be read in accordance with the correlation table in Annex II.

1. General. The consolidated Term Directive of 2006 replaced the original 1993 text following the latter's amendment by the Information Society Directive in 2001. The deadlines for transposition into national law contained in the abolished Directive all expired long before the adoption of the consolidated version and have therefore not be reproduced, although it is stated explicitly that they continue to apply. Annex I of the consolidated Directive sets out these dates in a table. Pursuant to art. 13(1) of the old Directive, the Member States were obliged to implement it into their national law by 1 July 1995. This date is also used as the base point for the application of the Directive in time according to art. 10(1) and (2). Thus, maintaining longer terms of protection is decided in reference to this date, as well as whether a particular work will be protected in at least one Member State. The amendments of the Information Society Directive had to be transposed by 22 December 2002. These outdated time limits may, depending on the circumstances, be relevant with regard to new, acceding EU Member States. Annex II of the consolidated Directive contains a table of correlations between the old and new article numbers. At some point a new consolidated version that combines Directive 2006/116/EC and Directive 2011/77/EU will have to be adopted, although there is currently no indication as to when that might take place.

[Entry into force]

Article 13

This Directive shall enter into force on the twentieth day following that of its publication in the Official Journal of the European Union.

1. General. Directive 2006/116/EC was published in the Official Journal on 27 December 2006 and entered into force on 16 January 2007. Amending Directive 2011/77/EU entered into force on 31 October 2011 (see art. 4 of the Term Extension Directive). No obligation to prepare an impact report as envisioned in other copyright directives is included in the Term Directive.

[Addressees]

Article 14

This Directive is addressed to the Member States.

1. General. According to art. 288 of the Treaty on the Functioning of the European Union (Treaty of Rome) (ex-art. 249 EC Treaty), Directives are binding as to the result to be achieved upon each Member State to which they are addressed, but leave to the national authorities the choice of form and methods. According to Annex XVII No. 9(f) to the EEA Agreement, the Term Directive, as amended by the Term Extension Directive, must be implemented in all EEA states. Therefore, not only the 28 EU Member States, but in addition Norway, Iceland and Liechtenstein are obliged to adjust their national legislation in accordance with the provisions of the two texts.

From Directive 2011/77/EU (*Term Extension Directive*):

[Transposition]

Article 2

(1) Member States shall bring into force the laws, regulations and administrative provisions necessary to comply with this Directive by 1 November 2013. They shall forthwith inform the Commission thereof.

When Member States adopt those measures, they shall contain a reference to this Directive or shall be accompanied by such a reference on the occasion of their official publication. The methods of making such reference shall be laid down by Member States.

(2) Member States shall communicate to the Commission the text of the main provisions of national law which they adopt in the field covered by this Directive.

1. General. The Term Extension Directive must be implemented by the Member States by 1 November 2013. Member States are encouraged to draw up and make public tables indicating the correlation between the provisions of the Term Extension Directive and their transposing national measures (recital 22 of the Term Extension Directive).

[Reporting]

Article 3

(1) By 1 November 2016, the Commission shall submit to the European Parliament, the Council and the European Economic and Social Committee a report on the application of this Directive in the light of the development of the digital market, accompanied, where appropriate, by a proposal for the further amendment of Directive 2006/116/EC.

(2) By 1 January 2012, the Commission shall submit a report to the European Parliament, the Council and the European Economic and Social Committee, assessing the possible need for an extension of the term of protection of rights to performers and producers in the audiovisual sector. If appropriate, the Commission shall submit a proposal for the further amendment of Directive 2006/116/EC.

1. General. Similar to other copyright Directives, the Term Extension Directive requires that the European Commission produce a report on its application by 1 November 2016. The possible need for further amendments of the Term Directive should then be assessed. By 1 January 2012 the Commission should prepare a report examining whether the term of protection of the rights of performers and producers in the audiovisual sector should be extended similar to those in the music industry (see art. 3(1)-(3)).

[Entry into force]

Article 4

This Directive shall enter into force on the 20th day following its publication in the Official Journal of the European Union.

1. General. The Term Extension Directive was published in the Official Journal on 11 October 2011 and entered into force on 31 October 2011.

[Addressees]

Article 5

This Directive is addressed to the Member States.

1. General. See art. 14 of the Term Directive.

DIRECTIVE 96/9/EC

(Database Directive)

of the European Parliament and of the Council of 11 March 1996 on the legal protection of databases

[Introductory remarks]

1. General. The Database Directive has created a two-tier protection regime for electronic and non-electronic databases. Member States are to protect databases by copyright as intellectual creations (Chapter 2), and provide for a sui generis right (database right) to protect the contents of a database in which the producer has substantially invested (Chapter 3). Both rights may apply cumulatively if the prerequisites for both regimes are fulfilled. The introduction of sui generis protection was considered necessary after supreme courts in the Netherlands and the US had held that copyright does not protect databases reflecting merely economic investment or intellectual effort (see *Feist* (US) and *Van Dale* (Netherlands)). Prior to implementation, intellectual property protection for non-original compilations existed in just a few Member States (the United Kingdom, Denmark, Sweden and the Netherlands). Many Member States provided only for unfair competition remedies, to be applied in special circumstances, or no remedies at all. However, the absence of a harmonized legal framework for unfair competition in Europe necessitated the introduction of a sui generis right to complement copyright protection for databases (recital 6).

2. Harmonization. The Directive is based on arts. 47(2), 55 and 95 of the EC Treaty, and is aimed at harmonizing the legal protection of databases across the European Community. The copyright chapter of the Directive harmonizes the originality standard for databases, which prior to the implementation differed greatly between Member States, especially between countries of the authors' right tradition where a measure of creativity, personal character or personal imprint was required, and the two Member States (Ireland and the UK) of the British copyright tradition where mere skill and labour sufficed. The sui generis database right serves in part to compensate the latter two States for having to raise the originality standard; databases resulting merely from skill and labour may no longer receive copyright protection, but will benefit from database right protection instead.

3. Legislative history. The Directive has its roots in the European Commission's Green Paper on Copyright and the Challenge of Technology (1988) in which the Commission first suggested that copyright might be inadequate in protecting database producers, and a special protection regime might be needed. On 13 May 1992, the Commission presented an Initial Proposal to the Council, which was accepted by the European Parliament in first reading subject to a large number of amendments. This led to an Amended Proposal, which was presented by the Commission on 4 October 1993. On 10 July 1995, the Council adopted a Common position, which was markedly different from the amended proposal, and accepted by the European Parliament in second reading on 14 December 1995. On 11 March 1996, the Directive was finally adopted. A report assessing the economic impact of the sui generis right pursuant to art. 16(3), was published by the European Commission on 12 December 2005 (Report on the Database Directive). The report is skeptical about the beneficial effect the introduction of the sui generis right has had on the production of databases in the Community. It proposes various future policy options, including repealing the Directive.

4. International context. (a) Database copyright. Art. 2(5) of the Berne Convention protects 'collections of literary or artistic works such as encyclopaedias and anthologies', but denies copyright protection to 'news of the day or to miscellaneous facts having the character of mere items of press information' (see art. 2 BC, notes 6 and 9). While the BC thus leaves open the question of copyright protection for compilations of unprotected facts, art. 5 of the WIPO Copyright Treaty and art. 10(2) TRIPS, more broadly, require protection for 'compilations of data or other material', which 'by reason of the selection or arrangement of their contents constitute intellectual creations' (see art. 5 WCT, note 2). **(b) Sui generis right.** The sui generis right is a legal invention of the European Commission, and has never become an international standard despite an attempt by WIPO to propose a 'WIPO Database Treaty' in 1996. Nevertheless, a number of countries outside the EU, especially those with trade-related ties with the EU such as the EEA states and Turkey, have also adopted the sui generis right. Variants of the right exist in Russia, South Korea and Mexico.

[Bibliography]

T. Aplin, 'The ECJ Elucidates the Database Right' (2005) *Intellectual Property Quarterly* 204-221

A.C. Beunen, *Protection for Databases: The European Database Directive and Its Effects in the Netherlands, France and the United Kingdom* (Wolf Legal Publishers 2007)

L.A. Bygrave, 'The Data Difficulty in Database Protection' (2012) EIPR 25

M.J. Davison, *The Legal Protection of Databases* (Cambridge University Press 2003)

M.J. Davison & P.B. Hugenholtz, 'Football Fixtures, Horse Races and Spin-offs: The ECJ Domesticates the Database Right' (2005) EIPR 113-118

E. Derclaye, 'What is a Database? A Critical Analysis of the Definition of a Database in the European Database Directive and Suggestions for an

International Definition' (2002) *Journal of World Intellectual Property* 981–1011

E. Derclaye, 'Database Sui Generis Right: What Is a Substantial Investment? A Tentative Definition' (2005) IIC 2-30

E. Derclaye, 'IPR on Information and Market Power: Comparing the European and American Protections of Databases' (2007) IIC 275-298

E. Derclaye, *The Legal Protection Of Databases: A Comparative Analysis* (Edward Elgar Publishing 2008)

J.L. Gaster, 'The New EU Directive Concerning the Legal Protection of Databases' (1997) 20(4) *Fordham International Law Journal* 1129-1150

J. Gaster, '"Obtinere" of Data in the Eyes of the ECJ. How to Interpret the Database Directive after *British Horseracing Board Ltd et al. v. William Hill Organisation Ltd.*' (2005) *Computer Law Review International (CRi)* 129-135

P.B. Hugenholtz, 'Implementing the Database Directive' in Jan J.C. Kabel & Gerard J.H.M. Mom (eds.), *Intellectual Property and Information Law, Essays in Honour of Herman Cohen Jehoram* (Kluwer Law International 1998)

A. Kur, et al., 'First Evaluation of Directive 96/9/EC on the Legal Protection of Databases' (2006) IIC 551-558

[Preamble]

The European Parliament and the Council of the European Union, Having regard to the Treaty establishing the European Community, and in particular Article 57 (2), 66 and 100a thereof,

Having regard to the proposal from the Commission,[1]

Having regard to the opinion of the Economic and Social Committee,[2]

Acting in accordance with the procedure laid down in Article 189b of the Treaty,[3]

(1) Whereas databases are at present not sufficiently protected in all Member States by existing legislation; whereas such protection, where it exists, has different attributes;

---

1. OJ No. C 156, 23 June 1992, p. 4 and OJ No. C 308, 15 November 1993, p. 1.
2. OJ No. C 19, 25 January 1993, p. 3.
3. Opinion of the European Parliament of 23 June 1993 (OJ No. C 194, 19 July 1993, p. 144), Common Position of the Council of 10 July 1995 (OJ No. C 288, 30 October 1995, p. 14), Decision of the European Parliament of 14 December 1995 (OJ No. C 17, 22 January 1996) and Council Decision of 26 February 1996.

(2) Whereas such differences in the legal protection of databases offered by the legislation of the Member States have direct negative effects on the functioning of the internal market as regards databases and in particular on the freedom of natural and legal persons to provide on-line database goods and services on the basis of harmonized legal arrangements throughout the Community; whereas such differences could well become more pronounced as Member States introduce new legislation in this field, which is now taking on an increasingly international dimension;

(3) Whereas existing differences distorting the functioning of the internal market need to be removed and new ones prevented from arising, while differences not adversely affecting the functioning of the internal market or the development of an information market within the Community need not be removed or prevented from arising;

(4) Whereas copyright protection for databases exists in varying forms in the Member States according to legislation or case-law, and whereas, if differences in legislation in the scope and conditions of protection remain between the Member States, such unharmonized intellectual property rights can have the effect of preventing the free movement of goods or services within the Community;

(5) Whereas copyright remains an appropriate form of exclusive right for authors who have created databases;

(6) Whereas, nevertheless, in the absence of a harmonized system of unfair-competition legislation or of case-law, other measures are required in addition to prevent the unauthorized extraction and/or re-utilization of the contents of a database;

(7) Whereas the making of databases requires the investment of considerable human, technical and financial resources while such databases can be copied or accessed at a fraction of the cost needed to design them independently;

(8) Whereas the unauthorized extraction and/or re-utilization of the contents of a database constitute acts which can have serious economic and technical consequences;

(9) Whereas databases are a vital tool in the development of an information market within the Community; whereas this tool will also be of use in many other fields;

(10) Whereas the exponential growth, in the Community and worldwide, in the amount of information generated and processed annually in all sectors of commerce and industry calls for investment in all the Member States in advanced information processing systems;

(11) Whereas there is at present a very great imbalance in the level of investment in the database sector both as between the Member States and between the Community and the world's largest database-producing third countries;

Hugenholtz

(12) Whereas such an investment in modern information storage and processing systems will not take place within the Community unless a stable and uniform legal protection regime is introduced for the protection of the rights of makers of databases;

(13) Whereas this Directive protects collections, sometimes called 'compilations', of works, data or other materials which are arranged, stored and accessed by means which include electronic, electromagnetic or electro-optical processes or analogous processes;

(14) Whereas protection under this Directive should be extended to cover non-electronic databases;

(15) Whereas the criteria used to determine whether a database should be protected by copyright should be defined to the fact that the selection or the arrangement of the contents of the database is the author's own intellectual creation; whereas such protection should cover the structure of the database;

(16) Whereas no criterion other than originality in the sense of the author's intellectual creation should be applied to determine the eligibility of the database for copyright protection, and in particular no aesthetic or qualitative criteria should be applied;

(17) Whereas the term 'database' should be understood to include literary, artistic, musical or other collections of works or collections of other material such as texts, sound, images, numbers, facts, and data; whereas it should cover collections of independent works, data or other materials which are systematically or methodically arranged and can be individually accessed; whereas this means that a recording or an audiovisual, cinematographic, literary or musical work as such does not fall within the scope of this Directive;

(18) Whereas this Directive is without prejudice to the freedom of authors to decide whether, or in what manner, they will allow their works to be included in a database, in particular whether or not the authorization given is exclusive; whereas the protection of databases by the sui generis right is without prejudice to existing rights over their contents, and whereas in particular where an author or the holder of a related right permits some of his works or subject matter to be included in a database pursuant to a non-exclusive agreement, a third party may make use of those works or subject matter subject to the required consent of the author or of the holder of the related right without the sui generis right of the maker of the database being invoked to prevent him doing so, on condition that those works or subject matter are neither extracted from the database nor re-utilized on the basis thereof;

(19) Whereas, as a rule, the compilation of several recordings of musical performances on a CD does not come within the scope of this Directive, both because, as a compilation, it does not meet the conditions for copyright protection and because it does not represent a substantial enough investment to be eligible under the sui generis right;

(20) Whereas protection under this Directive may also apply to the materials necessary for the operation or consultation of certain databases such as thesaurus and indexation systems;

(21) Whereas the protection provided for in this Directive relates to databases in which works, data or other materials have been arranged systematically or methodically; whereas it is not necessary for those materials to have been physically stored in an organized manner;

(22) Whereas electronic databases within the meaning of this Directive may also include devices such as CD-ROM and CD-i;

(23) Whereas the term 'database' should not be taken to extend to computer programs used in the making or operation of a database, which are protected by Council Directive 91/250/EEC of 14 May 1991 on the legal protection of computer programs;[4]

(24) Whereas the rental and lending of databases in the field of copyright and related rights are governed exclusively by Council Directive 92/100/EEC of 19 November 1992 on rental right and lending right and on certain rights related to copyright in the field of intellectual property;[5]

(25) Whereas the term of copyright is already governed by Council Directive 93/98/EEC of 29 October 1993 harmonizing the term of protection of copyright and certain related rights;[6]

(26) Whereas works protected by copyright and subject matter protected by related rights, which are incorporated into a database, remain nevertheless protected by the respective exclusive rights and may not be incorporated into, or extracted from, the database without the permission of the rightholder or his successors in title;

(27) Whereas copyright in such works and related rights in subject matter thus incorporated into a database are in no way affected by the existence of a separate right in the selection or arrangement of these works and subject matter in a database;

(28) Whereas the moral rights of the natural person who created the database belong to the author and should be exercised according to the legislation of the Member States and the provisions of the Berne Convention for the Protection of Literary and Artistic Works; whereas such moral rights remain outside the scope of this Directive;

(29) Whereas the arrangements applicable to databases created by employees are left to the discretion of the Member States; whereas, therefore nothing in this Directive prevents Member States from stipulating in their legislation that where a database is created by an employee in the execution of his duties or following the instructions

---

4. OJ No. L 122, 17 May 1991, p. 42. Directive as last amended by Directive 93/98/EEC (OJ No. L 290, 24 November 1993, p. 9.).

5. OJ No. L 346, 27 November 1992, p. 61.

6. OJ No. L 290, 24 November 1993, p. 9.

given by his employer, the employer exclusively shall be entitled to exercise all economic rights in the database so created, unless otherwise provided by contract;

(30) Whereas the author's exclusive rights should include the right to determine the way in which his work is exploited and by whom, and in particular to control the distribution of his work to unauthorized persons;

(31) Whereas the copyright protection of databases includes making databases available by means other than the distribution of copies;

(32) Whereas Member States are required to ensure that their national provisions are at least materially equivalent in the case of such acts subject to restrictions as are provided for by this Directive;

(33) Whereas the question of exhaustion of the right of distribution does not arise in the case of on-line databases, which come within the field of provision of services; whereas this also applies with regard to a material copy of such a database made by the user of such a service with the consent of the rightholder; whereas, unlike CD-ROM or CD-i, where the intellectual property is incorporated in a material medium, namely an item of goods, every on-line service is in fact an act which will have to be subject to authorization where the copyright so provides;

(34) Whereas, nevertheless, once the rightholder has chosen to make available a copy of the database to a user, whether by an on-line service or by other means of distribution, that lawful user must be able to access and use the database for the purposes and in the way set out in the agreement with the rightholder, even if such access and use necessitate performance of otherwise restricted acts;

(35) Whereas a list should be drawn up of exceptions to restricted acts, taking into account the fact that copyright as covered by this Directive applies only to the selection or arrangements of the contents of a database; whereas Member States should be given the option of providing for such exceptions in certain cases; whereas, however, this option should be exercised in accordance with the Berne Convention and to the extent that the exceptions relate to the structure of the database; whereas a distinction should be drawn between exceptions for private use and exceptions for reproduction for private purposes, which concerns provisions under national legislation of some Member States on levies on blank media or recording equipment;

(36) Whereas the term 'scientific research' within the meaning of this Directive covers both the natural sciences and the human sciences;

(37) Whereas Article 10(1) of the Berne Convention is not affected by this Directive;

(38) Whereas the increasing use of digital recording technology exposes the database maker to the risk that the contents of his database may be copied and rearranged electronically, without his authorization,

to produce a database of identical content which, however, does not infringe any copyright in the arrangement of his database;

(39) Whereas, in addition to aiming to protect the copyright in the original selection or arrangement of the contents of a database, this Directive seeks to safeguard the position of makers of databases against misappropriation of the results of the financial and professional investment made in obtaining and collection the contents by protecting the whole or substantial parts of a database against certain acts by a user or competitor;

(40) Whereas the object of this sui generis right is to ensure protection of any investment in obtaining, verifying or presenting the contents of a database for the limited duration of the right; whereas such investment may consist in the deployment of financial resources and/or the expending of time, effort and energy;

(41) Whereas the objective of the sui generis right is to give the maker of a database the option of preventing the unauthorized extraction and/or re-utilization of all or a substantial part of the contents of that database; whereas the maker of a database is the person who takes the initiative and the risk of investing; whereas this excludes subcontractors in particular from the definition of maker;

(42) Whereas the special right to prevent unauthorized extraction and/or re-utilization relates to acts by the user which go beyond his legitimate rights and thereby harm the investment; whereas the right to prohibit extraction and/or re-utilization of all or a substantial part of the contents relates not only to the manufacture of a parasitical competing product but also to any user who, through his acts, causes significant detriment, evaluated qualitatively or quantitatively, to the investment;

(43) Whereas, in the case of on-line transmission, the right to prohibit re-utilization is not exhausted either as regards the database or as regards a material copy of the database or of part thereof made by the addressee of the transmission with the consent of the rightholder;

(44) Whereas, when on-screen display of the contents of a database necessitates the permanent or temporary transfer of all or a substantial part of such contents to another medium, that act should be subject to authorization by the rightholder;

(45) Whereas the right to prevent unauthorized extraction and/or re-utilization does not in any way constitute an extension of copyright protection to mere facts or data;

(46) Whereas the existence of a right to prevent the unauthorized extraction and/or re-utilization of the whole or a substantial part of works, data or materials from a database should not give rise to the creation of a new right in the works, data or materials themselves;

(47) Whereas, in the interests of competition between suppliers of information products and services, protection by the sui generis right must not be afforded in such a way as to facilitate abuses of a dominant

position, in particular as regards the creation and distribution of new products and services which have an intellectual, documentary, technical, economic or commercial added value; whereas, therefore, the provisions of this Directive are without prejudice to the application of Community or national competition rules;

(48) Whereas the objective of this Directive, which is to afford an appropriate and uniform level of protection of databases as a means to secure the remuneration of the maker of the database, is different from the aim of Directive 95/46/EC of the European Parliament and of the Council of 24 October 1995 on the protection of individuals with regard to the processing of personal data and on the free movement of such data,[7] which is to guarantee free circulation of personal data on the basis of harmonized rules designed to protect fundamental rights, notably the right to privacy which is recognized in Article 8 of the European Convention for the Protection of Human Rights and Fundamental Freedoms; whereas the provisions of this Directive are without prejudice to data protection legislation;

(49) Whereas, notwithstanding the right to prevent extraction and/or re-utilization of all or a substantial part of a database, it should be laid down that the maker of a database or rightholder may not prevent a lawful user of the database from extracting and re-utilizing insubstantial parts; whereas, however, that user may not unreasonably prejudice either the legitimate interests of the holder of the sui generis right or the holder of copyright or a related right in respect of the works or subject matter contained in the database;

(50) Whereas the Member States should be given the option of providing for exceptions to the right to prevent the unauthorized extraction and/or re-utilization of a substantial part of the contents of a database in the case of extraction for private purposes, for the purposes of illustration for teaching or scientific research, or where extraction and/or re-utilization are/is carried out in the interests of public security or for the purposes of an administrative or judicial procedure; whereas such operations must not prejudice the exclusive rights of the maker to exploit the database and their purpose must not be commercial;

(51) Whereas the Member States, where they avail themselves of the option to permit a lawful user of a database to extract a substantial part of the contents for the purposes of illustration for teaching or scientific research, may limit that permission to certain categories of teaching or scientific research institution;

(52) Whereas those Member States which have specific rules providing for a right comparable to the sui generis right provided for in this Directive should be permitted to retain, as far as the new right is concerned, the exceptions traditionally specified by such rules;

---

7.   OJ No. L 281, 23 Novemeber 1995, p. 31.

(53) Whereas the burden of proof regarding the date of completion of the making of a database lies with the maker of the database;

(54) Whereas the burden of proof that the criteria exist for concluding that a substantial modification of the contents of a database is to be regarded as a substantial new investment lies with the maker of the database resulting from such investment;

(55) Whereas a substantial new investment involving a new term of protection may include a substantial verification of the contents of the database;

(56) Whereas the right to prevent unauthorized extraction and/or re-utilization in respect of a database should apply to databases whose makers are nationals or habitual residents of third countries or to those produced by legal persons not established in a Member State, within the meaning of the Treaty, only if such third countries offer comparable protection to databases produced by nationals of a Member State or persons who have their habitual residence in the territory of the Community;

(57) Whereas, in addition to remedies provided under the legislation of the Member States for infringements of copyright or other rights, Member States should provide for appropriate remedies against unauthorized extraction and/or re-utilization of the contents of a database;

(58) Whereas, in addition to the protection given under this Directive to the structure of the database by copyright, and to its contents against unauthorized extraction and/or re-utilization under the sui generis right, other legal provisions in the Member States relevant to the supply of database goods and services continue to apply;

(59) Whereas this Directive is without prejudice to the application to databases composed of audiovisual works of any rules recognized by a Member State's legislation concerning the broadcasting of audiovisual programmes;

(60) Whereas some Member States currently protect under copyright arrangements databases which do not meet the criteria for eligibility for copyright protection laid down in this Directive; whereas, even if the databases concerned are eligible for protection under the right laid down in this Directive to prevent unauthorized extraction and/or re-utilization of their contents, the term of protection under that right is considerably shorter than that which they enjoy under the national arrangements currently in force; whereas harmonization of the criteria for determining whether a database is to be protected by copyright may not have the effect of reducing the term of protection currently enjoyed by the rightholders concerned; whereas a derogation should be laid down to that effect; whereas the effects of such derogation must be confined to the territories of the Member States concerned,

Have adopted this Directive:

CHAPTER I. SCOPE

[Scope]

Article 1

(1) This Directive concerns the legal protection of databases in any form.

(2) For the purposes of this Directive, 'database' shall mean a collection of independent works, data or other materials arranged in a systematic or methodical way and individually accessible by electronic or other means.

(3) Protection under this Directive shall not apply to computer programs used in the making or operation of databases accessible by electronic means.

1. General. Art. 1 defines the general notion of database, and thereby determines the scope of the Directive. The definition applies both to the copyright provisions of the Directive (arts. 3-6), and to the provisions on sui generis protection (arts. 7-11). Note that a database that complies with the definition will only be protected by copyright or sui generis database right if the corresponding prerequisites (originality and substantial investment, respectively) are met.

2. Databases in any form (para. 1). The Directive is not merely concerned with electronic databases (recital 13), but with databases 'in any form' including non-electronic compilations (recital 14) such as card-based catalogues, telephone directories, encyclopaedias, and microfilm databases. According to the ECJ, the European legislature should 'give the term database as defined in the directive, a wide scope, unencumbered by considerations of a formal, technical or material nature' (*Fixtures/OPAP*). Similarly, art. 10(2) of the TRIPS Agreement provides for copyright protection of databases 'whether in machine readable or other form', and art. 5 of the WIPO Copyright Treaty calls for copyright protection of compilations of data or other material 'in any form'. Digital databases are protected both in on-line (internet-based) form and as off-line versions, such as databases on CD-ROM (recital 22).

3. Definition of database (para. 2). Art. 1(2) defines the notion of database. **(a) Collection of independent works, data or other materials.** A 'database' is any collection of works, data or other informational matter. A collection of works of authorship, such as an anthology, encyclopedias or multimedia work, therefore qualifies as a database. Note that the works collected need not be protected by copyright; a collection of works in the public domain (e.g., works in which copyright has expired) can also constitute a database. A database might even consist of 'other materials', that is, subject matter that is neither work nor data, such as sound recordings and non-original photographs that might be protected by neighbouring rights. The Explanatory Memorandum describes the contents of the database as '"information" in the widest sense of that term', while making it clear that the notion of database does not encompass collections of physical objects, such as stamp or butterfly collections. The definition does not provide for a minimum number of elements; this is for the courts to determine. According to the ECJ, the definition does not imply that a 'large number' of data be collected (*Fixtures/OPAP*). Case law from national courts in Europe indicates that the definition of database covers a wide variety of information products, such as telephone directories, collections of legal materials, real estate information websites, bibliographies, encyclopedias, address lists, company registries, exhibition catalogues, etc. **(b) Independent.** The elements (works, data or other materials) must be independent, 'that is to say, materials which are separable from one another without their informative, literary, artistic, musical or other value being affected' (*Fixtures/OPAP* (ECJ)). Therefore a literary work, a musical composition or a sound recording is not a database, even if it can be perceived as a collection of moving images, words, notes or sounds (recital 17). Thus a total overlap between the Directive and existing copyright and neighbouring rights law is avoided. For example, the data in a midi music file lacks sufficient independence (see *Midi files* (Germany)), whereas a hit parade (i.e. chart of bestselling music) does qualify as a database, because the individual chart listings do have independent information value (*Hit Balanz* (Germany)). **(c) Arranged in a systematic or methodical way.** The individual elements of the database must be arranged in a systematic or methodical way. A collection of random notes does not qualify as a database, nor does a hard disk containing unsorted data. The Explanatory Memorandum excludes from the definition of a database 'the mere stockage of quantities of works or materials in electronic form'. However, it is not necessary for the contents of a database to be physically stored in an organized manner (recital 21). A large number of unsorted data fixed on a hard disk, for example, will still qualify as a database if combined with database management software that arranges and enables retrieval of the stored data. **(d) Individually accessible.** The elements collected in the database must be individually accessible (that is, retrievable) by electronic or other means. Thus a website containing hyperlinks to a number of web pages was deemed a database because the links made the information on the sites individually accessible (*C. Villas* (Austria)). But perfect arrangement and accessibility does not always seem to be required. For example, the roughly indexed jobs section of a daily newspaper was held by a Dutch appeals court to qualify as a database (*Wegener* (Netherlands)). By contrast, in a Belgian case the description in writing of a sightseeing bus tour through Brussels was not deemed a database because the data could not be individually accessed (*Dochy/Nice Traveling* (Belgium)).

4. Database software (para. 3). The Directive does not protect the computer software driving the database as such. **(a) Computer programs excluded.** Computer programs are protected independently by the Computer Programs Directive. Art. 2 confirms in more general terms that the Directive does not deal with subject matter harmonized by previous directives.

(b) Thesaurus and index. But the Directive does apply to the materials necessary for the operation or consultation of certain databases such as thesaurus and indexation systems (recital 20). These bibliographic tools are protected as (parts of) a database.

[Limitations on the scope]

Article 2

This Directive shall apply without prejudice to Community provisions relating to:
    (a) the legal protection of computer programs;
    (b) rental right, lending right and certain rights related to copyright in the field of intellectual property;
    (c) the term of protection of copyright and certain related rights.

1. Scope. The Directive respects the acquis of previous directives and does not affect or alter the rules of these directives. Subject matter protected by copyright or neighbouring rights remains fully protected despite being incorporated in a database (recital 26; see also recital 18), regardless of whether a separate copyright or sui generis right in the database as such exists (recital 27). The Directive does not provide for a general limitation or exception to use works in databases. Moral rights of database creators also remain outside the scope of the Directive (recital 28). Subsequent Directives, in particular the Information Society Directive, are without prejudice to this Directive, except for the provisions on technological measures and rights management information (arts. 6 and 7 of the Information Society Directive) that do apply to subject matter protected by the Database Directive.

2. Previous directives unaffected. The provisions of the Directive are without prejudice to the three directives preceding it, the Computer Programs Directive, the Rental Right Directive and the Term Directive. **(a) Computer programs.** Computer programs are specifically dealt with in the Computer Programs Directive. Art. 1(3) expressly excludes computer programs from the definition of database. **(b) Rental rights, lending rights and related (neighbouring) rights.** The Directive does not amend the Rental Right Directive that harmonizes rental and lending rights for authors, performing artists, phonogram producers and film producers. Therefore, the author of a database that satisfies the test of art. 3.1 will enjoy these rights (recital 24), but not the maker (producer) of a database within the meaning of art. 7; the sui generis right does not comprise rights of lending and rental. **(c) Term of protection.** Databases that are protected by copyright will enjoy the terms harmonized by the Term Directive. Art. 10 sets a special term for the sui generis right to which the Term Directive does not apply.

CHAPTER II. COPYRIGHT

[Object of protection]

Article 3

(1) **In accordance with this Directive, databases which, by reason of the selection or arrangement of their contents, constitute the author's own intellectual creation shall be protected as such by copyright. No other criteria shall be applied to determine their eligibility for that protection.**

(2) **The copyright protection of databases provided for by this Directive shall not extend to their contents and shall be without prejudice to any rights subsisting in those contents themselves.**

1. **Copyright protection (para. 1).** Art. 3 harmonizes copyright protection for databases. The sui generis database right is dealt with in Chapter III, arts. 7-11. **(a) Author's own intellectual creation.** Databases are protected by copyright if by reason of the selection or arrangement of their contents they constitute the author's own intellectual creation. The standard of 'the author's own intellectual creation' can also be found in art. 1(3) of the Computer Programs Directive and art. 6 of the Term Directive. Although art. 3(1) does not expressly mention originality, it is assumed that this is the essential prerequisite. According to the ECJ a database is protected by copyright 'provided that the selection or arrangement of the data which it contains amounts to an original expression of the creative freedom of its author' (*Football Dataco and others* (ECJ)). This is a stricter test than the traditional British requirement of skill and labour ('sweat of the brow'). The ECJ has held that 'the significant labour and skill required for setting up [a] database cannot as such justify such a protection if they do not express any originality in the selection or arrangement of the data which that database contains' (*Football Dataco and others* (ECJ)). There is also no originality 'when the setting up of the database is dictated by technical considerations, rules or constraints which leave no room for creative freedom' (*Football Dataco and others* (ECJ)). Courts in author's rights countries often combine a test of originality (creativity) with an additional requirement of 'personal character' or 'personal imprint' (see e.g. *Van Dale* (Netherlands)). Whether this standard is on a par with *Football Dataco and others* remains to be seen. **(b) Selection or arrangement.** Databases will qualify for copyright protection only if by reason of the selection or arrangement of their contents, they constitute the author's own intellectual creation. A nearly identical test is laid down in art. 10(2) of the TRIPS Agreement and in art. 5 of the WIPO Copyright Treaty. The selection or arrangement of the elements of the database (or structure) must result from an act of creation. According to the ECJ, 'the criterion of originality is satisfied when, through the selection or arrangement of the data which it contains, its author expresses his creative ability in an original manner by making free and creative choices'. For example, a list of the author's

favourite restaurants in Amsterdam will probably qualify, while a list of the most expensive restaurants most likely will not. Completeness is not creative, nor is an arrangement of data based on objective criteria, such as alphabetical ordering. Note that selection and arrangement are not cumulative criteria. **(c) No other criteria.** Member States may not apply other (local) standards to determine whether a database qualifies for copyright protection. In particular no aesthetic or qualitative criteria should be applied (recital 16). The standard set by the Directive is clearly intended as full harmonization. Member States may not maintain or introduce more restrictive or more lenient standards that were previously applied in several Member States. Thus the Directive pre-empts the British skill and labour test that courts in the United Kingdom traditionally applied to compilations (*Football Dataco and others* (ECJ)). The same holds true for the protection of non-original writings ('geschriftenbescherming') that existed for over a century in the Netherlands, but was first rejected by the Dutch Supreme Court (*Ryanair/PR Aviation* (Netherlands), and shortly thereafter abolished in 2014. German courts have in the past regularly awarded copyright protection to low-originality 'small change' ('kleine Münze'), such as a lexicon of trademarks. In so far as such low-originality productions qualify as 'databases' they have now become subject to the higher standard of the Database Directive. For example, the Federal Supreme Court has denied copyright protection to a telephone directory because its contents did not reflect intellectual creation (*Deutsche Telekom* (Germany)). **(d) Non-database compilations.** Compilations that do not qualify as databases may still benefit from lower-threshold copyright regimes existing at the national level. In the light of the Directive's broad definition of 'database', this remaining category will probably be of limited practical importance.

2. No copyright in contents of the database (para. 2). Database copyright based on selection or arrangement does not extend to its contents, that is, the works, data or other elements as such. Art. 10(2) of the TRIPS Agreement contains similar language. Copyright protects only the expressive features or the structure (recital 15) of the database. Users that extract (part of) the contents of the database without appropriating the selection or arrangement as such do not infringe the copyright in the database (see e.g., *Meltwater* (United Kingdom)), but might infringe copyright in the individual elements of the database. Database copyright thus offers at best a thin layer of protection. **(a) No prejudice to rights in contents of the database.** The second part of para. 2 is inspired by art. 2(5) of the Berne Convention that deals with collections of works. The Initial Proposal of the Database Directive provided for a direct reference to art. 2(5) BC, but this was later deleted since the notion of database extends beyond a collection of works. Copyright protection of the database does not affect any pre-existing rights in the contents of the database, such as copyrights or neighbouring rights in works or phonograms collected in the database. A database producer cannot invoke copyright or sui generis database right to prevent the author of a work that was licensed non-exclusively to the producer from granting a subsequent licence to a third party (recital 18). Also, copyright protection of the database may co-exist with database right in its contents; both regimes may apply cumulatively to the same database. **(b) No special exceptions to permit incorporation into database.** Art. 4 of the Initial Proposal of the Database Directive provided for a special exception that would have permitted the incorporation of bibliographic data, short excerpts and summaries, but this was eventually deleted (see recital 26).

[Database authorship]

Article 4

(1) The author of a database shall be the natural person or group of natural persons who created the base or, where the legislation of the Member States so permits, the legal person designated as the rightholder by that legislation.

(2) Where collective works are recognized by the legislation of a Member State, the economic rights shall be owned by the person holding the copyright.

(3) In respect of a database created by a group of natural persons jointly, the exclusive rights shall be owned jointly.

1. General. Art. 4 is modelled on art. 2 of the Computer Programs Directive, except that it does not provide for a special rule for databases created by employees (see art. 2 Computer Programs Directive, notes 1 and 2). The Directive establishes a general rule of database authorship and, by implication, copyright ownership in art. 4(1), but leaves Member States considerable freedom to deviate from this rule.

2. Database authorship (para. 1). The author of a database shall be the natural person(s) who created the database. The wording of art. 4(1) suggests that a 'group' of natural persons may also qualify as the author, but as para. 3 clarifies what is meant here is joint authorship. Art. 4(1) does not explicitly state that authors are also initial owners of the copyright, but this can be inferred from art. 4(3) and recital 30. **(a) Legal persons as authors and owners.** Member States remain free to designate a legal person as the author or first owner of the copyright. For instance, in the Netherlands authorship and ownership vest directly in the employer of the author (usually a legal person) and in a legal person that publishes a work without indicating the actual creator. In the UK copyright vests directly in a legal person arranging for the creation of computer-generated works (see art. 2 Computer Programs Directive, note 1(c)). **(b) Database created by employees.** Databases are often created in employment relationships. The Initial Proposal would have allocated the economic rights directly to the employer of the creator of the database, like art. 2(3) of the Computer Programs Directive, but this rule was not included in the final Directive. Member States however remain free to stipulate in their legislation that where a databases are created by employees in the execution of their duties or following the instructions given by their employers, the employers shall be exclusively entitled to exercise all economic rights in the database so created, unless otherwise provided (recital 29). Such rules exist in several Member States.

3. Collective works (para. 2). In Member States where so-called collective works ('oeuvres collectives') enjoy special copyright status, like France, the economic rights (under copyright) in the database shall be allocated to the owner of the collective work, which in all likelihood will be a legal person (see art. 2 Computer Programs Directive, note 1(d)).

4. Joint ownership (para. 3). The copyright in a database that was jointly created by several natural persons will be owned jointly by those persons. Art. 4(3) does not require that the individual parts of the work not be capable of individual exploitation, as some Member States require. Nor does the Directive provide for special rules on the exercise of jointly owned copyrights. This too is left to the discretion of the Member States (see art. 2 Computer Programs Directive, note 2(b)).

[Restricted acts]

Article 5

In respect of the expression of the database which is protectable by copyright, the author of a database shall have the exclusive right to carry out or to authorize:
- **(a) temporary or permanent reproduction by any means and in any form, in whole or in part;**
- **(b) translation, adaptation, arrangement and any other alteration;**
- **(c) any form of distribution to the public of the database or of copies thereof. The first sale in the Community of a copy of the database by the rightholder or with his consent shall exhaust the right to control resale of that copy within the Community;**
- **(d) any communication, display or performance to the public;**
- **(e) any reproduction, distribution, communication, display or performance to the public of the results of the acts referred to in (b).**

1. General. Art. 5 enumerates the economic rights protected under database copyright. The rights are granted only to the 'author of a database', but clearly successors in title will enjoy these rights as well. The rights apply only in respect of 'the expression of the database', which probably means the same as 'the selection or arrangement of their contents' (art. 3) or 'the structure of the database' (recital 15). The rights do not extend to the individual elements of the database. The enumeration of exclusive rights in (a) to (e) applies to copyright protection of databases only, not to the sui generis database right which is exclusively dealt with in arts. 7-11 and the common provisions (arts. 12-17) of the Directive. The enumeration has not been amended or superseded by the Information Society Directive, since databases remain outside the scope of that Directive (see art. 1(2)(e) Information Society Directive). The enumeration is very broad, and by including a right of adaptation goes well beyond the Information Society Directive. It includes all economic rights relevant to databases, and even some rights that will rarely or ever be invoked by the author of a database, such as a performance right. Moral rights however are not included; this is left to the discretion of the Member States, taking into account art. 6bis of the BC (recital 28).

2. Reproduction right (art. 5(a)). Database authors enjoy a broad right of reproduction that includes temporary reproduction and therefore goes beyond the definition of the reproduction right in the BC (art. 9(1) BC), but appears to fall short of the even broader reproduction right of the Information Society Directive (art. 2) that also includes 'direct or indirect' reproduction. The wording of art. 5(a) is almost identical to that of art. 4(a), first sentence, of the Computer Programs Directive (see art. 4 Computer Programs Directive, note 2). Although art. 5(a) suggests a broad meaning of reproduction, it does not define reproduction. **(a) Temporary reproduction.** The reproduction right includes temporary reproductions, such as non-permanent copies made in random-access memory (RAM) or in temporary caches on computer servers or personal computers. The Directive does not provide for a (mandatory) exception allowing the making of such copies by intermediaries or lawful users, such as art. 5(1) of the Information Society Directive. Since the latter Directive does not affect the Database Directive, making such copies of databases appears not to be allowed. This is one of the incongruences addressed by the Commission's 2004 Staff Working Paper on Copyright Review. **(b) By any means and in any form.** These words clarify that copying onto a medium other than the original (e.g., scanning a database, i.e. converting it from paper form to digital medium) may be regarded as reproduction (see also art. 2 Information Society Directive, note 3). **(c) In whole or in part.** Reproduction of a part of a database will also amount to reproduction insofar as a relevant part of its expressive features (structure) is copied. This is a normal copyright principle, and most likely applies also to the other rights enumerated in art. 5. The Directive offers no guidance on what constitutes a relevant part of a database. However, the ECJ's *Infopaq International* decision interpreting the scope of the reproduction right enshrined in art. 2 Information Society Directive might offer guidance.

3. Adaptation (art. 5(b)). Database copyright includes the right of translation, adaptation, arrangement and any other alteration. The wording of art. 5(b) is reproduced literally from art. 4(b), first half sentence, of the

Computer Programs Directive (see art. 4 Computer Programs Directive, note 3). **(a) Translation.** Since copyright in a database concerns only its structure, not its contents, a translation right will exist mostly in theory. **(b) Other alteration.** An example of an adaptation covered by art. 5(b) might be the making of a database that reproduces the expressive features of a prior database, such as its menu structure, rubrics, visual design, and so on. **(c) Any subsequent reproduction, distribution, communication or display to the public of an adaptation (art. 5(e)).** Art. 5(e) clarifies that any further reproduction, distribution, communication to the public or display of an adaptation or alteration of a database will constitute a separate restricted act. This provision is most likely redundant, since this rule already follows from the general principles of copyright law.

4. Distribution (art. 5(c)). The rights granted to database authors include a right of distribution, similar to the distribution rights in other Directives (art. 4(c) Computer Programs Directive, art. 9 Rental Directive, art. 4 Information Society Directive). Although distribution usually refers to the sale of physical copies, the wording 'in any form' suggests that the term might also encompass distribution in electronic form. Exhaustion of the distribution right however may only occur in respect of the sale of physical copies; (recital 33). **(a) Community exhaustion.** Like similar rights in other directives, the distribution right is exhausted following the first sale in the Community of a copy of the database by the rightholder or with his consent (see art. 4 Computer Programs Directive, note 5(a)). Note that pursuant to the EEA Agreement, the exhaustion rule also applies to the first sale in the other countries of the European Economic Area. **(b) No electronic exhaustion.** Exhaustion is limited to the first sale of copies in physical form. Recital 33 clarifies that exhaustion does not occur in the case of on-line databases; the downloading of (parts of a) database does not give rise to exhaustion. For other copyright subject matter this is confirmed by art. 3(3) Information Society Directive (see art. 3(3) Information Society Directive, note 4). In respect of computer programs however the ECJ has opened the possibility of electronic exhaustion (*UsedSoft* (ECJ); see art. 4 Computer Programs Directive, note 4(e)). The clear language of recital 33 however arguably precludes application by analogy of the *UsedSoft* rule to databases. **(c) Rental and lending.** As the Directive leaves the provisions of the Rental Directive intact, it does not provide expressly for rights of rental and lending (recital 24). The Rental Directive applies to all copyright works (arts. 1(1) and 2(1)), including databases. Therefore database copyright also includes rights of rental and lending.

5. Any communication, display or performance to the public (art. 5(d)). The author of a database shall also have the exclusive right of communication to the public, public display and even public performance. This includes making databases available by means other than the distribution of copies (recital 31). Presumably this comprises making the database available 'in such a way that members of the public may access them from a place and at a time individually chosen by them' (art. 3(1) Information Society Directive), albeit such a right is not expressly mentioned in art. 5(d). **(a) Communication to the public.** The right of communication to the public covers a spectrum of acts whereby the database is transmitted to the public in non-tangible form, by wired or wireless means (see art. 3(1) Information Society Directive, note 2(a)). **(b) Public display.** The right of display (to the public) concerns displaying databases on viewing screens in public areas, such as airline arrival or departure information in airports. It might also have the broader meaning of covering the transmission of the database in such a way that its users may consult it on screens and terminals. In this sense it is equivalent to the right of making available to the public. **(c) Performance.** Since it is difficult to conceive how a database can be performed, this right will be of theoretical interest only. **(d) Public.** The Directive does not define the term public. Guidance may be found in the ECJ's jurisprudence regarding the right of communication to the public of art. 3(1) of the Information Society Directive (see art. 3(1) Information Society Directive, note 2(a)).

[Exceptions to restricted acts]

Article 6

(1) The performance by the lawful user of a database or of a copy thereof of any of the acts listed in Article 5 which is necessary for the purposes of access to the contents of the databases and normal use of the contents by the lawful user shall not require the authorization of the author of the database. Where the lawful user is authorized to use only part of the database, this provision shall apply only to that part.

(2) Member States shall have the option of providing for limitations on the rights set out in Article 5 in the following cases:

    (a) in the case of reproduction for private purposes of a non-electronic database;

    (b) where there is use for the sole purpose of illustration for teaching or scientific research, as long as the source is indicated and to the extent justified by the non-commercial purpose to be achieved;

    (c) where there is use for the purposes of public security of [or] for the purposes of an administrative or judicial procedure;

    (d) where other exceptions to copyright which are traditionally authorized under national law are involved, without prejudice to points (a), (b) and (c).

(3) In accordance with the Berne Convention for the protection of Literary and Artistic Works, this Article may not be interpreted in such a way as to allow its application to be used in a manner which unreasonably

prejudices the rightholder's legitimate interests or conflicts with normal exploitation of the database.

1. General. Art. 6 deals with exceptions to database copyright. Aside from the mandatory 'lawful user' exception of art. 6(1) and the prohibition on having a private copying exception apply to electronic databases (art. 6(2) (a)), it leaves Member States broad discretion to provide for exceptions to the economic rights granted under art. 5. Note that exceptions to database copyright will concern the use of the expressive features (structure, selection or arrangement) of the database, and not the individual elements of the database (recital 35).

2. Acts necessary for access to database and normal use (para. 1). Art. 6(1) provides that a lawful user may perform restricted acts that are necessary to access the database or for normal use. Since access to and use of a database normally entails acts of reproduction, art. 6(1) primarily concerns the reproduction right. Absent an express provision to this effect, the freedom of the lawful user to perform these acts (sometime termed the 'user right') might be merely implied, but could be limited or even ruled out altogether under the terms of a user license agreement. The wording of art. 6(1) ('shall not require') indicates that this is a mandatory limitation that all Member States must implement. More importantly, it may not be overridden by contract (art. 15). In this respect art. 6(1) goes further than art. 5(1) of the Information Society Directive. **(a) Authorized part of database.** If the user is authorized to use only part of the database, the 'user right' of art. 6(1) applies only to that part. This allows database producers to somewhat restrict the ambit of the lawful use exception. **(b) Lawful user.** The term lawful user is similar but not identical to the term lawful acquirer of art. 5(1) Computer Programs Directive (see art. 5 Computer Programs Directive, note 2(d); see also art. 5 Information Society Directive, note 2(f)). A lawful user will be any end user contractually authorized to use the database (recital 34). This will include users implicitly licensed, as will be the case for most websites offered freely on the Internet. But the term also applies to persons having legally acquired copies of the database, such as the purchaser of a database in paper form or on CD-ROM. Moreover it can be argued that a person or entity invoking a copyright exception is a lawful user and can therefore benefit from art. 6(1). The acquirer of an illegal copy of the database however will not be regarded as a lawful user. **(c) Necessity of act.** The act must be necessary for the purposes of accessing the databases and normal use. This is an objective requirement that does not require that the intended purpose can only be achieved by performing the restricted act (see art. 5 Computer Programs Directive, note 2(b)). Necessity does not mean that the act is absolutely indispensable or essential. **(d) Necessary acts to access the database.** Acts that are necessary to access the database include for instance searching (querying) and browsing on-line database and downloading the results of a search.

(e) Necessary acts for normal use. Whether an act is necessary for normal use will have to be determined both in the light of the terms and conditions of the user license agreement (recital 34) and, objectively, in the light of normal practice, particularly in cases where a user license is absent. Acts of browsing and downloading certainly constitute normal use, but are probably already excepted as acts necessary to access the database. Although back-up copies are not expressly mentioned, as in art. 5(2) Computer Programs Directive, it can be argued that making a back-up copy is necessary for normal use. **(f) No contrary contractual stipulation.** Any contractual provision contrary to art. 6(1) shall be null and void (art. 15).

3. Optional exceptions (para. 2). Art. 6(2) enumerates the exceptions that Member States may provide to limit database copyright. Note that the exceptions may only apply in respect of the structure (selection or arrangement) of the database. The catalogue of exceptions is optional and leaves Member States the freedom to maintain most exceptions traditionally found in national copyright laws. The exceptions listed in art. 6(2) have not been amended or superseded by the closed list of exceptions in arts. 5(1) and (2) of the Information Society Directive. **(a) Reproduction for private purposes.** Member States may permit reproduction for private purposes, but only as regards non-electronic database. Allowing private copying from digital versions of a database would have permitted the making of 'perfect' copies, and was therefore deemed too far-reaching. By contrast, art. 5(2)(b) Information Society Directive does allow exceptions for private copying from digital sources. Nonetheless, compensation of right owners (through a scheme of levies), as mandated by art. 5(2)(b) of the Information Society Directive, is not required here. In respect of electronic databases a levy is even ruled out since a levy scheme presupposes that copying is permitted. The Directive does not define what private purposes are. However, it is clear that copying for public or commercial purposes may not be exempted. **(b) Teaching or scientific research.** Member States may permit use of a database for the sole purpose of illustration in teaching or scientific research, subject to certain conditions (indication of source, non-commercial purpose). Permitted uses may affect all rights protected under art. 5, namely reproduction, adaptation, distribution and communication to the public. Uses must be justified by (that is, proportional to) the non-commercial purpose to be achieved. The wording of art. 6(2)(b) is inspired by art. 10(2) of the Berne Convention, reminiscent of art. 10(1)(d) of the Rental Right Directive and nearly identical to art. 5(3)(a) of the Information Society Directive (see art. 10(2) BC, note 3). Even though the educational or scientific purpose of the use must be non-commercial, this does not rule out that commercial entities, such as scientific institutes, benefit from the exception. The term scientific research covers both the natural sciences and the human sciences (recital 36). **(c) Public security, administrative or judicial procedure.** Art. 6(2)(c) permits excepting uses for the purposes of public security or of administrative or judicial procedure. Art. 5(3)(e) of the Information Society Directive allows for similar exceptions. **(d) Traditional exceptions.** Art. 6(2)(d) allows Member States to except other uses 'which are traditionally authorized under national law'. The likely meaning of this provision is that it permits the continued application in national law of exceptions that already applied to databases prior to the adoption of the Directive. If for instance a Member State's news reporting exception encompassed databases, the exception may survive. However, it can also be argued that the provision permits a broad range of exceptions that are generally applicable to copyright works. **(e) Without prejudice to points (a), (b) and (c).** Whether interpreted narrowly or more broadly, art. 6(2)(d) does not allow Member States to go beyond the limits set in points 6(2)(a), (b) and (c). For instance, a Member State that 'traditionally' allowed private copying from electronic databases is no longer free to do so. **(f) Quotation.** Recital 37 recalls that the quotation right enshrined in art. 10(1) BC is not affected by the Directive. It is however difficult to conceive how the quotation right might apply to databases given that database copyright is limited to the structure (selection or arrangement) of its contents, not to the contents themselves.

   4. Three-step test (para. 3). According to art. 6(3) any exception permitted under art. 6 may not unreasonably prejudice the rightholder's legitimate interests or conflict with normal exploitation of the database. These are two of three criteria of the so-called three-step test enshrined in art. 9(2) BC, art. 13 TRIPS Agreement, art. 10 WIPO Copyright Treaty and art. 5(5) Information Society Directive (see art. 10 WIPO Copyright Treaty, notes 1, 4 and 5, and art. 5 Information Society Directive, note 6). The express reference in art. 6(3) to the BC is somewhat misleading, since the three-step test in art. 9(2) BC only applies to exceptions to the reproduction right, whereas the exceptions permitted under art. 6 of the Directive apply to all economic rights granted pursuant to art. 5.

CHAPTER III. SUI GENERIS RIGHT

[Object of protection]

Article 7

   (1) Member States shall provide for a right for the maker of a database which shows that there has been qualitatively and/or quantitatively a substantial investment in either the obtaining, verification or presentation of the contents to prevent extraction and/or re-utilization of the whole or of a substantial part, evaluated qualitatively and/or quantitatively, of the contents of that database.

   (2) For the purposes of this Chapter:

   (a) 'extraction' shall mean the permanent or temporary transfer of all or a substantial part of the contents of a database to another medium by any means or in any form;

(b) 're-utilization' shall mean any form of making available to the public all or a substantial part of the contents of a database by the distribution of copies, by renting, by on-line or other forms of transmission. The first sale of a copy of a database within the Community by the rightholder or with his consent shall exhaust the right to control resale of that copy within the Community; Public lending is not an act of extraction or re-utilization.

(3) The right referred to in paragraph 1 may be transferred, assigned or granted under contractual licence.

(4) The right provided for in paragraph 1 shall apply irrespective of the eligibility of that database for protection by copyright or by other rights. Moreover, it shall apply irrespective of eligibility of the contents of that database for protection by copyright or by other rights. Protection of databases under the right provided for in paragraph 1 shall be without prejudice to rights existing in respect of their contents.

(5) The repeated and systematic extraction and/or re-utilization of insubstantial parts of the contents of the database implying acts which conflict with a normal exploitation of that database or which unreasonably prejudice the legitimate interests of the maker of the database shall not be permitted.

1. General. Chapter III (arts. 7-11) of the Directive concerns the sui generis database right. **(a) Purpose.** The sui generis right protects the investment of the database producer, that is, the human, technical and financial resources invested in the contents of the database (recitals 7 and 40). The right is meant to protect the investment in databases that are especially vulnerable to misappropriation if they exist in digital form (recital 39). The right is intended to protect 'financial and professional investment' (recital 39). This investment must be substantial. Whereas copyright protects only the original structure of the database (that is, the selection or arrangement of its contents), the sui generis right protects the contents themselves (see Introductory remarks, note 1). The sui generis right was initially devised as a safety net for databases that could not find protection under copyright (Initial Proposal of the Database Directive). Both rights, however, may apply cumulatively if the prerequisites for both regimes are fulfilled. The sui generis right is a right of intellectual property not primarily rooted in principles of natural justice, but rather in utilitarian arguments. The principal reason for introducing the sui generis right was to promote investment in the (then emerging) European database sector (recital 10). At the time, investment in the European database sector was well behind other countries, in particular the US (recital 11). Creating a 'stable and uniform legal protection regime' was considered a necessary precondition for investment in 'modern information storage and processing systems' in the EU (recital 12). **(b) Nature of sui generis (database) right.** The right prescribed by art. 7 is a sui generis intellectual property right (i.e., of its own kind). In other words, it is not a copyright and does not as such fit into any other general category of intellectual property rights. In view of its intended purpose to protect economic investment in database production, the sui generis right is more closely related to the neighbouring (related) rights of phonogram producers or film producers. Indeed in many Member States, including Germany, France, Spain, Portugal and Italy, the right has been transposed as a special neighbouring right. In other Member States, such as the Netherlands and Belgium, the right has been enacted in a special act, illustrating its sui generis status. The right has undergone an evolution between the Initial Proposal and the final adoption of the Directive. Initially conceived as a special rule of unfair competition, defined as a right to prevent 'unfair' extraction, it would have protected database producers only against unauthorized acts of commercial use. In the final version of the Directive the words 'unfair' and 'unauthorized' have disappeared. The sui generis right has become a full-fledged and fully transferable intellectual property right that applies not only in competitive situations, but can be invoked against 'any user who, through his acts, causes significant detriment, evaluated qualitatively or quantitatively, to the investment' (recitals 39 and 42). **(c) Transfer and licence.** The sui generis right may be transferred, assigned or granted under contractual licence (art. 7(3)). In all likelihood partial transfers or licences of the sui generis right that are limited to specific acts of exploitation are also permitted. The Directive does not mention formalities in relation to the transfer or licensing of the sui generis right, such as the requirement of a written deed; this is left to the discretion of the Member States.

2. Maker of a database. Art. 7(1) grants the sui generis right to the maker of a database, namely, the database producer. Recital 41 defines the maker of a database as the person who takes the initiative and the risk of investing. Subcontractors are excluded from this definition; producing a commissioned database will therefore not be rewarded with sui generis right, even if most of the 'sweat of the brow' is done by the commissioned party. To qualify as database maker a producer must be involved both in the initial organization of the database and in its financing. In cases of databases produced by not-for-profit organizations or amateurs, the required investment will be bearing the cost of database production. In many cases the maker of the database will be a legal person (company) rather than a natural person. This explains the absence in Chapter III of the Directive of special provisions regarding databases produced in employment relationships. If several (legal) persons collaborate in initiating and investing, this might result in joint ownership of the sui generis right. The Directive however does not give any guidance on this issue, and leaves this to the Member States.

3. Substantial investment. (a) General. The main prerequisite of the sui generis right is substantial investment. This is a threshold requirement. Absent substantial investment the right does not exist. Art. 7 does not define how much 'substantial' is or how this should be established. Recital 19 offers some limited guidance by explaining that 'as a rule, the compilation of several recordings of musical performances on a CD does not come within the scope of this Directive, both because, as a compilation, it does not meet the conditions for copyright protection and because it does not represent a substantial enough investment to be eligible under the sui generis right'. The example suggests that compiling a small number of items (e.g., a dozen recordings on a CD) will not qualify as substantial investment, at least not quantitatively. According to the German Federal Supreme Court 'substantial investment' is not a high standard. The standard is met if 'viewed objectively, the investment in the database is not wholly insignificant and easy to be made by anyone' (*Zweite Zahnarztmeinung II* (Germany)). The ECJ has yet to pronounce itself on the height of this threshold criterion. **(b) Qualitative or quantitative investment.** The investment protected must be qualitative or quantitative. According to the ECJ, 'the quantitative assessment refers to quantifiable resources and the qualitative assessment to efforts which cannot be quantified, such as intellectual effort or energy' (*Fixtures Marketing/Svenska Spel*). A qualitative investment may result from applying the skill of a professional, for example, a lexicographer selecting the key words for a dictionary or a website designer using his skills to develop an on-line database. If the intellectual effort invested in the database is both substantial and the result of creative selection or arrangement, the database will be protected by sui generis right and copyright. A quantitative investment will involve the deployment of financial resources and/or the expense of time, effort and energy (recital 40). Courts will usually assess this on the basis of invested financial resources (see *Deutsche Telekom* (Germany), *Lectiel/France Télécom* (France)). However, the financial costs of acquiring an entire database, or a licence thereto, may not be factored in (*Elektronischer Zolltarif* (Germany)). In practice many databases, resulting from both skill and labour, will reflect both qualitative and quantitative investment. Computer-generated databases will also qualify for protection if they are the result of substantial qualitative or quantitative investment. **(c) Obtaining, verification or presentation of the contents.** The substantial investment must be done in either the obtaining, verification or presentation of the contents of the database. *Obtaining*. Obtaining refers to the acts of seeking out existing independent materials, and collecting them in the database (*British Horseracing Board* (ECJ)), in other words to the gathering of pre-existing data, works or other materials. This does not include producing ('creating') data (see below, note (d)). *Verification*. Investment in the verification of the contents refers to the resources used, with a view to ensuring the reliability of the information contained in that database, to monitor the accuracy of the materials collected when the database was created and during its operation. However, the resources used for verification during the stage of creation of materials which are subsequently collected in a database may not be taken into account (*British Horseracing Board* (ECJ)). Verification thus involves the checking, correcting and updating of data that already exists in the database, but not the verification of 'created' data (see note (d)). *Presentation.* According to the ECJ, 'the expression "investment in ... the ... presentation of the contents" of the database concerns [...] the resources used for the purpose of giving the database its function of processing information, that is to say those used for the systematic or methodical arrangement of the materials contained in that database and the organisation of their individual accessibility' (*Fixtures Marketing/Svenska Spel*). Presentation therefore includes such activities as digitalizing analog files, producing a thesaurus or designing a user interface. **(d) Created data.** The sui generis right does not protect investment that is not directed towards the making of a database. As mentioned above, according to the ECJ, 'the expression "investment in ... the obtaining ... of the contents" of a database in Article 7(1) [...] must be understood to refer to the resources used to seek out existing independent materials and collect them in the database. It does not cover the resources used for the creation of materials which make up the contents of a database' (*British Horseracing Board* (ECJ) and *Fixtures Marketing/Svenska Spel* (ECJ); see also recital 46). In these cases the ECJ ruled out sui generis protection for such 'created' data as horse racing schedules and football fixture lists. Similarly, investment in the creation of web advertisements may not be taken into account (*Précom* (France)). However, facts observed, such as the scoring of a goal, are probably not 'created' data; subjective comments and interpretation, on the other hand, are (*Football Dataco/Stan James* (UK)). **(e) No rights in data per se.** The sui generis right protects the investment in the contents of the database, not the works, data or other compiled materials themselves (recital 46). The right is not to be seen as 'an extension of copyright protection to mere facts or data' (recital 45). **(f) Public sector databases.** Whether the sui generis right protects databases produced by state entities or other public authorities is not entirely clear. While some case law suggests that public bodies do indeed qualify for sui generis protection (see *Bodenrichtwertsammlung* (Germany), *Compass-Datenbank* (ECJ)), some commentators have argued that such bodies do not merit protection, since activities undertaken by public authorities are normally financed by public funds, and therefore not the result of 'investment'. Based on this argument the Dutch Council of State denied database right to the City of Amsterdam in a case involving an environmental database produced by the municipality (*Landmark* (Netherlands)). A preliminary reference to the ECJ that might have shed light on this issue was later withdrawn (*Sächsischer Ausschreibungsdienst* (Germany)).

4. Rights protected (para. 2). The sui generis right comprises two distinct rights: a right of extraction, which is somewhat similar to the reproduction right protected under copyright, and a right of reutilization, which might be described as a composite of a distribution right and a right of communication to the public. Together, both rights are meant to protect database producers' investment against harm, and secure remuneration (recitals 42 and 28). **(a) Extraction.** Extraction is defined as the permanent or temporary transfer of all or a substantial part of the contents of a database to another medium by any means or in any form. The right pertains to the downloading, copying, printing, or any other reproduction in any, permanent or temporary form. According to the ECJ extraction does not require an act of technical reproduction (e.g. 'cutting and pasting'). While consulting a database as such remains outside the scope of protection (*British Horseracing Board* (ECJ)), regularly and systematically consulting a database may give rise to (infringing) extraction (*Directmedia Publishing* (ECJ)). Solely retrieving the updated data from a database might also qualify as extraction (*Elektronischer Zolltarif* (Germany)). If the physical and technical characteristics of a sui generis protected database reappear in another database this may be seen as evidence of extraction, regardless of whether the extracted data are rearranged (*Apis-Hristovich* (ECJ)). **(b) Reutilization.** Reutilization is defined as any form of making available to the public all or a substantial part of the contents of a database by the distribution of copies, by renting, or by on-line or other forms of transmission. Reutilization 'must be understood broadly, as extending to any act, not authorised by the maker of the database protected by the sui generis right, of distribution to the public of the whole or a part of the contents of the database' (*Football Dataco/Sports Radar* (ECJ)). Reutilization covers both acts of physical distribution and other acts of communication to the public, notably by on-line transmission. According to the ECJ the provider of a 'dedicated meta search engine' that systematically searches and retrieves data from a sui generis protected database reutilizes the whole or a substantial part of that database (*Innoweb*). Although rental is covered by the reutilization right, the rental provisions of the Rental Directive do not apply. Moreover, public lending is not an act of extraction or reutilization, so sui generis right owners do not qualify for public lending rights. **(c) Exhaustion.** Like similar rights in other Directives, the right of reutilization is exhausted following the first sale in the Union of a copy of the database by the rightholder or with his consent. Likewise, exhaustion does not occur in respect of acts of on-line transmission (recital 43). See art. 5, notes 4(a) and (b). **(d) Viewing.** The Directive does not determine whether the on-screen display of the contents of a database is a restricted act. According to recital 44 this would be the case if the on-screen display 'necessitates the permanent or temporary transfer of all or a substantial part of such contents to another medium'. However, according to the ECJ the sui generis right does not cover the act of 'consulting' a database by an end user (*British Horseracing Board* (ECJ)). The ECJ appears to hold that once a producer makes its database available to the public, it has implicitly consented to members of the public viewing the contents of the database that are made available in that way. Note however that the Database Directive, in contrast with the Information Society Directive, does not provide for a mandatory exception permitting temporary copies by lawful users (see art. 5 Information Society Directive, note 2). **(e) No direct access to database required.** The terms extraction and reutilization must be interpreted as referring to any unauthorized act of appropriation and distribution to the public of the whole or a part of the contents of a database. Those terms do not imply direct access to the database concerned (*British Horseracing Board*, *Directmedia Publishing* (ECJ)). In other words, extracting data from a database that is itself a copy of another database may amount to infringement of the sui generis right in that database. On the other hand, the database right does not confer upon the database producer a patent-like monopoly. Producing an identical database without directly or indirectly extracting data from a previously existing database is not infringement. **(f) Substantial part.** The sui generis right will be infringed in case of extraction and/or reutilization of a substantial part of the contents of the database. Whether or not the ordering or arrangement of the contents are misappropriated is irrelevant for the purpose of applying the sui generis right (*Hit Balanz* (Germany)). What matters is whether a 'substantial' part has been used. The Directive however does not define this. According to the Explanatory Memorandum 'no fixed limits can be placed in this Directive as to the volume of material which can be used'. In considering what constitutes a substantial part of a database, it must be considered whether the human, technical and financial efforts put in by the maker of the database in obtaining, verifying and presenting those data constitute a substantial investment (*British Horseracing Board* (ECJ)). In other words, if the appropriated data do not reflect substantial investment on the part of the database producer, there is no infringement of the sui generis right (see recital 42). If a database consists of multiple parts that each qualify as a separate database, then the substantiality of the extraction or reutilization must be assessed relative to each sub-database (*Apis-Hristovich* (ECJ)). **(g) Qualitative and quantitative substantial part.** Whether or not a substantial part has been appropriated is to be evaluated qualitatively and/or quantitatively (for an explanation of these terms, see note 3(a)). The taking of relatively large amounts of data would normally amount to extraction of a quantitatively substantial part, whereas appropriating a relatively small amount would not. For example, according to the German Federal Supreme Court the extraction of 10% of the total reviews and 1.5 % of the number of dentists listed on an on-line dentist rating website did not amount to substantial extraction (*Zweite Zahnarztmeinung II* (Germany)). The intrinsic value of the data extracted does not constitute a relevant criterion for assessing whether the part in question is substantial, evaluated qualitatively. Even so, a quantitatively negligible part of the contents of a database may in fact represent, in terms of obtaining, verification or presentation, significant human, technical or financial investment (*British Horseracing Board* (ECJ)). In other words, the market value of the appropriated data is irrelevant, but the extraction or reutilization of a relatively small number of data may nevertheless amount to infringement if those data reflect substantial qualitative investment. **(h) Further investment by infringer irrelevant.** The sui generis right may be invoked regardless of whether the party that has extracted or reutilized a substantial part of the contents of the database has subsequently invested substantially in the derivative database (*Baukompass*

(Austria)). **(i) Repeated and systematic extraction of insubstantial parts.** The extraction of insubstantial parts of the database does not infringe the sui generis right. Thus, incidental browsing and piecemeal copying from databases, even committed by unauthorized users, are lawful acts. However the repeated and systematic extraction of insubstantial parts may amount to infringement (art. 7(5)). The ECJ has noted that the purpose of this provision is to prevent repeated acts by a user which would lead to 'the reconstitution of the database as a whole or, at the very least, of a substantial part of it' (*British Horseracing Board* (ECJ)). In other words, the systematic extraction of insubstantial parts will amount to infringement only if the aggregate parts are substantial. The second half-sentence of art. 7(5) partly reproduces the three-step test (see art. 6, note 4). According to the German Federal Supreme Court, posting (deep) hyperlinks to on-line newspaper articles collected in a database by copying the headlines is not covered by art. 7(5), because there was no conflict with a normal exploitation of the database (*Paperboy* (Germany)). Note, however, as mentioned above, that the ECJ has held that the provider of a 'dedicated meta search engine' that systematically searches and retrieves data from a database reutilizes the whole or a substantial part of that database (*Innoweb*). **(j) Place where infringing act occurs.** In cases of cross-border infringement, difficult questions may arise regarding the locus of the infringing act(s). According to ECJ, the 'mere fact that the website containing the data in question is accessible in a particular national territory is not a sufficient basis for concluding that the operator of the website is performing an act of re-utilisation [in that jurisdiction]'. However, there will be an act of re-utilization in that Member State 'where there is evidence from which it may be concluded that the act discloses an intention on the part of the person performing the act to target members of the public [in that Member State]' (*Football Dataco/Sports Radar*).

5. Relation to copyright and other rights in contents of database (para. 4). The sui generis right applies irrespective of the eligibility of the database, or its contents, for protection by copyright or by other rights (art. 7(4)). In other words, sui generis right may co-exist with copyrights or neighbouring rights in the database. The Initial Proposal would have excluded such cumulation; sui generis protection would have applied only if the database were not protected by copyright. Art. 7(4) also underscores that the sui generis right in the database shall not affect underlying copyrights or neighbouring rights in its contents.

[Rights and obligations of lawful users]

Article 8

(1) **The maker of a database which is made available to the public in whatever manner may not prevent a lawful user of the database from extracting and/or re-utilizing insubstantial parts of its contents, evaluated**

qualitatively and/or quantitatively, for any purposes whatsoever. Where the lawful user is authorized to extract and/or re-utilize only part of the database, this paragraph shall apply only to that part.

(2) A lawful user of a database which is made available to the public in whatever manner may not perform acts which conflict with normal exploitation of the database or unreasonably prejudice the legitimate interests of the maker of the database.

(3) A lawful user of a database which is made available to the public in any manner may not cause prejudice to the holder of a copyright or related right in respect of the works or subject matter contained in the database.

1. General. Art. 8 guarantees lawful users of a database that has been made available to the public certain minimum user rights that may not be overridden by contract (art. 15). Notwithstanding contractual provisions to the contrary, lawful users may extract and reutilize insubstantial parts of the contents of the database. Since such acts are normally outside the scope of the sui generis right, the purpose of art. 8 is clearly to prevent contractual expansion of database protection beyond the scope of the sui generis right. See art. 6, note 2. The insubstantial extraction or reutilization may be done 'for any purposes whatsoever', that is, for private and commercial purposes. The lawful user's rights may be invoked not only against the database producer but also against its successor in title (recital 49), such as a licensed distributor.

2. Lawful user. A lawful user will be any end user who is contractually authorized to use the database (recital 34). This will include users implicitly licensed, as will be the case for most website offered freely on the Internet. But the term also applies to persons having legally acquired copies of the database, such as the purchaser of a database in paper form or on a CD-ROM (see art. 6, note 2(b)). It can be argued that art. 8 may also be invoked by the successor in title to a lawful user. Where the lawful user is authorized to extract and/or reutilize only part of the database, the user's right shall apply only to that part (art. 8(1), second sentence). See art. 9, note 1(b); see also art. 5 Computer Programs Directive, note 2(d), regarding the similar, but not necessarily identical notion of the 'law acquirer' of a computer program.

3. No prejudice to database producer or other right owners. Art. 8(2) and 8(3) admonish that a lawful user may not perform acts which unreasonably prejudice the legitimate interests of the maker of the database or cause prejudice to the holder of a copyright or related right in the contents of the database (see recital 49). Read by themselves these provisions would expand the rights of database producers and other content owners in relation to lawful users far beyond the scope of the sui generis right, copyright or neighbouring rights. The likely meaning of these provisions, therefore, is to limit the scope of the non-overridable 'user right' of the lawful user provided by art. 8(1), much in the same way as the three-step test limits the scope of exceptions to exclusive rights.

[Exceptions to the sui generis right]

Article 9

Member States may stipulate that lawful users of a database which is made available to the public in whatever manner may, without the authorization of its maker, extract or re-utilize a substantial part of its contents:

  (a) in the case of extraction for private purposes of the contents of a non-electronic database;

  (b) in the case of extraction for the purposes of illustration for teaching or scientific research, as long as the source is indicated and to the extent justified by the non-commercial purpose to be achieved;

  (c) in the case of extraction and/or re-utilization for the purposes of public security or an administrative or judicial procedure.

1. General. (a) Few exceptions allowed. The Directive allows for only limited statutory exceptions in respect of the sui generis right (see note 2). Art. 9 leaves no room for many limitations traditionally found in copyright law, such as journalistic freedoms, quotation rights and library privileges (but see note (c) below). Apparently, the user's freedom to extract and reutilize insubstantial parts of the database was considered, by the European legislature, to be sufficient. Where sui generis right and copyright overlap, as for instance in the case of an encyclopaedia, this may lead to incongruences. Users are prevented from effectively invoking copyright exceptions insofar as these exceptions are not recognized in art. 9 (see, for example *Wegener* (Netherlands)). The short catalogue of exceptions to the sui generis right is exhaustive. In principle, no other exceptions are allowed. However, its is argued that art. 13 leaves some room to the Member States for additional limitations grounded in the laws or interests recognized in that provision (see note (d)). **(b) Lawful users.** Only 'lawful' users may benefit from the exceptions permitted under art. 9. This is unusual, because elsewhere in the law of intellectual property limitations usually apply to all users, whether lawful or not (except in the case of computer programs, see art. 5(1) Computer Programs Directive). For instance, the catalogue of optional exceptions to database copyright of art. 6(2) does not require lawful use. The Directive provides no guidance on how to interpret the term lawful user in this context. Clearly, it must have a broader meaning than in art. 8, which focuses on the contractual relationship between database producer and user. By contrast art. 9 deals with users that would normally not have a contractual relationship with the database producer. The likely meaning of the term then is a user who has gained access to or acquired a copy of the database without breaking the law. This would exclude for instance a 'hacker' having illegally gained access to the database. **(c) Traditional exceptions.** Recital 52 makes an exception for 'those Member States which have specific rules providing for a right comparable to the sui generis right' to retain 'the exceptions traditionally specified by such rules'. This obviously refers to the catalogue rule that already existed in the Nordic countries before the adoption of the Directive. In those countries exceptions that applied to the catalogue right (that is, normal copyright exceptions) may be carried over to the sui generis right. **(d) Other exceptions.** Art. 13 arguably leaves some room for additional limitations grounded in any of the laws or interests recognized in that provision as not being prejudiced by the Directive. Notably, the public interest in granting access to public documents (freedom of information) may legitimize a statutory limitation on sui generis protection of public databases, as is the case in the Netherlands.

2. Optional exceptions. Art. 9 expressly allows exceptions to the sui generis right in only three cases. This catalogue of exceptions is exhaustive, but not mandatory. Member States may elect not to implement any or all of the exceptions mentioned. **(a) Extraction for private purposes.** Art. 9 permits an exception for private extraction, but only from non-electronic databases. Art. 6(2)(a) allows a similar exception under copyright (see art. 6, note 3(a)). Such an exception might, for instance, allow private photocopying from an almanac, but not downloading from a web-based database. Compensation of right owners, as required by art. 5(2)(b) of the Information Society Directive, is not required here. **(b) Extraction for teaching or scientific research.** Member States may also permit extraction for the sole purpose of illustration for teaching or scientific research, subject to certain restrictions (indication of course, non-commercial purpose). Art. 6(2)(b), more broadly, allows the use for similar purposes of a database protected under copyright (see art. 6, note 3(b)). **(c) Public security, administrative or judicial procedure.** Exceptions permitting uses for the purposes of public security or for the purposes of an administrative or judicial procedure are similarly allowed. Art. 6(2)(c) allows a similar exception under copyright (see art. 6, note 3(c)).

[Term of protection]

Article 10

   (1) The right provided for in Article 7 shall run from the date of completion of the making of the database. It shall expire fifteen years from the first of January of the year following the date of completion.

   (2) In the case of a database which is made available to the public in whatever manner before expiry of the period provided for in paragraph 1, the term of protection by that right shall expire fifteen years from the first of January of the year following the date when the database was first made available to the public.

(3) Any substantial change, evaluated qualitatively or quantitatively, to the contents of a database, including any substantial change resulting from the accumulation of successive additions, deletions or alterations, which would result in the database being considered to be a substantial new investment, evaluated qualitatively or quantitatively, shall qualify the database resulting from that investment for its own term of protection.

1. General. Art. 10 determines the term (duration) of the sui generis right. The term of the sui generis right is fifteen years from the date of completion of the database (art. 10(1)), or if later, after it is first made available to the public (art. 10(2)). This term can be extended ad infinitum upon each additional substantial investment in the contents of the database (art. 10(3)). The Initial Proposal would have limited the term to only ten years, but in the end a longer basic term of fifteen years was established. This is still substantially shorter than the copyright term of 70 years after the author's death mandated by the Term Directive, which does not apply to the sui generis right.

2. Fifteen years from date of completion (para. 1). The sui generis right 'shall run from the date of completion of the making of the database' (art. 10(1)). This language suggests that incomplete databases will not receive sui generis protection. It may be argued, however, that an incomplete database still merits sui generis protection if the legal prerequisites for protection are met, in other words, if it fulfils the definition of a database and is the result of substantial investment. For databases that are not made available to the public (see art. 10(2)), the protection expires fifteen years from the first of January of the year following the date of completion. The burden of proof regarding the date of completion of the making of a database lies with the maker of the database (recital 53).

3. Fifteen years from first making available to the public (para. 2). For databases that have been made available to the public, the term expires fifteen years from the first of January of the year following the date when the database was first made available to the public. Since the average database will not immediately be made available to the public upon completion, the total term of protection of the database will be more than 15 years, since the term of art. 10(2) may commence at any time as long as the term of art. 10(1) has not yet expired. The term of art. 10(2) will start running upon the first making available to the public of the database 'in whatever manner'. This includes all forms of reutilization (see art. 7, note 4(b)), including the distribution of copies and on-line transmission. Again, the Directive does not define the notion of public. This is left to the discretion of the Member States.

4. Prolonged protection after substantial change (para. 3). The term of sui generis protection will be prolonged after each additional substantial investment in the contents of the database. **(a) Substantial change.** Such a 'substantial change' may be the result of a series of insubstantial additions, deletions or alterations, as long as the aggregate changes are substantial. Thus, a regularly updated (dynamic) database is likely to receive perpetual protection (but see note (b) below). The burden of proof of such a substantial change lies with the database producer (recital 54). Even a mere 'substantial verification of the contents of the database' is enough to trigger a new term of protection, presumably even if this does not alter the contents of the database (recital 55). **(b) Dynamic databases.** The Directive does not clarify how to apply the term provisions to dynamic databases, in other words databases that are in constant flux. It is not clear whether such a database should be considered as a single database, or as a series of databases each with its own term of protection, commencing every time a substantial change to the database is made, as suggested by the Advocate-General in *British Horseracing Board* (ECJ). The ECJ has left this question unanswered.

[Beneficiaries of protection under the sui generis right]

Article 11

(1) The right provided for in Article 7 shall apply to database whose makers or rightholders are nationals of a Member State or who have their habitual residence in the territory of the Community.

(2) Paragraph 1 shall also apply to companies and firms formed in accordance with the law of a Member State and having their registered office, central administration or principal place of business within the Community; however, where such a company or firm has only its registered office in the territory of the Community, its operations must be genuinely linked on an ongoing basis with the economy of a Member State.

(3) Agreements extending the right provided for in Article 7 to databases made in third countries and falling outside the provisions of paragraphs 1 and 2 shall be concluded by the Council acting on a proposal from the Commission. The term of any protection extended to databases by virtue of that procedure shall not exceed that available pursuant to Article 10.

1. General. (a) Beneficiaries of sui generis right. Art. 11 names the beneficiaries of the sui generis right. Since this right is not a copyright, neighbouring right or other right of intellectual property covered by an international treaty, such as the BC, Rome Convention. Paris Convention or TRIPS Agreement, the rule of national treatment (assimilation principle) need not apply. Instead, the Directive has reserved sui generis protection to nationals or residents of a Member State (art. 11(1)), and to companies and firms formed in accordance with the law of a Member State and having their registered office, central administration or principal place of business within the Community (art.

11(2)). However, the Council of the European Union may extend protection to nationals or residents of third countries on the basis of special agreements (art. 11(3)). **(b) European Economic Area (EEA).** Pursuant to the EEA Agreement, arts. 11(1) and 11(2) also apply to the EEA countries that are not members of the European Union (Norway, Iceland and Liechtenstein).

2. EU nationals or residents (para. 1). The sui generis right shall apply to databases whose makers or rightholders are nationals of a Member State or who have their habitual residence in the territory of the Community (art. 11(1)). **(a) Maker or rightholders.** If the rightholder does not meet the criteria of art. 11(1) or 11(2), the database will receive sui generis protection nonetheless if its maker (producer) qualifies. Sui generis rights may therefore be assigned to non-Community persons or entities without forfeiting sui generis protection. **(b) Habitual residence.** The term habitual residence refers to either the domicile of the database producer or his place of establishment.

3. Companies established in the EU (para. 2). Companies and firms formed in accordance with the law of a Member State and having their registered office, central administration or principal place of business within the Community, will also benefit from the sui generis right (art. 11(2)). This rule is a direct application of art. 48 of the EC Treaty (ex art. 58). **(a) Companies or firms.** Companies or firms are 'companies or firms constituted under civil or commercial law, including cooperative societies, and other legal persons governed by public or private law, save for those which are non-profit-making'(art. 48 EC Treaty). **(b) No 'mailbox' firms.** Where a company or firm has only its registered office in the territory of the Community, its operations must be genuinely linked on an ongoing basis with the economy of a Member State (art. 11(2), second sentence). This prevents the circumvention of art. 11 by the setting up of 'mailbox' companies. The company's European office must engage in genuine economic activities in a Member State.

4. Extension to third countries (para. 3). (a) Reciprocity. Art. 11 's departure from the principle of national treatment was largely inspired by the US Semiconductor Chip Protection Act of 1984, that introduced sui generis protection for the 'topography' (that is, design) of semiconductor chips. Protection of non-US designers was made subject to reciprocity. Similarly, the Council of the European Union may extend sui generis protection to nationals or residents of third countries on the basis of special agreements with such countries (art. 11(3)). Certainly, material reciprocity will be required for any such agreement to come into existence. According to recital 56, such an extension will be granted 'only if such third countries offer comparable protection to databases produced by nationals of a Member State or persons who have their habitual residence in the territory of the Community'. It is not clear how closely the database protection regime in a third country must resemble the sui generis right. At present, only one extension has been granted, notably to the Isle of Man. **b) WIPO Draft Treaty.** An attempt to adopt a WIPO Treaty on the Protection of Databases that would have provided for multilateral sui generis database protection, failed at the 1996 WIPO diplomatic conference, largely due to a lack of support from the United States, and resistance from the developing nations.

CHAPTER IV. COMMON PROVISIONS

[Remedies]

Article 12

Member States shall provide appropriate remedies in respect of infringements of the rights provided for in this Directive.

1. General. Art. 12 instructs Member States to provide 'appropriate remedies' against infringement of the rights dealt with in the Directive, namely, database copyright and sui generis right. However, no remedies are specified; this is left to the discretion of the Member States. With regard to copyright Member States will find guidance in the enforcement chapter of the TRIPS Agreement (arts. 41-61), which prescribes both civil and criminal remedies and sanctions, but the TRIPS Agreement is not concerned with sui generis database protection. The more recent Enforcement Directive prescribes specific civil remedies that must be provided by the Member States in respect of both copyright and sui generis protection (art. 2(1) Enforcement Directive). The Enforcement Directive, however, does not include criminal sanctions. Member States are thus under no obligation to provide for criminal sanctions in respect of the sui generis right.

[Continued application of other legal provisions]

Article 13

This Directive shall be without prejudice to provisions concerning in particular copyright, rights related to copyright or any other rights or obligations subsisting in the data, works or other materials incorporated into a database, patent rights, trade marks, design rights, the protection of national treasures, laws on restrictive practices and unfair competition, trade secrets, security, confidentiality, data protection and privacy, access to public documents, and the law of contract.

1. General. (a) Other legal provision not affected. The Directive leaves intact other legal rules relevant to contents of a database, such as copyright, neighbouring right and other rights of intellectual property. Note that this only concerns rights relating to works and other subject matter incorporated into a database. It does not allow low-threshold copyright regimes, such as British copyright in 'skill and labour', Dutch protection of non-original writings or the Nordic 'catalogue rule', to survive in tandem with the Directive's harmonized rules on database copyright (*Football Dataco* (ECJ)). It remains to be seen whether and to what extent unfair competition remedies are similarly preempted by the Directive's sui generis right (see *Précom* (France)). The words 'in particular' indicate that the enumeration of legal domains in art. 13 is non-exhaustive. Art. 9 of the Computer Programs Directive contains a similar provision. Art. 13 also mentions a variety of legal domains that are not intended to protect intellectual property, but protect the interests of the general public, such as data protection law and access to public documents. **(b) Data protection.** Data protection law (which is often confused with sui generis database protection) will be applicable to databases containing personal data. The existence of sui generis protection does not in any way diminish or affect obligations on the part of the database producer to comply with national data protection laws pursuant to the Personal Data Protection Directive. **(c) Access to public documents.** The express reference in art. 13 to the law on access to public documents (freedom of information) may be seen as legitimizing a statutory limitation on sui generis protection of public databases, as is the case in the Netherlands (see art. 9, note 1(d)). **(d) Contract.** The reference to the law of contract is somewhat misleading. Art. 15 declares any contractual provision contrary to arts. 6(1) and 8 null and void.

[Application over time]

Article 14

(1) **Protection pursuant to this Directive as regards copyright shall also be available in respect of databases created prior to the date referred to [in] Article 16 (1) which on that date fulfil the requirements laid down in this Directive as regards copyright protection of databases.**

(2) **Notwithstanding paragraph 1, where a database protected under copyright arrangements in a Member State on the date of publication of this Directive does not fulfil the eligibility criteria for copyright protection laid down in Article 3 (1), this Directive shall not result in any curtailing in that Member State of the remaining term of protection afforded under those arrangements.**

(3) **Protection pursuant to the provisions of this Directive as regards the right provided for in Article 7 shall also be available in respect of databases the making of which was completed not more than fifteen years prior to the date referred to in Article 16 (1) and which on that date fulfil the requirements laid down in Article 7.**

(4) **The protection provided for in paragraphs 1 and 3 shall be without prejudice to any acts concluded and rights acquired before the date referred to in those paragraphs.**

(5) **In the case of a database the making of which was completed not more than fifteen years prior to the date referred to in Article 16 (1),**

the term of protection by the right provided for in Article 7 shall expire fifteen years from the first of January following that date.

1. General. Art. 14 contains transitional provisions. In principle the Directive has retroactive effect. Its rules shall apply not only to new databases but also to databases that already existed prior to the implementation deadline (1 January 1998). Art. 14 contains different transitional rules for copyright and sui generis protection. Arts. 14(1) and (2) deal with copyright, while arts. 14(3) and (5) concern the sui generis right. Art. 14(4) clarifies that the Directive shall be without prejudice to any acts concluded and rights acquired before the implementation date. The Directive does not comprise any special rules on the term of copyright protection; the general provisions of the Term Directive apply.

2. Retroactive effect: copyright (paras. 1 and 2). Copyright protection under the terms of the Directive shall apply to all databases created prior to the implementation deadline (January 1, 1998). Nevertheless, copyright protection for databases that do not meet these criteria, but were protected on the date of publication of the Directive (27 March 1996) under softer conditions, as in the United Kingdom, Ireland, the Nordic countries and the Netherlands, will not be lost or curtailed upon implementation. In other words, pre-existing old-style British copyrights in databases reflecting mere 'skill and labour', not intellectual creation, are not reduced to short-lived sui generis rights, but will expire after the full term of copyright has elapsed (recital 60).

3. Retroactive effect: sui generis right (paras. 3 and 5). Sui generis protection under the terms of the Directive shall be available for databases completed no more than fifteen years prior to the implementation deadline (1 January 1998). In other words, the sui generis right retroactively applies to all databases that were made on or after 1 January 1983 (see, for example, *Hit Balanz* (Germany)). Although the language of art. 14(5) is not very clear, the likely meaning of it is to grant to such pre-existing databases a full term of sui generis protection, commencing on 1 January 1998.

4. No prejudice to acts concluded before implementation (para. 4). The Directive affects only acts concluded after the implementation deadline. The provisions of art. 14 shall be without prejudice to any acts concluded and rights acquired before that date. The phrase 'acts concluded' refers, firstly, to acts of exploitation of databases that were legal prior to implementation, for instance because in the Member State where they occurred no database protection existed. Second, it refers to contracts concluded before the implementation deadline, for instance between database producers and distributors. These remain valid, even if the underlying rights (e.g., an old-style British database copyright) no longer comply with the prerequisites of the Directive (e.g., the database does not constitute an intellectual creation). Similarly, the Directive does not prejudice 'rights acquired'; an assignment of old-style

British database copyright therefore remains valid. Art. 14(4) is inspired by art. 9(2), second half-sentence of the Computer Programs Directive. Art. 10(2) Information Society Directive contains similar language.

[Binding nature of certain provisions]

Article 15

Any contractual provision contrary to Articles 6 (1) and 8 shall be null and void.

1. General. Arts. 6(1) and 8 grant certain minimum user rights to lawful users of a database. These rights may not be overridden by contract (see art. 6, note 2, and art. 8, note 1). Any contractual provision contrary to arts. 6(1) and 8 'shall be null and void'. The Directive however does not determine the consequences of such a nullity. Whether the nullity is absolute or relative (that is, only in respect of the user) is to be determined by the Member States.

2. Non-protected databases. The user rights guaranteed by arts. 6(1), 8 and 15 apply only in respect of databases that are protected by copyright or sui generis right pursuant to the Directive. The Directive does not preclude similar contractual limitations on users of non-protected databases (*Ryanair* (ECJ)).

[Final provisions]

Article 16

(1) Member States shall bring into force the laws, regulations and administrative provisions necessary to comply with this Directive before 1 January 1998. When Member States adopt these provisions, they shall contain a reference to this Directive or shall be accompanied by such reference on the occasion of their official publication. The methods of making such reference shall be laid down by Member States.

(2) Member States shall communicate to the Commission the text of the provisions of domestic law which they adopt in the field governed by this Directive.

(3) Not later than at the end of the third year after the date referred to in paragraph 1, and every three years thereafter, the Commission shall submit to the European Parliament, the Council and the Economic and Social Committee a report on the application of this Directive, in which, inter alia, on the basis of specific information supplied by the Member States, it shall examine in particular the application of the sui generis right, including Articles 8 and 9, and shall verify especially whether the application of this right has led to abuse of a dominant position or other interference with free competition which would justify appropriate measures being taken, including the establishment of non-voluntary

licensing arrangements. Where necessary, it shall submit proposals for adjustment of this Directive in line with developments in the area of databases.

1. Implementation deadline (para. 1). Member States were required to implement the provisions of the Directive by 1 January 1998. Most countries completed the implementation process in the course of 1998–1999.

2. Report (para. 3). As many other Directives, the Commission is required to submit regularly a report on the application of the Directive. The first review was published by the Commission on 12 December 2005 (Report on the Database Directive). The report is skeptical about the beneficial effect the introduction of the sui generis right has had on the production of databases in the Community. It proposes various policy options, including repealing the Directive. **(a) Abuse of dominant position.** The report mentioned in art. 15(3) should focus on the sui generis right, and more particularly on 'whether the application of this right has led to abuse of a dominant position or other interference with free competition'. This language reflects concerns by interested parties that the introduction of the sui generis right would lead to or strengthen information monopolies that might easily be abused, notwithstanding the fact that the provisions of the Directive are without prejudice to the application of Community or national competition law (recital 47). **(b) Compulsory licences.** To remedy the possible abuse of the sui generis right, the Initial Proposal would have provided for a scheme of compulsory licences. If certain data were available only from a single ('sole-source') database, the producer of that database would be compelled to license under fair and non-discriminatory terms the use of such data. A similar compulsory licence was proposed in respect of data held in government-controlled databases. These provisions were later deleted from the Directive following *Magill* (ECJ). All that is left is recital 47, admonishing that 'in the interests of competition between suppliers of information products and services, protection by the sui generis right must not be afforded in such a way as to facilitate abuses of a dominant position, in particular as regards the creation and distribution of new products and services which have an intellectual, documentary, technical, economic or commercial added value …'.

[Addressees]

Article 17

This Directive is addressed to the Member States.

1. General. According to art. 249 EC-Treaty, Directives are binding, as to the result to be achieved, upon each Member State to which it is addressed, but shall leave to the national authorities the choice of form and method.

2. European Economic Area (EEA). Pursuant to the EEA Agreement, the Directive also applies to the EEA countries that are not members of the European Union, namely, Norway, Iceland and Liechtenstein.

DIRECTIVE 2001/29/EC

(Information Society Directive)

of the European Parliament and of the Council of 22 May 2001 on the harmonisation of certain aspects of copyright and related rights in the information society

[Introductory Remarks]

1. Legislative History. In 1988, the European Commission's Green Paper on 'Copyright and the Challenge of Technology' initiated copyright legislation at the European Union level. Over the next years, six Directives harmonized the legal protection of computer programs (Computer Programs Directive), rental rights, lending rights and the main neighbouring rights (the Rental Right Directive), satellite broadcasting and cable retransmission (the Satellite and Cable Directive), the duration of protection of authors' and neighbouring rights (the Term Directive), the legal protection of databases (the Database Directive) as well as the 'droit de suite' (the Resale Right Directive) in the Member States of the European Union. These so-called 'first generation' Directives address sectorial issues of copyright harmonization, as they apply only to certain categories of works (computer programs, databases) or rights (rental right, 'droit de suite'), focus on a particular situation (satellite broadcasting, cable retransmission) or address a particular feature of protection (duration). The Information Society Directive initiated the 'second generation' of European copyright Directives which harmonize copyright law more horizontally. The Directive harmonizes several essential rights of authors and those of four neighbouring rightholders, as well as limitations and exceptions to these rights. It also harmonizes the protection of technological measures and of rights management information as well as – to a lesser extent – sanctions and remedies. Another example of such 'second generation' legislation is the Enforcement Directive. Thereafter, European copyright legislation turned to specific problems again (as in the Term Extension, the Orphan Works or the Collective Rights Management Directive). The Commission had tabled its initial proposal for the Information Society Directive on 10 December 1997, and an amended proposal on 21 May 1999. The Common Position followed on 28 September 2000, and the Information Society Directive was finally adopted on 22 May 2001. The most controversial provisions during the legislative process had been the limitations contained in art. 5 and the exact contours of the anti-circumvention provisions in art. 6.

2. Implementation of the WCT and the WPPT. The Information Society Directive implements two international treaties that were concluded in December 1996: the WCT and the WPPT. However, in many areas, the Directive goes well beyond the international obligations of both treaties. During the drafting process, several provisions of the Directive – in particular arts. 5

and 6 – were highly controversial. The Directive has sometimes been called the 'most-lobbied Directive in European history'.

[Bibliography]

S. Bechtold, *Vom Urheber- zum Informationsrecht: Implikationen des Digital Rights Management* (2002)

S. Bechtold, 'Digital Rights Management in the United States and Europe' (2004) 52 *American Journal of Comparative Law* 323

S. van Gompel, 'Creativity, Autonomy and Personal Touch' in Mireille van Eechoud (ed.), *The Work of Authorship* (Amsterdam University Press 2014)

L. Guibault, 'Why Cherry-picking Never Leads to Harmonisation: The Case of the Limitations on Copyright under Directive 2001/29/EC' (2010) *Journal of Intellectual Property, Information Technology and E-Commerce Law* 55

P.B. Hugenholtz, 'Why the Copyright Directive is Unimportant and Possibly Invalid' (2000) *European Intellectual Property Review* 499

P.B. Hugenholtz, Lucie Guibault & Sjoerd van Geffen, *The Future of Levies in a Digital Environment* (IViR 2003)

K. Klafkowska-Waniowska, 'Public Communication Right: Towards the Full Harmonisation?' (2013) *European Intellectual Property Review* 751

M. Leistner, 'Copyright at the Interface between EU Law and National Law: Definition of "Work" and "Right of Communication to the Public"' (2015) *Journal of Intellectual Property Law and Practice* 626

B. Lindner & T. Shapiro (eds.), *Copyright in the Information Society: A Guide to National Implementation of the European Directive* (Edward Elgar 2011)

E. Rosati, 'Copyright in the EU: In Search of (In)flexibilities' (2014) *Journal of Intellectual Property Law & Practice* 585

E. Rosati, 'Towards an EU-wide Copyright? (Judicial) Pride and (Legislative) Prejudice' (2013) *Intellectual Property Quarterly* 47

M. Senftleben, *Copyright, Limitations and the Three-Step Test: An Analysis of the Three-Step Test in International and EC Copyright Law* (Kluwer Law International 2004)

J.-P. Triaille a.o., *Study on the Application of Directive 2001/29/EC on Copyright and Related Rights in the Information Society* (De Wolf 2013)

[Preamble]

The European Parliament and the Council of the European Union,
Having regard to the Treaty establishing the European Community, and
in particular Articles 47(2), 55 and 95 thereof,

Having regard to the proposal from the Commission,[1]

Having regard to the opinion of the Economic and Social Committee,[2]

Acting in accordance with the procedure laid down in Article 251 of
the Treaty,[3]

Whereas:

(1) The Treaty provides for the establishment of an internal market
and the institution of a system ensuring that competition in the internal
market is not distorted. Harmonisation of the laws of the Member States
on copyright and related rights contributes to the achievement of these
objectives.

(2) The European Council, meeting at Corfu on 24 and 25 June 1994,
stressed the need to create a general and flexible legal framework at
Community level in order to foster the development of the information
society in Europe. This requires, inter alia, the existence of an internal
market for new products and services. Important Community legislation
to ensure such a regulatory framework is already in place or its adoption
is well under way. Copyright and related rights play an important role in
this context as they protect and stimulate the development and marketing of new products and services and the creation and exploitation of
their creative content.

(3) The proposed harmonisation will help to implement the four
freedoms of the internal market and relates to compliance with the
fundamental principles of law and especially of property, including
intellectual property, and freedom of expression and the public interest.

(4) A harmonised legal framework on copyright and related rights,
through increased legal certainty and while providing for a high level
of protection of intellectual property, will foster substantial investment
in creativity and innovation, including network infrastructure, and lead
in turn to growth and increased competitiveness of European industry,
both in the area of content provision and information technology and

---

1. OJ No. C 108, 7 April 1998, p. 6 and OJ C 180, 25 July 1999, p. 6.
2. OJ No. C. 407, 28 December 1998, p. 30.
3. Opinion of the European Parliament of 10 February 1999 (OJ No. C 150, 28 May
   1999, p. 171), Council Common Position of 28 September 2000 (OJ No. C 344,
   1 December 2000, p. 1) and Decision of the European Parliament of 14 February
   2001 (OJ No. C 276, 1 October 2001, p. 24). Council Decision of 9 April 2001.

more generally across a wide range of industrial and cultural sectors. This will safeguard employment and encourage new job creation.

(5) Technological development has multiplied and diversified the vectors for creation, production and exploitation. While no new concepts for the protection of intellectual property are needed, the current law on copyright and related rights should be adapted and supplemented to respond adequately to economic realities such as new forms of exploitation.

(6) Without harmonisation at Community level, legislative activities at national level which have already been initiated in a number of Member States in order to respond to the technological challenges might result in significant differences in protection and thereby in restrictions on the free movement of services and products incorporating, or based on, intellectual property, leading to a refragmentation of the internal market and legislative inconsistency. The impact of such legislative differences and uncertainties will become more significant with the further development of the information society, which has already greatly increased transborder exploitation of intellectual property. This development will and should further increase. Significant legal differences and uncertainties in protection may hinder economies of scale for new products and services containing copyright and related rights.

(7) The Community legal framework for the protection of copyright and related rights must, therefore, also be adapted and supplemented as far as is necessary for the smooth functioning of the internal market. To that end, those national provisions on copyright and related rights which vary considerably from one Member State to another or which cause legal uncertainties hindering the smooth functioning of the internal market and the proper development of the information society in Europe should be adjusted, and inconsistent national responses to the technological developments should be avoided, whilst differences not adversely affecting the functioning of the internal market need not be removed or prevented.

(8) The various social, societal and cultural implications of the information society require that account be taken of the specific features of the content of products and services.

(9) Any harmonisation of copyright and related rights must take as a basis a high level of protection, since such rights are crucial to intellectual creation. Their protection helps to ensure the maintenance and development of creativity in the interests of authors, performers, producers, consumers, culture, industry and the public at large. Intellectual property has therefore been recognised as an integral part of property.

(10) If authors or performers are to continue their creative and artistic work, they have to receive an appropriate reward for the use of their work, as must producers in order to be able to finance this work. The investment required to produce products such as phonograms, films or multimedia products, and services such as 'on-demand' services, is

considerable. Adequate legal protection of intellectual property rights is necessary in order to guarantee the availability of such a reward and provide the opportunity for satisfactory returns on this investment.

(11) A rigorous, effective system for the protection of copyright and related rights is one of the main ways of ensuring that European cultural creativity and production receive the necessary resources and of safeguarding the independence and dignity of artistic creators and performers.

(12) Adequate protection of copyright works and subject-matter of related rights is also of great importance from a cultural standpoint. Article 151 of the Treaty requires the Community to take cultural aspects into account in its action.

(13) A common search for, and consistent application at European level of, technical measures to protect works and other subject-matter and to provide the necessary information on rights are essential insofar as the ultimate aim of these measures is to give effect to the principles and guarantees laid down in law.

(14) This Directive should seek to promote learning and culture by protecting works and other subject-matter while permitting exceptions or limitations in the public interest for the purpose of education and teaching.

(15) The Diplomatic Conference held under the auspices of the World Intellectual Property Organisation (WIPO) in December 1996 led to the adoption of two new Treaties, the 'WIPO Copyright Treaty' and the 'WIPO Performances and Phonograms Treaty', dealing respectively with the protection of authors and the protection of performers and phonogram producers. Those Treaties update the international protection for copyright and related rights significantly, not least with regard to the so-called 'digital agenda', and improve the means to fight piracy world-wide. The Community and a majority of Member States have already signed the Treaties and the process of making arrangements for the ratification of the Treaties by the Community and the Member States is under way. This Directive also serves to implement a number of the new international obligations.

(16) Liability for activities in the network environment concerns not only copyright and related rights but also other areas, such as defamation, misleading advertising, or infringement of trademarks, and is addressed horizontally in Directive 2000/31/EC of the European Parliament and of the Council of 8 June 2000 on certain legal aspects of information society services, in particular electronic commerce, in the internal market ('Directive on electronic commerce'),[4] which clarifies and harmonises various legal issues relating to information society services including electronic commerce. This Directive should be implemented

---

4.   OJ No. L 178, 17 July 2000, p. 1.

within a timescale similar to that for the implementation of the Directive on electronic commerce, since that Directive provides a harmonised framework of principles and provisions relevant inter alia to important parts of this Directive. This Directive is without prejudice to provisions relating to liability in that Directive.

(17) It is necessary, especially in the light of the requirements arising out of the digital environment, to ensure that collecting societies achieve a higher level of rationalisation and transparency with regard to compliance with competition rules.

(18) This Directive is without prejudice to the arrangements in the Member States concerning the management of rights such as extended collective licences.

(19) The moral rights of rightholders should be exercised according to the legislation of the Member States and the provisions of the Berne Convention for the Protection of Literary and Artistic Works, of the WIPO Copyright Treaty and of the WIPO Performances and Phonograms Treaty. Such moral rights remain outside the scope of this Directive.

(20) This Directive is based on principles and rules already laid down in the Directives currently in force in this area, in particular Directives 91/250/EEC,[5] 92/100/EEC,[6] 93/83/EEC,[7] 93/98/EEC,[8] and 96/9/EC,[9] and it develops those principles and rules and places them in the context of the information society. The provisions of this Directive should be without prejudice to the provisions of those Directives, unless otherwise provided in this Directive.

(21) This Directive should define the scope of the acts covered by the reproduction right with regard to the different beneficiaries. This should be done in conformity with the acquis communautaire. A broad definition of these acts is needed to ensure legal certainty within the internal market.

---

5. Council Directive 91/250/EEC of 14 May 1991 on the legal protection of computer programs (OJ No. L 122, 17 May 1991, p. 42). Directive as amended by Directive 93/98/EEC.
6. Council Directive 92/100/EEC of 19 November 1992 on rental right and lending right and on certain rights related to copyright in the field of intellectual property (OJ No. L 346, 27 November 1992, p. 61). Directive as amended by Directive 93/98/EEC.
7. Council Directive 93/83/EEC of 27 September 1993 on the coordination of certain rules concerning copyright and rights related to copyright applicable to satellite broadcasting and cable retransmission (OJ No. L 248, 6 October 1993, p. 15).
8. Council Directive 93/98/EEC of 29 October 1993 harmonising the term of protection of copyright and certain related rights (OJ L 290, 24 November 1993, p. 9).
9. Directive 96/9/EC of the European Parliament and of the Council of 11 March 1996 on the legal protection of databases (OJ No. L 77, 27 March 1996, p. 20).

(22) The objective of proper support for the dissemination of culture must not be achieved by sacrificing strict protection of rights or by tolerating illegal forms of distribution of counterfeited or pirated works.

(23) This Directive should harmonise further the author's right of communication to the public. This right should be understood in a broad sense covering all communication to the public not present at the place where the communication originates. This right should cover any such transmission or retransmission of a work to the public by wire or wireless means, including broadcasting. This right should not cover any other acts.

(24) The right to make available to the public subject-matter referred to in Article 3(2) should be understood as covering all acts of making available such subject-matter to members of the public not present at the place where the act of making available originates, and as not covering any other acts.

(25) The legal uncertainty regarding the nature and the level of protection of acts of on-demand transmission of copyright works and subject-matter protected by related rights over networks should be overcome by providing for harmonised protection at Community level. It should be made clear that all rightholders recognised by this Directive should have an exclusive right to make available to the public copyright works or any other subject-matter by way of interactive on-demand transmissions. Such interactive on-demand transmissions are characterised by the fact that members of the public may access them from a place and at a time individually chosen by them.

(26) With regard to the making available in on-demand services by broadcasters of their radio or television productions incorporating music from commercial phonograms as an integral part thereof, collective licensing arrangements are to be encouraged in order to facilitate the clearance of the rights concerned.

(27) The mere provision of physical facilities for enabling or making a communication does not in itself amount to communication within the meaning of this Directive.

(28) Copyright protection under this Directive includes the exclusive right to control distribution of the work incorporated in a tangible article. The first sale in the Community of the original of a work or copies thereof by the rightholder or with his consent exhausts the right to control resale of that object in the Community. This right should not be exhausted in respect of the original or of copies thereof sold by the rightholder or with his consent outside the Community. Rental and lending rights for authors have been established in Directive 92/100/EEC. The distribution right provided for in this Directive is without prejudice to the provisions relating to the rental and lending rights contained in Chapter I of that Directive.

(29) The question of exhaustion does not arise in the case of services and online services in particular. This also applies with regard to a

material copy of a work or other subject-matter made by a user of such a service with the consent of the rightholder. Therefore, the same applies to rental and lending of the original and copies of works or other subject-matter which are services by nature. Unlike CD-ROM or CD-I, where the intellectual property is incorporated in a material medium, namely an item of goods, every online service is in fact an act which should be subject to authorisation where the copyright or related right so provides.

(30) The rights referred to in this Directive may be transferred, assigned or subject to the granting of contractual licences, without prejudice to the relevant national legislation on copyright and related rights.

(31) A fair balance of rights and interests between the different categories of rightholders, as well as between the different categories of rightholders and users of protected subject-matter must be safeguarded. The existing exceptions and limitations to the rights as set out by the Member States have to be reassessed in the light of the new electronic environment. Existing differences in the exceptions and limitations to certain restricted acts have direct negative effects on the functioning of the internal market of copyright and related rights. Such differences could well become more pronounced in view of the further development of transborder exploitation of works and cross-border activities. In order to ensure the proper functioning of the internal market, such exceptions and limitations should be defined more harmoniously. The degree of their harmonisation should be based on their impact on the smooth functioning of the internal market.

(32) This Directive provides for an exhaustive enumeration of exceptions and limitations to the reproduction right and the right of communication to the public. Some exceptions or limitations only apply to the reproduction right, where appropriate. This list takes due account of the different legal traditions in Member States, while, at the same time, aiming to ensure a functioning internal market. Member States should arrive at a coherent application of these exceptions and limitations, which will be assessed when reviewing implementing legislation in the future.

(33) The exclusive right of reproduction should be subject to an exception to allow certain acts of temporary reproduction, which are transient or incidental reproductions, forming an integral and essential part of a technological process and carried out for the sole purpose of enabling either efficient transmission in a network between third parties by an intermediary, or a lawful use of a work or other subject-matter to be made. The acts of reproduction concerned should have no separate economic value on their own. To the extent that they meet these conditions, this exception should include acts which enable browsing as well as acts of caching to take place, including those which enable transmission systems to function efficiently, provided that the intermediary does not modify

the information and does not interfere with the lawful use of technology, widely recognised and used by industry, to obtain data on the use of the information. A use should be considered lawful where it is authorised by the rightholder or not restricted by law.

(34) Member States should be given the option of providing for certain exceptions or limitations for cases such as educational and scientific purposes, for the benefit of public institutions such as libraries and archives, for purposes of news reporting, for quotations, for use by people with disabilities, for public security uses and for uses in administrative and judicial proceedings.

(35) In certain cases of exceptions or limitations, rightholders should receive fair compensation to compensate them adequately for the use made of their protected works or other subject-matter. When determining the form, detailed arrangements and possible level of such fair compensation, account should be taken of the particular circumstances of each case. When evaluating these circumstances, a valuable criterion would be the possible harm to the rightholders resulting from the act in question. In cases where rightholders have already received payment in some other form, for instance as part of a licence fee, no specific or separate payment may be due. The level of fair compensation should take full account of the degree of use of technological protection measures referred to in this Directive. In certain situations where the prejudice to the rightholder would be minimal, no obligation for payment may arise.

(36) The Member States may provide for fair compensation for rightholders also when applying the optional provisions on exceptions or limitations which do not require such compensation.

(37) Existing national schemes on reprography, where they exist, do not create major barriers to the internal market. Member States should be allowed to provide for an exception or limitation in respect of reprography.

(38) Member States should be allowed to provide for an exception or limitation to the reproduction right for certain types of reproduction of audio, visual and audio-visual material for private use, accompanied by fair compensation. This may include the introduction or continuation of remuneration schemes to compensate for the prejudice to rightholders. Although differences between those remuneration schemes affect the functioning of the internal market, those differences, with respect to analogue private reproduction, should not have a significant impact on the development of the information society. Digital private copying is likely to be more widespread and have a greater economic impact. Due account should therefore be taken of the differences between digital and analogue private copying and a distinction should be made in certain respects between them.

(39) When applying the exception or limitation on private copying, Member States should take due account of technological and economic

developments, in particular with respect to digital private copying and remuneration schemes, when effective technological protection measures are available. Such exceptions or limitations should not inhibit the use of technological measures or their enforcement against circumvention.

(40) Member States may provide for an exception or limitation for the benefit of certain non-profit making establishments, such as publicly accessible libraries and equivalent institutions, as well as archives. However, this should be limited to certain special cases covered by the reproduction right. Such an exception or limitation should not cover uses made in the context of online delivery of protected works or other subject-matter. This Directive should be without prejudice to the Member States' option to derogate from the exclusive public lending right in accordance with Article 5 of Directive 92/100/EEC. Therefore, specific contracts or licences should be promoted which, without creating imbalances, favour such establishments and the disseminative purposes they serve.

(41) When applying the exception or limitation in respect of ephemeral recordings made by broadcasting organisations it is understood that a broadcaster's own facilities include those of a person acting on behalf of and under the responsibility of the broadcasting organisation.

(42) When applying the exception or limitation for non-commercial educational and scientific research purposes, including distance learning, the non-commercial nature of the activity in question should be determined by that activity as such. The organisational structure and the means of funding of the establishment concerned are not the decisive factors in this respect.

(43) It is in any case important for the Member States to adopt all necessary measures to facilitate access to works by persons suffering from a disability which constitutes an obstacle to the use of the works themselves, and to pay particular attention to accessible formats.

(44) When applying the exceptions and limitations provided for in this Directive, they should be exercised in accordance with international obligations. Such exceptions and limitations may not be applied in a way which prejudices the legitimate interests of the rightholder or which conflicts with the normal exploitation of his work or other subject-matter. The provision of such exceptions or limitations by Member States should, in particular, duly reflect the increased economic impact that such exceptions or limitations may have in the context of the new electronic environment. Therefore, the scope of certain exceptions or limitations may have to be even more limited when it comes to certain new uses of copyright works and other subject-matter.

(45) The exceptions and limitations referred to in Article 5(2), (3) and (4) should not, however, prevent the definition of contractual relations designed to ensure fair compensation for the rightholders insofar as permitted by national law.

(46) Recourse to mediation could help users and rightholders to settle disputes. The Commission, in cooperation with the Member States within the Contact Committee, should undertake a study to consider new legal ways of settling disputes concerning copyright and related rights.

(47) Technological development will allow rightholders to make use of technological measures designed to prevent or restrict acts not authorised by the rightholders of any copyright, rights related to copyright or the sui generis right in databases. The danger, however, exists that illegal activities might be carried out in order to enable or facilitate the circumvention of the technical protection provided by these measures. In order to avoid fragmented legal approaches that could potentially hinder the functioning of the internal market, there is a need to provide for harmonised legal protection against circumvention of effective technological measures and against provision of devices and products or services to this effect.

(48) Such legal protection should be provided in respect of technological measures that effectively restrict acts not authorised by the rightholders of any copyright, rights related to copyright or the sui generis right in databases without, however, preventing the normal operation of electronic equipment and its technological development. Such legal protection implies no obligation to design devices, products, components or services to correspond to technological measures, so long as such device, product, component or service does not otherwise fall under the prohibition of Article 6. Such legal protection should respect proportionality and should not prohibit those devices or activities which have a commercially significant purpose or use other than to circumvent the technical protection. In particular, this protection should not hinder research into cryptography.

(49) The legal protection of technological measures is without prejudice to the application of any national provisions which may prohibit the private possession of devices, products or components for the circumvention of technological measures.

(50) Such a harmonised legal protection does not affect the specific provisions on protection provided for by Directive 91/250/EEC. In particular, it should not apply to the protection of technological measures used in connection with computer programs, which is exclusively addressed in that Directive. It should neither inhibit nor prevent the development or use of any means of circumventing a technological measure that is necessary to enable acts to be undertaken in accordance with the terms of Article 5(3) or Article 6 of Directive 91/250/EEC. Articles 5 and 6 of that Directive exclusively determine exceptions to the exclusive rights applicable to computer programs.

(51) The legal protection of technological measures applies without prejudice to public policy, as reflected in Article 5, or public security. Member States should promote voluntary measures taken by

rightholders, including the conclusion and implementation of agreements between rightholders and other parties concerned, to accommodate achieving the objectives of certain exceptions or limitations provided for in national law in accordance with this Directive. In the absence of such voluntary measures or agreements within a reasonable period of time, Member States should take appropriate measures to ensure that rightholders provide beneficiaries of such exceptions or limitations with appropriate means of benefiting from them, by modifying an implemented technological measure or by other means. However, in order to prevent abuse of such measures taken by rightholders, including within the framework of agreements, or taken by a Member State, any technological measures applied in implementation of such measures should enjoy legal protection.

(52) When implementing an exception or limitation for private copying in accordance with Article 5(2)(b), Member States should likewise promote the use of voluntary measures to accommodate achieving the objectives of such exception or limitation. If, within a reasonable period of time, no such voluntary measures to make reproduction for private use possible have been taken, Member States may take measures to enable beneficiaries of the exception or limitation concerned to benefit from it. Voluntary measures taken by rightholders, including agreements between rightholders and other parties concerned, as well as measures taken by Member States, do not prevent rightholders from using technological measures which are consistent with the exceptions or limitations on private copying in national law in accordance with Article 5(2)(b), taking account of the condition of fair compensation under that provision and the possible differentiation between various conditions of use in accordance with Article 5(5), such as controlling the number of reproductions. In order to prevent abuse of such measures, any technological measures applied in their implementation should enjoy legal protection.

(53) The protection of technological measures should ensure a secure environment for the provision of interactive on-demand services, in such a way that members of the public may access works or other subject-matter from a place and at a time individually chosen by them. Where such services are governed by contractual arrangements, the first and second sub-paragraphs of Article 6(4) should not apply. Non-interactive forms of online use should remain subject to those provisions.

(54) Important progress has been made in the international standardisation of technical systems of identification of works and protected subject-matter in digital format. In an increasingly networked environment, differences between technological measures could lead to an incompatibility of systems within the Community. Compatibility and interoperability of the different systems should be encouraged. It would be highly desirable to encourage the development of global systems.

(55) Technological development will facilitate the distribution of works, notably on networks, and this will entail the need for rightholders to identify better the work or other subject-matter, the author or any other rightholder, and to provide information about the terms and conditions of use of the work or other subject-matter in order to render easier the management of rights attached to them. Rightholders should be encouraged to use markings indicating, in addition to the information referred to above, inter alia their authorisation when putting works or other subject-matter on networks.

(56) There is, however, the danger that illegal activities might be carried out in order to remove or alter the electronic copyright-management information attached to it, or otherwise to distribute, import for distribution, broadcast, communicate to the public or make available to the public works or other protected subject-matter from which such information has been removed without authority. In order to avoid fragmented legal approaches that could potentially hinder the functioning of the internal market, there is a need to provide for harmonised legal protection against any of these activities.

(57) Any such rights-management information systems referred to above may, depending on their design, at the same time process personal data about the consumption patterns of protected subject-matter by individuals and allow for tracing of online behaviour. These technical means, in their technical functions, should incorporate privacy safeguards in accordance with Directive 95/46/EC of the European Parliament and of the Council of 24 October 1995 on the protection of individuals with regard to the processing of personal data and the free movement of such data.[10]

(58) Member States should provide for effective sanctions and remedies for infringements of rights and obligations as set out in this Directive. They should take all the measures necessary to ensure that those sanctions and remedies are applied. The sanctions thus provided for should be effective, proportionate and dissuasive and should include the possibility of seeking damages and/or injunctive relief and, where appropriate, of applying for seizure of infringing material.

(59) In the digital environment, in particular, the services of intermediaries may increasingly be used by third parties for infringing activities. In many cases such intermediaries are best placed to bring such infringing activities to an end. Therefore, without prejudice to any other sanctions and remedies available, rightholders should have the possibility of applying for an injunction against an intermediary who carries a third party's infringement of a protected work or other subject-matter in a network. This possibility should be available even where the acts carried out by the intermediary are exempted under Article 5. The

---

10. OJ No. L 281, 23 November 1995, p. 31.

conditions and modalities relating to such injunctions should be left to the national law of the Member States.

(60) The protection provided under this Directive should be without prejudice to national or Community legal provisions in other areas, such as industrial property, data protection, conditional access, access to public documents, and the rule of media exploitation chronology, which may affect the protection of copyright or related rights.

(61) In order to comply with the WIPO Performances and Phonograms Treaty, Directives 92/100/EEC and 93/98/EEC should be amended,

Have adopted this Directive:

CHAPTER I. OBJECTIVE AND SCOPE

[Scope]

Article 1

(1) This Directive concerns the legal protection of copyright and related rights in the framework of the internal market, with particular emphasis on the information society.

(2) Except in the cases referred to in Article 11, this Directive shall leave intact and shall in no way affect existing Community provisions relating to:

    (a) the legal protection of computer programs;

    (b) rental right, lending right and certain rights related to copyright in the field of intellectual property;

    (c) copyright and related rights applicable to broadcasting of programmes by satellite and cable retransmission;

    (d) the term of protection of copyright and certain related rights;

    (e) the legal protection of databases.

1. Scope (para. 1). As a horizontal copyright Directive of the 'second generation' (see introductory remarks), the Directive has a broad field of application. It concerns the protection of works and other protected subject matter created by authors and neighbouring rightholders. The reference to the information society in art. 1(1) does not restrict the application of the Directive to the Internet. Although the Directive focuses on various copyright-related aspects of digitization and communications networks, many of its articles apply to traditional areas of copyright law as well (in particular arts. 2-5 and 8). At the same time, the Directive does not harmonize all aspects of copyright law in the information society. For example, it does not deal with moral rights, the adaptation right, collecting societies, and it only partly deals with levy systems.

2. Relationship to other Directives (para. 2). (a) General. This paragraph concerns the relationship between this Directive and earlier European copyright directives. In general, the paragraph attempts to preserve the acquis communautaire and to limit changes of earlier European copyright Directives as much as possible. On the general relationship between this Directive and other legal provisions, see art. 9. **(b) Computer Programs Directive (para. 2(a)).** The Directive does not alter any provisions of the Computer Programs Directive. Therefore, as far as computer programs are concerned, the rights of reproduction and distribution as well as the limitations to these rights are defined in arts. 4–6 of the Computer Programs Directive and not in arts. 2, 4, 5 of this Directive. In particular, art. 5(1) of the Directive does not apply to computer programs (see art. 5, note 2(a)). Furthermore, technological measures protecting computer programs are protected in art. 7(1)(c) of the Computer Programs Directive. Art. 6 of this Directive does not apply (see art. 6, note 1(c)). The provisions of the Computer Programs Directive constitute a lex specialis in relation to the provisions of the present Directive (*UsedSoft, Nintendo and others* (ECJ)). **(c) Rental Right Directive (para. 2(b)).** The rights harmonized in arts. 2-4 of the Directive do not include rental and lending rights. In this regard, the Rental Right Directive applies. Insofar as the Rental Right Directive harmonizes neighbouring rights in its arts. 7-10, that Directive applies as well. However, art. 2 of this Directive grants a right of reproduction to performers and other neighbouring rightholders (see art. 2, note 4(b)), and art. 3(2) of this Directive grants a right of making available to the public for neighbouring rightholders. These rights complement the related rights laid down in art. 8 of the Rental Right Directive. Although both directives sometimes use the same terminology, their interpretation may differ (concerning the concept of communication to the public, *SCF*; *Phonographic Performance (Ireland)* (ECJ)). The anti-circumvention provisions of arts. 6 and 7 of this Directive apply to neighbouring rightholders as well. The modifications of the Rental Right Directive (old) by art. 11(1) of the present Directive have become obsolete with the adoption of the new Rental Right Directive. **(d) Satellite and Cable Directive (para. 2(c)).** The Directive does not alter or affect the provisions of the Satellite and Cable Directive. While the Satellite and Cable Directive provides for minimal harmonization of certain transmissions related to satellite and cable networks, this Directive has a much broader scope (*SGAE* (ECJ)). **(e) Term Directive (para. 2(d)).** The modification of the (old) Term Directive by art. 11(2) of this Directive has become obsolete with the adoption of the new Term Directive and the Term Extension Directive. The new Term Directive remains unaffected by this Directive. **(f) Database Directive (para. 2(d)).** The Directive leaves the provisions of the Database Directive intact. However, the anti-circumvention provisions of arts. 6 and 7 of the Directive protect database authors and sui generis rightholders as well (see art. 6, note 5(h)).

3. General definitions. (a) General. Although the Directive defines several technical terms it uses (such as 'technological measures' in art. 6(3)), this is not the case for all terms. **(b) Rightholder.** In particular, the Directive does not define the term rightholder as used in arts. 4(2), 5(2)(a), (b) and (e), 5(5),

6(3) and (4), 7(2) as well as arts. 8(2) and (3). Other European intellectual property directives use the term as well without providing a clear definition. The Enforcement Directive, for example, uses the term rightholder without defining it. Art. 3(1) of the Rental Right Directive lists the author, performer, phonogram producer and the producer of the first fixations of films under the heading 'rightholders'. As far as the Directive is concerned, art. 6(3) shows that the term 'rightholder' may cover authors, neighbouring rightholders as well as the rightholder of the 'sui generis' database right provided for in arts. 7 et seq. of the Database Directive. Therefore, the term rightholder as used by the Directive includes at least the author of a work or other protected subject matter. It also includes the four categories of European neighbouring right-holders (performers, phonogram producers, producers of the first fixations of films and broadcasting organizations), as far as their rights are covered by the Directive and not excluded by art. 1(2). **(c) Rightholder and licensee.** It is questionable whether the term 'rightholder' also includes licensees of the original rightholders listed in art. 1, note 3(b). While this question has no practical consequences in some cases, in other cases – in particular when the rightholder is entitled to receive fair compensation (art. 5(2)(a), (b) and (e)) or when his interests must be protected (art. 5(5)) – it becomes relevant. This Directive remains silent on this issue. Other directives do not provide a decisive answer either. On the one hand, the heading and wording of art. 3(1) Rental Rights Directive seem to suggest that only original rightholders are covered by the term 'rightholder'. On the other hand, art. 3(c) of the Collective Rights Management Directive includes licensees in its definition of the term 'rightholder'. **(d) Author and neighbouring rightholder.** The Directive also does not define what the requirements for an author or one of the four European neighbouring rightholders (performers, phonogram producers, producers of the first fixations of films and broadcasting organizations) are. At a European level, rules on initial ownership of copyright exist only with regard to cinematographic and audiovisual works (art. 1(5) Satellite and Cable Directive, art. 2(2) Rental Right Directive, art. 2 Term Directive), computer programs (art. 2 Computer Programs Directive) and databases (art. 4 Database Directive). However, regarding the principal director of a cinematographic work, the ECJ has concluded from art. 2(2) Rental Right Directive that such director is also an author as far as the exploitation rights of the present Directive are concerned (*Luksan* (ECJ)).

4. Interpretation in ECJ case law. In recent years, the ECJ has become increasingly active in interpreting the Directive. In its case law, some general trends can be observed. First, the exploitation rights of the Directive must be interpreted broadly, as the goal of the Directive is to establish a high level of protection (*SGAE*; *Infopaq International*; *Football Association Premier League and others* (ECJ)). Secondly, the ECJ has noted that copyright ex-ceptions must be interpreted strictly. This is not only due to the three-step test as laid down in art. 5(5), but also because this is generally the case with provisions of a directive which derogate from a general principle established by that directive (*Infopaq International*; *Infopaq International II*; *Painer, Public Relations Consultations Association*; *ACI Adam and others* (ECJ)) In later decisions, the ECJ has deviated from a very strict interpretation of copyright exceptions, noting that the interpretation may not hamper the development of new technologies and must achieve a fair balance between the interests of rightholders, users, and society at large (*Football Association Premier League and others*; *Public Relations Consultations Association* (ECJ)). Thirdly, the ECJ has ruled on several occasions that various concepts of the Directive (e.g. ownership, originality standard in art. 2, what constitutes a reproduction in art. 2 and a distribution or public in art. 3, fair compensation in art. 5(2)(b), parody, or who is an author) must be given an autonomous and uniform European interpretation, thereby contributing to the further consolidation of European copyright law (*Luksan*; *Football Association Premier League and others*; *Infopaq International*; *SGAE*; *Padawan*; *DR and TV2 Danmark*; *Luksan*; *Donner*; *Dimensione Direct Sales and Labianca*; *Deckmyn and Vrijheidsfonds* (ECJ); but see *Stichting de Thuiskopie, Amazon.com International Sales and others, VG Wort and others* (ECJ), which leave broad discretion to Member States in the implementation of art. 5(2)b); and *Painer* (ECJ) which leaves broad discretion to Member States in the implementation of art. 5(3)(e)). Fourthly, the ECJ has stressed that provisions of the Directive must, as far as possible, be interpreted in a manner consistent with international law, in particular the Berne Convention, the WCT, WPPT, the TRIPS Agreement, the Rome Convention and the Charter of Fundamental Rights of the EU (*Football Association Premier League and others*; *SCF*; *Donner*; *UPC Telekabel Wien* (ECJ)). **5. Legal basis.** The preamble cite arts. 53(1), 62 and 114 TFEU (equivalent to arts. 47(2), 55 and 95 EC Treaty) as the legal basis for this Directive (see also *Laserdisken II* (ECJ)).

CHAPTER II. RIGHTS AND EXCEPTIONS

[Reproduction right]

Article 2

Member States shall provide for the exclusive right to authorise or prohibit direct or indirect, temporary or permanent reproduction by any means and in any form, in whole or in part:

    (a) for authors, of their works;
    (b) for performers, of fixations of their performances;
    (c) for phonogram producers, of their phonograms;
    (d) for the producers of the first fixations of films, in respect of the original and copies of their films;
    (e) for broadcasting organisations, of fixations of their broadcasts, whether those broadcasts are transmitted by wire or over the air, including by cable or satellite.

1. General. Earlier European copyright directives have harmonized exploitation rights only with respect to certain categories of works, neighbouring rights, the 'sui generis' database right, rental and lending rights as well as satellite broadcasting and cable retransmission. Chapter II of the Directive harmonizes exploitation rights more generally. Art. 2 harmonizes the right of reproduction, art. 3 the right of communication and of making available to the public, and art. 4 harmonizes the right of distribution. Art. 2 does not apply if the work being reproduced is a computer program or a database. In these cases, art. 4 of the Computer Programs Directive and art. 5 of the Database Directive apply (see art. 1, note 2(a) and (e)). However, it should be noted that the Information Society Directive does not harmonize all exploitation rights, such as, for example, the adaptation right (*Art & Allposters International* (ECJ)).

2. Originality standard. (a) Definitions. Various European copyright directives have specified standards of originality for particular work categories to be eligible for copyright protection: for computer programs in art. 1(3) Computer Programs Directive, for databases in art. 3(1) Database Directive and for photographs in art. 6(1) Term Directive. **(b) Interpretation by the ECJ.** However, no directive has established a general standard of originality that is applicable to all copyrightable works. In recent years, the ECJ has attempted, through judicial interpretation, to harmonize the originality requirement in European copyright law. The justification for such harmonization is that it is impossible to determine the scope of exploitation rights, which are harmonized at the European level, unless the originality standard is also harmonized. Arguably, the court has now interpreted the European copyright directives as containing an autonomous standard of originality which covers all conceivable categories of works. Starting with its *Infopaq International* decision, the court has held that a work has to be the expression of the own intellectual creation of its author in order to be eligible for copyright protection (*Infopaq International*; *BSA*; *Football Association Premier League and others*; *Football Dataco and others*; *Nintendo and others* (ECJ)). This test was slightly modified in *Painer* (ECJ) in which the court noted that an intellectual creation needs to reflect the author's personality. This is the case if the author was able to express his creative abilities by making free and creative choices. It is not sufficient if the work is dictated by technical considerations, rules or constraints which leave no room for creative freedom (*BSA*; *Football Dataco*; *SAS Institute* (ECJ)). Whether a particular subject matter fulfils these requirements is for national courts to determine (*Infopaq International*; *BSA*; *Painer*; *SAS Institute* (ECJ)). **(c) Application to particular cases.** The ECJ has applied its test in various cases. While individual words as such do not constitute copyrightable elements, their choice, sequence and combination can (*Infopaq International*; *SAS Institute* (ECJ)). A graphical user interface of a software program does not meet the criterion of originality if the components of the interface do not permit the author to express his creativity in an original manner, but are dictated by their technical function. However, in general, a graphical user interface may be copyrightable if the standard of originality is met (*BSA* (ECJ)). Similarly, the functionalities of a computer program, including its data file formats and programming languages, cannot be copyrighted as such (*SAS Institute* (ECJ)). A portrait photograph can be copyrightable. The ECJ has held in *Painer* that the Directive does not vary the scope of protection granted according to the degree of creative freedom an author enjoys when creating the work. As a result, a portrait photograph receives the same level of protection by art. 2(a) of the Directive as other works (*Painer* (ECJ)). **(d) Effect on national laws.** The ECJ's standard of originality has also implications for national copyright laws, e.g. with regard to applied art (*Geburtstagszug* (Germany)) or the 'skill, judgment and labour' test and the closed catalogue of copyrightable subject matter under UK copyright law.

3. Reproduction by any means and in any form. The right of reproduction encompasses reproductions in both analogue and digital form. It does not matter by which means or on what kind of carrier material the reproduction is created. A reproduction also occurs if the form of the work is substantially changed during the copying process (as with the reproduction of an architectural work in a photography). Creating a digital version from an analogue original constitutes a reproduction of the work, as does the subsequent digital copying of the digital version. Examples of reproductions include photographs, photocopies, copying by hand, CD or DVD ripping, as well as copies of works in the RAM memory of a computer (but see note 3(b) and art. 5(1)).

4. Types of reproduction. The term 'reproduction' is an autonomous concept of European Union law which must be given a uniform interpretation throughout the European Union (*Football Association Premier League and others* (ECJ)). Art. 2 distinguishes reproductions into three categories: direct or indirect, temporary or permanent and whole or partial. **(a) Direct or indirect.** Following the examples of art. 10 RC and art. 7 of the Rental Right Directive (old version), the right of reproduction in art. 2 of the Directive also covers reproductions that necessitate some intermediary copying (such as the recording of a broadcast). **(b) Temporary or permanent.** *General.* As the right of reproduction in art. 4(a) of the Computer Programs Directive, the right of reproduction in art. 2 of the Directive applies to both permanent and temporary copies. This is particularly relevant for digital technologies and has been the focus of lengthy debates, both during the negotiations of the WCT and WPPT and in many countries worldwide (see the Agreed Statement to art. 1(4) WCT and for comment art. 1 WCT, note 5).The mere existence of the exception contained in art. 5(1) suggests that art. 2 defines the general scope of the right of reproduction very broadly. *RAM copies.* The right of reproduction extends to transient fragments of a work within a satellite decoder's memory or on a television screen, if those fragments contain elements which are the expression of the author's own intellectual creation

(*Football Association Premier League and others* (ECJ)). Although the right of reproduction is defined very broadly in art. 2, its effect is limited with regard to certain kinds of transient and incidental reproductions as defined and mandatorily exempt from the exclusive reproduction right in art. 5(1). Moreover, art. 5(2)(d) provides for an optional exception for certain ephemeral recordings of works made by broadcasting organizations. However, arts. 2 and 5 of the Information Society Directive only apply if the work being copied is not a computer program or a database. If it is a computer program or a database, then arts. 4-6 of the Computer Programs Directive and arts. 5-6 of the Database Directive apply (see art. 1, note 2(a) and (e) and art. 5, note 1(e)). **(c) In whole or in part.** The question of whether and to what extent partial digital copies of a work should be covered by the right of reproduction has been subject of an extensive debate. In general, the right of reproduction may cover partial reproductions of works, as long as the part being reproduced is still a copyrightable work (see art. 2, note 2). If a partial reproduction is covered by art. 2, the limitations of art. 5 may still apply. **(d) Mere use of a work.** It is widely accepted that the mere use of a work does not fall within the scope of any exploitation right under copyright law. However, the more the scope of the right of reproduction is extended, the more it covers the 'mere use' of a work such as Internet browsing or consuming digital audio or video works. The Directive limits this undesirable overextension of the right of reproduction in art. 5(1). See also *Football Association Premier League and others* (ECJ). **(e) Law of conflicts**. The Directive does not explicitly address questions of law of conflicts (see art. 3, note 2(b)).

5. Rightholders. (a) General. Art. 2 grants the right of reproduction to authors and the four categories of European neighbouring rightholders. The Directive does not define these entities. Regarding the principal director of a cinematographic work, the ECJ has concluded from art. 2(2) Rental Right Directive that such director is also an author as far as the exploitation rights of the present Directive are concerned (*Luksan* (ECJ)). Despite art. 14bis BC, Member States may not deny such director the exploitation rights and allocate them, e.g., to the producer of the work. Member States may, however, lay down a rebuttable presumption of transfer in favour of the producer (*Luksan* (ECJ); see also art. 1, note 3(d)). **(b) Neighbouring rightholders.** Art. 7 of the Rental Right Directive (old) used to harmonize the right of reproduction for the four European neighbouring rights. However, art. 11(1)(a) of the Directive has repealed that article. Instead, art. 2 of the Directive now applies to neighbouring rightholders as well. Art. 11 of the Directive has not repealed the fixation right of art. 7 of the Rental Right Directive (new). Therefore, the distinction between the first fixation of a work and subsequent reproductions of the work (which can also be found in international treaties such as arts. 7(1)(b) and (c) RC, art. 13 RC and art. 6–7 WPPT) continues to exist for European neighbouring rights. Performers and broadcasting organizations benefit from both the fixation right in art. 7 of the Rental Right Directive and the right of reproduction in art. 2 of the present Directive. However, phonogram producers and producers of the first fixations of films only benefit from the right of reproduction in art. 2 of the Directive. Art. 7 of the Rental Right Directive does not apply to them.

[Right of communication to the public of works and right of making available to the public other subject-matter]

Article 3

(1) Member States shall provide authors with the exclusive right to authorise or prohibit any communication to the public of their works, by wire or wireless means, including the making available to the public of their works in such a way that members of the public may access them from a place and at a time individually chosen by them.

(2) Member States shall provide for the exclusive right to authorise or prohibit the making available to the public, by wire or wireless means, in such a way that members of the public may access them from a place and at a time individually chosen by them:

    (a) for performers, of fixations of their performances;

    (b) for phonogram producers, of their phonograms;

    (c) for the producers of the first fixations of films, of the original and copies of their films;

    (d) for broadcasting organisations, of fixations of their broadcasts, whether these broadcasts are transmitted by wire or over the air, including by cable or satellite.

(3) The rights referred to in paragraphs 1 and 2 shall not be exhausted by any act of communication to the public or making available to the public as set out in this Article.

1. General. Art. 3 harmonizes the right of communication to the public for authors and introduces the right of making available to the public for authors and neighbouring rightholders. It implements art. 8 WCT as well as arts. 10 and 14 WPPT, largely using the wording of these provisions. As a result, art. 3 must be interpreted in compliance with these provisions and other relevant international treaties, such as the Berne and Rome Conventions and the TRIPS Agreement (*Football Association Premiere League and others*; *SCF* (ECJ)).

2. Authors (para. 1). Art. 3(1) harmonizes the right of communication to the public and introduces the right of making available to the public for authors. **(a) Right of communication to the public.** *General.* Before the Directive was enacted, the right of communication to the public had been harmonized only with regard to databases (art. 5(d) of the Database Directive) and satellite broadcasting (art. 2 of the Satellite and Cable Directive; for limits to this harmonization, see *Egeda*, *SGAE* (ECJ)). According to art. 1(2) of the Directive, these provisions remain in force, but are supplemented by a general harmonization of the right of communication to the public. The concept of 'communication to the public' in art. 8(2) of the Rental Right Directive may differ from the concept of the same terminology in the present Directive (*SCF*; *Phonographic Performance (Ireland)*, *OSA* (ECJ)). As far as art. 3 of the present Directive is concerned, the term 'communication to the public' must be interpreted broadly, as the goal of the Directive is to establish a high level of protection (*SGAE*; *Football Association Premier League and others*; *BSA*; *ITV Broadcasting and others*; *OSA*; *Svensson and others* (ECJ)). *Communication*. Art. 3(1) harmonizes the general right of communication to the public. This right encompasses a wide variety of non-tangible disseminations of the work, including wired and wireless transmissions. The right only covers communication to a public not present at the place where the communication originates, such as broadcasting, cable and online transmissions or television broadcasting (*BSA*; *ITV Broadcasting and others*; *OSA* (ECJ)). It does not cover local communication to the public, such as public representation, live performance, recitation and display (*Football Association Premier League and others*; *Circul Globus Bucureşti* (ECJ)). Recital 23 and the more narrow understanding of the 'communication to the public' in the BC and WCT (see arts. 11(1)(i), 11ter(1)(i) and 14(1)(ii) BC and the reference in art. 8 WCT) support this interpretation (*Football Association Premier League and others* (ECJ)). The decisive factor is whether the communication is transmitted to a public located in a place different from the communication's place of origination. Therefore, art. 3 does not harmonize the rights of public performance, recitation and display. However, if such public performance and so forth is transmitted via technical means, for example to an audience in an adjacent room, such transmission is covered by the right of communication to the public. As recital 27 points out, the mere provision of physical facilities for enabling or making a communication does not in itself constitute a communication as defined in art. 3(1) (*SGAE* (ECJ)). For a communication to the public, it is sufficient if the work is made available in such a way that the persons forming the public may access it, irrespective of whether they actually do access it (*SGAE*; *Svensson* (ECJ)). *Public*. The work has to be communicated to the public. The Directive does not include a definition of who the public is. Still, the term 'public' must be given an autonomous and uniform interpretation throughout the European Union (*SGAE* (ECJ)). The term refers to an indeterminate number of potential listeners and implies a fairly large number of persons (*SGAE*; *SCF*; *ITV Broadcasting and others*; *OSA*; *Svensson and others* (ECJ)). The communication may not be restricted to specific individuals belonging to a private group, and a public may consist both of persons who are accessing the work at the same time and of persons who are accessing the work consecutively (*SGAE*; *SCF* (ECJ)). It is also relevant whether the communication is of a profit-making nature or not; however, a profit-making nature is not an essential condition for the existence of a communication to the public (*Football Association Premier League and others*; *SCF*; *Phonographic Performance (Ireland)*; *ITV Broadcasting and others* (ECJ)). The distribution of a television signal by a hotel to its guest rooms constitutes communication to the public, even if the works are only watched in the private context of hotel rooms (*SGAE* (ECJ)). In general, in order for there to be a 'communication to the public', the work broadcast needs to be transmitted to a new public, i.e. a public which was not taken into account by the authors when they authorized its use for communication to the original public (*Football Association Premier League and others*; *OSA*; *Airfield and Canal Digitaal*; *Svensson and others*; *SGAE*; *ITV Broadcasting and others*; *BestWater International* (ECJ)). As a result, providing a hyperlink on a website to a copyrighted work which is freely available on another website or including such work in a frame of a website does not constitute a 'communication to the public' within the meaning of art. 3(1), as the work is not communicated to a new public by the hyperlink or frame (*Svensson and others*; *BestWater International* (ECJ)). This is only the case if the hyperlink enables users to circumvent access restrictions put in place by the site on which the work appears (*Svensson and others* (ECJ)). The near-simultaneous retransmission of television broadcasts over the Internet (streaming) can constitute a communication to the public within the meaning of art. 3(1) (*ITV Broadcasting and others* (ECJ)). In such case in which a different means of transmission for the protected works are used, it is not necessary that the streaming service reaches a new public which could not watch the broadcast on their television sets, as both broadcasting and streaming are different means of transmission (*ITV Broadcasting and others* (ECJ)). However, merely using technical means to ensure or improve reception of an original transmission does not constitute a communication to the public (*ITV Broadcasting and others*; *Football Association Premier League and others*; *Airfield and Canal Digitaal* (ECJ)). *Communication to the public and distribution*. If an act of communication to the public also involves a transfer of ownership of the copy of a work, such act is treated as a distribution within the meaning of art. 4, not as a communication to the public within the meaning of art. 3 (*UsedSoft* (ECJ)). This is of particular importance when it comes to exhaustion of the distribution right (compare art. 3(3) with art. 4(2)). **(b) Right of making available to the public.** *General*. Art. 3(1) introduces the authors' right of making available to the public, which is a special case of the general right of communication to the public. Having its roots in art. 8 WCT, characterising features of this right include the making available of the work, the limitation of the right to making works available to the public, and the possibility of members of the public to access the work on demand. *Making available*. The right of making available to the public covers the act of providing a work to the public. If a user subsequently retrieves the work, the user's act is not covered by the right of making available, but may constitute a reproduction of the work according to art. 2, as long as the requirements for the right of reproduction are met and the retrieval is not a mere use of a work (see art. 2, note 3(d)). *Public*. The Directive does not further define what constitutes a public (see art. 3, note 2(a)). *Access on demand*. The right of making available to the public requires that members of the public may access the work from a place and at a time individually chosen by them, namely, on demand (*SCF*; *C More Entertainment* (ECJ)). The author's exclusive right applies irrespective of whether and how often the work is actually accessed. The mere possibility of the public accessing the work suffices. Examples include the offer to download a work from a public website or to receive a movie from a pay-per-view TV channel. If the work is offered in a way that the member of the public does not have individual control over when and from where to access the work (for example, normal TV and radio broadcasting, streaming content over the Internet, Internet radio stations and possibly near-on-demand pay TV), the right of making available to the public does not apply (*C More Entertainment* (ECJ)). Rather, the more general right of communication to the public may apply. *Applicable to computer programs.* Although art. 1(2) of the Directive states that earlier European copyright Directives remain in force, this does not mean that the Directive cannot regulate aspects that lie within the general subject area of earlier Directives, but were not harmonized in those Directives. However, a television broadcast of a running computer program is not a communication to the public of the graphical user interface, as the TV viewers cannot use features of the interface (*BSA* (ECJ)). *Law of conflicts.* If a work is made available to the public in one Member State, but is accessed from another Member State, the issue is then which law to apply. The present Directive does not explicitly address questions of law of conflicts. It should be noted, in this respect, that an application of the country of origin's law (as well as a harmonization of substantive law as undertaken by art. 1(2)(b) of the Satellite and Cable Directive) would require a comprehensive harmonization across Member States regarding copyright limitations, rights ownership, transfer of rights, scope of protection and collective management of rights – issues which the present Directive does not address to a large extent. For these reasons, it may seem appropriate to apply the law of the country or the countries in which the work that has been publicly communicated can be, or was intended to be, received. In a decision on the Database Directive which may also be important for this Directive, the ECJ ruled that if a website operator targets material infringing the sui generis database right to recipients based in another EU Member State, the act of infringement takes place, at least, in the EU Member State where those recipients are located (*Football Dataco/Sports Radar* (ECJ)). **(c) Authors.** While the Directive does not define who an author is, the ECJ has concluded from art. 2(2) Rental Right Directive that the principal director of a cinematographic work is also an author as far as the exploitation rights of this Directive are concerned (*Luksan* (ECJ)). Despite art. 14bis BC, Member States may not deny such director the exploitation rights and allocate them, e.g., to the producer of the work. Member States may, however, lay down a rebuttable presumption of transfer in favour of the producer (*Luksan* (ECJ); see also art. 1, note 3). **(d) Level of harmonization.** Art. 3(1) fully harmonizes the right of communication to the public, so that Member States are not allowed to extend national protection beyond the scope of art. 3(1), as interpreted by the ECJ (*Svensson and others* (ECJ)). However, art. 3(2) does not preclude Member States from granting broadcasting organizations a right of communication to the public which goes beyond the right of making available to the public as granted in art. 3(2)(d) (*C More Entertainment* (ECJ)).

3. Neighbouring rightholders (para. 2). This provision implements arts. 10 and 14 WPPT, but grants the right of making available to the public (see art. 3, note 2(b)) not only to performers and phonogram producers, but also to producers of the first fixations of films and to broadcasting organizations. Unlike arts. 10 and 14 WPPT, art. 3(2) covers not only audio works, but also audiovisual works. Art. 3(2) does not grant neighbouring rightholders the more general right of communication to the public. However, performers, phonogram producers and broadcasting organizations may benefit from the right of communication to the public as codified in art. 8 of the Rental Right Directive and art. 4 of the Satellite and Cable Directive, which remain in force (see art. 1(2)). The concept of communication to the public in art. 8(2) Rental Right Directive may diverge from the concept in this Directive (*SCF*; *OSA* (ECJ)).

4. No exhaustion (para. 3). (a) General. The right of distribution as introduced by art. 4(1) of the present Directive is exhausted if the first sale of a work is made with the rightholder's consent within the EEA (see art. 4, note 3). According to art. 3(3) of the Directive, the principle of exhaustion applies to neither the right of communication to the public nor the right of making available to the public. If authors have made their works available to the public within the EEA, they may still prevent third parties from making their works available subsequently within (or outside) the EEA. As recital 29 of the Directive points out, communicating and making works available to the public are regarded as services. The principle of exhaustion does not apply to services (*Coditel I* and *II* (ECJ) and *Christiansen* (ECJ)), but only to the trading of tangible goods (see also art. 4, note 3(b)). A national law that treats the public performance of a musical work without payment of royalties as infringement although royalties have already been paid to the author for the reproduction of the work in another Member State does not violate arts. 28 and 49 EC Treaty (*Tournier* (ECJ)). **(b) Online transmission as a substitute to physical distribution.** The Directive does not apply the principle of exhaustion to the rights of communication and making available to the public. According to recital 29, in these cases the 'question of exhaustion does not arise'. This then raises the issue to what extent exhaustion takes place in cases where the online transmission of a work is a functional equivalent to the physical distribution of a work. Recital 29 seems to exclude exhaustion in these cases as well, since it goes on to state that '[t]his also applies with regard to a material copy of a work or other subject-matter made by a user of such a service with the consent of the rightholder.' However, it could be argued that exhaustion does take place at least with regard to a material copy made by the user with the consent of the rightholder, provided such user does not retain a dataset of the work in question after he has sold the material copy. On the other hand, one might argue that due to difficulties of proof, the control interests of the rightholder should prevail even in these cases. While the ECJ held in *UsedSoft* that the exhaustion of the distribution right in art. 4(2) of the Computer Programs Directive concerns both tangible and intangible copies of a computer program, it neither drew conclusions on the right of communication to the public nor the distribution right as laid down in this Directive. Rather, the court treats the Computer Programs Directive, which does not know a separate right of communication to the public, as a lex specialis to this Directive (*UsedSoft*; *Nintendo and others* (ECJ)). More recent case law by the ECJ suggests that the court might not be willing to extend the exhaustion principle to online transmissions (*Art & Allposters* (ECJ); see also art. 4, note 3(f)).

[Distribution right]

Article 4

(1) Member States shall provide for authors, in respect of the original of their works or of copies thereof, the exclusive right to authorise or prohibit any form of distribution to the public by sale or otherwise.

(2) The distribution right shall not be exhausted within the Community in respect of the original or copies of the work, except where the first sale or other transfer of ownership in the Community of that object is made by the rightholder or with his consent.

1. General. Earlier European copyright directives have harmonized the right of distribution only for certain categories of works (for computer programs in art. 4(1)(c) Computer Programs Directive and for databases in art. 5(1)(c) Database Directive) and for neighbouring rightholders (in art. 9 Rental Right Directive). By implementing art. 6 WCT, art. 4 of the present Directive harmonizes the author's right of distribution more generally, but leaves the other provisions in force (see art. 1(2)). As recital 28 points out, the harmonization of the right of distribution is without prejudice to the rental and lending rights as harmonized in the Rental Right Directive. Art. 4 of the present Directive does not influence the provisions on the rental and lending rights in any manner.

2. Right of distribution (para. 1). (a) Distribution to the public. *General.* The 'distribution to the public … by sale' in art. 4(1) of the Directive must be construed as having the same meaning as the expression 'making available to the public through sale' in art. 6(1) of the WCT. The concept of 'distribution' must be interpreted as an autonomous concept of EU law (*Donner*; *Dimensione Direct Sales and Labianca* (ECJ)). *Difference between arts. 3 and 4.* The most important difference between art. 3 and art. 4 is that art. 3 applies to dissemination of works in non-tangible ways, whereas art. 4 applies to dissemination of tangible objects. This distinction between tangible and non-tangible dissemination is supported by recital 28 ('distribution of the work incorporated in a tangible article') and by the understanding of the term 'distribution' in international copyright law (see, for example, the Agreed Statement concerning arts. 6 and 7 WCT: 'the expressions 'copies' and 'original and copies' ... refer exclusively to fixed copies that can be put into circulation as tangible objects'). Unlike the right of communication to the public in art. 3, the right of distribution in art. 4 covers dissemination of fixations of the work that can be put into circulation as tangible objects. This includes, for example, the sale of books, magazines and journals as well as CDs and DVDs. Transmissions of works over a non-tangible medium (in particular on-line transmissions) are not covered by the right of distribution, but by the rights of communication or making available to the public in art. 3. The right of distribution also does not apply even if an online transmission can be viewed as a functional equivalent to a tangible offline transmission. It should be noted that the ECJ has held in *UsedSoft* that the distribution right of art. 4 of the Computer Programs Directive applies to both tangible and intangible distribution channels. But the court treats the Computer Programs Directive, which does not know a separate right of communication to the public, as a lex specialis to this Directive (*UsedSoft, Nintendo and others* (ECJ)). *Circulation of an existing tangible object.* In order to qualify for a distribution, a tangible object encompassing the work has to be put into circulation. It is not sufficient that, as the result of a dissemination, a new tangible object is created (see also art. 3, note 4(b)). *Public.* The Directive does not define what constitutes a public, although an autonomous interpretation of the term 'public' is necessary (see art. 3, note 2(a); *SGAE* (ECJ)). If a person sells a work to another acquainted person without first offering the work to the public, such act does not violate the author's right of distribution. **(b) By sale or otherwise.** Some European copyright directives build on a broad understanding of the term 'distribution' that, in general, also includes rental and lending (see, for example, art. 4(c) of the Computer Programs Directive, and also the wording 'by sale or otherwise' in art. 4(1) of the present Directive). However, according to art. 1(2) of the Directive, the provisions concerning the rental and lending right in arts. 2 and 3 Rental Right Directive remain intact. Therefore, the author's rental and lending rights are harmonized in arts. 2 and 3 of the Rental Right Directive, whereas the particular right of distribution is harmonized in art. 4 of the present Directive. A good is only distributed within the meaning of art. 4(1) if a transfer of ownership has occurred. The mere use or exhibition of such good without transfer of ownership is not sufficient. A broader expansion of the distribution right could only be implemented by the EU legislature (*Peek & Cloppenburg* (ECJ)). Distribution to the public consists of a series of acts ranging, at the very least, from the conclusion of a contract of sale to the performance thereof by delivery to a member of the public (*Donner*; *Blomqvist*; *Dimensione Direct*

Sales and Labianca (ECJ)). However, acts taking place before the conclusion of a contract can also be covered by the distribution right. In particular, contractual offers, intivations to submit an offer and non-binding advertisements fall under the series of acts taken with the objective of making a sale of that object and are therefore covered by the rightholder's distribution right (*Dimensione Direct Sales and Labianca*; *Donner*; *Blomqvist* (ECJ)). In cases of an (unauthorized) advertisement to sell, the rightholder's distribution right is infringed even if no purchase takes place afterwards (*Dimensione Direct Sales and Labianca* (ECJ)). **(c) Original or copies.** The right of distribution applies to both an original and copies, regardless of whether it is the author or a third party who has produced the copies. The original must be a tangible object (see art. 4, note 2(a)). However, if a good gets altered and sold thereafter, it may still violate the rightholder's distribution right (*Art & Allposters International* (ECJ)). **(d) Authors.** Art. 4 grants the right of distribution to authors only. While the Directive does not define who an author is, the ECJ has concluded from art. 2(2) Rental Right Directive that the principal director of a cinematographic work is also an author as far as the exploitation rights of this Directive are concerned (*Luksan* (ECJ); see also art. 1, note 3). Art. 4 does not grant the right of distribution to the four European neighbouring rightholders (performers, phonogram producers, producers of the first fixations of films and broadcasting organizations). For these rightholders, the right of distribution has already been harmonized by art. 9 of the Rental Right Directive. **(e) Not applicable to computer programs.** Art. 4 is not applicable to the distribution of computer programs, which is covered by art. 4(c) of the Computer Programs Directive (see also art. 1(2)(a)). Art. 4(c) Computer Programs Directive conceptualizes the rental right as part of the right of distribution, which is not true for art. 4 of the Directive (see art. 4, note 2(b)). The provisions of the Computer Programs Directive are a lex specialis to art. 4 of this Directive (*UsedSoft*; *Nintendo and others* (ECJ)). **(f) Conflict of laws.** As the distribution to the public may consist of a series of steps (from advertisement to the conclusion of a sales contract and the delivery of the work), the right of distribution may be infringed in several Member States in case of cross-border sales (*Donner*; *Blomqvist*; *Dimensione Direct Sales and Labianca* (ECJ)). If a customer in an EU Member State buys a copyright-infringing good from an online shop located outside the EU, the mere acquisition is sufficient proof that the good was intended to be put on sale in the EU. As a result, the distribution right may be violated once the good enters the EU (*Blomqvist* (ECJ)).

3. Exhaustion (para. 2). (a) General. The principle of exhaustion as enshrined in art. 4(2) limits the author's right of distribution granted in art. 4(1). According to this principle, if, for example, a book is sold within the EEA by the rightholder or with his consent, he may not prevent purchasers of this book from selling it or giving it away subsequently in the EEA, even if this subsequent purchase or gift takes place in another EEA Member State in which the rightholder has not offered the book for sale. The principle of exhaustion ensures that the right of distribution does not inhibit the free movement of goods in the internal market (see art. 34 TFEU). It applies not only to the area of the EU, but also to the entire EEA (see art. 4, note 3(f)). **(b) Exhaustion only applicable to the right of distribution.** In the understanding of the Directive, the principle of exhaustion applies to the right of distribution only. It does not apply to other exploitation rights, particularly not to the rights of communication and making available to the public (see art. 3, note 4). It also does not apply to the rental and lending rights as codified in the Rental Right Directive (see art. 1(2) of the Rental Right Directive). **(c) Exhaustion in case of first sale or other transfer of ownership.** According to art. 4(2), the right of distribution is exhausted if the 'first sale or other transfer of ownership' in the Community is made by the rightholder or with his consent. By including the term 'other transfer of ownership' (such as donation or exchange), the Directive deviates from earlier, more narrow definitions of the principle of exhaustion (see art. 4(c)(2) of the Computer Programs Directive, art. 9(2) of the Rental Right Directive for neighbouring rights and arts. 5(c)(2) and 7(2)(b)(2) of the Database Directive for databases, none of which include the wording 'other transfer of ownership' in the definition of the principle of exhaustion; see also art. 4, note 1(b)). The term 'sale' must be interpreted in a uniform and independent manner throughout the European Union (*UsedSoft* (ECJ) in the context of the Computer Programs Directive). **(d) No exhaustion without consent.** *General*. The right of distribution is only exhausted if the first sale of the object has been made by or with the consent of the rightholder (on the term rightholder, see art. 1, note 3). The consent by a licensee is only sufficient if the licensee him has obtained a licence for the area for which he seeks to grant consent. *European interpretation*. In order to achieve the purpose of copyright harmonization, interpreting the concept of consent is not a matter of applying national laws, but of interpreting art. 4(2) directly (*Davidoff* (ECJ) with respect to the similar consent requirement in art. 7(1) of the Trademark Directive). Usually, consent will be granted in an express statement. However, it is possible that consent may be inferred from facts and circumstances prior to, simultaneous with or subsequent to the placing of the work on the market (*Davidoff* (ECJ)). As the ECJ has decided in the area of trademark law, arts. 34 and 36 TFEU may necessitate an alteration of national rules of evidence in regards to who bears the burden of proof for the prerequisites of an exhaustion (*Van Doren* (ECJ)). **(e) Limited consent.** *General*. Another question is whether, and if so, to what extent a rightholder may limit his consent in geographical scope, time or modes of distribution and what effects such limitations have on the exhaustion of the right of distribution. *Consent limited in geographical scope*. Rightholders may not limit consent to the distribution in certain EEA Member States. Otherwise, they could prevent their distribution right from being exhausted in those Member States. Such limited consent violates arts. 34 and 36 TFEU (*Deutsche Grammophon, Musik-Vertrieb Membran, Dansk Supermarked* (ECJ)). If a rightholder consents to the distribution of his work in one EEA Member State, his right of distribution is automatically exhausted for the whole EEA ('European exhaustion', see also art. 4, note 3(f)). *Consent limited in time or modes of distribution.* In general, a rightholder may limit his consent to the distribution by a third party to a certain time frame or a certain mode of distribution (for example, only to a paperback edition). However, European copyright law does not adopt an explicit standpoint whether, if the licensee engages in an activity outside his limited licence, there is a violation of the rights of the rightholder. In the copyright laws of some Member States (such as, for example, Germany), this is the case. This leads to the question of whether a limited consent also means that the effects of the exhaustion are limited to the types of distribution to which the rightholder consented. The Directive – along with the other copyright directives – is silent on this issue. According to the German Supreme Court in civil matters, this question has to be answered by resorting to national copyright and contract law (*OEM-Version* (Germany)). *Consent limited to particular copies.* If the rightholder has only consented to the distribution of certain copies of the work, his right of distribution becomes exhausted only with respect to these particular copies. Consent must relate to each individual copy of the work in respect of which exhaustion is claimed (*Sebago* (ECJ) with respect to art. 7(1) of the Trademark Directive). *Consent limited in case of alterations.* If, after it has been marketed with the rightholder's consent, the good has undergone an alteration of its medium (e.g., transfer of a painting from paper poster onto canvas), the consent of the rightholder does not extend to the sale of the altered work. As a result, such sale infringes upon the distribution right which has not been exhausted. In this context, it does not matter whether the alteration leads to an additional copy of the work or not (*Art & Allposters International* (ECJ)). **(f) Online exhaustion.** While the ECJ held in *UsedSoft* that the exhaustion of the distribution right in art. 4(2) of the Computer Programs Directive concerns both tangible and intangible copies of a computer program, it neither drew conclusions for the right of communication to the public nor the distribution right as laid down in this Directive. Rather, the court treats the Computer Programs Directive, which does not know a separate right of communication to the public, as a lex specialis to this Directive (*UsedSoft*; *Nintendo and others* (ECJ)). More recent case law by the ECJ suggests that the court might not be willing to extend the exhaustion principle to online transmissions (*Art & Allposters International* (ECJ)). In particular, the court explicitly refers to an agreed statement of the contracting parties of WCT, according to which the distribution right, as defined in Art. 6(1) WCT, exclusively covers 'fixed copies that can be put into circulation as tangible objects' (see also art. 3, note 4(b)). **(g) No international exhaustion.** *Merely European exhaustion.* According to the clear wording of art. 4(2), the right of distribution is only exhausted if the first sale or other transfer of ownership is made 'in the Community' and not in a foreign country. Therefore, a first sale outside of the Community does not result in exhaustion of the right of distribution within the Community (see also recital 28) (*Laserdisken II, Art & Allposters International* (ECJ)). The

European Union is not required to establish a system of international exhaustion, nor is a Member State allowed to implement international exhaustion in its national copyright law (*Laserdisken II*; *Art & Allposters International* (ECJ)). In other words, if a rightholder consents to the distribution of his work in a country outside the EEA, this does not exhaust his right of distribution inside the EEA. The Information Society Directive has thus rejected the principle of international exhaustion. This is in line with the interpretation of the Trademark Directive by the ECJ (*Silhouette* (ECJ)). The prohibition of international exhaustion also applies to countries that have signed a free trade agreement with the EU (*Polydor* (ECJ)). *Exhaustion within the entire EEA, not only the EU.* According to the wording of art. 4(2), the right of distribution is only exhausted 'within the Community', that is, within the geographical area of the EU. However, because of Annex 17 No. 9(e) and Protocol 28 art. 2 to the EEA Agreement, the effect of exhaustion likewise extends to the EEA (that is, also to Norway, Iceland and Liechtenstein).

[Exceptions and limitations]

Article 5

(1) Temporary acts of reproduction referred to in Article 2, which are transient or incidental, which are an integral and essential part of a technological process and the sole purpose of which is to enable:

(a) a transmission in a network between third parties by an intermediary, or

(b) a lawful use

of a work or other subject-matter to be made, and which have no independent economic significance, shall be exempted from the reproduction right provided for in Article 2.

(2) Member States may provide for exceptions or limitations to the reproduction right provided for in Article 2 in the following cases:

(a) in respect of reproductions on paper or any similar medium, effected by the use of any kind of photographic technique or by some other process having similar effects, with the exception of sheet music, provided that the rightholders receive fair compensation;

(b) in respect of reproductions on any medium made by a natural person for private use and for ends that are neither directly nor indirectly commercial, on condition that the rightholders receive fair compensation which takes account of the application or non-application of technological measures referred to in Article 6 to the work or subject-matter concerned;

(c) in respect of specific acts of reproduction made by publicly accessible libraries, educational establishments or museums, or by archives, which are not for direct or indirect economic or commercial advantage;

    (d) in respect of ephemeral recordings of works made by broad-casting organisations by means of their own facilities and for their own broadcasts; the preservation of these recordings in official archives may, on the grounds of their exceptional documentary character, be permitted;

    (e) in respect of reproductions of broadcasts made by social institutions pursuing non-commercial purposes, such as hospitals or prisons, on condition that the rightholders receive fair compensation.

(3) Member States may provide for exceptions or limitations to the rights provided for in Articles 2 and 3 in the following cases:

    (a) use for the sole purpose of illustration for teaching or scientific research, as long as the source, including the author's name, is indicated, unless this turns out to be impossible and to the extent justified by the non-commercial purpose to be achieved;

    (b) uses, for the benefit of people with a disability, which are directly related to the disability and of a non-commercial nature, to the extent required by the specific disability;

    (c) reproduction by the press, communication to the public or making available of published articles on current economic, political or religious topics or of broadcast works or other subject-matter of the same character, in cases where such use is not expressly reserved, and as long as the source, including the author's name, is indicated, or use of works or other subject-matter in connection with the reporting of current events, to the extent justified by the informatory purpose and as long as the source, including the author's name, is indicated, unless this turns out to be impossible;

    (d) quotations for purposes such as criticism or review, provided that they relate to a work or other subject-matter which has already been lawfully made available to the public, that, unless this turns out to be impossible, the source, including the author's name, is indicated, and that their use is in accordance with fair practice, and to the extent required by the specific purpose;

    (e) use for the purposes of public security or to ensure the proper performance or reporting of administrative, parliamentary or judicial proceedings;

    (f) use of political speeches as well as extracts of public lectures or similar works or subject-matter to the extent justified by the informatory purpose and provided that the source, including the author's name, is indicated, except where this turns out to be impossible;

    (g) use during religious celebrations or official celebrations organised by a public authority;

(h) use of works, such as works of architecture or sculpture, made to be located permanently in public places;

(i) incidental inclusion of a work or other subject-matter in other material;

(j) use for the purpose of advertising the public exhibition or sale of artistic works, to the extent necessary to promote the event, excluding any other commercial use;

(k) use for the purpose of caricature, parody or pastiche;

(l) use in connection with the demonstration or repair of equipment;

(m) use of an artistic work in the form of a building or a drawing or plan of a building for the purposes of reconstructing the building;

(n) use by communication or making available, for the purpose of research or private study, to individual members of the public by dedicated terminals on the premises of establishments referred to in paragraph 2(c) of works and other subject-matter not subject to purchase or licensing terms which are contained in their collections;

(o) use in certain other cases of minor importance where exceptions or limitations already exist under national law, provided that they only concern analogue uses and do not affect the free circulation of goods and services within the Community, without prejudice to the other exceptions and limitations contained in this Article.

(4) Where the Member States may provide for an exception or limitation to the right of reproduction pursuant to paragraphs 2 and 3, they may provide similarly for an exception or limitation to the right of distribution as referred to in Article 4 to the extent justified by the purpose of the authorised act of reproduction.

(5) The exceptions and limitations provided for in paragraphs 1,2,3 and 4 shall only be applied in certain special cases which do not conflict with a normal exploitation of the work or other subject-matter and do not unreasonably prejudice the legitimate interests of the rightholder.

1. General. (a) Harmonization. Art. 5 enacts an exhaustive list of exceptions and limitations which the Member States must or may provide in their national copyright laws. The provision uses the terms 'exception', 'limitation' and 'to exempt' (see *VG Wort and others* (ECJ)), but leaves the technical implementation method to the Member States. Art. 5 is of particular significance due to its ambitious goal to harmonize copyright limitations across the European Union (see recital 31). To some extent, it falls short of this goal. The only mandatory limitation that art. 5 introduces is a limitation to the right of reproduction in art. 5(1). All other 20 limitations (to the right of reproduction in art. 5(2), to the rights of reproduction, communication and making available to the public in art. 5(3) and to the right of distribution in art. 5(4)) are optional. Due to the broad latitude left to the Member States regarding which limitation to implement in what way, art. 5 has not led to true harmonization of copyright limitations across the European Union. **(b) Exhaustive enumeration.** As recital 32 points out, art. 5 provides an exhaustive enumeration of limitations to the right of reproduction and the right of communication to the public. Member States are required to implement the limitation of art. 5(1) and are allowed to implement the limitations listed in art. 5(2) and (3). They are not allowed to implement any limitations that are not included in arts. 5(1) to 5(3). Existing limitations in national copyright laws must be modified or deleted insofar as they do not fall within the scope of the exhaustive list of art. 5. However, for analogue uses, there is a 'grandfather clause' in art. 5(3)(o) (see art. 5, note 4(p)). Furthermore, newer directives may introduce additional exceptions. Art. 6 Orphan Works Directive introduces two mandatory exceptions to the right of reproduction and the right of making available to the public which benefits libraries, archives and similar organizations. **(c) Exceptions or subjective rights.** In recent years, it has been increasingly questioned whether copyright limitations should be conceptualized as mere exceptions to the exclusive rights of authors and neighbouring rightholders or whether they grant beneficiaries real subjective rights. The Directive does not adopt an explicit position on this issue and uses the terms 'exception', 'limitation' and 'exempt[ion]' concurrently. **(d) Three-step test.** In addition to fulfilling the specific requirements set by art. 5(1)-(4), all copyright limitations implemented by Member States must pass the three-step test of art. 5(5) (see art. 5, note 6). Furthermore, recital 44 stresses that Member States should, while crafting their copyright limitations, 'duly reflect the increased economic impact that such exceptions ... may have in the context of the new electronic environment. Therefore, the scope of certain exceptions ... may have to be even more limited when it comes to certain new uses of copyright works and other subject matter.' **(e) Relationship to other copyright directives.** *General.* As art. 1(2) shows, limitations that may be found in earlier European copyright directives remain in force. This raises the question of whether, in such cases, the limitations of art. 5 of the Directive apply in addition to the existing limitations. *Computer Programs Directive.* Regarding computer programs, arts. 5 and 6 of the Computer Programs Directive list several limitations to the exploitation rights found in art. 4 of that Directive. These limitations remain in force, art. 1(2)(a) of the present Directive. The limitations of art. 5 of the present Directive arguably do not apply, as the ECJ regards the Computer Programs Directive a lex specialis to this Directive (*UsedSoft*; *Nintendo and others* (ECJ)). *Database Directive.* Regarding databases, arts. 6 and 9 of the Database Directive list several limitations to the exploitation rights found in arts. 5, 7 and 8 of the Database Directive. These limitations remain in force, art. 1(2)(a) of the present Directive. Similar to the situation regarding Computer Programs Directive, art. 5(1) of the present Directive does not apply in the database context. As the European Commission has pointed out, the list of limitations found in the Database Directive is exhaustive. (Staff Working Paper on Copyright Review). *Rental Right Directive*. Art. 10(1) of the Rental Right Directive lists several limitations to the neighbouring rights provided in arts. 6-9 of that Directive. Art. 10(2) of the Rental Right Directive states that Member States may provide for the same kinds of limitations with regard to neighbouring rightholders as they provide with regard to authors. *Orphan Works Directive*. Art. 6 Orphan Works Directive introduces two mandatory exceptions to the right of reproduction and the right of making available to the public which benefits libraries, archives and similar organizations. Thereby, that provision complements art. 5(2) and (3) of the present Directive. **(f) Interpretation.** Originally, the ECJ noted that the exception of art. 5(1) must be interpreted strictly. This is not only due to the three-step test as laid down in art. 5(5), but also because this is generally the case with provisions of a directive which derogates from a general principle established by that directive (*Infopaq International*; *Infopaq International II*; *Painer*; *Public Relations Consultations Association*; *ACI Adam and others* (ECJ)). In later decisions, however, the ECJ has deviated from a very strict interpretation of copyright exceptions, noting that the interpretation may not hamper the development of new technologies and must achieve a fair balance between the interests of rightholders, users, and society at large (*Football Association Premier League and others*; *Public Relations Consultations Association* (ECJ)). Also, in at least one decision the ECJ has expressed its opinion that although it is open to the Member States to introduce or not an exception of the open catalogue, Member States may not, however, define the limits thereof in an unharmonized manner, since this would be contrary to the harmonizing objective of this Directive, inasmuch as the limits of that exception could vary from one Member State to another and would therefore give rise to potential inconsistencies (*DR and TV2 Danmark* (ECJ)). **(g) Relationship to contract law.** In European copyright law, it is still an open question whether copyright limitations can be overridden by contractual agreements. Little legislation or case law exists concerning the question of whether a rightholder may, for example, prevent a user by contract from making copies for private purposes even if the national copyright law allows the user to make such copies. In two earlier copyright directives, explicit provisions dealing with this issue may be found. Art. 9(1)(2) of the Computer Programs Directive prohibits the contractual overriding of the limitations found in arts. 5(2), (3) and art. 6 of that Directive. Art. 15 of the Database Directive declares any contractual term that contradicts the limitations found in arts. 6(1) and 8 of that Directive void. The present Directive does not include any such provision that would make any of the limitations found in arts. 5(2) to 5(4) of the present Directive explicitly resistant against any contractual overriding. Rather, art. 9 states that the Directive shall be without prejudice to the law of contract, and recital 45 declares in quite clear terms that the limitations of arts. 5(2) to 5(4) can be overridden by contractual agreements. However, even the limitations in arts. 5(2) to 5(4) may not, under some circumstances, be overridden by contract as consumer protection statutes and statutes concerning mass-market contracts may forbid such practices. Furthermore, the ECJ has ruled that the right of fair compensation in art. 5(2)(b) cannot be waived by contract (*Luksan* (ECJ); see also art. 5, note 3(b)).

2. Mandatory limitation (para. 1). (a) General. Art. 5(1) provides the only copyright limitation in the Directive that Member States are required to implement (see art. 5, note 1(a)). This limitation has resulted from a long controversy whether and to what extent temporary copies that occur during the processing of copyrighted works by computer technologies should be covered by the right of reproduction. The discussions have been triggered by activities such as copying copyrighted works onto the internal memory (so-called 'RAM') of a computer, Internet browsing and the use of routers and proxy servers that are essential parts of the Internet. While it may seem appropriate to extend the right of reproduction to such activities, as copies of copyrighted materials are made in all these cases, one might also argue that the right of reproduction should not be overextended to cover the mere use of a work, which has traditionally not been within the scope of the exploitation rights (see art. 2, note 3(d)). Art. 5(1) exempts certain temporary reproductions that are transient or incidental from the right of reproduction found in art. 2. Even if all requirements of art. 5(1) are met, the conditions of art. 5(5) have also to be fulfilled (*Public Relations Consultations Association* (ECJ)). If all conditions of art. 5(1) and (5) are met, on-screen and cached copies that are created while browsing publicly available, authorized web pages can fall under the exception of art. 5(1), thereby not requiring another authorization from rightholder (*Public Relations Consultants Association* (ECJ)). Regarding computer programs, the special provision of art. 5(1) Computer Programs Directive applies (see art. 5, note 1(e)). **(b) Relationship to liability regulations.** Arts. 12-14 of the e-Commerce Directive address the liability of service providers for activities in network environments. These articles deal with, among other areas of law, copyright-infringing activities and exempt routing, caching and hosting of information from liability. As recital 16 of the Directive points out, the e-Commerce Directive and the present Directive provide a joint framework concerning the liability for copyright-related activities in network environments. In this framework, arts. 2 and 5(1) of the present Directive determine whether a certain activity constitutes a violation of the right of reproduction. If (and only if) such violation has been determined, arts. 12-14 of the e-Commerce Directive determine whether a service provider is liable for this activity. **(c) Temporary and transient or incidental.** Art. 5(1) applies to temporary copies only. These copies must either have a very short lifetime (that is, be transient) or they must at least have no particular significance from a copyright perspective (that is, be incidental). Examples of such temporary copies include reproductions of works in Internet routers, copies created during Web browsing (*Public Relations Consultations Association* (ECJ)) or, more generally, copies created in computer memory (RAM). Such copies usually have a very short lifetime. Other copies have a longer life lifetime, but are incidental reproductions. Copies created in proxy servers (see also art. 5 note 2(e)) and local caches of computer systems (*Public Relations Consultations Association* (ECJ)), for example, may last for hours, days or even longer. They are not transient, but incidental reproductions and may, as long as they are temporary (which is much longer than transient), qualify for the limitation in art. 5(1) as well (see also the examples given in recital 33). In sum, a reproduction is only transient if its duration is limited to what is technically necessary and if the process is automated so that the copy of the work is deleted automatically, without human intervention, upon completion of the process (*Infopaq International*; *Public Relations Consultations Association* (ECJ)). **(d) Integral and essential part of a technological process.** The limitation of art. 5(1) only applies to reproductions that exist due to technical necessities. Internet routers and proxy servers do not exist in order to make reproductions of copyrighted works, but due to network addressing, management and performance issues. By restricting art. 5(1) to reproductions that are technically predetermined, this limitation implements the three-step-test of art. 5(5) (see art. 5, note 6). While the technological process requirement does not mean that a process which involves human intervention or manual activation cannot be exempted by art. 5(1), no human interaction is allowed concerning the transient reproduction requirement (*Infopaq International, Public Relations Consultations Association* (ECJ) and art. 5, note 2(c)). It is irrelevant whether the technological process would also function without temporary reproductions of the work (*Infopaq International II* (ECJ)). On-screen copies and cached copies created as part of web browsing are an integral and essential part of a technological process in the meaning of art. 5(1) (*Public Relations Consultations Association* (ECJ)). The English version of the Directive originally published in the Official Journal included a typographic error. Later, the wording 'which are transient or identical [and] an integral and essential part of a technological process and whose sole purpose is to enable' was corrected to 'which are transient or identical, which are an integral and essential part of a technological process and the sole purpose of which is to enable' (OJ No. L 6/70, 10 January 2002). **(e) Transmission in a network by an intermediary (para. 1(a)).** Art. 5(1) exempts temporary and transient or incidental copies from the right of reproduction only if their sole purpose is either to enable a transmission in a network or to enable a lawful use. A typical example of a transmission in a network is an Internet router which directs copyrighted works from the sender to the recipient. A proxy server falls under art. 5(1)(a) as well, as its sole purpose is to facilitate the transmission of copyrighted works and other data over the network. Art. 5(1) also applies to other communications networks such as the telephone network and wireless networks. According to recital 33, the intermediary should neither modify the information transmitted nor interfere with the lawful use of technology. **(f) Lawful use (para. 1(b)).** Art. 5(1) also exempts temporary and transient or incidental copies whose sole purpose is to enable a lawful use. According to recital 33, a use should be considered lawful where it is authorized by the rightholder or not restricted by law. *Authorized by the rightholder.* A rightholder may give his explicit or implicit consent. If a rightholder, for example, offers a work on a web page for public download without any restrictions, such behaviour may be regarded as an implicit consent to the users' downloading of this work. Therefore, many copies that are created during web browsing are not covered by the right of reproduction. *Not restricted by law.* If a Member State has implemented a particular copyright limitation of those listed in arts. 5(2) and (3), and an ephemeral copy merely enables a user to benefit from this limitation, such copy does not violate the right of reproduction, as the copy is not restricted by law. Web browsing, for example, may also fall under art. 5(2)(b). Thereby, all transient or incidental copies that are created to enable web browsing are exempted from the right of reproduction by art. 5(1)(b) as long as they do not have any independent economic significance. In this regard, art. 5(1)(b) ensures that the right of reproduction cannot be used by rightholders to undermine the copyright limitations listed in arts. 5(2) and (3). The mere reception of television broadcasts in private circles is not restricted by EU legislation and is therefore a lawful use within the meaning of art. 5(1)(b) (*Football Association Premier League and others* (ECJ)). **(g) Work or other subject matter.** Art. 5(1) not only applies to copyrighted works, but also to other subjectmatter covered by European copyright Directives, in particular those covered by the four European neighbouring rights (see also art. 2(b) to (e)). **(h) No independent economic significance.** As a final requirement, for an ephemeral copy to be exempted from the right of reproduction, it must not have any separate and independent economic value (see recital 33). This application of the three-step-test (see art. 5(5)) demonstrates that art. 5(1) is directed at reproductions that only exist due to technical necessities (see art. 5, note 2(d)). While ephemeral copies may facilitate the use of a work, thereby contributing to the creation of some economic value, they may not have independent economic significance (*Football Association Premier League and others*; *Infopaq International II* (ECJ)).

3. Optional limitations to art. 2 (para. 2). (a) General. While Member States are required to implement the copyright limitation of art. 5(1), they are allowed, but not required, to implement the limitations to the right of reproduction found in art. 5(2). According to art. 5(4), these limitations can also be extended to the right of distribution. All limitations must pass the three-step test of art. 5(5) (*Infopaq International*; *Public Relations Consultations Association* (ECJ)). **(b) Fair compensation.** *General*. If a Member State decides to implement the limitations of arts. 5(2)(a), (b) or (e), it is required to provide for fair compensation for the rightholders. According to recital 36, Member States are allowed to provide for such compensation also in the case of the other limitations of art. 5(2). In fact, art. 5(5) may require the creation of a system of fair compensation even for limitations other than arts. 5(2)(a), (b) and (e) (see art. 5, note 6(g)). Although the Directive does not set up any detailed requirements on how the fair compensation system should be implemented, recital 35 lists some factors that have to be considered in determining the fair compensation. *Fair compensation versus equitable remuneration*. The term 'fair compensation' has not been used in earlier copyright directives. In the context of the rental right and the performers' neighbouring rights, the Rental Right Directive uses the term 'equitable remuneration'. By introducing the notion of 'fair compensation', the framers of the Directive attempted to bridge the gap between such (continental-European) Member States having levy systems that provide for 'equitable remuneration' and those (such as the UK and Ireland) that had so far resisted levies altogether. The concept of 'equitable remuneration' is founded in notions of natural justice and based on the theory, developed particularly in German copyright doctrine, that authors have a right to remuneration for each and every act of usage of their copyrighted works. In determining 'fair compensation', however, recital 35 states that 'a valuable criterion would be the possible harm to the rightholders resulting from the act in question'. ECJ case law seems to suggest that the conceptual difference between 'remuneration' and 'compensation' is not large (*VEWA*; *Luksan* (ECJ)). *Relationship to technological measures*. Recital 35 requires that the level of fair compensation take full account of the degree of use of technological measures (see art. 5, note 3(e)). *Rightholders*. In the cases of arts. 5(2)(a), (b) and (e)), fair compensation must be provided to rightholders. This term includes not only authors, but also the neighbouring rightholders listed in arts. 2(b) to (e) (see art. 1, note 3(d)). As the principal director of a cinematographic work is also an author (see art. 1, note 3(d)), he is entitled to a fair compensation payable under this exception (*Luksan* (ECJ)). *Waivability and presumption of transfer*. The ECJ has ruled in the context of the principal director of a cinematographic work that the right to fair compensation is neither waivable nor that a Member State is allowed to lay down a presumption of transfer of that right to another party (*Luksan* (ECJ)). *Three-step test*. If a Member State creates a system of fair compensation, the system must pass the three-step test as codified in art. 5(5). *De minimis cases*. Recital 35 states that, in certain de minimis cases, no obligation for payment may arise at all. Some commentators have argued that time and space-shifting constitute such de minimis cases. *Illegal copying*. The payment of fair compensation is not intended to compensate rightholders for acts of illegal copying. All cases in which such fair compensation is due (art. 5(2)(a), (b) and (e)) concern copying activities that are exempted from the right of reproduction, that is, are legitimate copying activities (see also art. 5, note 3(e)). **(c) Levy systems.** With the emergence of cassette recorders and photocopying machines since the 1950s, it became evident that private copying was a mass-scale phenomenon that was very difficult to control. Following two German Supreme Court decisions (*Grundig-Reporter* (Germany) and *Personalausweise* (Germany)), the German legislature created the first levy system in 1965. Under a levy system, copies for private and similar purposes are exempted from the right of reproduction, but rightholders are compensated indirectly by imposing a levy on all blank media and copying devices being sold. Levy systems may cover reprographic equipment (photocopiers, fax machines) and activities (copying, faxing) as well as audio and video recording equipment and media (audio and video cassettes). Increasingly, levy systems are extended to digital recording equipment (scanners, CD and DVD burners, computers, tablet PCs and other mobile devices) and media (hard drives as well as writable CD and DVD formats). Levy systems are not intended to compensate rightholders for acts of illegal copying such as file sharing since fair compensation is only due in cases of legitimate private copying (see art. 5, note 3(b)). Levy systems also do not cover reproductions that are made with the express or implied consent of rightholders (as is the case with many web-based downloads), as these reproductions fall outside the scope of any private copying regime in the first place. Today, the majority of Member States have implemented levy systems, although great differences between these systems exist. Despite various attempts since the 1990s, the legal framework of levy systems has not been harmonized at the EU level. Although these systems differ substantially in different Member States in their scope and operation, recitals 37 and 38 state that these differences do not create significant barriers to the internal market. For the relationship between levy systems and technological measures, see art. 5, note 3(e). **(d) Reprography (para. 2(a)).** *General.* Art. 5(2)(a) concerns reproductions on paper and similar analogue media (*VG Wort and others* (ECJ)). The reproduction should be made by a photographic technique or another process with similar effects. This does not per se preclude digital reproduction technologies. Only the result of the reproduction must appear on paper or a similar analogue medium (*VG Wort and others* (ECJ)). The reprography limitation requires that rightholders receive fair compensation (see art. 5, note 3(b)). It is not required that the reproduction be made by the person who ultimately benefits from the reproduction. Therefore, copy shops which offer services to persons who themselves fulfil the requirements of art. 5(2)(a) may benefit from the limitation as well. It is also not required that the reproduction be made for private purposes (but see art. 5(2)(b)). *Sheet music.* Reproductions of music scores are not covered by this limitation, due to their widespread copying in music circles and the resulting lobbying efforts by music publishers. According to the Austrian Supreme Court, a limitation that allows for the copying of sheet music for private purposes may, under certain conditions, violate the three-step test now codified in art. 5(5) (*Ludus tonalis* (Austria)). **(e) Reproductions for private use (para. 2(b)).** Art. 5(2)(b) allows Member States to exempt reproductions made by natural persons for private purposes from the right of reproduction found in art. 2. *Reproduction technology.* Unlike art. 5(2)(a), art. 5(2)(b) is not limited to reproductions on paper and similar media, but covers reproductions on any medium, including digital media such as hard drives, CDs and DVDs. The reproduction technology can be analogue or digital. *Natural person.* The reproduction must be made by a natural person. The Directive leaves open the question whether art. 5(2)(b) also covers the case that a natural person asks a copy shop or another third party to create the reproduction for him (see also art. 5, note 3(d)). *Private use*. A reproduction is only covered by art. 5(2)(b) if it is made for private use and for ends that are neither directly nor indirectly commercial. These requirements severely limit the scope of art. 5(2)(b). The reproduction must be made purely for private purposes. However, the Directive does not explain what commercial ends are. In this regard, determining the contours of the limitation is left to the Member States. *Fair compensation*. Art. 5(2)(b) only applies if the rightholders receive fair compensation (see art. 5, note 3(b)). The term 'rightholders' includes not only authors, but also the neighbouring rightholders listed in arts. 2(b) to (e) (see art. 1, note 3). *Case law*. In recent years, a rich body of case law has developed which interprets art. 5(2)(b) and identifies admissible 'fair compensation' schemes and levy systems. 'Fair compensation' is an autonomous concept of EU law which must be interpreted uniformly throughout the EU (*Padawan*; *VG Wort and others* (ECJ)). While Member States are free to introduce a private copying exception into their national copyright laws, if they do so, they are bound by this uniform interpretation of 'fair compensation' (*Padawan* (ECJ)). Fair compensation is a recompense for the (actual and possible) harm suffered by the author as a result of the introduction of the private copying exception; it must achieve a fair balance between the rightholders and users (recital 31 as well as *Padawan*; *Stichting de Thuiskopie*; *VG Wort and others* (ECJ)). Member States enjoy broad discretion when determining the design of a 'fair compensation' scheme (*Stichting de Thuiskopie*; *Amazon.com International Sales and others*; *VG Wort and others*; *Copydan Båndkopi* (ECJ)). This includes the determination of who owes the fair compensation (*VG Wort and others*; *Copydan Båndkopi* (ECJ)). Accordingly, levies on recording equipment and devices can be compatible with art. 5(2)(b) (*VG Wort and others*; *Padawan*; *Stichting de Thuiskopie*; *Amazon.com International Sales and others* (ECJ)). Whether a rightholder has authorized the reproduction of his work or not has no bearing on the fair compensation owed (*VG Wort and others*; *Copydan Båndkopi* (ECJ)). In order to implement a levy system, it is not necessary to show that natural persons have in fact made private copies and caused actual harm (*Padawan*; *Copydan Båndkopi* (ECJ)). Practical difficulties in identifying private users and requiring them to compensate rightholders may justify a general levy system on recording media that also covers media which are not used in any infringing way, provided that a right of reimbursement exists for such non-infringing recording media uses (*Amazon.com International Sales and others*; *Padawan*; *Copydan Båndkopi* (ECJ)). Such levy system is only appropriate, however, as far as private copying is concerned. The indiscriminate application of a levy to all types of digital reproduction equipment, devices and media – in particular to companies and professional users – does not comply with art. 5(2)(b) (*Padawan* (ECJ)). At the same time, levy systems may extend to multifunctional media for which making copies for private use is only an ancillary function (e.g.

cell phone storage). The relative importance of such function may affect the amount of fair compensation payable. Member States are not required to include every storage media and component into their national levy system, as long as the different treatment of storage media and components is justified (*Copydan Båndkopi* (ECJ)). A levy system may also cover reproductions of protected works made by a natural person with the aid of a device which belongs to a third party (*Copydan Båndkopi* (ECJ)). A Member State may create a levy system in which parts of the revenues are directed to social and cultural establishments set up for the benefit of the rightholders who are entitled to benefit from the 'fair compensation' (*Amazon.com International Sales and others* (ECJ)). In the case of cross-border sales of recording media and equipment, a Member State is not prevented from creating a levy system by the fact that a comparable levy has already been paid in another Member State (*Amazon.com International Sales and others* (ECJ)). If a Member State has decided to introduce a levy system, it must guarantee the effective recovery of the fair compensation for the rightholder (*Stichting de Thuiskopie* (ECJ)) in a case involving cross-border transactions). *Levy systems and illegal copying*. Art. 5(2)(b) does not allow Member States to create private copying exceptions which exempt reproductions made from unlawful sources from the rightholder's reproduction right. Accordingly, levy systems can only extend to reproductions made from lawful sources (*ACI Adam and others, Copydan Båndkopi* (ECJ)). *Relationship between levy systems and technological measures*. As indicated in the wording of art. 5(2)(b), any fair compensation must take 'account of the application or non-application of technological measures'. The more a work is protected by technological measures, the lower any levy for media and equipment that are used to copy this work should be. However, implementing technological measures may only affect the level of fair compensation owed, but does not mean that no fair compensation is due. If a rightholder decides not to use technological measures to protect his work, a Member State cannot exclude him from its fair compensation scheme (*VG Wort and others*; *Copydan Båndkopi* (ECJ)).

(f) Libraries etc. (para. 2(c)). Art. 5(2)(c) allows Member States to exempt reproductions made by certain non-profit institutions from the right of reproduction of art. 2. *Specific acts of reproductions*. Unlike arts. 5(2)(a), (b) and (e), this limitation does not apply 'in respect of reproductions' but 'in respect of specific acts of reproduction'. As recital 40 highlights, the limitation should be limited to certain special cases. The wording of art. 5(2)(c) thus points to the first prong of the three-step test set out in art. 5(5). A blanket provision that would exempt all reproductions in libraries from the right of reproduction is not permissible under art. 5(2)(c). Recital 40 demands that the limitation should not cover uses made in the context of online delivery of protected works. However, reproductions made in the course of an online library delivery of a work may be exempted by art. 5(2)(b), as the library makes the reproductions on behalf of a natural person, which is sufficient for art. 5(2)(b). *Institutions*. Art. 5(2)(c) lists libraries, educational establishments, museums and archives as institutions that may fall under this limitation without further defining them. Common to all these institutions is their non-profit purpose. They have scientific and/or educational goals. Examples of educational establishments are schools, universities and institutions of adult education. *Publicly accessible*. In order to qualify for art. 5(2)(c), the library, educational establishment or museum must be publicly accessible. However, archives do not need to be publicly accessible. This distinction can be derived from the wording of art. 5(2)(c) (at least in the English and German versions of the Directive; the French version is less clear in this regard) as well as from recital 40 ('... certain non-profit making establishments, such as publicly accessible libraries and equivalent institutions, as well as archives'). Although libraries, educational establishments and museums must be publicly accessible, this does not mean that no fee may be charged for the use of these institutions. Rather, it suffices that access to the institution is granted to the general public on a non-discriminatory basis. While the institutions must be publicly accessible, they do not have to be publicly funded. Private museums and schools may qualify for art. 5(2)(c) as long as the other requirements are met. *No commercial advantage*. The institution must not exist for direct or indirect economic or commercial advantage. Therefore, company libraries and archives (which may also be open to external visitors) are not covered by art. 5(2)(c). If the usage fee of an institution is intended not only to cover the expenses of this institution, but also to make some additional profit or to cover expenses of another institution or company, art. 5(2)(c) does not apply. *Public lending right*. Recital 40 stresses that, independent of art. 5(2)(c), Member States are free to derogate from the exclusive public lending right in accordance with art. 6 of the Rental Right Directive. *Orphan works*. Art. 6(1)(b) Orphan Works Directive complements art. 5(2) (c) of the present Directive insofar as it establishes an additional mandatory exception to the right of reproduction to the benefit of libraries, archives and similar organizations which have orphan works in their collections. **(g) Ephemeral recordings (para. 2(d)).** Art. 5(2)(d) allows Member States to exempt certain ephemeral recordings made by broadcasting organizations from the right of reproduction of art. 2. This provision implements art. 11bis(3) BC and arts. 15(1)(c) and (2) RC. It is similar to art. 10(1)(c) of the Rental Right Directive. The provision intends to facilitate the internal organization and the mission of broadcasting organizations. If a broadcasting organization is allowed to broadcast a work without the rightholder's consent (because, for example, art. 5(3)(c) applies), art. 5(2)(d) allows the broadcasting organization to make the reproductions that are necessary in order to broadcast the work. In some cases, art. 5(1)(b) may apply concurrently. *By own facilities and for own broadcasts*. The term 'by means of their own facilities' must be interpreted uniformly and independently throughout the European Union (*DR and TV2 Danmark* (ECJ)). In accordance with recital 41, the interpretation of which varies in different language versions of the Directive, a broadcaster's own facilities include the facilities of any third party acting on behalf of or under the responsibility of the broadcaster (*DR and TV2 Danmark* (ECJ)). Whether these conditions are met is for the national courts to assess (*DR and TV2 Danmark* (ECJ)). *Ephemeral recording.* The provision does not create any time frame after which the recording must be deleted. On the one hand, ephemeral recordings may have a longer life span than temporary reproductions as defined in art. 5(1). On the other hand, a long-term preservation of an ephemeral recording is only permissible if the requirements of art. 5(2)(d) are met. *Preservation.* An ephemeral recording may only be preserved without the rightholder's consent if it is of exceptional documentary character and is preserved in an official archive. Official archives cannot be operated by private broadcasting organizations. Only public broadcasting organizations may operate official archives. The limitation does not allow the broadcasting organizations to exploit the archived works later on without the rightholder's consent. Due to these hurdles, in practice, most broadcasting organizations acquire the right to archive works by contract. **(h) Hospitals and prisons. (para. 2(e)).** Art. 5(2)(e) allows Member States to exempt reproductions of broadcasts made by social institutions from the right of reproduction of art. 2. The social institution must have non-commercial purposes. Art. 5(2)(e) only allows the creation of these reproductions. If any subsequent distribution of these reproductions among patients, inmates and so on violates art. 4, art. 5(4) allows the Member States to exempt this activity from the right of distribution as well. Art. 5(2)(e) is only applicable if rightholders receive fair compensation (see art. 5, note 3(b)).

4. Optional limitations to art. 2 and 3 (para. 3). (a) General. In addition to the five optional limitations to the right of reproduction set out in art. 5(2), art. 5(3) lists 15 optional limitations which Member States may implement in regard to the right of reproduction and/or the rights of communication and making available to the public. According to art. 5(4), these limitations can also be extended to the right of distribution. All limitations must pass the three-step test codified in art. 5(5) (see art. 5, note 6) (*Infopaq International, Public Relations Consultations Association* (ECJ)). **(b) Teaching and research (para. 3(a)).** Art. 5(3)(a) allows Member States to exempt certain exploitations of a work for educational or scientific purposes from arts. 2 and 3. This limitation is similar to art. 10(1)(d) of the Rental Right Directive as well as arts. 6(2)(b) and 9(b) of the Database Directive. Yet, art. 5(3)(a) Directive is more nuanced as it includes a requirement to indicate the source unless this is impossible or not justified. *Illustration.* Art. 5(3)(a) exempts exploitations of a work only for the purpose of illustration and only to the extent justified by this purpose. As the wording 'sole purpose' indicates, if the exploitation simultaneously serves another purpose besides illustration for teaching or scientific research, it is not covered by art. 5(3)(a). *Teaching or scientific research.* The Directive does not further define the terms 'teaching' and 'scientific research', but stresses the non-commercial purpose that is sought to be achieved by the teaching or research. Recital 42 stresses that the non-commercial nature of teaching and scientific research should not hinge on the organizational structure and the means of funding. In the case of teaching, the exploitation (for example, the reproduction) does not have to be made during teaching. It is sufficient if the reproduction and so forth is made as a teaching material that will be used later. According to recital 42, distance-learning activities may benefit from art. 5(3)(a). *Indication of source.* Art. 5(3)(a) requires that the source, including the author's name, be indicated when using a work for illustrative purposes. By stressing the indication of the author's name, the provision regulates a particular aspect of the author's moral rights – the right of attribution – for a particular case, although moral rights in general are still an area of copyright law that has not been harmonized at a European level. Art. 5(3)(a) not only applies to works, but also to the subject matter of the four European neighbouring rights (see art. 2(b)-(e)). In these cases, instead of the author's name, the name of the respective neighbouring rightholder must be indicated. **(c) Disabled persons (para. 3(b)).** Art. 5(3)(b) allows Member States to exempt exploitations of a work from arts. 2 and 3 if they are done for the benefit of disabled persons, are of a non-commercial nature and are directly related to the disability (such as the reproduction of works in Braille for the blind). The provision does not require that the exploitation be made by the disabled person himself. Recital 43 stresses that Member States should remove all accessibility problems for disabled persons such as data format problems. **(d) Press (para. 3(c)).** Based on arts. 10(1) and 10bis BC and similar to art. 10(1)(b) of the Rental Right Directive, art. 5(3)(c) of the Directive allows Member States to exempt certain uses of works by the news media from arts. 2 and 3. *Published articles on current topics.* According to the first alternative of art. 5(3)(c), reproduction by the press as well as communication or making available to the public of certain articles can be exempted from arts. 2 and/or 3. The limitation covers articles that have already been published, works that have already been broadcast as well as other subject matter (such as those of the four European neighbouring rights) of the same character. The work must deal with a current economic, political or religious topic in order to qualify for the limitation. While any reproduction must be made by the 'press' (a term which is not further defined in the Directive) in order to fall under the limitation, a communication or making available to the public may be carried out by anyone. *Reporting of current events.* According to the second alternative of art. 5(3)(c), Member States may exempt the reproduction, communication and/ or making available to the public of works or other subject matter if these uses are made in connection with the reporting of current events. This applies, for example, to news reports citing or showing copyrighted works as part of the report. The limitation only applies to the extent justified by the informative purpose. *No express reservation.* An exploitation does not fall under any alternative of art. 5(3)(c) if such use has been expressly reserved by the rightholder. Since the exception concerns the use of a work, it may be argued that a rightholder must equip each individual article or other subject matter with an express reservation, rather than making a general reservation in, for example, a masthead. *Indication of source*. Both alternatives of art. 5(3)(c) only apply if the source, including the author's name, are indicated (see also art. 5, note 4(b)). In the second alternative of art. 5(3)(c), such indication is not required if it is impossible (e.g., due to the news reporting format or the extraordinary effort it would take to identify the source). **(e) Criticism and review (para. 3(d)).** Based on art. 10(1) BC, art. 5(3)(d) of the Directive allows Member States to provide for limitations to the rights of arts. 2 and 3 for quotation, criticism, review and similar purposes. The limitation is only applicable if the work or other subject matter has already been made available to the public with the consent of the rightholder (*Painer* (ECJ) concerning the French version of the Directive). The work or other protected subject matter listed does not have to be a literary work, but can also be a photograph (*Painer* (ECJ)). Although the Directive does not set a strict limit concerning the extent of a quotation, it requires that the quotation be in accordance with fair practice and that it be required by the specific purpose. In general, the exception must be interpreted strictly. While the exception generally requires the user to indicate the author's name, this is not required if the work has already been published in accordance with art. 5(3)(e), which does not require author indication (*Painer* (ECJ)). **(f) Public security (para. 3(e)).** This provision enables Member States, for example, to introduce copyrighted works into judicial proceedings without consent by the rightholders. As the limitation also covers reports about such proceedings, it may partially overlap with art. 5(3)(c). As the Directive does not specify the circumstances under which the interests of public security can be invoked, Member States enjoy a broad discretion when implementing this exception (*Painer*/ (ECJ)). However, they are bound by general principles of EU law, such as the principle of proportionality and the need for legal certainty. Furthermore, the exception must be interpreted strictly (*Painer* (ECJ)). As a result, the use of a work for the purposes of public security must not be dependent on discretionary human intervention by a user. Consequently, the media may not use, of their own volition, works by invoking the public security exception (*Painer* (ECJ)). **(g) Political speeches and public lectures (para. 3(f)).** Based on art. 2bis BC and similar to art. 5(3)(c), art. 5(3)(g) allows Member States to support a timely news reporting and shaping of the public opinion. The limitation covers political speeches as a whole or in part and extracts of public lectures. The reproduction of entire public lectures is not covered by art. 5(3)(g). The political speech and public lecture do not have to be published in written form in order to qualify for the limitation. The limitation also extends to similar works and subject matter. The limitation only applies if the source, including the author's name, is indicated, unless this is impossible (see art. 5, note 4(b)). **(h) Religious celebrations (para. 3(g)).** This traditional exception exempts religious celebrations as well as official celebrations that have been organized by a public authority from copyright. Typical examples are religious masses and other religious festivities and events, and the playing of music at State visits and other official occasions. However, the scope of this exception is limited to use during the celebration. **(i) Architecture and sculpture (para. 3(h))**. This limitation applies to works that are created with the purpose to locate them permanently in public places (for a definition of 'permanent' see *Verhüllter Reichstag* (Germany)). The term 'public place' should be understood broadly and includes, for example, public streets (for a limitation to views taken from the street see *Hundertwasser-Haus* (Germany)). **(j) Incidental inclusion (para. 3(i))**. Similar to art. 5(3)(o), art. 5(3)(i) allows Member States to introduce a 'de minimis' limitation into their national copyright laws. The Directive does not further define the boundary between an incidental and a significant inclusion of a work. The size of the included work, the intent of the person including the work and similar circumstances may determine this boundary. **(k) Advertising a public exhibition or sale of an artistic work (para. 3(j))**. If an artistic work is used for the purpose of advertising its public exhibition or sale, then such use can be exempt from copyright. However, this exception is limited to the extent that the use is necessary to promote the event, and it may likewise not include any other commercial use. Hence it appears that exhibition catalogues might be covered, if they are sold in connection with the exhibition or sale, but not if they are sold in the general book trade. **(l) Caricature, parody and pastiche (para. 3(k))**. Art. 5(3)(k) allows Member States to exempt of a work for the purposes of caricature, parody or style imitations from the rights set out in arts. 2 and 3. The concept of 'parody' is an autonomous concept of EU law and must be interpreted uniformly throughout the EU. The meaning and scope of the term must be determined by considering its usual meaning in everyday language, while taking into account the context and purpose of its use (*Deckmyn and Vrijheidsfonds* (ECJ)). Parody evokes an existing work while being noticeably different from it, and it constitutes an expression of humour and mockery. The concept of 'parody', within the meaning of that provision, is not subject to the conditions that the parody should display an original character of its own, other than that of displaying noticeable differences with respect to the original parodied work; that it could reasonably be attributed to a person other than the author of the original work itself; that it should relate to the original work itself or mention the source of the parodied work. However, the application of the parody exception must strike a fair balance, also taking into account fundamental rights, between the interests of rightholders and the freedom of expression of the users of copyrighted works (*Deckmyn and Vrijheidsfonds* (ECJ)). **(m) Demonstration of equipment (para. 3(l))**. An example of this limitation is the communication to the public of audiovisual works in TV sets in an electronics store. **(n) Building reconstruction (para. 3(m))**. According to art. 5(3)(m), any work that exists in the form of a building or a drawing or plan thereof may be used for the purpose of reconstructing the building without violating the exploitation rights found in arts. 2 and 3. The work or drawing may only be used for reconstructing the building, that is, after the building has been (partially) destroyed. Any initial construction of the building based on the drawing of a work necessitates the consent of the author of the drawing. **(o) Terminals in libraries (para. 3(n)).** Art. 5(3)(n) allows Member States to exclude certain on-the-spot consultations in libraries and similar institutions from the rights listed in arts. 2 and 3. *Institutions.* The limitation applies to all institutions listed in art. 5(2)(c) (see art. 5, note 3(f)). *Communication.* Member States may allow libraries and similar institutions to communicate or make available (see arts. 3(1) and (2)) works and other subject matter to individual members of the public. However, any communication directed towards the general public (such as public performances) is not covered by this limitation. Rather, the limitation covers computer, audio and video terminals that can be accessed by individual library users. These terminals have to be located on the premises of the respective institution. Therefore, an online access to the library collections from the user's home is not covered by the limitation. However, Member States may grant libraries a right to digitize their works in order to make them available in accordance with art. 5(3)(n). Such digitization does not violate the rightholder's reproduction right (*Eugen Ulmer* (ECJ); see also art. 5(2)(c)). The exception of art. 5(3)(n) does not extend to terminals which allow library users to print out works or store them on USB disks. However, such terminals may benefit from the exceptions of art. 5(2)(a) and (b) (*Eugen Ulmer* (ECJ)). *Purpose.* The user of the institution must access the work for the purpose of research or private study. *Works and other subject matter.* The limitation not only applies to works, but also to other protected subject matter such as those of the four European neighbouring rights. The works and other subject matter must reside in the collection of the respective institution. Art. 5(3)(n) does not cover any online use of a library's collection on another library's premises. *Not subject to purchase or licensing terms.* Art. 5(3)(n) does not apply if the work has been licensed by the library from the rightholder. A mere offer to enter into a license agreement by the rightholder is not sufficient (*Eugen Ulmer* (ECJ)). *Orphan works.* Art. 6(1)(a) Orphan Works Directive complements art. 5(3)(n) of the present Directive insofar as it establishes an additional mandatory exception to the right of making available to the public to the benefit of libraries, archives and similar organizations which have orphan works in their collections. **(p) Analogue uses of minor importance (para. 3(o)).** Art. 5(3)(o) includes a 'grandfather clause' which breaks with the concept of an exhaustive enumeration of copyright limitations in art. 5 (see art. 5, note 1(b)). However, this 'de minimis' limitation is restricted in several regards. Firstly, the limitation only applies to already-existing national copyright limitations. Second, the national limitation must concern only analogue uses. Third, the national limitation must not affect the free circulation of goods and service. Finally, art. 5(3)(o) only applies in cases of minor importance.

5. Optional limitations to art. 4 (para. 4). While arts. 5(2) and (3) concern limitations to the right of reproduction and the rights of communication and making available to the public, art. 5(4) regulates limitations to the right of distribution found in art. 4. Art. 5(4) does not provide an individual list of limitations, but refers to the limitations to the right of reproduction in arts. 5(2) and (3).

6. Three-step test (para. 5). (a) General. Apart from art. 5(1), all limitations listed in art. 5 are merely optional and leave ample flexibility to the Member States regarding what limitation to implement in which way. This flexibility is restricted by the three-step test of art. 5(5), which all copyright limitations must pass. First codified in art. 9(2) BC, later adopted in art. 13 TRIPS, art. 10 WCT and art. 16 WPPT and also reflected in art. 6(3) of the Computer Programs Directive and art. 6(3) of the Database Directive, art. 5(5) of the Directive prescribes the three-step test for all limitations listed in art. 5, including the mandatory limitation of art. 5(1) (*Infopaq International*; *Public Relations Consultations Association* (ECJ)). Art. 11(2) of the Directive introduces the three-step test to the Rental Right Directive. Compared to art. 9(2) BC, the scope of the three-step test in art. 5(5) of the Directive is considerably broader. Art. 9(2) BC only limits the right of reproduction and speaks only of the author's interests. Art. 5(5) of the Directive, just as art. 13 TRIPS, applies to all exploitation rights and speaks of the rightholder's interests in general. In some cases, art. 5(5) might prove to further limit the freedom Member States enjoy when implementing the copyright limitations of art. 5 of the Information Society Directive (for additional comment on the three-step test, see art. 9 BC, note 4(b) and art. 10 WCT, notes 1 et seq.).If an ephemeral reproduction fulfils all the conditions laid down in art. 5(1), it may thereby also pass the three-step test of art. 5(5) (*Football Association Premier League and others*; *Infopaq International II* (ECJ)). This raises the general question whether courts of Member States should or must apply art. 5(5) directly in each of their decisions, or whether this provision is only addressed to the legislatures of the Member States who are obliged to implement the exceptions of art. 5 in accordance with the three-step test. In *Public Relations Consultants Association*, the ECJ ruled that on-screen and cached copies that are created while browsing publicly available, authorized web pages fulfil the conditions of the three-step test as laid down in art. 5(5). **(b) Addressees.** Member States are required to take art. 5(5) into account when implementing the limitations listed in arts. 5(1) to 5(4). If a national court applies a national implementation of one of the limitations listed in arts. 5(1) to 5(4), it should also interpret the implementation as applied in the particular case in the light of art. 5(5). However, Member States are not required to transpose art. 5(5) literally into their national copyright laws. **(c) Special cases.** The wording 'shall only be applied in certain special cases' in art. 5(5), it can be argued, is not to be understood as though it required national legislatures to form special cases of the limitations listed in arts. 5(1) to 5(4). Some of the limitations are detailed enough to be implemented in national laws. Any further duty to form a special case of the already specialized limitation would abandon the overarching objective of art. 5, that is the harmonization of copyright limitations within the European Union. **(d) No conflict with normal exploitation.**

Any limitation must not deprive the rightholder of the general benefits of the right in question. According to the Austrian Supreme Court, a limitation that allows for the copying of sheet music for private purposes may, under certain conditions, violate the three-step test as it conflicts with the normal exploitation of the work (*Ludus tonalis* (Austria)). **(e) No unreasonable prejudice for the interests.** Any copyright limitation must not inappropriately tip the balance between the interests of rightholders and of third parties. In assessing whether a limitation unreasonably prejudices legitimate interests of rightholders, both the quantity and the quality of the potential prejudice must be assessed. It makes a difference, for example, whether a few reproductions are made for private purposes or whether they are made on a massive scale. **(f) Rightholder.** Unlike art. 9(2) BC, art. 5(5) of the Directive does not speak of the interests of the 'author' (and, as art. 2(6)(2) BC shows, of the 'successor in title'), but uses the more general term 'rightholder' (see art. 1, note 3). Therefore, not only the interests of authors, but also those of neighbouring rightholders have to be taken into account in the three-step test as implemented in art. 5(5). **(g) Compensation.** *General.* In weighing the different factors of the three-step test, the existence or non-existence of an equitable remuneration for the rightholders (by, for example, a levy system or a statutory licensing fee) may play an important role in justifying the copyright limitation. Art. 5(5) may necessitate a statutory system of equitable remuneration even if the limitation in question does not explicitly prescribe a system of fair compensation (which is only prescribed by arts. 5(2)(a), (b) and (e)). In this context, it should be noted that the concept of fair compensation is not entirely identical with the concept of equitable remuneration (see art. 5, note 3(b)). **(h) Case law.** On-screen copies and cached copies created as part of web browsing can fall under the exception of art. 5(1) and fulfil the requirements of art. 5(5) (*Public Relations Consultations Association* (ECJ)).

CHAPTER III. PROTECTION OF TECHNOLOGICAL MEASURES AND RIGHTS-MANAGEMENT INFORMATION

[Obligations as to technological measures]

Article 6

(1) Member States shall provide adequate legal protection against the circumvention of any effective technological measures, which the person concerned carries out in the knowledge, or with reasonable grounds to know, that he or she is pursuing that objective.

(2) Member States shall provide adequate legal protection against the manufacture, import, distribution, sale, rental, advertisement for sale or rental, or possession for commercial purposes of devices, products or components or the provision of services which:

    (a) are promoted, advertised or marketed for the purpose of circumvention of, or

(b) have only a limited commercially significant purpose or use other than to circumvent, or

(c) are primarily designed, produced, adapted or performed for the purpose of enabling or facilitating the circumvention of, any effective technological measures.

(3) For the purposes of this Directive, the expression 'technological measures' means any technology, device or component that, in the normal course of its operation, is designed to prevent or restrict acts, in respect of works or other subject-matter, which are not authorised by the rightholder of any copyright or any right related to copyright as provided for by law or the sui generis right provided for in Chapter III of Directive 96/9/EC. Technological measures shall be deemed 'effective' where the use of a protected work or other subject-matter is controlled by the rightholders through application of an access control or protection process, such as encryption, scrambling or other transformation of the work or other subject-matter or a copy control mechanism, which achieves the protection objective.

(4) Notwithstanding the legal protection provided for in paragraph 1, in the absence of voluntary measures taken by rightholders, including agreements between rightholders and other parties concerned, Member States shall take appropriate measures to ensure that rightholders make available to the beneficiary of an exception or limitation provided for in national law in accordance with Article 5(2)(a), (2)(c), (2)(d), (2)(e), (3) (a), (3)(b) or (3)(e) the means of benefiting from that exception or limitation, to the extent necessary to benefit from that exception or limitation and where that beneficiary has legal access to the protected work or subject-matter concerned.

(5) A Member State may also take such measures in respect of a beneficiary of an exception or limitation provided for in accordance with Article 5(2)(b), unless reproduction for private use has already been made possible by rightholders to the extent necessary to benefit from the exception or limitation concerned and in accordance with the provisions of Article 5(2)(b) and (5), without preventing rightholders from adopting adequate measures regarding the number of reproductions in accordance with these provisions.

(6) The technological measures applied voluntarily by rightholders, including those applied in implementation of voluntary agreements, and technological measures applied in implementation of the measures taken by Member States, shall enjoy the legal protection provided for in paragraph 1.

(7) The provisions of the first and second subparagraphs shall not apply to works or other subject-matter made available to the public on agreed contractual terms in such a way that members of the public may access them from a place and at a time individually chosen by them.

(8) When this Article is applied in the context of Directives 92/100/ EEC and 96/9/EC, this paragraph shall apply mutatis mutandis.

1. General. Art. 6 of the Directive implements arts. 11 WCT and 18 WPPT. **(a) Technological development.** For years, the recording and movie industries have accused file-sharing and content streaming distribution networks of enabling mass-scale piracy and severely hampering revenue opportunities. Various technological measures, for example copy-control technologies, promise to offer a secure framework for distributing copyrighted works, be it music, video or works in writing. Such measures attempt to ensure that rightholders receive adequate remuneration for the creation of the works that are distributed with them. They are supported by 'rights management information' that formally describe digital content and related parameters (see art. 7). Although technological measures promise to provide a high level of technological security, no commercially viable system will be 100% secure. Technological measures have been hacked in the past and this will not change in the foreseeable future. **(b) Emergence of anti-circumvention regulations.** In order to increase the overall security of content distribution systems, special anti-circumvention provisions were created in the 1990s and early 2000s. These provisions outlaw the circumvention of technological measures as well as the production and distribution of devices that may be used to circumvent such measures (so-called 'preparatory activities'). At an international level, anti-circumvention provisions can be found in arts. 11 WCT and 18 WPPT and, to some extent, in arts. 2, 3 and 6 of the Council of Europe's Convention on Cybercrime. In the EU, anti-circumvention provisions may be found in three Directives. First, art. 7(1)(c) of the Computer Programs Directive prohibits the circulation and 'possession for commercial purposes' of any tools that are solely intended to circumvent technological measures protecting a computer program. Second, art. 4 of the Conditional Access Directive prohibits the production, distribution and promotion of illicit devices that circumvent conditional access technologies used in the pay TV, broadcasting and Internet sector (see art. 6, note 1(c)). Finally, art. 6 of the present Directive contains the most general anti-circumvention provisions. Art. 6(1) prohibits the actual circumvention of any effective technological measure that is used by the rightholders of any copyright or neighbouring rights to protect their works. Art. 6(2) prohibits a wide range of preparatory activities. Art. 6(3) defines the term 'effective technological measure'. Art. 6(4) attempts to reconcile technological measures with copyright limitations. Art. 7 prohibits the removal or alteration of rights management information. **(c) Relationship to other directives.** *General.* The relationship between the anti-circumvention provisions of three directives – art. 7(1)(c) of the Computer Programs Directive, the Conditional Access Directive and art. 6 of the present Directive – is often either unclear or even inconsistent. The Computer Programs Directive, for example, protects technological measures more effectively than the present Directive. *Conditional Access Directive and*

Information Society Directive. Both the Conditional Access Directive and the present Directive outlaw the production, distribution and promotion of circumvention devices. Technically, both provisions address different kinds of technological measures and are therefore complementary. Whereas art. 6 of the present Directive is intended to deal with the unauthorized exploitation of a work protected by copyright the Conditional Access Directive is intended to protect against the unauthorized reception of conditional access services, which may or may not contain intellectual property. *Computer Programs Directive and Information Society Directive.* As far as the relationship between the Computer Programs Directive and the present Directive is concerned, art. 6 of the present Directive does not apply to technological measures protecting computer programs. In this regard, art. 7(1)(c) Computer Programs Directive applies alone (see also art. 1, note 2(a), art. 6, note 2(a), and recital 50). *Consumer Rights Directive.* According to Art. 6(1)(r) and (s) Consumer Rights Directive, a trader has to inform a consumer, in a distance or off-premises contract, about the functionality of technological measures as well as any relevant interoperability of digital content with hardware and software. **(d) No technology mandate.** As recital 48 points out, arts. 6 and 7 do not imply any obligation for technology and service providers to design their products and services so that they correspond to technological measures. Therefore, it is perfectly legal to manufacture and distribute an audio player that does not recognize any of the copy-protected audio formats available.

2. Definitions (para. 3). Art. 6(3) provides a general definition of the terms 'technological measure' and 'effective' that is applicable to both arts. 6(1) and (2). **(a) Technological measure (para. 3 sentence 1).** Art. 6(3) sentence 1 provides a very broad definition of the term 'technological measure' that is used by both art. 6(1) and (2). *Technology, device or component.* The definition of a technological measure encompasses both hardware and software implementations of security technologies. *Designed to prevent or restrict acts.* The technological measure must, in the normal course of its operation, be designed to prevent or restrict acts not authorized by the rightholder. Technological measures can be divided into three categories: first, technologies that protect access to and use of copyrighted works (for example, encryption technologies, digital containers, passwords and serial numbers as well as copy-control technologies); second, technologies that protect the integrity and authenticity of copyrighted works and devices (for example, hash functions, digital signatures and challenge response protocols); and third, technologies that prevent a third party from tampering with security features (for example, smart cards, code obfuscation, trusted computing technologies and other tamper-resistant hardware and software) (see also *Nintendo and others* (ECJ)). For the purposes of art. 6, it is irrelevant whether these measures are implemented in software or hardware or across different devices (*Nintendo and others* (ECJ)) and whether they are of a digital or analog nature. Analog protection measures (such as analogue outputs of DVD players) are technological measures as defined in art. 6(3) sentence 1 as well.

Technological measures and DRM. While art. 6 uses the term 'technological measure', quite often 'technological protection measure' is used as a synonym. While technological measures are individual technologies that protect works and other subject matter, the term DRM describes more complex protection systems. While technological measures characterise an individual technology that protects works and other subject matter, the term DRM characterises protection systems that use technological, contractual and statutory protection concurrently. *Technological measures and rights management information*. Despite the broad definition of art. 6(3) sentence 1, for some technologies it is unclear whether they fall under the definition. Digital watermarks, for example, are used to imbed rights management information (see art. 7) into digital works. If an attacker removes a watermark, such behaviour violates art. 7 (see art. 7, note 3(a)). However, digital watermarks may also be part of a copy control system (as the numbers of copies allowed may be coded into the digital watermark). If the watermark is removed, the copy control system is rendered ineffective. Such behaviour violates art. 6(1). The removal of a digital watermark may therefore be both the removal of a rights management information (art. 7(1)) and the circumvention of a technological measure (art. 6(1)). *In respect of works or other subject matter*. Art. 6 not only protects technological measures used in conjunction with copyrighted works. It also protects technological measures used in conjunction with the four European neighbouring rights (performers, phonogram producers, producers of the first fixations of films and broadcasting organizations) as well as the 'sui generis' database right of arts. 7 et seq. of the Database Directive. However, art. 6 does not apply to technological measures protecting computer programs. In this regard, art. 7(1)(c) of the Computer Programs Directive solely applies (see art. 6, note 1(c), art. 1, note 2(a) and recital 50). This distinction becomes problematic as the once clear line between computer programs and other works becomes more and more blurred with the advent of computer games, digital content wrapped in computer programs and similar hybrid works. In fact, the British High Court has applied the British implementations of art. 7(1)(c) of the Computer Programs Directive and art. 6 of the present Directive concurrently in a case that involved a region coding system which is part of Sony's video gaming console PlayStation 2. The Court assumed that the region coding system protects both a computer program and another work at the same time, without elaborating in detail what the other work might be (*Sony/Ball* (UK)). *Not authorized by the rightholder*. Technological measures are only protected against circumvention if they are designed to prevent or restrict acts which are not authorized by the rightholder. In practice, technological measures are not used or applied by the authors themselves, but rather by their agents or licensees acting with the author's consent. For comments on the term 'rightholder', see art. 1, note 2(a). If rightholders bundle their exploitation rights through licensing agreements in, for example, a record company, it is this licensee whose authorization or non-authorization counts for the purposes of art. 6(3) sentence 1. *Power to authorize*. Technological measures are only protected by art. 6 if they prevent or restrict acts that fall within the rightholder's power to authorize. If a technological measure prevents a certain activity that is neither protected by copyright law nor by any neighbouring right or the 'sui generis' database right, art. 6 does not forbid the circumvention of this technological measure, regardless of whether the 'rightholder' has authorized this activity. If, for example, a work has fallen into the public domain because the term of copyright protection has expired (see art. 1 of the Term Directive), any technological measure preventing the reproduction of the work does not benefit from art. 6. *Dual use technological measures.* The application of art. 6 is problematic regarding technological measures that protect, at the same time, some acts that are covered by copyright and some acts that are not (such as protecting a digital information product as a whole although only a part of the product qualifies for copyright protection). In general, in such 'dual use' cases, art. 6 probably applies as long as the technological measure is not misused primarily for the purpose to substitute the absence of copyright protection by technological protection. *Technological measures and anti-competitive effects.* Technological measures may also be used by rightholders to control competition on markets adjacent to their protected works. The legal protection provided by art. 6 must respect the principle of proportionality (see also recital 48) and should not prohibit devices or activities which have a commercially significant purpose or use other than to circumvent the technical protection (*Nintendo and others* (ECJ)). Technological measures much pursue the objective of preventing or eliminating acts not authorized by the rightholder with respect to the rights granted in arts. 2-4 of this Directive. They must not go beyond what is necessary for this purpose (*Nintendo and others* (ECJ)). Considering the principle of proportionality, the relative costs and levels of effectiveness of different types of technological measures have to be considered. In this regard, it is important to examine how often anti-circumvention devices are used for purposes which do not infringe the rights granted to rightholders in arts. 2-4 of this Directive (*Nintendo and others* (ECJ)). **(b) Effective technological measures (para. 3 sentence 2).** Art. 6(3) sentence 2 contains not so much a (tautological) definition of the term 'effective' as a circumscription of the term that is not very helpful. *Effectiveness.* A technological measure is deemed effective if it controls the use of a work through an access or copy-control mechanism. According to this understanding of the term 'effective', it is irrelevant whether a technological measure can be easily circumvented or whether great efforts are needed to circumvent the measure. From a technical point of view, the use of an encryption scheme that is based on 40 bit-long encryption keys cannot be considered an effective encryption scheme as it can be easily hacked. Nevertheless, such encryption scheme seems to fall under the term 'effective technological measure' in art. 6(3). The only limitation to the broad understanding of the term is the requirement that the technological measure achieve the protection objective and that it control the use of a work or other subject matter. Therefore, technological measures that are completely useless are not effective as described in art. 6(3) sentence 2. All other technological measures are covered by art. 6(3) as long as they achieve the protection objective and exercise at least some control over the use of a work. *Control of use through access or copy control.* The technological measure must control the use of a work or other subject matter through an access or copy control mechanism. The use of these terms is surprising. The mere use of a work is not covered by copyright law (see art. 2, note 3(d)). The European Union has enacted a separate directive concerning conditional access technologies (see note art. 6, note 1(c)). In order to align art. 6 with traditional copyright law, art. 6(3) sentence 2 might be understood as covering technological measures that control an act covered by an exploitation right granted by traditional copyright law (such as the right of reproduction, communication and making available to the public and of distribution). *Control by rightholder.* The technological measure must be used or at least authorized by a rightholder (see art. 6, note 2(a)). *Encryption, scrambling or other transformation.* Art. 6(3) sentence 2 lists several technologies that may be used in a technological measure.

3. Prohibition of actual circumvention (para. 1). Whereas art. 6(2) forbids certain preparatory activities, art. 6(1) prohibits the actual circumvention of technological measures. **(a) Circumvention.** A broad variety of activities may constitute circumvention of a technological measure. This may include the exploration of passwords and decryption keys, the manipulation of authentication protocols as well as physical attacks on hardware protection mechanisms. **(b) Effective technological measure.** The term 'effective technological measure' is defined in art. 6(3) (see art. 6, note 2). **(c) Knowledge or reasonable grounds to know.** The person circumventing an effective technological measure must know or have reasonable grounds to know that he is pursuing the objective to circumvent an effective technological measure. **(d) Security research.** In general, anti-circumvention provisions may create chilling effects on scientific security research. Practical experiments and tests are indispensable for evaluating the features and security level of any real-world implementation of a security system. One of the standard approaches to evaluating a real-world security system is to attempt to break it. If a researcher succeeds in breaking it, he publishes his procedure and results, thereby enabling other members of the security research community to understand the attack and build more secure systems. By impeding such security research, anti-circumvention provisions could have detrimental impact on technological innovation in the area of security systems. The Directive recognizes this tension in recital 48, according to which the anti-circumvention provision of art. 6 should not hinder research into cryptography. While this recital only mentions cryptography research, it can be assumed that the Directive does not intend to interfere with other areas of security research either. For a similar tension between art. 7 and information hiding research, see art. 7, note 3(d).

4. Prohibition of preparatory activities (para. 2). Art. 6(2) prohibits a wide variety of preparatory activities. **(a) Manufacture of devices etc.**

Devices, products or components. Art. 6(2) covers specialized software programs and unauthorized hardware dongles. It may also cover components that are harmless individually, but, in combination with other components, can be used to circumvent technological measures. *Import.* In addition to the manufacturing of such devices, art. 6(2) prohibits the import of such devices into the EU. It not only covers the commercial import, but also the import by private persons: as opposed to art. 7(1)(b), art. 6(2) not only covers the import for distribution, but the import in general. *Distribution.* It is unclear whether the term 'distribution' is used in the same manner as in art. 4. If this were the case, the term distribution would only cover the dissemination of tangible objects, but not any online transmission of circumvention tools (see art. 4, note 2(a)). Such reading is consistent with the overall classification of exploitation rights by the Directive. The Directive regards the communication and making available to the public (art. 3) as the provision of services, see art. 3 note 4(a). Therefore, in the context of art. 6(2), any online transmission of circumvention tools can be regarded as 'the provision of services' as set out in art. 6(2). *Advertisement for sale or rental.* A definition of the term 'advertising' may be found in art. 2(a) of the Misleading and Comparative Advertising Directive. *Possession for commercial purposes.* Art. 6(2) limits the prohibition to possession of circumvention tools for commercial purposes. In this regard, the provision refers to a phrase which has already been used in art. 7(1)(c) of the Computer Programs Directive. If a private user has installed a circumvention software on his computer or a circumvention circuit board in his pay TV decoder, he does not violate art. 6(2). However, as recital 49 points out, Member States may also prohibit the private possession of circumvention tools. **(b) Provision of services.** Art. 6(2) prohibits the provision of services such as commercial circumvention services and the online transmission of circumvention tools (see art. 6, note 4(a)). This may also cover printed or on-line instructions of how to circumvent technological measures. Even detailed instructions in computer magazines about how to circumvent a particular technological measure may fall under art. 6(2). **(c) Limitations in arts. 6(2) (a)-(c).** *General.* As recital 48 points out, the protection of technological measures must respect proportionality. The products or services must meet the requirements of either arts. 6(2)(a), (b) or (c) in order to qualify for the protection of art. 6(2). These limitations are an important safeguard not to establishing a prohibition of preparatory activities that is too far-reaching. *Only limited other purpose (para. 2(b)).* Many circumvention tools are neutral in their consequences in that they may not only be used to circumvent technologies, but also for legitimate purposes (e.g., electron microscopes, in-circuit emulators, logic analyzers or software debuggers). Art. 6(2)(b) attempts to solve this 'dual use' problem by exempting such dual use tools from art. 6(2). However, it should be noted that the solution found by art. 6(2)(b) only exempts tools that have a commercially significant other purpose. Tools with purposes other than of commercial significance, such as research tools with scientific significance, are not necessarily covered by art. 6(2)(b). On dual use technologies, see art. 6 note 2(a). **(d) Contributory infringement.** In principle, doctrines of contributory infringement stemming from national tort laws may be applied in the context of art. 6(2). **(e) Security research.** As recital 48 points out, the anti-circumvention provision of art. 6 should not hinder research into cryptography (see art. 6, note 3(d)). Very often, the development of a circumvention tool by a security researcher and other stages in security research will not fulfil the requirements of art. 6(2)(a), (b) or (c).

5. Relationship to copyright limitations (para. 4). (a) General tension. While copyright limitations such as those found in art. 5 are inherent components of any copyright regime, the protection by technological measures is potentially unlimited. Theoretically, technological measures enable content providers to protect their interests without paying adequate attention to interests of third parties or the society at large. Technological measures may protect digital content that is not copyrightable. They may prevent consumers from copying content for private purposes even if a copyright limitation allows them to do so without the rightholder's permission. In general, technological measures potentially confer a degree of control over access to and use of works that goes well beyond the rights afforded by copyright law. Just as copyright protection is limited in many respects, the protection by technological measures should be limited by equivalent mechanisms. **(b) Solution adopted by art. 6(4).** *General.* Art. 6(4) allows for the implementation of a wide variety of approaches to solving the tension between technological measures and copyright limitations. It allows Member States to take appropriate measures to help beneficiaries of copyright limitations benefiting from these limitations. The understanding of art. 6(4) is complicated by the fact that it uses the term 'measures' in four different contexts (voluntary measures by the rightholders, appropriate measures by the Member States, technological measures, and measures by the rightholders regarding the number of reproductions). Member States enjoy great freedom in two regards for implementing art. 6(4). First, the Directive does not state whether the obligations possible under art. 6(4) should be enacted as a statutory provision and whether the compliance with such obligations could be sought in court or should be left to alternative dispute resolution mechanisms. Second, the Directive leaves it to the Member States to decide what kind of obligations it will impose on rightholders under the umbrella of art. 6(4). Again, several possibilities exist. Rightholders may, for example, be required to make circumvention devices or services available to certain beneficiaries of copyright limitations (sometimes called a 'key escrow system' solution). They may also be required to adapt their technological measures so that it observes copyright limitations from the beginning (see recital 51). Another option is the mere statutory statement that rightholders have an obligation to cooperate with beneficiaries of copyright limitations. Yet another option is that rightholders are required to provide beneficiaries of a certain copyright limitation with several (copy-protected) copies of the work. However, there is one implementation approach which art. 6(4) specifically forbids, since the Directive does not allow beneficiaries of copyright limitations to circumvent technological measures and distribute tools needed for such circumvention on their own (here, the Directive deviates from the US Digital Millennium Copyright Act). This follows from the wording and system provided for in art. 6(4) and from the fact that art. 6(4) only limits the anti-circumvention provision of art. 6(1), but not the prohibition of preparatory activities in art. 6(2). *Limitations of the approach.* Art. 6(4) restricts the abilities of Member States to adopt appropriate legislation in three ways: first, art. 6(4)(1) states that 'voluntary measures taken by rightholders, including agreements between rightholders and other parties concerned' have priority over any legislative action (see art. 6, note 5(c)). Second, the ability of Member States to take legislative action differs among various copyright limitations. Regarding some limitations – such as copying privileges for libraries, researchers, museums, hospitals and disabled persons – Member States are, under certain conditions, obliged to take legislative action (art. 6(4)(1)). With regard to another copyright limitation – the privilege to make copies for private purposes – Member States are not obliged, but only entitled to take such action (art. 6(4)(2)). With regard to a third set of copyright limitations – including the privilege to quote existing works for purposes of criticism or review or to use them for parody purposes – Member States are not even entitled to take such action. Even the limitation concerning temporary copies in art. 5(1) falls in this third category. The most important restriction of the Member States, however, which was introduced very late in the legislative process, is that according to art. 6(4)(4), Member States are not allowed to take any legislative action at all, if the rightholder offers technologically protected content over the Internet, and access is conditioned on the formation of a contract. This gives rightholders the possibility to dispose of all copyright limitations. **(c) Mandatory measures to facilitate access (art. 6 (4)(1)).** Art. 6(4)(1) requires Member States, under certain conditions, to take appropriate measures to help beneficiaries of copyright limitations to benefit from these limitations. *Copyright limitations covered.* Art. 6(4)(1) only covers the limitations of arts. 5(2)(a), (c), (d), (e) and of arts. 5(3)(a), (b) and (e). *Appropriate measures by Member States.* The Directive does not define, nor is it discussed in the recitals, what such appropriate measures should look like in practice. For possibilities and implementation by the Member States, see note 5(b) and (c). *Legal access to the work.* Art. 6(4)(1) only applies if the beneficiary of the copyright limitation has legal access to the work or other subject matter. Art. 6(4)(1) does not grant beneficiaries a right of initial access to the work, nor does it grant any right to those having obtained illegal copies. *Absence of voluntary measures by rightholders.* Art. 6(4)(1) does not apply if rightholders have taken voluntary measures to reconcile technological measures with copyright limitations. For comments on the term 'rightholder', see art. 1, note 3. Art. 6(4)(1) lists agreements between rightholders and other parties concerned as an example. If, for example, rightholders reach an agreement with a library association that enables libraries to benefit from relevant copyright limitations in spite of technological measures, the Member States cannot take legislative action under art. 6(4)(1). The Directive does not provide clear guidelines on how long Member States have to wait before they can impose obligations on rightholders. Recital 51 merely requires Member States to wait for a 'reasonable period of time'. It is also unclear under which conditions the mere authority to impose obligations changes to a duty to impose obligations. It is questionable, for example, whether this duty only emerges once an abusive behaviour by a rightholder has become apparent. **(d) Optional measures to facilitate private copying (art. 6 (4)(2)).** Art. 6(4)(2) allows, but does not require, Member States, under certain conditions, to take appropriate measures to help beneficiaries of a particular copyright limitation benefiting from this limitation. *Copyright limitation covered.* Art. 6(4)(2) only covers the limitation of art. 5(2)(b). *Appropriate measures by the Member States.* By allowing the Member States to 'also take such measures', art. 6(4)(2) refers to the 'appropriate measures' described in art. 6(4)(1) (see art. 6, note 5(c)). *Absence of voluntary measures by rightholders.* Art. 6(4)(2) does not apply if rightholders have already made possible the reproduction for private use to the extent necessary to benefit from art. 5(2)(b). If, for example, the rightholder designs his technological measure in a way that reproductions for private use are not prevented, Member States are not allowed to take any legislative action under art. 6(4)(2). *In accordance with arts. 5(2)(b) and (5).* The reference to arts. 5(2)(b) and 5 and recital 52 are intended to emphasise that rightholders must, under all circumstances, receive fair compensation. *Measures regarding the number of reproductions.* Even if Member States are allowed to take appropriate measures under art. 6(4)(2), this does not prevent rightholders from using technological measures to limit the number of reproductions in accordance with art. 5(2)(b) and art. 5(5). **(e) Other copyright limitations.** The copyright limitations of arts. 5(1), 5(2)(c), (d) and (f) to (o) are not covered by the system of arts. 6(4)(1) and (2). Member States are not allowed to take appropriate measures in order to enable beneficiaries of these limitations to benefit from them. Therefore, rightholders have the power to override these limitations by using technological measures. Concerning the limited term of copyright protection, another system applies. If a work has fallen into the public domain because the term of copyright protection has expired (see art. 1 of the Term Directive), any technological measure preventing the reproduction of the work does not benefit from art. 6, (see art. 6, note 2(a)). **(f) Legal protection of art. 6 (4) measures (art. 6(4)(3)).** In complying with art. 6(4)(1) and (2), rightholders may use technological measures that allow beneficiaries of copyright limitations to carry out certain activities but prevent others. They may, for example, allow a certain number of reproductions for private use, but prevent reproductions beyond that number. According to art. 6(4)(3), such technological measures themselves are protected against circumvention. **(g) On-demand access (art. 6(4)(4)).** Art. 6(4)(4) is a major exception to the approach adopted in arts. 6(4)(1) and (2) (see art. 6, note 5(b)). Member States are not allowed to take appropriate measures described in arts. 6(4)(1) and (2) if the work or other protected subject matter is made available to the public on agreed contractual terms on an on-demand basis. The user has to enter into a contractual agreement before accessing the work or other subject matter, which includes mass-market contracts. Furthermore, the work or other subject matter must be offered for on-demand access, as described by the right of making available to the public in art. 3(2). The right of making available to the public covers all transmissions over the Internet, as long as the user is able to choose and initialize that transmission (see art. 3, note 2(b)). According to recital 53, non-interactive Internet transmissions do not fall under this provision. What constitutes a non-interactive transmission is unclear. Only live webcasting, webradio and similar transmissions where the user cannot choose the time of the transmission qualify for non-interactive transmissions. In this regard, it has been stated by some European Commission officials that art. 6(4)(4) is only intended to deal with video-on-demand and similar services. However, this is not what the broad wording of art. 6(4)(4) implies. **(h) Application to other directives (art. 6(4)(5)).** As art. 6(3) sentence 1 refers to the rightholder 'of any copyright or any right related to copyright ... or the sui generis right', art. 6 is applicable to technological measures that protect works, 'sui generis' databases as defined in art. 7 of the Database Directive, and the subject matter of the four European neighbouring rights as defined in arts. 7 et seq. of the Rental Right Directive. These Directives include limitations that are, in some cases, similar to the limitations listed in art. 5 of the present Directive, (see art. 10 of the Rental Right Directive and arts. 6 and 9 of the Database Directive). Art. 6(2)(b) of the Database Directive, for example, is comparable to art. 5(3)(a) of the present Directive. Art. 6(4)(5) of the present Directive states in this particular case that, if a database is protected by a technological measure, Member States are required under the conditions of art. 6(4)(1) to take appropriate measures to enable beneficiaries of art. 6(2)(b) of the Database Directive to benefit from this limitation. The mechanism of art. 6(4)(5) only applies under two conditions. First, it only applies to limitations found in the Rental Right Directive and the Database Directive that are comparable to a limitation found in art. 5 of the present Directive. Second, it only applies if the conditions set out in art. 6(4)(4) are not fulfilled. If these conditions are not fulfilled, limitations found in the Rental Right Directive and the Database Directive can be undermined by technological measures, as art. 6(4)(1) and (2) does not apply. **(i) Relationship to levy systems.** For comments on the relationship between technological measures and levy systems, see art. 5, notes 3(b), (c) and (e).

[Obligations concerning rights-management information]

Article 7

(1) Member States shall provide for adequate legal protection against any person knowingly performing without authority any of the following acts:

   (a) the removal or alteration of any electronic rights-management information;

   (b) the distribution, importation for distribution, broadcasting, communication or making available to the public of works or other subject-matter protected under this Directive or under Chapter III of Directive 96/9/EC from which electronic rights-management information has been removed or altered without authority,

if such person knows, or has reasonable grounds to know, that by so doing he is inducing, enabling, facilitating or concealing an infringement of any copyright or any rights related to copyright as provided by law, or of the sui generis right provided for in Chapter in of Directive 96/9/EC.

(2) For the purposes of this Directive, the expression 'rights-management information' means any information provided by rightholders which identifies the work or other subject-matter referred to in this Directive or covered by the sui generis right provided for in Chapter in of Directive 96/9/EC, the author or any other rightholder, or information about the terms and conditions of use of the work or other subject-matter, and any numbers or codes that represent such information.

The first subparagraph shall apply when any of these items of information is associated with a copy of, or appears in connection with the communication to the public of, a work or other subject-matter referred to in this Directive or covered by the sui generis right provided for in Chapter in of Directive 96/9/EC.

1. General. Art. 7 implements arts. 12 WCT and 19 WPPT. **(a) Rights management information.** In order to provide a secure distribution platform for digital content, DRM systems not only have to protect content against copying, they must also offer means to identify and manage content. For this purpose, DRM systems use so-called 'rights management information' or 'metadata' to formally describe digital content and related parameters. With rights management information, the rightholder is able to control meticulously which consumer may access and use content under what circumstances and for what purpose. In particular, rights management information enables the machine-readable identification and description of content, content providers and rightholders (expressed in systems such as DOI), of usage rules under which content may be accessed and used (expressed in 'rights expression languages' and 'rights data dictionaries'), and of users of protected content. Rights management information may be stored in the special headers of a digital content format. It may also be embedded directly into the content with digital watermarking technologies. **(b) Anti-circumvention provision.** The technological expression of rights in rights management information is not failsafe. Once in a while, attackers will succeed in altering or deleting rights management information. If such an attack is successful, the content may be used without paying the appropriate fee. In order to prevent such attacks, the law provides regulations which prohibit the manipulation or deletion of metadata.

2. Definitions (para. 2). (a) Rights management information (para. 2(1)). *Information identifying the work, author or usage terms.* The rights management information identifies the work or other subject matter, any of its rightholders or the terms and conditions of use of the work. Therefore, if contractual terms describing the conditions under which a work may be accessed and used (e.g. reproduction only for private purposes or no CD burning) are expressed in a machine-readable form, such information is protected against removal or alteration. Art. 7(2)(1) relates to subject matter protected by copyright, related rights and database right. Rights management information that identifies subject matter which is in the public domain is outside the scope of art. 7. *Information identifying the user.* From a technical point of view, rights management information can be used and is often used to identify the individual user of a work. However, due to privacy concerns, art. 7 does not apply to rights management information identifying consumers (see recital 57). The removal or alteration of rights management information identifying consumers is not prohibited by art. 7. Recital 57 points out that rights management information systems should incorporate privacy safeguards in accordance with European privacy directives. *Numbers or codes.* The protection offered by art. 7 not only applies to rights management information itself, but also to machine-readable codes expressing this information (such as numbering schemes). **(b) Electronic rights management information.** Although art. 7(2) deals with rights management information in general, arts. 7(1)(a) and (b) show that art. 7 only applies to electronic rights management information. Therefore, numbering systems such as ISBN do not benefit from the protection of art. 7 as long as they are applied to tangible objects. If such numbering systems are applied to digitized works, however, they are covered by art. 7. **(c) Connection between rights management information and the work (para. 2(2)).** Art. 7 applies if the rights management information is associated with a copy of the work. This may be achieved, for example, by using digital watermarks (see also art. 7, note 1(a)). Art. 7 also applies if the rights management information only appears in connection with the communication to the public (see art. 3(2)) of the work or other subject matter. Therefore, it suffices if the rights management information is not directly attached to the work, but is only retrieved from a central database once the work is transmitted. It is not necessary that the rights management information is visible to the user any time.

3. Prohibitions (para. 1). (a) Prohibited activities. *Removal or alteration (para. 1(1)).* Art. 7(1)(1) makes it illegal to remove or alter electronic rights management information. The removal of a watermark that contains such right management information or a code that links to such information may therefore violate art. 7(1)(1). It may also violate art. 6(1) at the same time (see art. 6, note 2(a)). *Distribution et al. (para. 1(2)).* Art. 7(1)(2) outlaws the distribution, importation for distribution, broadcasting, communication or making available to the public of manipulated works or other subject matter. The mere reproduction of a manipulated work or the passing on of such work to a friend is not prohibited by art. 7. *Activities not covered.* The distribution of false electronic rights management information is not prohibited by art. 7. Preparatory activities (such as the production of devices that may be used to remove rights management information) are not covered by art. 7 either. Art. 7 also does not require rightholders to use rights management information. Only if a rightholder decides to use rights management information do they enjoy the protection of art. 7. **(b) Without authority.** Art. 7 applies only if the rights management information is removed or altered without the rightholder's consent and the removal or alteration is not authorized or even prescribed by law (e.g., privacy regulations). **(c) Subjective requirements.** *Knowingly without authority.* The person must know positively that he acts without authority when he removes or alters the rights management information or distributes, imports, broadcasts, communicates or makes a manipulated work available to the public. *Person knows or has reasonable grounds to know.* Furthermore, the person must know or have reasonable grounds to know that his activity is inducing, enabling, facilitating or concealing an infringement of any copyright, neighbouring rights or the 'sui generis' right of art. 7 et seq. of the Database Directive. **(d) Information hiding research.** Similar to cryptography research (see art. 6, notes 3(d) and 4(e)), practical experiments and tests are indispensable in the areas of steganography research, research into digital watermarks and similar information hiding research.

CHAPTER IV. COMMON PROVISIONS

[Sanctions and remedies]

Article 8

(1) **Member States shall provide appropriate sanctions and remedies in respect of infringements of the rights and obligations set out in this Directive and shall take all the measures necessary to ensure that those sanctions and remedies are applied. The sanctions thus provided for shall be effective, proportionate and dissuasive.**

(2) **Each Member State shall take the measures necessary to ensure that rightholders whose interests are affected by an infringing activity carried out on its territory can bring an action for damages and/or apply for an injunction and, where appropriate, for the seizure of infringing material as well as of devices, products or components referred to in Article 6(2).**

(3) **Member States shall ensure that rightholders are in a position to apply for an injunction against intermediaries whose services are used by a third party to infringe a copyright or related right.**

1. General. Art. 8 implements the obligations that stem from art. 14(2) WCT and art. 23(2) WPPT. Internationally, more detailed provisions regarding the enforcement of copyright law may be found in art. 41 et seq. TRIPS. Art. 12 of the Database Directive includes a similar general provision regarding remedies. However, both art. 8 of the present Directive and art. 12 of the Database Directive are of relatively little importance. It was the Enforcement Directive that harmonized the enforcement of intellectual property law in detail.

2. Sanctions (para. 1). Art. 8(1) requires Member States to provide effective, proportionate and dissuasive sanctions and remedies in respect of infringements of the rights granted in arts. 2-4 and 6-7. The provision leaves ample freedom to Member States on how to implement these obligations. Further obligations regarding the enforcement of the rights and obligations set out in arts. 2-4 and 6-7 may be found in the Enforcement Directive, which is applicable concurrently (see art. 2(2) and recital 16 of the Enforcement Directive). Art. 8(1) does not require Member States to create an obligation for Internet service providers to communicate personal data in the context of copyright infringement proceedings against their users; but it also does not prevent them from doing so (*Promusicae* (ECJ)).

3. Damages, injunction, seizure (para. 2). Art. 8(2) requires Member States to provide rightholders with the possibility of bringing actions for damages and applying for injunctions and seizures. For comments on the term 'rightholder', see art. 1, note 3. Art. 8(2) only steps in if interests of a rightholder are affected. This requires a direct or indirect violation of any rights and obligations set out in arts. 2-4 and 6-7. It is not sufficient that some interests of rightholders are affected that are not harmonized by this Directive. The ability to apply for the seizure of infringing material covers, for example, illegal reproductions of a work, but also devices that can be used for preparatory activities as described in art. 6(2). Like art. 8 (1), art. 8(2) also does not require Member States to create an obligations for Internet service providers to communicate personal data in the context of copyright infringement proceedings against their users; but it also does not prevent them from doing so (*Promusicae* (ECJ)).

4. Injunction against intermediaries (para. 3). (a) General. Art. 8(3) obligates Member States to enable rightholders to apply for an injunction against intermediaries. According to recital 59, in communications networks, intermediaries are best placed to bring infringing activities to an end. This possibility, recital 59 continues, should be available even where the acts carried out by the intermediary are exempted under art. 5. If, for example, a user violates the right of reproduction, an Internet service provider who simply transmits the user's data may not be liable for damages under arts. 8(1), (2), because pursuant to art. 5(1) the right of reproduction has not been violated. However, according to art. 8(3) and recital 59, the rightholder may still apply for an injunction against the intermediary (see also art. 12(3) of the e-Commerce Directive and *LSG-Gesellschaft zu Wahrnehmung von*

Leistungsschutzrechten (ECJ)). Art. 11 of the Enforcement Directive leaves art. 8(3) of this Directive unaffected (see recital 23 of the Enforcement Directive). **(b) Effect on ISP liability.** As a result, art. 8(3) plays an important role in the development of liability law for content, host and access providers. Internet service providers as well as owners of an online social networking platform can be intermediaries within the meaning of art. 8(3) (*UPC Telekabel Wien*; *SABAM* v *Netlog* (ECJ)). Rightholders may be able to seek an injunction against an Internet service provider even without proving that one of the provider's customers actually accessed a protected work in an infringing way (*UPC Telekabel Wien* (ECJ)). Determining the scope and procedures of injunctions under art. 8(3) is a matter for national law, although limitations arising from this Directive and other EU law – in particular fundamental rights enshrined in the Charter of Fundamental Rights of the European Union – must be observed (*Scarlet Extended*; *SABAM* v *Netlog*; *UPC Telekabel Wien* (ECJ)). An injunction must strike a balance between the interests of rightholders (art. 17(2) of the Charter), the freedom of Internet service providers to conduct business (art. 16 of the Charter), and the freedom of information of Internet users (art. 11 of the Charter) (*UPC Telekabel Wien* (ECJ)). This can become problematic when the injunction of the national court is very broad and does not specify which measures the Internet service provider must take ('open-ended injunction'). Such injunctions can be valid if the Internet service provider can avoid penalties for breach of such injunction by showing that it has taken all reasonable measures, if Internet users can still lawfully access information, if the injunction makes it difficult, at least, to access unauthorized works, and if Internet users have the possibility to assert their rights before court (*UPC Telekabel Wien* (ECJ)). The *UPC Telekabel Wien* decision of the ECJ only addresses whether open-ended website-blocking injunctions are compatible with EU law. It does not answer the question of whether such injunctions are required under EU law. Read together, this Directive, the e-Commerce, the Enforcement Directive and the Charter for Fundamental Rights of the EU must be interpreted as precluding an injunction against an access or a hosting service provider that would require the provider to install a content filtering system actively monitoring all data traffic coming through its system for copyright infringements for an unlimited period at its own expense (*Scarlet*; *SABAM* v *Netlog* (ECJ)). This does not necessarily mean, though, that service providers cannot be obliged to install less comprehensive filtering and content blocking systems.

[Continued application of other legal provisions]
Article 9

This Directive shall be without prejudice to provisions concerning in particular patent rights, trade marks, design rights, utility models, topographies of semi-conductor products, type faces, conditional access,

access to cable of broadcasting services, protection of national treasures, legal deposit requirements, laws on restrictive practices and unfair competition, trade secrets, security, confidentiality, data protection and privacy, access to public documents, the law of contract.

1. General. Art. 9 recognizes that the provisions of this Directive and legal instruments of the EU and its Member States from other areas of law overlap on many issues. In general, apart from art. 11, this Directive does not repeal any existing EU rules. Rather, the Directive is applicable in addition to those rules. On the relationship between this Directive and earlier copyright directives, see art. 1(2). On the relationship between copyright limitations and contractual agreements, see art. 5, note 1(f).

[Application over time]

Article 10

(1) The provisions of this Directive shall apply in respect of all works and other subject-matter referred to in this Directive which are, on 22 December 2002, protected by the Member States' legislation in the field of copyright and related rights, or which meet the criteria for protection under the provisions of this Directive or the provisions referred to in Article 1(2).

(2) This Directive shall apply without prejudice to any acts concluded and rights acquired before 22 December 2002.

1. Works protected on 22 December 2002 (para. 1). According to art. 10(1), the Directive applies to all works and other subject matter (including the four European neighbouring rights and the 'sui generis' database right inarts. 7 et seq. of the Database Directive) which were protected by the legislation of the Member States on 22 December 2002. This is the date when Member States were required to have implemented the Directive (see art. 13(1)).

2. Acts and rights before 22 December 2002 (para. 2). The Directive does not apply to any acts concluded or rights acquired before the date when Member States were required to have implemented the Directive (see art. 13(1)). The wording 'rights acquired' primarily concerns the licence contracts in which rightholders grant their exploitation rights to third parties on an exclusive or nonexclusive basis.

[Technical adaptations]

Article 11

(1)   Directive 92/100/EEC is hereby amended as follows:

(a) **Article 7 shall be deleted;**

(b) **Article 10(3) shall be replaced by the following: '3. The limitations shall only be applied in certain special cases which do not conflict with a normal exploitation of the subject-matter and do not unreasonably prejudice the legitimate interests of the rightholder.'**

(2) Article 3(2) of Directive 93/98/EEC shall be replaced by the following: '2. The rights of producers of phonograms shall expire 50 years after the fixation is made. However, if the phonogram has been lawfully published within this period, the said rights shall expire 50 years from the date of the first lawful publication. If no lawful publication has taken place within the period mentioned in the first sentence, and if the phonogram has been lawfully communicated to the public within this period, the said rights shall expire 50 years from the date of the first lawful communication to the public.

However, where through the expiry of the term of protection granted pursuant to this paragraph in its version before amendment by Directive 2001/29/EC of the European Parliament and of the Council of 22 May 2001 on the harmonisation of certain aspects of copyright and related rights in the information society[11] the rights of producers of phonograms are no longer protected on 22 December 2002, this paragraph shall not have the effect of protecting those rights anew.'

1. Changes in the Rental Right Directive (para. 1). With the adoption of the new Rental Right Directive, this paragraph, which revised the old Rental Right Directive, has become obsolete.

2. Change in the Term Directive (para. 2). With the adoption of the new Term Directive and the Term Extension Directive, this paragraph, which revised the old Term Directive, has likewise become obsolete.

[Final provisions]

Article 12

(1) Not later than 22 December 2004 and every three years thereafter, the Commission shall submit to the European Parliament, the Council and the Economic and Social Committee a report on the application of this Directive, in which, *inter alia,* on the basis of specific information supplied by the Member States, it shall examine in particular the application of Articles 5, 6 and 8 in the light of the development of the digital market. In the case of Article 6, it shall examine in particular whether that Article confers a sufficient level of protection and whether

---

11. OJ No. L 167, 22 June 2001, p. 10.

acts which are permitted by law are being adversely affected by the use of effective technological measures. Where necessary, in particular to ensure the functioning of the internal market pursuant to Article 14 of the Treaty, it shall submit proposals for amendments to this Directive.

(2) Protection of rights related to copyright under this Directive shall leave intact and shall in no way affect the protection of copyright.

(3) A contact committee is hereby established. It shall be composed of representatives of the competent authorities of the Member States. It shall be chaired by a representative of the Commission and shall meet either on the initiative of the chairman or at the request of the delegation of a Member State.

(4) The tasks of the committee shall be as follows:

- (a) to examine the impact of this Directive on the functioning of the internal market, and to highlight any difficulties;
- (b) to organise consultations on all questions deriving from the application of this Directive;
- (c) to facilitate the exchange of information on relevant developments in legislation and case-law, as well as relevant economic, social, cultural and technological developments;
- (d) to act as a forum for the assessment of the digital market in works and other items, including private copying and the use of technological measures.

1. Report by the European Commission (para. 1). Similar to other copyright Directives, art. 12(1) of the Directive requires the European Commission to produce a report on the application of the Directive every three years, starting on 22 December 2004.

2. Relationship between copyright and neighbouring rights (para. 2). This paragraph reinforces the notion that the neighbouring rights protected by arts. 2, 3(2) and 6-8 do not restrict the protection of copyright in any way. Such a provision can already be found in arts. 1 RC and 1(2) WPPT.

3. Contact committee (para. 3 and 4). The contact committee consists of representatives of the component ministries of the Member States as well as of the European Commission.

[Implementation]

Article 13

(1) Member States shall bring into force the laws, regulations and administrative provisions necessary to comply with this Directive before 22 December 2002. They shall forthwith inform the Commission thereof.

When Member States adopt these measures, they shall contain a reference to this Directive or shall be accompanied by such reference on the occasion of their official publication. The methods of making such reference shall be laid down by Member States.

(2) Member States shall communicate to the Commission the text of the provisions of domestic law which they adopt in the field governed by this Directive.

1. General. Member States were required to have transposed this Directive into their national laws by 22 December 2002. Only Greece and Denmark had met the deadline. The Directive did not have any effect on acts of using protected works or other subject matter before the date by which it should have been transposed into national law (*VG Wort and others* (ECJ)).

[Entry into force]

Article 14

This Directive shall enter into force on the day of its publication in the Official Journal of the European Communities.

1. General. The Directive was published in the Official Journal on 22 June 2001 and went into force on that day.

[Addressees]

Article 15

This Directive is addressed to the Member States.

1. General. Art. 15 reinforces that Directives are binding upon EU Member States (see art. 249(3) EC Treaty). According to Annex 17 No. 9(e) to the EEA Agreement, all EEA Member States are required to implement the Directive. Therefore, the Directive is not only binding on the EU Member States, but also on Iceland, Liechtenstein and Norway.

DIRECTIVE 2001/84/EC

(Resale Right Directive)

of the European Parliament and of the Council of 27 September 2001 on the resale right for the benefit of the author of an original work of art

[Introductory remarks]

1. Legislative history. Directive 2001/84/EC (the Resale Right Directive) harmonizes the resale right, also known as droit de suite. The Directive has travelled a long and windy road from the Commission's first proposal of 13 March 1996 to its final adoption by the Council and the European Parliament on 27 September 2001. More than two years elapsed between the Commission's amended proposal of 12 March 1998 to the Council's Common Position of 19 June 2000. This delay can largely be explained by the staunch opposition by those Member States that did not provide for a resale right prior to the Directive (such as the United Kingdom and the Netherlands) and feared that the introduction of such a right might negatively affect national art markets. In the end this opposition could not prevent the adoption of the Directive, although is has led to an unusually generous transposition period of over four years. Member States were obliged to implement the provisions of the Directive before 1 January 2006 (art. 12). Moreover, Member States that did not apply the resale right on the date of entry into force of the Directive (13 October 2001, see art. 13) were not required until 1 January 2012 to apply the resale right for the benefit of the heirs of deceased artists (art. 8(2) and (3)). A report on the implementation and effects of the Directive was published by the European Commission on 14 December 2011 (Report on the Resale Right Directive); see art. 11(1).

2. Harmonization. (a) Need for harmonization. The Directive aims at harmonizing, and for some countries introducing, the artist's resale right (droit de suite) in the Member States. Existing disparities in the laws of the Member States concerned not only the categories of works to which the resale right applied, but also the persons entitled to receive royalties, the rates applied, the transactions subject to the payment of a royalty, and the basis on which these were calculated (recital 9). These disparities negatively affected the functioning of the internal market in works of art (recital 10), and had allegedly led to the displacement of sales of original works of art to Member States where no such right existed or low rates were applied. All this led to unequal treatment of artists depending on where their works were sold (recital 14). **(b) No complete harmonization.** The Directive does not harmonize every aspect of the resale right. Harmonization is limited to those aspects that directly affect the functioning of the internal market and were liable to create or maintain distorted conditions of competition (recital 15), such as the scope of the resale right, the categories of works of art subject to the right, the persons entitled to receive royalties, the rates applied, the transactions subject to payment of a royalty and the debtor of the resale right. However, Member States remained free to provide domestic rules concerning the exercise of the resale right, particularly with regard to the way it is managed, and the collection and distribution of royalties. **(c) Aim of the resale right.** The resale right is intended to ensure that authors of graphic and plastic works of art share in the economic success of their original works of art. Given the fact that authors of other categories of works benefit from the successive exploitation of their works (e.g. publishing, film production, television broadcasting), the resale right is intended to create for authors of graphic and plastic works similar economic conditions by giving them the possibility of sharing in the 'successive' exploitation of their works (see recital 3). **(d) The resale right is an integral part of copyright.** The resale right is characterized as an integral part of copyright, and an essential prerogative for authors (recital 4). Thus the resale right applies only to works that are protected by copyright, and exists without having to fulfil any formality.

[Bibliography]

J. Cave, 'An Overview of the European Artist's Resale Right Directive 2001/84/EC and Its Implementation in the UK via the Artist's Resale Right Regulations 2005' (2006) *Journal of Intellectual Property Law & Practice* 242-246

J. Collins, 'Droit de suite: An Artistic Stroke of Genius? A Critical Exploration of the European Directive and its Resultant Effects' (2012) EIPR 305-312

W. Duchemin, 'The Community directive on the resale right' (2002) 191 RIDA 3-131

S. Hughes, 'Droit de Suite: A Critical Analysis of the Approved Directive' (1997) EIPR 694-700

J. Wuenschel, 'Art. 95 EC Revisited: Is the Artist's Resale Right Directive a Community Act Beyond EC Competence' (2009) *Journal of Intellectual Property Law & Practice* 130-136

[Preamble]

The European Parliament and the Council of the European Union, Having regard to the Treaty establishing the European Community, and in particular Article 95 thereof,

Having regard to the proposal from the Commission,[1]

Having regard to the opinion of the Economic and Social Committee,[2]

Acting in accordance with the procedure laid down in Article 251 of the Treaty,[3] **and in the light of the joint text approved by the Conciliation Committee on 6 June 2001, Whereas:**

(1) In the field of copyright, the resale right is an unassignable and inalienable right, enjoyed by the author of an original work of graphic or plastic art, to an economic interest in successive sales of the work concerned.

(2) The resale right is a right of a productive character which enables the author/artist to receive consideration for successive transfers of the work. The subject-matter of the resale right is the physical work, namely the medium in which the protected work is incorporated.

(3) The resale right is intended to ensure that authors of graphic and plastic works of art share in the economic success of their original works of art. It helps to redress the balance between the economic situation of authors of graphic and plastic works of art and that of other creators who benefit from successive exploitations of their works.

(4) The resale right forms an integral part of copyright and is an essential prerogative for authors. The imposition of such a right in all Member States meets the need for providing creators with an adequate and standard level of protection.

(5) Under Article 151(4) of the Treaty the Community is to take cultural aspects into account in its action under other provisions of the Treaty.

(6) The Berne Convention for the Protection of Literary and Artistic Works provides that the resale right is available only if legislation in the country to which the author belongs so permits. The right is therefore optional and subject to the rule of reciprocity. It follows from the case-law of the Court of Justice of the European Communities on the application of the principle of non-discrimination laid down in Article 12 of the Treaty, as shown in the judgment of 20 October 1993 in Joined Cases C-92/92 and C-326/92 Phil Collins and Others,[4] that domestic provisions containing reciprocity clauses cannot be relied upon in order to deny nationals of other Member States rights conferred on national authors.

---

1. OJ No. C 178, 21 June 1996, p. 16 and OJ No. C 125, 23 April 1998, p. 8.
2. OJ No. C 75, 10 March 1997, p. 17.
3. Opinion of the European Parliament of 9 April 1997 (OJ No. C 132, 28 April 1997, p. 88), confirmed on 27 October 1999, Council Common Position of 19 June 2000 (OJ No. C 300, 20 October 2000, p. 1) and Decision of the European Parliament of 13 December 2000 (OJ No. C 232, 17 August 2001, p. 173). Decision of the European Parliament of 3 July 2001 and Decision of the Council of 19 July 2001.
4. [1993] ECR I-5145.

The application of such clauses in the Community context runs counter to the principle of equal treatment resulting from the prohibition of any discrimination on grounds of nationality.

(7) The process of internationalisation of the Community market in modern and contemporary art, which is now being speeded up by the effects of the new economy, in a regulatory context in which few States outside the EU recognise the resale right, makes it essential for the European Community, in the external sphere, to open negotiations with a view to making Article 14b of the Berne Convention compulsory.

(8) The fact that this international market exists, combined with the lack of a resale right in several Member States and the current disparity as regards national systems which recognise that right, make it essential to lay down transitional provisions as regards both entry into force and the substantive regulation of the right, which will preserve the competitiveness of the European market.

(9) The resale right is currently provided for by the domestic legislation of a majority of Member States. Such laws, where they exist, display certain differences, notably as regards the works covered, those entitled to receive royalties, the rate applied, the transactions subject to payment of a royalty, and the basis on which these are calculated. The application or non-application of such a right has a significant impact on the competitive environment within the internal market, since the existence or absence of an obligation to pay on the basis of the resale right is an element which must be taken into account by each individual wishing to sell a work of art. This right is therefore a factor which contributes to the creation of distortions of competition as well as displacement of sales within the Community.

(10) Such disparities with regard to the existence of the resale right and its application by the Member States have a direct negative impact on the proper functioning of the internal market in works of art as provided for by Article 14 of the Treaty. In such a situation Article 95 of the Treaty constitutes the appropriate legal basis.

(11) The objectives of the Community as set out in the Treaty include laying the foundations of an ever closer union among the peoples of Europe, promoting closer relations between the Member States belonging to the Community, and ensuring their economic and social progress by common action to eliminate the barriers which divide Europe. To that end the Treaty provides for the establishment of an internal market which presupposes the abolition of obstacles to the free movement of goods, freedom to provide services and freedom of establishment, and for the introduction of a system ensuring that competition in the common market is not distorted. Harmonisation of Member States' laws on the resale right contributes to the attainment of these objectives.

(12) The Sixth Council Directive (77/388/EEC) of 17 May 1977 on the harmonisation of the laws of the Member States relating to turnover

taxes – common system of value added tax: uniform basis of assessment,[5] progressively introduces a Community system of taxation applicable inter alia to works of art. Measures confined to the tax field are not sufficient to guarantee the harmonious functioning of the art market. This objective cannot be attained without harmonisation in the field of the resale right.

(13) Existing differences between laws should be eliminated where they have a distorting effect on the functioning of the internal market, and the emergence of any new differences of that kind should be prevented. There is no need to eliminate, or prevent the emergence of, differences which cannot be expected to affect the functioning of the internal market.

(14) A precondition of the proper functioning of the internal market is the existence of conditions of competition which are not distorted. The existence of differences between national provisions on the resale right creates distortions of competition and displacement of sales within the Community and leads to unequal treatment between artists depending on where their works are sold. The issue under consideration has therefore transnational aspects which cannot be satisfactorily regulated by action by Member States. A lack of Community action would conflict with the requirement of the Treaty to correct distortions of competition and unequal treatment.

(15) In view of the scale of divergences between national provisions it is therefore necessary to adopt harmonising measures to deal with disparities between the laws of the Member States in areas where such disparities are liable to create or maintain distorted conditions of competition. It is not however necessary to harmonise every provision of the Member States' laws on the resale right and, in order to leave as much scope for national decision as possible, it is sufficient to limit the harmonisation exercise to those domestic provisions that have the most direct impact on the functioning of the internal market.

(16) This Directive complies therefore, in its entirety, with the principles of subsidiarity and proportionality as laid down in Article 5 of the Treaty.

(17) Pursuant to Council Directive 93/98/EEC of 29 October 1993 harmonising the term of protection of copyright and certain related rights,[6] the term of copyright runs for 70 years after the author's death. The same period should be laid down for the resale right. Consequently, only the originals of works of modern and contemporary art may fall within the scope of the resale right. However, in order to allow the legal systems of Member States which do not, at the time of the adoption of

---

5. OJ No. L 145, 13 June 1977, p. 1. Directive as last amended by Directive 1999/85/EC (OJ No. L 277, 28 October 1999, p. 34).
6. OJ No. L 290, 24 November 1993, p. 9.

this Directive, apply a resale right for the benefit of artists to incorporate this right into their respective legal systems and, moreover, to enable the economic operators in those Member States to adapt gradually to the aforementioned right whilst maintaining their economic viability, the Member States concerned should be allowed a limited transitional period during which they may choose not to apply the resale right for the benefit of those entitled under the artist after his death.

(18) The scope of the resale right should be extended to all acts of resale, with the exception of those effected directly between persons acting in their private capacity without the participation of an art market professional. This right should not extend to acts of resale by persons acting in their private capacity to museums which are not for profit and which are open to the public. With regard to the particular situation of art galleries which acquire works directly from the author, Member States should be allowed the option of exempting from the resale right acts of resale of those works which take place within three years of that acquisition. The interests of the artist should also be taken into account by limiting this exemption to such acts of resale where the resale price does not exceed EUR 10000.

(19) It should be made clear that the harmonisation brought about by this Directive does not apply to original manuscripts of writers and composers.

(20) Effective rules should be laid down based on experience already gained at national level with the resale right. It is appropriate to calculate the royalty as a percentage of the sale price and not of the increase in value of works whose original value has increased.

(21) The categories of works of art subject to the resale right should be harmonised.

(22) The non-application of royalties below the minimum threshold may help to avoid disproportionately high collection and administration costs compared with the profit for the artist. However, in accordance with the principle of subsidiarity, the Member States should be allowed to establish national thresholds lower than the Community threshold, so as to promote the interests of new artists. Given the small amounts involved, this derogation is not likely to have a significant effect on the proper functioning of the internal market.

(23) The rates set by the different Member States for the application of the resale right vary considerably at present. The effective functioning of the internal market in works of modern and contemporary art requires the fixing of uniform rates to the widest possible extent.

(24) It is desirable to establish, with the intention of reconciling the various interests involved in the market for original works of art, a system consisting of a tapering scale of rates for several price bands. It is important to reduce the risk of sales relocating and of the circumvention of the Community rules on the resale right.

(25) The person by whom the royalty is payable should, in principle, be the seller. Member States should be given the option to provide for derogations from this principle in respect of liability for payment. The seller is the person or undertaking on whose behalf the sale is concluded.

(26) Provision should be made for the possibility of periodic adjustment of the threshold and rates. To this end, it is appropriate to entrust to the Commission the task of drawing up periodic reports on the actual application of the resale right in the Member States and on the impact on the art market in the Community and, where appropriate, of making proposals relating to the amendment of this Directive.

(27) The persons entitled to receive royalties must be specified, due regard being had to the principle of subsidiarity. It is not appropriate to take action through this Directive in relation to Member States' laws of succession. However, those entitled under the author must be able to benefit fully from the resale right after his death, at least following the expiry of the transitional period referred to above.

(28) The Member States are responsible for regulating the exercise of the resale right, particularly with regard to the way this is managed. In this respect management by a collecting society is one possibility. Member States should ensure that collecting societies operate in a transparent and efficient manner. Member States must also ensure that amounts intended for authors who are nationals of other Member States are in fact collected and distributed. This Directive is without prejudice to arrangements in Member States for collection and distribution.

(29) Enjoyment of the resale right should be restricted to Community nationals as well as to foreign authors whose countries afford such protection to authors who are nationals of Member States. A Member State should have the option of extending enjoyment of this right to foreign authors who have their habitual residence in that Member State.

(30) Appropriate procedures for monitoring transactions should be introduced so as to ensure by practical means that the resale right is effectively applied by Member States. This implies also a right on the part of the author or his authorised representative to obtain any necessary information from the natural or legal person liable for payment of royalties. Member States which provide for collective management of the resale right may also provide that the bodies responsible for that collective management should alone be entitled to obtain information,

Have adopted this Directive:

CHAPTER I. SCOPE

[Subject matter of the resale right]

Article 1

(1) **Member States shall provide, for the benefit of the author of an original work of art, a resale right, to be defined as an inalienable right, which cannot be waived, even in advance, to receive a royalty based on the sale price obtained for any resale of the work, subsequent to the first transfer of the work by the author.**

(2) **The right referred to in paragraph 1 shall apply to all acts of resale involving as sellers, buyers or intermediaries art market professionals, such as salesrooms, art galleries and, in general, any dealers in works of art.**

(3) **Member States may provide that the right referred to in paragraph 1 shall not apply to acts of resale where the seller has acquired the work directly from the author less than three years before that resale and where the resale price does not exceed EUR 10000.**

(4) **The royalty shall be payable by the seller. Member States may provide that one of the natural or legal persons referred to in paragraph 2 other than the seller shall alone be liable or shall share liability with the seller for payment of the royalty.**

1. **Definition of the resale right (para. 1). (a) Inalienable right.** The resale right is an inalienable (unassignable) right that cannot be waived, to receive a royalty based on the sale price obtained for any resale of an original work of art, subsequent to the first transfer of the work by the author. The right cannot be transferred, not even in advance, irrespective of whether it concerns a transfer for valuable consideration or not. Moreover, an artist cannot commit in a contract never to claim the royalty, not even before the royalty is due. **(b) Original work of art.** Pursuant to art. 1(1), the resale right applies only to original works of art. These works are more precisely defined in art. 2(1). An important characteristic of the resale right is that its subject matter is the physical work, namely the medium in which the protected work of art is incorporated (recital 2). Only in case of a resale of this object is a royalty due. **(c) Remuneration right.** The resale right is not an exclusive right, but a right to remuneration. The Directive characterizes the resale right as 'a right of a productive character' which enables the author/artist to receive consideration for successive transfers of the work (recital 2).

2. **Acts of resale (para. 2). (a) Resale.** The resale right applies only to acts of resale of an original work of art, subsequent to the first transfer of the work by the author. Therefore, no royalty is due when the author of an original work of art sells his own work. **(b) Resellers.** The resale right only applies to acts of resale involving, as sellers, buyers or intermediaries, art market professionals, such as salesrooms, art galleries and, in general,

any dealers in works of art. Acts of private resale are not covered by the resale right; see note (f). The list of art market professionals in art. 1(2) is non-exhaustive. **(c) Any resale.** The resale right applies to 'any' resale. Consequently, a royalty may have to be paid more than once for the same original work of art. Once the first transfer of the work by the author has taken place, a royalty is due each time a resale fulfilling the conditions laid down in art. 1(2) occurs. **(d) A transfer of the work by the author.** It is possible that the person who sells the author's work did not buy the work from the author but obtained it in some other way. Perhaps the author has made a donation. Even if in this case the beneficiary of the donation subsequently sells the original work of art that was donated by the author of this work, a royalty must be paid. Art. 1(1) clearly stipulates that the resale right applies to any resale subsequent to the first 'transfer' by the author. So, the legal character of this first transfer is of no importance. **(e) Resale by heirs.** It can be argued that the resale right also applies to the first resale by the heirs or devisees of the author of the work. An amendment to the Directive by the European Parliament that would have exempted the first resale by the author's heirs was not adopted. Note that ownership of the resale right and of the physical object in which the work is incorporated may be in different hands. The Directive does not concern the Member States' succession laws (recital 27). **(f) Private resale excluded.** No royalty must be paid in the event of a resale effected directly between persons acting in their private capacity without the participation of an art market professional and in case of acts of resale by persons acting in their private capacity to museums which are not for profit and which are open to the public (recital 18). **(g) Agreements with galleries.** Galleries often agree with artists not to buy their works but to offer the opportunity to exhibit them. In this situation the gallery will almost always receive a percentage based on the sale price obtained for the work. However if in these situations the work is sold no royalty will have to be paid because the sale will take place between the author and the buyer of his work.

   3. Acts of resale excluded (para. 3). Member States may provide that the resale right shall not apply to acts of resale where the seller has acquired the work directly from the author less than three years before that resale and where the resale price does not exceed EUR 10,000. Such situations are those where art galleries acquire works directly from authors who are often unknown, and then sell these works (recital 18). The purpose of this provision is not to discourage such galleries from buying works of unknown artists.

   4. The debtor of the resale right (para. 4). In principle, the person by whom the royalty is payable shall be the seller, that is, the person or undertaking on whose behalf the sale is concluded (recital 25). But Member States may derogate from this principle, by providing that one of the art market professionals, such as salesrooms, art galleries and, in general, any dealers in works of art, who are involved in acts of resale as buyers or intermediaries, shall alone be liable or shall share liability with the seller for the payment of the royalty. While the Directive makes provision about the person by whom the royalty is payable (i.e. the person liable for payment of the royalty to the author), it does not designate the person who must ultimately bear the cost of the royalty. According to the Court of Justice, art. 1(4) must be interpreted as not precluding the person by whom the resale royalty is payable, designated as such by national law, whether that is the seller or an art market professional involved in the transaction, from agreeing with any other person, including the buyer, that that other person will definitively bear, in whole or in part, the cost of the royalty, provided that a contractual arrangement of that kind does not affect the obligations and liability which the person by whom the royalty is payable has towards the author (*Christie's France* (ECJ)).

[Works of art to which the resale right relates]

Article 2

(1) For the purposes of this Directive, 'original work of art' means works of graphic or plastic art such as pictures, collages, paintings, drawings, engravings, prints, lithographs, sculptures, tapestries, ceramics, glassware and photographs, provided they are made by the artist himself or are copies considered to be original works of art.

(2) Copies of works of art covered by this Directive, which have been made in limited numbers by the artist himself or under his authority, shall be considered to be original works of art for the purposes of this Directive. Such copies will normally have been numbered, signed or otherwise duly authorised by the artist.

1. **Definition of original work of art (para. 1). (a) Definition and non-exhaustive enumeration.** Pursuant to art. 1(1), the resale right applies only to original works of art. These are defined in art. 2(1) as works of graphic or plastic art. Consequently, the resale right only applies to works of graphic or plastic art. The wording of art. 2(1) indicates that the enumeration in this provision of the different types of works of graphic or plastic art is non-exhaustive and only exemplary. It is important to underline that only works of graphic or plastic art protected by copyright can be subject to the resale right. Copies of works of art that have been produced in limited numbers, also qualify as original works of art (see art. 2(2) and note 2). **(b) Assistance of a third person.** The original work of graphic or plastic art need not be made entirely by the author himself. The resale right also applies when the author has been assisted by a third party, such as a master craftsman, for the material realization of his work, as would be the case for a sculpture cast in bronze. **(c) Original manuscripts of writers or composers.** The Directive harmonizes the categories of works that are subject to the resale right (recital 21). Recital 19 clarifies that the Directive does not apply to original

manuscripts of writers or composers. Member States therefore remain free to include such manuscripts as objects of the resale right. **(d) Architectural works and master copies of cinematographic works.** The resale right only relates to original works of graphic or plastic art. It can be argued that architectural works and master copies of cinematographic works cannot be qualified as such, and are therefore not subject to the resale right.

2. Copies of original works of art (para. 2). (a) Copies subject to the resale right. The resale right not only relates to an original work of graphic or plastic art made by the author in a single copy ('a unique copy'). It also applies to an original work of graphic or plastic art from which several copies are made, and even to those copies themselves. Copies are subject to the resale right if they have been made in limited numbers by the artist himself or under his authority. Such copies will normally have been numbered, signed or otherwise duly authorized by the artist. For instance copies of etchings and engravings will be considered to be original works of art, if they are signed by the author and numbered, and the total amount of copies made is also mentioned. Note that the number of copies made will often depend on the reproduction technique used. Certain art forms such as etching, engraving and lithography will inevitably lead to the making of several copies. However, para. 2, first sentence clearly requires that a limited number of copies have been made. Existing or professional customs may not be taken into account. **(b) Copies made after the death of the author.** The wording of para. 2, first sentence implies that the resale right will not relate to copies made after the death of the author, even if they have been made in limited numbers, when those copies are not made under the authority of the author.

CHAPTER II. PARTICULAR PROVISIONS

[Threshold]

Article 3

(1) **It shall be for the Member States to set a minimum sale price from which the sales referred to in Article 1 shall be subject to resale right.**

(2) **This minimum sale price may not under any circumstances exceed EUR 3000.**

1. Threshold (para. 1). The Directive offers Member States the possibility of setting a threshold below which no resale right is due. So Member States can set in their national legislation a minimum sale price from which sales shall be subject to the resale right. This may help avoid disproportionately high collection and administration costs compared with the profit for the artist (recital 22).

2. Minimum sale price (para. 2). Art. 3(2) provides that the minimum sale price the Member States may set and below which no resale right is due may not exceed EUR 3,000 Given art. 3(1), Member States are allowed to establish national thresholds lower than this Community threshold of EUR 3,000 By doing this they can promote the interests of new artists (recital 22). The minimum threshold rates foreseen by Member States vary between EUR 15 and EUR 3,000 (Report on the Resale Right Directive). The sale price referred to in art. 3 is without taxes (see art. 5).

[Rates]

Article 4

(1) The royalty provided for in Article 1 shall be set at the following rates:
- **(a) 4% for the portion of the sale price up to EUR 50000;**
- **(b) 3% for the portion of the sale price from EUR 50000.01 to EUR 200000;**
- **(c) 1% for the portion of the sale price from EUR 200000.01 to EUR 350000;**
- **(d) 0.5% for the portion of the sale price from EUR 350000.01 to EUR 500000;**
- **(e) 0.25% for the portion of the sale price exceeding EUR 500000. However, the total amount of the royalty may not exceed EUR 12500.**

(2) By way of derogation from paragraph 1, Member States may apply a rate of 5% for the portion of the sale price referred to in paragraph 1(a).

(3) If the minimum sale price set should be lower than EUR 3000, the Member State shall also determine the rate applicable to the portion of the sale price up to EUR 3000; this rate may not be lower than 4%.

1. Rates. This provision sets the rate of the resale right. The Directive provides a system that divides the sale price of the original work of art subject to the resale right into different price bands to which a degressive rate scale is applied. This schedule is aimed at reconciling the different interests of all the parties that operate on the market of original works of arts. It is also seen as necessary to reduce the risk of sales relocation and of the circumvention of the Community rules on the resale right (recital 24). It is clear that the risk of sales relocation especially exists in the case of sales that command the highest prices. The sale price referred to in art. 4 is without taxes (see art. 5).

2. Maximum amount (para. 1). Art. 4(1) sets the maximum amount of the resale royalty at EUR 12,500. This is intended to reduce the risk of sales relocating towards countries where a resale right is not known or not applied, especially in cases where the sale price of an original work of art is very high.

3. Derogation (para. 2). According to art. 4(1) the resale royalty shall be set at 4% for the portion of the sale price up to EUR 50,000. Art. 4(2) allows that by way of derogation, Member States may apply a rate of 5% for that first portion of the sale price. This derogation reflects the fact that several Members States already applied a rate of 5% before the implementation of the Resale Right Directive. It also takes into account that sales in this price band mainly concern the domestic market, making a difference of 1% at this level unlikely to have a significant impact on the internal market.

4. Minimum sale price (para. 3). Member States are free to set a minimum sale price for works that are subject to the resale right, but this may not exceed EUR 3,000. If a Member State sets a minimum sale price lower than EUR 3,000, it has to determine the rate applicable to the portion of the sale price up to EUR 3,000. This rate may not be lower than 4%, but Member States may elect to set a higher rate.

[Calculation basis]

Article 5

The sale prices referred to in Articles 3 and 4 are net of tax.

1. Sale price. The sale prices referred to in arts. 3 and 4 are without taxes. Thus, the sale price mentioned in these articles is the price the buyer has to pay including, depending on the kind of the resale (public or not), the (administration) costs, the fees of those involved in the resale like intermediaries or public servants, and so on. The sale price does not include taxes, like VAT.

[Persons entitled to receive royalties]

Article 6

(1) The royalty provided for under Article 1 shall be payable to the author of the work and, subject to Article 8(2), after his death to those entitled under him/her.

(2) Member States may provide for compulsory or optional collective management of the royalty provided for under Article 1.

1. Persons entitled (para. 1). (a) General rule. Pursuant to art. 6(1) the royalty provided for under the Directive shall be payable to the author of the work. After the author's death it shall be payable to those entitled under him. Member States are free to make their own legislative choice in determining the categories of persons capable of benefiting from the resale right after the death of the author of a work of art (*Fundación Gala-Salvador Dalí and*

VEGAP (ECJ)). According to the ECJ, while the Union legislature wanted those entitled under the author to benefit fully from the resale right after his death, it did not, in accordance with the principle of subsidiarity, consider it appropriate to take action through the Directive in relation to Member States' laws of succession, thus leaving to each Member State the task of defining the categories of persons capable of being considered, under national law, as those entitled. Art. 6(1) must therefore be interpreted as not precluding a provision of national law which reserves the benefit of the resale right to the artist's heirs at law alone, to the exclusion of testamentary legatees. The ECJ also stated that a national court, for the purposes of applying the national provision transposing art. 6(1), must take due account of all the relevant rules for the resolution of conflicts of laws relating to the transfer on succession of the resale right. After all, there is nothing in the Resale Right Directive to indicate that the European Union legislature intended to rule out the application of rules governing coordination between the various national laws relating to succession, in particular those of private international law which are intended to govern a conflict of laws (*Fundación Gala-Salvador Dalí and VEGAP* (ECJ)). **(b) Exception.** Art. 8(2) and (3) provides that those Member States that did not apply the resale right on 13 October 2001 (date of entry into force of the Directive; see art. 13) were not required, for a period expiring not later than 1 January 2012, to apply the resale right for the benefit of those entitled under the artist after his death. Austria, Ireland, Malta, the Netherlands and the UK made use of this exception (Report on the Resale Right Directive). As the derogation of art. 8(2) and (3) came to an end on 1 January 2012, the general rule that the royalty provided for under the Directive shall be payable to the author of the work and after his death to those entitled under him must also be applied in these countries without any exception.

2. Collective management of the resale right (para. 2). Member States are free to provide for compulsory or optional collective management of the resale right. While the majority of Member States provide for obligatory collective management of the resale right, a significant number of States have opted for optional collective management (Report on the Resale Right Directive). If Member States provide for collective management, they must ensure that collective societies operate transparently and efficiently (recital 28). The Directive also leaves Member States free to make arrangements for the collection and distribution of royalties, but in any case they must ensure that sums intended for authors who are nationals of other Member States are collected and distributed (see recital 28).

[Third-country nationals entitled to receive royalties]

Article 7

(1) Member States shall provide that authors who are nationals of third countries and, subject to Article 8(2), their successors in title shall

enjoy the resale right in accordance with this Directive and the legislation of the Member State concerned only if legislation in the country of which the author or his/her successor in title is a national permits resale right protection in that country for authors from the Member States and their successors in title.

(2) On the basis of information provided by the Member States, the Commission shall publish as soon as possible an indicative list of those third countries which fulfil the condition set out in paragraph 1. This list shall be kept up to date.

(3) Any Member State may treat authors who are not nationals of a Member State but who have their habitual residence in that Member State in the same way as its own nationals for the purpose of resale right protection.

1. Third-country nationals entitled only in case of reciprocity (para. 1). **(a) General rule.** From ECJ case law, based on the principle of non-discrimination laid down in art. 18(1) of the Treaty on the Functioning of the European Union, it can be concluded that nationals of Member States can claim the resale right that arises in connection with their works in other EU countries (see *Phil Collins* (ECJ)). But the question remains whether non-EU nationals are entitled to resale right. Art. 14ter(2) BC submits the resale right to the principle of reciprocity. Art. 7(1) of the Directive similarly requires reciprocity. Member States shall provide that authors who are nationals of third countries and their successors in title shall enjoy the resale right in accordance with the Directive and the legislation of the Member State concerned only if legislation in the country of which the author or his successor in title is a national permits resale right protection in that country for authors from the Member States and their successors in title. Clearly the protection afforded by this third country must be comparable to the protection offered by the Directive (recital 29). **(b) Exception.** Member States that did not apply the resale right on 13 October 2001 (date of the entry into force of the Directive; see art. 13) were not required, for a period expiring not later than 1 January 2012, to apply the resale right for the benefit of those entitled under the foreign artist after his death (see art. 8(2) and (3)). However this exception came to an end on 1 January 2012. Consequently, in these countries a distinction can no longer be made between the foreign artist himself and those entitled under him after his death. If in these countries the foreign artist is entitled to the resale right, then those entitled under him after his death will also be entitled.

2. Third-countries offering comparable protection (para. 2). On the basis of information provided by the Member States, the Commission must publish an indicative list of those third countries which afford a comparable protection to authors who are nationals of Member States. This list must be kept up to date. It has not yet been published.

3. Freedom to extend the protection (para. 3). Art. 7(3) leaves Member States the freedom to extend enjoyment of the resale right to authors who are not nationals of a Member State but who have their habitual residence in that State. If a Member State so decides, these foreign authors are to be treated in the same way as its own nationals.

[Term of protection of the resale right]

Article 8

(1) **The term of protection of the resale right shall correspond to that laid down in Article 1 of Directive 93/98/EEC.**

(2) **By way of derogation from paragraph 1, those Member States which do not apply the resale right on (the entry into force date referred to in Article 13), shall not be required, for a period expiring not later than 1 January 2010, to apply the resale right for the benefit of those entitled under the artist after his/her death.**

(3) **A Member State to which paragraph 2 applies may have up to two more years, if necessary to enable the economic operators in that Member State to adapt gradually to the resale right system while maintaining their economic viability, before it is required to apply the resale right for the benefit of those entitled under the artist after his/her death. At least 12 months before the end of the period referred to in paragraph 2, the Member State concerned shall inform the Commission giving its reasons, so that the Commission can give an opinion, after appropriate consultations, within three months following the receipt of such information. If the Member State does not follow the opinion of the Commission, it shall within one month inform the Commission and justify its decision. The notification and justification of the Member State and the opinion of the Commission shall be published in the Official Journal of the European Communities and forwarded to the European Parliament.**

(4) **In the event of the successful conclusion, within the periods referred to in Article 8(2) and (3), of international negotiations aimed at extending the resale right at international level, the Commission shall submit appropriate proposals.**

1. Term of protection (para. 1). The term of protection of the resale right corresponds to that laid down in the Term Directive (see art. 1 Term Directive). Art. 8(1) still refers to Directive 93/98/EEC. This directive was meanwhile repealed and replaced by Directive 2006/116/EC (Term Directive). Pursuant to art. 12(2) of that Directive, references made to the repealed Directive shall be construed as being made to the new Term Directive and should be read in accordance with the correlation table in Annex II of that Directive. Consequently, art. 8(1) of the Resale Right Directive should be read as meaning that the term of protection of the resale right shall correspond to that laid down in art. 1 of Directive 2006/116/EC. Since art. 8(1) does not mention art. 4 of the Term Directive (protection of previously unpublished works), no resale right can be invoked for works that are subject to that special protection (see Term Directive, art. 4).

2. Persons entitled after the author's death (para. 2). Pursuant to art. 6(1), the resale royalty shall be payable to the author of the work, and after his death to those entitled under him. However, according to art. 8(2) Member States that did not apply the resale right on 13 October 2001 (the date of the entry into force of the Directive; see art. 13) were not required until 1 January 2010 to apply the resale right for the benefit of those entitled under the artist after his death. This exception could also be applied to those entitled under a third-country national after his death (see art. 7, note 1(b)).

3. Extra term of two years (para. 3). Member States that did not apply the resale right on 13 October 2001 could decide not to apply the resale right for the benefit of those entitled under the artist after his death for a period expiring not later than 1 January 2010. Pursuant to art. 8(3) these Member States had another two years, if necessary, to enable their economic operators to adapt gradually to the resale right while maintaining their economic viability, before they were required to apply the resale right for the benefit of the successors mentioned in title. So an additional two-year transition period could be granted, if appropriate justification was presented. Austria, Ireland, Malta, the Netherlands and the UK made use of art. 8(2) and (3) (Report on the Resale Right Directive). But this derogation came to an end on 1 January 2012, at which point the Resale Right Directive had to be fully implemented in all Member States. Consequently, in these countries as from 1 January 2012 the resale right shall also be payable after the death of the author of the work to those entitled under him.

[Right to obtain information]

Article 9

The Member States shall provide that for a period of three years after the resale, the persons entitled under Article 6 may require from any art market professional mentioned in Article 1(2) to furnish any information that may be necessary in order to secure payment of royalties in respect of the resale.

1. Right to information. Member States must introduce appropriate procedures for monitoring transactions so as to ensure by practical means that the resale right is effectively applied by them (see recital 30). Therefore Member States must provide that, for a period of three years after the resale, the persons entitled to receive royalties may require from any art market professional to furnish any information necessary in order to secure payment of royalties in respect of the resale. This right to information may also be exercised by the author's authorized representative, such as a collecting society. Member States which provide for collective management of the resale right may even provide that the bodies responsible for collective management are exclusively entitled to obtain information (see recital 30). Clearly, the right to obtain information does not apply to acts of resale outside the scope of the resale right.

CHAPTER III. FINAL PROVISIONS

[Application in time]

Article 10

This Directive shall apply in respect of all original works of art as defined in article 2 which, on 1 January 2006, are still protected by the legislation of the Member States in the field of copyright or meet the criteria for protection under the provisions of this Directive at that date.

1. Application in time. The Directive, and the national provisions transposing it, apply in respect of all original works of art as defined in art. 2 that were created before the implementation deadline (1 January 2006; see art. 12(1)) and which on that date were still protected by copyright in the Member States or, if this was not the case, meet the criteria for protection under the provisions of the Directive on that same date (see art. 2).

[Revision clause]

Article 11

(1) The Commission shall submit to the European Parliament, the Council and the Economic and Social Committee not later than 1 January 2009 and every four years thereafter a report on the implementation and the effect of this Directive, paying particular attention to the competitiveness of the market in modern and contemporary art in the Community, especially as regards the position of the Community in relation to relevant markets that do not apply the resale right and the fostering of artistic creativity and the management procedures in the Member States. It shall examine in particular its impact on the internal market and the effect of the introduction of the resale right in those Member States that did not apply the right in national law prior to the entry into force of this Directive. Where appropriate, the Commission shall submit proposals for adapting the minimum threshold and the rates of royalty to take account of changes in the sector, proposals relating to the maximum amount laid down in Article 4(1) and any other proposal it may deem necessary in order to enhance the effectiveness of this Directive.

(2) A Contact Committee is hereby established. It shall be composed of representatives of the competent authorities of the Member States. It shall be chaired by a representative of the Commission and shall meet either on the initiative of the Chairman or at the request of the delegation of a Member State.

(3) The task of the Committee shall be as follows:

- **to organise consultations on all questions deriving from application of this Directive,**
- **to facilitate the exchange of information between the Commission and the Member States on relevant developments in the art market in the Community.**

1. Review by the European Commission (para. 1). The European Commission is to regularly report on the implementation and the effect of the Directive, in particular regarding those Member States that did not already provide for a resale right prior to its entry into force. The reports by the Commission may contain proposals to amend the Directive. A first report was published in 2011 (Report on the Resale Right Directive). The Commission notes that no clear patterns can be established to link the EU's loss of share in the global market for modern and contemporary art over the 2005-2010 period with the harmonization of provisions relating to the application of the resale right in the EU on 1 January 2006. Neither can any clear patterns be established that would indicate systematic trade diversion within the EU away from those Member States that introduced the right for living artists in 2006. Also nothing can be found to suggest that Member States that did not levy the royalty on the work of deceased artists have performed better over 2008-2010 than those that did. Nevertheless, the Commission recognizes that there are clear pressures on European art markets, in all price ranges, and for both the auction and dealer sectors. The report also expresses concern over the costs, efficiency and quality of the administration of the resale right, a matter on which differences exist between the Member States. The Commission proposes initiating a Stakeholder Dialogue, tasked with making recommendations for the improvement of the system of resale right collection and distribution in the EU (Report on the Resale Right Directive).

2. Contact Committee (paras. 2 and 3). A Contact Committee composed of representatives of the Member States is set up to discuss the application of the Directive and exchange information.

[Implementation]

Article 12

(1) Member States shall bring into force the laws, regulations and administrative provisions necessary to comply with this Directive before 1 January 2006. They shall forthwith inform the Commission thereof.

When Member States adopt these measures, they shall contain a reference to this Directive or shall be accompanied by such reference on the occasion of their official publication. The methods of making such a reference shall be laid down by the Member States.

(2) Member States shall communicate to the Commission the provisions of national law which they adopt in the field covered by this Directive.

1. Implementation. The Directive was to be transposed by the Member States before 1 January 2006. As the Directive entered into force on 13 October 2001 (see art. 13), the Member States enjoyed a transposition period of more than four years. Such a long transposition period is quite unusual for directives, but it was considered necessary for those Member States that did not already provide for resale rights, such as the UK and the Netherlands (see Introductory remarks).

[Entry into force]

Article 13

This Directive shall enter into force on the day of its publication in the Official Journal of the European Communities.

1. Date of entry into force. As the Directive was published in the Official Journal on 13 October 2001, it entered into force on that date.

[Addressees]

Article 14

This Directive is addressed to the Member States.

1. General. According to art. 288 of the Treaty on the Functioning of the European Union, Directives are binding, as to the result to be achieved, upon each Member State to which they are addressed, but shall leave to the national authorities the choice of form and methods.

DIRECTIVE 2012/28/EU

(Orphan Works Directive)

of the European Parliament and of the Council of 25 October 2012 on certain permitted uses of orphan works

[Introductory remarks]

1. General. The stated aim of the Orphan Works Directive is to allow mass digitization and making available of works and phonograms held in the collections of cultural heritage institutions. The Directive addresses the specific case of works and phonograms for which no right owner can be identified or located, also known as 'orphan' works and phonograms. Since the authorization of the right owner is necessary in order to digitize and make works available to the public, a solution had to be found to overcome the inability to clear rights and to permit certain uses of such orphan works and phonograms. The Directive creates a legal framework designed to prevent the infringement of rights from occurring and to favour the cross-border digitization and dissemination of works within the single market. The Directive achieves this essentially by targeting the specific problem of the legal determination of orphan work status and its consequences in terms of the permitted users and permitted uses of works or phonograms considered to be orphan works (recital 3). While the Directive does not address the broader issue of 'out-of-commerce' works, it does make reference to the Memorandum of Understanding on key principles on the digitization and making available of out-of-commerce works, signed on 20 September 2011 by representatives of European libraries, authors, publishers and collecting societies and witnessed by the Commission (recital 4).

2. Legislative history. The Orphan Works Directive harmonizes certain permitted uses of orphan works. The adoption process of this Directive went rather swiftly, just 18 months lapsed from the introduction of the Initial Proposal on 24 May 2011 to the adoption of the final text on 25 October 2012. The European Parliament accepted the Proposal in first reading subject to sixty-one amendments. The resulting Amended Proposal was presented on 5 September 2012 and adopted shortly thereafter. Member States were given two years to implement the provisions of the Directive into their national law, until 29 October 2014.

3. Need for harmonization. (a) Situation before the Directive. Before the adoption of the Directive, most Member States had done nothing to alleviate the cultural heritage institutions' problem of rights clearance of orphan works, despite the Commission's 2006 Recommendation on the digitisation and online accessibility of cultural content and digital preservation (Digitisation Recommendation). Only Denmark, Finland, Hungary, Sweden,

France and the United Kingdom had adopted measures dealing more or less directly with orphan works. In no case, however, did any of these measures enable the cross-border access to or use of orphan works. **(b) Reason for harmonization.** The different approaches to the recognition of orphan work status in the few Member States where the question had been addressed, or in most cases, the lack of any applicable procedure for the determination of the orphan status was seen as a potential obstacle to the functioning of the internal market and the use of, and cross-border access to, orphan works (recital 8). Moreover, it was felt that regulatory fragmentation as to orphan work status would lead to legal uncertainty as to whether a particular work is an orphan work or not. There might even be a risk of divergent decisions as to the status of any particular work. This would be detrimental to the property rights of those that own orphan works. The Commission was confident that ensuring legal certainty with respect to the use of orphan works could not be sufficiently achieved by the Member States and could therefore, by reason of the need for uniformity of the rules governing the use of orphan works, be better achieved at Union level (recital 25).

[Bibliography]

U. Suthersanen & M.M. Frabboni, 'Chapter 13 – The Orphan Works Directive' in I. Stamatoudi and P. Torremans (eds.), *Copyright Law of the European Union* (Edward Elgar 2014)

E. Rosati, 'The Orphan Works Directive, or Throwing a Stone and Hiding the Hand' (2013) 8(4) *Journal of Intellectual Property Law & Practice* 303-310

E.F. Schulze, 'Orphan Works and Other Orphan Material Under National, Regional and International Law: Analysis, Proposals and Solutions' (2012) 34(5) *European Intellectual Property Review* 313-323

K. de la Durantaye, 'How to Build an Orphanage, and Why' (2011) 2 JIPITEC

K. de la Durantaye, 'H Is for Harmonization: The Google Book Search Settlement and Orphan Works Legislation in the European Union' (2011) 55(1) *New York Law School Law Review* 157-175

S. van Gompel, 'Unlocking the Potential of Pre-Existing Content: How to Address the Issue of Orphan Works in Europe?' (2007) 38(6) *IIC International Review of Intellectual property and Competition Law* 669-702

S. van Gompel, 'Audiovisual Archives and the Inability to Clear Rights in Orphan Works' (2007) 4 *IRIS plus* 2

M.M.M. van Eechoud, P.B. Hugenholtz, S. van Gompel, L. Guibault & N. Helberger, *Harmonizing European Copyright Law* (Kluwer Law International 2009) 263

[Preamble]

THE EUROPEAN PARLIAMENT AND THE COUNCIL OF THE EUROPEAN UNION,

Having regard to the Treaty on the Functioning of the European Union, and in Articles 53(1), 62 and 114 thereof,

Having regard to the proposal from the European Commission,

After transmission of the draft legislative act to the national parliaments,

Having regard to the opinion of the European Economic and Social Committee [1],

Acting in accordance with the ordinary legislative procedure [2],

Whereas:

(1) Publicly accessible libraries, educational establishments and museums, as well as archives, film or audio heritage institutions and public-service broadcasting organisations, established in the Member States, are engaged in large-scale digitisation of their collections or archives in order to create European Digital Libraries. They contribute to the preservation and dissemination of European cultural heritage, which is also important for the creation of European Digital Libraries, such as Europeana. Technologies for mass digitisation of print materials and for search and indexing enhance the research value of the libraries' collections. Creating large online libraries facilitates electronic search and discovery tools which open up new sources of discovery for researchers and academics who would otherwise have to content themselves with more traditional and analogue search methods.

(2) The need to promote free movement of knowledge and innovation in the internal market is an important component of the Europe 2020 Strategy, as set out in the Communication from the Commission entitled 'Europe 2020: A strategy for smart, sustainable and inclusive growth', which includes as one of its flagship initiatives the development of a Digital Agenda for Europe.

(3) Creating a legal framework to facilitate the digitisation and dissemination of works and other subject-matter which are protected by copyright or related rights and for which no rightholder is identified or for which the rightholder, even if identified, is not located – so-called orphan works – is a key action of the Digital Agenda for Europe, as set out in the Communication from the Commission entitled 'A Digital Agenda for Europe'. This Directive targets the specific problem of the legal determination of orphan work status and its consequences in terms of the permitted users and permitted uses of works or phonograms considered to be orphan works.

(4) This Directive is without prejudice to specific solutions being developed in the Member States to address larger mass digitisation issues, such as in the case of so-called 'out-of-commerce' works. Such solutions take into account the specificities of different types of content and different users and build upon the consensus of the relevant stakeholders. This approach has also been followed in the Memorandum of Understanding on key principles on the digitisation and making available of out-of-commerce works, signed on 20 September 2011 by representatives of European libraries, authors, publishers and collecting societies and witnessed by the Commission. This Directive is without prejudice to that Memorandum of Understanding, which calls on Member States and the Commission to ensure that voluntary agreements concluded between users, rightholders and collective rights management organisations to licence the use of out-of-commerce works on the basis of the principles contained therein benefit from the requisite legal certainty in a national and cross-border context.

(5) Copyright is the economic foundation for the creative industry, since it stimulates innovation, creation, investment and production. Mass digitisation and dissemination of works is therefore a means of protecting Europe's cultural heritage. Copyright is an important tool for ensuring that the creative sector is rewarded for its work.

(6) The rightholders' exclusive rights of reproduction of their works and other protected subject-matter and of making them available to the public, as harmonised under Directive 2001/29/EC of the European Parliament and of the Council of 22 May 2001 on the harmonisation of certain aspects of copyright and related rights in the information society [3], necessitate the prior consent of rightholders to the digitisation and the making available to the public of a work or other protected subject-matter.

(7) In the case of orphan works, it is not possible to obtain such prior consent to the carrying-out of acts of reproduction or of making available to the public.

(8) Different approaches in the Member States to the recognition of orphan work status can present obstacles to the functioning of the internal market and the use of, and cross-border access to, orphan works. Such different approaches can also result in restrictions on the free movement of goods and services which incorporate cultural content. Therefore, ensuring the mutual recognition of such status is appropriate, since it will allow access to orphan works in all Member States.

(9) In particular, a common approach to determining the orphan work status and the permitted uses of orphan works is necessary in order to ensure legal certainty in the internal market with respect to the use of orphan works by publicly accessible libraries, educational establishments and museums, as well as by archives, film or audio heritage institutions and public-service broadcasting organisations.

(10) Cinematographic or audiovisual works and phonograms in the archives of public-service broadcasting organisations and produced by them include orphan works. Taking into account the special position of broadcasters as producers of phonograms and audiovisual material and the need to adopt measures to limit the phenomenon of orphan works in the future, it is appropriate to set a cut-off date for the application of this Directive to works and phonograms in the archives of broadcasting organisations.

(11) Cinematographic and audiovisual works and phonograms contained in the archives of public-service broadcasting organisations and produced by them, should for the purposes of this Directive be regarded as including cinematographic and audiovisual works and phonograms which are commissioned by such organisations for the exclusive exploitation by them or other co-producing public-service broadcasting organisations. Cinematographic and audiovisual works and phonograms contained in the archives of public-service broadcasting organisations which have not been produced or commissioned by such organisations, but which those organisations have been authorised to use under a licensing agreement, should not fall within the scope of this Directive.

(12) For reasons of international comity, this Directive should apply only to works and phonograms that are first published in the territory of a Member State or, in the absence of publication, first broadcast in the territory of a Member State or, in the absence of publication or broadcast, made publicly accessible by the beneficiaries of this Directive with the consent of the rightholders. In the latter case, this Directive should only apply provided that it is reasonable to assume that the rightholders would not oppose the use allowed by this Directive.

(13) Before a work or phonogram can be considered an orphan work, a diligent search for the rightholders in the work or phonogram, including rightholders in works and other protected subject-matter that are embedded or incorporated in the work or phonogram, should be carried out in good faith. Member States should be permitted to provide that such diligent search may be carried out by the organisations referred to in this Directive or by other organisations. Such other organisations may charge for the service of carrying out a diligent search.

(14) It is appropriate to provide for a harmonised approach concerning such diligent search in order to ensure a high level of protection of copyright and related rights in the Union. A diligent search should involve the consultation of sources that supply information on the works and other protected subject-matter as determined, in accordance with this Directive, by the Member State where the diligent search has to be carried out. In so doing, Member States could refer to the diligent search guidelines agreed in the context of the High Level Working Group on Digital Libraries established as part of the i2010 digital library initiative.

(15) In order to avoid duplication of search efforts, a diligent search should be carried out in the Member State where the work or phonogram was first published or, in cases where no publication has taken place, where it was first broadcast. The diligent search in respect of cinematographic or audiovisual works the producer of which has his headquarters or habitual residence in a Member State should be carried out in that Member State. In the case of cinematographic or audiovisual works which are co-produced by producers established in different Member States, the diligent search should be carried out in each of those Member States. With regard to works and phonograms which have neither been published nor broadcast but which have been made publicly accessible by the beneficiaries of this Directive with the consent of the rightholders, the diligent search should be carried out in the Member State where the organisation that made the work or phonogram publicly accessible with the consent of the rightholder is established. Diligent searches for the rightholders in works and other protected subject-matter that are embedded or incorporated in a work or phonogram should be carried out in the Member State where the diligent search for the work or phonogram containing the embedded or incorporated work or other protected subject-matter is carried out. Sources of information available in other countries should also be consulted if there is evidence to suggest that relevant information on rightholders is to be found in those other countries. The carrying-out of diligent searches may generate various kinds of information, such as a search record and the result of the search. The search record should be kept on file in order for the relevant organisation to be able to substantiate that the search was diligent.

(16) Member States should ensure that the organisations concerned keep records of their diligent searches and that the results of such searches, consisting in particular of any finding that a work or phonogram is to be considered an orphan work within the meaning of this Directive, as well as information on the change of status and on the use which those organisations make of orphan works, are collected and made available to the public at large, in particular through the recording of the relevant information in an online database. Considering in particular the pan-European dimension, and in order to avoid duplication of efforts, it is appropriate to make provision for the creation of a single online database for the Union containing such information and for making it available to the public at large in a transparent manner. This can enable both the organisations which are carrying out diligent searches and the rightholders easily to access such information. The database could also play an important role in preventing and bringing to an end possible copyright infringements, particularly in the case of changes to the orphan work status of the works and phonograms. Under Regulation (EU) No 386/2012 [4], the Office for Harmonization in the Internal Market ('the Office') is entrusted with certain tasks and activities, financed

by making use of its own budgetary means, aimed at facilitating and supporting the activities of national authorities, the private sector and the Union institutions in the fight against, including the prevention of, infringement of intellectual property rights. In particular, pursuant to point (g) of Article 2(1) of that Regulation, those tasks include providing mechanisms which help to improve the online exchange of relevant information between the Member States' authorities concerned and fostering cooperation between those authorities. It is therefore appropriate to rely on the Office to establish and manage the European database containing information related to orphan works referred to in this Directive.

(17) There can be several rightholders in respect of a particular work or phonogram, and works and phonograms can themselves include other works or protected subject-matter. This Directive should not affect the rights of identified and located rightholders. If at least one rightholder has been identified and located, a work or phonogram should not be considered an orphan work. The beneficiaries of this Directive should only be permitted to use a work or phonogram one or more of the rightholders in which are not identified or not located, if they are authorised to carry out the acts of reproduction and of making available to the public covered by Articles 2 and 3 respectively of Directive 2001/29/EC by those rightholders that have been identified and located, including the rightholders of works and other protected subject-matter which are embedded or incorporated in the works or phonograms. Rightholders that have been identified and located can give this authorisation only in relation to the rights that they themselves hold, either because the rights are their own rights or because the rights were transferred to them, and should not be able to authorise under this Directive any use on behalf of rightholders that have not been identified and located. Correspondingly, when previously non-identified or non-located rightholders come forward in order to claim their rights in the work or phonogram, the lawful use of the work or phonogram by the beneficiaries can continue only if those rightholders give their authorisation to do so under Directive 2001/29/EC in relation to the rights that they hold.

(18) Rightholders should be entitled to put an end to the orphan work status in the event that they come forward to claim their rights in the work or other protected subject-matter. Rightholders that put an end to the orphan work status of a work or other protected subject-matter should receive fair compensation for the use that has been made of their works or other protected subject-matter under this Directive, to be determined by the Member State where the organisation that uses an orphan work is established. Member States should be free to determine the circumstances under which the payment of such compensation may be organised, including the point in time at which the payment is due. For the purposes of determining the possible level of fair compensation, due account should be taken, inter alia, of Member States' cultural

promotion objectives, of the non-commercial nature of the use made by the organisations in question in order to achieve aims related to their public-interest missions, such as promoting learning and disseminating culture, and of the possible harm to rightholders.

(19) If a work or phonogram has been wrongly found to be an orphan work, following a search which was not diligent, the remedies for copyright infringement in Member States' legislation, provided for in accordance with the relevant national provisions and Union law, remain available.

(20) In order to promote learning and the dissemination of culture, Member States should provide for an exception or limitation in addition to those provided for in Article 5 of Directive 2001/29/EC. That exception or limitation should permit certain organisations, as referred to in point (c) of Article 5(2) of Directive 2001/29/EC and film or audio heritage institutions which operate on a non-profit making basis, as well as public-service broadcasting organisations, to reproduce and make available to the public, within the meaning of that Directive, orphan works, provided that such use fulfils their public interest missions, in particular the preservation of, the restoration of, and the provision of cultural and educational access to, their collections, including their digital collections. Film or audio heritage institutions should, for the purposes of this Directive, cover organisations designated by Member States to collect, catalogue, preserve and restore films and other audiovisual works or phonograms forming part of their cultural heritage. Public-service broadcasters should, for the purposes of this Directive, cover broadcasters with a public-service remit as conferred, defined and organised by each Member State. The exception or limitation established by this Directive to permit the use of orphan works is without prejudice to the exceptions and limitations provided for in Article 5 of Directive 2001/29/EC. It can be applied only in certain special cases which do not conflict with the normal exploitation of the work or other protected subject-matter and do not unreasonably prejudice the legitimate interests of the rightholder.

(21) In order to incentivise digitisation, the beneficiaries of this Directive should be allowed to generate revenues in relation to their use of orphan works under this Directive in order to achieve aims related to their public-interest missions, including in the context of public-private partnership agreements.

(22) Contractual arrangements may play a role in fostering the digitisation of European cultural heritage, it being understood that publicly accessible libraries, educational establishments and museums, as well as archives, film or audio heritage institutions and public-service broadcasting organisations, should be allowed, with a view to undertaking the uses permitted under this Directive, to conclude agreements with commercial partners for the digitisation and making available to the public

of orphan works. Those agreements may include financial contributions by such partners. Such agreements should not impose any restrictions on the beneficiaries of this Directive as to their use of orphan works and should not grant the commercial partner any rights to use, or control the use of, the orphan works.

(23) In order to foster access by the Union's citizens to Europe's cultural heritage, it is also necessary to ensure that orphan works which have been digitised and made available to the public in one Member State may also be made available to the public in other Member States. Publicly accessible libraries, educational establishments and museums, as well as archives, film or audio heritage institutions and public-service broadcasting organisations that use an orphan work in order to achieve their public-interest missions should be able to make the orphan work available to the public in other Member States.

(24) This Directive is without prejudice to the arrangements in the Member States concerning the management of rights such as extended collective licences, legal presumptions of representation or transfer, collective management or similar arrangements or a combination of them, including for mass digitisation.

(25) Since the objective of this Directive, namely ensuring legal certainty with respect to the use of orphan works, cannot be sufficiently achieved by the Member States and can therefore, by reason of the need for uniformity of the rules governing the use of orphan works, be better achieved at Union level, the Union may adopt measures, in accordance with the principle of subsidiarity as set out in Article 5 of the Treaty on European Union. In accordance with the principle of proportionality, as set out in that Article, this Directive does not go beyond what is necessary in order to achieve that objective,

HAVE ADOPTED THIS DIRECTIVE:

[Subject-matter and scope]

Article 1

(1) This Directive concerns certain uses made of orphan works by publicly accessible libraries, educational establishments and museums, as well as by archives, film or audio heritage institutions and public-service broadcasting organisations, established in the Member States, in order to achieve aims related to their public-interest missions.

(2) This Directive applies to:
  (a) works published in the form of books, journals, newspapers, magazines or other writings contained in the collections of publicly accessible libraries, educational establishments or museums as well as in the collections of archives or of film or audio heritage institutions;

    (b) **cinematographic or audiovisual works and phonograms contained in the collections of publicly accessible libraries, educational establishments or museums as well as in the collections of archives or of film or audio heritage institutions; and**

    (c) **cinematographic or audiovisual works and phonograms produced by public-service broadcasting organisations up to and including 31 December 2002 and contained in their archives;**

which are protected by copyright or related rights and which are first published in a Member State or, in the absence of publication, first broadcast in a Member State.

(3) This Directive also applies to works and phonograms referred to in paragraph 2 which have never been published or broadcast but which have been made publicly accessible by the organisations referred to in paragraph 1 with the consent of the rightholders, provided that it is reasonable to assume that the rightholders would not oppose the uses referred to in Article 6. Member States may limit the application of this paragraph to works and phonograms which have been deposited with those organisations before 29 October 2014.

(4) This Directive shall also apply to works and other protected subject-matter that are embedded or incorporated in, or constitute an integral part of, the works or phonograms referred to in paragraphs 2 and 3.

(5) This Directive does not interfere with any arrangements concerning the management of rights at national level.

1. Users of orphan works (para. 1). The Directive applies to the use of orphan works and phonograms by a specific set of institutions within the Member States in the pursuit of their public interest missions. Private individuals, as well as any other private enterprise or institution, not mentioned in the list remain outside the scope of the Directive and must obtain permission from the right owner prior to using the work or phonogram. Should the right owner remain unknown or un-locatable, the Directive provides no relief to other non-listed users (recital 6). Where it is impossible to obtain prior authorization because of the orphan status of a work or other subject-matter (recital 7), the decision to use or not an orphan work or phonogram will be made in practice following a risk assessment of the likelihood of seeing a right owner show up and claim damages for the unauthorized use of the work. **(a) Beneficiaries.** The institutions listed in art. 1 of the Directive are publicly accessible libraries, educational establishments or museums, as well as archives, film or audio heritage institutions and public-service broadcasting organizations (hereinafter collectively referred to as 'cultural heritage institutions'). This list is broader than that of art. 5(2)c of the Information Society Directive, which only covers publicly accessible libraries, educational establishments, museums and archives. The Orphan Works Directive would not be able to achieve its objective of facilitating the large-scale digitization of Europe's cultural heritage (recital 5) if some key institutions holding copyright protected works and other subject-matter in their collections were not included in the list. In addition to those institutions listed in the Information Society Directive, the institutions covered by the Orphan Works Directive are film or audio heritage institutions which operate on a non-profit making basis, as well as public-service broadcasting organizations. This would seem to exclude private broadcasting organizations. **(b) Established in the Member States**. In order to foster access by the Union's citizens to Europe's cultural heritage, orphan works that have been digitized and made available to the public in one Member State must also be made available to the public in other Member States. Beneficiary organizations that use an orphan work in order to achieve their public-interest missions should be able to make the orphan work available to the public in other Member States (recital 23). The geographical scope of the Directive is therefore the territory of the European Union, although the uses by institutions located in the countries of the European Economic Area (Norway, Liechtenstein and Iceland) are also covered; this means that only institutions located in one of the Member States (EEA country) can benefit from the exception created pursuant to art. 6 of the Directive and that the mutual recognition of the orphan work status (art. 4) only operates within the territory of the EEA. **(c) Public interest missions.** Contrary to art. 5(2)c of the Information Society Directive, the institutions listed in the Orphan Works Directive are not restricted by their non-profit purpose. Instead, recital 20 specifies that those organizations listed may use orphan works provided such use fulfils their public interest missions, in particular the preservation of, the restoration of, and the provision of cultural and educational access to their collections, including their digital collections. For the purposes of this Directive, film or audio heritage institutions cover organizations designated by Member States to collect, catalogue, preserve and restore films and other audiovisual works or phonograms forming part of their cultural heritage, whereas public-service broadcasters cover broadcasters with a public-service remit as conferred, defined and organized by each Member State. It is not clear from the text of the Directive, however, what other specific factors must be taken into consideration to allow the institutions mentioned in the article to qualify as pursuing a public-interest mission or whether such public-interest mission must be laid down in a law or other regulatory instrument.

2. Subject-matter covered (para. 2). General. Art. 1(2) defines three categories of 'works' covered by the Directive. These include (1) works published in the form of books, journals, newspapers, magazines or other writings (art. 1(2)(a)); (2) cinematographic or audiovisual works and phonograms (art. 1(2)(b)) that are contained in the collections of publicly accessible libraries, educational establishments or museums as well as in the collections of archives or of film or audio heritage institutions; and (3) cinematographic or audiovisual works and phonograms (art. 1(2)(c)) produced by public-service broadcasting organizations up to and including 31 December 2002 and contained in their archives (see below). The term 'works' in art. 1(2)(a) arguably refers to printed matter, including the electronic versions thereof. Photographs and artworks are not expressly mentioned. These are covered only insofar as they are embedded in books, journals, newspapers, magazines or other writings (see para. 4 below). This interpretation follows from the Commission's Impact Assessment accompanying the Proposal of the Orphan Works Directive, which stresses that the Directive's focus should be on the print sector as opposed to the image and photography sectors. The Parliamentary reports contain references to the fact that the scope of application must cover not only works, but also other protected subject-matter, as the Directive would otherwise have no meaningful effect for the beneficiary film or audio heritage institutions, or the public-service broadcasting organizations concerned. The remainder of the Directive refers to 'works' and 'phonograms', rather than to the individual categories of works and other subject-matter. This is presumably a measure of economy of language, where all copyright protected items, including books, journals, newspapers, magazines or other writings, as well as cinematographic or audiovisual works, are jointly referred to as 'works', and where phonograms are the only category of subject-matter protected by related rights expressly covered by the Directive, to the apparent exclusion of fixations of films and broadcast signals. Compared to the text of the Proposal, which left some ambiguity on its application to related rights, the last sentence of this paragraph clearly states that the subject-matter covered by the Directive is that which is protected by copyright or related rights.

(a) Special regime for works held by public-service broadcasters. Recital 10 clarifies that cinematographic or audiovisual works and phonograms in the archives of public-service broadcasting organizations and produced by them may include orphan works. Taking into account the special position of broadcasters as producers of phonograms and audiovisual material and the need to adopt measures to limit the phenomenon of orphan works in the future, the EU legislator considered it appropriate to set a cut-off date for the application of this Directive to works and phonograms in the archives of broadcasting organizations. Art. 1(2) sets this for the cinematographic and audiovisual works and phonograms contained in the archives of public-service broadcasting organizations at 31 December 2002. The reason for establishing such a cut-off date is to reduce the occurrence of orphan works within the public broadcaster's collections. With respect to works produced by public-service broadcasting organizations themselves, recital 11 specifies that these works should be regarded as including cinematographic and audiovisual works and phonograms which are commissioned by such organizations for the exclusive exploitation by them or other co-producing public-service broadcasting organizations. Cinematographic and audiovisual works and phonograms contained in the archives of public-service broadcasting organizations which have not been produced or commissioned by such organizations, but which those organizations have been authorized to use under a licensing agreement, should not fall within the scope of this Directive. Although it is stated neither in the Explanatory Memorandum accompanying the Proposal of the Orphan Works Directive nor anywhere else, the restriction to subject-matter commissioned or produced by the public organizations is presumably meant to constrain the application of the Directive to works and phonograms that are within the exploitation mandate of the public-service broadcasting organization, since the right to use works produced or commissioned by third party organizations is governed by the licensing agreement concluded with such third party organizations. **(b) First publication or broadcast.** The Directive applies to works first published in a Member State or, in the absence of publication, first broadcast in a Member State. The need to specify that, in the absence of publication, the country where the work was first broadcast also constitutes a point of attachment of protection, arises because of the limited meaning of 'publication' in art. 3(3) of the Berne Convention. According to this provision acts of communication to the public where no copy is made available to the public do not constitute a 'publication'.

3. Unpublished works (para. 3). In line with the previous paragraph, para. 3 clarifies that the Directive also applies to works and phonograms, which have neither been published or broadcast, but which have been made publicly accessible by the cultural heritage institutions referred to in para. 1 with the consent of the right owner. The application of the Directive is under the condition, however, that it can reasonably be assumed that the right owner would not oppose the uses permitted under art. 6 of the Directive, which include the reproduction of works and their making available to the public but only in order to achieve aims related to the organization's public-interest mission. Since the Directive applies to a vast array of works and phonograms held in the collections of different types of institutions, it is not inconceivable that some works contained in the collections of cultural heritage institutions were never published or broadcast, but have been made publicly accessible with the consent of the rightholders. This would be the case, for example, of a unique recording of a live concert, a rare film documentary or a single issue of an art or poetry book, held in the collection of an institution and made accessible with the consent of the right owner. Absent this provision, an unpublished manuscript on display at a library or archive would fall outside the scope of the Directive. The Directive however does not indicate how an institution will be able to prove that unidentifiable or unlocatable rightholders may or may not have authorized specific uses, especially when dealing with works created in the pre-digital era. Furthermore cultural heritage institutions may, pursuant to this provision, limit the application of this paragraph to works and phonograms that have been deposited with those organizations before the implementation deadline, that is, 29 October 2014. The rationale for the inclusion of this provision in the Directive was to provide a safety net to address concerns on moral rights and to limit the use of unpublished works to the past.

4. Embedded works (para. 4). The application of the Directive to works and other protected subject-matter that are embedded or incorporated in, or constitute an integral part of, the works or phonograms is the only indirect reference to other categories of works than those enumerated in para. 2. Other categories of works might include, according to the Directive's Annex, works of fine art, photographs, illustrations, designs, architecture, and sketches of these and other works and other such works, but only so long as they 'are contained in books, journals, newspapers and magazines or other works'. In the course of the legislative process, an amendment had been proposed to include photographs and artworks in the definition of 'works published in the form of books, journals, newspapers, magazines or other writings' (art. 1(2) (a)). Since this proposed amendment was rejected, the works or phonograms that are not expressly mentioned in para. 2 only fall within the scope of the Directive provided they are embedded or incorporated into another work or phonogram that is listed in para. 2. Standalone photographs, illustrations and the like will therefore not be the object of separate determination as to their orphan status, nor be amenable for use by cultural heritage institutions pursuant to art. 6 of the Directive.

5. Non-interference with arrangements (para. 5). The Commission's original proposal stated in recital 20 that 'This Directive should be without prejudice to existing arrangements in the Member States concerning the management of rights such as extended collective licences'. This text created some unease among certain Member States, especially the Nordic countries and others who envisaged the establishment of an extended licensing system as a way to facilitate mass digitization while eliminating the problem of orphan works. The word 'existing' in the recital implied that the creation of any new arrangement concerning the management of rights would have run counter to the Directive. The opposition of these few Member States was strong enough to change the ambit of the provision entirely: from a restrictive recital, it became a permissive provision in the body of the Directive. As a result, the Directive does not stand in the way of existing or yet to be implemented arrangements for the collective rights management including those in the form of extended collective licensing arrangements, as specified by recital 24.

[Orphan works]

Article 2

(1) A work or a phonogram shall be considered an orphan work if none of the rightholders in that work or phonogram is identified or, even if one or more of them is identified, none is located despite a diligent search for the rightholders having been carried out and recorded in accordance with Article 3.

(2) Where there is more than one rightholder in a work or phonogram, and not all of them have been identified or, even if identified, located after

a diligent search has been carried out and recorded in accordance with Article 3, the work or phonogram may be used in accordance with this Directive provided that the rightholders that have been identified and located have, in relation to the rights they hold, authorised the organisations referred to in Article 1(1) to carry out the acts of reproduction and making available to the public covered respectively by Articles 2 and 3 of Directive 2001/29/EC.

(3) Paragraph 2 shall be without prejudice to the rights in the work or phonogram of rightholders that have been identified and located.

(4) Article 5 shall apply mutatis mutandis to the rightholders that have not been identified and located in the works referred to in paragraph 2.

(5) This Directive shall be without prejudice to national provisions on anonymous or pseudonymous works.

1. Definition of orphan works (para. 1) The definition of orphan works in art. 1(1) makes explicit reference to the obligation to conduct a diligent search in accordance with art. 3. The determination of the orphan status of works, and with it the possibility to use these works pursuant to art. 6, are therefore premised on the inability to identify or locate any of the rightholders despite a diligent search. In other words, without evidence that a diligent search was conducted in accordance with art. 3, a work will not be conferred orphan status, even if none of the authors are identified or located.

2. Multiple ownership and orphan status (para. 2). The Commission's proposal originally stated that 'where a work has more than one right owner, and one of the right owners has been identified and located, that work shall not be considered an orphan work.' During the Parliamentary debates, the point was made that this wording would create a situation in which a majority of works, particularly in the audiovisual sphere, would be rendered inaccessible. The final text of art. 2(3) makes it clear that the rights of identified and located right owners remain unaffected. Recital 17 states that 'if at least one rightholder has been identified and located, a work or phonogram should not be considered an orphan work'. The same recital specifies that the beneficiaries of this Directive should only be permitted to use a work or phonogram that is 'partly' orphan (e.g. for which one or more of the rightholders are not identified or not located), if they are authorized to carry out the acts of reproduction and of making available to the public by those rightholders that have been identified and located, including the rightholders of works and other protected subject-matter which are embedded or incorporated in other works or phonograms. Rightholders that have been identified and located can give this authorization only in relation to the rights that they themselves hold, either because the rights are their own rights or because the rights were transferred to them, and should not be able to authorize under this Directive any use on behalf of rightholders that have not been identified and located. This paragraph also clarifies that the work or phonogram may only be used in accordance with this Directive provided that the rightholders who have been identified and located give their permission to carry out the acts mentioned in arts. 2 and 3 of the Information Society Directive. It is important to note this cross-reference is to the provisions of the Information Society Directive, rather than to art. 6 of this Directive. In practice, it may well mean that one rightholder's objection to the reproduction and making available of his part of the work can suffice to prevent the reproduction and making available of the entire work. Consider, for example, the rights of the screenplay writer in a cinematographic work even if no other rightholders were identified or located, the screenplay writer would be in a position to stop the re-use of the whole film.

3. Rights of identified and located owners unaffected (para. 3) Perhaps superfluously, para. 3 stresses that the rights of right owners who have been identified and located after a diligent search remain unaffected. This certainly includes the exclusive rights mentioned in arts. 2 and 3 of the Information Society Directive, but presumably also refers to remuneration rights that exist in many Member States (for private copying, public lending, reprography, educational use, etc.). Nothing in this Directive should prevent identified and located right owners from benefiting from any rights on their work.

4. End of orphan status for works of unidentified or unlocated authors (para. 4) The wording of this paragraph is not very straightforward The provision ensures in essence that, in case of multiple ownership of rights on a work or phonogram only parts of which have been declared orphan, the right owners who had not been identified or located but who later resurface have at all times the possibility to put an end to the orphan status of their rights in that work or phonogram.

5. National provisions on anonymous or pseudonymous works unaffected (para. 5) It is not uncommon for an author to publish a work anonymously or under a pseudonym. The anonymous or pseudonymous character of a work may influence the possibility to identify and locate the right owner. The Directive gives precedence in this case to the national provisions governing anonymous and pseudonymous works. The laws of most Member States contain rules on how to establish the identity of anonymous and pseudonymous authors, and how to apply for compulsory licences for the use of such works. In practice, the difficulty for cultural heritage institutions will lie in trying to ascertain whether a work is indeed anonymous or pseudonymous, or whether it is truly orphaned, thus falling within the scope of application of the Directive.

[Diligent search]

Article 3

(1) For the purposes of establishing whether a work or phonogram is an orphan work, the organisations referred to in Article 1(1) shall ensure

that a diligent search is carried out in good faith in respect of each work or other protected subject-matter, by consulting the appropriate sources for the category of works and other protected subject-matter in question. The diligent search shall be carried out prior to the use of the work or phonogram.

(2) The sources that are appropriate for each category of works or phonogram in question shall be determined by each Member State, in consultation with rightholders and users, and shall include at least the relevant sources listed in the Annex.

(3) A diligent search shall be carried out in the Member State of first publication or, in the absence of publication, first broadcast, except in the case of cinematographic or audiovisual works the producer of which has his headquarters or habitual residence in a Member State, in which case the diligent search shall be carried out in the Member State of his headquarters or habitual residence.

In the case referred to in Article 1(3), the diligent search shall be carried out in the Member State where the organisation that made the work or phonogram publicly accessible with the consent of the rightholder is established.

(4) If there is evidence to suggest that relevant information on rightholders is to be found in other countries, sources of information available in those other countries shall also be consulted.

(5) Member States shall ensure that the organisations referred to in Article 1(1) maintain records of their diligent searches and that those organisations provide the following information to the competent national authorities:

(a) the results of the diligent searches that the organisations have carried out and which have led to the conclusion that a work or a phonogram is considered an orphan work;

(b) the use that the organisations make of orphan works in accordance with this Directive;

(c) any change, pursuant to Article 5, of the orphan work status of works and phonograms that the organisations use;

(d) the relevant contact information of the organisation concerned.

(6) Member States shall take the necessary measures to ensure that the information referred to in paragraph 5 is recorded in a single publicly accessible online database established and managed by the Office for Harmonization in the Internal Market ('the Office') in accordance with Regulation (EU) No 386/2012. To that end, they shall forward that information to the Office without delay upon receiving it from the organisations referred to in Article 1(1).

1. General. This article lays down the criteria that a search should meet in order to qualify as diligent, and as a result of which the beneficiaries are permitted to use the works declared orphan in accordance with art. 6 of the

Directive. The obligation to carry out a diligent search for the works or phonograms contained in the collections of the cultural heritage institutions met severe opposition from the institutions concerned because they felt that this would put an undue burden on their financial and personnel resources and that this would render any dissemination of works impossible. Despite these objections, the Directive was designed on the premise that cultural heritage institutions are obliged to conduct a diligent search to ascertain the status of works or phonograms in their collections. Diligent search under this Directive must be conducted according to the following parameters: (1) the diligent search for each work must obey the principle of good faith; (2) it must be done by consulting appropriate sources in the Member State of first publication of the work or another relevant country; and (3) the procedure and results of the search must be recorded with the competent national authorities. Recital 19 specifies that 'if a work or phonogram has been wrongly found to be an orphan work, following a search which was not diligent, the remedies for copyright infringement in Member States' legislation, provided for in accordance with the relevant national provisions and Union law, remain available'.

2. Diligent search in good faith (para. 1). A diligent search must be carried out in good faith in respect of each work or other protected subject-matter. The obligation to carry out a diligent search for each work was qualified, between the initial proposal for a Directive and the final text, by the expression 'in good faith'. Strong protest from representatives of libraries, museums and other memory institutions against the obligation in the proposal to conduct a search in respect of 'each work' were to no avail. Cultural heritage institutions argued unsuccessfully that large-scale release of orphan works would be impossible if the Directive insisted on a diligent search for the right-holder of 'each work' that is contained within a film, book or sound recording. The EU legislator clearly intended to minimise the risk that an institution would digitize without permission a work the right owners of which can be traced, by requiring the search to be in 'good faith' and 'diligent', both of which were deemed well-understood legal principles. In addition, the Annex to the Directive gives a list of minimum sources that need to be consulted in order for an institution to be able to qualify the search as 'diligent'. Recital 13 reiterates the requirement of art. 3(1), but adds that 'Member States should be permitted to provide that such diligent search may be carried out by the organizations referred to in this Directive or by other organizations. Such other organizations may charge for the service of carrying out a diligent search'. In addition, recital 14 refers Member States to the diligent search guidelines agreed in the context of the European Digital Libraries Initiative Guidelines (High Level Working Group on Digital Libraries). The diligent search must be carried out prior to the use, which means that users should withhold from any act of reproduction and making available of the works or phonograms until their status has been ascertained. This requirement may prove in practice to be a serious obstacle to the digitization efforts of cultural heritage institutions.

3. Appropriate sources for diligent search (para. 2). The procedure for carrying out a diligent search is not further defined in the Directive, save for the specification in para. 1 that such search be conducted by consulting the 'appropriate sources for the category of works and other protected subject-matter in question'. According to para. 2, the sources that are appropriate for each category of works or phonogram in question are to be determined by each Member State, in consultation with rightholders and users, and shall include at least the relevant sources listed in the Annex. The fact that right-holders and (especially) users (e.g. cultural heritage institutions) could have their say in the establishment of the procedure was the political compromise that made the obligation of carrying out a diligent search for each work acceptable to the cultural heritage institutions. The Annex lists, per category of work and phonogram, the general sources that should be consulted as part of a diligent search. Generally speaking, these sources include for all categories of works and phonograms in the respective country: the relevant legal deposit, the databases of publishers' and authors' associations, existing indexes and catalogues and the databases of relevant collecting societies. Collective rights management organizations (CRMOs) across Europe are indeed in the best position to provide information about the identity and location of right owners on works or phonograms. Unfortunately no obligation has been put, under this Directive, on CRMOs to cooperate with cultural heritage institutions that wish to obtain information as part of the required diligent search efforts. It is also unclear whether the provisions of chapter 5 of the Collective Rights Management Directive on transparency and reporting will be sufficient to ensure effective cooperation between the CRMOs and the cultural heritage institutions.

4. Diligent search in country of first publication (para. 3). Recital 15 explains that in order to avoid duplication of search efforts, a diligent search should be carried out in the Member State where the work or phonogram was first published or, in cases where no publication has taken place, where it was first broadcast. The form of publication (in print or digital) is irrelevant. **(a) Country of first publication.** A cultural heritage institution is in principle not allowed to declare orphan a work or phonogram published or broadcast in another Member State. It is unclear, however, in which Member State the diligent search must take place in case of translations. **(b) Cinematographic works.** The diligent search in respect of cinematographic or audiovisual works the producer of which has his headquarters or habitual residence in a Member State should be carried out in that Member State. In the case of cinematographic or audiovisual works, which are co-produced by producers established in different Member States, the diligent search should be carried out in each of those Member States. With regard to works and phonograms which have neither been published nor broadcast but which have been made publicly accessible by the beneficiaries of this Directive with the consent of the rightholders, the diligent search should be carried out in the Member State where the organization that made the work or phonogram publicly accessible with the consent of the rightholder is established. Diligent searches for the rightholders in works and other protected subject-matter that are embedded or incorporated in another work or phonogram should be carried out in the Member State where the diligent search for the work or phonogram containing the embedded or incorporated work or other protected subject-matter is carried out. Diligent searches for the rightholders in works and other protected subject-matter that are embedded or incorporated in another work or phonogram should be carried out in the Member State where the diligent search for the work or phonogram containing the embedded or incorporated work or other protected subject-matter is carried out (recital 15).

5. Information from other countries (para. 4). Recital 15 repeats the requirement laid down in art. 3(4) that 'sources of information available in other countries should also be consulted if there is evidence to suggest that relevant information on rightholders is to be found in those other countries'. Other countries in this paragraph may mean countries outside the European Union. The Directive does not specify what type of evidence would suggest that relevant information on rightholders is to be found in other countries. One could think for example of sources of information located in a former colony or in a neighbouring country as a result of geo-political changes (e.g. countries of former Yugoslavia or Czechoslovakia). Arguably, in view of the wording of the provision, the failure to consult information sources in those other countries could affect the 'diligent' character of the search. It is unclear whether the possibility offered under para. 1 of this article and recital 15 to entrust another organization to carry out the diligent search in these other countries also applies to diligent searches carried out in other countries. Considering that the procedure to be followed is left to the discretion of the Member State it is reasonable to assume that if the national rules laying down the procedure for a good faith diligent search allow a search to be carried out by such another organization, this option should be open for a search in another country. The final responsibility and burden to prove that the search was diligent would lie in all cases with the cultural heritage institution that claims the benefit of the application of the provisions flowing from the implementation of the Directive.

6. Duty to maintain records (para. 5). (a) General. This article puts an administrative burden on the Member States and on the organizations benefiting from the provisions under the Directive, in that it requires that search records be kept on file in order for the relevant organization to be able to substantiate that the search was diligent (recital 15). Member States must therefore ensure that the organizations concerned keep records of their diligent searches (e.g. the information sources consulted), the results of such searches (consisting in particular of any finding that a work or phonogram is to be considered an orphan work within the meaning of this Directive), as well as information on the change of status (e.g. end of orphan status by rightholders), and on the use which those organizations make of orphan works. These records are collected and made available to the public at large, in particular through the recording of the relevant information in an online database (recital 16). **(b) Competent national authorities.** The obligation, introduced in the last stages of the legislative process towards the adoption of the Directive, to appoint a 'competent national authority' for the registration of search information and results was met with scepticism by the Member States, as the Directive does not specify what qualifies as a competent national authority. The Directive leaves it to the Member States to decide how to implement this requirement, for example by entrusting their national library, patent office, intellectual property office or copyright board with the task of maintaining the registry. The rationale behind this measure probably rests on the belief that the information concerning diligent searches, their results and the rightholders that put an end to the orphan status of a work will flow more efficiently between the Member States and the central database of the Office for Harmonization in the Internal Market (OHIM), if one entity per country is in charge of gathering the information and transmitting it to the OHIM.

7. Online database (para. 6). The OHIM is charged with maintaining the central database. The choice of OHIM, which occurred in the final stage of the legislative process, was not obvious due to its lack of prior experience in the field of copyright and neighbouring rights. Nevertheless, the EU legislator seems to have opted for this organization mainly for budgetary and organizational reasons (recital 16).

[Mutual recognition of orphan work status]

Article 4

A work or phonogram which is considered an orphan work according to Article 2 in a Member State shall be considered an orphan work in all Member States. That work or phonogram may be used and accessed in accordance with this Directive in all Member States. This also applies to works and phonograms referred to in Article 2(2) in so far as the rights of the non-identified or non-located rightholders are concerned.

1. General. Art. 4 establishes the principle of mutual recognition whereby a work deemed to be an orphan work after a diligent search carried out in accordance with art. 3 is to be considered an orphan work in all Member States. Recital 23 stresses the need to ensure that orphan works which have been digitized and made available to the public in one Member State may also be made available to the public in other Member States. **a) Principle of mutual recognition.** The Directive does not provide any specific information on the definition of 'mutual recognition', it is a concept that has been present in European law for a long time. It originates from the *Cassis de Dijon* (ECJ) decision in which the Court decided that goods that were lawfully marketed in one Member State could also be introduced in other Member States. Instead of harmonizing Member States' law, the principle of mutual recognition operates a horizontal transfer of sovereignty of Member States regarding the orphan work status to the 'home state' of the orphan work. It remains unclear how the provision on mutual recognition in art. 4 will apply between Member States who opt to implement the Directive through other mechanisms than an obligation to conduct a diligent search for the rightholders. This is the case for example of countries like the Denmark, Finland, Sweden, and the UK who chose to solve the problem of mass-digitization of works, including that of orphan works, by allowing the conclusion of extended collective licences. Such licences are freely negotiated between collective rights management organizations and cultural heritage institutions, and 'extended' by law to apply to non-members of the collective rights management organization. Such contractual arrangements are safeguarded under art. 7 of the Directive. By addressing mass-digitization through extended collective licensing, no diligent search takes place; there is, therefore, no orphan status for works or phonograms in the collections of cultural heritage institutions that can be 'mutually recognised'. **(b) Use in all Member States**. Once the orphan status has been conferred on a work in one Member State, such status is automatically recognized in all other Member States. As a consequence of the automatic recognition of the orphan status of a work, all other Member States thereby accept that the work can be used and accessed in their own territory. Although art. 4 does not specifically refer to it, it is logical to assume that the use and access to orphan works in each Member State will occur pursuant to the national implementation of art. 6 of this Directive. **(c) Application to rights of non-identified or non-located owners.** This sentence confirms the application of the principle of mutual recognition of the orphan status of parts of works created by multiple authors only some of whom could not be identified or located.

[End of orphan work status]

Article 5

Member States shall ensure that a rightholder in a work or phonogram considered to be an orphan work has, at any time, the possibility of putting an end to the orphan work status in so far as his rights are concerned.

1. End of orphan work status. This provision deals with the possibility of a rightholder putting an end to the orphan status of a work. Recital 17 specifies that when previously non-identified or non-located rightholders come forward in order to claim their rights in the work or phonogram, the lawful use of the work or phonogram by the beneficiaries can continue only if those rightholders give their authorization to do so under the Information Society Directive in relation to the rights that they hold. Putting an end to the orphan status of a work therefore requires an action from the rightholder in accordance with the procedures prescribed by the national law. The form and content of those national procedures is as yet unknown. Deviations between national laws may occur. The question arises as to whether the end of the orphan work status in one Member State automatically leads to the end of the orphan work status in all Member States, as the mutual recognition principle would imply. Unfortunately the Orphan Works Directive contains no mutual recognition rule regarding the end of the orphan work status. However it can reasonably expected that the termination of the orphan work status works in the same way as obtaining that status, meaning that as soon as the orphan work status is ended in one Member States, the work has automatically lost orphan work status in all other Member States as well. The possibility to come forward is unrestricted in time. Consequently, the obligation of art. 6(5) to pay compensation for past uses is in principle also unrestricted in time under the Directive. Finally, the term 'rightholder' has not been specified. It should therefore be understood in its general sense, as covering both the original author, as original copyright owner, and an assignee or an heir.

[Permitted uses of orphan works]

Article 6

(1) Member States shall provide for an exception or limitation to the right of reproduction and the right of making available to the public provided for respectively in Articles 2 and 3 of Directive 2001/29/EC to ensure that the organisations referred to in Article 1(1) are permitted to use orphan works contained in their collections in the following ways:

    (a) by making the orphan work available to the public, within the meaning of Article 3 of Directive 2001/29/EC;

    (b) by acts of reproduction, within the meaning of Article 2 of Directive 2001/29/EC, for the purposes of digitisation, making available, indexing, cataloguing, preservation or restoration.

(2) The organisations referred to in Article 1(1) shall use an orphan work in accordance with paragraph 1 of this Article only in order to achieve aims related to their public-interest missions, in particular the preservation of, the restoration of, and the provision of cultural and educational access to, works and phonograms contained in their collection. The organisations may generate revenues in the course of such uses, for the exclusive purpose of covering their costs of digitising orphan works and making them available to the public.

(3) Member States shall ensure that the organisations referred to in Article 1(1) indicate the name of identified authors and other rightholders in any use of an orphan work.

(4) This Directive is without prejudice to the freedom of contract of such organisations in the pursuit of their public-interest missions, particularly in respect of public-private partnership agreements.

(5) **Member States shall provide that a fair compensation is due to rightholders that put an end to the orphan work status of their works or other protected subject-matter for the use that has been made by the organisations referred to in Article 1(1) of such works and other protected subject-matter in accordance with paragraph 1 of this Article. Member States shall be free to determine the circumstances under which the payment of such compensation may be organised. The level of the compensation shall be determined, within the limits imposed by Union law, by the law of the Member State in which the organisation which uses the orphan work in question is established.**

1. Permitted uses of orphan works (para. 1). This provision creates a new exception for the benefit of the organizations referred to in art. 1(1) of the Directive with respect to the uses of orphan works contained in their collections. This is the first exception on copyright and related rights to be introduced in Union law since the adoption of art. 5 of the Information Society Directive. Contrary to the exceptions and limitations enumerated in that Directive, the exception in this article is mandatory. It is also couched in very specific terms leaving Member States little leeway in the implementation of the provision in national law. This provision makes explicit reference to the exclusive rights granted under arts. 2 and 3 of the Information Society Directive, although the wording of the current provision is more detailed. The works covered are those that are contained in the collections of the organizations, as described in art. 2 of this Directive, presumably excluding works on loan or displayed on a temporary basis. **(a) Making available.** The wording of art. 6(1)(a) could give rise to interpretation as regards the scope of activities permitted under the exception with respect to orphan works, and whether such acts concern only online activities or other forms of communication to the public as well. Arguably this provision should be read in conjunction with recital 19 of the Public Sector Information Directive (Directive 2013/37/EC), which applies to libraries, museums and archives. Recital 19 of that Directive refers in turn to the Council conclusions of 10 May 2012 on the digitisation and online accessibility of cultural material and digital preservation (OJ C 169, 15.6.2012, p. 5), which suggest that only online activities are envisaged as forms of dissemination of the digitized material. Assuming that the legislator intended to refer specifically to the right of making available to the public, understood as covering all acts of making available such subject-matter to members of the public not present at the place where the act of making available originates, then it would have been more consistent to refer in this Directive to art. 3(2) of the Information Society Directive, rather than to art. 3 generally, which harmonizes the author's right of communication to the public. **(b) Reproduction.** The exception of art. 6(1)(b) of this Directive is much more precise than its equivalent under art. 5(2)(c) of the Information Society Directive, which applies to 'specific acts of reproduction made by publicly accessible libraries, educational establishments or museums, or by archives, which are not for direct or indirect economic or commercial advantage' (see *Eugen Ulmer* (ECJ)). This article spells out the acts permitted under the new exception as including reproductions 'for the purposes of digitisation, making available, indexing, cataloguing, preservation or restoration', but does not restrict such acts solely to non-commercial purposes.

2. Use in accordance with public-interest mission (para. 2). (a) Public interest mission. The reference to the public-interest mission of the organizations benefiting from the exception under this article should be read in conjunction with art. 1(1) and recital 20 (see comment above). In contrast with art. 1(1) however, this article specifies that among the uses permitted to achieve aims related to an organization's public interest mission are in particular the preservation of, the restoration of, and the provision of cultural and educational access to works and phonograms contained in its collection. **(b) Cost recovery.** Art. 6(2) expressly states that cultural heritage institutions may generate revenues in the course of such uses, for the exclusive purpose of covering their costs of digitizing orphan works and making them available to the public. The possibility to generate revenues from the activities of use is seen as an incentive to digitization (recital 21). This provision should be read in conjunction with art. 6(2)(c) and recital 23 of the Public Sector Information Directive, the latter of which states: 'Libraries, museums and archives should also be able to charge above marginal costs in order not to hinder their normal running. In the case of such public sector bodies the total income from supplying and allowing re-use of documents over the appropriate accounting period should not exceed the cost of collection, production, reproduction, dissemination, preservation and rights clearance, together with a reasonable return on investment. For the purpose of libraries, museums and archives and bearing in mind their particularities, the prices charged by the private sector for the re-use of identical or similar documents could be considered when calculating a reasonable return on investment.'

3. Name of identified author (para. 3). In case of multiple authorship of a work that is declared part-orphan, this requirement is established in deference to the moral right of attribution of the identified author(s).

4. Contracts in pursuit of public-interest mission unaffected (para. 4). Recital 22 states that contractual arrangements may play a role in fostering the digitization of European cultural heritage, it being understood that publicly accessible libraries, educational establishments and museums, as well as archives, film or audio heritage institutions and public-service broadcasting organizations, should be allowed, with a view to undertaking the uses permitted under this Directive, to conclude agreements with commercial partners for the digitization and making available to the public of orphan works. Those agreements may include financial contributions by such partners. Such agreements should not impose any restrictions on the beneficiaries of this Directive as to their use of orphan works and should not grant the commercial partner any rights to use, or control the use of, the orphan works. This is in line with art. 11 and recital 30 of the Public Sector Information Directive.

5. Payment of fair compensation (para. 5). The obligation to pay fair compensation to right owners who come forward and put an end to the orphan status of a work or phonogram was among the most debated provisions of the Proposal for a Directive, for organizations feared being confronted with significant claims for past uses of works of reappearing authors. Fair compensation for the use of the work can also be payable to the rightholders (e.g. publishers) depending on the type and extent of the use of the work. Member States must make provision for fair compensation, but it is up to Member States to determine the circumstances under which such payment is to be organized. In determining the possible level of fair compensation, recital 18 states that due account should be taken of Member States' cultural promotion objectives, of the non-commercial nature of the use made by the organizations in question in order to achieve aims related to their public-interest missions, such as promoting learning and disseminating culture, and of the possible harm to rightholders. Member States may elect to regulate the level of fair compensation or to leave it for agreement between a rightholder and the beneficiary institution. In the event of a dispute arising from the determination of the payment of fair compensation under the terms of the Directive, Member States are free to set up an alternative dispute resolution system.

[Continued application of other legal provisions]

Article 7

This Directive shall be without prejudice to provisions concerning, in particular, patent rights, trade marks, design rights, utility models, the topographies of semi-conductor products, type faces, conditional access, access to cable of broadcasting services, the protection of national treasures, legal deposit requirements, laws on restrictive practices and unfair competition, trade secrets, security, confidentiality, data protection and privacy, access to public documents, the law of contract, and rules on the freedom of the press and freedom of expression in the media.

1. Continued application. This provision specifies how Member States may permit certain additional uses under specific conditions. The Directive therefore leaves intact other legal forms of protection for works and phonograms, and provides an extensive but non-exhaustive list of some of those mechanisms. More importantly, this provision must be read in conjunction with recital 24 according to which this Directive is 'without prejudice to the arrangements in the Member States concerning the management of rights such as extended collective licences, legal presumptions of representation or transfer, collective management or similar arrangements or a combination of them, including for mass digitisation'.

[Application in time]

Article 8

(1) This Directive shall apply in respect of all works and phonograms referred to in Article 1 which are protected by the Member States' legislation in the field of copyright on or after 29 October 2014.

(2) This Directive shall apply without prejudice to any acts concluded and rights acquired before 29 October 2014.

1. Immediate application (para. 1). As with the other directives on copyright and neighbouring rights, being informed by the goal of harmonization, this Directive applies to existing works protected on or after the day the transposition term expired, i.e. 29 October 2014. Were the Directive to apply only to future works, there would be no actual harmonization for many decades, and the orphan works problem would effectively remain unresolved. Consequently, the implementation of the Directive might alter existing rights and obligations.

2. Preservation of rights (para 2). The phrase 'acts concluded' can be contrasted with the phrases 'acts of exploitation performed' and 'any contracts concluded' used in art. 13(2) and (6) of the Rental Right Directive. The second condition is for 'rights acquired.' In principle, such national copyrights are 'rights acquired' which should survive implementation of the Directive.

[Transposition]

Article 9

(1) Member States shall bring into force the laws, regulations and administrative provisions necessary to comply with this Directive by 29 October 2014. They shall forthwith communicate to the Commission the text of those provisions.

When Member States adopt those provisions, they shall contain a reference to this Directive or shall be accompanied by such a reference on the occasion of their official publication. The methods of making such reference shall be laid down by Member States.

(2) Member States shall communicate to the Commission the text of the main provisions of national law which they adopt in the field covered by this Directive.

1. Transposition. Member States were given a period of 24 months, expiring on 29 October 2014, to transpose the Directive in their national laws. The choice of method of transposition of the obligations under this Directive into national law was left to the national authorities.

[Review clause]

Article 10

The Commission shall keep under constant review the development of rights information sources and shall by 29 October 2015, and at annual intervals thereafter, submit a report concerning the possible inclusion in the scope of application of this Directive of publishers and of works or other protected subject-matter not currently included in its scope, and in particular stand-alone photographs and other images.

By 29 October 2015, the Commission shall submit to the European Parliament, the Council and the European Economic and Social Committee a report on the application of this Directive, in the light of the development of digital libraries.

When necessary, in particular to ensure the functioning of the internal market, the Commission shall submit proposals for amendment of this Directive.

A Member State that has valid reasons to consider that the implementation of this Directive hinders one of the national arrangements concerning the management of rights referred to in Article 1(5) may bring the matter to the attention of the Commission together with all relevant evidence. The Commission shall take such evidence into account when drawing up the report referred to in the second paragraph of this Article and when assessing whether it is necessary to submit proposals for amendment of this Directive.

1. General. As other directives in the field, art. 10 contains a review clause for monitoring the impact of the Directive. Only the third sentence, according to which the Commission shall submit proposals for amendment of this Directive if necessary to ensure the functioning of the internal market, is commonly found in other directives. Moreover, in contrast with other directives that set review intervals at three or five years, this article foresees an annual review process starting already after the first year from the date of implementation of the Directive in national law. This interval is particularly short in view of the fact that approximately one third of the Member States did not meet the implementation deadline. **(a) Information sources.** The Commission plans to periodically review the development of rights information sources. This review exercise should provide the occasion to examine whether the list of sources provided in Annex to the Directive and in national law are workable in practice, hopefully with a view to adapting the list if needed. **(b) Inclusion of other subject-matter.** The Commission also plans to periodically monitor the need to include in the scope of application of this Directive other works or other protected subject-matter not currently included in its scope, and in particular stand-alone photographs and other images. As a percentage, photographs and other images are indeed in the most common orphans. **(c) Negative effect on national arrangements.** The possibility for Member States to notify the Commission of the negative impact of the Directive on national arrangements concerning the management of rights may prove to be particularly important, for those Member States, such as the Nordic countries, that have set up a system of extended collective licensing for uses by cultural heritage institutions.

[Entry into force]

Article 11

This Directive shall enter into force on the day following that of its publication in the Official Journal of the European Union.

1. Entry into force. The Directive was published in the Official Journal on 27 October 2012 and went into force on that day.

[Addressees]

Article 12

This Directive is addressed to the Member States.

1. Addressees. According to art. 288 TFEU, Directives are binding as to the result to be achieved upon each Member State to which they are addressed. Art. 12 confirms that the Directive is addressed to Member States. This may seem superfluous in the context of the adoption of secondary legislation for the European Union, but it is good to realize that the implementation of the obligations flowing from this instrument is the sole responsibility of the Member States rather than that of cultural heritage institutions or any other stakeholder involved in the digitization and dissemination of works and phonograms. Member States will be held accountable if the provisions of national laws implementing this Directive are not complied with.

ANNEX

The sources referred to in Article 3(2) include the following:
(1) for published books:
  (a) **legal deposit, library catalogues and authority files maintained by libraries and other institutions;**
  (b) **the publishers' and authors' associations in the respective country;**
  (c) **existing databases and registries, WATCH (Writers, Artists and their Copyright Holders), the ISBN (International Standard Book Number) and databases listing books in print;**

    (d) the databases of the relevant collecting societies, in particular reproduction rights organisations;

    (e) sources that integrate multiple databases and registries, including VIAF (Virtual International Authority Files) and ARROW (Accessible Registries of Rights Information and Orphan Works);

(2) for newspapers, magazines, journals and periodicals:

    (a) the ISSN (International Standard Serial Number) for periodical publications;

    (b) indexes and catalogues from library holdings and collections;

    (c) legal deposit;

    (d) the publishers' associations and the authors' and journalists' associations in the respective country;

    (e) the databases of relevant collecting societies including reproduction rights organisations;

(3) for visual works, including fine art, photography, illustration, design, architecture, sketches of the latter works and other such works that are contained in books, journals, newspapers and magazines or other works:

    (a) the sources referred to in points (1) and (2);

    (b) the databases of the relevant collecting societies, in particular for visual arts, and including reproduction rights organisations;

    (c) the databases of picture agencies, where applicable;

(4) for audiovisual works and phonograms:

    (a) legal deposit;

    (b) the producers' associations in the respective country;

    (c) databases of film or audio heritage institutions and national libraries;

    (d) databases with relevant standards and identifiers such as ISAN (International Standard Audiovisual Number) for audiovisual material, ISWC (International Standard Music Work Code) for musical works and ISRC (International Standard Recording Code) for phonograms;

    (e) the databases of the relevant collecting societies, in particular for authors, performers, phonogram producers and audiovisual producers;

    (f) credits and other information appearing on the work's packaging;

    (g) databases of other relevant associations representing a specific category of rightholders.

DIRECTIVE 2014/26/EU

(Collective Rights Management Directive)

of the European Parliament and of the Council of 26 February 2014 on collective management of copyright and related rights and multi-territorial licensing of rights in musical works for online use in the internal market

[Introductory remarks]

1. Legislative history. Harmonization of collective rights management has been subject to study and debate since the Follow-up to the Green Paper on Copyright and the Challenge of Technology of 1991. In the Green Paper on Copyright and Related Rights in the Information Society of 1995 and its Follow-up of 1996, the Commission still found it premature to initiate Community action in this area. It stressed the importance of transparency, non-discrimination and effectiveness of collective management organizations (CMOs), but concluded that such conditions could be left to the market to develop alongside existing competition rules. In 2004 the European Parliament's Resolution on a Community framework for CMOs urged the Commission to take action to harmonize, democratise and create transparency in the area of collective rights management while taking account of the cultural and social role of CMOs. In its Communication on the Management of Copyright and Related Rights in the Internal Market of 2004, the Commission for the first time recognized that an internal market in collective rights management could be achieved only if the monitoring of CMOs under competition law were complemented by Community legislation on the efficiency, transparency and accountability of CMOs. These aspects were considered to impede the full potential of the internal market as regards the cross-border trade of goods and provision of services based on copyright and related rights. Surprisingly, when in 2005 it came to adopting a relevant measure, the Commission's focus shifted in terms of both substance and form. It adopted the Online Music Recommendation, a non-binding legal instrument that was chiefly aimed at creating competition between CMOs engaged in cross-border licensing of copyright and related rights for legitimate online music services. The Commission's choice for a soft law over a legislative approach met with fierce criticism from the European Parliament. The Parliament found that the Commission had circumvented the democratic process by adopting a recommendation without prior consultation and without the formal involvement of Parliament and the Council. It further expressed concerns about the legal uncertainty for rightholders and users resulting from the non-binding nature of the measure and about the potentially negative implications on local repertoires and cultural diversity resulting from the increased concentration of rights in a few larger CMOs. In 2012 the Commission published its Proposal of the Collective Rights Management Directive and an impact assessment report. After discussion in the European Parliament the proposal was amended and subsequently adopted on 26 February 2014. The Member States are obliged to implement the provisions of the Directive by 10 April 2016.

2. Aim and structure of Directive. The Directive has two complementary objectives. **(a) Good governance.** First, the Directive aims to ensure a high standard of governance by increasing transparency and efficiency in the functioning of CMOs. To this end it lays down rules concerning access to the activities of CMOs, their supervisory framework and the modalities for their governance, including rules on financial management, transparency and reporting. These rules codify some of the earlier competition law rulings on CMOs by the Commission and the ECJ. Furthermore, they implement the Commission's action plan laid down in the Communication on the Management of Copyright and Related Rights in the Internal Market of 2004 and provide general and binding application to some of the rules on good governance contained in the Online Music Recommendation. The substantive rules on good governance are laid down in Title II, while Title IV sets out measures of enforcement, including a mandatory supervisory framework by national competent authorities. **(b) Multi-territorial licensing.** The Directive further aims to improve the multi-territorial licensing by CMOs of authors' rights in musical works for online use. Recitals 38 and 39 explain that the Online Music Recommendation of 2005 has failed to sufficiently encourage the widespread multi-territorial licensing of online rights in musical works and to address the specific demands of multi-territorial licensing. As a result, the online market for music services in the EU is still fragmented. The Directive therefore aims to the support the creation of a digital single market for online music services by laying down rules on multi-territorial licensing of online rights in musical works in Title III. These rules build on the provisions of the Online Music Recommendation, but the Directive now confers binding legal effect on them.

3. Scope of Directive. (a) Substantive scope. The Directive applies to all CMOs established in the EU, with the exception of Title III, which applies only to EU-based CMOs managing authors' rights in musical works for online use on a multi-territorial basis. In the proposal for the directive the Commission explains that in areas other than the collective management of authors' rights in musical works, multi-territorial licensing has not given rise to any difficulties that need to be addressed. The Directive further applies to entities owned or controlled by CMOs that carry out management activities and, in part, to independent management entities established in the EU. Member States are free to apply the Directive to CMOs established outside the EU which operate in that Member State (recital 10). **(b) Level of harmonization.** While the proposal for the directive suggested that the Directive is a 'minimum harmonization' legal instrument, recital 9 clarifies that only Title II involves minimum harmonization. It provides that Member

States are free to subject CMOs established in their territories to more stringent standards than those laid down in Title II, provided that such standards are compatible with EU law. This seems to imply that Titles I, III, IV and V provide for maximum harmonization rules. In comparison to other directives in the field of copyright law, this Directive stands out because of its detailed provisions and exceptional length, comprising a total of 58 recitals, 45 articles and one Annex.

4. Legislative power. The Directive has as legal bases art. 50(1) TFEU on the freedom of establishment as regards a particular activity, art. 53(1) TFEU on the coordination of rules concerning the taking-up and pursuit of activities as self-employed persons and art. 62 TFEU on the freedom to provide services. Recital 3 also makes express reference to art. 167 TFEU, which obliges the Union to take cultural aspects into account and to respect and to promote cultural diversity. In 2012, the French Senate, the Luxembourg Chamber of Deputies, the Polish Sejm and the Swedish Parliament submitted reasoned opinions that the proposed directive did not comply with the principle of subsidiarity in art. 5 TFEU, as its provisions were overly prescriptive and detailed. In its opinion, the European Economic and Social Committee responded to these objections, stating that the 'minimum' provisions set out in the proposal 'leave Member States significant leeway for transposition, to allow them to respond to the expectations of authors and creators and to promote culture and its dissemination to the best of their ability'. On this point, recital 55 notes that the principles of proportionality and subsidiarity are complied with, since the Directive does not go beyond what is necessary to achieve its objectives and those objectives cannot be sufficiently achieved by Member States but, by reason of their scale and effects, can be better achieved at EU level.

[Bibliography]

A. Dietz, 'The Proposal of the EU Commission for a Directive on Collecting Societies and Cultural Diversity – a Missed Opportunity' (2014) *Auteurs & Media* 90-97

J. Drexl, 'Competition in the Field of Collective Management: Preferring "Creative Competition" to Allocative Efficiency in European Copyright Law' in P.L.C. Torremans (ed.), *Copyright Law: A Handbook of Contemporary Research* (Edward Elgar 2007) 255-282

M.M. Frabboni, 'Collective Management of Copyright and Related Rights: Achievements and Problems of Institutional Efforts Towards Harmonisation' in E. Derclaye (ed.) *Research Handbook on the Future of EU Copyright* (Edward Elgar 2009) 373-400

M.M. Frabboni, 'The Changing Market for Music Licences: A Redefinition of Collective Interests and Competitive Dynamics' in A. Flanagan & and

M.L. Montagnani (eds.), *Intellectual Property Law: Economics and Social Justice Perspectives* (Edward Elgar 2010) 144-162

D. Gervais (ed.), *Collective Management of Copyright and Related Rights* (3rd edn., Kluwer Law International 2015)

F. Gotzen, 'Multi-territorial Licences between Judge and Legislator. From the "Cisac" Cases to Directive 2014/26' (2014) 241 RIDA 94-161

C.B. Graber, 'Collective Rights Management, Competition Policy and Cultural Diversity: EU Lawmaking at a Crossroads' (2012) 4(1) *WIPO Journal* 35-43

L. Guibault, 'Collective Rights Management Directive' in I. Stamatoudi & P.L.C. Torremans (eds.), *Copyright Law in the European Union* (Edward Elgar 2014) 696-795

L. Guibault & S. van Gompel, 'Collective Management in the European Union' in D. Gervais (ed.), *Collective Management of Copyright and Related Rights* (3rd edn., Kluwer Law International 2015)

J.P. Quintais, 'Proposal for a Directive on Collective Rights Management and (Some) Multi-territorial Licensing' (2013) *European Intellectual Property Review* 65-73

T. Riis, 'Collecting Societies, Competition and the Services Directive' (2011) *Journal of Intellectual Property Law & Practice* 482-493

F. Trumpke, J. Drexl, R.M. Hilty & S. Nérisson, 'Comments of the Max Planck Institute for Intellectual Property and Competition Law on the Proposal for a Directive of the European Parliament and of the Council on Collective Management of Copyright and Related Rights and Multi-Territorial Licensing of Rights in Musical Works for Online Uses in the Internal Market COM (2012) 372' (2013) IIC 322-351

[Recitals]

THE EUROPEAN PARLIAMENT AND THE COUNCIL OF THE EUROPEAN UNION,

Having regard to the Treaty on the Functioning of the European Union, and in particular Articles 50(1) and 53(1) and Article 62 thereof,

Having regard to the proposal from the European Commission,

After transmission of the draft legislative act to the national parliaments,

Having regard to the opinion of the European Economic and Social Committee,[1]

---

1. OJ C 44, 15.2.2013, p. 104.

Acting in accordance with the ordinary legislative procedure,[2]

Whereas:

(1) The Union Directives which have been adopted in the area of copyright and related rights already provide a high level of protection for rightholders and thereby a framework wherein the exploitation of content protected by those rights can take place. Those Directives contribute to the development and maintenance of creativity. In an internal market where competition is not distorted, protecting innovation and intellectual creation also encourages investment in innovative services and products.

(2) The dissemination of content which is protected by copyright and related rights, including books, audiovisual productions and recorded music, and services linked thereto, requires the licensing of rights by different holders of copyright and related rights, such as authors, performers, producers and publishers. It is normally for the rightholder to choose between the individual or collective management of his rights, unless Member States provide otherwise, in compliance with Union law and the international obligations of the Union and its Member States. Management of copyright and related rights includes granting of licences to users, auditing of users, monitoring of the use of rights, enforcement of copyright and related rights, collection of rights revenue derived from the exploitation of rights and the distribution of the amounts due to rightholders. Collective management organisations enable rightholders to be remunerated for uses which they would not be in a position to control or enforce themselves, including in non-domestic markets.

(3) Article 167 of the Treaty on the Functioning of the European Union (TFEU) requires the Union to take cultural diversity into account in its action and to contribute to the flowering of the cultures of the Member States, while respecting their national and regional diversity and at the same time bringing the common cultural heritage to the fore. Collective management organisations play, and should continue to play, an important role as promoters of the diversity of cultural expression, both by enabling the smallest and less popular repertoires to access the market and by providing social, cultural and educational services for the benefit of their rightholders and the public.

(4) When established in the Union, collective management organisations should be able to enjoy the freedoms provided by the Treaties when representing rightholders who are resident or established in other Member States or granting licences to users who are resident or established in other Member States.

---

2. Position of the European Parliament of 4 February 2014 (not yet published in the Official Journal) and decision of the Council of 20 February 2014.

(5) There are significant differences in the national rules governing the functioning of collective management organisations, in particular as regards their transparency and accountability to their members and rightholders. This has led in a number of instances to difficulties, in particular for non-domestic rightholders when they seek to exercise their rights, and to poor financial management of the revenues collected. Problems with the functioning of collective management organisations lead to inefficiencies in the exploitation of copyright and related rights across the internal market, to the detriment of the members of collective management organisations, rightholders and users.

(6) The need to improve the functioning of collective management organisations has already been identified in Commission Recommendation 2005/737/EC.[3] That Recommendation set out a number of principles, such as the freedom of rightholders to choose their collective management organisations, equal treatment of categories of rightholders and equitable distribution of royalties. It called on collective management organisations to provide users with sufficient information on tariffs and repertoire in advance of negotiations between them. It also contained recommendations on accountability, rightholder representation in the decision-making bodies of collective management organisations and dispute resolution. However, the Recommendation has been unevenly followed.

(7) The protection of the interests of the members of collective management organisations, rightholders and third parties requires that the laws of the Member States relating to copyright management and multi-territorial licensing of online rights in musical works should be coordinated with a view to having equivalent safeguards throughout the Union. Therefore, this Directive should have as a legal base Article 50(1) TFEU.

(8) The aim of this Directive is to provide for coordination of national rules concerning access to the activity of managing copyright and related rights by collective management organisations, the modalities for their governance, and their supervisory framework, and it should therefore also have as a legal base Article 53(1) TFEU. In addition, since it is concerned with a sector offering services across the Union, this Directive should have as a legal base Article 62 TFEU.

(9) The aim of this Directive is to lay down requirements applicable to collective management organisations, in order to ensure a high standard of governance, financial management, transparency and reporting. This should not, however, prevent Member States from maintaining or imposing, in relation to collective management organisations established

---

3. Commission Recommendation 2005/737/EC of 18 May 2005 on collective cross-border management of copyright and related rights for legitimate online music services (OJ L 276, 21.10.2005, p. 54).

in their territories, more stringent standards than those laid down in Title II of this Directive, provided that such more stringent standards are compatible with Union law.

(10) Nothing in this Directive should preclude a Member State from applying the same or similar provisions to collective management organisations which are established outside the Union but which operate in that Member State.

(11) Nothing in this Directive should preclude collective management organisations from concluding representation agreements with other collective management organisations – in compliance with the competition rules laid down by Articles 101 and 102 TFEU – in the area of rights management in order to facilitate, improve and simplify the procedures for granting licences to users, including for the purposes of single invoicing, under equal, non-discriminatory and transparent conditions, and to offer multi-territorial licences also in areas other than those referred to in Title III of this Directive.

(12) This Directive, while applying to all collective management organisations, with the exception of Title III, which applies only to collective management organisations managing authors' rights in musical works for online use on a multi-territorial basis, does not interfere with arrangements concerning the management of rights in the Member States such as individual management, the extended effect of an agreement between a representative collective management organisation and a user, i.e. extended collective licensing, mandatory collective management, legal presumptions of representation and transfer of rights to collective management organisations.

(13) This Directive does not affect the possibility for Member States to determine by law, by regulation or by any other specific mechanism to that effect, rightholders' fair compensation for exceptions or limitations to the reproduction right provided for in Directive 2001/29/EC of the European Parliament and of the Council[4] and rightholders' remuneration for derogations from the exclusive right in respect of public lending provided for in Directive 2006/115/EC of the European Parliament and of the Council[5] applicable in their territory as well as the conditions applicable for their collection.

(14) This Directive does not require collective management organisations to adopt a specific legal form. In practice, those organisations operate in various legal forms such as associations, cooperatives or

---

4. Directive 2001/29/EC of the European Parliament and of the Council of 22 May 2001 on the harmonisation of certain aspects of copyright and related rights in the information society (OJ L 167, 22.6.2001, p. 10).

5. Directive 2006/115/EC of the European Parliament and of the Council of 12 December 2006 on rental right and lending right and on certain rights related to copyright in the field of intellectual property (OJ L 376, 27.12.2006, p. 28).

limited liability companies, which are controlled or owned by holders of copyright and related rights or by entities representing such rightholders. In some exceptional cases, however, due to the legal form of a collective management organisation, the element of ownership or control is not present. This is, for example, the case for foundations, which do not have members. None the less, the provisions of this Directive should also apply to those organisations. Similarly, Member States should take appropriate measures to prevent the circumvention of the obligations under this Directive through the choice of legal form. It should be noted that entities which represent rightholders, and which are members of collective management organisations, may be other collective management organisations, associations of rightholders, unions or other organisations.

(15) Rightholders should be free to entrust the management of their rights to independent management entities. Such independent management entities are commercial entities which differ from collective management organisations, inter alia, because they are not owned or controlled by rightholders. However, to the extent that such independent management entities carry out the same activities as collective management organisations, they should be obliged to provide certain information to the rightholders they represent, collective management organisations, users and the public.

(16) Audiovisual producers, record producers and broadcasters license their own rights, in certain cases alongside rights that have been transferred to them by, for instance, performers, on the basis of individually negotiated agreements, and act in their own interest. Book, music or newspaper publishers license rights that have been transferred to them on the basis of individually negotiated agreements and act in their own interest. Therefore audiovisual producers, record producers, broadcasters and publishers should not be regarded as 'independent management entities'. Furthermore, authors' and performers' managers and agents acting as intermediaries and representing rightholders in their relations with collective management organisations should not be regarded as 'independent management entities' since they do not manage rights in the sense of setting tariffs, granting licences or collecting money from users.

(17) Collective management organisations should be free to choose to have certain of their activities, such as the invoicing of users or the distribution of amounts due to rightholders, carried out by subsidiaries or by other entities that they control. In such cases, those provisions of this Directive that would be applicable if the relevant activity were carried out directly by a collective management organisation should be applicable to the activities of the subsidiaries or other entities.

(18) In order to ensure that holders of copyright and related rights can benefit fully from the internal market when their rights are being managed collectively and that their freedom to exercise their rights is

not unduly affected, it is necessary to provide for the inclusion of appropriate safeguards in the statute of collective management organisations. Moreover, a collective management organisation should not, when providing its management services, discriminate directly or indirectly between rightholders on the basis of their nationality, place of residence or place of establishment.

(19) Having regard to the freedoms established in the TFEU, collective management of copyright and related rights should entail a rightholder being able freely to choose a collective management organisation for the management of his rights, whether those rights be rights of communication to the public or reproduction rights, or categories of rights related to forms of exploitation such as broadcasting, theatrical exhibition or reproduction for online distribution, provided that the collective management organisation that the rightholder wishes to choose already manages such rights or categories of rights.

The rights, categories of rights or types of works and other subject-matter managed by the collective management organisation should be determined by the general assembly of members of that organisation if they are not already determined in its statute or prescribed by law. It is important that the rights and categories of rights be determined in a manner that maintains a balance between the freedom of rightholders to dispose of their works and other subject-matter and the ability of the organisation to manage the rights effectively, taking into account in particular the category of rights managed by the organisation and the creative sector in which it operates. Taking due account of that balance, rightholders should be able easily to withdraw such rights or categories of rights from a collective management organisation and to manage those rights individually or to entrust or transfer the management of all or part of them to another collective management organisation or another entity, irrespective of the Member State of nationality, residence or establishment of the collective management organisation, the other entity or the rightholder. Where a Member State, in compliance with Union law and the international obligations of the Union and its Member States, provides for mandatory collective management of rights, rightholders' choice would be limited to other collective management organisations.

Collective management organisations managing different types of works and other subject-matter, such as literary, musical or photographic works, should also allow this flexibility to rightholders as regards the management of different types of works and other subject-matter. As far as non-commercial uses are concerned, Member States should provide that collective management organisations take the necessary steps to ensure that their rightholders can exercise the right to grant licences for such uses. Such steps should include, inter alia, a decision by the collective management organisation on the conditions attached to the exercise of that right as well as the provision to their members of information on those conditions. Collective management organisations should inform rightholders of their choices and allow them to exercise the rights related to those choices as easily as possible. Rightholders who have already authorised the collective management organisation may be informed via the website of the organisation. A requirement for the consent of rightholders in the authorisation to the management of each right, category of rights or type of works and other subject-matter should not prevent the rightholders from accepting proposed subsequent amendments to that authorisation by tacit agreement in accordance with the conditions set out in national law. Neither contractual arrangements according to which a termination or withdrawal by rightholders has an immediate effect on licences granted prior to such termination or withdrawal, nor contractual arrangements according to which such licences remain unaffected for a certain period of time after such termination or withdrawal, are, as such, precluded by this Directive. Such arrangements should not, however, create an obstacle to the full application of this Directive. This Directive should not prejudice the possibility for rightholders to manage their rights individually, including for non-commercial uses.

(20) Membership of collective management organisations should be based on objective, transparent and non-discriminatory criteria, including as regards publishers who by virtue of an agreement on the exploitation of rights are entitled to a share of the income from the rights managed by collective management organisations and to collect such income from the collective management organisations. Those criteria should not oblige collective management organisations to accept members the management of whose rights, categories of rights or types of works or other subject-matter falls outside their scope of activity. The records kept by a collective management organisation should allow for the identification and location of its members and rightholders whose rights the organisation represents on the basis of authorisations given by those rightholders.

(21) In order to protect those rightholders whose rights are directly represented by the collective management organisation but who do not fulfil its membership requirements, it is appropriate to require that certain provisions of this Directive relating to members be also applied to such rightholders. Member States should be able also to provide such rightholders with rights to participate in the decision-making process of the collective management organisation.

(22) Collective management organisations should act in the best collective interests of the rightholders they represent. It is therefore important to provide for systems which enable the members of a collective management organisation to exercise their membership rights by participating in the organisation's decision-making process. Some collective management organisations have different categories of members, which may represent different types of rightholders, such as producers

and performers. The representation in the decision-making process of those different categories of members should be fair and balanced. The effectiveness of the rules on the general assembly of members of collective management organisations would be undermined if there were no provisions on how the general assembly should be run. Thus, it is necessary to ensure that the general assembly is convened regularly, and at least annually, and that the most important decisions in the collective management organisation are taken by the general assembly.

(23) All members of collective management organisations should be allowed to participate and vote in the general assembly of members. The exercise of those rights should be subject only to fair and proportionate restrictions. In some exceptional cases, collective management organisations are established in the legal form of a foundation, and thus have no members. In such cases, the powers of the general assembly of members should be exercised by the body entrusted with the supervisory function. Where collective management organisations have entities representing rightholders as their members, as may be the case where a collective management organisation is a limited liability company and its members are associations of rightholders, Member States should be able to provide that some or all powers of the general assembly of members are to be exercised by an assembly of those rightholders. The general assembly of members should, at least, have the power to set the framework of the activities of the management, in particular with respect to the use of rights revenue by the collective management organisation. This should, however, be without prejudice to the possibility for Member States to provide for more stringent rules on, for example, investments, mergers or taking out loans, including a prohibition on any such transactions. Collective management organisations should encourage the active participation of their members in the general assembly. The exercise of voting rights should be facilitated for members who attend the general assembly and also for those who do not. In addition to being able to exercise their rights by electronic means, members should be allowed to participate and vote in the general assembly of members through a proxy. Proxy voting should be restricted in cases of conflicts of interest. At the same time, Member States should provide for restrictions as regards proxies only if this does not prejudice the appropriate and effective participation of members in the decision-making process. In particular, the appointment of proxy-holders contributes to the appropriate and effective participation of members in the decision-making process and allows rightholders to have a true opportunity to opt for a collective management organisation of their choice, irrespective of the Member State of establishment of the organisation.

(24) Members should be allowed to participate in the continuous monitoring of the management of collective management organisations. To that end, those organisations should have a supervisory function

appropriate to their organisational structure and should allow members to be represented in the body that exercises that function. Depending on the organisational structure of the collective management organisation, the supervisory function may be exercised by a separate body, such as a supervisory board, or by some or all of the directors in the administrative board who do not manage the business of the collective management organisation. The requirement of fair and balanced representation of members should not prevent the collective management organisation from appointing third parties to exercise the supervisory function, including persons with relevant professional expertise and rightholders who do not fulfil the membership requirements or who are represented by the organisation not directly but via an entity which is a member of the collective management organisation.

(25) For reasons of sound management, the management of a collective management organisation must be independent. Managers, whether elected as directors or hired or employed by the organisation on the basis of a contract, should be required to declare, prior to taking up their position and thereafter on a yearly basis, whether there are conflicts between their interests and those of the rightholders that are represented by the collective management organisation. Such annual statements should be also made by persons exercising the supervisory function. Member States should be free to require collective management organisations to make such statements public or to submit them to public authorities.

(26) Collective management organisations collect, manage and distribute revenue from the exploitation of the rights entrusted to them by rightholders. That revenue is ultimately due to rightholders, who may have a direct legal relationship with the organisation, or may be represented via an entity which is a member of the collective management organisation or via a representation agreement. It is therefore important that a collective management organisation exercise the utmost diligence in collecting, managing and distributing that revenue. Accurate distribution is only possible where the collective management organisation maintains proper records of membership, licences and use of works and other subject-matter. Relevant data that are required for the efficient collective management of rights should also be provided by rightholders and users and verified by the collective management organisation.

(27) Amounts collected and due to rightholders should be kept separately in the accounts from any own assets the organisation may have. Without prejudice to the possibility for Member States to provide for more stringent rules on investment, including a prohibition of investment of the rights revenue, where such amounts are invested, this should be carried out in accordance with the general investment and risk management policy of the collective management organisation. In order to maintain a high level of protection of the rights of rightholders and to ensure that any income that may arise from the exploitation of such

rights accrues to their benefit, the investments made and held by the collective management organisation should be managed in accordance with criteria which would oblige the organisation to act prudently, while allowing it to decide on the most secure and efficient investment policy. This should allow the collective management organisation to opt for an asset allocation that suits the precise nature and duration of any exposure to risk of any rights revenue invested and does not unduly prejudice any rights revenue owed to rightholders.

(28) Since rightholders are entitled to be remunerated for the exploitation of their rights, it is important that management fees do not exceed justified costs of the management of the rights and that any deduction other than in respect of management fees, for example a deduction for social, cultural or educational purposes, should be decided by the members of the collective management organisation. The collective management organisations should be transparent towards rightholders regarding the rules governing such deductions. The same requirements should apply to any decision to use the rights revenue for collective distribution, such as scholarships. Rightholders should have access, on a non-discriminatory basis, to any social, cultural or educational service funded through such deductions. This Directive should not affect deductions under national law, such as deductions for the provision of social services by collective management organisations to rightholders, as regards any aspects that are not regulated by this Directive, provided that such deductions are in compliance with Union law.

(29) The distribution and payment of amounts due to individual rightholders or, as the case may be, to categories of rightholders, should be carried out in a timely manner and in accordance with the general policy on distribution of the collective management organisation concerned, including when they are performed via another entity representing the rightholders. Only objective reasons beyond the control of a collective management organisation can justify delay in the distribution and payment of amounts due to rightholders. Therefore, circumstances such as the rights revenue having been invested subject to a maturity date should not qualify as valid reasons for such a delay. It is appropriate to leave it to Member States to decide on rules ensuring timely distribution and the effective search for, and identification of, rightholders in cases where such objective reasons occur. In order to ensure that the amounts due to rightholders are appropriately and effectively distributed, without prejudice to the possibility for Member States to provide for more stringent rules, it is necessary to require collective management organisations to take reasonable and diligent measures, on the basis of good faith, to identify and locate the relevant rightholders. It is also appropriate that members of a collective management organisation, to the extent allowed for under national law, should decide on the use of any amounts that

cannot be distributed in situations where rightholders entitled to those amounts cannot be identified or located.

(30) Collective management organisations should be able to manage rights and collect revenue from their exploitation under representation agreements with other organisations. To protect the rights of the members of the other collective management organisation, a collective management organisation should not distinguish between the rights it manages under representation agreements and those it manages directly for its rightholders. Nor should the collective management organisation be allowed to apply deductions to the rights revenue collected on behalf of another collective management organisation, other than deductions in respect of management fees, without the express consent of the other organisation. It is also appropriate to require collective management organisations to distribute and make payments to other organisations on the basis of such representation agreements no later than when they distribute and make payments to their own members and to non-member rightholders whom they represent. Furthermore, the recipient organisation should in turn be required to distribute the amounts due to the rightholders it represents without delay.

(31) Fair and non-discriminatory commercial terms in licensing are particularly important to ensure that users can obtain licences for works and other subject-matter in respect of which a collective management organisation represents rights, and to ensure the appropriate remuneration of rightholders. Collective management organisations and users should therefore conduct licensing negotiations in good faith and apply tariffs which should be determined on the basis of objective and non-discriminatory criteria. It is appropriate to require that the licence fee or remuneration determined by collective management organisations be reasonable in relation to, inter alia, the economic value of the use of the rights in a particular context. Finally, collective management organisations should respond without undue delay to users' requests for licences.

(32) In the digital environment, collective management organisations are regularly required to license their repertoire for totally new forms of exploitation and business models. In such cases, and in order to foster an environment conducive to the development of such licences, without prejudice to the application of competition law rules, collective management organisations should have the flexibility required to provide, as swiftly as possible, individualised licences for innovative online services, without the risk that the terms of those licences could be used as a precedent for determining the terms for other licences.

(33) In order to ensure that collective management organisations can comply with the obligations set out in this Directive, users should provide those organisations with relevant information on the use of the rights represented by the collective management organisations. This obligation should not apply to natural persons acting for purposes outside their

trade, business, craft or profession, who therefore fall outside the definition of user as laid down in this Directive. Moreover, the information required by collective management organisations should be limited to what is reasonable, necessary and at the users' disposal in order to enable such organisations to perform their functions, taking into account the specific situation of small and medium-sized enterprises. That obligation could be included in an agreement between a collective management organisation and a user; this does not preclude national statutory rights to information. The deadlines applicable to the provision of information by users should be such as to allow collective management organisations to meet the deadlines set for the distribution of amounts due to rightholders. This Directive should be without prejudice to the possibility for Member States to require collective management organisations established in their territory to issue joint invoices.

(34) In order to enhance the trust of rightholders, users and other collective management organisations in the management of rights by collective management organisations, each collective management organisation should comply with specific transparency requirements. Each collective management organisation or its member being an entity responsible for attribution or payment of amounts due to rightholders should therefore be required to provide certain information to individual rightholders at least once a year, such as the amounts attributed or paid to them and the deductions made. Collective management organisations should also be required to provide sufficient information, including financial information, to the other collective management organisations whose rights they manage under representation agreements.

(35) In order to ensure that rightholders, other collective management organisations and users have access to information on the scope of activity of the organisation and the works or other subject-matter that it represents, a collective management organisation should provide information on those issues in response to a duly justified request. The question whether, and to what extent, reasonable fees can be charged for providing this service should be left to national law. Each collective management organisation should also make public information on its structure and on the way in which it carries out its activities, including in particular its statutes and general policies on management fees, deductions and tariffs.

(36) In order to ensure that rightholders are in a position to monitor and compare the respective performances of collective management organisations, such organisations should make public an annual transparency report comprising comparable audited financial information specific to their activities. Collective management organisations should also make public an annual special report, forming part of the annual transparency report, on the use of amounts dedicated to social, cultural and educational services. This Directive should not prevent a collective

management organisation from publishing the information required by the annual transparency report in a single document, for example as part of its annual financial statements, or in separate reports.

(37) Providers of online services which make use of musical works, such as music services that allow consumers to download music or to listen to it in streaming mode, as well as other services providing access to films or games where music is an important element, must first obtain the right to use such works. Directive 2001/29/EC requires that a licence be obtained for each of the rights in the online exploitation of musical works. In respect of authors, those rights are the exclusive right of reproduction and the exclusive right of communication to the public of musical works, which includes the right of making available. Those rights may be managed by the individual rightholders themselves, such as authors or music publishers, or by collective management organisations that provide collective management services to rightholders. Different collective management organisations may manage authors' rights of reproduction and communication to the public. Furthermore, there are cases where several rightholders have rights in the same work and may have authorised different organisations to license their respective shares of rights in the work. Any user wishing to provide an online service offering a wide choice of musical works to consumers needs to aggregate rights in works from different rightholders and collective management organisations.

(38) While the internet knows no borders, the online market for music services in the Union is still fragmented, and a digital single market has not yet been fully achieved. The complexity and difficulty associated with the collective management of rights in Europe has, in a number of cases, exacerbated the fragmentation of the European digital market for online music services. This situation is in stark contrast to the rapidly growing demand on the part of consumers for access to digital content and associated innovative services, including across national borders.

(39) Commission Recommendation 2005/737/EC promoted a new regulatory environment better suited to the management, at Union level, of copyright and related rights for the provision of legitimate online music services. It recognised that, in an era of online exploitation of musical works, commercial users need a licensing policy that corresponds to the ubiquity of the online environment and is multi-territorial. However, the Recommendation has not been sufficient to encourage the widespread multi-territorial licensing of online rights in musical works or to address the specific demands of multi-territorial licensing.

(40) In the online music sector, where collective management of authors' rights on a territorial basis remains the norm, it is essential to create conditions conducive to the most effective licensing practices by collective management organisations in an increasingly cross-border context. It is therefore appropriate to provide a set of rules prescribing

basic conditions for the provision by collective management organisations of multi-territorial collective licensing of authors' rights in musical works for online use, including lyrics. The same rules should apply to such licensing for all musical works, including musical works incorporated in audiovisual works. However, online services solely providing access to musical works in sheet music form should not be covered. The provisions of this Directive should ensure the necessary minimum quality of cross-border services provided by collective management organisations, notably in terms of transparency of repertoire represented and accuracy of financial flows related to the use of the rights. They should also set out a framework for facilitating the voluntary aggregation of music repertoire and rights, thus reducing the number of licences a user needs to operate a multi-territory, multi-repertoire service. Those provisions should enable a collective management organisation to request another organisation to represent its repertoire on a multi-territorial basis where it cannot or does not wish to fulfil the requirements itself. There should be an obligation on the requested organisation, provided that it already aggregates repertoire and offers or grants multi-territorial licences, to accept the mandate of the requesting organisation. The development of legal online music services across the Union should also contribute to the fight against online infringements of copyright.

(41) The availability of accurate and comprehensive information on musical works, rightholders and the rights that each collective management organisation is authorised to represent in a given territory is of particular importance for an effective and transparent licensing process, for the subsequent processing of the users' reports and the related invoicing of service providers, and for the distribution of amounts due. For that reason, collective management organisations granting multi-territorial licences for musical works should be able to process such detailed data quickly and accurately. This requires the use of databases on ownership of rights that are licensed on a multi-territorial basis, containing data that allow for the identification of works, rights and rightholders that a collective management organisation is authorised to represent and of the territories covered by the authorisation. Any changes to that information should be taken into account without undue delay and the databases should be continually updated. Those databases should also help to match information on works with information on phonograms or any other fixation in which the work has been incorporated. It is also important to ensure that prospective users and rightholders, as well as collective management organisations, have access to the information they need in order to identify the repertoire that those organisations are representing. Collective management organisations should be able to take measures to protect the accuracy and

integrity of the data, to control their reuse or to protect commercially sensitive information.

(42) In order to ensure that the data on the music repertoire they process are as accurate as possible, collective management organisations granting multi-territorial licences in musical works should be required to update their databases continuously and without delay as necessary. They should establish easily accessible procedures to enable online service providers, as well as rightholders and other collective management organisations, to inform them of any inaccuracy that the organisations' databases may contain in respect of works they own or control, including rights – in whole or in part – and territories for which they have mandated the relevant collective management organisation to act, without however jeopardising the veracity and integrity of the data held by the collective management organisation. Since Directive 95/46/EC of the European Parliament and of the Council[6] grants to every data subject the right to obtain rectification, erasure or blocking of inaccurate or incomplete data, this Directive should also ensure that inaccurate information regarding rightholders or other collective management organisations in the case of multi-territorial licences is to be corrected without undue delay. Collective management organisations should also have the capacity to process electronically the registration of works and authorisations to manage rights. Given the importance of information automation for the fast and effective processing of data, collective management organisations should provide for the use of electronic means for the structured communication of that information by rightholders. Collective management organisations should, as far as possible, ensure that such electronic means take into account the relevant voluntary industry standards or practices developed at international or Union level.

(43) Industry standards for music use, sales reporting and invoicing are instrumental in improving efficiency in the exchange of data between collective management organisations and users. Monitoring the use of licences should respect fundamental rights, including the right to respect for private and family life and the right to protection of personal data. In order to ensure that these efficiency gains result in faster financial processing and ultimately in earlier payments to rightholders, collective management organisations should be required to invoice service providers and to distribute amounts due to rightholders without delay. For this requirement to be effective, it is necessary that users provide collective management organisations with accurate and timely reports on the use of works. Collective management organisations should not be required to accept users' reports in proprietary formats when widely used industry

6. Directive 95/46/EC of the European Parliament and of the Council of 24 October 1995 on the protection of individuals with regard to the processing of personal data and on the free movement of such data (OJ L 281, 23.11.1995, p. 31).

standards are available. Collective management organisations should not be prevented from outsourcing services relating to the granting of multi-territorial licences for online rights in musical works. Sharing or consolidation of back-office capabilities should help the organisations to improve management services and rationalise investments in data management tools.

(44) Aggregating different music repertoires for multi-territorial licensing facilitates the licensing process and, by making all repertoires accessible to the market for multi-territorial licensing, enhances cultural diversity and contributes to reducing the number of transactions an online service provider needs in order to offer services. This aggregation of repertoires should facilitate the development of new online services, and should also result in a reduction of transaction costs being passed on to consumers. Therefore, collective management organisations that are not willing or not able to grant multi-territorial licences directly in their own music repertoire should be encouraged on a voluntary basis to mandate other collective management organisations to manage their repertoire on a non-discriminatory basis. Exclusivity in agreements on multi-territorial licences would restrict the choices available to users seeking multi-territorial licences and also restrict the choices available to collective management organisations seeking administration services for their repertoire on a multi-territorial basis. Therefore, all representation agreements between collective management organisations providing for multi-territorial licensing should be concluded on a non-exclusive basis.

(45) The transparency of the conditions under which collective management organisations manage online rights is of particular importance to members of collective management organisations. Collective management organisations should therefore provide sufficient information to their members on the main terms of any agreement mandating any other collective management organisation to represent those members' online music rights for the purposes of multi-territorial licensing.

(46) It is also important to require any collective management organisations that offer or grant multi-territorial licences to agree to represent the repertoire of any collective management organisations that decide not to do so directly. To ensure that this requirement is not disproportionate and does not go beyond what is necessary, the requested collective management organisation should only be required to accept the representation if the request is limited to the online right or categories of online rights that it represents itself. Moreover, this requirement should only apply to collective management organisations which aggregate repertoire and should not extend to collective management organisations which provide multi-territorial licences for their own repertoire only. Nor should it apply to collective management organisations which merely aggregate rights in the same works for the purpose of being able to license jointly both the right of reproduction and the right

of communication to the public in respect of such works. To protect the interests of the rightholders of the mandating collective management organisation and to ensure that small and less well-known repertoires in Member States can access the internal market on equal terms, it is important that the repertoire of the mandating collective management organisation be managed on the same conditions as the repertoire of the mandated collective management organisation and that it is included in offers addressed by the mandated collective management organisation to online service providers. The management fee charged by the mandated collective management organisation should allow that organisation to recoup the necessary and reasonable investments incurred. Any agreement whereby a collective management organisation mandates another organisation or organisations to grant multi-territorial licences in its own music repertoire for online use should not prevent the first-mentioned collective management organisation from continuing to grant licences limited to the territory of the Member State where that organisation is established, in its own repertoire and in any other repertoire it may be authorised to represent in that territory.

(47) The objectives and effectiveness of the rules on multi-territorial licensing by collective management organisations would be significantly jeopardised if rightholders were not able to exercise such rights in respect of multi-territorial licences when the collective management organisation to which they have granted their rights did not grant or offer multi-territorial licences and furthermore did not want to mandate another collective management organisation to do so. For this reason, it would be important in such circumstances to enable rightholders to exercise the right to grant the multi-territorial licences required by online service providers themselves or through another party or parties, by withdrawing from their original collective management organisation their rights to the extent necessary for multi-territorial licensing for online uses, and to leave the same rights with their original organisation for the purposes of mono-territorial licensing.

(48) Broadcasting organisations generally rely on a licence from a local collective management organisation for their own broadcasts of television and radio programmes which include musical works. That licence is often limited to broadcasting activities. A licence for online rights in musical works would be required in order to allow such television or radio broadcasts to be also available online. To facilitate the licensing of online rights in musical works for the purposes of simultaneous and delayed transmission online of television and radio broadcasts, it is necessary to provide for a derogation from the rules that would otherwise apply to the multi-territorial licensing of online rights in musical works. Such a derogation should be limited to what is necessary in order to allow access to television or radio programmes online and to material having a clear and subordinate relationship to the original broadcast

produced for purposes such as supplementing, previewing or reviewing the television or radio programme concerned. That derogation should not operate so as to distort competition with other services which give consumers access to individual musical or audiovisual works online, nor lead to restrictive practices, such as market or customer sharing, which would be in breach of Article 101 or 102 TFEU.

(49) It is necessary to ensure the effective enforcement of the provisions of national law adopted pursuant to this Directive. Collective management organisations should offer their members specific procedures for handling complaints. Those procedures should also be made available to other rightholders directly represented by the organisation and to other collective management organisations on whose behalf it manages rights under a representation agreement. Furthermore, Member States should be able to provide that disputes between collective management organisations, their members, rightholders or users as to the application of this Directive can be submitted to a rapid, independent and impartial alternative dispute resolution procedure. In particular, the effectiveness of the rules on multi-territorial licensing of online rights in musical works could be undermined if disputes between collective management organisations and other parties were not resolved quickly and efficiently. As a result, it is appropriate to provide, without prejudice to the right of access to a tribunal, for the possibility of easily accessible, efficient and impartial out-of-court procedures, such as mediation or arbitration, for resolving conflicts between, on the one hand, collective management organisations granting multi-territorial licences and, on the other, online service providers, rightholders or other collective management organisations. This Directive neither prescribes a specific manner in which such alternative dispute resolution should be organised, nor determines which body should carry it out, provided that its independence, impartiality and efficiency are guaranteed. Finally, it is also appropriate to require that Member States have independent, impartial and effective dispute resolution procedures, via bodies possessing expertise in intellectual property law or via courts, suitable for settling commercial disputes between collective management organisations and users on existing or proposed licensing conditions or on a breach of contract.

(50) Member States should establish appropriate procedures by means of which it will be possible to monitor compliance by collective management organisations with this Directive. While it is not appropriate for this Directive to restrict the choice of Member States as to competent authorities, nor as regards the ex-ante or ex-post nature of the control over collective management organisations, it should be ensured that such authorities are capable of addressing in an effective and timely manner any concern that may arise in the application of this Directive. Member States should not be obliged to set up new

competent authorities. Moreover, it should also be possible for members of a collective management organisation, rightholders, users, collective management organisations and other interested parties to notify a competent authority in respect of activities or circumstances which, in their opinion, constitute a breach of law by collective management organisations and, where relevant, users. Member States should ensure that competent authorities have the power to impose sanctions or measures where provisions of national law implementing this Directive are not complied with. This Directive does not provide for specific types of sanctions or measures, provided that they are effective, proportionate and dissuasive. Such sanctions or measures may include orders to dismiss directors who have acted negligently, inspections at the premises of a collective management organisation or, in cases where an authorisation is issued for an organisation to operate, the withdrawal of such authorisation. This Directive should remain neutral as regards the prior authorisation and supervision regimes in the Member States, including a requirement for the representativeness of the collective management organisation, in so far as those regimes are compatible with Union law and do not create an obstacle to the full application of this Directive.

(51) In order to ensure that the requirements for multi-territorial licensing are complied with, specific provisions on the monitoring of their implementation should be laid down. The competent authorities of the Member States and the Commission should cooperate with each other to that end. Member States should provide each other with mutual assistance by way of exchange of information between their competent authorities in order to facilitate the monitoring of collective management organisations.

(52) It is important for collective management organisations to respect the rights to private life and personal data protection of any rightholder, member, user and other individual whose personal data they process. Directive 95/46/EC governs the processing of personal data carried out in the Member States in the context of that Directive and under the supervision of the Member States' competent authorities, in particular the public independent authorities designated by the Member States. Rightholders should be given appropriate information about the processing of their data, the recipients of those data, time limits for the retention of such data in any database, and the way in which rightholders can exercise their rights to access, correct or delete their personal data concerning them in accordance with Directive 95/46/EC. In particular, unique identifiers which allow for the indirect identification of a person should be treated as personal data within the meaning of that Directive.

(53) Provisions on enforcement measures should be without prejudice to the competencies of national independent public authorities established by the Member States pursuant to Directive 95/46/EC to monitor

compliance with national provisions adopted in implementation of that Directive.

(54) This Directive respects the fundamental rights and observes the principles enshrined in the Charter of Fundamental Rights of the European Union ('the Charter'). Provisions in this Directive relating to dispute resolution should not prevent parties from exercising their right of access to a tribunal as guaranteed in the Charter.

(55) Since the objectives of this Directive, namely to improve the ability of their members to exercise control over the activities of collective management organisations, to guarantee sufficient transparency by collective management organisations and to improve the multi-territorial licensing of authors' rights in musical works for online use, cannot be sufficiently achieved by Member States but can rather, by reason of their scale and effects, be better achieved at Union level, the Union may adopt measures in accordance with the principle of subsidiarity as set out in Article 5 of the Treaty on European Union. In accordance with the principle of proportionality, as set out in that Article, this Directive does not go beyond what is necessary in order to achieve those objectives.

(56) The provisions of this Directive are without prejudice to the application of rules on competition, and any other relevant law in other areas including confidentiality, trade secrets, privacy, access to documents, the law of contract and private international law relating to the conflict of laws and the jurisdiction of courts, and workers' and employers' freedom of association and their right to organise.

(57) In accordance with the Joint Political Declaration of 28 September 2011 of Member States and the Commission on explanatory documents,[7] Member States have undertaken to accompany, in justified cases, the notification of their transposition measures with one or more documents explaining the relationship between the components of a directive and the corresponding parts of national transposition instruments. With regard to this Directive, the legislator considers the transmission of such documents to be justified.

(58) The European Data Protection Supervisor was consulted in accordance with Article 28(2) of Regulation (EC) No 45/2001 of the European Parliament and of the Council[8] and delivered an opinion on 9 October 2012.

HAVE ADOPTED THIS DIRECTIVE:

---

7. OJ C 369, 17.12.2011, p. 14.
8. Regulation (EC) No 45/2001 of the European Parliament and of the Council of 18 December 2000 on the protection of individuals with regard to the processing of personal data by the Community institutions and bodies and on the free movement of such data (OJ L 8, 12.1.2001, p. 1).

TITLE I. GENERAL PROVISIONS

[Subject-matter]

Article 1

This Directive lays down requirements necessary to ensure the proper functioning of the management of copyright and related rights by collective management organisations. It also lays down requirements for multi-territorial licensing by collective management organisations of authors' rights in musical works for online use.

1. General. Art. 1 contains no substantive rule, but merely sets out the subject-matter of the Directive, thereby unfolding its twofold objective of providing a harmonized framework for the good governance of CMOs and for the multi-territorial licensing by CMOs of authors' rights in musical works for online use. It serves as a prelude to art. 2, which sets out in more detail in which parts of the Directive these two objectives are being addressed.

2. Unregulated matters. While having the regulation of CMOs as its object, recital 12 makes clear that this Directive does not interfere with arrangements concerning the management of rights in the Member States such as individual management, extended collective licensing, mandatory collective management, legal presumptions of representation and transfer of rights to CMOs. It further does not affect the possibility for Member States to regulate and establish the conditions applicable for the collection of rightholders' fair compensation for exceptions or limitations to the reproduction right in the Information Society Directive and rightholders' remuneration for derogations from the exclusive lending right in the Rental Right Directive applicable in their territory (recital 13). Recital 11 states that nothing in this Directive should preclude CMOs from concluding representation agreements with other CMOs to facilitate, improve and simplify the procedures for granting licences to users and to offer multi-territorial licences also in areas other than those referred to in Title III.

[Scope]

Article 2

(1) Titles I, II, IV and V with the exception of Article 34(2) and Article 38 apply to all collective management organisations established in the Union.

(2) Title III and Article 34(2) and Article 38 apply to collective management organisations established in the Union managing authors' rights in musical works for online use on a multi-territorial basis.

(3) The relevant provisions of this Directive apply to entities directly or indirectly owned or controlled, wholly or in part, by a collective

management organisation, provided that such entities carry out an activity which, if carried out by the collective management organisation, would be subject to the provisions of this Directive.

(4) Article 16(1), Articles 18 and 20, points (a), (b), (c), (e), (f) and (g) of Article 21(1) and Articles 36 and 42 apply to all independent management entities established in the Union.

1. General. Art. 2 delineates the scope of the Directive.

2. All CMOs established in the EU (para. 1). Titles I, II, IV and V, with the exception of arts. 34(2) and 38, contain general provisions on subject-matter, scope and definitions; organizational and transparency provisions; provisions on complaint and dispute resolution procedures; and reporting and final provisions. Art. 2(1) states that these rules apply to all CMOs established in the EU, no matter in which sector they are active.

3. CMOs granting multi-territorial licences (para. 2). Title III and arts. 34(2) and 38 deal specifically with multi-territorial licensing of online rights in musical works by CMOs. Art. 2(2) specifies that these provisions apply to CMOs established in the EU managing authors' rights in musical works for online use on a multi-territorial basis. EU-based CMOs which grant or offer to grant multi-territorial licences for online use of author's rights in musical works are consequently bound by the entire Directive, as they fall within the scope of both art. 2(1) and (2). All other CMOs established in the EU are subject only to Titles I, II, IV and V, with the exception of arts. 34(2) and 38. Member States may choose to apply the Directive to CMOs established outside the EU but operating in their territories (recital 10).

4. Other entities carrying out collective management activities (para. 3). Art. 2(3) extends the scope of the Directive to entities that are directly or indirectly owned or controlled by CMOs and carry out collective management activities that fall within the reach of the Directive. Recital 17 gives the example of entities carrying out the invoicing of users or the distribution of amounts due to rightholders on behalf of CMOs.

5. Independent management entities (para. 4). Art. 2(4) subjects so-called 'independent management entities' established in the EU to specific provisions of the Directive, involving obligations to conduct licensing negotiations in good faith (art. 16(1)), transparency rules (arts. 18, 20, 21(1) (a)-(c) and (e)-(g)), mechanisms for compliance control (art. 36), and rules on the processing of personal data (art. 42). Recital 16 explains that independent management entities carry out similar activities as CMOs, which would justify obliging them to provide certain information to rightholders they represent, CMOs, users and the public. Definitions of 'CMOs' and 'independent management entities' are contained in art. 3(a) and (b).

[Definitions]

Article 3

For the purposes of this Directive, the following definitions shall apply:

(a) 'collective management organisation' means any organisation which is authorised by law or by way of assignment, licence or any other contractual arrangement to manage copyright or rights related to copyright on behalf of more than one rightholder, for the collective benefit of those rightholders, as its sole or main purpose, and which fulfils one or both of the following criteria:

    (i) it is owned or controlled by its members;

    (ii) it is organised on a not-for-profit basis;

(b) 'independent management entity' means any organisation which is authorised by law or by way of assignment, licence or any other contractual arrangement to manage copyright or rights related to copyright on behalf of more than one rightholder, for the collective benefit of those rightholders, as its sole or main purpose, and which is:

    (i) neither owned nor controlled, directly or indirectly, wholly or in part, by rightholders; and

    (ii) organised on a for-profit basis;

(c) 'rightholder' means any person or entity, other than a collective management organisation, that holds a copyright or related right or, under an agreement for the exploitation of rights or by law, is entitled to a share of the rights revenue;

(d) 'member' means a rightholder or an entity representing rightholders, including other collective management organisations and associations of rightholders, fulfilling the membership requirements of the collective management organisation and admitted by it;

(e) 'statute' means the memorandum and articles of association, the statute, the rules or documents of constitution of a collective management organisation;

(f) 'general assembly of members' means the body in the collective management organisation wherein members participate and exercise their voting rights, regardless of the legal form of the organisation;

(g) 'director' means:

    (i) where national law or the statute of the collective management organisation provides for a unitary board, any member of the administrative board;

    (ii) where national law or the statute of the collective management organisation provides for a dual board, any member of the management board or the supervisory board;

(h) 'rights revenue' means income collected by a collective management organisation on behalf of rightholders, whether deriving from an exclusive right, a right to remuneration or a right to compensation;

(i) 'management fees' means the amounts charged, deducted or offset by a collective management organisation from rights revenue or from any income arising from the investment of rights revenue in order to cover the costs of its management of copyright or related rights;

(j) 'representation agreement' means any agreement between collective management organisations whereby one collective management organisation mandates another collective management organisation to manage the rights it represents, including an agreement concluded under Articles 29 and 30;

(k) 'user' means any person or entity that is carrying out acts subject to the authorisation of rightholders, remuneration of rightholders or payment of compensation to rightholders and is not acting in the capacity of a consumer;

(l) 'repertoire' means the works in respect of which a collective management organisation manages rights;

(m) 'multi-territorial licence' means a licence which covers the territory of more than one Member State;

(n) 'online rights in musical works' means any of the rights of an author in a musical work provided for under Articles 2 and 3 of Directive 2001/29/EC which are required for the provision of an online service.

1. General. Art. 3 is important because the Directive's scope of application largely hinges on the definitions it provides. Some terms, such as 'multi-territorial licence', have been defined earlier in the Online Music Recommendation. The same holds for the term 'repertoire', which is defined here as the works in respect of which a CMO manages rights. That this term refers only to copyright protected works and not to subject-matter protected by related rights has to do with the fact that 'repertoire' is used solely as a technical legal term in the context of Title III, which regulates multi-territorial licensing of authors' rights in musical works for online use. Only in recitals 1 to 6 is the term used in a more general fashion, extending also to the subject-matter protected by related rights. The terms 'rights revenue' and 'management fees' are defined in accordance with the Commission's *CISAC* and *IFPI Simulcasting* decisions. Some terms in art. 3 are explicitly defined broadly, so as to ensure that the Directive has sufficiently wide reach. The term 'statute', for example, not only relates to the statute of a CMO, but also to the memorandum and articles of association, the rules or documents of constitution of a CMO.

2. Definition of collective management organization (sub a). The definition of 'CMOs' is key to the Directive's aim and objectives, as it determines which organizations fall within or outside its scope of application. A too broad or narrow definition of 'CMOs' would have direct effect on the Directive's reach. This may explain why the Directive has not adopted existing definitions of 'collecting societies' in art. 1(4) of the Satellite and Cable Directive, which is broad and perhaps too unspecific, or 'collective rights manager' in the Online Music Recommendation, which contains detailed language about the activities of CMOs. The latter would entail the risk that CMOs could escape the obligations under the Directive if they alter their services because of technological changes, new business models or simply to avoid control of their activities. A definition that relies on membership structures of CMOs (like the one contained in the initial proposal) holds a similar risk of circumvention, as it allows CMOs to switch legal forms to avoid the application of the Directive. The Directive has therefore adopted a purpose-oriented definition. Art. 3(a) defines a CMO as any organization set up 'to manage copyright or rights related to copyright on behalf of more than one rightholder, for the collective benefit of those rightholders, as its sole or main purpose'. The definition further indicates that a CMO can be 'authorised by law or by way of assignment, licence or any other contractual arrangement' and that it must either be 'owned or controlled by its members', be 'organised on a not-for-profit basis', or both. Accordingly, the definition leaves open whether CMOs have been mandated by law or by rightholders directly. Moreover, it ensures that the operation of the Directive extends to CMOs regardless of their legal form. It applies to CMOs established as associations, cooperatives or limited liability companies, which are controlled or owned by members (i.e. rightholders or entities representing them, such as other CMOs, associations of rightholders, unions or other organizations), as well as to CMOs operating as foundations, which do not have members and therefore are not under a membership structure, but which are organized on a not-for-profit basis (recital 14).

3. Definition of independent management entity (sub b). Pursuant to art. 2(4), only few provisions of the Directive apply to independent management entities. The Directive must therefore clearly spell out how these entities differentiate from CMOs, as this provision could otherwise turn into an escape clause for CMOs trying to avoid the application of most of the Directive by claiming to be independent management entities. The definition of 'independent management entity' follows the definition of CMO insofar as the purpose and mandate of the organizations are concerned. It also applies to 'any organisation which is authorised by law or by way of assignment, licence or any other contractual arrangement to manage copyright or rights related to copyright on behalf of more than one rightholder, for the collective benefit of those rightholders, as its sole or main purpose'. Independent management entities differ from CMOs in that they are 'organised on a for-profit basis' and are 'neither owned nor controlled, directly or indirectly, wholly or in part, by rightholders'. No explicit examples of independent management entities are given, but recital 16 names organizations that should not be regarded as independent management entities. The recital lists audiovisual producers, record producers, broadcasters and book, music or newspaper publishers, because they license rights that have been transferred to them on the basis of individually negotiated agreements and act in their own interest; and authors' and performers' managers and agents acting as intermediaries and representing rightholders in their relations with CMOs, because they do not manage rights in the sense of setting tariffs, granting licences or collecting money from users.

4. Definition of rightholder and member (sub c and d). CMOs may represent different types of rightholders, such as authors, performers and producers who enjoy rights in their own names, but also publishers who by virtue of an agreement on the exploitation of rights are entitled to a share of the income from the rights managed by CMOs and to collect such income from CMOs (recital 20). To ensure that all these rightholders fall within the scope of application of the Directive, art. 3(c) defines 'rightholder' as 'any person or entity, other than a CMO, that holds a copyright or related right or, under an agreement for the exploitation of rights or by law, is entitled to a share of the rights revenue'. The definition of 'member' of a CMO is more narrowly construed as a rightholder or an entity representing rightholders that fulfils the membership requirements of the CMO and is admitted by it. In practice, CMOs manage rights of their members, but sometimes also of rightholders who are not members but who have a legal relationship by law or by way of assignment, licence or other contractual arrangement with them. The Directive contains rules allowing members of CMOs to take part and vote in the general assembly of members and to participate in the continuous monitoring of the management of CMOs. To protect rightholders whose rights are directly represented by CMOs but who do not fulfil their membership conditions, art. 7 obliges certain provisions of the Directive relating to members to be also applied to such rightholders.

5. Definition of user (sub k). The Directive defines 'user' in a broad fashion as any person or entity that is carrying out acts which, from the point of view of right owners, would require their authorization or payment of remuneration or compensation. Persons acting in the capacity of consumers are excluded from this definition. These are 'natural persons acting for purposes outside their trade, business, craft or profession' (recital 33), which is in accordance with the definition of 'consumer' in e.g. art. 2(1) of the Consumer Rights Directive.

6. Definition of online rights in musical works (sub n). This definition is relevant for the provisions on multi-territorial licensing of authors' rights in musical works for online use in Title III. 'Online rights in musical works' are defined as 'any of the rights of an author in a musical work which are required for the provision of an online service'. The 'musical work' involves both the musical composition and the lyrics. Recitals 37 and 40 clarify that 'online services' include music services that allow consumers to download music or to listen to it in streaming mode and services providing access to films or games in which musical works are incorporated. Online services solely providing access to musical works in sheet music form are excluded from the definition (recital 40). The definition of art. 3(n) directly refers to the rights of reproduction and communication to the public, including the making available right, in arts. 2 and 3 of the Information Society Directive. Often the licensing of each of these rights is required for the exploitation of musical works in online services. Recital 37 forewarns that different rightholders and CMOs may be involved in the management of those rights.

TITLE II. COLLECTIVE MANAGEMENT ORGANISATIONS

CHAPTER 1. REPRESENTATION OF RIGHTHOLDERS AND MEMBERSHIP AND ORGANISATION OF COLLECTIVE MANAGEMENT ORGANISATIONS

[General principles]

Article 4

Member States shall ensure that collective management organisations act in the best interests of the rightholders whose rights they represent and that they do not impose on them any obligations which are not objectively necessary for the protection of their rights and interests or for the effective management of their rights.

1. General. Art. 4 instructs Member States to adopt measures requiring CMOs to act in the best interests of rightholders whose rights they represent and to not impose any obligations that run counter to the protection of those interests. The rights and obligations ensuing from this general norm are set out in further detail in the other provisions of Title II.

[Rights of rightholders]

Article 5

(1) Member States shall ensure that rightholders have the rights laid down in paragraphs 2 to 8 and that those rights are set out in the statute or membership terms of the collective management organisation.

(2) Rightholders shall have the right to authorise a collective management organisation of their choice to manage the rights, categories of rights or types of works and other subject-matter of their choice, for the territories of their choice, irrespective of the Member State of nationality, residence or establishment of either the collective management

organisation or the rightholder. Unless the collective management organisation has objectively justified reasons to refuse management, it shall be obliged to manage such rights, categories of rights or types of works and other subject-matter, provided that their management falls within the scope of its activity.

(3) Rightholders shall have the right to grant licences for non-commercial uses of any rights, categories of rights or types of works and other subject-matter that they may choose.

(4) Rightholders shall have the right to terminate the authorisation to manage rights, categories of rights or types of works and other subject-matter granted by them to a collective management organisation or to withdraw from a collective management organisation any of the rights, categories of rights or types of works and other subject-matter of their choice, as determined pursuant to paragraph 2, for the territories of their choice, upon serving reasonable notice not exceeding six months. The collective management organisation may decide that such termination or withdrawal is to take effect only at the end of the financial year.

(5) If there are amounts due to a rightholder for acts of exploitation which occurred before the termination of the authorisation or the withdrawal of rights took effect, or under a licence granted before such termination or withdrawal took effect, the rightholder shall retain his rights under Articles 12, 13, 18, 20, 28 and 33.

(6) A collective management organisation shall not restrict the exercise of rights provided for under paragraphs 4 and 5 by requiring, as a condition for the exercise of those rights, that the management of rights or categories of rights or types of works and other subject-matter which are subject to the termination or the withdrawal be entrusted to another collective management organisation.

(7) In cases where a rightholder authorises a collective management organisation to manage his rights, he shall give consent specifically for each right or category of rights or type of works and other subject-matter which he authorises the collective management organisation to manage. Any such consent shall be evidenced in documentary form.

(8) A collective management organisation shall inform rightholders of their rights under paragraphs 1 to 7, as well as of any conditions attached to the right set out in paragraph 3, before obtaining their consent to its managing any right or category of rights or type of works and other subject-matter.

A collective management organisation shall inform those rightholders who have already authorised it of their rights under paragraphs 1 to 7, as well as of any conditions attached to the right set out in paragraph 3, by 10 October 2016.

1. General. Art. 5(1) instructs Member States to adopt measures to safeguard the rights of rightholders vis-à-vis CMOs laid down in art. 5(2)-(8) and to ensure that those rights are specified in the statute or membership terms of CMOs.

2. Right of rightholders to authorize CMOs of their choice to manage rights or works of their choice (para. 2). The first sentence of art. 5(2) offers rightholders a large freedom of choice when it comes to the management of their rights. **(a) Right of choice of CMO.** Art. 5(2) gives rightholders the choice to which CMO they will entrust the management of their rights. In principle, this can also be multiple CMOs. Art. 5(2) confirms that this freedom of choice exists 'irrespective of the Member State of nationality, residence or establishment of either the CMO or the rightholder CMOs'. Thus, rightholders are free to entrust any CMO in the EU with the management of their rights and CMOs may not refuse their services to rightholders on grounds of nationality. This codifies the Commission's *GEMA I* and *GVL* decisions and the ECJ's *GVL* and *Phil Collins* cases, which affirm, inter alia, that CMOs which refuse to accept the membership of nationals of other Member States infringe the principle of non-discrimination in art. 18 TFEU and the prohibition of discrimination under Community competition law, as derived from art. 102(c) TFEU. **(b) Right to select the rights, types of works and territories for collective administration.** Art. 5(2) also grants rightholders the right to select the (categories of) rights or types of works and other subject-matter which they want a CMO of their choice to manage on their behalf, and to pick the territories to which their authorization will extend. This means that rightholders can choose to have a CMO of their choice manage all or only certain rights, categories of rights or types of works, for all or only certain territories. This can involve, for example, rights of communication to the public or reproduction rights, or categories of rights related to forms of exploitation such as broadcasting, theatrical exhibition or reproduction for online distribution (recital 19). Again, this codifies existing case law. In the Commission's *GEMA I* and *Daft Punk* decisions and the ECJ's *SABAM II* case, the practice of CMOs to require as a condition of membership an exclusive assignment of all present and future rights for all categories of works for worldwide exploitation was held to be an abuse of the CMO's dominant position contrary to art. 102 TFEU, given that such practice corresponds to the imposition of an unfair trading condition. Therefore, CMOs were ordered to allow their members more freedom in controlling the individual forms of exploitation of their rights in every single country in the world. **(c) Right not to manage rights collectively.** It is implicit in art. 5(2) that rightholders may also choose not to entrust any CMO with the management of their rights, but to rather manage them individually. They can also choose to manage parts to their rights individually and parts collectively. Recital 19 confirms this, but adds that the rightholder's choice may be limited in cases where a Member State, in compliance with Union law and the international obligations of the Union and its Member States, provides for mandatory collective management of rights. As observed, the Directive does not interfere with arrangements concerning the management of rights in the Member States, including mandatory collective management (recital 12).

3. Obligation to manage rights on the part of CMOs (para. 2). The second sentence of art. 5(2) puts an obligation on CMOs to manage such rights, categories of rights or types of works and other subject-matter which rightholders entrust them with, provided that their management falls within the scope of its activity. This obligation also extends to other CMOs which sign up as a member and fulfil the CMO's membership requirements (art. 6(2)). The rationale for this rule is to ensure that CMOs will not 'cherry-pick' by refusing their services to smaller rightholders and other CMOs with a less profitable repertoire. CMOs can refuse management only for objectively justified reasons. One objective reason is that the mandate of the CMO does not cover the management of particular rights, categories of rights or types of works and other subject-matter. Recital 19 explains that, unless the mandate of the CMO is determined in its statute or prescribed by law, the rights, categories of rights or types of works and other subject-matter managed by the CMO should be determined by the CMO's general assembly of members. It must do so in a manner that maintains a balance between the freedom of rightholders to dispose of their works and other subject-matter and the ability of the CMO to manage the rights effectively, taking into account in particular the category of rights managed by the organization and the creative sector in which it operates.

4. Flexibility to grant licences for non-commercial uses (para. 3). To give flexibility to rightholders in the management of their repertoire without jeopardizing their membership of CMOs which represent them, art. 5(3) grants rightholders the right to decide on the licensing of any (categories of) rights or types of works and other subject-matter for non-commercial uses. This offers rightholders the possibility to make (parts of) their repertoire available under Creative Commons or other non-commercial licences. CMOs must take the necessary steps to effectuate this right, inter alia, by taking a decision on the conditions attached to the exercise of this right and by informing their members about those conditions (recital 19).

5. Withdrawal of rights or termination of authorization (para. 4). Taking due account of the balance between the freedom of rightholders to dispose of their repertoire and the ability of the CMO to manage the rights effectively, art. 5(4) gives rightholders the right to terminate their authorization to a CMO or to withdraw from a CMO any (categories of) rights or types of works and other subject-matter of their choice, for the territories of their choice. The right is effectuated by serving reasonable notice within a term not longer than six months. Art. 5(4) codifies the Commission's *GEMA I* and *GEMA II* decisions, which laid down a similar right. A right to withdraw online rights in musical works is also part of the Online Music Recommendation. Pursuant to the last sentence of art. 5(4), CMOs may decide that the termination or withdrawal will take effect only at the end of the financial year.

6. Amounts due under earlier licences granted (para. 5). The Directive does not, as such, preclude contractual arrangements according to which a termination or withdrawal has an immediate effect on earlier licences granted or which leave such licences unaffected for a certain period of time after the termination or withdrawal, unless such contractual arrangements create an obstacle to the full application of this Directive (recital 19). Art. 5(5) therefore provides that, if there are amounts due to a rightholder under licences granted or for acts of exploitation which occurred before such termination or withdrawal took effect, the rightholder shall retain his rights with respect to deductions from the rights revenue (art. 12), the distribution of amounts due (arts. 13 and 28), information on the management of rights (arts. 18 and 20), and the recourse to effective and timely complaints procedures (art. 33).

7. No mandatory assignment of rights to another CMO (para. 6). Art. 5(6) prohibits CMOs from restricting the rights of termination and withdrawal by requiring, as a condition for the exercise of those rights, that the rightholder entrusts the management of the retracted rights and repertoire to another CMO. Unless mandatory collective management is prescribed by law, rightholders always retain the right to manage their repertoire individually (recital 19).

8. Express consent required per individual right, category of rights and type of works (para. 7). To give full effect to the rights enshrined in art. 5(2) and (4), art. 5(7) sets out that rightholders must give consent specifically for each right or category of rights or type of works and other subject-matter which they authorize a CMO to manage. Any such consent must be evidenced in documentary form. Recital 19 explains that this should not prevent the rightholders from accepting proposed subsequent amendments to their authorization by tacit agreement in accordance with the conditions set out in national law. The required consent is further impossible to obtain from rightholders who have not authorized a CMO to manage their rights, but whose rights are nevertheless represented by the CMO by way of a national system of extended collective licensing, mandatory collective licensing, legal presumptions of representation or transfer of rights to CMOs. The Directive explicitly leaves such national arrangements concerning the management of rights untouched (recital 12). Art. 5(7) applies only to cases where rightholders have authorized a CMO to manage their rights.

9. Information to rightholders about their rights vis-à-vis CMOs (para. 8). Pursuant to art. 5(8), CMOs must inform new and existing members of their rights under art. 5(1)-(7), as well as of any conditions attached to the right set out in art. 5(3). Rightholders who have not yet authorized the CMO must to be informed of their rights before the CMO obtains their consent to manage any right or category of rights or type of works and other subject-matter. Rightholders who have already authorized the CMO must be informed of their rights by 10 October 2016. This may be done via the website of the CMO (recital 19).

[Membership rules of collective management organisations]

Article 6

(1) Member States shall ensure that collective management organisations comply with the rules laid down in paragraphs 2 to 5.

(2) A collective management organisation shall accept rightholders and entities representing rightholders, including other collective management organisations and associations of rightholders, as members if they fulfil the membership requirements, which shall be based on objective, transparent and non-discriminatory criteria. Those membership requirements shall be included in the statute or membership terms of the collective management organisation and shall be made publicly available. In cases where a collective management organisation refuses to accept a request for membership, it shall provide the rightholder with a clear explanation of the reasons for its decision.

(3) The statute of a collective management organisation shall provide for appropriate and effective mechanisms for the participation of its members in the organisation's decision-making process. The representation of the different categories of members in the decision-making process shall be fair and balanced.

(4) A collective management organisation shall allow its members to communicate with it by electronic means, including for the purposes of exercising members' rights.

(5) A collective management organisation shall keep records of its members and shall regularly update those records.

1. General. Art. 6 sets out conditions to the membership rules of CMOs that are organized as associations, cooperatives or limited liability companies. CMOs organized as foundations do not have members. Art. 6(1) instructs Member States to adopt measures requiring CMOs to comply with the provisions on membership rules of CMOs in art. 6(2)-(5). As observed, the Directive does not require CMOs to adopt a specific legal form (recital 14).

2. Objective, transparent and non-discriminatory membership requirements (para. 2). Art. 6(2) repeats that CMOs must accept rightholders and entities representing rightholders, including other CMOs, as members if they fulfil their membership requirements. This largely echoes the obligation on the part of CMOs to manage rights which rightholders entrust them with and that fall within the scope of their activity (art. 5(2)). The membership requirements of CMOs must be based on objective, transparent and non-discriminatory criteria. The same criteria should govern the rules of CMOs relating to publishers who by virtue of an agreement on the exploitation of rights are entitled to a share of the income from the rights managed by CMOs and to collect such income from CMOs (recital 20). This implies, inter alia, that in their membership requirements, CMOs may not discriminate between rightholders on grounds of their nationality or place of residence. On the other hand, CMOs may refuse membership to rightholders whose rights, categories of rights or types of works or other subject-matter fall outside their scope of activity. In cases where a request for membership is refused, the CMO must provide the rightholder with a clear explanation of the reasons for its decision. Art. 6(2) requires CMOs to include the membership requirements in their statutes or membership terms and to make them publicly available. The latter obligation also follows from art. 21.

3. Participation of members in the CMO's decision-making process (para. 3). To ensure that CMOs act in the best collective interests of the rightholders they represent and that members can exercise their membership rights, art. 6(3) requires the statutes of CMOs to provide for appropriate and effective mechanisms for the participation of their members in the CMO's decision-making process. It further states that the representation of the different categories of members in the decision-making process must be fair and balanced. This is to prevent one category of members, which may represent a specific group of rightholders, from having a decisive voice in the CMO's decision-making process (recital 22). Art. 8 grants members a right to participate in and vote at the general assembly of members.

4. Facilitating electronic communication (para. 4). CMOs must provide facilities for their members to allow them to communicate with the CMO by electronic means, for instance via e-mail, including for the purposes of exercising members' rights. In accordance with art. 7(1), such facilities must also be provided to rightholders whose rights are directly represented by the CMOs but who are not their members.

5. Records of members of CMOs (para. 5). Pursuant to art. 6(5), CMOs must keep records of their members and regularly update those records. The records kept by a CMO should allow for the identification and location of its members and the rightholders whose rights it represents on the basis of authorizations given by those rightholders (recital 20). This aims to ensure, inter alia, that CMOs are able to diligently and accurately distribute and pay amounts due to rightholders (art. 13) and to enable them to give relevant information about the rights they represent to rightholders, other CMOs and users on request (art. 20). Indirectly, these records of represented rightholders also help to alleviate the orphan works problem.

[Rights of rightholders who are not members of the collective management organisation]

Article 7

(1) Member States shall ensure that collective management organisations comply with the rules laid down in Article 6(4), Article 20, Article 29(2) and Article 33 in respect of rightholders who have a direct legal

relationship by law or by way of assignment, licence or any other contractual arrangement with them but are not their members.

(2) Member States may apply other provisions of this Directive to the rightholders referred to in paragraph 1.

1. General. Because the Directive leaves national systems of extended collective licensing, mandatory collective licensing and legal presumptions of representation or transfer of rights to CMOs untouched (recital 12) and because the Directive also applies to CMOs that have no members, such as CMOs organized as foundations (recital 14), the activities of CMOs also extend to rightholders whose rights are directly represented by a CMO but who are not their members. For this reason, it was deemed appropriate to require that some of the Directive's provisions relating to members also be applied to such rightholders (recital 21).

2. Rules applicable to non-member rightholders (paras. 1 and 2). Art. 7(1) instructs Member States to require CMOs to allow rightholders whose rights are directly represented by them but who are not their members to communicate with them by electronic means (art. 6(4)); to provide such rightholders, on request, with information on (the types of) works or other subject-matter they represent, the rights they manage and the territories they cover (art. 20); to provide such rightholders with information about the main terms of an agreement with a CMO they have mandated to grant multi-territorial licences for online rights in musical works (art. 29(2)); and to grant such rightholders recourse to their complaints procedures (art. 33). Art. 7(2) allows Member States to apply other provisions of this Directive to non-member rightholders whose rights are directly represented by CMOs. Recital 21 explains that Member States may, for example, choose to also provide such non-member rightholders with rights to participate in the CMO's decision-making process.

[General assembly of members of the collective management organisation]

Article 8

(1) Member States shall ensure that the general assembly of members is organised in accordance with the rules laid down in paragraphs 2 to 10.

(2) A general assembly of members shall be convened at least once a year.

(3) The general assembly of members shall decide on any amendments to the statute and to the membership terms of the collective management organisation, where those terms are not regulated by the statute.

(4) The general assembly of members shall decide on the appointment or dismissal of the directors, review their general performance and

approve their remuneration and other benefits such as monetary and non-monetary benefits, pension awards and entitlements, rights to other awards and rights to severance pay.

In a collective management organisation with a dual board system, the general assembly of members shall not decide on the appointment or dismissal of members of the management board or approve their remuneration and other benefits where the power to take such decisions is delegated to the supervisory board.

(5) In accordance with the provisions laid down in Chapter 2 of Title II, the general assembly of members shall decide at least on the following issues:

(a) the general policy on the distribution of amounts due to rightholders;

(b) the general policy on the use of non-distributable amounts;

(c) the general investment policy with regard to rights revenue and to any income arising from the investment of rights revenue;

(d) the general policy on deductions from rights revenue and from any income arising from the investment of rights revenue;

(e) the use of non-distributable amounts;

(f) the risk management policy;

(g) the approval of any acquisition, sale or hypothecation of immovable property;

(h) the approval of mergers and alliances, the setting-up of subsidiaries, and the acquisition of other entities or shares or rights in other entities;

(i) the approval of taking out loans, granting loans or providing security for loans.

(6) The general assembly of members may delegate the powers listed in points (f), (g), (h) and (i) of paragraph 5, by a resolution or by a provision in the statute, to the body exercising the supervisory function.

(7) For the purposes of points (a) to (d) of paragraph 5, Member States may require the general assembly of members to determine more detailed conditions for the use of the rights revenue and the income arising from the investment of rights revenue.

(8) The general assembly of members shall control the activities of the collective management organisation by, at least, deciding on the appointment and removal of the auditor and approving the annual transparency report referred to in Article 22.

Member States may allow alternative systems or modalities for the appointment and removal of the auditor, provided that those systems or modalities are designed to ensure the independence of the auditor from the persons who manage the business of the collective management organisation.

(9) All members of the collective management organisation shall have the right to participate in, and the right to vote at, the general assembly

of members. However, Member States may allow for restrictions on the right of the members of the collective management organisation to participate in, and to exercise voting rights at, the general assembly of members, on the basis of one or both of the following criteria:

(a) duration of membership;

(b) amounts received or due to a member,

provided that such criteria are determined and applied in a manner that is fair and proportionate.

The criteria laid down in points (a) and (b) of the first subparagraph shall be included in the statute or the membership terms of the collective management organisation and shall be made publicly available in accordance with Articles 19 and 21.

(10) Every member of a collective management organisation shall have the right to appoint any other person or entity as a proxy holder to participate in, and vote at, the general assembly of members on his behalf, provided that such appointment does not result in a conflict of interest which might occur, for example, where the appointing member and the proxy holder belong to different categories of rightholders within the collective management organisation.

However, Member States may provide for restrictions concerning the appointment of proxy holders and the exercise of the voting rights of the members they represent if such restrictions do not prejudice the appropriate and effective participation of members in the decision-making process of a collective management organisation.

Each proxy shall be valid for a single general assembly of members. The proxy holder shall enjoy the same rights in the general assembly of members as those to which the appointing member would be entitled. The proxy holder shall cast votes in accordance with the instructions issued by the appointing member.

(11) Member States may decide that the powers of the general assembly of members may be exercised by an assembly of delegates elected at least every four years by the members of the collective management organisation, provided that:

(a) appropriate and effective participation of members in the collective management organisation's decision-making process is ensured; and

(b) the representation of the different categories of members in the assembly of delegates is fair and balanced.

The rules laid down in paragraphs 2 to 10 shall apply to the assembly of delegates mutatis mutandis.

(12) Member States may decide that where a collective management organisation, by reason of its legal form, does not have a general assembly of members, the powers of that assembly are to be exercised by the body exercising the supervisory function. The rules laid down in

paragraphs 2 to 5, 7 and 8 shall apply mutatis mutandis to such body exercising the supervisory function.

(13) Member States may decide that where a collective management organisation has members who are entities representing rightholders, all or some of the powers of the general assembly of members are to be exercised by an assembly of those rightholders. The rules laid down in paragraphs 2 to 10 shall apply mutatis mutandis to the assembly of rightholders.

1. General. The general assembly of members is the body in a CMO wherein members participate and exercise their voting rights, regardless of the legal form of the CMO (art. 3(f)). Art. 8(1) instructs Member States to adopt measures to ensure that a CMO's general assembly of members is organized in accordance with the rules laid down in art. 8(2)-(10). These rules establish how the general assembly of members of a CMO should be run and determine the minimum powers which it must possess.

2. General assembly to be convened at least annually (para. 2). In order not to undermine the powers conferred on the general assembly of members, it is necessary to ensure that the general assembly meets regularly (recital 22). Art. 8(2) reinforces this by requiring that a general assembly of members shall be convened at least once a year.

3. Powers of the general assembly (paras. 3 to 8). Under the Directive, the general assembly of members is a powerful decision-making organ. This is evident from recitals 22 and 23, which state that the most important decisions in the CMO need to be taken by the general assembly and that it should, at least, have the power to set the framework of the activities of the management, in particular with respect to the use of rights revenue by the CMO. Art. 8(3), (4), (5) and (8) thus establish four powers that the general assembly of members of a CMO must possess as a minimum. **(a) Amending the CMO's statute and membership terms (para. 3).** Pursuant to art. 8(3), the general assembly shall decide on any amendments to the statute and to the membership terms of the CMO. **(b) Appointing, dismissing and reviewing the CMO's directors (para. 4).** Art. 8(4) requires that the general assembly shall also decide on the appointment or dismissal of the directors of the CMO, review their general performance and approve their remuneration and other benefits. Directors are any members of the administrative board if the CMO has a unitary board, or any members of the management board or supervisory board if the CMO has a dual board (art. 3(g)). In CMOs with a dual board, the general assembly shall not decide on the appointment or dismissal of members of the management board or approve their remuneration and other benefits where the power to take such decisions is delegated to the supervisory board. **(c) Deciding on the use of rights revenue by the CMO (paras. 5 to 7).** Art. 8(5) states that the general assembly shall at least also decide on the CMO's general policies on the distribution of amounts due to rightholders, the use of non-distributable amounts, and the investment of and deductions from rights revenue and any income arising therefrom. Art. 8(7) permits Member States to require the general assembly to determine more detailed conditions for the use of the rights revenue and the income arising from the investment thereof. Art. 8(5) further requires that the general assembly shall at least also decide on the use of non-distributable amounts, the CMO's risk management policy and the approval of other activities that may affect the CMO's financial situation, such as the acquisition or sale of immovable property, the creation of mergers and alliances, and the taking out or granting of loans. Art. 8(6) permits the general assembly to delegate specific powers to the body exercising the supervisory function (see art. 9). Recital 23 explains that more stringent rules may be provided on investments, mergers or taking out loans, including a prohibition on such transactions. **(d) Controlling the CMO's activities (para. 8).** To control the activities of the CMO, art. 8(8) requires that the general assembly shall at least also decide on the appointment and removal of the auditor and approving the annual transparency report (art. 22). Alternative systems or modalities for the appointment and removal of the auditor may be allowed, on condition that they are designed to ensure the independence of the auditor from the persons who manage the business of the CMO.

4. Right to participate in and vote at the general assembly (para. 9). Art. 8(9) provides that all members of the CMO shall have the right to participate in and vote at the general assembly. This right may be restricted only on the basis of the duration of membership and/or the amounts received or due to a member, provided that such criteria are determined and applied in a fair and proportionate manner and are included in the CMO's statute or membership terms. Recital 23 incites CMOs to encourage the active participation of their members in the general assembly and to enable them to exercise their rights by electronic means, so as to facilitate voting also for members who do not attend the general assembly.

5. Right to appoint another person or entity as proxy holder (para. 10). Art. 8(10) gives all members of a CMO the right to appoint any other person or entity as a proxy holder to participate in and vote at the general assembly on their behalf. This may not however cause a conflict of interest, which might occur where the appointing member and proxy holder belong to different categories of rightholders within the CMO. Member States may further restrict proxies, but only if this does not prejudice the appropriate and effective participation of members in the CMO's decision-making process. In particular, such restrictions should not deny rightholders a true opportunity to opt for a CMO where they can effectively exercise membership rights (recital 23). Restrictions are permitted that require proxies to be in writing or to be allocatable only to other members of the CMO, not to outsiders. To avoid publishers or producers getting control of a CMO by demanding a permanent proxy from rightholders signing contracts with them, art. 8(10) limits the validity of each proxy to a single general assembly. It further provides that proxy holders must enjoy the same rights in the general assembly as the appointing members and that their votes must be cast in accordance with the instructions issued by the appointing members.

6. Other bodies upon which the general assembly's powers can be conferred (paras. 11 to 13). Member States may decide that the powers of the general assembly may be exercised by an assembly of delegates elected at least every four years by members of the CMO. In accordance with art. 6(3), appropriate and effective participation of members in the CMO's decision-making process must be ensured and the representation of the different categories of members in the assembly of delegates must be fair and balanced (art. 8(11)). In cases where a CMO is established in the legal form of a foundation, and thus has no members and no general assembly of members, Member States may further decide that the powers of that assembly are to be exercised by the body exercising the supervisory function, as established in accordance with art. 9 (art. 8(12)). Where a CMO has entities representing rightholders as members, Member States may decide that all or some of the powers of the general assembly of members are to be exercised by an assembly of those rightholders (art. 8(13)). This is the case, e.g., where a CMO is organized as a limited liability company and has associations of rightholders as their members (recital 23). In these instances, the rules relating to the general assembly of members apply mutatis mutandis to such assembly of delegates, body exercising the supervisory function and assembly of rightholders.

[Supervisory function]

Article 9

(1) **Member States shall ensure that each collective management organisation has in place a supervisory function for continuously monitoring the activities and the performance of the duties of the persons who manage the business of the organisation.**

(2) **There shall be fair and balanced representation of the different categories of members of the collective management organisation in the body exercising the supervisory function.**

(3) **Each person exercising the supervisory function shall make an annual individual statement on conflicts of interest, containing the information referred to in the second subparagraph of Article 10(2), to the general assembly of members.**

(4) **The body exercising the supervisory function shall meet regularly and shall have at least the following powers:**

    (a) **to exercise the powers delegated to it by the general assembly of members, including under Article 8(4) and (6);**

(b) to monitor the activities and the performance of the duties of the persons referred to in Article 10, including the implementation of the decisions of the general assembly of members and, in particular, of the general policies listed in points (a) to (d) of Article 8(5).

(5) The body exercising the supervisory function shall report on the exercise of its powers to the general assembly of members at least once a year.

1. General. Art. 9(1) instructs Member States to require CMOs to have in place a supervisory function, but it does not demand that each CMO has a separate supervisory body. Pursuant to recital 24, CMOs should have a supervisory function appropriate to their organizational structure.

2. Body exercising the supervisory function (para. 2). Depending on the organizational structure of the CMO, the supervisory function may be exercised by a separate body, e.g. a supervisory board, or by some or all of the directors in the administrative board who do not manage the business of the CMO (recital 24). Pursuant to art. 9(2), the different categories of members of a CMO must be represented in the body exercising the supervisory function in a fair and balanced manner, but recital 24 explains that this should not prevent the CMO from appointing third parties to exercise the supervisory function, including relevant professionals and non-member rightholders who are represented in the CMO indirectly.

3. Powers of the body exercising the supervisory function (para. 4). The body exercising the supervisory function of a CMO must at least have the power to monitor the activities and the performance of the duties of the persons who manage the business of the CMO referred to in art. 10. This includes the monitoring of the implementation of the decisions of the general assembly and, in particular, of the general policies listed in art. 8(5)(a)-(d). Further, it must exercise the powers delegated to it by the general assembly of members, including under art. 8(4) and (6). Depending on the legal form of the CMO, additional powers may accrue to it. As observed, pursuant to art. 8(12), Member States may decide to confer the powers of the general assembly of members on the body exercising the supervisory function in cases where a CMO is organized as a foundation and thus has no members.

4. Meeting and reporting obligations (paras. 3 to 5). The body exercising the supervisory function must meet regularly and report on the exercise of its powers to the general assembly at least once a year (art. 9(4) and (5)). This reporting obligation does not apply in cases where a CMO, due to its legal form as a foundation, has no general assembly of members and Member States have conferred the powers of that assembly on the body exercising the supervisory function pursuant to art. 8(12). Each person exercising the supervisory function is further required to make an annual individual statement on conflicts of interest to the general assembly (art. 9(3)). This statement must contain the information referred to in art. 10(2).

[Obligations of the persons who manage the business of the collective management organisation]

Article 10

(1) Member States shall ensure that each collective management organisation takes all necessary measures so that the persons who manage its business do so in a sound, prudent and appropriate manner, using sound administrative and accounting procedures and internal control mechanisms.

(2) Member States shall ensure that collective management organisations put in place and apply procedures to avoid conflicts of interest, and where such conflicts cannot be avoided, to identify, manage, monitor and disclose actual or potential conflicts of interest in such a way as to prevent them from adversely affecting the collective interests of the rightholders whom the organisation represents.

The procedures referred to in the first subparagraph shall include an annual individual statement by each of the persons referred to in paragraph 1 to the general assembly of members, containing the following information:

(a) any interests in the collective management organisation;

(b) any remuneration received in the preceding financial year from the collective management organisation, including in the form of pension schemes, benefits in kind and other types of benefits;

(c) any amounts received in the preceding financial year as a rightholder from the collective management organisation;

(d) a declaration concerning any actual or potential conflict between any personal interests and those of the collective management organisation or between any obligations owed to the collective management organisation and any duty owed to any other natural or legal person.

1. General. Art. 10 instructs Member States to ensure that each CMO takes all necessary measures to warrant that its managers conduct their business in a sound, prudent and appropriate manner. To this end, CMOs must put in place and apply sound administrative and accounting procedures, internal control mechanisms and procedures to avoid conflicts of interest. It does not lay down specific obligations, except that managers of CMOs must give annual individual statements on conflicts of interest (art. 10(2)). This obligation extends to managers who are elected as directors to the board of a CMO as well as to managers who are hired or employed by the CMO on the basis of a contract (recital 25).

2. Annual individual statement on conflicts of interest (para. 2). Each manager of a CMO must give an annual individual statement to the general assembly of members on actual or potential conflicts of interest that may affect the collective interests of rightholders whom the CMO represent (art. 10(2)). Recital 25 suggests that managers must also give such statement prior to taking up their position. The statement must contain information on the managers' interests in the CMO, the remuneration they received in the preceding financial year from the CMO, the amounts they received in the preceding financial year as rightholders from the CMO and a declaration on actual or potential conflicts between the interests of the CMO and any direct or indirect interest on their parts. Member States may require CMOs to make such statements public or to submit them to public authorities (recital 25).

CHAPTER 2. MANAGEMENT OF RIGHTS REVENUE

[Collection and use of rights revenue]

Article 11

(1) Member States shall ensure that collective management organisations comply with the rules laid down in paragraphs 2 to 5.

(2) A collective management organisation shall be diligent in the collection and management of rights revenue.

(3) A collective management organisation shall keep separate in its accounts:

(a) rights revenue and any income arising from the investment of rights revenue; and

(b) any own assets it may have and income arising from such assets, from management fees or from other activities.

(4) A collective management organisation shall not be permitted to use rights revenue or any income arising from the investment of rights revenue for purposes other than distribution to rightholders, except where it is allowed to deduct or offset its management fees in compliance with a decision taken in accordance with point (d) of Article 8(5) or to use the rights revenue or any income arising from the investment of rights revenue in compliance with a decision taken in accordance with Article 8(5).

(5) Where a collective management organisation invests rights revenue or any income arising from the investment of rights revenue, it shall do so in the best interests of the rightholders whose rights it represents, in accordance with the general investment and risk management policy referred to in points (c) and (f) of Article 8(5) and having regard to the following rules:

(a) where there is any potential conflict of interest, the collective management organisation shall ensure that the investment is made in the sole interest of those rightholders;

(b) **the assets shall be invested in order to ensure the security, quality, liquidity and profitability of the portfolio as a whole;**

(c) **the assets shall be properly diversified in order to avoid excessive reliance on any particular asset and accumulations of risks in the portfolio as a whole.**

1. General. Because CMOs collect, manage and distribute revenue which is ultimately due to rightholders, it is important that they exercise the utmost diligence in collecting, managing and distributing that revenue (recital 26). Art. 11 therefore instructs Member States to adopt measures requiring CMOs to comply with the rules on collection and use of rights revenue in art. 11(2)-(5), while arts. 12 and 13 deal specifically with deductions and the distribution of rights revenue. Recital 33 states that this Directive is without prejudice to the possibility for Member States to require CMOs established in their territory to issue joint invoices for the purpose of collecting rights revenue.

2. Diligent collection and management of rights revenue (paras. 2 to 4). Art. 11(2) requires CMOs to be diligent in the collection and management of rights revenue. In view of that, they must keep separate accounts of the revenues collected and due to rightholders and of their own assets and income from other activities (art. 11(3)). Art. 11(4) further prohibits CMOs from using rights revenue or any income arising from the investment thereof for purposes other than distribution to rightholders. This is different only where the general assembly of members in accordance with art. 8(5) has decided that the CMO may deduct or offset its management fees or use part of the revenues collected and due to rightholders for another purpose.

3. Investment of rights revenue (para. 5). To avoid unnecessary risks to the revenues collected and due to rightholders, art. 11(5) requires CMOs to employ a secure and efficient investment strategy in accordance with their general investment and risk management policy (art. 8(5)(c) and (f)). CMOs that invest rights revenue must do so in the best interests of the rightholders whose rights they represent. In case of potential conflicts of interest, investments must be made in the sole interest of those rightholders. CMOs must further ensure that the security, quality, liquidity and profitability of the portfolio as a whole is guaranteed and that the assets are properly diversified so as to avoid excessive reliance on any particular asset and accumulations of risks in the portfolio. Recital 27 allows Member States to provide for more stringent rules on investment, including a prohibition of investment of rights revenue.

[Deductions]

Article 12

(1) Member States shall ensure that where a rightholder authorises a collective management organisation to manage his rights, the collective

management organisation is required to provide the rightholder with information on management fees and other deductions from the rights revenue and from any income arising from the investment of rights revenue, before obtaining his consent to its managing his rights.

(2) Deductions shall be reasonable in relation to the services provided by the collective management organisation to rightholders, including, where appropriate, the services referred to in paragraph 4, and shall be established on the basis of objective criteria.

(3) Management fees shall not exceed the justified and documented costs incurred by the collective management organisation in managing copyright and related rights.

Member States shall ensure that the requirements applicable to the use and the transparency of the use of amounts deducted or offset in respect of management fees apply to any other deductions made in order to cover the costs of managing copyright and related rights.

(4) Where a collective management organisation provides social, cultural or educational services funded through deductions from rights revenue or from any income arising from the investment of rights revenue, such services shall be provided on the basis of fair criteria, in particular as regards access to, and the extent of, those services.

1. General. Art. 12 lays down rules on deductions from revenues collected by CMOs and due to rightholders, such as management fees and deductions for social, cultural or educational purposes. CMOs must be transparent towards rightholders about the rules governing such deductions and any decision to use the rights revenue for collective distribution, such as scholarships (recital 28). Art. 12(1) therefore obliges CMOs to provide advance information on management fees and other deductions to rightholders who intend to entrust them with the management of their rights. This somewhat resembles the Commission's *IFPI Simulcasting* decision, which required CMOs to apply a transparent pricing policy to users by separating the administration costs from the royalty rates and to identify them separately when charging a licence fee. Along similar lines, art. 12(1) now also requires CMOs to adopt a transparent rights revenue policy towards rightholders. Recital 28 reiterates that any deduction other than in respect of management fees must be decided by the general assembly of members in accordance with art. 8(5)(d). Deductions must further be reasonable in relation to the services provided by the CMO to rightholders and be based on objective criteria (art. 12(2)).

2. Management fees (para. 3). Pursuant to art. 12(3), management fees may not exceed the justified and documented costs incurred by the CMO in managing the rights. Any other deductions made to cover the CMO's management costs are subject to the same rules applicable to the use and transparency of management fees.

3. Deductions for social, cultural or educational purposes (para. 4). Art. 12(4) requires CMOs which provide social, cultural or educational services funded through deductions from the revenues collected and due to rightholders to provide such services on the basis of fair criteria. In particular, rightholders should have access to and enjoy such services on a non-discriminatory basis. Recital 28 affirms that the Directive does not affect deductions under national law, such as deductions for the provision of social services by CMOs to rightholders, provided that they comply with Union law and the provisions of this Directive.

[Distribution of amounts due to rightholders]

Article 13

(1) Without prejudice to Article 15(3) and Article 28, Member States shall ensure that each collective management organisation regularly, diligently and accurately distributes and pays amounts due to rightholders in accordance with the general policy on distribution referred to in point (a) of Article 8(5).

Member States shall also ensure that collective management organisations or their members who are entities representing rightholders distribute and pay those amounts to rightholders as soon as possible but no later than nine months from the end of the financial year in which the rights revenue was collected, unless objective reasons relating in particular to reporting by users, identification of rights, rightholders or matching of information on works and other subject-matter with rightholders prevent the collective management organisation or, where applicable, its members from meeting that deadline.

(2) Where the amounts due to rightholders cannot be distributed within the deadline set in paragraph 1 because the relevant rightholders cannot be identified or located and the exception to that deadline does not apply, those amounts shall be kept separate in the accounts of the collective management organisation.

(3) The collective management organisation shall take all necessary measures, consistent with paragraph 1, to identify and locate the rightholders. In particular, at the latest three months after the expiry of the deadline set in paragraph 1, the collective management organisation shall make available information on works and other subject-matter for which one or more rightholders have not been identified or located to:

(a) the rightholders that it represents or the entities representing rightholders, where such entities are members of the collective management organisation; and

(b) all collective management organisations with which it has concluded representation agreements.

The information referred to in the first subparagraph shall include, where available, the following:

    (a) the title of the work or other subject-matter;

    (b) the name of the rightholder;

    (c) the name of the relevant publisher or producer; and

    (d) any other relevant information available which could assist in identifying the rightholder.

The collective management organisation shall also verify the records referred to in Article 6(5) and other readily available records. If the abovementioned measures fail to produce results, the collective management organisation shall make that information available to the public at the latest one year after the expiry of the three-month period.

(4) Where the amounts due to rightholders cannot be distributed after three years from the end of the financial year in which the collection of the rights revenue occurred, and provided that the collective management organisation has taken all necessary measures to identify and locate the rightholders referred to in paragraph 3, those amounts shall be deemed non-distributable.

(5) The general assembly of members of a collective management organisation shall decide on the use of the non-distributable amounts in accordance with point (b) of Article 8(5), without prejudice to the right of rightholders to claim such amounts from the collective management organisation in accordance with the laws of the Member States on the statute of limitations of claims.

(6) Member States may limit or determine the permitted uses of non-distributable amounts, inter alia, by ensuring that such amounts are used in a separate and independent way in order to fund social, cultural and educational activities for the benefit of rightholders.

1. General. Art. 13(1) requires CMOs to regularly, diligently and accurately distribute and pay amounts due to rightholders in accordance with their general policy on distribution, as agreed upon by the general assembly of members (see art. 8(5)(a)). The amounts due must be distributed and paid to rightholders as soon as possible but no later than nine months from the end of the financial year in which the rights revenue was collected, unless objective reasons can justify delay in the distribution and payment. Because accurate distribution is possible only when CMOs have access to relevant usage and rights management data, such objective reasons relate in particular to untimely reporting of relevant information by users (art. 17) and possible setbacks in identifying rights, rightholders or matching information on works and other subject-matter with rightholders. Circumstances such as the rights revenue having been invested for a fixed period are not valid reasons for a delay in distributing and paying amounts due to rightholders (recital 29). It is left to Member States to decide on rules ensuring timely distribution in cases where objective reasons occur. Rules on the distribution of amounts due to rightholders pursuant to representation agreements or accruing from multi-territorial licences for online rights in musical works are included in arts. 15(3) and 28.

2. Amounts due to unidentifiable or unlocatable rightholders (paras. 2 and 3). Art. 13(2) requires CMOs to keep separate accounts of the amounts due to rightholders that cannot be timely distributed because the relevant rightholders cannot be identified or located. CMOs are obliged to take all necessary measures to identify and locate the rightholders. Within three months after the expiry of the deadline in art. 13(1), they must make available relevant information on works and subject-matter for which one or more rightholders have not been identified or located to rightholders which they represent and CMOs with which they have concluded representation agreements (art. 13(3)). They must further verify the records referred to in art. 6(5) and other readily available records, including e.g. the European database on orphan works referred to in art. 3(6) of the Orphan Works Directive and perhaps the databases mentioned in the Annex of the Orphan Works Directive. If these measures fail to produce results, the CMOs must make the relevant information publicly available one year after the expiry of the three-month period at the latest. Member States may provide for more stringent rules (recital 29).

3. Use of non-distributable amounts (paras. 4 to 6). Amounts due to rightholders shall be deemed non-distributable if they cannot be distributed after three years from the end of the financial year in which the collection of the rights revenue occurred and the CMO has taken all necessary measures to identify and locate the rightholders (art. 13(4)). In accordance with art. 8(5)(b), the general assembly of members of a CMO shall decide on the use of the non-distributable amounts. This is without prejudice to the right of rightholders to claim such amounts from the CMO in accordance with the laws of Member States on the statute of limitations of claims (art. 13(5)). Member States may limit or determine the permitted uses of non-distributable amounts. They may, for example, provide that such amounts be applied to fund social, cultural and educational activities for the benefit of rightholders (art. 13(6)).

CHAPTER 3. MANAGEMENT OF RIGHTS ON BEHALF OF OTHER COLLECTIVE MANAGEMENT ORGANISATIONS

[Rights managed under representation agreements]

Article 14

Member States shall ensure that a collective management organisation does not discriminate against any rightholder whose rights it manages under a representation agreement, in particular with respect to applicable tariffs, management fees, and the conditions for the collection of the rights revenue and distribution of amounts due to rightholders.

1. General. It is a long-standing practice that CMOs manage rights and collect revenue from their exploitation under representation agreements with other CMOs. Recital 30 confirms that such practice should continue to exist under this Directive. To protect the rights of members of other contracting CMOs, art. 14 prohibits CMOs from discriminating against any rightholder whose rights it manages under a representation agreement. In particular, CMOs should apply the same tariffs, the same management fees, and the same conditions for the collection and distribution of the rights revenue to the rightholders of other CMOs as those applicable to their own members. This principle of non-discrimination in treatment between members and other represented rightholders follows from art. 18 TFEU and from the case law of the ECJ and the Commission, as discussed above in relation to art. 5(2).

[Deductions and payments in representation agreements]

Article 15

(1) Member States shall ensure that a collective management organisation does not make deductions, other than in respect of management fees, from the rights revenue derived from the rights it manages on the basis of a representation agreement, or from any income arising from the investment of that rights revenue, unless the other collective management organisation that is party to the representation agreement expressly consents to such deductions.

(2) The collective management organisation shall regularly, diligently and accurately distribute and pay amounts due to other collective management organisations.

(3) The collective management organisation shall carry out such distribution and payments to the other collective management organisation as soon as possible but no later than nine months from the end of the financial year in which the rights revenue was collected, unless objective reasons relating in particular to reporting by users, identification of rights, rightholders or matching of information on works and other subject-matter with rightholders prevent the collective management organisation from meeting that deadline.

The other collective management organisation, or, where it has as members entities representing rightholders, those members, shall distribute and pay the amounts due to rightholders as soon as possible but no later than six months from receipt of those amounts, unless objective reasons relating in particular to reporting by users, identification of rights, rightholders or matching of information on works and other subject-matter with rightholders prevent the collective management organisation or, where applicable, its members from meeting that deadline.

1. General. Art. 15 sets rules on deductions and payments in representation agreements between CMOs. These rules deviate somewhat from the general rules on deductions in art. 12 and the payment schemes contained in art. 13(1).

2. No deductions other than in respect of management fees (para. 1). Art. 15(1) derogates from art. 12 with respect to deductions from the revenue collected and due to rightholders pursuant to a representation agreement. It provides that, other than in respect of management fees, CMOs may not make deductions from such rights revenue, unless the other CMO that is party to the representation agreement expressly consents to such deductions. This implies that without the express consent of the other CMO, no deductions to the rights revenue collected on behalf of another CMO can be made for social, cultural or educational purposes.

3. Payment to other CMOs (para. 2). Art. 15(2) obliges CMOs to regularly, diligently and accurately distribute and pay amounts due to other CMOs. This echoes the general obligation under art. 13(1), which pursuant to art. 15(2) must also be applied in relation to distribution and payments under representation agreements.

4. Payments to and from other CMOs (para. 3). Art. 15(3) applies the rule of art. 13(1), second subparagraph, to the distribution and payments of the amounts due to other CMOs pursuant to a representation agreement. This ensures that CMOs distribute and make such payments to other CMOs no later than when they distribute and make payments to their own members and to non-member rightholders whom they represent (recital 30). The other CMO in turn must distribute the amounts due to the rightholders it represents without delay. Art. 15(3), second subparagraph, requires the recipient CMO to distribute and pay the amounts due to rightholders as soon as possible but no later than six months from receipt of those amounts. Here too, objective reasons may justify delay in the distribution and payment. These reasons are identical to the ones discussed above in relation to art. 13(1).

CHAPTER 4. RELATIONS WITH USERS

[Licensing]

Article 16

(1) Member States shall ensure that collective management organisations and users conduct negotiations for the licensing of rights in good faith. Collective management organisations and users shall provide each other with all necessary information.

(2) Licensing terms shall be based on objective and non-discriminatory criteria. When licensing rights, collective management organisations shall not be required to use, as a precedent for other online services, licensing terms agreed with a user where the user is providing a new type

of online service which has been available to the public in the Union for less than three years.

Rightholders shall receive appropriate remuneration for the use of their rights. Tariffs for exclusive rights and rights to remuneration shall be reasonable in relation to, inter alia, the economic value of the use of the rights in trade, taking into account the nature and scope of the use of the work and other subject-matter, as well as in relation to the economic value of the service provided by the collective management organisation. Collective management organisations shall inform the user concerned of the criteria used for the setting of those tariffs.

(3) Collective management organisations shall reply without undue delay to requests from users, indicating, inter alia, the information needed in order for the collective management organisation to offer a licence.

Upon receipt of all relevant information, the collective management organisation shall, without undue delay, either offer a licence or provide the user with a reasoned statement explaining why it does not intend to license a particular service.

(4) A collective management organisation shall allow users to communicate with it by electronic means, including, where appropriate, for the purpose of reporting on the use of the licence.

1. General. Chapter 4 of Title II provides rules on the relationship between CMOs and users. Art. 16(1) serves as a general prelude, instructing Member States to adopt measures requiring CMOs and users to conduct negotiations for the licensing of rights in good faith and to provide each other with all necessary information. These are basic principles that may guide or serve as reference for the rules on the licensing of rights (art. 16(2)-(4)) and the obligation for users to inform CMOs about the use of the rights they represent (art. 17).

2. Licensing terms (para. 2). The first sentence of the first subparagraph of art. 16(2) lays down the general principle that licensing terms are based on objective and non-discriminatory criteria. However, to foster an environment conducive to the development of CMOs licensing their repertoire for new online exploitation models, the second sentence of art. 16(2) includes one exception to this rule. CMOs shall not be required to use, as a precedent for other online services, licensing terms agreed with users providing new types of online services which have been available in the EU for less than three years. Recital 32 explains that CMOs should be able to promptly grant individualized licences to innovative online services, without the risk that the terms of those licences be used as a precedent for determining the terms for other licences. As this is without prejudice to the application of competition law rules, CMOs cannot rely on this exception if this would amount to an abuse of their dominant position (art. 102 TFEU).

3. Tariffs (para. 2). The second subparagraph of art. 16(2) states that rightholders shall receive appropriate remuneration for the use of their rights. This does not however seem to constitute a substantive right, but rather an objective. To ensure that rightholders receive appropriate remuneration for the use of their rights, the second sentence requires that tariffs for exclusive rights and remuneration rights be reasonable in relation to, inter alia, the economic value of the use of the rights in trade and of the service provided by the CMO. This language reflects the case law of the ECJ on remuneration and the setting of tariffs. From this case law it can be inferred that tariffs must be applied in a non-discriminatory manner (*Tournier*; *Lucazeau*) and be based on objective criteria (*Sena*; *Kanal 5 and TV 4*). In order to be appropriate, the rightholders' remuneration for the use of their rights must further be reasonable in relation to the economic value of the service provided (*Kanal 5 and TV 4*; *Football Association Premier League and others*; *OSA*). This depends on factors such as the actual and potential audience reached by that service and the language versions applied. Art. 16(2) further adds that account must be taken of the nature and scope of the use of the work and other subject-matter in establishing the economic value of the use of the rights in trade. For reasons of transparency, CMOs are obliged to duly inform users of the criteria they apply for setting tariffs.

4. Obligations of CMOs vis-à-vis users (paras. 3 and 4). Art. 16(3) requires CMOs to reply without undue delay to users' requests for licences. They are required to indicate, inter alia, the information they will need from the user in order to enable them to offer a licence. The Directive does not, as such, oblige CMOs to contract with users, as this was considered to violate the exclusive rights of rightholders. However, the second subparagraph of art. 16(3) requires CMOs, upon receipt of all relevant information, to either offer a licence or to provide reasoned explanation for why they do not intend to license a particular service. This must be done without undue delay. Art. 16(4) requires CMOs to allow users to communicate with them by electronic means, including, where appropriate, for the purpose of reporting on the use of the licence.

[Users' obligations]

Article 17

Member States shall adopt provisions to ensure that users provide a collective management organisation, within an agreed or pre-established time and in an agreed or pre-established format, with such relevant information at their disposal on the use of the rights represented by the collective management organisation as is necessary for the collection of rights revenue and for the distribution and payment of amounts due to rightholders. When deciding on the format for the provision of such information, collective management organisations

and users shall take into account, as far as possible, voluntary industry standards.

1. General. Art. 17 instructs Member States to adopt measures to ensure that users deliver relevant information at their disposal to CMOs. This concerns information on the use of the rights represented by the CMO as is necessary for the collection of rights revenue (art. 11) and the distribution and payment of amounts due to rightholders (art. 13). The information must be supplied within an agreed or pre-established time which should allow CMOs to meet the deadlines set for the distribution of amounts due to rightholders (recital 33). It must further be provided in an agreed or pre-established format which takes into account, as far as possible, voluntary industry standards. The information required should be limited to what is reasonable, necessary and at the users' disposal in order to enable CMOs to perform their functions, taking into account the specific situation of small and medium-sized enterprises (recital 33). The obligation to supply relevant information does not apply to any natural person acting for purposes outside his or her trade, business, craft or profession, as the definition of 'user' (art. 3(k)) specifically excludes consumers.

CHAPTER 5. TRANSPARENCY AND REPORTING

[Information provided to rightholders on the management of their rights]

Article 18

(1) Without prejudice to paragraph 2 of this Article and Article 19 and Article 28(2), Member States shall ensure that a collective management organisation makes available, not less than once a year, to each rightholder to whom it has attributed rights revenue or made payments in the period to which the information relates, at least the following information:

    (a) any contact details which the rightholder has authorised the collective management organisation to use in order to identify and locate the rightholder;

    (b) the rights revenue attributed to the rightholder;

    (c) the amounts paid by the collective management organisation to the rightholder per category of rights managed and per type of use;

    (d) the period during which the use took place for which amounts were attributed and paid to the rightholder, unless objective reasons relating to reporting by users prevent the collective management organisation from providing this information;

    (e) deductions made in respect of management fees;

    (f)   deductions made for any purpose other than in respect of management fees, including those that may be required by national law for the provision of any social, cultural or educational services;

    (g)   any rights revenue attributed to the rightholder which is outstanding for any period.

(2) Where a collective management organisation attributes rights revenue and has as members entities which are responsible for the distribution of rights revenue to rightholders, the collective management organisation shall provide the information listed in paragraph 1 to those entities, provided that they do not have that information in their possession. Member States shall ensure that the entities make at least the information listed in paragraph 1 available, not less than once a year, to each rightholder to whom they have attributed rights revenue or made payments in the period to which the information relates.

1. General. Art. 18 instructs Member States to require CMOs to provide individual rightholders with certain information on the management of their rights at least once a year. The minimum information to be supplied is listed in art. 18(1) and includes the amounts attributed and paid to the rightholders and the deductions made. In cases where the distribution or payment of amounts due to individual rightholders is performed via an entity representing rightholders which is a member of the CMO, as is permitted under art. 13, these transparency obligations also apply to such entities (art. 18(2)). Recital 34 explains that the aim of these transparency rules is to enhance the trust of rightholders in the management of rights by CMOs.

[Information provided to other collective management organisations on the management of rights under representation agreements]

Article 19

Member States shall ensure that a collective management organisation makes at least the following information available, not less than once a year and by electronic means, to collective management organisations on whose behalf it manages rights under a representation agreement, for the period to which the information relates:

    (a)   the rights revenue attributed, the amounts paid by the collective management organisation per category of rights managed, and per type of use, for the rights it manages under the representation agreement, and any rights revenue attributed which is outstanding for any period;

    (b)   deductions made in respect of management fees;

    (c)   deductions made for any purpose other than in respect of management fees as referred to in Article 15;

   (d)   **information on any licences granted or refused with regard to works and other subject-matter covered by the representation agreement;**

   (e)   **resolutions adopted by the general assembly of members in so far as those resolutions are relevant to the management of the rights under the representation agreement.**

1. General. Art. 19 instructs Member States to require CMOs to provide other CMOs on whose behalf they manage rights under a representation agreement with certain information on the management of rights under that agreement at least once a year and by electronic means. The minimum information that must be supplied is listed. The aim of this transparency rule is to enhance the mutual trust of CMOs in the management of rights pursuant to representation agreements (recital 34).

[Information provided to rightholders, other collective management organisations and users on request]

Article 20

Without prejudice to Article 25, Member States shall ensure that, in response to a duly justified request, a collective management organisation makes at least the following information available by electronic means and without undue delay to any collective management organisation on whose behalf it manages rights under a representation agreement or to any rightholder or to any user:

   (a)   **the works or other subject-matter it represents, the rights it manages, directly or under representation agreements, and the territories covered; or**

   (b)   **where, due to the scope of activity of the collective management organisation, such works or other subject-matter cannot be determined, the types of works or of other subject-matter it represents, the rights it manages and the territories covered.**

1. General. Art. 20 instructs Member States to require CMOs to provide information on their scope of activity and the repertoire that they represent, in response to a duly justified request. The requested information must be made available by electronic means and without undue delay. Recital 35 leaves it to Member States to determine whether, and to what extent, CMOs may charge reasonable fees for providing information on request.

2. Information to be provided upon request. The information that a CMO must provide under art. 20 includes at least information on the works or other subject-matter it represents, the rights it manages, directly or under representation agreements, and the territories covered. This basically requires a CMO to be (fully) transparent about the mandate that it possesses in relation to the specific repertoire that it represents. Where, due to its scope of activity, a CMO cannot determine the works or other subject-matter, it suffices if that CMO supplies general information on its field and scope of operation (i.e. the types of works or of other subject-matter it represents, the rights it manages and the territories covered).

3. Persons eligible to make a request for information. A request for information under art. 20 can be made by any CMO on whose behalf the CMO manages rights under a representation agreement or by any rightholder or any user. **(a) Other CMOs.** The text of art. 20 suggests that CMOs with which the CMO has not (yet) concluded representation agreements are not eligible to make a request for information under art. 20. Given that the entire business model of CMOs is built around the information they hold on the management of rights, it would go too far to require CMOs to submit relevant information on their scope of mandate to any other CMO so requesting. Although an exchange of information between CMOs must likely take place before CMOs can enter into a representation agreement, this can be done on a mutual and voluntary basis and does not need to involve a requirement to submit any (commercially sensitive) information upon request. **(b) Rightholders.** By contrast, art. 20 seemingly allows any rightholder to make a request for information without requiring a membership or other type of relationship to exist between the rightholder and the CMO. This must probably be explained in the light of the flexibility offered to rightholders under art. 5(2) to entrust the management of their rights to the CMO of their choice. In order for rightholders to make an informed decision about the CMO that is best suited for the task, they need to obtain relevant information about the scope of activities and the relative strength of the various CMOs in their field. In view of this, the requirement to submit information upon request is almost certainly to be understood as extending not to all rightholders, but only to rightholders within the specific field of operation of the CMO. **(c) Users.** The text of art. 20 also permits any user to make a request for information. Again, this probably relates to any user within the specific field of activity of the CMO only. Yet, it is uncertain whether CMOs are required to submit information upon request only to users with whom they have licensing arrangements or also to other users and perhaps even prospective users. Formally speaking, prospective users do not qualify as 'users' within the definition of art. 3(k) for the reason that they are not yet 'carrying out acts subject to the authorization of rightholders'. At the same time, they would be 'users' in the legal sense if they were to start their activities, even if they would not have the prior authorization of the rightholders or CMOs representing them. As a general rule, it could be argued that only users who have a legitimate interest to obtain information should be eligible to request such information. In this line of reasoning, prospective users must probably not be denied the right to request information, as they need information about the scope of activity of a CMO and the repertoire it represents so as to ascertain whether a licence from that CMO is required for the use they intend to make. In view of the underlying objective of the Directive to foster the dissemination of content by creating an adequate collective licensing framework (recital 2), it could be argued that prospective users should also qualify as recipients of the information requestable under art. 20. Indeed, under a corresponding provision relating to requests for multi-territorial repertoire information, prospective users are explicitly listed as beneficiaries in an accompanying recital (see art. 25, note 1). Even so, the requirement to submit information upon request is a relatively far-reaching obligation on the part of CMOs. In light of the aim of transparency that this provision intends to achieve, it art. 20 may be interpreted as requiring CMOs to provide information only to users who have a legitimate interest to obtain information and only for the specific purposes for which the request is made.

4. Provision on confidentiality of information. Although art. 20 does not expressly permit this, in order to guarantee the confidentiality of (commercially sensitive) information that is handed over to the requesting person or entity, it seems reasonable to allow CMOs to submit the information upon request subject to an obligation of secrecy. In this respect, recital 56 explicitly states that the provisions of this Directive are without prejudice to the application of relevant law in other areas, including confidentiality and trade secrets.

[Disclosure of information to the public]

Article 21

(1) Member States shall ensure that a collective management organisation makes public at least the following information:

    (a) its statute;

    (b) its membership terms and the terms of termination of authorisation to manage rights, if these are not included in the statute;

    (c) standard licensing contracts and standard applicable tariffs, including discounts;

    (d) the list of the persons referred to in Article 10;

    (e) its general policy on distribution of amounts due to rightholders;

    (f) its general policy on management fees;

    (g) its general policy on deductions, other than in respect of management fees, from rights revenue and from any income arising from the investment of rights revenue, including deductions for the purposes of social, cultural and educational services;

    (h) a list of the representation agreements it has entered into, and the names of the collective management organisations with which those representation agreements have been concluded;

    (i) the general policy on the use of non-distributable amounts;

(j) **the complaint handling and dispute resolution procedures available in accordance with Articles 33, 34 and 35.**

(2) The collective management organisation shall publish, and keep up to date, on its public website the information referred to in paragraph 1.

1. General. Art. 21 instructs Member States to require CMOs to publicly disclose information on their structure and on the way in which they carry out their activities. It lists in detail the information that must be made public as a minimum, including their statutes and membership terms, standard tariffs and licensing contracts and their general policies on management fees, deductions and tariffs. Member States may require CMOs to disclose other information. The information must be published and kept up-to-date on the CMO's public website.

[Annual transparency report]

Article 22

(1) Member States shall ensure that a collective management organisation, irrespective of its legal form under national law, draws up and makes public an annual transparency report, including the special report referred to in paragraph 3, for each financial year no later than eight months following the end of that financial year.

The collective management organisation shall publish on its website the annual transparency report, which shall remain available to the public on that website for at least five years.

(2) The annual transparency report shall contain at least the information set out in the Annex.

(3) A special report shall address the use of the amounts deducted for the purposes of social, cultural and educational services and shall contain at least the information set out in point 3 of the Annex.

(4) The accounting information included in the annual transparency report shall be audited by one or more persons empowered by law to audit accounts in accordance with Directive 2006/43/EC of the European Parliament and of the Council[9].

The audit report, including any qualifications thereto, shall be reproduced in full in the annual transparency report.

For the purposes of this paragraph, accounting information shall comprise the financial statements referred to in point 1(a) of the Annex and any financial information referred to in points (g) and (h) of point 1 and in point 2 of the Annex.

---

9. Directive 2006/43/EC of the European Parliament and of the Council of 17 May 2006 on statutory audits of annual accounts and consolidated account, amending Council Directives 78/660/EEC and 83/349/EEC and repealing Council Directive 84/253/EEC (OJ L 157, 9.6.2006, p. 87).

1. General. Art. 22 instructs Member States to require CMOs to draw up and publish an annual transparency report. This aims to ensure that rightholders are able to monitor and compare the respective performances of CMOs (recital 36). The annual transparency report should consist of a report comprising comparable audited financial information specific to the CMO's activities, as set out in detail in points 1 and 2 of the Annex, and a special report on the use of the amounts deducted for the purposes of social, cultural and educational services containing the information set out in point 3 of the Annex. The annual transparency report must be published online within eight months from the end of the financial year and remain publicly available on the CMO's website for at least five years. Furthermore, the annual transparency report must be approved by the general assembly of members (art. 8(8)). Art. 22 is silent on the language in which the transparency report must be drawn up. This suggests that a CMO is free to publish the report in the language of the Member State where it is settled. To some degree, this may impair the objective of creating transparency about the CMO's performance to rightholders from other Member States, but it is conceivable that the more competitive CMOs will deliberately choose to also publish their transparency reports in other language versions, so as to attract foreign rightholders to entrust them with the management of their rights, categories of rights or types of works and other subject-matter, as provided for in art. 5(2).

TITLE III. MULTI-TERRITORIAL LICENSING OF ONLINE RIGHTS IN MUSICAL WORKS BY COLLECTIVE MANAGEMENT ORGANISATIONS

[Multi-territorial licensing in the internal market]

Article 23

Member States shall ensure that collective management organisations established in their territory comply with the requirements of this Title when granting multi-territorial licences for online rights in musical works.

1. General. Art. 23 instructs Member States to adopt measures requiring CMOs established in their territory to comply with the requirements of Title III when granting multi-territorial licences for online rights in musical works. These are licences required for the provision of an online music service which cover the territory of more than one Member State (art. 3(m)). In accordance with the definition of 'online rights in musical works' (art. 3(n)), this involves the licensing of author's rights in musical works for online use only. The use of musical works in online services often requires the licensing of the rights of reproduction and communication to the public, including the making available right, in arts. 2 and 3 of the Information Society Directive.

Pursuant to the definition of art. 3(n), Title III does not apply to the multi-territorial licensing of related rights of performers or phonogram producers. Online services that solely provide access to musical works in the form of sheet music are also excluded from its scope of application (see art. 3, note 6). Title III imposes requirements additional to the ones laid down in Title II. CMOs granting multi-territorial licences for online rights in musical works must consequently abide by the requirements of both Title II and Title III.

2. Requirements of Title III. Title III seeks to improve the legal framework of multi-territorial licensing in the internal market in two ways. **(a) 'Passport system'.** First, arts. 24 to 28 set out the conditions under which CMOs may engage in multi-territorial licensing services. These provisions subject CMOs granting multi-territorial licences for online rights in musical works to a number of functional, technical and operational requirements and additional standards of good governance, so as to ensure the necessary minimum quality of cross-border licensing by CMOs in terms of their capacity to process multi-territorial licences, the transparency of the repertoire they represent and the accuracy of financial flows related to the use of online rights. **(b) Obligation to represent repertoire of other CMOs.** For CMOs that are not willing or, due to the inability to meet the requirements of arts. 24 to 28, are unable to grant multi-territorial licences directly in their own music repertoire, arts. 29 to 31 establish a system allowing CMOs to request other CMOs to represent their online music repertoire on a multi-territorial basis. The latter CMOs are obliged to agree to such a request if they are already granting multi-territorial licences for the same category of online rights in musical works on behalf of one or more other CMOs. Once a representation agreement has been concluded, the mandated CMO is required to manage the online rights of the mandating CMO on a non-discriminatory basis and on the same conditions as those which it applies to the management of its own repertoire.

3. Aims. The provisions of Title III aim to support the creation of a single European digital market for online music services. This should respond to the rapidly growing demand on the part of consumers for access to digital content and associated innovative services, including across national borders (recital 38). The development of legal online music services across the EU is further considered to contribute to the fight against online infringements of copyright (recital 40).

[Capacity to process multi-territorial licences]

Article 24

(1) Member States shall ensure that a collective management organisation which grants multi-territorial licences for online rights in musical works has sufficient capacity to process electronically, in an efficient and transparent manner, data needed for the administration of such licences, including for the purposes of identifying the repertoire and monitoring its

use, invoicing users, collecting rights revenue and distributing amounts due to rightholders.

(2) For the purposes of paragraph 1, a collective management organisation shall comply, at least, with the following conditions:

    (a) to have the ability to identify accurately the musical works, wholly or in part, which the collective management organisation is authorised to represent;

    (b) to have the ability to identify accurately, wholly or in part, with respect to each relevant territory, the rights and their corresponding rightholders for each musical work or share therein which the collective management organisation is authorised to represent;

    (c) to make use of unique identifiers in order to identify rightholders and musical works, taking into account, as far as possible, voluntary industry standards and practices developed at international or Union level;

    (d) to make use of adequate means in order to identify and resolve in a timely and effective manner inconsistencies in data held by other collective management organisations granting multi-territorial licences for online rights in musical works.

1. General. Art. 24 aims to ensure the necessary minimum quality of cross-border licensing by CMOs in terms of their capacity to process multi-territorial licences. It instructs Member States to require that CMOs can engage in the multi-territorial licensing of online rights in musical works only if they have sufficient capacity to electronically process data needed for the administration of such licences. This includes data required for identifying the repertoire and monitoring its use, invoicing users, collecting rights revenue and distributing amounts due to rightholders. CMOs should be able to process such detailed data quickly, accurately and in an efficient and transparent manner. Art. 24(2) stipulates minimum conditions with which CMOs granting multi-territorial licences for musical works must comply.

2. Data to be processed for multi-territorial licensing (para. 2). Art. 24(2) requires that CMOs granting multi-territorial licences for online rights must be able to accurately identify the musical works, rights and rightholders that they are authorized to represent for each of the territories covered by the authorization. This requires the use of adequate rights management databases that should be continually updated without undue delay (recital 41). They should use adequate means to timely and effectively identify and resolve inconsistencies between their databases and those held by other CMOs granting multi-territorial licences for online rights in musical works. They must further use unique identifiers to identify rightholders and musical works, such as fingerprinting techniques. These should be based as far as possible on voluntary industry standards and practices developed at international or EU level.

[Transparency of multi-territorial repertoire information]

Article 25

(1) **Member States shall ensure that a collective management organisation which grants multi-territorial licences for online rights in musical works provides to online service providers, to rightholders whose rights it represents and to other collective management organisations, by electronic means, in response to a duly justified request, up-to-date information allowing the identification of the online music repertoire it represents. This shall include:**

    (a) **the musical works represented;**

    (b) **the rights represented wholly or in part; and**

    (c) **the territories covered.**

(2) **The collective management organisation may take reasonable measures, where necessary, to protect the accuracy and integrity of the data, to control their reuse and to protect commercially sensitive information.**

1. Obligation to provide information on request (para. 1). Echoing the general obligation under art. 20, but now in relation to CMOs granting multi-territorial licences for online rights in musical works, art. 25 instructs Member States to require CMOs granting such licences to provide up-to-date information on the online music repertoire they represent in response to a duly justified request by online service providers, rightholders whose rights they represent and other CMOs. This includes information on the musical works and rights represented and the territories covered. Importantly, recital 41 explicitly states that prospective users and rightholders, as well as CMOs, should also have access to this information.

2. Protection of data and commercially sensitive information (para. 2). Pursuant to art. 25(2), CMOs may take reasonable measures, where necessary, to protect the accuracy and integrity of the data, to control their reuse or to protect commercially sensitive information. This is without prejudice to the application of relevant laws on, inter alia, confidentiality, trade secrets, privacy and access to documents (recital 56).

[Accuracy of multi-territorial repertoire information]

Article 26

(1) **Member States shall ensure that a collective management organisation which grants multi-territorial licences for online rights in musical works has in place arrangements to enable rightholders, other collective management organisations and online service providers to request a correction of the data referred to in the list of conditions under Article 24(2) or the information provided under Article 25, where such rightholders,**

collective management organisations and online service providers, on the basis of reasonable evidence, believe that the data or the information are inaccurate in respect of their online rights in musical works. Where the claims are sufficiently substantiated, the collective management organisation shall ensure that the data or the information are corrected without undue delay.

(2) The collective management organisation shall provide rightholders whose musical works are included in its own music repertoire and rightholders who have entrusted the management of their online rights in musical works to it in accordance with Article 31 with the means of submitting to it in electronic form information concerning their musical works, their rights in those works and the territories in respect of which the rightholders authorise the organisation. When doing so, the collective management organisation and the rightholders shall take into account, as far as possible, voluntary industry standards or practices regarding the exchange of data developed at international or Union level, allowing rightholders to specify the musical work, wholly or in part, the online rights, wholly or in part, and the territories in respect of which they authorise the organisation.

(3) Where a collective management organisation mandates another collective management organisation to grant multi-territorial licences for the online rights in musical works under Articles 29 and 30, the mandated collective management organisation shall also apply paragraph 2 of this Article with respect to the rightholders whose musical works are included in the repertoire of the mandating collective management organisation, unless the collective management organisations agree otherwise.

1. Correction of rights management data (para. 1). To ensure that the data processed under art. 24 and the information provided under art. 25 are as accurate as possible, art. 26(1) instructs Member States to oblige CMOs granting multi-territorial licences in musical works to correct that data or that information without undue delay upon a sufficiently substantiated claim by rightholders, CMOs or online service providers that the data or the information are inaccurate in respect of their online rights in musical works. Such claims should be substantiated by reasonable evidence, so as to prevent that the accuracy and integrity of the data held by CMOs is jeopardized. Recital 42 states that this procedure corresponds to the Personal Data Protection Directive, which grants to every data subject the right to obtain rectification, erasure or blocking of inaccurate or incomplete data (see also art. 42). CMOs must put in place easily accessible arrangements that enable requests for the correction of relevant data or information to be made.

2. Electronic submission of rights management data (paras. 2 and 3). Recital 42 stresses the importance of information automation for the fast and effective processing of data. In view of that, art. 26(2) and (3) require CMOs to provide for the use of electronic means for the structured communication of information on online music repertoire by rightholders. This involves information on the musical works, the online rights and the territories covered by their authorizations. CMOs should ensure, as far as possible, that such electronic means conform to relevant voluntary industry standards or practices regarding the exchange of data developed at international or EU level.

[Accurate and timely reporting and invoicing]

Article 27

(1) **Member States shall ensure that a collective management organisation monitors the use of online rights in musical works which it represents, wholly or in part, by online service providers to which it has granted a multi-territorial licence for those rights.**

(2) **The collective management organisation shall offer online service providers the possibility of reporting by electronic means the actual use of online rights in musical works and online service providers shall accurately report the actual use of those works. The collective management organisation shall offer the use of at least one method of reporting which takes into account voluntary industry standards or practices developed at international or Union level for the electronic exchange of such data. The collective management organisation may refuse to accept reporting by the online service provider in a proprietary format if the organisation allows for reporting using an industry standard for the electronic exchange of data.**

(3) **The collective management organisation shall invoice the online service provider by electronic means. The collective management organisation shall offer the use of a least one format which takes into account voluntary industry standards or practices developed at international or Union level. The invoice shall identify the works and rights which are licensed, wholly or in part, on the basis of the data referred to in the list of conditions under Article 24(2), and the corresponding actual uses, to the extent that this is possible on the basis of the information provided by the online service provider and the format used to provide that information. The online service provider may not refuse to accept the invoice because of its format if the collective management organisation is using an industry standard.**

(4) **The collective management organisation shall invoice the online service provider accurately and without delay after the actual use of the online rights in that musical work is reported, except where this is not possible for reasons attributable to the online service provider.**

(5) **The collective management organisation shall have in place adequate arrangements enabling the online service provider to challenge the accuracy of the invoice, including when the online service provider**

receives invoices from one or more collective management organisations for the same online rights in the same musical work.

1. General. Art. 27 aims to ensure the necessary minimum quality of cross-border licensing by CMOs in terms of the accuracy of financial flows related to the use of rights. It does so by imposing obligations on CMOs to monitor use of rights and on users to report actual use of works and by regulating the invoicing of online service providers. With respect to music use, sales reporting and invoicing, the Directive strongly encourages the use of industry standards, which it considers to be instrumental in improving efficiency in the exchange of data between CMOs and users. The idea is that such efficiency gains will lead to faster financial processing and ultimately result in earlier payments to rightholders. To improve management services and rationalize investments in data management tools, CMOs may also outsource particular services or share or consolidate back-office capabilities (recital 43).

2. Monitoring use of online rights in musical works (para. 1). Art. 27(1) instructs Member States to require CMOs to monitor the use of online rights in musical works which they represent by online service providers to which they have granted a multi-territorial licence for those rights. Recital 43 reminds Member States that monitoring the use of licences should, of course, respect fundamental rights, including the right to respect for private and family life and the right to protection of personal data. This reflects the ECJ's case law barring general monitoring obligations imposed on internet service providers on the ground of considerations based on fundamental rights (see *Scarlet Extended* and *SABAM v Netlog*).

3. Obligation to report actual use of musical works (para. 2). Art. 27(2) requires online service providers to provide CMOs with accurate and timely reports on their actual use of musical works. To facilitate this, CMOs must offer them the possibility of reporting the use by electronic means. They must allow for at least one method of reporting which takes into account voluntary industry standards or practices developed at international or EU level for the electronic exchange of such data. CMOs enabling online service provider to report using an industry standard may refuse to accept users' reports in proprietary formats.

4. Invoicing online service providers (paras. 3 to 5). Art. 27(4) requires CMOs to invoice online service providers accurately and without delay after they have reported on their actual use of works. The invoicing can be delayed only for reasons attributable to the online service provider, such as incorrect or incomplete reporting. Invoicing must occur by electronic means (art. 27(3)). The CMO's invoices must identify the works and rights which are licensed and the corresponding actual uses, to the extent that this is possible on the basis of the report by the online service provider. CMOs should offer the use of at least one format which takes into account voluntary industry standards or practices developed at international or EU level. An online service provider may not refuse to accept the invoice because of its format if the CMO is using an industry standard. Art. 27(5) obliges CMOs to put in place adequate arrangements for online service providers to challenge the accuracy of invoices, e.g., invoices received from one or more CMOs for the same online rights in the same musical work.

[Accurate and timely payment to rightholders]

Article 28

(1) Without prejudice to paragraph 3, Member States shall ensure that a collective management organisation which grants multi-territorial licences for online rights in musical works distributes amounts due to rightholders accruing from such licences accurately and without delay after the actual use of the work is reported, except where this is not possible for reasons attributable to the online service provider.

(2) Without prejudice to paragraph 3, the collective management organisation shall provide at least the following information to rightholders together with each payment it makes under paragraph 1:

   (a) the period during which the uses took place for which amounts are due to rightholders and the territories in which the uses took place;

   (b) the amounts collected, deductions made and amounts distributed by the collective management organisation for each online right in any musical work which rightholders have authorised the collective management organisation, wholly or in part, to represent;

   (c) the amounts collected for rightholders, deductions made, and amounts distributed by the collective management organisation in respect of each online service provider.

(3) Where a collective management organisation mandates another collective management organisation to grant multi-territorial licences for the online rights in musical works under Articles 29 and 30, the mandated collective management organisation shall distribute the amounts referred to in paragraph 1 accurately and without delay, and shall provide the information referred to in paragraph 2 to the mandating collective management organisation. The mandating collective management organisation shall be responsible for the subsequent distribution of such amounts and the provision of such information to rightholders, unless the collective management organisations agree otherwise.

1. Distribution of income from multi-territorial licences: general rule (paras. 1 and 2). Art. 28(1) instructs Member States to require CMOs granting multi-territorial licences for online rights in musical works to distribute amounts due to rightholders accruing from such licences accurately and without delay after the actual use of the work is reported. The payment can be delayed only for reasons attributable to the online service provider, such as an incorrect or incomplete reporting. With each payment, CMOs must specify the period and territories of use to which the payment pertains and the amounts collected, deductions made and amounts distributed in respect of each online service provider and for each online right in any musical work represented by them (art. 28(2)).

2. Distribution of income from multi-territorial licences under a mandate (para. 3). Art. 28(3) contains an exception to the general rule in paras. 1 and 2 for the situation where a CMO has mandated another CMO to grant multi-territorial licences for the online rights in musical works under arts. 29 and 30. In such situation, the mandated CMO must distribute the amounts due to rightholders accruing from multi-territorial licences accurately and without delay to the mandating CMO, together with the information referred to in art. 28(2). The mandating CMO is then responsible for the subsequent distribution of the amounts and the provision of information to rightholders, unless the CMOs have agreed otherwise.

[Agreements between collective management organisations for multi-territorial licensing]

Article 29

(1) Member States shall ensure that any representation agreement between collective management organisations whereby a collective management organisation mandates another collective management organisation to grant multi-territorial licences for the online rights in musical works in its own music repertoire is of a non-exclusive nature. The mandated collective management organisation shall manage those online rights on a non-discriminatory basis.

(2) The mandating collective management organisation shall inform its members of the main terms of the agreement, including its duration and the costs of the services provided by the mandated collective management organisation.

(3) The mandated collective management organisation shall inform the mandating collective management organisation of the main terms according to which the latter's online rights are to be licensed, including the nature of the exploitation, all provisions which relate to or affect the licence fee, the duration of the licence, the accounting periods and the territories covered.

1. General. Art. 29 sets out a legal construction for facilitating the voluntary aggregation of music repertoire and rights required for the provision of online music services. It does so by enabling a CMO to request another CMO to represent its repertoire on a multi-territorial basis where it is not willing or not able to grant multi-territorial licences directly in its own music repertoire. This so-called 'passport' system contributes to reducing the number of licences an online music provider needs in order to operate a multi-territory, multi-repertoire music service. This should facilitate the development of new online services and result in a reduction of transaction costs being passed on to consumers (recital 44).

2. Non-exclusive mandate (para. 1). Art. 29(1) instructs Member States to require that any representation agreement between CMOs that follow the 'passport' construction is of a non-exclusive nature. This should ensure that CMOs have the choice to join different hubs for multi-territorial licensing of their repertoire and that users seeking multi-territorial licences have the choice to obtain licences from several licensing hubs (recital 44). Recital 46 further stipulates that a CMO which has mandated another CMO to grant multi-territorial licences in its own music repertoire should not be prevented from continuing to grant licences limited to the territory of the Member State where it is established, in its own repertoire and in any other repertoire which it may be authorized to represent in that territory.

3. Management on a non-discriminatory basis (para. 1). Art. 29(1) requires the mandated CMO to manage the online rights of the mandating CMO on a non-discriminatory basis. This means that it may not differentiate between its own repertoire and that of the mandating CMO when granting multi-territorial licences for online rights in musical works. This obligation is elaborated in more detail in art. 30(3) and (4).

4. Transparency requirements (paras. 2 and 3). To ensure transparency of the management of online rights by the mandated CMO, art. 29(2) requires the mandating CMO to inform its members of the main terms of the representation agreement concluded, including its duration and the costs of the services provided by the mandated CMO. In accordance with art. 7(1), such information must also be provided to rightholders whose rights are directly represented by the CMOs but who are not their members. The mandated CMO, on its part, must inform the mandating CMO of the main terms according to which it will license the online rights of the mandating CMO. Information should be provided, inter alia, on the nature of the exploitation, all provisions which relate to or affect the licence fee, the duration of the licence, the accounting periods and the territories covered (art. 29(3)).

[Obligation to represent another collective management organisation for multi-territorial licensing]

Article 30

(1) Member States shall ensure that where a collective management organisation which does not grant or offer to grant multi-territorial

licences for the online rights in musical works in its own repertoire requests another collective management organisation to enter into a representation agreement to represent those rights, the requested collective management organisation is required to agree to such a request if it is already granting or offering to grant multi-territorial licences for the same category of online rights in musical works in the repertoire of one or more other collective management organisations.

(2) The requested collective management organisation shall respond to the requesting collective management organisation in writing and without undue delay.

(3) Without prejudice to paragraphs 5 and 6, the requested collective management organisation shall manage the represented repertoire of the requesting collective management organisation on the same conditions as those which it applies to the management of its own repertoire.

(4) The requested collective management organisation shall include the represented repertoire of the requesting collective management organisation in all offers it addresses to online service providers.

(5) The management fee for the service provided by the requested collective management organisation to the requesting organisation shall not exceed the costs reasonably incurred by the requested collective management organisation.

(6) The requesting collective management organisation shall make available to the requested collective management organisation information relating to its own music repertoire required for the provision of multi-territorial licences for online rights in musical works. Where information is insufficient or provided in a form that does not allow the requested collective management organisation to meet the requirements of this Title, the requested collective management organisation shall be entitled to charge for the costs reasonably incurred in meeting such requirements or to exclude those works for which information is insufficient or cannot be used.

1. Obligation to accept the mandate of a requesting CMO (paras. 1 and 2). To prevent discriminatory treatment and to enable small and medium-sized CMOs to effectively include their repertoires within existing or future hubs for multi-territorial licensing of online rights in musical works, art. 30(1) instructs Member States to require CMOs which already grant or offer to grant multi-territorial licences to agree to a request by any CMO which does not grant or offer to grant such licences to represent the online rights in its repertoire. This obligation is not absolute. To ensure that this requirement is not disproportionate and does not go beyond what is necessary, it is restricted in three ways (recital 46). First, the requested CMO is only required to accept representation if the request is limited to the (categories of) online rights that it represents itself. Secondly, this requirement only applies to CMOs aggregating repertoire and not to CMOs providing multi-territorial licences for their own repertoire only. Thirdly, the requirement does not apply to CMOs aggregating rights in the same works for the purpose of being able to license jointly the rights of reproduction and of communication to the public in respect of such works. For reasons of clarity and expedition, art. 30(2) requires the requested CMO to respond to the requesting CMO in writing and without undue delay.

2. Obligation to apply the same conditions to the mandated repertoire (paras. 3 and 4). To protect the interests of rightholders of the mandating CMO and to ensure that small and less well-known repertoires in Member States can access the internal market on equal terms (recital 46), art. 30(3) obliges the mandated CMO to manage the represented repertoire of the mandating CMO on the same conditions as those which it applies to the management of its own repertoire. Art. 30(4) further explicates that the represented repertoire of the mandating CMO must be included in all offers of the mandated CMO to online service providers.

3. Management fee (para. 5). The management fee charged by the mandated CMO for the service provided to the mandating CMO may not exceed the costs reasonably incurred by it (art. 30(5)). Recital 46 states that such management fee should allow the mandated CMO to recoup the necessary and reasonable investments incurred.

4. Information requirement (para. 6). Art. 30(6) requires the requesting CMO to make available to the requested CMO information relating to its own music repertoire required for the provision of multi-territorial licences for online rights in musical works. The penalty for not meeting this requirement is serious. Where information is provided in a form that is inapt for the requested CMO to meet the requirements of Title III, the costs reasonably incurred in meeting such requirements may be charged. Those works for which the information provided is insufficient or cannot be used may further be excluded by the requested CMO.

[Access to multi-territorial licensing]

Article 31

Member States shall ensure that where a collective management organisation does not grant or offer to grant multi-territorial licences for online rights in musical works or does not allow another collective management organisation to represent those rights for such purpose by 10 April 2017, rightholders who have authorised that collective management organisation to represent their online rights in musical works can withdraw from that collective management organisation the online rights in musical works for the purposes of multi-territorial licensing in respect of all territories without having to withdraw the online rights in musical works for the purposes of mono-territorial licensing, so as to

grant multi-territorial licences for their online rights in musical works themselves or through any other party they authorise or through any collective management organisation complying with the provisions of this Title.

1. General. Art. 31 contemplates the situation where rightholders have authorized a CMO to represent their online rights in musical works but that CMO does not (offer to) grant multi-territorial licences for online rights in musical works or does not mandate another CMO to do so. Recital 47 notes that in such circumstances the objectives and effectiveness of the rules on multi-territorial licensing by CMOs would be significantly jeopardized if rightholders were not able to exercise such rights in respect of multi-territorial licences. Art. 31 provides relief by enabling rightholders in such circumstances to withdraw their online rights from the CMO.

2. Right of withdrawal of online rights in musical works for multi-territorial licensing. Art. 31 instructs Member States, in situations where a CMO has not allowed for the multi-territorial licensing of online rights in musical works by 10 April 2017, to grant rightholders the right to withdraw from the CMO their online rights in musical works for the purposes of multi-territorial licensing in respect of all territories without having to withdraw the same rights from that CMO for the purposes of mono-territorial licensing. Nevertheless, pursuant to art. 5(4), rightholders may choose to also withdraw their online rights in musical works for mono-territorial licensing or to terminate their authorization to the CMO altogether. The general right of termination of authorization and withdrawal of rights in art. 5(4) is however subject to a term of notice of maximum six months, while art. 31 does not mention any term of notice. This seems to imply that, if a CMO does not (offer to) grant multi-territorial licences by 10 April 2017, rightholders can immediately withdraw from the CMO their online rights in musical works for the purposes of multi-territorial licensing by giving notification of the withdrawal to the CMO. This would enable rightholders to grant multi-territorial licences for online rights in musical works themselves, through another party they authorize or through any CMO complying with the provisions of Title III.

3. Burden of proof. Art. 31 does not further specify who has the burden of proof that a CMO does not grant or offer to grant multi-territorial licences for online rights in musical works. In cases of dispute, however, it seems reasonable to give rightholders the benefit of the doubt and to require CMOs to provide evidence of their multi-territorial licensing practices, as they are in the best position to give information about the licences they grant to users. That would also do justice to the aim of art. 31, which is to protect the interests of rightholders in cases where CMOs fail to offer multi-territorial licences to online music services.

[Derogation for online music rights required for radio and television programmes]

Article 32

The requirements under this Title shall not apply to collective management organisations when they grant, on the basis of the voluntary aggregation of the required rights, in compliance with the competition rules under Articles 101 and 102 TFEU, a multi-territorial licence for the online rights in musical works required by a broadcaster to communicate or make available to the public its radio or television programmes simultaneously with or after their initial broadcast as well as any online material, including previews, produced by or for the broadcaster which is ancillary to the initial broadcast of its radio or television programme.

1. General. Recital 48 contends that there is need for a derogation from the rules that would otherwise apply to the multi-territorial licensing of online rights in musical works for certain online activities of broadcasters. It explains that broadcasters generally rely on a licence from a local CMO for the broadcasting of television and radio programmes which include musical works, but that an additional licence for online rights in musical works is often needed to also allow them to make such television or radio broadcasts available online. A derogation of the rules of Title III for particular online transmissions of television and radio broadcasts was deemed necessary to prevent broadcasters from having to acquire the licences required for the use of musical works in their services from several passport entities, which could make the provision of these services more cumbersome. Such derogation ensures that CMOs may continue to license online rights in musical works to broadcasters directly and not through passport entities. Arguably, this provides leeway to voluntary agreements of CMOs creating a one stop shop for the licensing of online rights for particular uses, akin to the already expired IFPI Simulcasting agreement (for simulcasting), Santiago agreement (for public performance of music on the internet) and BIEM Barcelona agreement (for the mechanical reproduction of music on the internet). Such agreements have the benefit that broadcasters do not have to contract with a multitude of licensing hubs to acquire the necessary licences required for their online uses, but can obtain a licence for such uses from a single CMO.

2. Derogation from Title III for aggregation of online rights required by broadcasters. Art. 32 provides that the requirements of Title III do not apply to the voluntary aggregation of online rights in musical works by CMOs for the purpose of granting multi-territorial licences to broadcasters for the purposes of certain acts of communication or making available to the public of their radio or television programmes. The derogation is limited to multi-territorial licences allowing broadcasters to provide online access to television or radio programmes simultaneously with or after their initial broadcast (e.g. simulcasting and catch-up television) and online material produced by or for broadcasters which is ancillary to the initial broadcast of their radio or television programmes (e.g. online previews, supplements or reviews of the programmes concerned). The multi-territorial licensing practice permitted under art. 32 must comply with the competition rules under arts. 101 and 102 TFEU. To understand what this requires, recourse can be made to the Commission's *IFPI Simulcasting* and *CISAC* decisions and the ECJ's *CISAC* case, which provide guidance on how representation agreements between CMOs for the voluntary aggregation of rights can be brought into conformity with EU competition law. Recital 48 further clarifies that any licensing agreements based on art. 32 should not lead to restrictive practices, such as market or customer sharing, or distorted competition with other services providing consumers access to individual musical or audiovisual works online.

3. Reasons for derogation. The Directive does not explain why a special exemption is warranted for facilitating the licensing of online rights in musical works for certain online activities of broadcasters but not for online activities of other music services. Recital 48 merely assumes that broadcasters require such a derogation. A possible reason is that, in line with the objective of the Satellite and Cable Directive, art. 32 was introduced to eliminate copyright-related barriers to online trans-frontier broadcasting services within the EU. This might explain the derogation of the rules of Title III to enable the creation of one stop shop models for the multi-territorial licensing of online rights in musical works for certain online broadcasting activities. Since the rules of Title III apply only in relation to author's rights in musical works, however, the Directive leaves quite some room for introducing similar multi-territorial licensing regimes in other areas (recital 11). Such licensing regimes could for example be introduced in relation to related rights for performers and phonogram producers or to enable the multi-territorial licensing of online rights in e-books or images.

TITLE IV. ENFORCEMENT MEASURES

[Complaints procedures]

Article 33

(1) **Member States shall ensure that collective management organisations make available to their members, and to collective management organisations on whose behalf they manage rights under a representation agreement, effective and timely procedures for dealing with complaints, particularly in relation to authorisation to manage rights and termination or withdrawal of rights, membership terms, the collection of amounts due to rightholders, deductions and distributions.**

(2) **Collective management organisations shall respond in writing to complaints by members or by collective management organisations on**

whose behalf they manage rights under a representation agreement. Where the collective management organisation rejects a complaint, it shall give reasons.

1. General. To ensure the effective enforcement of provisions of national law adopted pursuant to this Directive, art. 33(1) instructs Member States to require CMOs to make effective and timely complaints procedures available to their members and to other CMOs on whose behalf they manage rights. Such complaints procedures must also be made available to rightholders whose rights are directly represented by the CMOs but who are not their members (art. 7(1)). The procedures must allow for handling complaints particularly in relation to authorization to manage rights, a termination or withdrawal of rights, membership terms, the collection of amounts due to rightholders, deductions and distributions. CMOs must respond to complaints in writing and give reasons where they reject a complaint (art. 33(2)). The CMOs' complaints procedures are without prejudice to the right to proceed before a court (art. 35(2)).

[Alternative dispute resolution procedures]

Article 34

(1) Member States may provide that disputes between collective management organisations, members of collective management organisations, rightholders or users regarding the provisions of national law adopted pursuant to the requirements of this Directive can be submitted to a rapid, independent and impartial alternative dispute resolution procedure.

(2) Member States shall ensure, for the purposes of Title III, that the following disputes relating to a collective management organisation established in their territory which grants or offers to grant multi-territorial licences for online rights in musical works can be submitted to an independent and impartial alternative dispute resolution procedure:

(a) disputes with an actual or potential online service provider regarding the application of Articles 16, 25, 26 and 27;

(b) disputes with one or more rightholders regarding the application of Articles 25, 26, 27, 28, 29, 30 and 31;

(c) disputes with another collective management organisation regarding the application of Articles 25, 26, 27, 28, 29 and 30.

1. Optional alternative dispute resolution (para. 1). Art. 34(1) offers Member States the possibility to provide that disputes that may arise between CMOs, members of CMOs, rightholders or users on the provisions of national law adopted pursuant to this Directive can be submitted to a rapid, independent and impartial alternative dispute resolution procedure, such as mediation or arbitration. It neither prescribes a specific manner in which such alternative dispute resolution should be organized, nor determines which body should carry it out, provided that its independence, impartiality and efficiency are guaranteed (recital 49). Such access to an alternative dispute resolution procedure is without prejudice to the right of parties to settle disputes before a court (art. 35(2)).

2. Mandatory alternative dispute resolution for conflicts on multi-territorial licensing (para. 2). To ensure the effectiveness of the rules on multi-territorial licensing of online rights in musical works under Title III, art. 34(2) orders Member States to provide for the possibility of easily accessible, independent and impartial alternative dispute resolution procedures for resolving conflicts between CMOs granting multi-territorial licences established in their territory, on the one hand, and actual or potential online service providers, rightholders or other CMOs, on the other hand. Art. 34(2) accurately lists which disputes on the application of the provisions of the Directive can be resolved in alternative dispute resolution procedures.

[Dispute resolution]

Article 35

(1) Member States shall ensure that disputes between collective management organisations and users concerning, in particular, existing and proposed licensing conditions or a breach of contract can be submitted to a court, or if appropriate, to another independent and impartial dispute resolution body where that body has expertise in intellectual property law.

(2) Articles 33 and 34 and paragraph 1 of this Article shall be without prejudice to the right of parties to assert and defend their rights by bringing an action before a court.

1. Dispute resolution by a court or specialized body (para. 1). To enable the independent, impartial and effective resolution of commercial disputes between CMOs and users on, inter alia, existing or proposed licensing conditions or a breach of contract, art. 35(1) requires Member States to ensure that such disputes can be submitted to a court or an independent and impartial dispute resolution body with expertise in intellectual property law.

2. Right to bring an action before a court (para. 2). Art. 35(2) provides that the complaints procedures (art. 33), alternative dispute resolution procedures (art. 34) and dispute resolution procedures before independent and impartial bodies with expertise in intellectual property law (art. 35(1)) are without prejudice to the right of parties to assert and defend their rights by instituting a proceeding before a court. The right of access to a tribunal is guaranteed in the Charter of Fundamental Rights of the European Union (see recital 54).

[Compliance]

Article 36

(1) Member States shall ensure that compliance by collective management organisations established in their territory with the provisions of national law adopted pursuant to the requirements laid down in this Directive is monitored by competent authorities designated for that purpose.

(2) Member States shall ensure that procedures exist enabling members of a collective management organisation, rightholders, users, collective management organisations and other interested parties to notify the competent authorities designated for that purpose of activities or circumstances which, in their opinion, constitute a breach of the provisions of national law adopted pursuant to the requirements laid down in this Directive.

(3) Member States shall ensure that the competent authorities designated for that purpose have the power to impose appropriate sanctions or to take appropriate measures where the provisions of national law adopted in implementation of this Directive have not been complied with. Those sanctions and measures shall be effective, proportionate and dissuasive.

Member States shall notify the Commission of the competent authorities referred to in this Article and in Articles 37 and 38 by 10 April 2016. The Commission shall publish the information received in that regard.

1. General. Recital 50 notes that Member States should establish appropriate procedures by means of which it will be possible to monitor compliance by CMOs with this Directive. In practice, Member States have in place vastly diverging procedures for the supervision of the CMOs established in their territory, varying from strict supervisory regimes to 'de minimis' types of control. To respect the diversity of the Member States' customary practice in relation to supervising the activities of CMOs, the Directive remains neutral as regards the existing regimes in the Member States for prior authorization, supervision and requirements for the representativeness of CMOs, in so far as those regimes are compatible with EU law and do not create an obstacle to the full application of this Directive (recital 50).

2. Competent authorities to monitor compliance by national CMOs (para. 1). Art. 36(1) orders Member States to have in place competent authorities designated for the purpose of monitoring compliance by CMOs with provisions of national law adopted pursuant to this Directive. **(a) No requirements as to the type of bodies or nature of control.** The Directive

van Gompel

does not oblige Member States to set up new competent authorities. They further remain free to choose the (type of) competent authority and the ex-ante or ex-post nature of control over CMOs. Member States must only ensure that the authorities to which they assign the task of supervising CMOs are capable of addressing in an effective and timely manner any concern arising in the application of this Directive (recital 50). **(b) Supervision limited to national CMOs.** The supervision of CMOs by a national competent authority is limited to the CMOs established in its territory. It may not subject CMOs established in other Member States to its supervision, even if they provide their services in its territory. That would be incompatible with the freedom to provide services under art. 56 TFEU, which according to settled case law of the ECJ precludes the application of any national rules which have the effect of making the provision of services between Member States more difficult than the provision of services purely within a Member State (see *Centro Europa 7* (ECJ)). A national competent authority may however request the competent authorities of any other Member State to take action against a noncompliant CMO established in that Member State but acting within its own territory (see art. 37(2)). In theory, Member States could extend the supervision to any CMO established outside the EU but operating in their territories (recital 10), but it is questionable whether such supervision would really be practicable and effective.

3. Procedures to notify competent authorities (para. 2). To enable members of a CMO, rightholders, users, CMOs and other interested parties to notify the competent authorities of activities or circumstances which, in their opinion, constitute a breach of the provisions of national law adopted pursuant to this Directive, art. 36(2) orders Member States to ensure that procedures are put in place for this purpose. Recital 50 notes that such procedures must allow for the reporting of any such breaches, whether made by CMOs or users.

4. Powers of the competent authorities (para. 3). To give the competent authorities some teeth, the first subparagraph of art. 36(3) requires Member States to ensure that they have the power to impose appropriate sanctions or to take appropriate measures where provisions of national law adopted pursuant to this Directive have not been complied with. The Directive however does not provide for specific types of sanctions or measures, but only requires that they shall be effective, proportionate and dissuasive. Recital 50 provides some examples of sanctions or measures that Member States may impose, such as orders to dismiss directors who act negligently, inspections at the premises of CMOs or, in cases where authorization is required for a CMO to operate, the withdrawal of such authorization.

5. Notification to the Commission (para. 3). The second subparagraph of art. 36(3) requires Member States to notify the Commission of their competent authorities. This information will subsequently be published by the Commission.

[Exchange of information between competent authorities]

Article 37

(1) In order to facilitate the monitoring of the application of this Directive, each Member State shall ensure that a request for information received from a competent authority of another Member State, designated for that purpose, concerning matters relevant to the application of this Directive, in particular with regard to the activities of collective management organisations established in the territory of the requested Member State, is responded to without undue delay by the competent authority designated for that purpose, provided that the request is duly justified.

(2) Where a competent authority considers that a collective management organisation established in another Member State but acting within its territory may not be complying with the provisions of the national law of the Member State in which that collective management organisation is established which have been adopted pursuant to the requirements laid down in this Directive, it may transmit all relevant information to the competent authority of the Member State in which the collective management organisation is established, accompanied where appropriate by a request to that authority that it take appropriate action within its competence. The requested competent authority shall provide a reasoned reply within three months.

(3) Matters as referred to in paragraph 2 may also be referred by the competent authority making such a request to the expert group established in accordance with Article 41.

1. General. The streamlining of rules on multi-territorial licensing of online rights in musical works will likely result in an increased provision of cross-border services by CMOs. Art. 37 provides rules to enable the national supervisory authorities to adjust to this increased international playing field within which CMOs operate. These rules aim to facilitate the monitoring of CMOs within the application of this Directive (recital 51).

2. Obligation to respond to requests for information by authorities from other Member States (para. 1). Art. 37(1) instructs each Member State to require that its national competent supervisory authority shall respond without undue delay to a request for information received from a competent supervisory authority of another Member State concerning matters relevant to the application of this Directive. Such matters concern in particular the activities of CMOs established in the territory of the requested Member State. Only requests which are not duly justified may be ignored.

3. Submission of information and requests for action to authorities from other Member States (para. 2). Art. 36(1) prevents national supervisory authorities from directly controlling any CMOs established in other Member States (see art. 36, note 2(b)). To nevertheless allow such authority to act against a CMO established in another Member State but operating within its territories in cases where such CMO allegedly violates the rules laid down in this Directive, art. 37(2) allows it to transmit all relevant information relating to such violation to the competent supervisory authority of the Member State in which the CMO is established. This may be accompanied where appropriate by a request to that authority to take appropriate action within its competence against the CMO. Art. 37(2) obliges the requested supervisory authority to provide a reasoned reply within three months.

4. Reference of requests for action to the expert group (para. 3). Art. 37(3) allows the national competent supervisory authority making a request pursuant to art. 37(2) to also refer the matter to the expert group established in accordance with art. 41. This may aid this expert group in fulfilling its task of monitoring the impact of the transposition of this Directive on the functioning of CMOs and highlighting any difficulties.

[Cooperation for the development of multi-territorial licensing]

Article 38

(1) The Commission shall foster a regular exchange of information between the competent authorities designated for that purpose in Member States, and between those authorities and the Commission, on the situation and development of multi-territorial licensing.

(2) The Commission shall conduct regular consultations with representatives of rightholders, collective management organisations, users, consumers and other interested parties on their experience with the application of the provisions of Title III of this Directive. The Commission shall provide competent authorities with all relevant information that emerges from those consultations, within the framework of the exchange of information provided for in paragraph 1.

(3) Member States shall ensure that by 10 October 2017, their competent authorities provide the Commission with a report on the situation and development of multi-territorial licensing in their territory. The report shall include information on, in particular, the availability of multi-territorial licences in the Member State concerned and compliance by collective management organisations with the provisions of national law adopted in implementation of Title III of this Directive, together with an assessment of the development of multi-territorial licensing of online rights in musical works by users, consumers, rightholders and other interested parties.

(4) On the basis of the reports received pursuant to paragraph 3 and the information gathered pursuant to paragraphs 1 and 2, the Commission shall assess the application of Title III of this Directive. If necessary, and where appropriate on the basis of a specific report, it shall consider further steps to address any identified problems. That assessment shall cover, in particular, the following:

(a) **the number of collective management organisations meeting the requirements of Title III;**

(b) **the application of Articles 29 and 30, including the number of representation agreements concluded by collective management organisations pursuant to those Articles;**

(c) **the proportion of repertoire in the Member States which is available for licensing on a multi-territorial basis.**

1. General. Art. 38 lays down specific provisions on the monitoring of the implementation of the requirements for multi-territorial licensing set out in Title III.

2. Exchange of information (paras. 1 and 2). The Commission must gather information on the situation and development of multi-territorial licensing by fostering a regular exchange of information between the competent supervisory authorities in Member States and between those authorities and the Commission (art. 38(1)) and conducting regular consultations with representatives of rightholders, CMOs, users, consumers and other interested parties (art. 38(2)). To facilitate the exchange of information, the Commission must provide competent supervisory authorities with relevant information emerging from those consultations.

3. National reports of competent authorities (para. 3). By 10 October 2017, all national competent supervisory authorities must issue a report on the situation and development of multi-territorial licensing in their territory to the Commission.

4. Assessment of the application of Title III (para. 4). On the basis of all the information gathered and reports received, the Commission must execute an assessment of the application of Title III of this Directive. That assessment should concentrate, in particular, on the number of CMOs meeting the requirements of Title III, the number of representation agreements between CMOs for the voluntary aggregation of rights (arts. 29 and 30), and the proportion of repertoire in the Member States which is available for multi-territorial licensing.

TITLE V. REPORTING AND FINAL PROVISIONS

[Notification of collective management organisations]

Article 39

By 10 April 2016, Member States shall provide the Commission, on the basis of the information at their disposal, with a list of the collective management organisations established in their territories.

Member States shall notify any changes to that list to the Commission without undue delay.

The Commission shall publish that information and keep it up to date.

1. General. Art. 39 requires Member States to provide the Commission with a list of the CMOs established in their territories by 10 April 2016 and to notify it without undue delay of any changes to that list. No similar requirement applies in relation to independent management entities. The Commission shall publish an up-to-date list of all CMOs.

[Report]

Article 40

By 10 April 2021, the Commission shall assess the application of this Directive and submit to the European Parliament and to the Council a report on the application of this Directive. That report shall include an assessment of the impact of this Directive on the development of cross-border services, on cultural diversity, on the relations between collective management organisations and users and on the operation in the Union of collective management organisations established outside the Union, and, if necessary, on the need for a review. The Commission's report shall be accompanied, if appropriate, by a legislative proposal.

1. General. The Commission must assess the application of the Directive by 10 April 2021 and, if appropriate, suggest legislative changes.

[Expert group]

Article 41

An expert group is hereby established. It shall be composed of representatives of the competent authorities of the Member States. The expert group shall be chaired by a representative of the Commission and shall meet either on the initiative of the chairman or at the request of the delegation of a Member State. The tasks of the group shall be as follows:

    (a) **to examine the impact of the transposition of this Directive on the functioning of collective management organisations and independent management entities in the internal market, and to highlight any difficulties;**

    (b) **to organise consultations on all questions arising from the application of this Directive;**

    (c) **to facilitate the exchange of information on relevant developments in legislation and case-law, as well as relevant economic, social, cultural and technological developments, especially in relation to the digital market in works and other subject-matter.**

1. General. Art. 41 establishes an expert group composed of representatives of the competent supervisory authorities of the Member States as instituted in accordance with art. 36(1). The expert group shall examine the impact of the transposition of this Directive on the functioning of CMOs and independent management entities in the internal market, and highlight any difficulties. In this respect, it is important that any requests for action against CMOs which allegedly violate the rules of this Directive are brought to its attention (see art. 37, note 4). It shall further organize consultations on any questions arising from the application of this Directive and facilitate the exchange of information on relevant developments in legislation and case law and in relation to the digital market in works and other subject-matter.

[Protection of personal data]

Article 42

The processing of personal data carried out within the framework of this Directive shall be subject to Directive 95/46/EC.

1. General. To ensure that CMOs respect the rights to private life and personal data protection of any rightholder, member, user and other individual whose personal data they process, art. 42 subjects the processing of personal data carried out within the framework of this Directive to the Personal Data Protection Directive (see also art. 26, note 1). In accordance with the latter Directive, recital 52 notes that rightholders should be given appropriate information about the processing of their data, the recipients of those data, time limits for the retention of such data in any database, and the way in which rightholders can exercise their rights to access, correct or delete their personal data. It also adds that unique identifiers which allow for the indirect identification of a person must be treated as personal data within the meaning of that Directive. Recital 53 further underlines that the provisions on enforcement measures in Title IV are without prejudice to the competencies of national data protection authorities established pursuant to the Personal Data Protection Directive to monitor compliance with national provisions adopted in implementation of that Directive.

[Transposition]

Article 43

(1) Member States shall bring into force the laws, regulations and administrative provisions necessary to comply with this Directive by 10 April 2016. They shall immediately inform the Commission thereof.

When Member States adopt those measures, they shall contain a reference to this Directive or shall be accompanied by such reference on

the occasion of their official publication. **The methods of making such reference shall be laid down by Member States.**

(2) Member States shall communicate to the Commission the text of the main measures of national law which they adopt in the field covered by this Directive.

1. Implementation deadline (para. 1). The deadline for implementation of the Directive is 10 April 2016.

2. References in transposition measures (para. 1). Member States must accompany the notification of their transposition measures with documentation of the relationship between the components of this Directive and the corresponding parts of national transposition laws or regulations. This is in accordance with the Joint Political Declaration of 28 September 2011 of Member States and the Commission on explanatory documents (recital 57).

[Entry into force]

Article 44

This Directive shall enter into force on the twentieth day following that of its publication in the Official Journal of the European Union.

1. General. The Directive entered into force on 9 April 2014.

[Addressees]

Article 45

This Directive is addressed to the Member States.

1. General. According to art. 288 TFEU, Directives are binding, as to the result to be achieved, upon each Member State to which it is addressed, but shall leave to the national authorities the choice of form and methods.

ANNEX

(1) Information to be provided in the annual transparency report referred to in Article 22(2):

    (a) **financial statements comprising a balance-sheet or a statement of assets and liabilities, an income and expenditure account for the financial year and a cash-flow statement;**

    (b) **a report on the activities in the financial year;**

    (c) **information on refusals to grant a licence pursuant to Article 16(3);**

   (d) a description of the legal and governance structure of the collective management organisation;

   (e) information on any entities directly or indirectly owned or controlled, wholly or in part, by the collective management organisation;

   (f) information on the total amount of remuneration paid to the persons referred in Article 9(3) and Article 10 in the previous year, and on other benefits granted to them;

   (g) the financial information referred to in point 2 of this Annex;

   (h) a special report on the use of any amounts deducted for the purposes of social, cultural and educational services, containing the information referred to in point 3 of this Annex.

(2) Financial information to be provided in the annual transparency report:

   (a) financial information on rights revenue, per category of rights managed and per type of use (e.g. broadcasting, online, public performance), including information on the income arising from the investment of rights revenue and the use of such income (whether it is distributed to rightholders or other collective management organisations, or otherwise used);

   (b) financial information on the cost of rights management and other services provided by the collective management organisation to rightholders, with a comprehensive description of at least the following items:

      (i) all operating and financial costs, with a breakdown per category of rights managed and, where costs are indirect and cannot be attributed to one or more categories of rights, an explanation of the method used to allocate such indirect costs;

     (ii) operating and financial costs, with a breakdown per category of rights managed and, where costs are indirect and cannot be attributed to one or more categories of rights, an explanation of the method used to allocate such indirect costs, only with regard to the management of rights, including management fees deducted from or offset against rights revenue or any income arising from the investment of rights revenue in accordance with Article 11(4) and Article 12(1), (2) and (3);

    (iii) operating and financial costs with regard to services other than the management of rights, but including social, cultural and educational services;

    (iv) resources used to cover costs;

     (v) deductions made from rights revenues, with a breakdown per category of rights managed and per type of use and the purpose of the deduction, such as costs relating to the management of rights or to social, cultural or educational services;

(vi) the percentages that the cost of the rights management and other services provided by the collective management organisation to rightholders represents compared to the rights revenue in the relevant financial year, per category of rights managed, and, where costs are indirect and cannot be attributed to one or more categories of rights, an explanation of the method used to allocate such indirect costs;

(c) financial information on amounts due to rightholders, with a comprehensive description of at least the following items:

(i) the total amount attributed to rightholders, with a breakdown per category of rights managed and type of use;

(ii) the total amount paid to rightholders, with a breakdown per category of rights managed and type of use;

(iii) the frequency of payments, with a breakdown per category of rights managed and per type of use;

(iv) the total amount collected but not yet attributed to rightholders, with a breakdown per category of rights managed and type of use, and indicating the financial year in which those amounts were collected;

(v) the total amount attributed to but not yet distributed to rightholders, with a breakdown per category of rights managed and type of use, and indicating the financial year in which those amounts were collected;

(vi) where a collective management organisation has not carried out the distribution and payments within the deadline set in Article 13(1), the reasons for the delay;

(vii) the total non-distributable amounts, along with an explanation of the use to which those amounts have been put;

(d) information on relationships with other collective management organisations, with a description of at least the following items:

(i) amounts received from other collective management organisations and amounts paid to other collective management organisations, with a breakdown per category of rights, per type of use and per organisation;

(ii) management fees and other deductions from the rights revenue due to other collective management organisations, with a breakdown per category of rights, per type of use and per organisation;

(iii) management fees and other deductions from the amounts paid by other collective management organisations, with a breakdown per category of rights and per organisation;

     (iv) **amounts distributed directly to rightholders originating from other collective management organisations, with a breakdown per category of rights and per organisation.**

(3) **Information to be provided in the special report referred to in Article 22(3):**

     (a) **the amounts deducted for the purposes of social, cultural and educational services in the financial year, with a breakdown per type of purpose and, for each type of purpose, with a breakdown per category of rights managed and per type of use;**

     (b) **an explanation of the use of those amounts, with a breakdown per type of purpose including the costs of managing amounts deducted to fund social, cultural and educational services and of the separate amounts used for social, cultural and educational services.**

1. General. The annex provides detailed instructions of information that CMOs need to include in the annual transparency report they must draw up and publish pursuant to art. 22. The list of information to be provided is mostly self-explanatory. Nonetheless, it is worth pointing out that the annex requires CMOs to make a breakdown per category of rights managed and – with the exception of costs – per type of use (e.g. broadcasting, online, public performance), when providing financial information on rights revenue, deductions made from rights revenue, operating and financial costs and total amounts collected, attributed and paid to rightholders. Where costs cannot be directly attributed to one or more categories of rights, CMOs must provide an explanation of the method used to allocate such indirect costs. The required breakdown of financial information enables rightholders to monitor and compare the performance of a CMO not just in general terms, but in respect of each type of use for each of the categories of rights it manages. This may assist rightholders in making informed decisions about the CMO to which they will entrust the management of the rights, categories of rights or types of works and other subject-matter of their choice, for the territories of their choice (see art. 5(2)). It remains to be seen, however, how specific CMOs can be in breaking down rights revenue, deductions, costs and amounts collected, attributed and paid to rightholders. In practice, it might be difficult to split up and accurately divide financial data between types of uses and categories of rights managed. Furthermore, confidentiality issues may arise if a CMO must report on rights revenue for a specific type of use that it has licensed only to a single user and the licensing contract contains a non-disclosure clause on the licensing fee and licensing conditions. In such a case, the CMO has no choice but to either ignore the reporting obligation for that specific type of use or to break the confidentiality agreement.

APPENDIX

List of Abbreviations

List of References

1. **International Legislation**
   Conventions and Agreements
   International Documents

2. **European Legislation**
   Treaty
   Regulations
   Directives
   Proposals
   Explanatory Memoranda
   Recommendations
   Reports
   Green Papers and Other Preparatory Documents

3. **WTO Panel Reports**

4. **European Court of Human Rights Decisions**

5. **European Court of Justice Decisions**

6. **Commission Decisions**

7. **EFTA Court Decisions**

8. **National Court Decisions**
   Austria
   Belgium
   Denmark
   Finland
   France
   Germany
   Netherlands
   Norway
   Sweden
   Switzerland
   United Kingdom
   United States

LIST OF ABBREVIATIONS

AMI	Tijdschrift voor auteurs-, media- en informatierecht
art.	Article
arts.	Articles
BC	Berne Convention for the Protection of Literary and Artistic Works
BGE	Bundesgerichtsentscheide (Switzerland)
BGH	Bundesgerichtshof (German Supreme Court)
BGHZ	Entscheidungen des Bundesgerichtshofs in Zivilsachen (Decisions of the Federal Supreme Court in Civil Matters)
BIRPI	International Bureaux for the Protection of Intellectual Property
CFI	Court of First Instance
CMO	collective management organisation
CRi	Computer Law Review – International
D.	Recueil Dalloz (France)
DOI	Digital Object Identifier
DRM	Digital Rights Management
e.g.	for example
EC	European Communities
ECC	European Commercial Cases
ECDR	European Copyright and Design Reports
ECJ	European Court of Justice
ECR	European Court of Justice Reporter
EEA	European Economic Area
EFTA	European Free Trade Association
EIPR	European Intellectual Property Review
et al.	et alii (and others)
et seq.	et sequens; as follows
etc.	etcetera
EMLR	Entertainment and Media Law Reports
EU	European Union
EWCA	England and Wales Court of Appeal
EWHC	High Court of England and Wales
FSR	Fleet Street Reports
GRUR	Gewerblicher Rechtsschutz und Urheberrecht (Germany)
GRUR Int.	Gewerblicher Rechtsschutz und Urheberrecht – Internationaler Teil
i.e.	id est; that is
IIC	International Review of Intellectual Property and Competition Law
ILO	International Labour Organization
I.R.D.I.	Intellectuele Rechten Droits Intellectuels
ISBN	International Standard Book Number
MMR	Multimedia und Recht

List of abbreviations

NJ	Nederlandse Jurisprudentie
NJW	Neue Juristische Wochenschrift
OGH	Oberster Gerichtshof (Austria)
ÖBl	Österreichische Blätter für Gewerblichen Rechtsschutz und Urheberrecht
p.m.a.	post mortem auctoris
para.	paragraph
PC	Paris Convention for the Protection of Industrial Property
RC	International Convention for the Protection of Performers, Producers of Phonograms and Broadcasting Organisations (Rome Convention)
RPC	Reports of Patent Cases
RG	Reichsgericht (German Supreme Court of the Reich)
RGZ	Entscheidungen des Reichsgerichts in Zivilsachen (Decisions of the Reichsgericht in Civil Matters)
RIDA	Revue Internationale du Droit d'Auteur
sec.	section
S.Ct.	Supreme Court
TFEU	Treaty on the Functioning of the European Union
TRIPS	Agreement on Trade-Related Aspects of Intellectual Property Rights
UCC	Universal Copyright Convention
UK	United Kingdom
UNESCO	United Nations Educational, Scientific and Cultural Organization
USA	United States of America
USPQ	United States Patents Quarterly
WCT	WIPO Copyright Treaty
WLR	Weekly Law Reports
WIPO	World Intellectual Property Organisation
WPPT	WIPO Performances and Phonograms Treaty
WTO	World Trade Organisation

LIST OF REFERENCES

1. International Legislation

Conventions and Agreements

Beijing Treaty	Beijing Treaty on Audiovisual Performances
Berne Convention	Berne Convention for the Protection of Literary and Artistic Works
Convention on Cybercrime	Council of Europe, Convention on Cybercrime
EEA Agreement	Agreement on the European Economic Area
Geneva Convention	Convention for the Protection of Producers of Phonograms Against Unauthorized Duplication of Their Phonograms
Locarno Convention	Locarno Convention on jurisdiction and the enforcement of judgments in civil and commercial matters
Marrakesh Treaty	Marrakesh Treaty to Facilitate Access to Published Works for Persons Who Are Blind, Visually Impaired or Otherwise Print Disabled
Paris Convention	Paris Convention for the Protection of Industrial Property
Rome Convention	International Convention for the Protection of Performers, Producers of Phonograms and Broadcasting Organisations
TRIPS Agreement	Agreement on Trade-Related Aspects of Intellectual Property Rights
Vienna Convention	Vienna Convention on the Law of Treaties
WIPO Copyright Treaty	World Intellectual Property Organisation Copyright Treaty
WIPO Performances and Phonograms Treaty	World Intellectual Property Organisation Performances and Phonograms Treaty
WTO Agreement	Agreement establishing the World Trade Organization

List of references

International documents

RC Conference Proceedings	Actes de la Conférence diplomatique sur la protection internationale des artistes interprètes ou exécutants, des producteurs de phonogrammes et des organismes de radiodiffusion, Geneva, ILO, UNESCO and BIRPI, 1968
UNESCO-WIPO Model Provisions of 1982	UNESCO-WIPO Model Provisions for National Laws on the Protection of Expressions of Folklore Against Illicit Exploitation and other Prejudicial Actions of 1982

2. European Legislation

Treaties

EC Treaty	Treaty Establishing the European Community (Consolidated Version)
TFEU	Treaty on the Functioning of the European Union, OJ No. C 83/47, March 30, 2010

Regulations

Community Designs Regulation	Council Regulation (EC) No. 6/2002 of 12 December 2001 on Community designs, OJ No. L 3/1, 5 January 2002
Regulation on Customs Enforcement	Regulation (EU) No 608/2013 of the European Parliament and of the Council of 12 June 2013 concerning customs enforcement of intellectual property rights and repealing Council Regulation (EC) No 1383/2003, OJ No. L 181/15, 29 June 2013
Regulation (EU) No 1215/2012	Council Regulation (EU) No 1215/2012 of the European Parliament and of the Council of 12 December 2012 on jurisdiction and the recognition and enforcement of judgments in civil and commercial matters, OJ No. L 351/1 of 20 December 2012

Regulation Rome I	Regulation (EC) No 593/2008 of the European Parliament and of the Council of 17 June 2008 on the law applicable to contractual obligations (Rome I), OJ No. L 177/6, 4 July 2008
Regulation Rome II	Regulation (EC) No 864/2007 of the European Parliament and of the Council of 11 July 2007 on the law applicable to non-contractual obligations (Rome II), OJ No. L 199/40, 31 July 2007

Directives

Audiovisual Media Services Directive	Directive 2010/13/EU of the European Parliament and of the Council of 10 March 2010 on the coordination of certain provisions laid down by law, regulation or administrative action in Member States concerning the provision of audiovisual media services (Audiovisual Media Services Directive) (codified version), OJ No. L 95/1, 15 April 2010, codifying Council Directive 89/552/EEC as amended by Directives 97/36/EC and 2007/65/EC
Collective Rights Management Directive	Directive 2014/26/EU of the European Parliament and of the Council of 26 February 2014 on collective management of copyright and related rights and multi-territorial licensing of rights in musical works for online use in the internal market, OJ No. L 84/72, 20 March 2014
Computer Programs Directive	Directive 2009/24/EC of the European Parliament and of the Council of 23 April 2009 on the legal protection of computer programs (codified version), OJ No. L 111/16, 5 May 2009, (replacing Council Directive 91/250/EEC of 14 May 1991 on the legal protection of computer programs, OJ No. L 122/42, 17 May 1991)
Computer Programs Directive (old version)	Council Directive 91/250/EEC of 14 May 1991 on the legal protection of computer programs, OJ No. L 122/42, 17 May 1991

List of references

Conditional Access Directive	Directive 98/84/EC of the European Parliament and of the Council of 20 November 1998 on the legal protection of services based on, or consisting of, conditional access, OJ No. L 320/54, 28 November 1998
Consumer Rights Directive	Directive 2011/83/EU of the European Parliament and of the Council of 25 October 2011 on consumer rights, amending Council Directive 93/13/EEC and Directive 1999/44/EC of the European Parliament and of the Council and repealing Council Directive 85/577/EC and Directive 97/7/EC of the European Parliament and of the Council, OJ No. L 304/64, 22 November 2011
Database Directive	Directive 96/9/EC of the European Parliament and of the Council of 11 March 1996 on the legal protection of databases, OJ No. L 77/20, 27 March 1996
Designs Directive	Directive 98/71/EC of the European Parliament and of the Council of 13 October 1998 on the legal protection of designs, OJ No. L 289/28, 28 October 1998
e-Commerce Directive	Directive 2000/31/EC of the European Parliament and of the Council of 8 June 2000 on certain legal aspects of information society services, in particular electronic commerce, in the Internal Market (Directive on electronic commerce), OJ No. L 178/1, 17 July 2000
Enforcement Directive	Directive 2004/48/EC on the enforcement of intellectual property rights, OJ No. L 195/16, 2 June 2004
Information Society Directive	Directive 2001/29/EC of 22 May 2001 on the harmonisation of certain aspects of copyright and related rights in the information society, OJ No. L 167/10, 22 June 2001
Misleading and Comparative Advertising Directive	Directive 2006/114/EC of the European Parliament and of the Council of 12 December 2006 concerning misleading and comparative advertising, OJ No. L 376/21, 27 December 2006

Orphan Works Directive	Directive 2012/28/EU of the European Parliament and of the Council of 25 October 2012 on certain permitted uses of orphan works, OJ No. L 299/5, 27 October 2012
Personal Data Protection Directive	Directive 95/46/EC of the European Parliament and of the Council of 24 October 1995 on the protection of individuals with regard to the processing of personal data and on the free movement of such data, OJ No. L 281/31, 23 November 1995
Public Sector Information Directive	Directive 2013/37/EU of the European Parliament and of the Council of 26 June 2013 amending Directive 2003/98/EC on the re-use of public sector information, OJ No. L 175/1, 27 June 2013
Rental Right Directive	Directive 2006/115/EC of the European Parliament and of the Council of 12 December 2006 on rental right and lending right and on certain rights related to copyright in the field of intellectual property (codified version), OJ No. L 376/28, 27 December 2006 (replacing Council Directive 92/100/EEC of 19 November 1992 on rental right and lending right and on certain rights related to copyright in the field of intellectual property, OJ No. L 346/61, 27 November 1992)
Rental Right Directive (old version)	Council Directive 92/100/EEC of 19 November 1992 on rental right and lending right and on certain rights related to copyright in the field of intellectual property, OJ No. L 346/61, 27 November 1992
Resale Right Directive	Directive 2001/84/EC of the European parliament and of the Council of 27 September 2001on the resale right for the benefit of the author of an original work of art, OJ No. L 272/32, 13 October 2001
Satellite and Cable Directive	Council Directive 93/83/EEC of 27 September 1993 on the coordination of certain rules concerning copyright and rights related to copyright applicable to satellite broadcasting and cable retransmission, OJ No. L 248/15, 6 October 1993

List of references

Television without Frontiers Directive	Council Directive 89/552/EEC of 3 October 1989 on the coordination of certain provisions laid down by Law, Regulation, or Administrative Action in Member States concerning the pursuit of television broadcasting activities, OJ No. L 298/23, 17 October 1989
Term Directive	Directive 2006/116/EC of the European Parliament and of the Council of 12 December 2006 on the term of protection of copyright and certain related rights (codified version), OJ No. L 372/12, 27 December 2006 (replacing Council Directive 93/98/EEC of 29 October 1993 harmonizing the term of protection of copyright and certain related rights, OJ No. L 290/9, 24 November 1993), as amended by Directive 2011/77/EU of the European Parliament and of the Council of 27 September 2011 amending Directive 2006/116/EC on the term of protection of copyright and certain related rights, OJ No. L 265/1, 11 October 2011
Term Extension Directive	Directive 2011/77/EU of the European Parliament and of the Council of 27 September 2011 amending Directive 2006/116/EC on the term of protection of copyright and certain related rights, OJ No. L 265/1, 11 October 2011
Term Directive (old version)	Council Directive 93/98/EEC of 29 October 1993 harmonizing the term of protection of copyright and certain related rights, OJ No. L 290/9, 24 November 1993
Trademark Directive	Directive 2008/95/EC of the European Parliament and of the Council of 22 October 2008 to approximate the laws of the Member States relating to trade marks (codified version), OJ No. L 299/25, 8 November 2008 (replacing Council Directive 89/104/EEC of 21 December 1988 to approximate the laws of the Member States relating to trade marks, OJ No. L 40/1, 11 February 1989, as amended)

Universal Service Directive	Directive 2002/22/EC of the European Parliament and of the Council of 7 March 2002 on universal service and users' rights relating to electronic communications networks and services, OJ No. L 108/51, 24 April 2002

Proposals

Amended Proposal of the Computer Programs Directive	Amended Proposal for a Council Directive on the Legal Protection of Computer Programs, OJ No. C 320/22, 20 December 1990
Amended Proposal of the Information Society Directive	Amended proposal for a European Parliament and Council Directive on the harmonisation of certain aspects of copyright and related rights in the Information Society, OJ No. C 180/6, 26 June 1999
Amended Proposal of the Rental Right Directive	Amended proposal for a Council Directive on rental right and lending right and on certain rights related to copyright in the field of intellectual property, COM (92) 159 final, 30 April 1992
Initial Proposal of the Computer Programs Directive	Proposal for a Council Directive on the Legal Protection of Computer Programs, OJ No. C 91/4, 12 April 1989
Initial Proposal of the Database Directive	Proposal for a Council Directive on the Legal Protection of Databases, COM (92) 24 final
Initial Proposal of the Information Society Directive	Proposal for a European Parliament and Council Directive on the harmonization of certain aspects of copyright and related rights in the Information Society, OJ No. C 108/6, 7 April 1998
Initial Proposal of the Rental Right Directive	Proposal for a Council Directive on rental right, lending right, and on certain rights related to copyright, COM (90) 586 final, 24 January 1991
Proposal of the Collective Rights Management Directive	Proposal for a Directive of the European Parliament and of the Council on collective management of copyright and related rights and multi-territorial licensing of rights in musical works for online uses in the internal market, COM (2012) 372 final, 11 July 2012

List of references

Proposal of the Orphan Works Directive	Proposal for a Directive of the European Parliament and of the Council on certain permitted uses of orphan works, COM(2011) 289 final
Proposal of the Resale Right Directive (codified version)	Proposal for a Directive of the European Parliament and of the Council on rental right and lending right and on certain rights related to copyright in the field of intellectual property (Codified version), COM (2006) 226 final, 22 May 2006
Proposal of the Term Directive	Proposal for a European Parliament and Council Directive amending Directive 2006/116/EC of the European Parliament and of the Council on the term of protection of copyright and related rights, Doc COM(2008) 464 final, 16 July 2008
Proposal of the Term Directive (old version)	Proposal for a Council Directive harmonizing the term of protection of copyright and certain related rights, COM(92) 33 final, 23 March 1992
Proposed Directive on Criminal Measures	Proposal for a European Parliament and Council Directive on criminal measures aimed at ensuring the enforcement of intellectual property rights, Doc. COM(2005)276 final, 12 July 2005
Proposed Rome II	Proposal for a Regulation of the European Parliament and the Council on the Law applicable to non-contractual obligations ('ROME II'), Doc. COM(2003) 427 final, 22 July 2003

Explanatory Memoranda

Explanatory Memorandum to the Amended Proposal of the Computer Programs Directive	Explanatory Memorandum to the Amended Proposal for a Council Directive on the legal protection of computer programs, Doc. COM/90/509FINAL – SYN 183, 18 October 1990
Explanatory Memorandum to the Computer Programs Directive	Explanatory Memorandum to the Proposal for a Council Directive on the Legal Protection of Computer Programs COM(88) 816 final-SYN 183, 5 January 1989

Explanatory Memorandum of the Information Society Directive	Explanatory Memorandum to the Proposal for a European Parliament and Council Directive on Harmonisation of Certain Aspects of Copyright and Related Rights in the Information Society, COM (97) 628 final, 10 December 1997
Explanatory Memorandum to the Proposal for the Term Directive (old version)	Explanatory Memorandum to Proposal for a Council Directive harmonizing the term of protection of copyright and certain related rights, COM(92) 33 final, 23 March 1992
Explanatory Memorandum to the Proposal for the Term Extension Directive	Explanatory Memorandum to Proposal for a European Parliament and Council Directive amending Directive 2006/116/EC of the European Parliament and of the Council on the term of protection of copyright and related rights, Doc COM(2008) 464 final, 16 July 2008

Recommendations

Online Music Recommendation	Commission Recommendation 2005/737/EC of 18 May 2005 on collective cross-border management of copyright and related rights for legitimate online music services, OJ No. L 276/54, 21 October 2005
Digitisation Recommendation	Commission Recommendation 2006/585/EC of 24 August 2006 on the digitisation and online accessibility of cultural material and digital preservation, OJ No. L 236/28, 31 August 2006

Reports

Report on the Computer Programs Directive	Report from the Commission to the Council, the European Parliament and the Economic and Social Committee on the implementation and effects of Directive 91/250/EEC on the legal protection of computer programs, COM(2000) 199 final, 10 April 2000
Report on the Database Directive	European Commission, 'First evaluation of Directive 96/9/EC on the legal protection of databases', DG Internal Market and Services Working Paper, Brussels, 12 December 2005

List of references

Report on Public Lending Right	Report from the Commission to the Council, the European Parliament and the Economic and Social Committee on the Public Lending Right in the European Union, COM (2002) 502 final, 12 September 2002
Report on the Resale Right Directive	Report from the Commission to the Council, the European Parliament and the Economic and Social Committee on the Implementation and Effect of the Resale Right Directive, COM(2011) 878 final, 14 December 2011
Report on the Satellite and Cable Directive	Report from the European Commission on the application of Council Directive 93/83/EEC on the coordination of certain rules concerning copyright and rights related to copyright applicable to satellite broadcasting and cable retransmission, COM (2002) 430 final, Brussels, 26 July 2002

Green Papers and Other Preparatory Documents

Communication on the Management of Copyright and Related Rights	Communication from the Commission to the Council, the European Parliament and the European Economic and Social Committee on the Management of Copyright and Related Rights in the Internal Market, COM (2004) 261 final, Brussels, 16 April 2004
Follow-up to the Green Paper on Copyright and Related Rights in the Information Society	Communication from the Commission, Follow-up to the Green Paper on Copyright and Related Rights in the Information Society, COM (96) 568 final, Brussels, 20 November 1996
Follow-up to the Green Paper on Copyright and the Challenge of Technology	Communication from the Commission, Follow-up to the Green Paper: Working Programme of the Commission in the field of Copyright and Neighbouring Rights, COM (90) 584 final, Brussels, 17 January 1991
Green Paper on Television without Frontiers	European Commission, 'Television without Frontiers', Green Paper, COM (84) def, Brussels, 14 June 1984
Green Paper on Copyright and the Challenge of Technology	European Commission, 'Copyright and the Challenge of Technology', Green Paper, COM (88) 172 final, Brussels, 7 June 1988.

Green Paper on Copyright and Related Rights in the Information Society	European Commission, 'Copyright and Related Rights in the Information Society', Green Paper, COM (95) 382 final, Brussels, 19 July 1995
Resolution on a Community framework for CMOs	Parliament Resolution on a Community framework for collective management societies in the field of copyright and neighbouring rights, 2002/2274(INI), P5_TA(2004)0036, Brussels, 15 January 2004
Staff Working Paper on Copyright Review	Commission Staff Working Paper on the Review of the EC legal Framework in the Field of Copyright and Related Rights SEC(2004) 995, Brussels, 19 July 2004

3. WTO Panel Reports

Canada – Term of Patent Protection	WTO Dispute Settlement Panel, WT/DS114/R of 17 March 2000
United States – Section 110(5) of the US Copyright Act	WTO Dispute Settlement Panel, WT/DS160/R of 15 June 2000

4. European Court of Human Rights Decisions

Ashby Donald	*Ashby Donald and Others* v *France*, European Court of Human Rights 10 January 2013, No. 36769/08
Neij& Sunde v. Sweden	*Fredrik Neij and Peter Sunde Kolmisoppi* v *Sweden*, European Court of Human Rights 19 February 2013, No. 40397/12

5. European Court of Justice Decisions

ACI Adam and others	*ACI Adam BV and Others* v *Stichting de Thuiskopie and Stichting Onderhandelingen Thuiskopie vergoeding*, ECJ 10 April 2014, case C-435/12, EU:C:2014:254
Airfield and Canal Digitaal	*Airfield NV and Canal Digitaal BV* v *Belgische Vereniging van Auteurs, Componisten en Uitgevers CVBA (Sabam); and Airfield NV v Agicoa Belgium BVBA*, ECJ 13 October 2011, joined cases C-431/09 and C-432/09, ECR [2011] I-9363

List of references

Amazon.com International Sales and others	*Amazon.com International Sales Inc. and Others* v *Austro-Mechana Gesellschaft zur Wahrnehmung mechanisch-musikalischer Urheberrechte Gesellschaft mbH*, ECJ 11 July 2013, Case C-521/11, EU:C:2013:515
Apis-Hristovich	*Apis-Hristovich EOOD* v *Lakorda AD*, ECJ 5 March 2009, case C-545/07, ECR [2009] I-01627
Art & Allposters International	*Art & Allposters International BV* v *Stichting Pictoright,* ECJ 22 January 2015, Case C-419/13; EU:C:2015:27
BestWater International	*BestWater International GmbH* v *Michael Mebes and Stefan Potsch,* ECJ 21 October 2014, Case C-348/13, EU:C:2014:2315
Blomqvist	*Martin Blomqvist* v *Rolex SA*, ECJ 6 February 2014, case C-98/13, EU:C:2014:55
Bonnier Audio and Others	*Bonnier Audio AB and Others* v *Perfect Communication Sweden AB*, ECJ 19 April 2012, case C-461/10, EU:C:2012:219
British Horseracing Board	*British Horseracing Board* v *William Hill Organization*, ECJ 9 November 2004, case C-203/02, ECR [2004] I-10415
BSA	*Bezpečnostní softwarová asociace – Svaz softwarové ochrany* v *Ministerstvo kultury*, ECJ 22 December 2010, case C-393/09, ECR [2010] I-13971
Butterfly	*Butterfly Music Srl* v *Carosello Edizioni Musicali e Discografiche Srl (CEMED)*, ECJ 29 June 1999, case C-60/98, ECR [1999] I-3939
C More Entertainment	*C More Entertainment AB* v *Linus Sandburg,* ECJ 26 March 2015, case C-279/13, EU:C:2015:199
Cassis de Dijon	*Rewe-Zentral AG* v *Bundesmonopolverwaltung für Branntwein.* ECJ 20 February 1979, case 120/78, ECR [1979] 649
Centro Europa 7	*Centro Europa 7 Srl* v *Ministero delle Comunicazioni e Autorità per le garanzie nelle comunicazioni and another*, ECJ 31 January 2008, case C-380/05, ECR [2008] I-349

Christie's France	*Christie's France SNC v Syndicat national des antiquaries,* ECJ 26 February 2015, Case C-41/14, EU:C:2015:119
Christiansen	*Warner Brothers Inc. et al. v E.V. Christiansen,* ECJ 17 May 1988, case 158/86, ECR [1988] 2605
CISAC	*International Confederation of Societies of Authors and Composers (CISAC) v European Commission,* ECJ 12 April 2013, case T-442/08
Circul Globus Bucureşti	*Circul Globus Bucureşti (Circ & Variete Globus Bucureşti) v Uniunea Compozitorilor şi Muzicologilor din România – Asociaţia pentru Drepturi de Autor (UCMR – ADA),* ECJ 24 November 2011, case C-283/10, ECR [2011] I-12031
CISAC	*International Confederation of Societies of Authors and Composers (CISAC) v European Commission,* CFI (Sixth Chamber) 12 April 2013, case T-442/08, EU:T:2013:188
Coditel I	*Coditel v Ciné Vog Films,* ECJ 19 March 1980, case 62/79, ECR [1980] 881
Coditel II	*Coditel v Ciné Vog Films,* ECJ 6 October 1982, case 262/81, ECR [1982] 3381
Commission/Council	*Commission v Council of the European Union,* ECJ 4 September 2014, Case C-114/12, EU:C:2014:2151
Commission/Ireland	*Commission v Ireland,* ECJ 11 January 2007, , case C-175/05, ECR [2007] I-00003
Commission/Italy,	*Commission v Italy,* ECJ 26 October 2006, case C-198/05, ECR [2006] I-00107
Commission/Portugal	*Commission v Portugal,* , case C-53/05, ECR [2006] I-06215
Commission/Portugal II	*Comission v Portugal,* ECJ 13 July 2006, case C-61/05, ECR [2006] I-6779
Commission/Spain	*Commission v Spain,* ECJ 26 October 2006, case C-36/05, ECR [2006] I-10313
Compass-Datenbank	*Compass-Datenbank GmbH v Republik Österreich,* ECJ 12 July 2012, case C-138/11, EU:C:2012:449

List of references

Copydan Båndkopi	*Copydan Båndkopi*, ECJ 5 March 2015, case C-463/12, EU:C:2015:144
Dansk Supermarked	*Dansk Supermarked* v *Imerco*, ECJ 22 January 1981, case 58/80, ECR [1981] 181
Davidoff	*Zino Davidoff* v *A&G Imports*, ECJ 20 November 2001, joined cases 414/99 to 416/99, ECR [2001] I-8691
Deckmyn and Vrijheidsfonds	*Johan Deckmyn and Vrijheidsfonds VZW* v *Helena Vandersteen and Others*. ECJ 3 September 2014, case C-201/13, EU:C:2014:2132
Deutsche Grammophon	*Deutsche Grammophon* v *Metro* SB, ECJ 8 June 1971, case 78/70, ECR [1971] 487
Dimensione Direct Sales and Labianca	*Dimensionse Direct Sales Srl and others* v *Knoll International SpA*, ECJ 13 May 2015, case C-516/13, EU:C:2015:315
Directmedia Publishing	*Directmedia Publishing GmbH* v *Albert-Ludwigs-Universität Freiburg*. ECJ 9 October 2008, case C-304/07, ECR [2008] I-07565
Donner	Criminal proceedings against *Titus Alexander Jochen Donner* ECJ 21 June 2012, case C-5/11, EU:C:2012:370
DR and TV2 Danmark	*DR and TV2 Danmark A/S* v *NCB – Nordisk Copyright Bureau*, ECJ 26 April 2012, case C-510/10, EU:C:2012:244
eDate Advertising and Martinez	*eDate Advertising GmbH* v *X* and *Martinez* v *MGN Ltd.*, ECJ 25 October 2011, cases C-509/09 and C-161/10, ECR [2011] I-10269
Egeda	*Entidad de Gestión de Derechos de los Productores Audiovisuales (Egeda)* v *Hostelería Asturiana SA (Hoasa)*, ECJ 8 February 2000, case C-293/98, ECR [2000] I-629
Eugen Ulmer	*Technische Universität Darmstadt* v *Eugen Ulmer KG*, ECJ 11 September 2014, case C-117/13, EU:C:2014:2196
Faccini Dora	*Paola Faccini Dora* v *Recreb*, ECJ 14 July 1994, case C-91/92, ECR [1994] I-3325
Fixtures Marketing/ Svenska Spel	*Fixtures Marketing Ltd* v *Svenska Spel AB*,, ECJ 9 November 2004, case C-338/02, ECR [2004] I-10497

Fixtures Marketing/OPAP	*Fixtures Marketing Ltd* v *Organismos prognostikon agonon podosfairou AE (OPAP)*, ECJ 9 November 2004, case C-444/02, ECR [2004] I-10549
Flos	*Flos* v *Semeraro*, ECJ 27 January 2011, case C-168/09, ECR [2011] I-181
Folien Fischer and Fofitec	*Folien Fischer and Fofitec* v *Ritrama*, ECJ 25 October 2012, case C-133/11, EU:C:2012:664
Football Association Premier League and others	*Football Association Premier League Ltd and Others* v *QC Leisure and Others; and Karen Murphy* v *Media Protection Services Ltd*, ECJ 4 October 2011, joined cases C-403/08 and C-429/08, ECR [2011] I-9083
Football Dataco and others	*Football Dataco Ltd and Others* v *Yahoo! UK Ltd and Others*, ECJ 1 March 2012, case C-604/10, EU:C:2012:115
Football Dataco/Sports Radar	*Football Dataco Ltd and Others* v *Sportradar GmbH and Sportradar AG*. ECJ 18 October 2012, case C-173/11, EU:C:2012:642
Francovich	*Francovich et al.* v *Italian Republic*, ECJ 19 November 1991, cases C-6/90 and 9/90, ECR [1991] I-5357
Fundación Gala-Salvador Dalí and VEGAP	*Fundación Gala-Salvador Dalí and Visual Entidad de Gestión de Artistas Plásticos (VEGAP)* v *Société des auteurs dans les arts graphiques et plastiques (ADAGP) and Others*, ECJ 15 April 2010, case C-518/08, ECR [2010] I-03091
G v Cornelius de Visser	*G* v *Cornelius de Visser* ECJ 15 March 2012, case C-292/10, EU:C:2012:142
GVL	*GVL* v *Commission*, ECJ 2 March 1983, case 7/82, ECR [1983] 483
Hejduk	*Pez Hejduk* v *EnergieAgentur.NRW GmbH*, ECJ 22 January 2015, case C-441/13, EU:C:2015:28
Hi Hotel HCF	*Hi Hotel HCF* v *Uwe Spoering*, ECJ 3 April 2014, case C-387/12, EU:C:2014:215
IMS Health	*NDC Health Corporation and NDC Health* v *IMS Health Inc. and Commission*, ECJ 29 April 2004, case C-481/01, ECR [2002] I-3401

List of references

Infopaq International	*Infopaq International A/S v Danske Dag-blades Forening*, ECJ 16 July 2009, case C-5/08, ECR [2009] I-06569
Infopaq International II	*Infopaq International A/S v Danske Dag-blades Forening*, ECJ 17 January 2012, case C-302/10, EU:C:2012:16
Innoweb	*Innoweb BV v Wegener ICT Media BV and Wegener Mediaventions BV.* ECJ 19 December 2013, case C-202/12, EU:C:2013:850
ITV Broadcasting and others	*ITV Broadcasting Ltd and Others v TV-CatchUp Ltd*, ECJ 7 March 2013, C-607/11, EU:C:2013:147
Kanal 5 and TV 4	*Kanal 5 Ltd and TV 4 AB v Föreningen Svenska Tonsättares Internationella Musik-byrå (STIM) upa*, ECJ 11 December 2008, case C-52/07, ECR [2008] I-9275
Lagardère	*Lagardère Active Broadcast v Société pour la Perception de la rémunération équitable (SPRE) and Others*, ECJ 14 July 2005, case C-192/04, ECR [2005] I-07199
Laserdisken	*Foreningen af danske Videogramdistributører v Laserdisken*, ECJ 22 September 1998, case C-61/97, ECR [1998] I-5171
Laserdisken II	*Laserdisken Aps v Kulturministeriet*, ECJ 15 September 2006, case C-479/04, ECR [2006] I-8098
LSG-Gesellschaft zur Wahrnehmung von Leistungsschutzrechten	*LSG-Gesellschaft zur Wahrnehmung von Leistungsschutzrechten GmbH v Tele2 Telecommunication GmbH*, ECJ 19 February 2009, case C-557/07, EU:C:2009:107
Lucazeau	*François Lucazeau and others v Société des Auteurs, Compositeurs et Editeurs de Musique (SACEM) and others*, ECJ 13 July 1989, cases 110/88, 241/88 and 242/88, ECR [1989] 2811
Luksan	*Martin Luksan v Petrus Van der Let*, ECJ 9 February 2012, case C-277/10, EU:C:2012:65
Magill	*Radio Telefis Eireann (RTE) and Independent Television Publications Ltd (ITP) v Commission*, ECJ 6 April 1995, joined cases C-241/91 and C-242/91, ECR [1995] I-743

Marleasing   *Marleasing* v *Comercial Internacional de
                          Alimentación*, ECJ 23 November 1990, case
                          C-106/89, ECR [1990] I-4135

Micro Leader   *Micro Leader Business* v *EC*, CFI (3rd
                          chamber) 16 December 1999, case T-198/98,
                          ECR [1999] II-3989

Microsoft   *Microsoft Corp.* v *Commission of the Euro-
                          pean Communities*, CFI (Grand Chamber) 17
                          September 2007, case T-201/04, ECR [2007]
                          II-03601

Metronome Musik   *Metronome Musik* v *Music Point Hokamp*,
                          ECJ 18 April 1998, case C-200/96, ECR
                          [1998] I-1953

Musik-Vertrieb Membran *Musik-Vertrieb Membran GmbH et al* v
                          GEMA, ECJ 20 January 1981, joined cases 55
                          and 57/80, ECR [1981] 147

Nintendo and others   *Nintendo Co. Ltd and Others* v *PC Box Srl
                          and 9Net Srl*, ECJ 23 January 2014, case
                          C-355/12, EU:C:2014:25

OSDDTOE   *Organismos Sillogikis Diacheirisis Dimiour-
                          gon Theatrikon kai Optikoakoustikon Ergon* v
                          *Divani Akropolis Anonimi Xenodocheiaki kai
                          Touristiki Etaireai* , ECJ 18 March 2010, case
                          . C-136/09, ECR [2010] I-37

OSA   *OSA – Ochranný svaz autorský pro
                          práva k dílům hudebním o.s.* v *Léčebné lázně
                          Mariánské Lázně a.s.*, ECJ 27 February 2014,
                          case C-351/12, EU:C:2014:110

Padawan   *Padawan SL* v *Sociedad General de Autores y
                          Editores de España (SGAE)*, ECJ 21 October
                          2010, case C-467/08, ECR [2010] I-10055

Painer   *Eva-Maria Painer* v *Standard VerlagsGmbH,
                          Axel Springer AG, Süddeutsche Zeitung
                          GmbH, Spiegel-Verlag Rudolf Augstein
                          GmbH & Co KG, Verlag M. DuMont
                          Schauberg Expedition der Kölnischen Zeitung
                          GmbH & Co KG*, ECJ 1 December 2011, case
                          C-145/10, ECR [2011] I-12533

List of references

Patricia

*EMI-Electrola GmbH v Patricia Im- und
Export Verwaltungsgesellschaft mbH et al.,*
ECJ 24 January 1989, case 341/87, ECR
[1989] 79

Peek & Cloppenburg

Peek & Cloppenburg KG v Cassina SpA, ECJ
17 April 2008, case C-456/06, ECR 2008
I-02731

Phil Collins

Phil Collins v Imtrat, ECJ 20 October 1993,
joined cases C-92/92 and C-326/92, ECR
[1993] I-5145

Pinckney

Peter Pinckney v KDG Mediatech, ECJ 3
October 2013, case C-170/12, EU:C:2013:635

Polydor

Polydor v Harlequin, ECJ 9 February 1982,
case 270/80, ECR [1982] 329

Phonographic Perfor-
mance (Ireland)

*Phonographic Performance (Ireland) Ltd v
Ireland,* ECJ 15 March 2012, case C-162/10,
EU:C:2012:141

Promusicae

*Productores de Música de España (Promu-
sicae) v Telefónica de España SAU,* ECJ 29
January 2008, case C-275/06, ECR [2008]
I-00271

Public Relations Consult-
ants Association

*Public Relations Consultants Association
Ltd v Newspaper Licensing Agency Ltd and
Others,* ECJ 5 June 2014, case C-360/13,
EU:C:2014:1195

Ricordi

Land Hessen v Ricordi, ECJ 6 June 2002,
case C-360/00 ECR [2002] I-5089

Ryanair

Ryanair Ltd v PR Aviation BV, ECJ 15 January 2015, case C-30/14, EU:C:2015:10

SABAM II

BRT v SABAM II, ECJ 30 January 1974, case
127/73, ECR [1973] 51

SABAM /Netlog

*Belgische Vereniging van Auteurs, Compon-
isten en Uitgevers CVBA (SABAM) v Netlog
NV,* ECJ 16 February 2012, case C-360/10,
EU:C:2012:85

SAS Institute

*SAS Institute Inc. v World Programming
Ltd.,* ECJ 2 May 2012, case C-406/10,
EU:C:2012:259

Scarlet Extended	*Scarlet Extended SA v Société belge des auteurs, compositeurs et éditeurs SCRL (SABAM)*. ECJ 24 November 2011, case C-70/10, ECR [2011] I-11959
SCF	*Societá Consortile Fonografici (SCF) v Marco del Corso*, ECJ 15 March 2012 case C-135/10, EU:C:2012:140
Sebago	*Sebago and Ancienne Maison Dubois et fils SA v GB-Unic SA*, ECJ 1 July 1999, case C-173/98, ECR [1999] I-4103
Sena	*Stichting ter Exploitatie van Naburige Rechten v Nederlandse Omroep Stichting*, ECJ 6 February 2003, case C-245/00, ECR [2003] I-1251
SGAE	*Sociedad General de Autores y Editores de España (SGAE) v Rafael Hoteles SA*, ECJ 7 December 2006, case C-306/05, ECR [2006] I-11519
Shevill	*Fiona Shevill, Ixora Trading Inc., Chequepoint SARL and Chequepoint International Ltd v Presse Alliance SA*, ECJ 7 March 1995, case C-68/93, ECR [1995] I-415
Silhouette	*Silhouette International Schied v Hartlauer Handelsgesellschaft*, ECJ 16 July 1998, case C-355/96, ECR [1998] I-4799
Sony Music Entertainment	*Sony Music Entertainment (Germany) GmbH v Falcon Neue Medien Vertrieb GmbH*, ECJ 20 January 2009, case C-240/07, ECR [2009] I-263
Stichting de Thuiskopie	*Stichting de Thuiskopie v Opus Supplies Deutschland GmbH and Others*. ECJ 16 June 2011, case C-462/09, ECR [2011] I-05331
Svensson and others	*Nils Svensson and Others v Retriever Sverige AB*, ECJ 13 February 2014, case C-466/12, EU:C:2014:76
Tod's	*Tod's SpA, Tod's France SARL v Heyraud SA*, ECJ 30 June 2005, case C-28/04, ECR [2005] I-5781

List of references

| *UPC Telekabel Wien* | *UPC Telekabel Wien GmbH v Constantin Film Verleih GmbH and Wega Filmproduktionsgesellschaft mbH*, ECJ 27 March 2014, case C-314/12, EU:C:2014:192 |

Uradex — *Uradex SCRL v Union Professionnelle de la Radio et de la Télédistribution (RTD), Société intercommunale pour la diffusion de la télévision (Brutélé)*, ECJ 1 June 2006, Case C-169/05, ECR 2006 I-04973

UsedSoft — *UsedSoft GmbH v Oracle International Corp*, ECJ 3 July 2012, case C-128/11, EU:C:2012:407

Tournier — *Ministère Public v Tournier*, ECJ 13 July 1989, case 395/87, ECR [1989] 2521

VEWA — *Vereniging van Educatieve en Wetenschappelijke Auteurs (VEWA) v Belgische Staat*, ECJ 30 June 2011, case C-271/10, ECR 2011 p. I-5815

Van Doren — *Van Doren + Q v Lifestyle sports + sportswear*, ECJ 8 April 2003, case C-244/00, ECR [2003] 3051

VG Wort and others — *Verwertungsgesellschaft Wort (VG Wort) v Kyocera and Others (C-457/11) and Canon Deutschland GmbH (C-458/11), and Fujitsu Technology Solutions GmbH (C-459/11) and Hewlett-Packard GmbH (C-460/11) v Verwertungsgesellschaft Wort (VG Wort)*, ECJ 27 June 2013, joined cases C-457/11 to C-460/11, EU:C:2013:426

Wintersteiger — *Wintersteiger AG v Products 4U Sondermaschinenbau GmbH*, ECJ 19 April 2012, case 523/10, EU:C:2012:220

6. Commission Decisions

CISAC — Commission Decision of 16 July 2008, case COMP/C2/38.698, C (2008) 3435 final, Brussels, 16 July 2008, also reported in [2009] 4 *Common Market Law Reports* 12

Daft Punk — Commission Decision of 6 August 2002, case COMP/37.219

GEMA I	Commission Decision 71/224/EEC of 2 June 1971, OJ No. L 134/15, 20 June 1971
GEMA II	Commission Decision 72/268/EEC of 6 July 1972, OJ No. L 166/22, 24 July 1972
GVL	Commission Decision 81/1030/EEC of 29 October 1981, OJ No. L 370/49, 28 December 1981
IFPI Simulcasting	Commission Decision 2003/300/EC of 8 October 2002, case COMP/C2/38.014, OJ No. L 107/58, 30 April 2003

7. EFTA Court Decisions

Maglite	*Mag Instrument* v *California Trading Company*, EFTA Court, advisory opinion, 3. 12. 1997, case E-2/97, IIC 1998, 316

8. National Court Decisions

Austria

C. Villas	Oberster Gerichtshof, OGH (Austrian Supreme Court), 10 July 2001, GRUR Int. 2002, 452, IIC 2003, 223
Gemeinschaftsantenne-Feldkirch	Oberster Gerichtshof, OGH (Austrian Supreme Court), 25 June 1974, case 4 Ob 321/74, GRUR Int. 1975, 68, IIC 1976, 125
Baukompass	Oberster Gerichtshof, OGH (Austrian Supreme Court), 27 November 2001, case 4 Ob 251/01, GRUR Int. 2002, 940, MMR 2002, 376, ÖBl 2002, 10
HWP WIN	*K**** GmbH* v *A***** GmbH* , Oberster Gerichtshof, OGH (Austrian Supreme Court), 23 May 2000, case 4 Ob 30/00, [2002] ECDR (29) 311
Ludus tonalis	Oberster Gerichtshof, OGH (Austrian Supreme Court), 31 January 1995, case 4 Ob 143/94, GRUR Int. 1995, 729
Meteo-data	Oberster Gerichtshof, OGH (Austrian Supreme Court), 17 December 2002, case 4 Ob 248/02, GRUR Int. 2003, 863

List of references

| *Sicherheitsanweisung für Flugpassagiere* | Oberster Gerichtshof, OGH (Austrian Supreme Court), *18 May 1999, case 4 Ob 130/99, GRUR Int. 2000, 447* |

TerraCAD — Oberster Gerichtshof, OGH (Austrian Supreme Court), 12 July 2005, case 4 Ob 45/05d, IIC 2007, 347

Thermenhotel — Oberster Gerichtshof, OGH (Austrian Supreme Court), 16 June 1998, case 4 Ob 146/98, GRUR Int. 1999, 279, IIC 2000, 223

Website Layout — Oberster Gerichtshof, OGH (Austrian Supreme Court), 24 April 2001, [2003] ECC 3, [2003] ECDR (24) 253

Belgium

Dochy/Nice Traveling — *A. Dochy and NV Open Tours* v *BVBA Nice Traveling*, Court of Appeals Brussels, 5 June 2007, I.R.D.I. 2008, 95-99, Auteurs & Media, 2008-1, 37-40

Musikwiedergabe — Cour de cassation, 11 May 1998, GRUR Int. 2001, 347

Finland

Adobe Systems — *Adobe Systems Inc.* v *A Software Distributor*, Supreme Court, Finland, 3 October 2003, [2004] ECDR (30) 303

France

Boldini — *Société Canal publicité promotion SA et autre v Société civile Auteurs dans les arts graphiques et plastiques ADAGP et autres*, Cour de cassation, première chambre civile, 27 February 2007, (2007) RIDA 212, 299, Propriétés intellectuelles 2007, 212

Huston — *Angelica, Daniel, Walter Huston, SACD et al. v la Société Turner Entertainment, La Société exploitation de la cinquième chaîne (La Cinq) et al*, Cour de cassation, 28 May 1991, (1991) RIDA 149, 197, IIC 1992, 702

IPEM   *Brennet, IPEM* v *Texport*, Cour d'appel de
                             Paris (Paris Court of Appeals), 19 December
                             1984, GRUR Int. 1985, 680

Lectiel/France Télécom   *Lectiel* v. *France Télécom*, Cour de cassation
                             (French Supreme Court), 23 March 2010,
                             (2010) RIDA 225, 373

Le Printemps   *S.A.C.E.M.* v *S.A. Le Printemps*, Cour de
                             cassation 23 November 1971, D. 1972, 95,
                             IIC 1974, 102

Précom   *Précom, Ouest France Multimedia* v *Direct
                             Annonces*, Court of Cassation, 5 March 2009,
                             (2009) RIDA 221, 491

Société Nomai   *Société Nomai* v *Société Iomega Corporation*,
                             Cour d'appel de Paris (Paris Court of Ap-
                             peals), 12 December 1997, [1998] ECC 281

UFC Que Choisir   *UFC Que Choisir* v *Films Alian Sarde* Cour
                             d'Appel de Paris (Paris Court of Appeals), 22
                             April 2005, (2006) RIDA 207, 374, IIC 2006,
                             112

Germany

August Fourteen   Bundesgerichtshof (Federal Supreme Court),
                             16 April 1975, case I ZR 40/73, BGHZ 64,
                             183, GRUR 1975, 561, IIC 1976, 134

Betriebssytem   Bundesgerichtshof (Federal Supreme Court),
                             4 October 1990, case I ZR 139/89, BGHZ
                             112, 264, NJW 1991, 1231

Bodenrichtwertsammlung   Bundesgerichtshof (Federal Supreme Court),
                             20 July 2006, case I ZR 185/03, GRUR 2007,
                             137

Bora Bora   Bundesgerichtshof (Federal Supreme Court),
                             10 July 1986, case I ZR 128/84, GRUR 1986,
                             887, GRUR Int. 1987, 40, IIC 1988, 411

Buchhaltungsprogramm   Bundesgerichtshof (Federal Supreme Court),
                             14 July 1993, case GRUR 1994, 39, 1995, IIC
                             1995, 127

Deutsche Telekom   Bundesgerichtshof (Federal Supreme Court),
                             6 May 1999, case I ZR 199/96, Multimedia
                             und Recht 1999, 470

List of references

Die Zauberflöte	Bundesgerichtshof (Federal Supreme Court), 20 November 1986, case I ZR 188/84, GRUR 1987, 814
Dongle	OLG Karlsruhe (Court of Appeals of Karlsruhe), 1 October 1996, case 6 U 40/95, ZUM-RD 1997, 340, IIC 1996, 740
ElektronischerPress-espiegel	Bundesgerichtshof (Federal Supreme Court), 11 July 2002, case I ZR 255/00, BGHZ 151, 300, GRUR 2002, 963
Elektronischer Zolltarif	Bundesgerichtshof (Federal Supreme Court), 29 June 2009, case I ZR 191/05, GRUR 2009, 852
Emile Zola	Reichsgericht (Supreme Court of the Reich), 20 September 1930, case I 91/30, RGZ 130, 1
Folgerecht bei Auslandsbezug	Bundesgerichtshof (Federal Supreme Court), 16 June 1994, case I ZR 24/92, BGHZ 126, 252, GRUR 1994, 789, IIC 1995, 573
Geburtstagszug	Bundesgerichtshof (Federal Supreme Court), 13 November 2013, case I ZR 143/12, BGHZ 199, 52, GRUR 2014, 175, IIC 2014, 831
Gold Rush	Bundesgerichtshof (Federal Supreme Court), 19 May 1972, case I ZR 42/71, GRUR Int. 1973, 49, 4 IIC 1973, 245
Grundig-Reporter	Bundesgerichtshof (Federal Supreme Court), 18 May 1955, case I ZR 8/54, BGHZ 17, 266, GRUR 1955, 492
Half-Life 2	Bundesgerichtshof (Federal Supreme Court), 11 February 2010, case I ZR 178/08, IIC 2011, 484
Heise	OLG München (Court of Appeals of Munich), 28 July 2005, case 29 U 2887/05, MMR 2005, 774 = GRUR-RR 2005, 372
Hit Bilanz	Bundesgerichtshof (Federal Supreme Court) 21 July 2005, case I ZR 290/02 GRUR 2005, 857
Holzhandelsprogramm	Bundesgerichtshof (Federal Supreme Court), 20 January 1994, case I ZR 267/91, GRUR 1994, 363, IIC 1995, 720

Hundertwasser-Haus	Bundesgerichtshof (Federal Supreme Court), 5 June 2003, case I ZR 192/00, GRUR 2003, 1035, IIC 2004, 351
Inkasso-Programm	Bundesgerichtshof (Federal Supreme Court), 9 May 1985, case I ZR 52/83, BGHZ 94, 276, GRUR 1985, 1041, IIC 1986, 681
Jeannot	Bundesgerichtshof (Federal Supreme Court), 23 June 1978, case I ZR 112/77, BGHZ 72, 63, GRUR 1978, 639, IIC 1979, 769
Kabelfernsehen II	Bundesgerichtshof (Federal Supreme Court), 4 June 1987, case I ZR 117/85, GRUR 1988, 206, IIC 1989, 251
Kabelfernsehen in Abschattungsgebieten	Bundesgerichtshof (Federal Supreme Court), 7 November 1980, case I 24/79, ZR BGHZ 79, 350, GRUR 1981, 413, IIC 1982, 104
Kandinsky III	Bundesgerichtshof (Federal Supreme Court), 2 March 1973, case I ZR 132/71, GRUR 1973, 602, IIC 1974, 98
Kauf auf Probe	Bundesgerichtshof (Federal Supreme Court), 7 June 2001, case I ZR 21/99, GRUR 2001, 1036
Kopienversanddienst	Bundesgerichtshof (Federal Supreme Court), 25 February 1999, case I ZR 118 /96, BGHZ 141, 13, GRUR 1999, 707
Laras Tochter	Bundesgerichtshof (Federal Supreme Court), 29 April 1999, case I ZR 65/96, BGHZ 141, 267, GRUR 1999, 984, IIC 2000, 1050
Lepo Sumera	Bundesgerichtshof (Federal Supreme Court), 29 March 2001, case I ZR 182/98, BGHZ 147, 178, GRUR 2001, 1134, GRUR Int. 2002, 170
Man spricht deutsh	Bundesgerichtshof (Federal Supreme Court), 13 October 2004, GRUR 2005, 48
Microchip	Bundesgerichtshof (Federal Supreme Court), 1 July 2010, case I ZR 32/09, EIPR 2011, 461
Midi files	Landgericht München (Regional Court of Munich), 30 March 2000, Computer und Recht 2000, 389

List of references

OEM-Version	Bundesgerichtshof (Federal Supreme Court), 6 July 2000, case *I ZR 244/97*, GRUR 2001, 153
Paperboy	Bundesgerichtshof (Federal Supreme Court), 17 July 2003, case I ZR 259/00, BGHZ 156, 1, NJW 2003, 3406, IIC 2004, 1097, CRi 2003, 184
Personalausweise	Bundesgerichtshof (Federal Supreme Court), 29 May 1964, case Ib ZR 4/63, BGHZ 42, 118, GRUR 1965, 104
Puccini	Bundesgerichtshof (Federal Supreme Court), 11 July 1985, case I ZR 50/83, BGHZ 95, 229, GRUR 1986, 69
Sächsischer Ausschreibungsdienst	Bundesgerichtshof (Federal Supreme Court), 28 September 2006, case I ZR 261/03, GRUR 2007, 500
U-Boot photo	OLG Hamburg (Court of Appeals of Hamburg), 3 March 2004, case 5 U 159/03, ZUM-RD 2004, 303
Verhüllter Reichstag	Bundesgerichtshof (Federal Supreme Court), 24 January 2002, case I ZR 102/99, BGHZ 150, 6, GRUR 2002, 605, IIC 2003, 570
Wetterführungspläne	Bundesgerichtshof (Federal Supreme Court), 24 October 2000, case X ZR 72/98, GRUR 2001, 155, IIC 2002, 668
Zweite Zahnarztmeinung II	Bundesgerichtshof (Federal Supreme Court), 1 December 2010, case I ZR 196/08

Netherlands

Amstelveen	*De Stichting tot Exploitatie Centrale Antenne-inrichting Amstelveen* v *Columbia Pictures Industries Inc. et.al.*, Hoge Raad (Supreme Court of the Netherlands), 25 May 1984, NJ 1984, 679, Auteursrecht/AMR 1984, 59, GRUR Int. 1985, 124
BUMA/Chellomedia	*Vereniging BUMA* v *Chellomedia Programming B.V.,* Hoge Raad (Supreme Court of the Netherlands), 19 June 2009, ECLI:NL:HR:2009:BH7602, IER 2010, 24, NJ 2009, 290

Cassina	*Cassina S.p.a et.al. v Jacobs Meubelen BV et.al.*, Hoge Raad (Supreme Court of the Netherlands), 26 May 2000, NJ 2000, 671, Ars Aequi 2001, 677, GRUR Int. 2002, 1050
De Nederlandse Dagbladpers	*De Nederlandse Dagbladpers v Staat der Nederlanden*, District Court of The Hague, 2 March 2005, AMI 2005, 103
Landmark	*College B&W Amsterdam v Landmark*, Afdeling Bestuursrechtspraak Raad van State (Council of State, Administrative Law Div.), 29 April 2009, AMI 2009, 233
Norma/NL Kabel	*Stichting Naburige Rechten Organisatie voor Musici en Auteurs (Norma) v Vereniging NLKabel, et.al.*, Hoge Raad (Supreme Court of the Netherlands), ECLI:NL:HR:2014:735, RvdW 2014, 520, AMI 2014, 94
Ryanair/PR Aviation	*Ryanair Ltd. v PR Aviation B.V,* Hoge Raad (Supreme Court of the Netherlands), 17 January 2014, Ars Aequi AA20140847
Small Cable Networks	*Centraal Antennesysteem Pastoor Schelstraeteweg UA et.al. v Vereniging BUMA,* Hoge Raad (Supreme Court of the Netherlands), 24 December 1993, NJ 1994, 641, GRUR Int. 1995, 83, IIC 1996, 565
Stichting Leenrecht	*Stichting Leenrecht v Vereniging van Openbare Bibliotheken (VOB),* Hoge Raad (Supreme Court of the Netherlands), 23 November 2012, NJ 2013, 381
Van Dale	*Van Dale Lexicografie B.V. v Rudolf Jan Romme,* Hoge Raad (Supreme Court of the Netherlands), 4 January 1991, NJ 1991, 608, English translation in: E.J. Dommering & P.B. Hugenholtz (eds.), *Protecting Works of Fact,* Deventer/Boston 1991, p. 93 et seq.
VOB	*Vereniging Openbare Bibliotheken (VOB) v Stichting Leenrecht a.o,* Rechtbank Den Haag (District Court of The Hague), 1 April 2015, case C/09/445039/ HA ZA 13-690
Vredestein	*Vredestein Fietsbanden BV v Stichting Ring 65,* Hoge Raad (Supreme Court of the Netherlands), 11 May 2001, Informatierecht/ AMI 2001, 97, GRUR Int. 2002, 10

List of references

Wegener

Wegener Uitgeverij Gelderland-Overijssel BV et.al. v *Hunter Select BV*, Court of Appeal Leeuwarden, 27 November 2002, AMI 2003, 59-63

Norway

Napster.no

TONO et al. v *Frank Bruvik*, Norwegian Supreme Court, 27 January 2005, case 2004/882, CRi 2005, 60, GRUR Int. 2005, 522

Sweden

Yapon

Yapon AB v *Ekstrom*, Supreme Court, Sweden, 22 November 2002, [2002] ECDR (14) 155; Court of Appeal for Skane and Blekinge, 14 October 1997, [2002] ECDR (13) 149

Switzerland

Gemeinschaftsantenne Altdorf

Schweizerisches Bundesgericht, 20 March 1984, BGE 110 II 61, GRUR Int. 1985, 412

The Gold Rush

Schweizerisches Bundesgericht, 3 November 1970, BGE 96 II 409, GRUR Int. 1972, 25, IIC 1971, 315

United Kingdom

Bodley Head v *Flegon*

Bodley Head v *Alec Flegon and another*, High Court of Justice, (Chancery Division) 16/17 and 25 November 1971, (1972) FSR 21, (1972) RPC 587, (1972) WLR 680

Experience Hendrix

Experience Hendrix LLC v *Purple Haze Records Ltd and Lawrence Miller*, Court of Appeal (Civ Division) [2007] EWCA Civ 501

Football Dataco/Stan James

Football Dataco & Others v *Stan James Plc & Others and Sportradar GmbH & Others*, Court of Appeal (Civ. Division), 6 February 2013, [2013] EWCA Civ 27

IBCOS v Barclays	*IBCOS Computers Ltd and another v Barclays Mercantile Highland Finance Ltd and others*, High Court of Justice (Chancery Division), 24 February 1994, [1994] FSR 275
Mars/Teknowledge	*Mars v Teknowledge,* High Court of Justice (Chancery Division), 11 June 1999, [2000] FSR 138
Meltwater	The Newspaper Licensing Agency & others v Meltwater & the PRCA, High Court of Justice (Chancery Division), 26 November 2010, [2010] EWHC 3099
Navitaire	*Navitaire Inc. v Easyjet Airline Co.*, High Court of Justice, (Chancery Division), 30 July 2004, [2004] EWHC 1725, [2005] ECDR 17
Norowzian/Arks II	*Norowzian v Arks Ltd and another,* Court of Appeal (Civ Division), 4 November 1999, [1999] EWCA Civ 3014
SAS Institute (High Court 2010)	*SAS Institute Inc v World Programming Ltd*, High Court of Justice (Chancery Division), 23 July 2010, [2010] EWHC 1829 (Ch), [2010] ECDR (15) 297, [2011] RPC 1
SAS Institute (High Court 2013)	*SAS Institute Inc v World Programming Ltd*, High Court of Justice (Chancery Division), 25 January 2013, [2010] EWHC 69 (Ch), [2013] RPC 17
SAS Institute (Court of Appeal 2013)	*SAS Institute Inc v World Programming Ltd*, Court of Appeal, 21 November 2013, [2013] EWCA Civ 1482, [2014] RPC 8
Sony/Ball	*Kabushiki Kaisha Sony Computer Entertainment Inc. et al. v Ball et al.*, High Court of Justice (Chancery Division), 19 July 2004, [2004] EWHC 1738, [2004] ECDR (33) 323, [2005] ECC 24, [2005] FSR 9
Sony/Owen	*Sony Computer Entertainment Inc. v Owen*, High Court of Justice, (Chancery Division), 23 January 2002, [2002] EMLR 742, [2002] ECDR 298

List of references

United States

A&M Records	*A&M Records, Inc.* v *Napster, Inc.*, 239 F.3d 1004 (9th Cir. 2001), *on remand to* A&M Records, Inc. v Napster, Inc., 2001 WL 227083 (ND Cal. 2001), affirmed by *A&M Records, Inc.* v *Napster, Inc.*, 284 F.3d 1091 (9th Cir. 2002)
Computer Associates	*Computer Associates International, Inc.* v *Altai Inc*, United States Court of Appeal, Second Circuit, 22 June 1992, 932 F.2d 693, 23 USPQ 2d. 1241
Eldred	*Eldred* v *Ashcroft*, United States Supreme Court, 15 January 2003, 537 US 186
Feist	*Feist Publications, Inc.* v. *Rural Telephone Service Co., Inc.,* United States Supreme Court, 27 March 1991, 111 S.Ct. 1282 (1991)
Oracle/Google	*Oracle America, Inc.* v *Google Inc.*, 750 F.3d 1339 (C. A. Fed. (Cal.) 2014), 9 May 2014
Mai Systems Corp.	*Mai Systems Corp.* v *Peak Computer, Inc.*, 991 F.2d 511 (9th Cir. 1993)
Religious Tech. Ctr.	*Religious Technology Center* v *Netcom On-Line Communication Services, Inc.*, 907 F.Supp. 1361 (N.D. Cal. 1995)

INDEX

professional Resale 1/2, 1/4, 9/
Right to information
value WPPT 15/3; Database 7/4
Marrakesh Treaty Introduction/2;
BC 9/1, 11/1, 20/2; WCT 11/3
mass digitization Orphan
Introductory remarks/1, 1/5,
4/1, 7/1
mass-market
contracts InfoSoc 5/1, 6/5
program Programs 5/2
master
**copies of cinematographic
works** Resale 2/1
tape WPPT 3/4
material reciprocity Introduc-
tion/6; BC Introductory
remarks/1, 14ter/1, 14ter/3;
Database 11/4
materials BC 9/4, 10/3; RC 15/2,
15/3, 15/4, 15/5, 20/1; Rental
11/4; Database 1/3, 1/4, 7/3,
13/1; InfoSoc 5/2
mathematical concepts TRIPS
9/3
maximum
harmonization Term Introductory remarks/2
protection BC 7/3, 19/No
maximum protection
means
for decryption WPPT 2/7;
SatCab 1/4, 1/6
of redress BC 5/1, 6bis/4, 16/3;
WPPT 5/1, 5/6
mechanical licence BC 14/1
mediators SatCab 11/1, 11/2
medium BC 9/2; WPPT 2/8, 16/4;
Programs 4/2, 4/4, 5/3; Rental
6/1; SatCab 1/6; Database 5/2,
7/4; InfoSoc 4/2, 5/3; Resale
1/1
metadata InfoSoc 7/1
method
of operation TRIPS 9/3

of reproduction BC 9/2
microfilm Database 1/2
microwave system SatCab 1/6
minimum
protection BC 1/2, 6/2, 6bis/1,
7/1, 17/3; RC 7/1, 14/1,
15/1, 21/1; GC 2/4; WPPT
1/5, 3/2, 16/1, 16/2, 17/3;
TRIPS 14/1; SatCab 6/1
rights BC passim; WCT 3/1,
3/5; WPPT 3/1; TRIPS 11/1,
13/1, 14/2, 14/4; SatCab 4/1
sale price Resale 3/1, 3/2, 4/4
minor reservations doctrine
WCT 10/2, 10/6
miscellaneous facts BC 2/9; WCT
3/3, 11/2
Misleading Advertising Directive
InfoSoc 6/4
mode BC 2/2; WCT 3/2, 4/2; RC
26/1; InfoSoc 4/3
modification BC 6bis/2; WCT
12/2, 12/4, 13/Application;
WPPT 5/1
**of existing electronic rights
management information
WCT** 12/2
monistic theory BC 6bis/1
moral rights BC passim; WCT
1/4, 12/4, 14/2; RC 1/2, 7/8,
10/6, 13/6; WPPT 1/3, 5/1,
5/2, 5/5, 17/1, 21/2, 22/1, 22/3;
TRIPS 9/2; Programs 1/1, 2/1,
2/2; SatCab 12/1; Term 9/1;
Database 2/1, 5/1; InfoSoc 1/1,
5/4
after the death of the author
BC 6bis/3; Term 9/1
most-favoured-nation treatment
BC 20/2; TRIPS Introductory
remarks/2, 10/3
moving images Rental 2/3; Term
3/4; Database 1/4
multi-territorial licensing
Introduction/7; CollRights

Index